WELLES-TURNER MEMORIAL
GLASTONBURY, CT   W9-BKW-716

DISCARDED BY
WELLES-TURNER
MEMORIAL LIBRARY
GLASTONBURY, CT

The MANTLE
of COMMAND

ALSO BY NIGEL HAMILTON

Royal Greenwich: A Guide and History to London's Most Historic Borough
(with Olive Hamilton)

*Nigel Hamilton's Guide to Greenwich: A Personal Guide to the Buildings and
Walks of One of England's Most Beautiful and Historic Areas*

*The Brothers Mann: The Lives of Heinrich and Thomas Mann,
1871–1950 and 1875–1955*

Monty: The Making of a General, 1887–1942

Master of the Battlefield: Monty's War Years, 1942–1944

Monty: Final Years of the Field-Marshal, 1944–1976

Monty: The Man Behind the Legend

JFK: Reckless Youth

Monty: The Battles of Field Marshal Bernard Law Montgomery

The Full Monty: Montgomery of Alamein, 1887–1942

Bill Clinton, An American Journey: Great Expectations

Montgomery: D-Day Commander

Bill Clinton: Mastering the Presidency

Biography: A Brief History

How to Do Biography: A Primer

*American Caesars: Lives of the Presidents from
Franklin D. Roosevelt to George W. Bush*

The MANTLE of COMMAND

FDR AT WAR
1941–1942

Nigel Hamilton

HOUGHTON MIFFLIN HARCOURT
BOSTON · NEW YORK
2014

This one is for my grandchildren, spread across the world:
Sophie, Oskari, Toby, and Matthew

Copyright © 2014 by Nigel Hamilton

All rights reserved

For information about permission to reproduce selections from this book,
write to Permissions, Houghton Mifflin Harcourt Publishing Company,
215 Park Avenue South, New York, New York 10003.

www.hmhco.com

Library of Congress Cataloging-in-Publication Data
Hamilton, Nigel.
The mantle of command : FDR at war, 1941–1942 / Nigel Hamilton.
pages cm
Includes bibliographical references and index.
ISBN 978-0-547-77524-1 (hardcover)
1. World War, 1939–1945 — United States. 2. Roosevelt, Franklin D. (Franklin Delano),
1882–1945 3. World War, 1939–1945 — United States — Biography. 4. World War, 1939–1945 —
Diplomatic history. 5. Command of troops — United States — Case studies. 6. World War,
1939–1945 — Campaigns. 7. Great Britain — Foreign relations — United States.
8. United States — Foreign relations — Great Britain. I. Title.
D753.H25 2014
940.54'1273 — dc23   2013045586

Typeset in Minion
Maps by Mapping Specialists, Ltd.

Printed in the United States of America
DOC 10 9 8 7 6 5 4 3 2 1

The author is grateful for permission to quote from the following: *War Diaries, 1939–1945: Field
Marshal Lord Alanbrooke,* edited by Alex Danchev and Daniel Todman, reprinted by permission of
David Higham Associates. Diary of Lord Halifax, 1941–1942, reprinted by permission of the Borth-
wick Institute for Archives, University of York. Diary of Thomas C. Hart, reprinted by permission of
the Operational Archives Branch, Naval Historical Center, Washington, D.C. Letters and diaries of
Margaret Lynch Suckley, reprinted by permission of the Wilderstein Preservation, Rhinebeck, N.Y.

Contents

vi | *Contents*

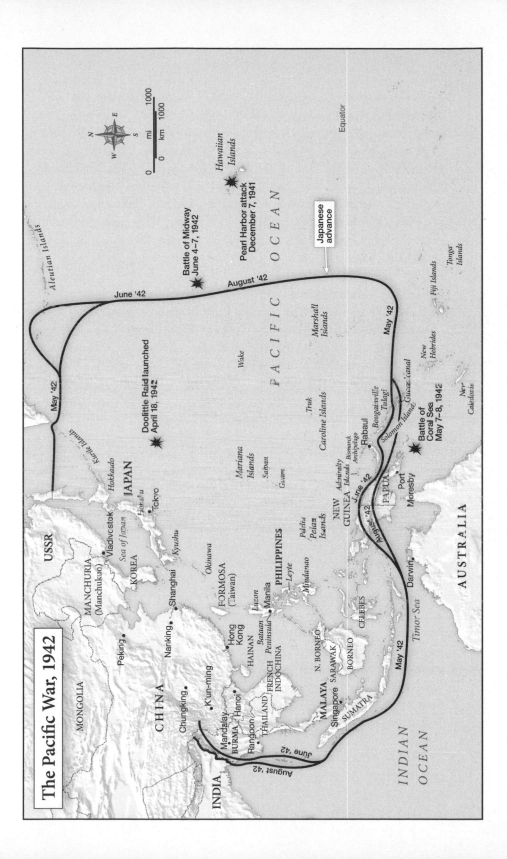

The Pacific War, 1942

USSR

MONGOLIA

MANCHURIA
(Manchukuo)

Peking

CHINA

Chungking

K'un-ming

Nanking

Shanghai

Vladivostok

KOREA

Sea of Japan

Hokkaido

Honshu

Tokyo

JAPAN

Kyushu

Kurile Islands

Aleutian Islands

Okinawa

FORMOSA
(Taiwan)

Hong Kong

HAINAN

Hanoi

FRENCH
INDOCHINA

THAILAND

Rangoon

Mandalay

BURMA

INDIA

August '42

June '42

May '42

Singapore

MALAYA

SARAWAK

N. BORNEO

SUMATRA

BORNEO

CELEBES

Luzon

Manila

Bataan
Peninsula

PHILIPPINES

Leyte

Mindanao

Palau
Pelau
Islands

NEW
GUINEA

Admiralty
Islands

Bismarck
Archipelago

Rabaul

New
Britain

Bougainville

Solomon Islands

Talagi

Guadalcanal

PAPUA

Port
Moresby

Darwin

Timor Sea

AUSTRALIA

INDIAN
OCEAN

Mariana
Islands

Saipan

Guam

Caroline Islands

Truk

Palau
Islands

Wake

Marshall
Islands

PACIFIC OCEAN

Doolittle Raid launched
April 18, 1942

Battle of Midway
June 4–7, 1942

Pearl Harbor attack
December 7, 1941

Hawaiian
Islands

Equator

Battle of
Coral Sea
May 7–8, 1942

New
Hebrides

New
Caledonia

Fiji Islands

Tonga
Islands

Japanese
advance

May '42

June '42

August '42

May '42

June '42

August '42

N E S W

mi 1000

km 1000

0

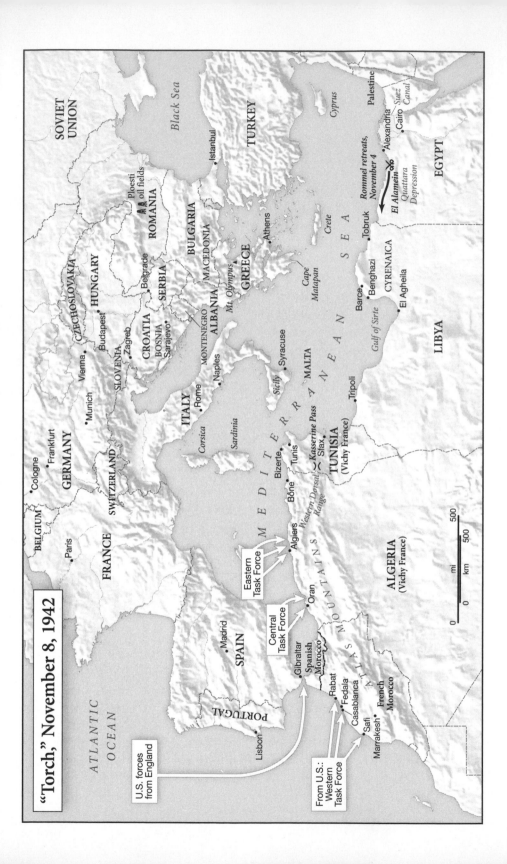

"Torch," November 8, 1942

SOVIET UNION

Black Sea

ATLANTIC OCEAN

TURKEY

Cyprus

Palestine
Cairo *Suez Canal*
Alexandria

EGYPT

Istanbul

Rommel retreats, November 4
El Alamein
Quattara Depression

CZECHOSLOVAKIA
HUNGARY
Budapest
Vienna
ROMANIA
Ploesti
oil fields
Belgrade
SERBIA
BULGARIA
MACEDONIA
ALBANIA
MONTENEGRO
CROATIA
BOSNIA
Sarajevo
Zagreb
SLOVENIA

GERMANY
Cologne
Frankfurt
Munich
SWITZERLAND

BELGIUM
Paris
FRANCE

GREECE
Athens
Mt. Olympus
Crete
Cape Matapan

M E D I T E R R A N E A N   S E A

Gulf of Sirte

Tobruk
Benghazi
Barce
CYRENAICA
El Aghella

LIBYA

ITALY
Rome
Naples
Corsica
Sardinia
Sicily
Syracuse
MALTA

Bizerte
Tunis
Bône
Kasserine Pass
Sfax
Western Dorsal Range
TUNISIA
(Vichy France)

Tripoli

ALGERIA
(Vichy France)

Algiers

Eastern Task Force

Oran

Central Task Force

Gibraltar
Spanish Morocco
Rabat
Fedala
Casablanca
Safi
Marrakesh
French Morocco

A T L A S   M O U N T A I N S

SPAIN
Madrid

PORTUGAL
Lisbon

U.S. forces from England

From U.S.: Western Task Force

mi   500
km   500
0
0

Prologue

WE CAN VIEW World War II from many angles, military to moral. Many fine books have been written about the struggle — perhaps the most famous being Winston Churchill's *The Second World War*, in six volumes, which helped the former British prime minister to win the Nobel Prize in Literature.

The Mantle of Command: FDR at War is my attempt to retell the story of the military direction of the Second World War from a different perspective: that of President Franklin Delano Roosevelt, in his role as U.S. commander in chief.

Following Pearl Harbor there were many calls for Roosevelt to hand over direction of America's world war to a military man: a professional like General Douglas MacArthur, the former U.S. Army chief of staff, who was serving in the Philippines. FDR rejected such calls — arguing that, as U.S. president, he was the U.S. commander in chief, and the Constitution made him so. As Alexander Hamilton had written in *Federalist* No. 74, the President of the United States was to have "the supreme command and direction of the military and naval forces, as first general and admiral" of the nation. This Roosevelt was, whether people liked it or not. "What is clearer than that the framers meant the President to be the *chief executive* in peace," he said to his doctor, Ross McIntire, "and in war the *commander in chief*?"[1]

Nevertheless, the military challenges facing Roosevelt as commander in chief were greater than any that had confronted his predecessors: America assailed by a coalition of three twentieth-century military empires — Hitler's Third Reich, Mussolini's Italian Empire, and Hirohito's Empire of Japan — seeking, in a Tripartite Pact, to remake the modern world in their own image. To this end they had revolutionized warfare: Nazi *Blitzkrieg* in Europe, and dazzling, ruthless amphibious invasions in the Far East by the Japanese.

How Roosevelt responded to those challenges as his nation's military commander is thus the burden of my new account. It is a story that, astonishingly, has never really been chronicled. Roosevelt himself did not live to tell it, as he had hoped he would, in retirement;[2] Churchill, surviving the war, did, in incomparable prose — but very much from his own point of view.

Succeeding generations of writers and historians have certainly addressed Roosevelt's career, but primarily as statesman and politician rather than as commander in chief. As far as the military direction of the war was concerned, such writers tended to ignore or downplay the President's role, focusing instead on Allied global strategy or on Roosevelt's subordinates and field commanders: General Marshall, Admiral King, General Arnold, Admiral Nimitz, General MacArthur, General Eisenhower, General Patton, General Bradley, and other World War II warriors.[3] As a result, the popular image of President Roosevelt has become one of a great and august moral leader of his nation: an inspiring figure on a world stage, but one who largely delegated the "business of war" to others — including Winston Churchill.

General George C. Marshall, for example, once remarked to the chief of staff of the British Army, General Alan Brooke, that Brooke was lucky to see the Prime Minister almost every day in London; in Washington, by contrast, Marshall — who was chief of staff of the U.S. Army — often did not see the President "for a month or six weeks."[4]

Marshall was exaggerating; moreover, he was expressing a very different frustration from the one the majority of writers have taken him to mean. Marshall was, in reality, complaining that President Roosevelt was making *all* the major military decisions at the White House, rather than allowing Marshall to make them at the War Department — and worse still, not allowing his U.S. Army chief of staff to contest them, or give advice, unless by appointment with the President.

This was a deliberate stratagem, as I hope *The Mantle of Command* will demonstrate. Deference to the military by political leaders in World War I had permitted the senseless battles of attrition on the Western Front. For this reason the President was unwilling to delegate something as important as world war to "professionals." Keeping General Marshall and Admiral Ernest King as separate though equal supplicants, the President intentionally sought to assert his ultimate authority as commander in chief: a power he kept strictly within the parameters of the U.S. Constitution, but which brooked no real opposition to his wishes or decisions — until the fateful day in 1942 when his military officials attempted a quasi mutiny, which is the centerpiece of this book.

The story of how America's commander in chief conducted World War II in the aftermath of Pearl Harbor, then, is almost the polar opposite of what we have been led, for the most part, to believe.[5] It is also more freighted, since the stakes for America and the free world in 1942 were perhaps the most serious in global history.

Tracing afresh how Roosevelt dealt with the military challenges he faced as commander in chief following the Japanese attack on Pearl Harbor allows us to see him in perhaps his greatest hour — setting and maintaining the moral agenda of the United Nations (as he christened the Allied powers), while slowly but surely turning defeat into relentless victory. His handling of General MacArthur and the manner in which he kept the Filipino forces fighting as allies of an embattled America, rather than giving in to the Japanese, was but one of his extraordinary achievements of the succeeding months as, swatting the persistent machinations and rumblings of near treason in the U.S. War Department, Roosevelt finally overruled his subordinates and, ordering into battle the largest American amphibious invasion force in the nation's history, his legions set out from shores three thousand miles apart to turn the tide of war against Hitler — astonishing the world, as they did so, and giving rise to the slogan that would hearten millions across Europe: "The Americans are coming!"

Side by side with this perspective, *The Mantle of Command* seeks to tell another story that has been largely downplayed or obscured in the decades since World War II: namely the collapse of the British Empire in the weeks and months after Pearl Harbor.

As prime minister of Great Britain, Winston S. Churchill had become an emblem of his island country's noble resistance to Nazi tyranny in 1940 and 1941 — so much so that writers and historians, following in the literary footsteps of Churchill's own multivolume account, have tended to overlook his often suspect leadership thereafter. In particular, Churchill's imperialist obsession over India, and the crisis this led to in his military relations with President Roosevelt in the spring of 1942, have been largely ignored in terms of their significance.

A third perspective that I feel has been neglected or underappreciated in relation to Franklin Delano Roosevelt was his modus operandi in the White House — and the consequences this has had for the writing of history. Paralyzed from the waist down after contracting polio in 1921, the President led a very different life from that of the British war leader. Winston Churchill was from childhood a romantic historian and journalist who loved to travel and put everything he thought or witnessed on paper — indeed, he made his living, his entire life, primarily by his writing. He also loved speechifying, holding forth with inimitable turns of phrase and perception to gatherings small and large. As his own doctor observed, he was not a good listener — and many of his worst mistakes as his nation's war leader stemmed from this.

Franklin Roosevelt, by contrast, was a very good listener. Though he could, as his mother's only child, be perfectly content on his own, reading or pasting items into his beloved stamp albums, Roosevelt also loved getting to know people, and enjoyed true conversation. He had earlier edited his university's newspaper; as a politician in a democracy made vibrant by an unfettered press and deeply partisan Congress, however, he came to distrust paper save as annotated records to be kept locked in his "'Safe' and Confidential Files" in his eventual presidential library at Hyde Park on the Hudson. These were the documents he thought he would eventually employ to reconstruct, once the war was over, the greatest drama of his life: his struggle to impose a moral, postimperial vision on his coalition wartime partners, and how he had been compelled by circumstances to supplant the United Kingdom as guardian of the world's democracies.

The President did not live to write that work. Reassembling from surviving documents his role as commander in chief seventy years later is thus considerably harder than it has been for writers seeking to portray and chronicle Churchill as wartime British prime minister. Piecing together the evidence not only from archival records but authentic wartime diaries, as well as the testimony of President Roosevelt's last surviving Map Room officer, I hope nevertheless that I've been able to restore for the reader something of the drama, the issues, and the confrontations Roosevelt faced, as well as the historic decisions he had to make as commander in chief in the aftermath of Pearl Harbor.

• • •

From the vantage point of Roosevelt's Oval Study, Oval Office, and his ground-floor Map Room at the White House, as well as his mansion at Hyde Park and Shangri-la (his presidential retreat, or camp, in the Maryland hills), the true story of FDR's conduct of the war bears little semblance to the picture Winston Churchill was at pains to chart in later years. Nor was it always perceived by outsiders, who found themselves charmed by Franklin Roosevelt's easy manner, and were not witnesses to the Commander in Chief's iron glove. General "Vinegar Joe" Stilwell, for example, had "retained the family's Republicanism and joined naturally in the exhilarating exercise of Roosevelt-hating" for his New Deal policies, in the words of his biographer; the general's contempt for the President got no better once war began. As Stilwell sniffed in his diary, Roosevelt was a "rank amateur in all military matters,"[6] and "completely hypnotized by the British," who had "his ear, while we have the hind tit."[7] Churchill's right-hand military man, Field Marshal Sir Alan Brooke, reflected in later years that, in contrast to his own master, the "President had no military knowledge and was aware of this fact and consequently relied on Marshall and listened to Marshall's advice."[8]

How little Sir Alan Brooke, as a British officer, knew! Churchill did, however — especially once his beloved British Empire began to collapse. It was not for nothing that the Prime Minister, waving goodbye to the President's plane some weeks after the successful American landings in Northwest Africa which turned the tide of World War II, remarked to the U.S. vice consul in Marrakesh: "If anything happened to that man, I couldn't stand it. He is the truest friend; he has the furthest vision; he is the greatest man I have ever known."[9]

The Mantle of Command, then, focuses for the first time on Roosevelt's *military* odyssey in the aftermath of Pearl Harbor — the personal, strategic, staffing, and command decisions he was called upon to make, in the context of the challenges he faced. In the interests of brevity I have focused on fourteen episodes, beginning with the President's historic meeting with Prime Minister Churchill on August 9, 1941, aboard their battleships in Placentia Bay, off the coast of Newfoundland, and ending with the first major landing of American troops on the threshold of Europe, in North Africa in late 1942. This time frame reveals Roosevelt's evolution from noncombatant supporter of Churchill, to become the master of the Allied effort, a commander in chief who took control of the war not only from his ally but from his own generals.

How accurately President Roosevelt read the demented mind of the Nazi führer; how, after ensuring U.S. naval victory in the Pacific, he turned his attention back toward Europe; how he overruled his generals and insisted upon American landings in French Northwest Africa in 1942, rather than a suicidal "Second Front" assault on the coast of mainland France — these marked a remarkable reversal of fortune for the Allies, and testify to Roosevelt's extraordinary military leadership: the saga reaching its climax as he sent into battle the massive American air, army, and naval forces that, on November 8, 1942, stunned Hitler and changed the course of World War II.

The tough challenges that came thereafter are the subject of another book. In the meantime, though, I hope these fourteen episodes will allow us to better understand the global test that Franklin Roosevelt faced as his country's military leader in the months following America's terrible defeat in Hawaii — and perhaps better appreciate the wisdom of Churchill's valedictory remark, seven decades ago.

PART ONE

Placentia Bay

1

Before the Storm

THE "PLAN OF ESCAPE," as Roosevelt called it, was simple. It was also deceitful — the sort of adventure that the President, confined to the White House by the burden of his responsibilities as well as his wheelchair, loved. He would pretend to go on a fishing trip on his 165-foot presidential yacht, the USS *Potomac,* similar to the vacation he had taken earlier in the spring. In reality he would secretly transfer from the "floating White House" to an American battleship or cruiser lying off the New England coast, then race up to Canadian waters to meet with the embattled British prime minister, Mr. Winston Churchill: the man who for more than a year had been leading his country in a lonely struggle against the Third Reich, following the fall of France and most of Europe.

FDR had suggested such a meeting several times since January 1941, when his emissary, Harry Hopkins, first put the idea to Churchill on a visit to London. The purpose was, according to Roosevelt's own account (which he dictated for the historical record and a magazine article — one that, sadly, he never completed), "to talk over the problem of the defeat of Germany."[1]

The proposed date "mentioned at that time," the President stated in his narrative, was to be "March or April" of that spring. However, the tortuous passage of the vast Lend-Lease bill through Congress and other important legislation made it impossible for him to leave Washington before the early summer, "and by that time the war in Greece — and later the war in Crete — prevented Churchill," Roosevelt explained. "The trip was mentioned again in May and June," the President narrated — but talk of such a meeting was overshadowed by a more momentous event than Hitler's predations in the Mediterranean. For on June 22, 1941, the German invasion of Russia began — Hitler launching several million mobilized German troops in a do-or-die effort to smash the Soviet Union before turning back to the problematic invasion of England.[2]

And — the U.S. secretary of war, Colonel Henry Stimson, feared — eventual war with the United States.[3]

Three weeks later a date for the Anglo-American summit "was finally decided"; it would take place, the President and Prime Minister concurred, in a mutually agreed upon location between August 8 and 10, 1941.[4] The initial site chosen was the British island of Bermuda. Canada, though, considered by the President to be safer, met with final approval by both leaders.

An official U.S. presidential visit to the capital city of Ottawa was mooted as cover for the meeting, with a secret side trip to the coast allowing Roosevelt to meet Churchill on his arrival. A problem was foreseen, however, in other British Dominion premiers asking to join the powwow. Such a gathering would have raised all sorts of political questions back in Washington, where a suspicious, isolationist Congress would have had to be informed — and involved.

It had thus been decided that only the President and Mr. Churchill would meet, aboard their anchored battleships — preferably in a protected sixty-mile-wide gulf off the Newfoundland coast called Placentia Bay, named for a French naval station that had existed there before the British conquest. Though the waters were Canadian, the naval station at Argentia had been ceded to the United States for ninety-nine years as a quid pro quo in the previous year's "destroyers for bases" deal to help Britain fight the Nazis. Following its acquisition it had been expanded to provide U.S. Army Air Force protection, and was already handling U.S. Navy minesweepers. Shore-based communications could also be provided, if required. From the President's perspective, however, it would above all be an *American* venue — putting the Prime Minister at a disadvantage, in the same way that visitors to Louis XIV were made to climb a thousand steps at Versailles before meeting the French monarch.

"Escape," for the President, meant, of course, *from* something, namely the American press: mainstay of the nation's vigilant democracy, but also a millstone in terms of executive privacy and confidentiality — and security. If word of the prospective meeting leaked, it would endanger not only the President's life but the Prime Minister's as well, drawing German U-boats in the North Atlantic to the area.

More threatening to Roosevelt's presidential authority in a time of continuing isolationism, though, would be the fierce debate aroused across America about the purpose of such a meeting. The majority of the American public (as expressed in opinion polls, which Roosevelt watched carefully)[5] remained resolutely opposed to being drawn into the war raging in Europe. At the height of the previous year's election campaign, the President had given his "most solemn assurance" that there was "no secret treaty, no secret obligation, no secret commitment, no secret understanding in any shape or form, direct or indirect, with any other Government, to involve this nation in any war or for any other purpose."[6] In the summer of 1941 there were still isolationists aplenty — encouraged by Hitler's turn to the east — watching to see that the President kept his word. Only Congress could declare war — or alter the terms of the November 1939 Neutrality Act.[7] For the President to end or breach American neutrality without congressional backing would risk his impeachment.

It was for personal reasons as well that the President was anxious to keep away the press and other voyeurs. He wanted the meeting to be intimate: an opportunity to finally get to know in person the British prime minister, with whom he had begun secretly corresponding in 1939, when Hitler invaded Poland and Churchill was made First Lord of the Admiralty. Once Churchill had become prime minister in May 1940, the President had continued to bypass his own U.S. ambassador to London, the nefarious appeaser and isolationist Joseph P. Kennedy, and the communications between Roosevelt and Churchill had become more and more grave, as the President first agreed to provide American mothballed warships to the British, then brokered through Congress the vast Lend-Lease deal to provide munitions, aircraft, and weapons on credit. Instead of being grateful, however, the Prime Minister kept asking for more — indeed, to the President's irritation, Churchill had recently told Roosevelt's emissary in London, Harry Hopkins, that he would be bringing all his military chiefs with him to the Placentia Bay summit. The President therefore had no option but, on Hopkins's advice, to take with him his *own* service chiefs: stern General George Marshall, chief of staff of the U.S. Army; bluff but more junior Major General Henry "Hap" Arnold, chief of the U.S. Army Air Forces (the Army Air Corps and GHQ Air Force, which was still a division of the U.S. Army);[8] and Admiral Harold

R. "Betty" Stark, quiet, bespectacled chief of naval operations. As commander of the Atlantic Fleet, responsible for the small presidential contingent's safe naval passage to Newfoundland, the irascible and somewhat anti-British Admiral Ernest "Ernie" King would be a party to the summit, too.

On a very hot August 3, 1941, Roosevelt left Washington by train. That evening he embarked on the presidential yacht (which had a crew of fifty-four) at New London's submarine base, in Connecticut — unaccompanied by the three Associated Press journalists who typically followed Roosevelt in a separate vessel on other such "fishing trips."

The USS *Potomac* motored north, anchoring that night off Martha's Vineyard, across the water from Cape Cod. At dawn the next morning Roosevelt secretly sped away by launch from the two-deck, 376-ton motor yacht, leaving a group of U.S. Secret Service stand-ins to impersonate him and his private guests when it continued its stately way up the Cape Cod Canal. From the shore the white vessel would be (and was) seen and waved to by peacetime summer holidaymakers. In truth the U.S. commander in chief was by then aboard the flagship of Admiral King's Atlantic Fleet, the USS *Augusta:* a ninety-two-hundred-ton, six-hundred-feet-long Northampton Class heavy cruiser, manned by more than a thousand sailors and armed with nine eight-inch guns, eight five-inch guns, and six torpedo tubes, lurking off Martha's Vineyard.

Admiral Stark and General Marshall were already onboard when the President arrived. A handful of other members of the presidential party, including General Arnold, had embarked on an accompanying heavy cruiser, the New Orleans–class USS *Tuscaloosa*. Escorted by four new American destroyers, the VIPs then sailed north toward a summit that, the officers finally became aware, promised to make history.

Speeding at times at thirty-two knots, the American presidential party raced through patchy fog to reach the Newfoundland rendezvous ahead of time. Roosevelt had not even told his secretary of war, Colonel Stimson, about the conference, nor his secretary of the navy, Mr. Frank Knox — nor even his secretary of state, Mr. Cordell Hull, who was on medical leave. The President had not even told his secretary, Grace Tully! He had only informed General Marshall and Admiral Stark three days before departure — with orders that General Arnold, the air force commander, be invited to attend but not informed of the purpose or destination of the voyage before embarking on the USS *Tuscaloosa*. There was to be no fraternization, or planning, before the meeting: nothing that could later be denounced as preparatory to a secret agreement or alliance.

By contrast, Prime Minister Winston Churchill had great plans for just such an affiliation.

Buoyed by excitement and hope, Winston Spencer Churchill — son, after all, of an American mother — had ordered his chiefs of staff to draw up a "Future Strategy Paper," setting out how Britain could win the war if the United States became an ally. He had also proudly sent secret signals to the prime ministers of all the Dominions of the British Empire to let them know of the impending conference — stating that, although none of them had been invited, he "hoped that from the meeting some momentous agreement might be reached."[9] Setting off "with a retinue which Cardinal Wolsey might have envied" (as his private secretary sarcastically noted in his diary),[10] the Prime Minister had even written in excitement to Queen Elizabeth, consort of the monarch, to tell her of his great expectations.

"I must say, I do not think our friend would have asked me to go so far, for what must be a meeting of world notice, unless he had in mind some further forward step," Churchill confided, explaining why he was leaving his country at such a critical time.[11] He had ordered grouse and rare turtle soup as among the provisions he would take, as well as a full military band. He would travel aboard his latest radar-equipped forty-three-thousand-ton battleship, HMS *Prince of Wales*. As he had presumptuously signaled to the President from Scapa Flow, Scotland, on August 4, 1941: "We are just off. It is twenty-seven years ago today that Huns began their last war. We must make a good job of it this time. Twice ought to be good enough."[12]

Churchill's hope that the President was about to declare war on Nazi Germany, or was going to promise to solicit the backing of the U.S. Congress for such a declaration, or was perhaps willing to engineer a casus belli (as Churchill himself had been accused of doing in 1915, over munitions he had ordered to be taken aboard the ill-fated neutral American liner, the SS *Lusitania*), was understandable, but completely erroneous. Roosevelt had no intention whatsoever of entering hostilities in Europe to save the British Empire — especially its colonial empire. Instead, he wished merely to get the measure of the British arch-imperialist — and see if he might bend him to a different purpose.

Poor Churchill, who rested up on the voyage and barely interacted with his own chiefs of staff, had no idea what was coming. Nor, ironically, did the U.S. chiefs of staff, who were not told the object of the meeting, or their roles, beyond that of advising the President.

Roosevelt genuinely respected his chiefs of staff as spokesmen of the armed services they directed, but the truth was, he had as yet little or no faith in their military, let alone their political, judgment. Almost everything they and their war departments had forecast or recommended to him as commander in chief since May 1941 had turned out wrong.[13] The "preparations" that the War Department had reported for a German drive through Spain and Northwest Africa to Dakar, prior to an anticipated assault on South America,[14] had proven but a ruse. Instead, the Führer had invaded the Soviet Union, on June 22, with more than three million troops, thirty-six hundred tanks, and six hundred thousand vehicles, supported by twenty-five hundred aircraft.

Far from conquering Russia in a matter of weeks, however, as forecast both by the secretary of war, the U.S. War Department,[15] and the U.S. military attaché in Moscow,[16] the vast 180-division German Wehrmacht and Luftwaffe forces sent into battle looked by early August as if they were meeting stiff resistance in the Soviet Union.[17] Moreover, far from abandoning their hold on the Middle East — as American military observers were still advising the British to do, but the President was not[18] — the British were holding General Erwin Rommel at bay in North Africa. British forces, in fact, had successfully driven into Iraq and Syria to deter Vichy French assistance to Hitler. As a result, neither Turkey nor Portugal, nor Spain, had moved a finger to help Hitler.[19] Even Marshal Pétain's egregious puppet government in Vichy had refused to alter the terms of its 1940 surrender to Hitler and permit French military cooperation with the Nazis. Hitler, the President was convinced, was not going to have things his own way.

It was not only the predictions of the U.S. War Department that were wrong, the President felt. The advice given by the U.S. Navy Department had seemed to him, as a former assistant secretary of the navy, to be strategically unsound — as well as psychologically naïve. The chief of naval operations and his director of plans favored a one-ocean navy operating solely in the Atlantic, with U.S. forces in the Philippines and Pacific Islands left to defend themselves against potential Japanese attack.[20] By contrast, the President had been determined to bluff both Hitler and the Japanese emperor, Hirohito, by keeping one U.S. fleet in the Pacific to deter Japan — still embroiled in a vicious land war on the Chinese main-land — from new conquests, while using the other U.S. fleet in the Atlantic to assert its naval authority over the waters of the Western Hemisphere. Hitler, the President was certain, had his hands full in Russia, and would not dare declare war on the United States as long as the U.S. was seen to be strong. In the meantime, moreover, the President would do his best to cajole Congress into expansion of the U.S. Armed Forces, to be ready for war once it came — as, inevitably, he was sure it must.

Roosevelt's firm belief about Russian resistance — backed by advice from old Russia hands like Joseph Davies, the former U.S. ambassador to Moscow — had been mocked by senior officers in the War Department. However, Harry Hopkins's latest signals from Moscow, where he had met personally with Marshal Stalin, had given Roosevelt renewed confidence in his own judgment. The President had therefore decided, in his own mind, America's best course of action — but it was not yet something he was willing to share with his chiefs of staff or his cabinet. Nor with Winston Churchill, the political leader of a foreign, fading colonial power.

To the surprise of his military advisers, then, the Commander in Chief had ordered all plans for U.S. military operations against the Azores, the defense of Brazil, as well as possible U.S. occupation of Vichy French territories in the Caribbean (which could be used as German naval bases) to be shelved. Instead, on July 9, 1941, he had formally instructed the secretary of war to draw up, in concert with the navy, a secret military plan or estimate: what exactly it would ultimately require of Congress and the U.S. military in terms of men, money, and machines to win the war against Hitler — and possibly the Japanese — if war came the following year, 1942, or, preferably, in 1943. That report was not due to be completed until September 1941. Thus, as the President set off for his sea summit with Churchill, his purpose was not to declare war on Germany, as the Prime Minister evidently hoped, but to see how war could be *avoided* for the moment.

With the press fooled as to Roosevelt's whereabouts, and his own staff, the cabinet, and even the U.S. chiefs of staff kept deliberately in the dark about the purpose of the powwow with Churchill, the most extraordinary drama now took place. Only the President — who seemed almost absurdly confident — appeared to have any idea what was going on, or of what was intended or likely to happen.

"There is I fear little chance of my getting to Campobello," the President had apologized in a letter to his elderly mother, who was summering at the Roosevelt camping estate off the coast of Newfoundland — but "I am feeling really well & the war is now encouraging to my peace of mind — in spite of the deceits & wiles of the Japs."[21]

To his distant cousin Daisy (an outwardly prim spinster with whom he had formed a quite intimate friendship over the past decade), Roosevelt was more jokey. "Strange thing happened this morning," he wrote her *en voyage* on August 5 — for he, his doctor, and his personal staff, even his beloved little Scottie, Fala, had "suddenly found ourselves transferred with all our baggage & mess crew from the little 'Potomac' to the Great Big Cruiser 'Augusta'! And then, the island of Martha's Vineyard disappeared in the distance, and as we head out into the Atlantic all we can see is our protecting escort, a heavy cruiser and four destroyers. Curiously enough the Potomac still flies my flag & tonight will be seen by thousands as she passes quietly through the Cape Cod Canal, guarded on shore by Secret Service and State Troopers while in fact the Pres. will be about 250 miles away. Even at my ripe old age I feel a thrill in making a get-away — especially from the American press. It is a smooth sea & a lovely day."[22]

The President was, in short, enjoying himself, hugely. Having bypassed Secretary Hull — who did not learn of the trip until Roosevelt was aboard the USS *Augusta*[23] — the President had secretly summoned Hull's undersecretary, Sumner Welles: the handsome professional diplomat, six feet three inches tall, who had attended the same school and college as FDR and had been a page boy at Roosevelt's wedding. Welles was, the President instructed, to travel separately, joining the U.S. team in Newfoundland. In the meantime Welles was ordered to start drafting a declaration of the President's postwar peace aims.

Postwar peace aims?

It was this document, not a putative agreement to enter the war, that the President had determined would make history. Although Roosevelt had, at the last minute, decided to take extra people to the meeting, they would still amount to less than half the number the British were bringing. Churchill had signaled that his party would include twenty-eight officers, military planners, and backup clerks, as well as (unbeknown to the President) two journalists and five photographers. By contrast, the President had limited himself to General Marshall, Admiral Stark, General Arnold, Admiral King, and only a handful of their staff; also his White House doctor, his appointments secretary, and his secret-intelligence officer[24] —

advisers to the President who would, as Roosevelt made clear, be under strict orders to say nothing that would in any way commit the U.S. military, beyond its current Western Hemisphere patrol and military-supply duties under the congressionally authorized Lend-Lease.

In short, any talk of operational military cooperation with the British, let alone an alliance, was *streng verboten,* the President told his military contingent when they finally assembled in his cabin onboard the USS *Augusta,* shortly after their arrival in Placentia Bay on August 7, 1941. They were merely to *listen* to the British.

Marshall, Stark, and Arnold were stunned.

As General Arnold noted in his diary on August 4 aboard the *Tuscaloosa* as it steamed north from New York, where he had boarded, he hadn't even brought enough clothes for the trip. "Thank God there is a laundry aboard. Where are we going? And why? Certainly the crew and the ship's officers do not know. Twice I was about to be informed and twice someone came up and I heard nothing."[25]

When the pioneering airman — the first to fly over the U.S. Capitol, and two-time winner of the Mackay Trophy — was brought by launch to the USS *Augusta,* off Martha's Vineyard, Admiral King, commander of the Atlantic Fleet and the man in charge of the secret expedition, had thrown a fit. "King quite mad because we came aboard his ship and he knew nothing about it. He gave us a look, got mad and went out to cool off prior to our getting in his office," Arnold noted.[26] They did not like each other.

Once King had finally cooled down, however, "Marshall and Stark came in. Marshall told us of our 'Brenner Pass' conference ahead" — a mocking reference to Hitler's earlier meeting with Mussolini to concert Axis strategy, and then his recent meeting at the beginning of June 1941, prior to Operation Barbarossa, the invasion of Russia — an offensive that the Führer had somehow failed to mention in advance to his main ally, lest the Italians leak the date and details! The Anglo-American version, General Arnold now learned from Marshall and Stark, would take place off Newfoundland and begin, General Marshall explained, on Saturday, August 9 — with Arnold ordered to remain on the *Tuscaloosa,* away from Marshall and Stark — lest they form a military triumvirate, as in ancient Rome, and spoil the President's plan.

It seemed a strange way to prepare for modern war, let alone fight one.

But then, unknown to the somewhat "unsophisticated" air force general,[27] or even to Stark and Marshall, that was precisely the President's point.

Churchill's plan, concocted with his chiefs of staff before setting out from Scotland, was very different.

Acting as both British prime minister and minister of defense (a position he had created for himself, thus making himself military as well as political supremo), Churchill had decided in advance that he should first present to the American team his own strategic overview of the current war — and his plans for winning it. This would be followed by carefully drawn-up military proposals in the "Future Strategy Paper," a formal document his chiefs of staff would present to the American team as to how to achieve military victory — with American help.

Such an agenda for the summit had by no means been agreed to by the President, however. In fact, the scheme had not even been communicated to him — leaving the British "war party" somewhat anxious as they rehearsed in advance the ceremony of piping the President aboard the HMS *Prince of Wales* (a ceremony, given the President's disability, requiring a reversal of normal naval procedure: British officers would have to file past and salute the President, rather than vice versa).

"The programme is quite unknown at present," the Prime Minister's military assistant noted in his diary on August 8, 1941. "All that is certain is that the Prime Minister will call on the President and the President will call on the Prime Minister, but whether they will be accompanied by their Chiefs of Staff or whether the Chiefs of Staff will go separately will not be known till we reach harbour and there is an opportunity to consult the wishes of the Americans. . . . The Chiefs of Staff met once during the day, at noon. There is little more they can do now until the meetings start."[28]

Onboard the USS *Augusta*, things were not much clearer.

On August 6, steaming through fog and with its radar malfunctioning, the huge cruiser had put out its antimine paravanes, which "made a lot of noise," the President noted in his diary-style letter to his cousin that afternoon, revealing they were "off Halifax and in the submarine area — Tho' there have been no reports of them in these waters recently." Visibility was good, but Roosevelt had gotten word that morning of a "leak" in London regarding the meeting — though "it seems to be pure guesswork," he told Daisy, unworried. "I went up to the deck above — alone in the bow & the spray came over as it has before."[29]

The President seemed entirely in his element, "smiling and cheerful," as Admiral Stark described him[30] — the former assistant secretary of the U.S. Navy in a previous world war now the nation's commander in chief; commander in chief, moreover, not only of the country's navy, but its army and burgeoning air force too.

Emerging on deck at 11:00 a.m. the next day, August 7, the President was glad he'd overruled Churchill's suggestion that they meet at an alternative British location. Under U.S. management, Argentia was bustling with American activity. "[F]ound several destroyers & patrol planes at this new base of ours," Roosevelt boasted to Daisy, " — one of the eight [bases] I got last August in exchange for the 50 destroyers. It is a really beautiful harbor, high mountains, deep water & fjord-like arms of the sea. Soon after we anchored, in came one of our old battleships accompanied by two destroyers — & on one of the latter F[ranklin] Jr. is asst. navigator — so I have ordered him to act as my Junior Naval Aide while I am here," he confided proudly, referring to his son. The "old battleship" was the World War I–era thirty-thousand-ton dreadnought USS *Arkansas*: three times the size of the *Augusta*, mounting a dozen twelve-inch guns and carrying three floatplanes.

"It was a complete surprise to him & to me to meet thus," the President told Daisy. In fact, loath to show favoritism, the President, who hoped to spend the afternoon fishing and to see how the naval station was progressing, soon summoned his chief of the Army Air Forces, General Arnold, and ordered that his other son, Elliott, an Army Air Corps navigator currently stationed at Gander, "80 miles from here," should "join me as Junior Military Aide. Again, pure luck, but very nice."[31]

The President was fortunate in his fishing sally, too — catching "toad fish, dog fish and halibut," General Arnold noted in his diary.[32] Arnold had earlier upset the President by his reluctance to recommend selling, let alone giving, warplanes to Britain, concerned that it would slow deliveries to his own U.S. Air Corps; in fact, "I felt I was about to lose my job," Arnold later recalled as, "looking directly at me," the President had said "there were places to which officers who did not 'play ball' might be sent — such as Guam."[33] In the end it was only on General Marshall's recommendation that the President had relented, and finally, a few weeks before, had forwarded Arnold's name to Congress for promotion from mere colonel to the rank of permanent major general. Relieved to be back in presidential favor, Arnold dutifully congratulated the President on his angling success.

Arnold possessed one advantage over his colleagues, however: he was the only one to have met — indeed stayed — with Prime Minister Churchill in England, that spring. His personal report to the Commander in Chief at the White House — advocating more airplane production and assistance to the British in countering the continuing German bombing of London and other British cities — had saved his career, which was slated to end that fall, after the usual two-year stint. But though he had genuinely admired the courage of Londoners enduring the Blitz — pounded by upwards of five hundred German bombers each night — the experience of being bombed had only increased Arnold's determination to build up America's own heavy-bomber air force, not dissipate its strength by giving most of U.S. airplane production to the Brits. To his boss, General Marshall, Arnold had therefore said that morning: "We must be prepared to put a [U.S.] force into the war if and when we enter. The people will want action and not excuses. We will be holding the sack. Time then will be just as important to us as it is to the British now."[34]

This was a new, more assertive Hap Arnold, aviator and spokesman for air power. As commander in chief, however, the President was determined not to allow the military to decide American policy, which he was intent on holding strictly in his own hands. The airman was thus summoned a second time that afternoon, to the *Augusta,* at 4:30 p.m. "Sort of heavy seas, almost fell into sea when little boat went down," Arnold recorded, "and gangway to big ship went up." Having spoken to General Marshall, Arnold then filed into Roosevelt's cabin, along with Admiral King, Admiral Stark, General Marshall, General James Burns, Colonel Harvey Bundy, and General Edwin "Pa" Watson, the President's elderly appointments secretary and longtime military aide.

Welcoming the officers for the first time on the trip as a group, the Commander in Chief then made clear that the meeting with Mr. Churchill and his staff was to be informal and informational — i.e., neither strategic nor political. The United States was not, repeat not, at war with Germany, and had no congressional mandate to go to war. Nevertheless, it was the policy of the U.S. government to aid both Britain and Russia in their struggle to deal with the Axis menace in Europe, as it was to aid China in its struggle with the expansionist Empire of Japan. Making sure that military aid was manufactured and successfully delivered to Great Britain, Russia, and

China was the point at issue — *without incurring war.* Indeed, it was the President's purpose to dissuade the Axis powers and Japan from risking war with the United States as the U.S. ramped up military production, by *deterrence:* i.e., showing strength rather than weakness. There was to be no collective summit of the U.S. chiefs of staff with the British chiefs of staff; rather, they would simply meet one-on-one with their counterparts, to find out what the British needed in the way of weaponry and help.

The officers got the message. No politics. And absolutely *no* mention of U.S. military strategy, let alone U.S. entry into the war.

"Discussed: convoys," Arnold noted in his diary, and "defense of convoys: US responsibility for getting [Lend-Lease] cargoes safely delivered . . . [L]ine of [U.S.] responsibility extends east of the Azores and east of Iceland; duties and responsibilities of Navy; what British may want from [U.S.] Navy, ships from Maritime Commission; tanks from Army, airplanes; troops in Iceland, Marines, relief by soldiers; airplanes to Russia; aid to Philippines, B-17s, P-40s, tanks, AA guns." The only nod to future strategy related to the question of Japan, whose government's most secret war plans had been revealed by "Magic," the U.S. Army's Signals Intelligence decryption of the supposedly unbreakable Japanese "Purple" diplomatic code. The United States would, the President stated, "turn deaf ear if Japan goes into Thailand but not if it goes into Dutch East Indies."[35]

In later years, General Marshall would look back at the lack of preparation for the Placentia Bay conference with disbelief. Claiming he "had no knowledge" of the impending discussions with the British "until we were well up the coast on the cruiser *Augusta,*" Marshall had had no time to assemble papers or even files in advance. At the President's firm insistence, he'd found, the rendezvous was to be "largely a get-together for the first time, an opportunity to meet the British chiefs of staff, and to come to some understanding with them as to how they worked and what their principal problems were."[36]

Having given his pep talk, the President meanwhile sent his lieutenants back to their quarters — with no instructions even to meet again the next day.

General Arnold was not the only one to be amazed. With nothing to do on August 8, since Churchill's battleship was delayed by heavy weather in mid-Atlantic, Admiral Stark and Admiral King commandeered a Catalina navy patrol plane and flew up to the Avalon Peninsula, while General Marshall suggested to Arnold that they inspect the growing U.S.-

Canadian air base at Gander Lake, the final staging post for U.S. aircraft being delivered by air to the United Kingdom.[37] As they circled Placentia Bay in their twin-engine Grumman Goose seaplane on their return, they saw that even *more* U.S. vessels and floatplanes had arrived in the harbor. "We now have corvettes, destroyers, destroyer leaders, cruisers, one battleship, two tankers, one aircraft tender, about 18 [four-engined] PBYs and PBYMs," Arnold noted. Moreover, as they disembarked and transferred back to their warships "we saw a large 4-engine flying boat arrive. Where from? The U.S.? What for? Carrying two distinguished passengers? Who?" he recorded the questions running through his and Marshall's minds.[38]

One passenger, they learned, was the undersecretary of state, Sumner Welles. Was the President preparing a diplomatic surprise, then, despite his assurances the previous day? Was he contemplating a more formal alliance with the Prime Minister, who was due to arrive first thing the next morning — even American entry into the war?

It was a measure of General Arnold's naïveté — and the success of the President's insistence on keeping his military team lodged on different vessels, with no orders but to listen to the British war needs once Churchill's party arrived — that the primary U.S. air force general had absolutely no idea what was going on. "I can't make up mind as yet whether most of us are window dressing for the main actors," he would write several days later.[39] For the moment, however, finding "everyone taking a nap" onboard the *Tuscaloosa*, he was completely in the dark.[40]

Sumner Welles, for his part, experienced no such puzzlement. A consummate professional of the "striped pants brigade," the assistant secretary of state was both counselor and confidant to the President — who trusted him more than the secretary of state, Cordell Hull, who, a former congressman and senator, was very much a distinguished political appointee.

To Welles the President had stated, before leaving Washington, that he wanted "some kind of public statement of objectives."[41] It should be, he explained, a draft declaration that would "hold out hope to the enslaved peoples of the world,"[42] based upon his famous "four freedoms" address (of speech and worship; from want and fear).[43] That would be all the President wanted of a concrete, or formal, nature from the conference. Such a peace communiqué would quieten the isolationists at home, and give the Prime Minister something positive to take back to Britain.

It would also serve to mask, the President intended, America's complete military unpreparedness for war.

The fact was, for all the outward show of U.S. naval and air strength to impress the British visitors on their arrival at Placentia Bay, the United States had no army to speak of — at least no army capable of mounting anything other than a minor operation overseas; no air force with the capacity to deter a determined enemy, let alone support its own ground troops; and no navy able to operate effectively in one ocean, let alone in two.[44] As the official historians of the U.S. Army later put it, "the United States Army's offensive combat strength was still close to zero."[45]

Worse still, according to General Marshall, the U.S. Army was now in a "desperate plight" unless the Selective Service Bill, or draft, was extended for a further six months. Its belated preparations for possible war were in imminent danger of being put back "a year and a half or two years," if its current eight hundred thousand draftees were sent home, once the draft lapsed. Letting these trainees go home would result in "the complete destruction of the fabric of the army that we had built up," Marshall told the President — who had meanwhile heard from the Speaker that there were insufficient Democratic votes in the House of Representatives to pass the extension bill; in fact, at the very moment when the President was secretly steaming to Placentia Bay on August 6, the majority leader had reported to the White House that he simply had not enough votes to pass the new bill.[46]

Yet to Welles and to Averell Harriman — the U.S. Lend-Lease administrator who had accompanied the undersecretary of state in the flying boat from the capital — the President looked and sounded refreshed, indeed positively ebullient, during their three-hour talk.[47] "Father looked well, and was obviously enjoying his break in routine," Roosevelt's son Elliott also found when, along with his brother Franklin Jr., he was ushered into the presence of the nation's commander in chief.[48]

Captain Elliott Roosevelt had recently been scouting potential bases for air ferry and delivery routes across the Northern Hemisphere. Like General Arnold, he'd stayed with Churchill at Chequers, the British premier's official country residence, on a visit to England. In Elliott's account, published five years later, the President now rehearsed over lunch with his sons the next day's meeting with the Prime Minister: a meeting that he saw primarily as morale-boosting. "*You* were there," the President said to Elliott. "You saw the people. You've even told me how they look — gray and thin and strained. A meeting like this one will do a world of good for British morale," his father asserted — adding that the British would be concerned over "Lend-Lease schedules" now that Russia, too, would be receiving American military aid. "They'll be worried about how much of our production we're going to divert to the Russians," the President predicted — the British still convinced Hitler was going to win on the Eastern Front. "I know already how much faith the P.M. has in Russia's ability to stay in the war," Roosevelt remarked — snapping his fingers to indicate zilch.[49]

"I take it you have more faith than that?" his son queried.

Roosevelt did — his confidence buoyed after receiving Hopkins's recent cables from Moscow. Although the war on the Eastern Front would help England, it wouldn't save Britain in the long run, the President told his son.

"'The P.M. is coming here tomorrow because — although I doubt that he'll show it — he knows that without America, England can't stay in the war. . . . Of course,' my father went on, 'Churchill's greatest concern is how soon we will be in the war. He knows very well that so long as American effort is confined to production, it will do no more than keep England in. He knows that to mount an offensive, he needs American troops. . . . Watch and see if the P.M. doesn't start off by demanding that we immediately declare war against the Nazis.'"[50]

Elliott, who had been the first of Roosevelt's sons to join the U.S. Armed Forces, would become increasingly ambivalent in the ensuing years about Britain's national interests, and may have been dramatizing the conversation he recalled with his father. However, the gist of it was probably correct, judging by contemporary accounts — especially the President's next assertion: namely that the "British Empire is at stake here."[51]

To his sons, FDR portrayed the British and the Germans as having been engaged in a struggle over trade for decades: a struggle that had turned into a new war between the revived German Empire and the ailing British Empire: a war the United States could not simply exploit out of greed — "what will profit us most greatly," as isolationists such as his former ambassador to London, Joseph P. Kennedy, advocated — since its outcome would affect the very future of the world. This did not mean that the U.S. should favor, let alone save, Britain as a *colonial* empire, however.

The United States had a noble Constitution, deriving from its Declaration of Independence from Britain, which the President was proud to uphold, and which as president he felt bound to embody, as far as was possible, in his foreign policy: that "all men are created equal, that they are endowed by their Creator with certain unalienable Rights, that among these are Life, Liberty and the pursuit of Happiness." This fundamental striving for "Liberty" made the U.S. a natural enemy of Nazism. "Leaving to one side for the moment that Nazism is hateful," he told Elliott, "and that our natural interests, our *hearts,* are with the British," there was, he confided to his son, "another angle. We've got to make clear to the British from the very outset that we don't intend to be simply a good-time Charlie who can be used to help the British Empire out of a tight spot, and then be forgotten forever." Taken aback, Elliott had feigned incomprehension.

"I think I speak as America's President when I say that America won't help England in this war," Roosevelt made clear to his son, "simply so that she will be able to ride roughshod over colonial peoples."[52]

Elliott, five years later, claimed to have been astonished at this revelation. "I think," he recalled telling his father, "I can see there will be a little fur flying here and there in the next few days."[53]

Early next morning, Saturday, August 9, 1942, the grand bout began — heralded by the arrival of the Prime Minister's battleship.

Normally, Churchill rose late, liking to work in bed, dictating to a secretary. This time, however, the Prime Minister was up soon after dawn, standing on the admiral's bridge aboard HMS *Prince of Wales* — "eager and restless as a boy, longing for the first sight of the Stars and Stripes," as one of the two journalists he'd unwisely brought with him recorded. "Just out of bed, his sandy hair still ruffled by the pillow, he stood watching the sea that stretched to the New World. In a few hours ceremony and anthems would begin, but in that quiet opening of the day, like a warrior awakened from his tent, he stood unarmed at dawn, surveying the scene, wondering maybe what the day would bring forth."[54]

Things soon went wrong. The battle-scarred *Prince of Wales* (which had narrowly avoided being sunk by the German battleship *Bismarck* in May) was due to anchor in Placentia Bay at 9:00 a.m. When, preceded by an American destroyer and shadowed by two U.S. flying boats circling above, the ship's company fell in at 8:30 a.m. — marines with fixed bayonets, Mr. Churchill standing in his dark-blue uniform as Lord Warden of the Cinque Ports, and a marine band ready to play — the huge thirty-five-thousand-ton battleship began to tilt and "started turning to starboard," Churchill's military assistant, Colonel Jacob, recorded in his diary that night. To Jacob's surprise, "we found ourselves heading out again."[55]

The two nations were, it appeared, observing different times — the U.S. following Eastern Standard Time, the British observing Newfoundland Time.

"We kicked our heels for an hour and a half," Jacob noted, "and then went through the whole process again," steaming slowly past the anchored vessels of the American armada: the men called to attention as they passed each vessel, until they reached a central body of clear water and the USS *Augusta*.[56]

The British band played "The Star-Spangled Banner," while across the water they heard "God Save the King." "The Prime Minister stood with the Chiefs of Staff and others at the after end of the Quarter Deck," Colonel Jacob noted, "and through our glasses we could see President Roosevelt under an awning just below the Bridge of the 'Augusta.'"[57] Dropping anchor some three hundred yards away, the formalities continued with the piping aboard of Admiral King's chief of staff, stepping up the gangway from a launch. There followed, for Churchill, another wait of one and a half hours before he was invited to board the President's gleaming cruiser.

For his part, the President had slept well, and was almost as excited as Churchill — though for a different reason. "All set for the big day tomorrow," he'd written his cousin the night before. "I wish you could see this scene. By the way," he cautioned, "don't ever give any times or places or names or numbers of ships!"[58]

Anxious not to be blindsided by any misunderstanding, Roosevelt had ordered Harry Hopkins to transfer immediately from the *Prince of Wales* — on which he had sailed with Churchill, following his dramatic air journey to the Kremlin — to the USS *Augusta* after the British battleship anchored. General Arnold, too, was summoned from his quarters on the *Tuscaloosa*. The airman was "received on deck by President, Stark, Marshall, King, Watson, Elliott Roosevelt, and F. Roosevelt, Jr.," as Arnold noted in his diary. "First to appear from below Sumner Welles then A. Harriman; soon a boat from the *Prince of Wales*, Harry Hopkins came aboard."[59]

Hopkins had earlier cabled the President a long report of his tête-à-tête with Stalin in Moscow — telling the President that the Russians were not about to cave in. Now, in person, he was anxious to confirm to the President and the chiefs of staff that he had not been whitewashing the Russian situation, as the U.S. Army chief of staff feared. Contrary to General Marshall's military intelligence reports from Europe—most especially those of the U.S. military attaché in Moscow—there was absolutely no doubt in Hopkins's mind that Hitler's invasion of Russia had by then nowhere near succeeded. "The Russians are confident, claim 2,500 plane output a month without counting 15 training planes a day," Arnold wrote in his diary, impressed. "Stalin claims the Russians have 24,000 tanks."[60]

Twenty-four *thousand?* Marshall was skeptical, since Hopkins was no military expert, yet the President chose to trust his emissary's judgment, at that moment, more than Marshall's—perhaps because it was what he wanted to hear. Hopkins also reported that Stalin had begged him—as had Churchill, in May—to ask the President to enter the conflict and declare war on Germany.

For President Roosevelt, Hopkins's verbal summary on the USS *Augusta* that morning became the keystone he needed in putting into effect the latest plan he'd concocted the day before with Welles and Harriman. If the Soviet Union was to hold out until the following year, when America would be fully armed and ready for combat in Europe, it was in America's best interests—as the President had drummed into his staff at the White House throughout July—to provide as much weaponry and aid as possible to the Russians, rather than giving all foreign aid to Britain, let alone enter the war on Britain's behalf, with all the military responsibilities and commitments this would require. Neither Stalin nor Churchill, ironically, seemed to have any idea how puny were current U.S. armed forces, at least with regard to offensive capacity, outside the continental United States. Moreover, the Selective Service extension bill was hanging by a thread in Washington, and the vast majority of the nation (between 75 and 80 percent, according to polls)[61] remained unwilling to go to war to save Britain's imperial possessions—and even less willing to go to war to save Russia's Communist empire, however much they might distrust Hitler.

Swearing his chiefs of staff once again to silence in terms of U.S. military strategy, the President made clear that he alone, as president and commander in chief, would be in charge of the two-day meeting. There would be no U.S. military "team": only a commander in chief backed by his various army, navy, and air officers as advisers.

• • •

Having cleared the air, the President was helped to his feet by his sons, acting as his equerries, ready to receive the British prime minister and his entourage.

Promptly at 11:00 a.m. on August 10, 1941, the admiral's barge of the HMS *Prince of Wales* approached the USS *Augusta*. As the bullheaded, chubby-faced Prime Minister in his peaked cap mounted the gangway, stepped onto the deck, and walked forward to shake hands with the waiting President, standing upright by the guardrail beside his son Elliott — Mr. Roosevelt a head taller than his British counterpart and dressed in a light-gray Palm Beach suit and hat — the introductory ceremonies came to a climax: the Prime Minister handing over a letter of introduction from his sovereign, King George VI, who had met and stayed with President Roosevelt at Hyde Park two years before.

Ironically, tall Lord Halifax, the man King George VI would have preferred to see as prime minister on the resignation of Neville Chamberlain the year before, was now in Washington, demoted from foreign secretary to British ambassador to the United States. Instead, as the Prime Minister of Great Britain, there stood little Winston Spencer Churchill — short, pudgy, menacing, and pugnacious — who had yearned all his life for the post, and had finally got it. Like most of the world, the King, however, had quickly responded to Churchill's rhetoric, if not his style of decision-making. The King's letter, when the President read it through, was brief but nicely phrased. He was glad, George VI wrote, "that you have an opportunity at last of getting to know my Prime Minister. I am sure you will agree that he is a very remarkable man, and I have no doubt that your meeting will prove of great benefit to our two countries in pursuit of our common goal."[62]

"Our common goal" was delicately put — neither mincing nor presumptuous. "We all met on the top deck and were duly photographed & then Churchill stayed on board & lunched with me alone," the President confided to his cousin afterwards.[63]

The Lion of England was, if not on American soil, then under American custodial protection.

At their private luncheon the President was polite, but noncommittal.

As Roosevelt's aide and speechwriter Robert Sherwood would describe, "If either of them could be called a student of Machiavelli, it was Roosevelt; if either was a bull in a china shop, it was Churchill."[64]

Certainly Churchill was bullish. He began by stating how privileged he felt to meet Mr. Roosevelt at last in person. The President corrected him, however, pointing out that they *had* already met. Did Churchill not remember the occasion? It had been twenty-three years earlier, at a Gray's Inn dinner during World War I, when Churchill was a British cabinet minister and minister of munitions. Roosevelt had been in London on an official visit as assistant U.S. secretary of the navy. Churchill had ignored him.

Strike one to the President.

When Churchill then admitted that, in addition to the twenty-eight members of his military, diplomatic, and scientific staff, he had also brought along two British journalists and a five-man camera crew, in direct contravention of Roosevelt's instructions regarding "no media," the President was understandably irritated. Given his own determined efforts to escape the American press and preserve privacy as well as secrecy, the Prime Minister's faux pas seemed extraordinarily gauche. Churchill quickly assured the President that the journalists would not be permitted to board any U.S. vessel, or to interview the President or any American officers, or to publish any account of the meeting when they returned, at least not until the following year.

Strike two to the President.

This agreed, the President, as host, ran over the agenda for the two days of meetings — making it clear that the get-together was not, repeat not, to be seen as a formal conference of political and military leaders gathering to make war. The President and Prime Minister were meeting merely to *discuss* matters as leaders of their respective countries: the one neutral, the other at war with Germany. Each U.S. chief of staff would be permitted to meet with his British opposite number to learn more of British needs — but with no roundtable discussion or semblance of a formal conference that could in any way be construed by people at home as an alliance. Most important of all, the President announced, he wanted to issue with the Prime Minister a joint declaration of principles, or war aims, in order to inspire the peoples of the "enslaved" countries and others.

For Winston Churchill, the President's easy charm — he began straightway calling him Winston — belied a steely American assurance that was close to arrogance: a projection of intelligent confidence in his own judgment that was hard to dent. The President was like a player holding all the cards — at least the cards that mattered — with little indication that he had any intention of declaring war on anyone.

Understandably, Churchill's heart sank. Hopkins had seen his own role as that of catalyst between "two prima donnas," but was unable to do much to relieve the tension. The summit thus lurched into second gear — Hopkins hoping food and libation might ease the encounter.

To Elliott Roosevelt, who was invited for coffee after the "tête-à-tête" luncheon, the atmosphere seemed little better. He found the two world leaders "politely sparring," as they sat facing each other. "My information, Franklin, is that the temper of the American people is strongly in our favor," Churchill claimed. "That in fact they are ready to join the issue."

"If you are interested in American opinion, I recommend you read the *Congressional Record* every day, Winston," the President retaliated tartly.

"Two ideas were clashing head-on," Elliott recalled: "the P.M. clearly was motivated by one governing thought, that we should declare war on Nazi Germany straightaway; the President was thinking of public opinion, American politics, all the intangibles that lead to action and at once betray it."

Finally, "after draining his glass, the P.M. heaved himself to his feet. It was close to two-thirty." The quasi papal audience was clearly over. "Father mentioned he was sending, on behalf of our Navy, gifts to the officers and men of the *Prince of Wales* and her three escorting destroyers," Elliott recalled. "The P.M. acknowledged this information with a nod and a short word, and left" — leaving Sir Alexander Cadogan, his chief diplomatic civil servant as undersecretary of the Foreign Office, to meet with Undersecretary Welles. They could discuss the President's proposed declaration of principles and other matters — such as the threat from Japan.

Given the prohibition against alcohol being served on U.S. naval vessels, it had been, the diminutive Cadogan wrote in his diary, "a very unsatisfactory, dry, déjeuner à la fourchette"[65] — the Prime Minister so disappointed he had simply gone to bed with a stiff drink, once back onboard the *Prince of Wales*.

The Prime Minister could be forgiven for feeling disappointed, even humiliated.

Surely, he reasoned in his bunk, he had not sailed more than two thousand miles through heavy seas, often without air or sea escort (the ocean had turned too rough for the British destroyers to keep up), simply to be given American *food parcels* for his crew: an orange, two apples, half a pound of cheese, and two hundred cigarettes in each seaman's package? He therefore hoped his second meeting with the President, when dining aboard the *Augusta* that evening, would prove more productive.

Harry Hopkins had sent a personal message over to the *Prince of Wales,* informing the Prime Minister that he had "just talked to the President." Mr. Roosevelt was, Hopkins wrote, "very anxious, after dinner tonight, to invite in the balance of the [U.S.] staff and wants to ask you to talk very informally to them about your general appreciation of the war. . . . I imagine there will be twenty-five people altogether. The President, of course, does not want anything formal about it."[66]

The President had also asked whether, as per their lunch conversation, the Prime Minister would be the one willing to try his hand at a first draft of the declaration of principles, in his inimitable English, so that it could become a true Anglo-American document: not a declaration of war, but a declaration of peace — at least, the peace they were seeking in confronting the Nazi menace, and after.[67]

To his cousin later that day the President described Churchill as "a tremendously vital person & in many ways is an English Mayor La Guardia!" — likening Churchill to the diminutive mayor of New York, an authoritarian, excitable, liberal Republican. "Don't say I said so!" Roosevelt enjoined Daisy, since the comparison was in some ways unflattering.

The President did not mean the description maliciously, however. He had, after all, recently made La Guardia his first director of civilian defense. "I like him," he confided to Daisy his feelings about Churchill, " — and lunching alone broke the ice both ways."[68]

The idea of getting Churchill to write a first draft of the President's declaration of principles was certainly brilliant, though; it would force Churchill to own the project as much as the President did. The stratagem may well have issued from Hopkins's fertile brain and his psychological understanding of the Prime Minister's ego — flattering him by the request for a draft couched in high, stirring English prose, as well as a peroration before the American chiefs of staff that would impress them.

Hopkins, often on the point of death because of the stomach cancer he had suffered,[69] had, after all, heard the Prime Minister give a number of spellbinding *tour d'horizon* talks on his two visits to Britain that year: Churchill's rhetoric full of memorable metaphors and demonstrating a command of history and language, with an Olympian perspective that raised him head and shoulders above any English-speaking contemporary. Moreover, in asking Churchill to produce the first draft of a joint declaration of principles, the President would be putting the Prime Minister on the spot, since Churchill, as supplicant at the American court, could scarcely refuse. Vanity, Hopkins assured the President, would do the rest.

Roosevelt left nothing to chance, however. Dinner aboard the USS *Augusta* comprised hors d'oeuvres, broiled chicken, buttered sweet peas, spinach omelet, candied sweet potatoes, mushroom sauce, current jelly and hot rolls, with tomato salad, then cheese and crackers to follow. After dinner there was conversation — and once again, in talking to Churchill, the President emphasized the need for an articulation of common peace aims, or "joint Anglo-American declaration of principles," as Sir Alec Cadogan noted of the evening.[70]

Churchill was, in truth, incensed by the repeated request; he wanted an American declaration of *war,* not a declaration of principles. As a guest of the President of the United States, however, he could only plead — and plead he was determined to do, with all the words at his command.

The President, however, was as well known for his mastery of defensive as for aggressive tactics. In asking Churchill to speak to the whole American contingent, Roosevelt had felt it better to let the Prime Minister show his hand openly, rather than keep it cached, lest there be even a hint of behind-the-scenes transaction.

To remind the gathering that war in Europe involved more than just a commitment to Great Britain, Roosevelt insisted that Hopkins, who had given the President a typed report of his trip to Moscow that afternoon, first entertain the assembled dignitaries with his eyewitness account of his stay in the Kremlin and his one-on-one interviews with the Russian dictator, Joseph Stalin — the "ghost" at the table, so to speak.

It was the Prime Minister of Great Britain whom the assembled brass really wanted to hear, Roosevelt knew, however — and once Hopkins had spoken and the tables were cleared, Winston S. Churchill, the King's First Minister of Great Britain and Northern Ireland, rose to deliver his "strategic overview."

The longer the evening had progressed, the more Churchill — who had been given special dispensation to drink — had imbibed, and the more loquacious, even lyrical, he had become. The President's military aide, General Watson, afterward admitted, for example, that he had been "curious as to whether he [Churchill] was a drunk." As Churchill finally stood before the roomful of generals, he certainly assumed "a broader stance" than before — whether to steady himself or to marshal his thoughts, General Watson was unsure. Drunk or sober, the effect was remarkable, once he began his speech. "He held the floor that evening and he talked," Elliott described. "Nor were the rest of us silent because we were bored. He held us enthralled even when we were inclined to disagree with him."[71]

Even the President was impressed, according to Elliott. "My experience of him in the past," the younger Roosevelt observed, "had been that he dominated every gathering he was part of; not because he insisted on it so much as that it always seemed his natural due. But not tonight. Tonight Father listened."[72]

Watching Laurence Olivier and Vivian Leigh at the screening of the film *Lady Hamilton* the night before, onboard the *Prince of Wales,* one of the two banished British journalists had seen Churchill actually weep — the sight of which deeply moved the newsman. Olivier was a consummate British actor, but watching Winston Churchill, the journalist had found himself even more affected than by the screen icon. "I thought that in some extraordinary way he belongs definitely to an older England, to the England of the Tudors, a violent swashbuckling England perhaps, but a warm and emotional England too, an England as yet untouched by the hardness of an age of steel," H. V. Morton afterward recalled. Why, Morton asked himself, did both ordinary and extraordinary people find themselves "so firmly held," when Churchill spoke — "so silent until the last word?" He wondered if the enchantment might not lie in the fact that Churchill's voice was "not of an industrialist, but of one who has, so to speak, missed the Industrial Revolution and speaks to us as if from the deck of the *Golden Hind.* Churchill's voice is also classless. . . . Like the Elizabethans, he speaks not as an Etonian but as an Englishman."[73]

Sir Alec Cadogan — who *was* an Etonian, and the son of an earl — was disappointed, having heard his master speak in public so often before, but Morton's was an apt insight, and one that chimed with Roosevelt's growing respect for the Prime Minister. The President was skeptical of Churchill's judgment in terms of military operations against the Germans, which thus far in the war had not produced a single victory on the battlefield. Roosevelt was far from impressed, moreover, by the Prime Minister's choice of subordinates, since the British chiefs on first acquaintance appeared that evening to be a polite, characterless, minion-like group of yes men. Rather, the President's admiration belied a sort of compassion: a recognition by Roosevelt of Churchill's *courage*: his tenacity, in a sea of mediocrity, in trying to make the best of the impossible situation he'd inherited from his mealy-mouthed, appeasement-minded predecessor, Neville Chamberlain — who had definitely *not* impressed the President. And admiration, too, for the Prime Minister's remarkable intellect, amounting almost to genius: his insistent, valiant efforts to place the problems of the world within a wider, historical and moral, framework.

Not only was Churchill's knowledge of history formidable, laced with a seemingly photographic memory for lines of poetry and idiosyncratic detail, but alongside his romantic exaggerations the Prime Minister could be disarmingly honest. Churchill thus admitted, freely, to his military audience — both his own countrymen and his American listeners — that his island nation, the previous summer, had been wholly unprepared for German invasion. "Hitler and his generals were too stupid," the Prime Minister asserted. "They never knew. Or else they never dared." According to Elliott, the subtext of this confession was an appeal for the United States, with all its military power, manpower, and industrial potential, to enter the war — Churchill's underlying message being: "It's your only chance! You've got to come in beside us! If you don't declare war, I say, without waiting for them to strike the first blow, they'll strike it after we've gone under, and the first blow will be their last as well!" Though his American listeners "could detect the underlying appeal," Elliott noted, they could not fail to be moved by the Prime Minister's personal courage and determination never to give in. Churchill's "whole bearing," Elliott Roosevelt recalled, "gave the impression of an indomitable force that would do all right, thank you, even if we didn't heed his warning."[74]

The President, sitting at the head of the table, with the Prime Minister on his right, impressed Alec Cadogan, meanwhile, who was placed on Mr. Roosevelt's left. In his diary that night he noted the President's "great, and natural, charm."[75] Listening to Churchill's studded rhetoric, the President seemed content to remain quiet, save when interrupting to ask about Russia, and how long the Prime Minister thought it would hold out (not long, Churchill answered, once Hitler took Moscow and the Germans reached the Urals, perhaps striking even beyond).

The President chose not to argue. If war came to the United States — and as president he was determined to hold off that evil day — it was as well his chiefs of staff see for themselves who was at the helm of the fading British Empire: not only as England's political leader but as a military strategist and commander in chief.

Britain had now been at war for two long years — and had learned many lessons, Churchill confessed. In contrast to World War I he characterized the struggle as "a mobile war, in the air, on the land, and at sea," a war in which science and mechanical science were playing a crucial role.[76] The British could not, and would not, give up their position in the Middle East; for by fighting the Germans at the farthest point from their bases in Germany, the British Commonwealth forces had the best chance of meeting their adversaries "on even terms."[77] Meanwhile, in the air, with enough bombers manufactured in Britain as well as those purchased or leased from the United States, they could "bring home to the Germans the horrors of war, just as the Germans had brought it home to the British." If the United States would take over full convoy protection across the whole North Atlantic, this would enable the Royal Navy to send destroyers to the South Atlantic; if the U.S. would join Britain in "sending an ultimatum to Japan," it could halt Japanese expansion. And if, in the successful aftermath, a new League of Nations could be set up, then the world could perhaps learn the lessons of Versailles, and start afresh, on a new page of history . . ."[78]

"[N]ot his best," Sir Alec Cadogan noted in his diary,[79] but to the President it was exactly what he had hoped for. No businessman would want to enter a partnership, Roosevelt felt, with such a diffuse, fading imperial power; but by investing in the company, so to speak, he might well help it stave off bankruptcy. Lend-Lease was, in fact, doing that; the next step would be military. But not yet. Not when the United States was, in all truth, still a military mouse, despite its roar.

As Mr. Churchill rehearsed Britain's strategy — to hang on to its collapsing colonial empire in the Middle East, India, Burma, Singapore, Malaya, and Hong Kong, and to harass Hitler's Third Reich from its margins, in the hope that something might turn up, as in the parlance of Mr. Micawber — it was impossible for President Roosevelt and his chiefs of staff not to shake their heads at the Prime Minister's mix of sentiment, myopia, and imagination. And luck! For not only had Hitler *not* invaded Britain when the country was at its most vulnerable, after the Dunkirk evacuation in May 1940, but something else *had* come up. Not an American entry into the war, as Churchill had so ardently wanted, but something in some ways even more fortunate for Britain and for America: Hitler's crazed decision, after failing to bomb the English into submission in the Battle of Britain, to attack Russia.

No one but a Nazi madman could have undertaken such a gamble. Assuming — as the President did, especially after hearing Hopkins's full report — that the Soviets would hold out, even if they had to retreat to the Urals, Hitler's mistake would inevitably mean the survival of Great Britain. Though not necessarily the survival of the British colonial empire, which was, in President Roosevelt's eyes, a different matter.

As he listened and occasionally prompted the Prime Minister to comment on how he saw certain issues — the Russian campaign, the threat of an expanding Japanese Empire in the Far East — the President felt more and more strongly that America's moment of destiny was approaching. Despite the fact that American isolationists were currently fanning public fears and dictating congressional attitudes, the United States was going to have to fight eventually, the President was certain. Secret decrypts made it quite clear that the Japanese were hell-bent on war, just as the Germans had been — and no amount of Chamberlain-style diplomacy, appeasement, or negotiating would placate them.[80] Yet the war that Winston Churchill was seeking — a war that preserved Britain's colonial empire, while smashing Hitler and Hirohito's empires — was not what President Roosevelt saw in America's tea leaves. If and when war came, America must fight for its *own* role in the sun, as leader of a postimperial, democratic world. America would thus become not just the arsenal of democracy, but — as the world's most prosperous nation by far — the senior partner in a new world order, with open borders and open markets.

To Churchill's consternation, then, once the Prime Minister sat down, the President announced that the dinner was over. It was 11:30 — and the President was going to bed. The British visitors were promptly seen off the ship at 11:45, and reaching his cabin onboard the *Prince of Wales,* the Prime Minister, too, retired. He was exhausted by his own peroration, the disappointments of the day — and the President's request that he begin the drafting of a joint declaration of peace aims.

"Considering all the tales of my reactionary, Old World outlook, and the pain this is said to have caused the President," Churchill later wrote, he was proud to say it was he, not the President, who now produced the "first draft" of the declaration of principles that the President had requested, and that it was "a British production cast in my own words."[81]

As David Reynolds, the British historian, later revealed, this was not, strictly speaking, the case.[82] In truth, the next morning, as Sir Alec Cadogan was enjoying his breakfast of "bacon and eggs" in the admiral's cabin, he was summoned by the Prime Minister, who was already up and on deck. "He wanted an immediate draft of the 'joint declaration,' which he outlined verbally." Cadogan then "worked up a text, about which Churchill 'expressed general but not very enthusiastic approval,' but it was typed up virtually unchanged for the Prime Minister to give to the President."[83]

The first draft was, then, a Cadogan production, rather than the Prime Minister's. Moreover, Churchill later misrepresented his own feelings about the very idea of such a document.[84] For what Churchill could not bring himself to admit, when penning his epic account of his war service, in 1949, was that this declaration was emphatically *not* what he had sailed all the way from Scapa Flow to Placentia Bay to obtain. Nor was it what Churchill wanted to subscribe to, as the prime minister of Great Britain and a servant of the British colonial empire. Biting his tongue, however, he approved Cadogan's first iteration of the joint declaration — and turned to Plan B, set for 11:00 a.m. that Sunday morning, August 10, 1941: the arrival of the President of the United States on the *Prince of Wales,* and a rousing church service.

At first the program went without hitch. As the crews of the two great warships prepared for the difficult maneuver, the clouds above Placentia Bay parted, the sun shone, and the shoreline reminded some who were present of the spare beauty of the Western Isles of Scotland.

An American destroyer wedged lengthways between the main deck of the USS *Augusta* and the stern of HMS *Prince of Wales* allowed the President, his small staff, and three hundred American sailors to be piped aboard the British battleship for divine services without transferring to barges. There then followed a ceremony that Churchill had planned and rehearsed in detail with the crew of the *Prince of Wales* and his own staff, right down to the choice of hymns, even before their arrival in Canadian waters.

The President, an Episcopalian, was delighted to participate in the religious ceremony — even sending a presidential invitation to each member of his own staff to attend. Loath to allow Churchill to control the media rendering of the event, however, Roosevelt had wisely sent for his own camera crew — a group of American army film cameramen and still photographers working in Gander, who had been ordered to fly immediately to Argentia by Grumman floatplane. Churchill might want to give the appearance of an alliance, but President Roosevelt was determined that the imagery reflect his joint declaration of principles of peace — and how better than by showing men worshiping God together?

With the Royal Marine Band playing in the background, the President of the United States was "received with 'honors,'" as he wrote his cousin that night, then "inspected the guard and walked aft to the quarter deck" — where, behind desks draped with the Stars and Stripes and Union Jack, he and the Prime Minister faced almost a thousand sailors grouped under the menacing fourteen-inch guns of the after-turret. The Prime Minister wore the dark blue uniform of the Royal Yacht Squadron, the President a blue double-breasted suit, "without a hat. It is a very great effort for the President to walk, and it took him a long time to get from the gangway to his chair, leaning on a stick and linking his arm with that of one of his sons who is acting as his A.D.C.," Churchill's military assistant recorded in his diary that night. "We heard that this was the longest walk that the President had ever taken since his illness many years ago."[85] As the President "slowly approached the assembled company," wrote another British officer, "it was obvious to everybody that he was making a tremendous effort and that he was determined to walk along that deck even if it killed him."[86]

Recorded on film, the service was profoundly affecting to those who took part — as it was to those who saw it on newsreels across America and the free world in the days and weeks afterward. Urged by their captain to "raise steam in an extra boiler so as to give the hymns extra value,"[87] the British sailors — intermingled with their American guests and sharing with them their hymnals — sang "O God, Our Help in Ages Past," "Onward, Christian Soldiers," and — at the President's urging — "Eternal Father, Strong to Save," better known as "For Those in Peril on the Sea." Six months later the huge warship would be attacked and sunk by Japanese planes in the South China Sea, its captain and many hundreds of the crew drowned.

H. V. Morton noticed once again how the Prime Minister's "handkerchief stole from its pocket" — for it was almost impossible not to be touched by emotion. "A British & an American chaplain did the prayers," the President himself described to Daisy.[88] With their caps off, "it was difficult," Morton later recalled, "to say who was American and who was British; and the sound of their voices rising together in the hymn was carried far out over the sea. In the long, frightful panorama of this War, a panorama of guns and tanks crushing the life out of men, of women and children weeping and of homes blasted into rubble by bombs, there had been no scene like this." It was, he wrote, "a scene, it seemed, from another world, conceived on lines different from anything known to the pageant-masters of the Axis."[89]

Aboard the *Prince of Wales,* as the divine service ended, the President seemed wonderfully confident. "Captain Leach read the lesson — and then we were all photographed — front, sides & rear!" he described to Daisy. "Next I inspected the P. of W. in my [wheel]chair, then sherry in the Ward Room & then a 'beautiful' lunch of about 40 — Toasts followed by two speeches."[90]

Churchill had certainly ordered nothing but the best for his guests, given the dire situation in an England suffering grave food shortages and universal rationing. The menu for the President and his entourage featured smoked salmon, caviar, turtle soup, freshly shot roast Scottish grouse, dessert, coffee, wines and liqueurs, with mood music played by the Royal Marine Band. In addition to the formal toasts to the King and to the President, there was even a risqué joke by Hopkins and welcome news that the German battleship *Tirpitz* had been espied in the dockyard at Kiel, meaning it would not have time to put to sea and prey upon the Prime Minister on his return voyage.

Afterward the President was introduced to the Prime Minister's junior staff. To the chagrin of the British chiefs of staff, however, that was it. As Churchill's military aide lamented, "it had been the intention that the Chiefs of Staff should have a short meeting with the American Chiefs of Staff at which to hand over the Future Strategy Paper. However, this went by the board as Admiral Stark and General Marshall decided to go back to their ships with the President."[91]

The luncheon, intended as the prelude to joint military discussions, had been for naught — the President determined not to be snared by Churchill into a position that isolationists back in the U.S. could interpret as having even the semblance of an alliance.

Once aboard the USS *Augusta* the President then held "a military & naval conference in my cabin"[92] — adamant to ensure that no hint of a military alliance was being suggested, or any whisper of U.S. "war plans" being given to emissaries of a foreign country. His chiefs of staff still seemed bewildered by his tactics, but were too loyal to protest.

Despite the President's ban on joint discussions among the chiefs, however, it was impossible to stop junior staff officers from confiding in one another. At a junior meeting with Colonel Harvey Bundy, General Marshall's director of plans, for example, Colonel Jacob, Churchill's military assistant, learned to his consternation just how different were British and American ideas for conducting the war against Germany.

Some weeks previously, it appeared, the President had ordered a secret new review to be drawn up — later called the Victory Plan — of what
the U.S. Army and Navy Departments would deem necessary in a war to
defeat the Third Reich. A preliminary report had been presented to the
President before he'd left Washington, and Colonel Bundy now unwisely
shared the gist of it with his counterpart — who was both amazed and
disbelieving. "The Americans are busy trying to draw up a scheme of
the forces which they would ultimately raise, and the possible theatres in
which they might be utilised. They are tentatively aiming at an Army of 4
million men."

Colonel Jacob was shocked. *Four million men?* "We did our best to
point out to Bundy that this was possibly a wasteful use of manpower
and manufacturing capacity; it hardly seemed conceivable that large scale
land fighting could take place on the Continent of America, and shipping
limitations would make it quite impossible for large forces to be transferred quickly to other theatres."[93]

Colonel Charles Lindbergh, one of the leaders of the America First
isolationist movement, would have been appalled to know that such secret discussions regarding possible American "intervention" in "other
theaters" were being aired; he would have been even more appalled to
discover the sheer magnitude of the army the U.S. military was proposing
in order to win the war against Germany. Colonel Jacob certainly was —
for the American notion of defeating Hitler was almost diametrically opposed to that of the British.

"The day has been almost entirely wasted from the point of view of
joint discussion," Jacob lamented in his diary. "We have been here two
days and have not yet succeeded in getting the opposite sets of Chiefs of
Staff together round a table," he recorded in frustration — unaware that
this was happening on the President's specific orders. "We have thus given
away the strength of our position, which lies in the fact that our three
Chiefs of Staff present a unified front of the strategical questions, while it
is quite clear that theirs do not. We have played into their hands by allowing the discussions to proceed in separate compartments."[94]

The President's stratagem worked magnificently — the British were
unable to present their "Future Strategy Paper," while their U.S. hosts remained wholly uncommitted either to enter the war, or to follow "unified" British strategic military policy: a policy that assumed there would
be no major ground forces landed on the continent of Europe, and that

Hitler could merely be forced into submission by peripheral harassment and aerial bombing — if only the United States provided enough bombers. (The RAF's request, Arnold learned from his opposite number, Air Vice Marshal Freeman, was for ten thousand heavy bombers — the entire output of the U.S.)[95]

As Colonel Jacob rued immediately after the conference, "neither the American Navy nor the Army go much on the heavy bomber" — the mainstay of Britain's only plan to defeat Hitler. Neither the U.S. Navy nor Army "seems to realize the value of a really heavy and sustained aerial offensive on Germany."[96]

Given that England had itself successfully survived the world's most sustained bomber offensive in human history — the Blitz — for an entire year, the notion that Nazi Germany could be defeated by the same tactics in reverse seemed nonsensical to General Marshall and Admiral Stark, the U.S. Army and Navy chiefs of staff — indeed, even to General Arnold, who *did* believe in an important role for heavy bombers in modern war.[97] Yes, heavy bombers could savage an enemy's manufacturing and supply chain to its armies. Even Arnold could not visualize, however, the war against Hitler being *won* by bombers . . .

Thanks to the President's injunction against a formal meeting between the two nations' joint chiefs of staff, however, the difference between British and American military strategy in conducting a full-scale war against Nazi Germany could, at least, safely be deferred.

Thus, when finally the British chiefs of staff managed to present their hollow-sounding "Future Strategy Paper" on Monday, August 11, the day the *Prince of Wales* was supposed to depart, all the U.S. chiefs of staff would say was that they would study the paper "with interest," and respond later.[98] For the only matter the President was determined to nail down was his declaration of principles.

Once the Cadogan draft of the declaration was handed over to the American team, Sumner Welles and the President took over.

Together with Harry Hopkins, Welles was perhaps the President's most trusted senior adviser. He "looks exactly as if he had stepped out of a film," Jacob felt — the sort of film in which Welles would probably be playing "a business lawyer."[99]

The comparison was apposite, for Welles was indeed acting the business lawyer in world politics. In the quiet of the President's cabin, he and

Roosevelt got down to the business of war and peace: pens poised as they went over the preliminary draft of what would become the Atlantic Charter.

"I am very doubtful about the utility of attempts to plan the peace before we have won the war," the Prime Minister had confided his fundamental unwillingness to his foreign secretary, Anthony Eden, in May 1941[100] — but given that it was what the President requested, Churchill had not dared refuse. In its contorted language the first draft reflected the Prime Minister's reluctance to draw up a charter at all, and his attempt to twist it, if he could, into a declaration of war. The preamble had thus opened by claiming that the U.S. president and the British prime minister were meeting at Placentia "to concert and resolve the means of providing for the safety of their respective countries in face of Nazi and German aggression . . ."

This, clearly, suggested an alliance — which was the last thing the President wanted American isolationists to infer. With Sumner Welles at his side, Roosevelt went through the document with the utmost care, taking out anything that could provide free ammunition to his opponents in America — isolationists waiting all too keenly to pounce on the President for any sign he had entered into an unconstitutional agreement with Great Britain and its colonial empire. By evening the American draft two was ready to be given to Churchill — who had gone ashore for a couple of hours to clear his head, but was due to come over to the USS *Augusta* at 7:00 p.m.

The previous night "Churchill had talked without interruption, except for questions," Elliott Roosevelt recalled[101] — the Prime Minister "talking, talking, talking," as irascible Admiral King put it.[102] "Tonight," however, as the Prime Minister arrived for his informal, private dinner with the President in the admiral's cabin of the *Augusta*, "there were other men's thoughts being tossed into the kettle, and the kettle correspondingly began to bubble up and — once or twice — nearly over. You sensed that two men accustomed to leadership had sparred, had felt each other out, and were now readying themselves for outright challenge, each of the other."[103]

The first bone of contention was the British Empire: its restrictive trade agreements, and its colonialism. "Of course," the President opened his attack, "of course, after the war, one of the preconditions of any lasting peace will have to be the greatest possible freedom of trade." Churchill countered by pointing out Britain had long-established trade agreements with its Dominions and colonies. "Yes. Those Empire trade agreements are a case in point," the President agreed.

"It's because of them that the people of India and Africa, of all the colonial Near East and Far East, are still as backward as they are."

Churchill's face, according to Elliott Roosevelt's account, went red with fury. "Mr. President, England does not propose for a moment to lose its favored position among the British Dominions. The trade that has made England great shall continue, and under conditions prescribed by England's ministers."[104]

The President's challenge had been met by Churchill—Roosevelt acknowledging "there is likely to be some disagreement between you, Winston, and me. I am firmly of the belief that if we are to arrive at a stable peace it must involve the development of backward countries. Backward peoples. How can this be done? It can't be done, obviously, by eighteenth-century methods."

Churchill, according to Elliott, became even more furious. "Who's talking eighteenth-century methods?" he snapped.

"Whichever of your ministers recommends a policy which takes wealth in raw materials out of a colonial country, but which returns nothing to the people of that country in consideration," the President explained patiently. "*Twentieth*-century methods involve bringing industry to these colonies. *Twentieth*-century methods include increasing the wealth of a people by increasing their standard of living, by educating them, by bringing them sanitation—by making sure that they get a return for the raw wealth of their community."[105]

At the mention of India, Churchill became, Elliott described, "apoplectic." "Yes," the President had added blithely, ignoring Churchill's rage as he piled accusation upon accusation. "I can't believe that we can fight a war against fascist slavery, and at the same time not work to free people all over the world from a backward colonial policy."[106]

Backward colonial policy? This then was the battle royal the Placentia Bay meeting had built up to, and though Churchill—"a real old Tory, isn't he? A real old Tory, of the old school," Roosevelt described his opponent to Elliott afterward[107]—would give no quarter, the President knew he'd made his point, and had the upper hand, "& now I'm ready for bed after dining Winston Churchill, his civilian aides & mine," the President finished his account of the day's doings for Daisy.[108]

Churchill, by contrast, went to bed with the aching realization that, despite all his oratory, the President of the United States was even *less* likely to enter into an alliance with Great Britain than when the Prime Minister had set sail from Scapa Flow.

The third day, Monday, August 11, 1941, the sparring continued.

"A day of very poor weather but good talks," the President wrote. "My staff came at 12, lunched, & we worked over joint statement. They went and Churchill returned at 6:30 & we had a delightful dinner of five: H. Hopkins, Elliott, F. Jr., Churchill & myself."[109]

Roosevelt was clearly delighted — getting what he wanted by his usual mixture of presidential charm, dogged insistence, occasional compromise, and sincere American hospitality. All day, fresh versions of the declaration of principles sped between the two warships — the President cutting out any implications of military or political alliance, the Prime Minister refusing to relent on "imperial preferences" in postwar trade agreements, and threatening to delay the declaration a further week while he submitted it to the governments of the British Dominions if the President insisted upon that article.

Feeling magnanimous, Roosevelt gave way. The core of his demand had gone unchallenged, after all: that the British government and the U.S. president sought "no territorial" or other "aggrandizement," in fact no "territorial changes that do not accord with the freely expressed wishes of the people concerned." The text of the declaration specifically committed the signatories to "respect the right of all peoples to choose the form of government under which they will live": a postwar peace aim that guaranteed an eventual end to the British colonial system — indeed caused British colonial administrators across the globe to shudder when they read the terms of the Atlantic Charter in the weeks that followed.

In the meantime, however, the President was ecstatic. He had got what he wanted — and not given Churchill what he so dearly hoped for.

For his part, the Prime Minister was resigned to defeat. It was disappointing, but the summit had at least brought the two men together. At dinner on Monday evening harmony finally reigned. "We talked about everything except the war!" the President related to his cousin, "& Churchill said it was the nicest evening he had had!"[110]

At some deeper level, Churchill was well aware the British Empire was doomed as a colonial enterprise, though he prayed the crumbling of the once-proud imperial edifice that had controlled a quarter of the world would not happen on his watch. Elliott Roosevelt afterward claimed that, at the summit, he saw "very gradually, and very quietly, the mantle of leadership was slipping from British shoulders to American." He had seen it vividly when, the night before, Churchill got to his feet and "brandished a stubby forefinger under Father's nose. 'Mr. President,'" he had cried, "'I believe you are trying to do away with the British Empire. Every idea you entertain about the structure of the postwar world demonstrates it. But in spite of that' — and his forefinger waved — 'in spite of that, we know that you constitute our only hope. And' — his voice sank dramatically — '*you* know that *we* know it. *You* know that *we* know that without America, the Empire won't stand.'"[111]

In sending the final, revised draft of the declaration of principles to the war cabinet in London by secret cipher on the evening of August 11, 1941, Churchill felt ashamed of what he had been forced to concede. With trepidation he therefore went to bed, wondering what the cabinet's response would be.

"Am I going to like it?" he asked his private secretary, "rather like a small boy about to take medicine," Colonel Jacob noted in his diary, when the response eventually came in.[112]

The British cabinet *did* — mercifully for the President.

In actuality, Roosevelt's hand was much weaker than Winston Churchill had realized. Not only was the United States in no position to wage war on anyone, at that time, but the President's political position was a great deal less powerful than the Prime Minister knew. Reports of a secret meeting with the leader of a belligerent nation were bound to arouse isolationist ire across America — making American intervention in the war even less likely. News of a joint declaration of principles, by contrast, would not.[113] In this sense the President had played a masterly hand.

"W.S.C. to lunch," the President wrote to Daisy the next day, "with Lord Beaverbrook [Churchill's minister of munitions], who landed by plane this A.M. at Gander Lake from Scotland." Churchill had brought with him "approval of statement by his cabinet & King — & after a few minor changes we gave final OKs & drew up the letter to Stalin, & arranged for release dates," the President chronicled.[114]

The Atlantic Charter, as it was swiftly called, was a historic document: a declaration in the great tradition of the American Bill of Rights, guaranteeing the rights of all nations — *including British colonies* — to self-determination, not conquest by rule of force. If the United States were to go to war, it would this time be for a noble cause.

"They left at 3:30, their whole staff having come to say goodbye — It was a very moving scene as they received full honors going over the side," back to their battle-scarred battleship, the President described to Daisy.[115] Then, at 5:00 p.m. that evening, August 12, 1941, after "great activity" getting the battleship ready to weigh anchor, the ill-fated HMS *Prince of Wales* steamed out of Placentia Bay with salutes given as it passed the ships of the U.S. flotilla — strains of the Royal Marine Band still playing as it headed across the still water.[116]

In Placentia Bay, meanwhile, the President breathed a sigh of relief. "At 5 p.m. sharp the P. of W. passed out of the harbor, past all our ships," he described the scene to his cousin. On his desk was the Atlantic Charter. "Ten minutes later we too stood out of the harbor with our escort, homeward bound. So end these four days that I feel have contributed to things we hold dear."[117]

PART TWO

Pearl Harbor

2

The U.S. Is Attacked!

PEARL HARBOR DAY BEGAN quietly. We were expecting quite a large party for luncheon," Eleanor Roosevelt later recalled, "and I was disappointed but not surprised when Franklin sent word a short time before lunch that he did not see how he could possibly join us."[1]

This was not unusual; the President and First Lady led somewhat separate lives. They lived together upstairs at the White House, but on opposite sides of the Central Hall. Their marriage, since FDR's affair with Eleanor's secretary and then his affliction with polio in 1921, had become one of duty, parenthood, and convenience — though they did respect one another, in the manner of English aristocrats. Eleanor acknowledged that in the White House the President "had been increasingly worried for some time and frequently at the last moment would tell me that he could not come to some large gathering that had been arranged. People naturally wanted to listen to what he had to say," she allowed, "but the fact that he carried so many secrets in his head made it necessary for him to watch everything he said, which in itself was exhausting."[2]

Mrs. Roosevelt's explanation seemed, in retrospect, a trifle jejune — yet was closer to the mark on December 7, 1941, than even she, as First Lady, recognized. A veritable army of conspiracy theorists in subsequent decades would come to suspect the Commander in Chief of having received secret warning of the Japanese attack on Pearl Harbor via American, or even British, intelligence — and of having withheld it in order to embroil the United States in war, against the will of the American people.[3] These were grave, posthumous charges — and they rested on undeniable truths. Had not the President received, late on the evening of December 6, 1941, decrypts of a top-secret Japanese signal from Tokyo to its imperial ambassador in Washington, suggesting that "peace" negotiations over U.S.-

Japanese problems in Southeast Asia — where Japan had seized control of southern China and also Indochina — were coming to an end? Had not Roosevelt remarked to his White House assistant, Harry Hopkins, within the hearing of the young officer delivering the decrypt to the President, that "this means war"? Had not the President immediately sought to telephone the chief of naval operations (CNO) of the United States, to discuss that secret intelligence? And had not the President said that "it certainly looked as though the Japanese were terminating negotiations"?

More tellingly still, had not the final fourteenth paragraph of the secret Japanese signal, decoded by American cryptographers early the next morning, been delivered to the President at 9:00 a.m. on Sunday, December 7, 1941, as he lay in bed having his breakfast, in the room next to his study? Had not the secretary of state, Mr. Cordell Hull, received the very same decrypt that morning, along with Mr. Henry Stimson and Mr. Frank Knox, the U.S. secretaries of war and of the navy, meeting together at the Munitions Building on the Mall? And had not Mr. Hull said to his colleagues he was "very certain that the Japs are planning some deviltry"[4] — for even as they read over the fourteenth paragraph of the formal diplomatic "note" that the Japanese ambassadors were being ordered to deliver, had not *further* decrypts been delivered by special messenger? Had not this Japanese cable from Tokyo instructed the ambassadors to present the formal government message, ending all efforts at diplomacy, to the "United States government (if possible to the secretary of state) at 1 p.m. on the 7th, your time"? Why that specific day and hour? Was not mention of an exact moment — lunchtime on a Sunday in Washington, D.C., but dawn of December 8 in the Philippines, and 6:30 a.m. in Hawaii — enough to ring a very loud bell in the minds of the top Roosevelt administration officials? And had not the very last decrypted postscript added a final instruction, to immediately destroy all secret documents and codebooks at the Japanese Embassy, which was then to shut down?

What more warning did the government of the United States *require,* for heaven's sakes? Why had decrypts of Purple communications by the U.S. Magic team (so called for their almost miraculous monitoring and deciphering of Japanese diplomatic radio signals) been denied to the naval and army-air commanders in chief in Hawaii? Why, in sum, had the President and his staff not *warned* the many thousands of brave U.S. servicemen — in the navy, the army, the air corps — who were to lose their lives a few hours later?

It *had,* surely, to be a conspiracy, or so the army of conspiracy theorists would say. After all, how could the Japanese Imperial Navy's First Air Fleet (a veritable armada of modern aircraft carriers — no less than six in number — and two battleships, three cruisers, nine destroyers, as well as eight fueling tankers and twenty-three submarines, totaling almost three dozen vessels) leave Hitokappu Bay in Japan and make its way across thirty-five hundred miles of the Pacific without U.S. detection? Surely the defense forces of the United States could not *all* have been asleep — especially when there was ample intelligence warning beforehand?

The reality of "Pearl Harbor day" — the longest and worst day of President Roosevelt's life — was somewhat different.

On receiving a Magic decrypt of the "pilot" message and the first thirteen parts of the alarming but mysterious Japanese Purple signal being sent from the Japanese foreign minister, Mr. Shigenori Togo, to Ambassador Kichisaburo Nomura in Washington, D.C., at 10:00 p.m. on the night of December 6, 1941, the President had indeed tried to call Admiral Harold "Betty" Stark, his CNO, at Stark's residence at the Naval Observatory in Georgetown.

The admiral, the President was told, was out at the theater with his wife, attending a performance of Romberg's popular operetta *The Student Prince* — famed for its rousing "Drinking Song." It was thus only at 11:30 p.m. that the President had finally spoken to Betty, once the admiral had returned home and had had time himself to read the still-incomplete message. They had agreed, on the telephone, that the news the Japanese were ending peace negotiations looked bleak for America — the two men speculating on what would be contained in the final part of the communiqué, yet to come. A declaration of war with Britain and the Netherlands, whose oil fields the Japanese military were eyeing with impatient, predatory interest, now that the United States had cut off American oil exports following the Japanese invasion of Indochina earlier that summer? Or war, even, with the United States — beginning with an invasion of the Philippines?

Over the past months the President had, as commander in chief, overridden the advice of Admiral Stark and deliberately augmented the U.S. fleet based at Pearl Harbor, at the very center of the Pacific. He had stationed another U.S. fleet at Manila, and — against the reluctance of General Marshall, the U.S. Army chief of staff — had ordered reinforcements of the most modern U.S. warplanes, ammunition, and troops to be sent out urgently to the Philippines as a deterrent against further Japanese predations in Southeast Asia.

Clearly, as the latest decrypts of Japanese diplomatic signals and cumulative American secret intelligence reports were indicating, the President's policy of deterrence had not worked. In fact the very opposite seemed to be the consequence. Like belated British and French rearmament in 1939, America's end of appeasement and its more muscular approach toward Japanese military conquest in Southeast Asia appeared to be producing the contrary effect to the one intended: convincing the leaders of the Japanese militocracy that further "peace" negotiations with the Americans, posing as the guardians of tranquility in the Far East in order to get their way, were pointless. Only a preemptive Japanese attack, similar to Hitler's assault on the West on May 10, 1940, could hope to defeat the United States before it reinforced its Far Eastern bases even further.

Japanese militarists were not mistaken in fearing belated American rearmament. The simple fact was: given the output of the U.S. economy — which was estimated to be more than five times that of Japan — America could only get more powerful. A flight of thirteen of the latest long-range, almost indestructible B-17 Flying Fortress bombers and reconnaissance airplanes, for example, was that day taking off from San Francisco, bound for the Philippines, on the President's orders. And a ship convoy carrying some twenty thousand U.S. troops and military equipment for the Philippines was due to leave San Francisco on December 8, on the President's instructions. The United States was waking up after its long slumber in the Orient.

Rather than continue diplomatic negotiations and allow a more powerful U.S. presence to be built in the Pacific, the Japanese were going to go to war — this was the incontrovertible conclusion of the initial decrypt. The first thirteen paragraphs of the intended Japanese note were dark and disappointing to the President and to his chief of naval operations, Admiral Stark. How much more potent would U.S. forces in the Pacific and Far East become as a deterrent, if only negotiations between the Japanese and U.S. governments could be dragged out still longer, they agreed. Yet the Japanese were not fools. They had done the sums — indeed, for weeks now American intelligence had tracked a vast fleet of warships and military troop transports assembling in Shanghai, then putting to sea. Clearly they were readying to invade somewhere in Southeast Asia, once they terminated negotiations.

Increasingly fatalistic, the President had composed a final appeal for "peace" to Emperor Hirohito. Despite the objection of his secretary of war, Roosevelt had dispatched it in a special personal telegram that was to be delivered by the U.S. ambassador in Tokyo on the evening of December 6 (December 7 in Japan) — a message the President had phrased with great care, so that if leaked or afterward published, it could be appreciated by all as a plea for peace, not war.[5]

In the cable, the President of the United States had assured the Emperor of Japan that the U.S. had no thought of "invading Indo-China" if the Japanese, as the U.S. requested, withdrew its occupation troops. Nervousness about Japanese intentions was understandably rife across Southeast Asia, Roosevelt had pointed out. "None of the peoples" of the Philippines, the East Indies, Malaya, and Thailand could be expected to "sit indefinitely or permanently on a keg of dynamite," he'd written. "I address myself to your Majesty . . . so that Your Majesty may, as I am doing, give thought in this indefinite emergency to ways of dispelling the dark clouds. I am confident that both of us, for the sake of the peoples not only of our own great countries but for the sake of humanity in neighboring territories, have a sacred duty to restore traditional amity and prevent further death and destruction."[6]

It was futile, of course. Unknown to the President, the Japanese foreign minister, Mr. Togo, did not even allow the U.S. ambassador, Joseph Grew, to take the cablegram to the Emperor's palace, lest it upset Japanese war operations already in train.

Togo's reasoning was straightforward: as commander in chief of Japan's Imperial Armed Forces, His Highness Emperor Hirohito had already been informed of Japanese invasion plans, and on December 3 had not only signed off on multipronged amphibious landings all across Southeast Asia — assaulting Malaya, Singapore, the Dutch East Indies, and the Philippines — but a top-secret sneak attack on the main military base of the United States at Pearl Harbor in Hawaii.[7] As one Pearl Harbor historian would later note, "attempting to stop Operation Hawaii at this point would have been rather like commanding Niagara Falls to flow uphill."[8] All was set; once the senior Japanese naval commander, Admiral Yamamoto, obtained the signed imperial order to proceed, his chief of staff noted smugly that, at the very moment when the Japanese ambassador would be performing his appointed tasks in Washington, pretending to be continuing negotiations as part of the Japanese plot or charade, "the biggest hand will be at their throat in four days to come."[9]

Admiral Yamamoto's chief of staff was not exaggerating. The surprise left hook at the American jugular at Pearl Harbor was designed not to win the war overnight, but to administer a savage first shock, ensuring that the Americans could not interfere with massive Japanese invasion forces about to strike across the whole of Southeast Asia, far to the north. The presence of *those* assault troopships could not be — and were not intended to be — concealed. Eight Japanese cruisers, thirty-five transport ships, and twenty destroyers had been observed and reported by the British Admiralty moving toward Kra on December 6, indicating an impending invasion of Singapore, Malaya, or Indonesia (Dutch East Indies) — or all three. And possibly the Philippines, too.

The President had thus gone to bed at the White House, after midnight on December 6, with foreboding. He slept fitfully. Then, at 9:00 a.m. on the morning of December 7, he received from a U.S. naval intelligence courier, Lieutenant Schulz, the top-secret Magic decrypt containing the missing fourteenth paragraph of the Japanese government's official "response" to Secretary Hull's American message of November 26. Hull's message had urged the Empire of Japan to unequivocally cease and desist in its military occupation of southern China and Indochina, in order that U.S.-Japanese relations could be put back upon a peaceful course. The final Japanese paragraph ended, the President noted, with bleak and ominous words. Since "efforts towards the establishment of peace through the creation of a New [Japanese] Order in Asia" had failed over the preceding weeks, the ambassadors were to inform the U.S. government, "it is impossible to reach an agreement through further negotiations."

So this was it. The decrypt was pretty much what the President had expected — it "looked as though the Japs are going to sever negotiations, break off negotiations" he remarked to his naval aide, Captain Beardall[10] — but it did not specifically indicate hostilities would result, or when or where they would take place. Hostilities, nevertheless, were clearly coming — the fleet of Japanese warships and transports openly poised to strike at British and Dutch territories in Southeast Asia, and perhaps the Philippines. Reading the first part of the Japanese message the night before, the President's assistant, Harry Hopkins, had remarked: "since war was undoubtedly going to come at the convenience of the Japanese it was too bad that we could not strike the first blow and prevent any sort of surprise."[11]

"No, we can't do that," the President had retorted. "We are a democracy and a peaceful people"[12] — even if his cabinet, disappointed by continuous American appeasement of the Japanese military government, and sickened by reports of Japanese atrocities in the countries they had over-run, favored preemptive war. Roosevelt had overridden their advice — repeating the well-known story of President Lincoln, when he polled his own cabinet members on whether to go ahead with the Emancipation Proclamation. As the cabinet members all said no, Lincoln had summa-rized: "Seven nays and one aye, the ayes have it"!

Asking, in the same vein, if they thought the country would back him if the United States were to attack the Japanese Navy preemptively, Roos-evelt's own cabinet members had voted unanimously yes. "The Nays have it," Roosevelt had concluded the cabinet meeting — refusing to go down the preemptive route.[13]

Despite mounting evidence of further Japanese aggression being pre-pared, then, the President had simply refused to budge. Not only did isolationists hold the whip hand in Congress and across the nation, he had reminded Hopkins, but preemptive military attack was not in Amer-ica's historical, moral vocabulary. Raising his voice, he'd claimed that the United States' policy of nonaggression — of only responding if and when itself attacked — had over the centuries been to America's advantage; "we have a good record," he'd summed up[14] — despite his anxiety.

The latest decrypt, however, was not the end of communications from Tokyo to its embassy in Washington, the President soon learned. A few minutes after 10:00 a.m. a courier arrived with *more* decrypts. These included instructions to deliver the entire fourteen-part message to the State Department that day at one o'clock, Washington time, *precisely*. The concluding part of the message thanked the dual Japanese ambassadors, Admiral Nomura and Mr. Kurusu, for their patient and devoted service to the Emperor — and ordered them to destroy, after reading the message, the cipher machine, all codes, and all secret documents remaining at the embassy.

It was clear to President Roosevelt, as he read this, that Japan was going to war not simply with Britain and the Dutch, but with the United States also — and that war could start any time after 1:00 p.m.

Understandably, then, the President forswore lunch with his wife and her thirty guests downstairs at the White House. After speaking on the tele-phone with his civilian war council — Secretaries Hull, Knox, and Simp-son, who had seen the same decrypts, messengered to them at their meet-ing in the Munitions Building on the Mall — Roosevelt resigned himself to his doctor's painful treatment of his sinus problem. "The damp weather, though mild that day, had made his sinus bad, which necessitated daily treatment of his nose," Eleanor recalled. "I always worried about this constant treatment for I felt that while it might help temporarily, in the long run it must cause irritation."[15]

On the Magic decrypt delivery list, beginning with the President and the civilian secretaries of state, war, and the navy, there followed the names of the chiefs of staff of the U.S. Army and Navy—though not the Air Corps (recently renamed the United States Army Air Forces), as befitted its still-lowly status in the nation's armed forces. The response of the chiefs of staff to the latest information, however, proved, in the light of history, as poor as that of their civilian masters. General Marshall, for reasons that remain unclear, later claimed not even to have received the decrypt of the first part of the Japanese note the night before; thus, when the missing fourteenth paragraph, followed by the instructions to the Japanese ambassadors about the 1:00 p.m. presentation and subsequent shutdown of the embassy, was hand-delivered to Marshall at his official residence at Fort Myer, the general was out riding and couldn't be contacted. Only at 11:15 a.m. did General Marshall, once alerted, reach his office at the Munitions Building on the Mall. Since he had not seen the earlier, thirteen-part decrypt, it took him a further twenty-five minutes to read and digest the whole message—leading up to its ominous climax regarding destruction of codes, and time of delivery of the Japanese government note.

Finally, at 11:40 a.m., the penny dropped. When General Marshall called Admiral Stark in his office at the Navy Department building next door, the admiral—who was under the mistaken impression there was a Magic decrypting office in Hawaii[16]—did not feel more Washington alerts than had already been sent would help naval commanders in the Philippines, Panama, Hawaii, and the West Coast.[17]

Stark's deputy must have questioned the wisdom of this, however, for Admiral Stark soon called back, and on second thought agreed to add his imprimatur to a cable General Marshall had drafted[18]—even though it threatened to reveal, if the Japanese intercepted the signal, Magic's breaking of the Japanese secret code. Certainly neither officer dared use the "scrambler" telephone to contact the overseas commanders.[19]

"The Japanese are presenting at 1 P.M. Eastern Standard Time, today, what amounts to an ultimatum," Marshall's cable disclosed to the recipient field commanders at midday—a presentation that was now only an hour away. "Also they are under orders to destroy their code machine immediately. Just what significance the hour set may have we do not know, but be on the alert accordingly."[20]

In the meantime, the Japanese ambassador, one of his aides at the embassy later recalled, "peeked into the office where the typing was being done, hurrying the men."[21] It was no use, however; they simply could not get the fourteen-part official note ready in time for 1:00 p.m. presentation to the U.S. State Department. The Japanese government's whole scheme — to hand over the official note only twenty minutes before the arrival of their warplanes over America's moored Pacific Fleet in Battleship Row in Pearl Harbor, Hawaii, thus leaving the Americans virtually no time to defend themselves — would be ruined.

Flustered, Ambassador Nomura telephoned Secretary Hull's office a few minutes after the 1:00 p.m. deadline, asking for a brief extension of the audience he had requested, to 1:45 p.m.[22] This the secretary of state, knowing what was in the note but not knowing what specific "deviltry" it portended, granted, after calling the President.

A guest at an official dinner the previous night, Mrs. Charles Hamlin, had noticed that Mr. Roosevelt "looked very worn . . . and after the meat course he was excused and wheeled away. He had an extremely stern expression."[23] Given the incoming decrypts and approaching winds of war, this was understandable. But the following morning the President's physician, Admiral McIntire, did not think the President unduly stressed, given the circumstances — indeed it was one of Franklin Roosevelt's most attractive traits, he reflected, that the President seldom showed irritation, though his humor could be sharp. He certainly took his medicine — the clearing of his nostrils and sinus ducts — like a man. He seemed more resigned than tense as he waited for news from Secretary Hull of Ambassador Nomura's visit.

Roosevelt had reason to be resigned, rather than nervous. He had spent the last several years as president trying to preserve America's stature as a neutral nation in a world of dictators and competing military empires — while holding off a phalanx of isolationists at home, headed by Senator Burton K. Wheeler and Colonel Lindbergh, opposed to anything but defense of the homeland. Like an expert juggler, Roosevelt had managed this feat without committing the United States to war — a destructive social behavior he had come to despise since his experience in World

War I, when he was still young and at the height of his physical and mental energies.

Roosevelt's character in the intervening years had certainly changed; as president he had become more opaque and manipulative, yet more compassionate, too. He rather liked Admiral Nomura, whom he'd known during the last war; despite the Magic decrypts he was reading, the President remained certain the ambassador, like the Emperor, was now but a pawn of the militarists in the Japanese government, headed by Admiral Hideki Tojo. Fortunately for the United States, the President felt sure, America was not only more economically powerful than Japan, but cleverer, too. The Magic decrypts were giving the U.S. a huge advantage, making it possible not only to read the mind of the Japanese militocracy, but their diplomatic instructions, several hours before they were read by the intended recipients. By steadying the hand of gung-ho American interventionists at home — including most members of his cabinet — and sending strict instructions to commanders in the Pacific and Far East not to provoke any kind of incident that could lead the Japanese to declare war as a response ("If hostilities cannot repeat cannot be avoided, the United States desires that Japan commit the first act," Admiral Stark had signaled in a war-warning to his fleet commanders on November 28),[24] the President had, it seemed, forced the Japanese government to make the first military move. In that way — the same way in which he had forced Winston Churchill to agree to the Atlantic Charter in August, before there could be any question of a U.S. alliance with Britain — America would be in the right, morally speaking, if war came.

So confident was the President in holding to this position of *moral* superiority that when the Chinese ambassador came to see him, as scheduled, in his study at 12:30 that day, Roosevelt had shown him the text of his personal appeal to Emperor Hirohito, dispatched the previous evening. "I got him there; that was a fine, telling phrase," FDR congratulated himself on his language. (The Chinese ambassador, Hu Shih, had a PhD in philosophy, and was an expert on linguistics, being credited with developing a Chinese vernacular.) "That will be fine for the record," he'd added, knowing he'd done everything possible to avoid war, short of appeasement.[25]

For the record? Responding to Dr. Shih's curious look, the President had explained: "If I do not hear from the Mikado by Monday evening, that is, Tuesday morning in Tokyo, I plan to publish my letter to the Mikado with my own comments. There is only one thing that can save the situation and avoid war, and that is for the Mikado to exercise his prerog-ative" — and cancel Japan's war preparations. "If he does not," the President went on, "there is no averting war. I think that something nasty will develop in Burma, or the Dutch East Indies, or possibly even in the Philippines." Referring to the impending visit of the Japanese ambassadors to the State Department, he remarked: "Now these fellows are rushing to get an answer to Secretary Hull's most recent notes; in fact, I have just been told that those fellows have asked for an appointment to see Secretary Hull this noon. They have something very nasty under way."[26]

The President was thus still thinking as a president — not as a commander in chief. His meeting with the Chinese ambassador ended after forty minutes, at 1:10 p.m.

Hearing from Secretary Hull that the Japanese ambassadorial visit had been delayed for almost an hour, the President then summoned Harry Hopkins, his adviser, and the two men ate a sandwich at his desk in the Oval Study on the second floor of the private residence of the White House, looking out over the National Mall, the Washington Monument, and the Lincoln Memorial.

According to Hopkins's account, written later that evening, the two men talked of "things far removed from war."[27]

Half an hour passed. The telephone rang. The President picked it up himself, expecting it to be Mr. Hull at the State Department, announcing the delayed arrival of the Japanese ambassadors.

It wasn't.

It was Mr. Frank Knox, the secretary of the navy, phoning from his office in the Navy Department on the Mall.[28] He was there with the chief of naval operations, Admiral Stark, and Stark's chief of war plans, Rear Admiral Turner. They had urgent news. The Navy Department in California had just monitored an emergency radio message being broadcast in Honolulu: "Air raid Pearl Harbor. This is no drill."[29]

Pearl Harbor?

Harry Hopkins questioned the veracity of the telephoned report. Not because he disbelieved news of a Japanese attack, but because he found it difficult to believe — despite the decoding of the Japanese note — that the Japanese would be so stupid as to target a primary American territory, instead of starting with the invasion of British and Dutch colonial possessions in Southeast Asia, as Washington expected.

That scenario — attacks by the Japanese on Burma, Singapore, Siam,

Malaya, the Dutch East Indies, without going to war with the United States — had been the President's constant dilemma over the past four months. For the plain political reality in America was: if the Japanese were clever, and attacked only British and Dutch territories in the Far East, Congress could not be counted on to declare war on Japan — leaving the Japanese to "pick off" any country it wished in Southeast Asia, much as Hitler had done in Europe.

It now seemed clear that it had been Japan's intention to attack the United States straight away, judging by the Magic decrypts of their communications to their ambassadors that morning. But Pearl Harbor, thousands of miles from Malaya and the Philippines? Would the Japanese dare strike at America's primary military and naval base in the Pacific, with ample U.S. fighter planes covering the islands, and bombers able to attack approaching Japanese warships from multiple Hawaiian airfields? Surely, Hopkins argued, it must be a mistake.

Pearl Harbor, Hopkins pointed out to the President, was *six thousand miles* away from the Japanese invasion fleet that the U.S. military was currently tracking off Cambodia Point. Not only was Hawaii an American island archipelago, but the impregnable headquarters — army, naval, and air — of the powerful U.S. Pacific Fleet: a fleet of aircraft carriers, battleships, cruisers, destroyers, and submarines, dominating the entire Central Pacific, together with U.S. bombers, patrol planes, fighter aircraft, radar! It seemed ridiculous. And yet . . .

Hopkins noted Roosevelt's pained expression.

Roosevelt had sailed almost since he could walk; had been assistant secretary of the United States Navy for nearly eight years, from 1913 to 1920. He had devoured the works of America's greatest naval strategist, Rear Admiral Alfred Thayer Mahan. Though he had never served as a commissioned officer, Roosevelt knew the navy forwards and backwards — in fact, he felt so committed to it that he had even asked to leave his post as assistant secretary and be permitted to join the service as an ordinary seaman in 1918, as the United States turned the tide of World War I in Europe. To his chagrin the U.S. Navy had by then — thanks in part to him — half a million sailors in its ranks, and had not needed a father of five, aged thirty-six — however able a seaman.

Assistant Navy Secretary Franklin D. Roosevelt's aggressive spirit and sheer energy had nevertheless become legendary in President Wilson's administration — his driving enthusiasm leading, among other achievements, to the laying of an innovative two-hundred-mile-long mine barrier in 1918, all the way from Scotland to Norway across the North Sea, to inhibit German submarines from getting into the Atlantic (or back if they succeeded).[30] Moreover, he was still so much a navy man that his army chief of staff once asked if, as president, he would mind not referring to the navy as "us" and the army as "they."[31]

More to the point: President Roosevelt had himself visited Hawaii in the summer of 1934, in his second year in the White House, aboard the new heavy cruiser USS *Houston*. There he'd been greeted by a crowd of some sixty thousand residents. He'd toured both Big Island and Oahu — the first U.S. president ever to do so. He'd witnessed a military review by some fifteen thousand U.S. troops — the largest ever on the islands. No less than a hundred army and navy planes had performed a fly-past — forming the letters "FR" in the sky. Joseph Poindexter (since 1934 the governor of the territory) had wined and dined Roosevelt at Washington Place, in Honolulu. "Concerning Hawaii as the American outpost of the Pacific," a reporter at the *Honolulu Star Bulletin* had written, "the president is anxious to confer with the heads of the military units first hand to determine for himself the defense needs here. His visit may later lead to an increase in the size of the army and navy posts. As the time approaches for the release [independence] of the Philippines, the president desires full preparedness information regarding the bulwark in the Pacific."[32]

Departing from the Hawaiian Islands, the President had congratulated "the efficiency and fine spirit of the Army and Navy forces of which I am Commander-In-Chief." These American forces constituted "an integral part of our national defense, and I stress the word 'defense.' They must ever be considered an instrument of continuing peace," he'd emphasized, "for our Nation's policy seeks peace and does not look to imperialistic aims."[33]

Little had changed, from President Roosevelt's point of view, in the intervening seven years. Except that America's "bulwark" in the Pacific had increasingly become a thorn in Japan's side — not least because the British and Dutch, as well as Australia and New Zealand, so utterly depended on American naval and air power in the Pacific as a deterrent to Japanese expansion. Should the Japanese seek to redefine their war in Asia, Pearl Harbor would doubtless offer a tempting target — much as Russia's Port Arthur had done in the run-up to the Russo-Japanese War of 1904–5. Then, too, the Japanese had launched a preemptive, sneak attack to trap the enemy's most powerful battleships in a seemingly inviolable harbor, before war was even declared, and to destroy it in situ. Ironically, the name of the defending admiral, in 1904, had been Stark . . .

Looking at Hopkins, the President now shook his head. Harry "the Hop" Hopkins might be skeptical, but the President felt in his very bones the news was right; it was Hopkins who was wrong. An air raid on Pearl Harbor it could well be — the Fort Sumter of World War II.

Belatedly, all *too* belatedly, in the early afternoon of Sunday, December 7, 1941, the pieces of the puzzle began to come together in Roosevelt's mind: in particular, the whereabouts of the fleet of Japanese aircraft carriers that had left port in Japan on November 26, and which had thereafter kept radio silence — a fleet whose whereabouts were currently unknown to American military and naval intelligence.

The President's immediate intuition, as well as his naval experience, thus told him what Hopkins, his closest civilian adviser, could not credit.

No, the President contradicted Hopkins. This was "just the kind of unexpected thing the Japanese would do."[34] A warrior nation defined by its history and culture, the Japanese had no qualms or reticence on moral grounds. If they were to embrace world war rather than a negotiated settlement, would it not make sense for them to strike preemptively at the very heart of America's Pacific defense?

What exactly President Franklin Roosevelt should *do* was unclear, however — just as Joseph Stalin had been unsure, on the morning of June 22, 1941, how to react when unconfirmed reports reached the Kremlin that Hitler's vast 180-division army had attacked Russia across the German frontier, aiming for Leningrad and Moscow.

Stalin had done nothing. In fact, in his suspicious wisdom, the Russian leader had rejected President Roosevelt's repeated warnings of impending German invasion in the long weeks prior to the Nazi invasion, dismissing them as an attempt by the capitalist Western nations to sow discord between the two signatories to the Hitler-Stalin Pact, who'd promised not to attack one another. Stalin had refused to credit first reports of the invasion. (It was even said he'd ordered his men to literally shoot the messenger, a German deserter.) And this barely five months before . . .

President Roosevelt's own case was different — yet bore uncomfortable similarities. It was true that the President, in contrast to Stalin, had heeded all intelligence warnings he'd gotten via Magic decrypts; it was true that, on his specific authority, all U.S. forces in the Pacific, the Philippines, and the Far East, including Hawaii, had been on war alert since November 27. But there were other aspects of the story that were more tellingly similar — such as the matter of supposed deterrence.

Fearing Nazi attack, despite the nonaggression pact he'd signed with Hitler in 1939, Stalin had accelerated Soviet arms production as he became more concerned about the Führer's intentions. In fact Stalin had even invited German officers to inspect Russian Ilyushin aircraft and manufacturing plants in Moscow, Rybinsk, Perm, and other cities as far as the Urals, to convince the Germans that they would be making a big mistake in attacking the Soviet Union — Artem Mikoyan (brother of the foreign minister) warning the Germans they had been "shown everything we have and are capable of. Anyone attacking us will be smashed by us."[35] Stalin had, meanwhile, bent over backwards not to give Hitler a casus belli — instructing Russian forces on the border with the Third Reich not to do anything provocative. Like Roosevelt, Stalin had even rejected the notion of a preemptive attack on Hitler's massing armies in Poland.[36] Worse still, four days before the German attack, Stalin had turned down General Georgy Zhukov's request for an official order that would put Russian forces on the border on full alert. "Do you want a war as you are not sufficiently decorated or your rank is not high enough?" Stalin had ridiculed the request. "It's all Timoshenko's work. He ought to be shot," Stalin had remarked to his Politburo colleagues — dismissing the Russian defense minister's protest that the Soviet Union's forces, in the pursuit of deterrence, were now neither prepared to attack nor to defend. "Timoshenko is a fine man, with a big head," Stalin had mocked his adviser, "but apparently a small brain" — illustrating how small by showing his own thumb. "Germany on her own will never fight Russia," he'd declared in one of the greatest mispredictions of the twentieth century. After he'd walked out of the meeting, he "stuck his pock-marked face" back around the door and in a loud voice sneered: "If you're going to provoke the Germans on the frontier by moving troops there without our permission, then heads will roll, mark my words."[37]

President Roosevelt was nowhere near as coarse as his Russian counterpart — yet the fact was, his "deterrent" posturing had proved just as vain as Stalin's. By compelling the Japanese to fire the first shot, yet refusing to allow U.S. forces to take preemptive action — indeed almost *inviting* a "midnight" Japanese attack by forbidding anything that could be construed as a hostile or threatening act in the Pacific and North Pacific —

had not the President, like Russia's leader, doomed his forces to receive the first blow?

How big a blow was it, though? More reports of the air attack on Pearl Harbor came in over succeeding minutes. They seemed genuine — indicating the start of hostilities, rather than a feint to draw American attention away from the South China Sea.

Still the Japanese ambassadors failed to arrive at the State Department, however. What did *that* mean?

Mr. Hull, the secretary of state, wished to cancel the meeting with Admiral Nomura altogether, he told the President by phone at 2:00 p.m., but at 2:05 the President ordered Hull to "receive their reply formally and coolly and bow them out"[38] — i.e., pretend he did not already know the details of the message they were bringing him, or that Pearl Harbor had already been bombed. That way, Japanese perfidy — continuing the ritual of negotiation, while embarking on a sneak attack — would be all the more unmistakable, once the President announced it.

The secretary of state assured the President he would do so. Yet far from quietly receiving the Japanese ambassadors, Hull lambasted them when they finally entered his office, at 2:20 p.m. "In all my fifty years of public life," he told Admiral Nomura and his assistant ambassador, Saburo Kurusu — who were made to remain standing while the secretary read through their fourteen-point note, in English — "I have never seen a document that was more crowded with infamous falsehoods and distortions — infamous falsehoods and distortions on a scale so huge that I never imagined until today that any Government on this planet was capable of uttering them."[39]

If the secretary of state hoped thereby to shame Admiral Nomura and Mr. Kurusu in their oriental treachery, however, it was to prove short-lived schadenfreude — for Pearl Harbor was under devastating Japanese air and undersea attack as they spoke. In fact, at 2:00 p.m. the President had anxiously called his secretary of war, Henry Stimson, who'd gone home to his mansion outside Washington for lunch. "Have you heard the news?" Roosevelt had asked. Incredibly, the secretary had still heard nothing. "They have attacked Hawaii," the President told him. "They are now bombing Hawaii!"

"Well that was an excitement indeed," Stimson jotted in his diary.[40] Excitement soon turned to horror, however. Less than half an hour later, according to Hopkins's memorandum that night, Admiral Stark, the CNO, called the President from his office at the Navy Department on the Mall. Not only could he officially confirm the aerial assault on Pearl Harbor, Hopkins recorded, but he had grave news. He stated, in Hopkins's words, "that it was a very severe attack and that some damage had already been done to the fleet and that there was some loss of life."[41]

"Some" damage to the fleet? "Some" loss of life?

Giving permission to Admiral Stark to execute War Plan 46 — effectively authorizing U.S. forces to begin unrestricted submarine and naval war in the Far East and in the Pacific — the President immediately called his press secretary, Steve Early, at his home. "The Japanese have attacked Pearl Harbor from the air," the President told him, "and all naval and military activities on the island of Oahu, the principal American base in the Hawaiian Islands. You had better tell the press right away." He added (erroneously at this point) that "a second air-attack is reported on Manila air and naval bases." Then he asked, almost innocently: "Have *you* any news?"

Early's response was almost comical: "None to compare with what you have just given me, sir."[42] The press secretary immediately called the three main U.S. press agencies (AP, UP, and INS) via the White House telephone switchboard, and gave them, at 2:22 p.m., the President's first statement: "The Japs have attacked Pearl Harbor, all military activities on Oahu Island. A second air-attack is reported on Manila air and naval bases."[43]

In actuality, Manila itself had still not been attacked — but a second wave of bombers had descended on Pearl Harbor, and the island's Hickam and Wheeler airfields, a full hour after the first assault. Newly developed shallow-water torpedoes had been used, with devastating results against almost no defensive action. As Admiral Stark reported, it was like a massacre of the innocents.

The conference of advisers that had been planned for 3:00 p.m. at the White House to discuss the President's dilemma — whether, and how, to appeal to Congress for action, if Japan went ahead with an invasion of British or Dutch territories — was now redundant, as the President clarified, once his war council — or quasi war-cabinet, now — assembled in his office: Secretaries Hull, Knox, and Stimson, as well as General Marshall. (Admiral Stark remained at the Navy Department, communicating with Hawaii. General Arnold was at the time in California — unreachable, it was explained, as he was out shooting grouse!)

America was now effectively at war, even if war had not been declared — as the President acknowledged shortly after 3:00 p.m., when taking a call from the U.S. ambassador in England, John Winant. Winant was staying with Winston Churchill at the British prime minister's official country residence, Chequers, together with Lend-Lease administrator Averell Harriman; they had just heard an announcement of the Japanese attack at the end of the nine o'clock BBC evening news.

Like Hopkins, Winston Churchill, suffering one of his periodic bouts of depression, had first failed to believe the news. "He didn't have much to say throughout dinner and was immersed in his thoughts, with his head in his hands part of the time," Harriman afterward recalled — the Prime Minister showing no sign of having understood when the BBC newscaster, Alvar Lidell, referred to reports of an air raid on Pearl Harbor.[44] Churchill's security chief, Commander Tommy Thompson, was equally at a loss, imagining the announcer had said "Pearl River" — wherever that was! Shocked to the core, Harriman and Winant, as Americans, had understood exactly the name of the location the BBC announcer had mentioned — yet as guests of the Prime Minister, they were unwilling to contradict Commander Thompson. It was only when the butler, Sawyers, entered, as in an Edwardian play, that the news was taken seriously. "It's quite true," the butler confirmed, "we heard it ourselves outside [i.e., in the servants' quarters]."[45]

Winant later recalled how the dinner guests looked at each other "incredulously. Then Churchill jumped to his feet and started for the door with the announcement, 'We shall declare war on Japan.' There is nothing half-hearted or unpositive about Churchill," Winant wrote, " — certainly not when he is on the move. Without ceremony I too left the table and followed him out of the room. 'Good God,' I said, 'you can't declare war on a radio announcement.'"[46]

Instead, Winant suggested that he himself should telephone the President to seek confirmation, which he promptly did — offering his sympathies, when told by the President that there had been significant loss of life, and ships sunk. He then passed the phone to Mr. Churchill, telling the President he would recognize the speaker by his voice.

"Mr. President, what's this about Japan?" asked Churchill.

"It's quite true," the President confirmed. "They have attacked us at Pearl Harbor. We are all in the same boat now."[47]

To the President, Mr. Churchill now announced that he wished to declare war immediately on Japan, as he'd told Winant. The President demurred.

They must take things calmly, Roosevelt declared, step by step. He himself would ask Congress for a declaration of war against Japan, the next morning. Churchill promised he would then ask Parliament for a similar declaration, which would "follow the President's within the hour."

Aware in part that he should not burden the President with more at this moment, Churchill rang off. His own mood, however, had shifted from depression to exultation. More than two years into the war, Britain was no longer alone! The United States would now protect British interests in the Far East, as well as safeguarding the sea-lanes to Australia and New Zealand!

All week the President had squirmed and struggled to avoid the Prime Minister's appeals for a mutual commitment to go to war with Japan, if Japan attacked only British and Dutch territories. Now, however, the United States would be at war, and of its own volition: the world's largest economy, untouched as yet by hostilities, bombing, or even blackouts. Even Churchill's two American guests, not knowing the extent of the disaster suffered at Pearl Harbor, seemed "exalted," Churchill later wrote, " — in fact they almost danced for joy," he claimed.[48]

In Washington, the atmosphere among the war council members in the President's Oval Study was very different, however. It was, as yet, "not too tense," Hopkins summarized later that night,[49] since the true extent of the destruction and casualties suffered at Pearl Harbor was, at 3:00 p.m., still unknown. All present agreed that hostilities had been bound to come to the United States sooner or later, and that this way the President, given his unwillingness to "fire the first shot," would be exonerated in the court of public opinion, as well as history.

As the minutes ticked by, however — with fresh reports arriving of the damage inflicted by the second Japanese air attack on Pearl Harbor — the mood in the White House became less confident. It was clear this was not going to turn into an American victory, or even a brave performance in defense of the nation's main Pacific base. Calls "kept coming in, indicating more and more damage to the fleet. The President handled the calls personally," Hopkins noted, "on the telephone with whoever was giving the dispatches. Most of them came through the Navy."[50]

The meeting soon broke up, as General Marshall wanted to return to his headquarters in the Munitions Building — saying he had already ordered General MacArthur to execute "all the necessary movement required in event of an outbreak of hostilities with Japan," including a U.S. air attack on Japanese installations on Taiwan.[51]

Grace Tully, the President's secretary, had meantime arrived from her apartment on Connecticut Avenue; she recalled there was such "noise and confusion" and so many "calls on a telephone in the second floor hall" that she herself moved into the President's bedroom, next to the Oval Study, and took them down in shorthand, then typed them for the President in a tiny office room next door. "The news was shattering," she recalled. "I hope I shall never again experience the anguish and near hysteria of that afternoon" — "each report more terrible than the last, and I could hear the shocked unbelief in Admiral Stark's voice as he talked to me. . . . The Boss [Roosevelt] maintained greater outward calm than anybody else but there was rage in his very calmness. With each new message he shook his head grimly and tightened the expression of his mouth."[52]

There was good reason. Word from the U.S. Army Air Corps in Hawaii was just as terrible as from the Navy — its planes blitzed on the ground, before they had even been able to take off.

It was clear the U.S. Armed Forces at Pearl Harbor — forces the President had himself inspected seven years before as commander in chief, and which he had much reinforced since then — had been caught with their pants down.

As ever more humiliating news came through from Hawaii, President Roosevelt felt something of the same disbelief, even guilt, that had paralyzed Stalin the previous June, following the German invasion of Russia. With shock and near panic gripping those around him in the White House, however, the President did not dare show his feelings.

At the White House there was certainly embarrassment, even shame, at the ever-bleaker news coming from Hawaii — with inevitable questions arising as to how far the President was himself responsible for the catastrophe. Had he not insisted, against the advice of his war council, upon pursuing a meandering course of initial appeasement of Japan, followed by belated military posturing in pursuit of supposed deterrence and moral high grounding — all carried out in spite of intelligence decrypts pointing to hardening Japanese attitudes and, finally, ominous signs of imminent Japanese hostilities? Overruling his team, had not the President refused to order a preemptive American attack on Japanese forces clearly massing for a new invasion in Southeast Asia? Moreover, had he not discouraged the British from carrying out such a preemptive attack on the Japanese fleet approaching Singapore, when they were in a good position to do so?

Given Roosevelt's character, and his absolute authority over the members of his cabinet, there was, however, no call for the President's resignation — something that had never taken place in American history. Nor, to judge by FDR's demeanor, did the President feel he should resign. He looked grave, but far from despair. In any event, there was simply no one who could take his place as chief executive — certainly not his vice president, Henry Wallace, the former secretary of agriculture.

Given the President's role as commander in chief, though, how was it possible that the President's *military* team had not foreseen such a sneak attack, over the months of increasing tension between Japan and the United States? How had the eventuality of an attack on Pearl Harbor not been taken seriously by Generals Marshall and Arnold and Admiral Stark?

Roosevelt had personally chosen and appointed them, as his professional chiefs of the U.S. Army, Army Air Forces, and Navy. Ironically, each one *had* considered the possibility, in the past, of such a sneak attack, and each had attempted, in his own feeble way, to guard against it. "Thinking out loud, should not Hawaii have some big bombers?" General Marshall had asked his operations and planning officers in the summer of 1940, more than a year before the Pearl Harbor debacle. "It is possible that opponents in the Pacific would be four fifths of the way to Hawaii before we knew they had moved. Would five or ten flying fortresses at Hawaii alter this picture?"[53] For his part, Admiral Stark had written to Admiral Husband Kimmel, commander in chief of the Pacific Fleet, as recently as November 25, 1941, to say the Japanese naval forces were at sea and capable of a "surprise aggressive movement in any direction."[54] And General Arnold, on an inspection of air defenses in Hawaii as far back as September 1939, had noted the lack of a supreme commander to ensure integration of air, navy, and army forces on the islands, as well as the vulnerability of battleships moored in Pearl Harbor to aerial attack — as he'd openly remarked in a press conference on the West Coast.[55] Moreover, on his visit to Britain during the Blitz in the spring of 1941 Arnold had been expressly shown (as he'd noted carefully in his diary) the way British aircraft were always kept *dispersed* on their airfields, to minimize damage from surprise attacks. Yet none of the U.S. chiefs had actually visited Pearl Harbor since then. Nor had they asked to see integrated plans or evidence of *rehearsals* for the defense of Hawaii if attacked by naval aircraft, launched from enemy flattops or carriers.

Pearl Harbor had, in sum, been considered inviolable: a vital way station in ferrying aircraft to defend the Philippines, and a platform to service the Pacific Fleet, but too far from Japan to be attacked itself, save by submarines, which could not get past the harbor boom, and would not be able to launch their torpedoes in such shallow water unseen, if they did — a fact that explained Admiral Kimmel's failure to reverse his predecessor's decision not to have antitorpedo nets lowered around his battleships. Thus, in their loyal concern to carry out the President's policy of deterrence in the Far East by building up forces in the Philippines primarily for show, backed by the might of the Pacific Fleet at Hawaii, but with no intention of using such forces aggressively, the chiefs of staff had arguably failed their commander in chief and their country.

Whoever was to blame for Pearl Harbor's unpreparedness for a sneak attack, the question now was what, as U.S. commander in chief, President Roosevelt could *do* about it.

Tragically, the Hawaiian Air Force — as the USAAF group in the islands was called — appeared to have been caught unarmed, literally: the planes' gun breaches empty, and the aircraft standing huddled on the nearby airfields, wingtip to wingtip, to guard against possible sabotage by some of the 150,000 Japanese immigrants and Japanese American citizens living in the islands — a third of the entire population. As a result, the U.S. airplanes were effectively wiped out by Japanese attack planes and bombers, while not a single significant American warship survived the attack in Battleship Row without major damage — four of the eight battleships moored there being sunk. Moreover, there was still the possibility that the news from Hawaii would get even worse, if the Japanese mystery fleet were to catch the rest of Admiral Kimmel's remaining Pacific Fleet warships out at sea, where his two aircraft carriers were returning from weekend maneuvers and nearing home. "Within the first hour," Grace Tully later confessed, "it was evident that the Navy was dangerously crippled, that the Army and Air Force were not fully prepared to guarantee safety from further shattering setbacks in the Pacific. It was easy to speculate that a Jap invasion force might be following their air strike at Hawaii — or that the West Coast might be marked for similar assault."[56]

Speculation mixed fact and fantasy. A telephone call by the President to Governor Poindexter in Honolulu was interrupted by the sounds of planes and antiaircraft fire in the background, suggesting a third Japanese air raid and causing the President to bark aloud to the people in his office: "My God, there's another wave of Jap planes over Hawaii right this minute."[57] American gunners were, unfortunately, mistakenly firing at the few surviving U.S. planes that attempted to take off, either to seek combat or search for the invaders.

However exaggerated such alarums and panic, the stream of incoming reports, taken collectively, gave a growing indication that a veritable catastrophe had taken place in Hawaii: the destruction of virtually the entire American fleet moored at Pearl Harbor, as well as most of the U.S. Army Air Forces' planes.

At times the President felt such disappointment with his chiefs of staff he would readily have fired them. (In contrast to the chief of the decrypting department at the Navy Security Section, Commander Laurance Safford, who wanted to get his gun and "shoot Stark" for the admiral's failure to warn Manila and Hawaii more urgently, given the early decrypting of the Japanese diplomatic note.)[58]

With whom could the President replace his chiefs of staff, though? Almost everything General Marshall, Admiral Stark, and General Arnold had done, or not done, to prepare America for combat in the Pacific and Far East had failed — miserably. But Secretaries Stimson and Knox — both of them Republicans — had not done much better. "Knox, whose Navy had suffered the worst damage, and Stimson were cross-examined closely on what had happened," Grace Tully recalled, "on what might happen next and on what they could do to repair to some degree the disaster."[59] To which they responded: nothing.

Finally, in the "hysteria" at the White House, the President managed to collect his thoughts and focus on the address he would have to give to Congress the next day, requesting an official U.S. declaration of war on Japan. "Shortly before 5:00 o'clock the Boss called me to his study. He was alone, seated before his desk on which were two or three neat piles of information of the past two hours. The telephone was close by his hand," Ms. Tully later described. "He was wearing a gray sack jacket and was lighting a cigarette as I entered the room. He took a deep drag and addressed me calmly."[60]

Hundreds were already gathering in the dusk beyond the White House gates — incredulous at the news being put out by radio stations. Some were singing patriotic songs. Others held candles, in prayer.

"Sit down, Grace. I'm going before Congress tomorrow. I'd like to dictate my message," the President said. "It will be short."[61]

It was short: barely 390 words. "Yesterday December 7, 1941," he began, "a day which will live in world history, the United States was simultaneously and deliberately attacked by naval and air forces of the Empire of Japan . . ."[62]

"As soon as I transcribed it, the President called Hull back to the White House," and the two men "went over the draft," Ms. Tully remembered.[63]

Hull was now seventy years old, and easily unnerved or irritated. With his white hair and courtly demeanor, the handsome former senator from Tennessee had been secretary of state since 1933, but the news that, after so many months of mounting tension and decrypted warnings of Japanese perfidy, the army, navy, and air forces of the United States had all been caught completely unawares, infuriated him. Magic decrypts had indicated throughout the year not only that Japan was preparing for war with the United States, but was doing everything possible to determine the "total strength of the U.S." and train fifth-columnists in America to work on anti-Semites, labor union members, blacks, Communists, and "all persons or organizations which either openly or secretly oppose the war."[64] To his staff, in his office, Mr. Hull had therefore expressed "with great emphasis his disappointment that the armed forces in Hawaii had been taken so completely by surprise," as well as his "bitter feelings" over the invidious way Ambassadors Nomura and Kurusu had behaved. The secretary had thus already prepared his own statement to the press, which duly went out at 6:00 p.m., denouncing the Japanese for their "infamously false and fraudulent" professions of desire for peace, while preparing for "new aggressions upon nations and peoples with which Japan was professedly at peace, including the United States."[65]

With the latest information coming in to the State Department that Japan had formally announced it was at war with the United States, Hull now begged the President to give the American people the whole history of Japan's treachery, not merely a 390-word request to Congress to declare war. As Grace Tully recalled, "The Secretary brought with him an alternative message drafted by Sumner Welles, longer and more comprehensive in its review of the circumstances leading to the state of war."[66] As Hopkins noted that night, Hull's draft was certainly a "a strong document," but one "that might take half an hour to read."[67]

The President didn't like it. What *more* justification did Congress need in order to declare war? Would such a review not simply lead people to question the administration's past efforts? Japan had openly announced that hostilities existed with the United States. It would be enough for the President to say, on record and before Congress, that the nation had been attacked, without warning, at the very moment Japanese diplomats were bringing their response to the latest American peace proposal. In other words, a briefer address would give no member of Congress the excuse to criticize the President or his administration, including Secretary Hull, for not having done yet more to appease or dissuade the Japanese government from going to war.

Hull was unconvinced, but the President was sure in his own mind. The fact of the Japanese sneak attack spoke for itself. The President's own longwinded speech before the governing board of the Pan American Union earlier that year, May 27, 1941, was a case in point. Intended as a refutation of the claims of Colonel Lindbergh and other America First isolationists, it had been a methodical account of the growing threat facing the United States from the Third Reich. It had failed completely. Isolationist sentiment in America had actually increased in the aftermath of the President's exhaustive state of emergency proclamation that day, not diminished. Accusations of warmongering had refused to die down, making it even harder for the President to draw up his contingency plans for war. Only three days before the Japanese attack, Colonel Robert McCormick, the virulently right-wing opponent of Roosevelt's New Deal policy, had published the guts of the President's top-secret "Victory Program," under the headline "FDR'S WAR PLANS," in his newspaper, the *Chicago Tribune*. The article had called the President's plan "a blueprint for total war on a scale unprecedented in at least two oceans and three continents, Europe, Africa and Asia" — a revelation so inflammatory that the President, while denying the existence of such a plan, had called J. Edgar Hoover to ask him to instigate an immediate FBI investigation into the source of the leak.

No, Roosevelt felt, better to let the plain fact of Japanese aggression speak for itself: thus ending the reign of isolationist loudmouths in the country forever. Especially as reports of the sheer scale of the American military disaster multiplied.

That evening, more than a hundred journalists, photographers, radio reporters, and technicians crowded into the small White House press room — the normal capacity of which was twelve — desperate for more information.

By 5:58 p.m. Steve Early, the White House press secretary, confirmed "the report of heavy damages and loss of life" in the sneak attack.[68] "The telegraph boys fairly came out of the cracks, the floor was tangled with a black spaghetti of wires, the motion picture lights were on, cameras were busy, men were telephoning, a radio receiver blared," wrote one White House correspondent. "Men with chattering hand motion-picture machines climbed over and under desks . . . and they were followed by others carrying glaring lamps on black cords."[69]

The Treasury secretary, Henry Morgenthau, had already doubled the size of the small Secret Service detail at the White House. When he sought permission for half a battalion of troops, along with tanks, to be stationed around the Executive Mansion, however, the President told Morgenthau to drop the idea. The Japanese might possibly invade Hawaii, 2,676 miles away, but it would take them longer to get to Pennsylvania Avenue, he argued.[70] Instead, the President ordered that U.S. troops be sent to protect the Japanese Embassy on Massachusetts Avenue, and gave instructions for all the White House lights to be turned *on* as darkness fell.

The White House should be seen, still, as a beacon of democratic hope, not as a military barracks, the President explained — and he asked that the members of his full cabinet assemble with him in his study at 8:30 p.m., to be followed then by the leaders of Congress at 9:00.

As the terrible afternoon and early evening of December 7, 1941, had worn on, Eleanor Roosevelt had "stayed in my sitting room and did my mail and wrote letters." Nevertheless, she recalled, "one ear was alert to the people coming and going to and from my husband's study. He went down in the late afternoon to have his nose treated, and at seven o'clock [Solicitor General] Charles Fahy came to see him for a short time," to discuss the legal terms required of the declaration of war, and the status of Japanese diplomats in the interim. "Again in the evening he had supper in his study, with James [Roosevelt], who was then a captain in the Marines, Harry Hopkins, and Grace Tully."[71]

Hopkins, Grace Tully recalled later, was in a state of sustained shock, indeed "looked just like a walking cadaver, just skin and bones."[72] The "phone was ringing constantly," Hopkins noted, for his part. Admiral Stark "continued to get further and always more dismal news about the attack on Hawaii. We went over the speech again briefly and the President made a few corrections" — including the change from "world history" to "infamy."[73]

"The Cabinet met promptly at 8.30," in Roosevelt's study, or Blue Room, over the South Portico — the members summoned from across the Washington area and the nation. "All members were present. They formed a ring completely around the President, who sat at his desk. The President was in a very solemn mood and told the group this was the most serious Cabinet session since Lincoln met with the Cabinet at the outbreak of the Civil War."[74]

It was an apt analogy. The members of the war council already knew the worst. "The news coming from Hawaii is very bad," Secretary Stimson had by then noted in his diary. "It has been staggering to see our people there, who have been warned long ago and were standing on the alert, should have been so caught by surprise."[75] Secretary Hull, by contrast, blamed Stimson and Knox. He had told his staff at the State Department that he had, "time after time" in recent months, "warned our military and naval men," with all the vigor at his command, "that there was constant danger of attack by Japan" — and how "deeply" he regretted his "warnings had not been taken more seriously." As the note-taker recorded, the initial reaction at the State Department had been that the Japanese attack had been "exceedingly stupid," for it would "instantaneously and completely" unite the American people. "However, after it became evident that our armed forces had suffered tremendous damage in Hawaii, there was less feeling that the Japanese had been stupid."[76] Worse still, reports were coming in of a massive Japanese air raid on the Philippines — with the destruction of pretty much all of General MacArthur's air force at Clark Field, despite *nine hours* of prior warning.

Other cabinet members, however, were still in the literal as well as proverbial dark. "I'm just off the plane from Cleveland. For God's sake, what happened?" asked the attorney general, Francis Biddle. "Mr. President, several of us have just arrived by plane. We don't know anything except a scare headline 'Japs Attack Pearl Harbor.' Could you tell us?" asked another.[77]

As best he currently knew, the President brought the full cabinet — including Vice President Wallace — up to date, recounting the final hours of negotiation. "And finally while we were alert — at eight o'clock," he recounted, "a great fleet of Japanese bombers bombed our ships in Pearl Harbor, and bombed all our airfields." He confided that the "casualties, I am sorry to say, were extremely heavy. . . . It looks as if out of eight battleships, three have been sunk, and possibly a fourth. Two destroyers were blown up while they were in drydock. Two of the battleships are badly damaged. Several other smaller vessels have been sunk or destroyed. The drydock itself has been damaged. Other portions of the fleet are at sea, moving towards what is believed to be two plane carriers, with adequate naval escort."[78]

The President's summary of U.S. naval losses was all too accurate. His belief that Admiral Kimmel's remaining naval forces — his carriers — were moving toward battle with the Japanese Navy, however, was overly optimistic.

In truth, neither the Japanese nor the American fleet commanders were anxious to join battle at sea. Enough, for the moment, was enough.

The same held true for the President's plans for his appearance before Congress the following day. Rocked by the disaster at Pearl Harbor, the President was reluctant to ask Congress for a declaration of war on Nazi Germany in addition to Japan. Thus when, in his study, the President read out to the cabinet members the draft of his proposed speech to Congress, Secretary Stimson objected that the declaration only covered war with Japan. It was, Stimson wrote in his diary that night, too simple, "based wholly upon the treachery of the present attack." Although in that respect it was "very effective," Stimson allowed, it did not "attempt to cover the long standing indictment of Japan's lawless conduct in the past. Neither did it connect her in any way with Germany," as he and Secretary Hull felt it should — in fact Stimson claimed "we know from the interceptions and other evidence that Germany had pushed Japan into this."[79]

Hitler as Hirohito's éminence grise? The President was unimpressed, and "stuck to his guns," in Hopkins's words, that night[80] — as if more determined than ever to avoid the moniker "warmonger." There was no evidence of collusion between Germany and Japan, Roosevelt countered — despite the suspicions voiced by his military team, such as Admiral Stark's remark to Rear Admiral Bloch in Hawaii, asking about an enemy submarine reported to have been sunk in the harbor: "is it German?"[81] As President he would continue to take one step at a time.

No sooner was his meeting with the cabinet over than the ten invited leaders of Congress — interventionists and former isolationists alike — now herded into the Blue Room.

It was 9:00 p.m. — with yet more bad news streaming in from the Far East. Word had come from Britain that Malaya had been invaded. Hong Kong, Bangkok, and Singapore had also been bombed. The American Pacific islands of Guam and Midway were under attack. Japanese carrier planes were confirmed as having bombed the Philippines — in fact, they seemed to have annihilated General MacArthur's air force at Clark airfield. If anything, the picture was worsening.

Labor Secretary Frances Perkins later recalled how, when she arrived in haste from the airport, the President did not even look up. "He was living off in another area. He wasn't noticing what went on on the other side of the desk. . . . His face and lips were pulled down, looking quite gray. . . . It was obvious to me that Roosevelt was having a dreadful time just accepting the idea that the Navy could be caught off guard. His pride in the Navy was so terrific that he was having actual physical difficulty in getting out the words that put him on record as knowing that the Navy was caught unawares, that bombs dropped on ships that were not in fighting shape and not prepared to move, but were just tied up."[82] And on top of that, the destruction of Hawaii's army air forces.

The mood began with collective shock, but soon gave way to congressional fury, as the President repeated the account that he had already given the cabinet, and then took questions.

Asked about losses suffered by the Japanese, the President was evasive. "It's a little difficult. We think we got some of their submarines, but we don't know," he responded lamely but truthfully. "We know some Japanese planes were shot down." Quoting his own experience in World War I, he cautioned against premature assumptions, or wishful thinking. "One fellow says he got fifteen of their planes and somebody else says five. . . . I should say that by far the greater loss has been sustained by us, although we have accounted for some Japanese." About the rumor that a Japanese carrier had been sunk off the Panama Canal Zone, he was dismissive — "Don't believe it," he warned; the U.S. forces there were "on the alert, but very quiet."[83] It had been, in short, an unmitigated naval and air disaster for the United States in the Pacific.

Unconfirmed reports had come in that the Japanese government had already proclaimed a state of hostilities with America, the President went on. With this in mind, he wished to ask the members of the Senate and House for authority to address Congress the next day, at 12:30 p.m. — though he did not read out his proposed speech, mindful that it would only spur more discussion, and leak within minutes.[84] Assured he would be invited to speak to a joint assembly of Congress, he now had to field more questions from the senators and congressmen about how the fleet and garrison at Pearl Harbor had been so unprepared.

"Hell's fire, we didn't do anything!" asserted Senator Tom Connally, a member of the Foreign Relations Committee from Texas, banging his fist on FDR's desk.

"That's about it," responded the President glumly.

"Well, what did we *do?*" Connally asked the navy secretary, Frank Knox, directly. "Didn't you say last month that we could lick the Japs in two weeks? Didn't you say that our navy was so well prepared and located that the Japanese couldn't hope to hurt us at all? When you made those public statements, weren't you just trying to say what an efficient secretary of the navy you were?"

Poor Knox knew not how to answer. Nor did the President help him out — he merely listened to the verbal attack with "a blank expression on his face."

Connally kept up his assault on the navy secretary — asking why "all the ships at Pearl Harbor" were so "crowded" together, and wanting to know about the log chain he'd heard had been pulled across the harbor entrance, so they could not get out.

"To protect us against Japanese submarines," Knox explained.

"Then you weren't thinking of an air attack?"

"No," the secretary admitted.

Connally was almost apoplectic by this time. "I am amazed by the attack by Japan, but I am still more astounded at what happened to our Navy. They were all asleep. Where were our patrols? They knew these negotiations were going on."

Knox fell silent. Attempting vainly to calm the temper of his meeting, the Chief Executive confided it was "a terrible disappointment to be President" in such "circumstances," in the aftermath of an attack that had "come most unexpectedly."[85]

The meeting went on for two long hours: accusations and disbelief at U.S. military incompetence leaving the President not only weary, but concerned lest the nation now descend into a witch-hunt as to whom to blame.

Fortunately Roosevelt was rescued by one of the legislators. "Well, Mr. President, this nation has a job ahead of it," a member of the delegation summed up, "and what we have to do is roll up our sleeves and win this war."[86]

Most, however, left the White House with unresolved feelings of guilt, anger, disappointment. And anxiety over the country's next steps.

After walking back to the Treasury, next door, at 11:25 p.m., Secretary

Morgenthau railed, like Secretary Hull, against the ineptitude of the professional armed forces — epitomized by the security at the White House, where he still counted only three men guarding the side of the mansion! He had then gone straight back to the Blue Room, and told the President in person that the "whole back of the White House — only three men. Anybody could take a five ton truck with 20 men and they could take the White House without any trouble."[87] It seemed endemic — Pearl Harbor merely the symbol of America's wider complacency. Inside the Treasury, Secretary Morgenthau was accosted by one of his senior staff. "Has there been negligence," the staffer asked, "or is it just the fortunes of war?"[88]

Morgenthau was unsure. The disaster was "just unexplainable," he answered, tormented. The Japanese "walked in just as easily as they [the Germans] did in Norway." At least "they didn't do it in the Philippines," where it was expected. "Let Stimson take the credit for that," Morgenthau remarked, not comprehending how devastating had been the destruction of MacArthur's air force planes, on the ground, as in Hawaii — but with nine hours' warning. He shook his white head; "all the explanations I have heard," he puzzled aloud, "just don't make sense." Hawaii was supposed to be "impregnable. I mean that has been sold to us," the Treasury secretary lamented. "They haven't learned anything here. They have the whole Fleet in one place — the whole fleet in this little Pearl Harbor base. The whole Fleet was there." And if, at the cabinet and congressional leaders' meeting, Secretary Knox had been distraught over the damage to the Pacific fleet, so had Secretary Stimson been over his precious army air forces. "He kept mumbling that all the planes were in one place," Morgenthau recounted to his staff.[89] How an entire Japanese fleet could sneak in, approach within a hundred or two hundred miles, as the President had described, and then make off, without being seen — let alone caught — was beyond the seventy-four-year-old. "Was it a terrible shock to the President?" asked his wife, who had come to take him home. To which Morgenthau could only sigh: "Must be — must be."[90]

The assistant secretary of state, Adolf Berle, noted in his diary: "It was a bad day all around; and if there is anyone I would not like to be, it is Chief of Naval Intelligence."[91]

Another candidate was, however, the devastated commander of the U.S. Pacific Fleet, Admiral Kimmel — who earlier that day had been hit by a spent bullet that crashed through the window of his operations room overlooking Pearl Harbor and ended on his chest, tarnishing his spotless white uniform. As Admiral Kimmel confided to his communications director, Commander Maurice Curts: "It would have been merciful, had it killed me."[92]

"His reaction to any event was always to be calm," the First Lady later described the President's temperament. Instead of getting agitated, he would batten down his hatches, emotionally. "If it was something that was bad, he just became almost like an iceberg."[93]

It had always been so, but now, late on the night of the Pearl Harbor attack, the President had trouble repressing his emotions. After the members of Congress left the White House, only Cordell Hull, the secretary of state, remained. They were joined by Sumner Welles — who arrived with yet *another* draft declaration of war "which the President did not like," Hopkins noted that night, "although Hull pressed very strongly that he use it."[94]

It was Hull's third attempt. "Hull's message," Hopkins noted, "was a long-winded dissertation on the history of Japanese relations leading up to the blow this morning. The President was very patient with them and I think in order to get them out of the room perhaps led them to believe he would give serious consideration to their draft. Waiters brought in beer and sandwiches, and at 12.30 the President cleared everybody out and said he was going to bed."[95]

Whatever his intentions, the President's living nightmare was not quite over. He had asked his son James, a liaison officer on the staff of Colonel William Donovan, to bring his boss to the White House. Known as "Wild Bill," Donovan was Roosevelt's recently handpicked chief of foreign intelligence, under the cover title "coordinator of information" (COI). For his part, however, Donovan had not been listening to his information; like half of America that Sunday, it seemed, he'd been watching a ball game — in Donovan's case in New York City's Polo Grounds (capacity fifty-four thousand) — when summoned to the White House.

The President had also decided to ask CBS reporter Edward R. Murrow, who with his wife had dined with Eleanor that night (a meal of scrambled eggs and pudding, served by the First Lady), to stay and speak with him privately, too.

When the two visitors thus finally went into the President's study, shortly after midnight, the extra chairs for the members of Congress were still out, and the President was still eating his sandwich along with a bottle of beer, alone at his desk.

"Gray with fatigue," the President gave his visitors a frank account of the past weeks — and past hours. His chiefs of staff had sent multiple warnings to all U.S. bases in the Pacific and Far East, yet, as he put it, "They caught our ships like lame ducks! Lame ducks, Bill. We told them, at Pearl Harbor and everywhere else, to have the lookouts manned," Donovan later recalled the President's words. "But they still took us by surprise."[96] Murrow, for his part, remembered how appalled the President was by the destruction of U.S. airplanes. "Several times the President pounded his fist on the table, as he told of the American planes that had been destroyed 'on the ground, by God, on the ground!'" As Murrow remembered, the very "idea seemed to hurt him."[97]

Given both Murrow's and Donovan's work in London, following the German invasion of the West, the President wanted to know from them, firsthand, whether they thought the people of the United States would rally in the same way the British had during the Blitz. Both men stated that they thought Americans would.

With that assurance, at 1:00 a.m. the President finally called it a day — the longest day of his life.

3

Hitler's Gamble

THE CAPITAL OF the United States buzzed with rumor, dread, and disbelief.

"The news of the shocking extent of the casualties and the damage to capital ships spread rapidly through Washington," Robert Sherwood, the President's speechwriter, later chronicled — even though the press were encouraged not to print the numbers of casualties, nor the extent of the destruction at Pearl Harbor. "The jittery conduct of some of our most eminent Government officials was downright disgraceful. They were telephoning the White House, shouting that the President must tell the people the full extent of this unmitigated disaster — that our nation had gone back to Valley Forge — that our West Coast was now indefensible and we must prepare to establish our battle lines in the Rocky Mountains or on the left bank of the Mississippi or God knows where." Sherwood wondered for a while whether Hitler might even be right: "that our democracy had become decadent and soft, that we could talk big, but there were too many of us who simply did not know how to stand up under punishment."[1]

Ignoring such hysteria and riding in an open car, as if to his inauguration, the President was driven to Capitol Hill late in the morning of December 8, 1941, and insisted he walk rather than be wheeled to the podium for the joint session. Congressmen and senators rose to their feet, giving him a standing ovation. Holding the lectern, facing a battery of microphones broadcasting his words to the world, the President delivered his address, beginning with the words: "Yesterday, December 7, 1941 — a date which will live in infamy — the United States of America was suddenly and deliberately attacked by naval and air forces of the Empire of Japan."

The speech — which included mention of the further Japanese attacks that had taken place in Malaya, Hong Kong, Guam, and the Philippine Islands — was a tour de force. Even Sherwood, who had not had a hand in the address, was amazed. There was, he later wrote, none of Winston Churchill's "eloquent defiance in this speech. There was certainly no trace of Hitler's hysterical bombast. And there was no doubt in the minds of the American people of Roosevelt's confidence. I do not think there was another occasion in his life when he was so completely representative of the whole people."[2]

The speech lasted only six minutes: six minutes that, in a way no one could ever have quite predicted, changed the world. "No matter how long it may take us to overcome the premeditated invasion, the American people in their righteous might will win through to absolute victory," the President closed. "I believe that I interpret the will of the Congress and of the people when I assert that we will not only defend ourselves to the uttermost but will make it very certain that this form of treachery shall never again endanger us.

"Hostilities exist. There is no blinking at the fact that our people, our territory, and our interests are in grave danger.

"With confidence in our armed forces — with the unbounding determination of our people — we will gain the inevitable triumph — so help us God." And with that, the President asked Congress to declare that, "since the unprovoked and dastardly attack by Japan on Sunday, December 7, 1941, a state of war has existed between the United States and the Japanese Empire."[3]

War, then, had come to the United States — war with Japan, not with Germany.

Ignoring this, within hours of hearing of the Pearl Harbor disaster, Winston S. Churchill decided he should travel to Washington to see President Roosevelt — Churchill informing the head of state in England, King George VI, as well as his own staff and colleagues, that he would meet with the President of the United States again, in person, so they could coordinate the "whole plan of Anglo-American defence and attack."[4] When cautioned by Admiral Pound, the First Sea Lord, that he must be careful not to be too assertive, given that the United States was not yet at war with Germany, the Prime Minister reacted "with a wicked leer in his eye," as Pound recalled.

"Oh! That was the way we talked to her while we were wooing her,"

Churchill quipped; "now that she is in the harem we talk to her quite differently!"[5]

In actuality Churchill was much more diplomatic. "Would it not be wise for us to have another conference?" he suggested cautiously in a cable to the President. "We could review the whole war plan in the light of reality and new facts, as well as the problems of production and distribution," he explained. "I could if desired start from here in a day or two, and come by warship to Baltimore or Annapolis. Voyage would take about eight days and I would arrange to stay a week so that everything important could be settled between us." He would bring, he added ominously, however, his three chiefs of staff and their staffs, just as he had done at the Newfoundland meeting. "Please let me know at earliest what you feel about this."[6]

Given the date of his cable — December 9, 1941 — and the fact that Hitler still appeared not to have made up his mind whether to declare war on the United States, the President felt this was jumping the gun, literally as well as metaphorically. President Roosevelt "was pretty sure that Germany and Italy would declare war almost immediately," the British ambassador, Lord Halifax, noted, however, in his secret diary, having called on the President before lunch.[7] But a visit planned by Churchill, when no German declaration of war against America had yet been made? Lord Halifax was not a little embarrassed by his prime minister's importuning.

The President, Halifax reported back to London, "was genuinely pleased at the idea of another meeting, and very grateful, I think for the suggestion at this particular moment." However, "publicity could not be avoided" — which would endanger Churchill's safety — and the President "thought it far too big a risk to take unless there is no other alternative."[8]

"I had a slight feeling," Halifax added — employing convoluted English that bespoke his discomfort in having to warn his own prime minister — "that with all these quite genuine anxieties went a certain feeling, the strength of which I could not exactly assess, that he was not quite sure if your coming here might not be rather too strong medicine in the immediate future for some of his public opinion that he still feels he has to educate up to the complete conviction of the oneness of the struggle against both Germany and Japan. I wouldn't overstate it," he apologized, "but I think it was definitely in his mind from something he said at the beginning before he switched on to laying the main weight of his argument on to security."[9]

The majority of Americans, the diplomat meant, still did not see the attack on Pearl Harbor as a casus belli against Hitler — however much the Prime Minister yearned for U.S. help in that struggle. "I seem to be conscious," Halifax added, voicing his own concern as ambassador in Washington, "of a still lingering distinction in some quarters of the public mind between war with Japan and war with Germany."[10]

This was putting the matter mildly. All eyes in America, and public fury, were directed toward Japan — not Germany.

Halifax's cautionary tone was confirmed the next day, December 10, 1941, when in the U.S. Senate the outspoken isolationist Hiram Johnson "stopped another hearing upon another AEF" — the American Expeditionary Force that the President wished to prepare for service overseas. Senator Johnson's adamant and unrepentant feeling was, as he explained to his son at the time, "we ought not to prepare an expeditionary force for Europe."[11]

Nothing the President could say would stop Churchill from coming, however. As to the date for such get-together with the Prime Minister, Lord Halifax reported that President Roosevelt "did pretty well satisfy me that it was almost physically impossible for him to make it earlier" than after the New Year. "He feels he cannot go away immediately with a possible crystallisation of the position vis-à-vis Germany very close."[12]

Besides, the British ambassador pointed out, the President had a raft of legislative and executive matters to attend to in the wake of war with Japan; "he is preparing large appropriation demands on Congress. On all this side of it he really is the only person that can pull all the strands together." Given Churchill's dual role as prime minister and minister of defense, making him Britain's quasi commander-in-chief, Churchill would, Halifax was sure, be understanding, and tame his impetuosity. "You will easily judge his difficulties arising from the immediate position on the defence side. Then he has to prepare in the last two weeks of this month the next annual budget, and also his annual message to Congress, which he will deliver on either the third or the fifth of January." Nevertheless, Halifax didn't want the Prime Minister to feel that he, as ambassador, had been remiss in personally communicating to the President Churchill's urgent request for a conference. "I pressed him as hard as I could about the importance of your meeting as quickly as it could be managed, and I don't think that he was other than perfectly genuine about the reasons that made an earlier date than he gave impracticable." Finally, in mitigation of his failure, Halifax added: "They are terribly shaken here, as you can well suppose, and fully realize that they have been caught napping. I think they realise too what it means."[13]

Churchill was furious to be balked. Halifax was, as he later put it, "a man compounded of charm. He is no coward," he allowed, "no gentleman is, but there is something," he noted, "that runs through him like a yellow streak; grovel, grovel, grovel. Grovel to the Indians [Halifax had been viceroy of India in 1926–31], grovel to the Germans, grovel to the Americans."[14]

Churchill's remark was nasty, but not unmerited. Halifax's role as Neville Chamberlain's foreign secretary had been execrable, and now he was thwarting the wishes of his own prime minister, who wished to come immediately to Washington to direct the next phase of the war against Hitler — who had, however, still not declared war on the United States.

Churchill groaned. He'd sent Halifax to Washington in January 1941 in large part to get rid of a rival — Lord Halifax having been King George VI's preferred choice when Chamberlain resigned in May 1940. He was, moreover, still Churchill's "heir apparent," were Churchill to be forced to resign by continuing British failures on the field of battle. Of this, Lord Halifax — an aristocrat and snob from his bald head and withered arm to his toes — was well aware. "I have never liked Americans," Halifax had confided before leaving London. "In the mass I have always found them dreadful."[15] "In the end we had to go," his wife, Lady Halifax, later lamented, "and I don't think I have ever felt more miserable."[16]

In the months since he'd arrived, however, Halifax had found himself entranced by Roosevelt's graciousness toward him. In comparison with Churchill, the President seemed most charming — yet with a steely underlay, the hidden hand of a strong presidential will. It was clear that, beneath all the politeness with which Roosevelt received Halifax at the White House to discuss Churchill's request, he had no wish to see the Prime Minister at this point, or to allow such a visit to become publicly known before the New Year, lest remaining isolationists cry foul and claim the President was conspiring to go to war with Germany, just at the moment when all attention should be paid to the war that Japan had begun against America in the Pacific. The response that the President drafted to be sent to the Prime Minister on December 10, 1941, was thus negative.

"In August," the President pointed out, thinking back to their Atlantic Charter meeting off Newfoundland, "it was easy to agree on obvious main items — Russian aid, Near East aid and new form Atlantic convoy — but I question whether situation in Pacific area is yet clear enough to make determination of that decisive character. Delay of even a couple of weeks might be advantageous" — a point he reiterated, given the time necessary in order to get "a clearer picture" of the situation in the Pacific. "I suggest we defer decision on your visit for one week. Situation ought to be much clearer then."[17]

Since the message sounded so circular — repetitive and somewhat negative in tone for a new ally — Roosevelt withheld it for several hours.

It was just as well. A report now came through that rocked the President at the White House, when his naval aide, Captain Beardall, brought it to him in his study. And stunned the Prime Minister, at his annex apartment next to 10 Downing Street in London.

"We got the bad news about the Prince of Wales and the Repulse," Lord Halifax jotted in his diary. "This is very bad, especially following after Hawaii."[18]

Britain's only real naval fleet in Southeast Asia, the battleships HMS *Repulse* and *Prince of Wales* — the very ship on whose deck the President and his military advisers had sung such rousing Christian hymns in August — were reported sunk, with great loss of life.

Churchill himself was devastated, since it was he who had sent the two latest battleships out to Singapore without their accompanying aircraft carrier, HMS *Illustrious,* which had put in for repairs at Ceylon. Field Marshal Smuts, the former South African premier, had warned Churchill on November 18, 1941, that the ships would be vulnerable to concentrated Japanese attack, in the case of war — "If Japanese are really nippy there is here an opening for a first-class disaster." The night before the ships were sunk Churchill had finally discussed with his advisers whether the battleships should "go to sea and vanish among the innumerable islands" or even seek safety in Hawaii.[19] No decision had been made, however, and when Churchill answered the phone next morning, Admiral Pound, the First Sea Lord, was on the line. "His voice sounded odd," Churchill later wrote. "He gave a sort of cough and gulp, and at first I could not hear quite clearly. 'Prime Minister, I have to report to you that the *Prince of Wales* and the *Repulse* have both been sunk by the Japanese — we think by aircraft. [Fleet Admiral] Tom Phillips is drowned.' . . .

"I was thankful to be alone," Churchill recalled. "In all the war I never received a more direct shock. . . . As I turned over and twisted in bed the full horror of the news sank in upon me. There were no British or American capital ships in the Indian Ocean or the Pacific except the American survivors of Pearl Harbor, who were hastening back to California. Over all this vast expanse of waters Japan was supreme, and we everywhere were weak and naked."[20]

The President's heart went out to Churchill and the British, who now had no hope of defending their British territories and Dominions in the Far East from invasion without American help — help that, thanks to America's own disaster at Pearl Harbor, could not be given.

It is possible the two men spoke by scrambler telephone; at any event the Prime Minister signaled the President at 6:00 p.m., December 10, London time, that he wasn't worried about his own security in making the voyage to America. There was, however, "great danger in our not having a full discussion on the highest level about the extreme gravity of the naval position" — and he offered again to meet the President either in Bermuda, or to fly on to Washington from Bermuda. It was no longer a matter of whether or not Germany would declare war. It was a question of whether British territories in the Far East — including Australia — could be defended, now that Churchill's fleet was sunk. "I feel it would be disastrous to wait for another month before we settled common action in face of new adverse situation particularly in Pacific." He admitted he'd "hoped to start tomorrow night," even without having been invited, "but will postpone my sailing till I have received rendezvous from you."[21]

Given the magnitude of Britain's new naval disaster, on top of Pearl Harbor, there was little the President could say, other than to repeat that there was still no way he himself could leave Washington before his State of the Union address to Congress, set for January 5, 1942. Once again he therefore sought to postpone Churchill's visit.

"I wholly agree about the gravity of naval position especially in Pacific," he allowed in his second draft reply, attempting to be courteous. "We are both of us reduced to defensive fighting in Pacific Islands and Malaya. At this moment you cannot help us there and we cannot help you except with very small naval forces now retiring southward from Philippines. Only small reinforcements on both sides can be sent to that area immediately. My first impression," the President stated, getting to the point, "is that full discussion would be more useful in a few weeks hence than immediately."[22]

Even this wording the President thought too negative, though, at a time of such fresh disaster for the British — and in a surge of compassion and goodwill, he assured Churchill that, were the Prime Minister to venture across the Atlantic, he would be "Overjoyed to have you here at the White House," adding, "If you come, give consideration to Canadian route, Bermuda route with plane from there, or sea route all the way."[23] Having decided that this signal, too, was too longwinded, he simply sent word: "Delighted to have you here at White House."[24]

Sheikh Churchill, his pasha-like mood crushed by the loss of Britain's two latest battleships and the death of so many brave sailors, gratefully accepted. Moreover, his instinct was right. The next day, December 11, 1941, before the Prime Minister set off from the River Clyde to see the President, the Führer made the second greatest blunder of his life — a mistake that would, in due course, end his odious life.

The Nazi leader had read translations of President Roosevelt's previous speeches, provided to him by his minister of propaganda, Dr. Joseph Goebbels. Whether Hitler read a transcript of President Roosevelt's first wartime Fireside Chat, broadcast from the White House at 10:00 p.m. on December 9, 1941, is unclear, but doubtful. Had he done so, though, it would have caused him to question his own assumption — for the Führer had become convinced that the President was going to have his hands full dealing with war in the Pacific and Southeast Asia, now, and would be forced to withdraw his naval forces from the Atlantic. In this case, Hitler convinced himself, Germany had nothing to fear from declaring war on America.

Roosevelt's broadcast from the White House, recorded in the Diplomatic Reception Room next to a fake fireplace, had made it abundantly clear, however, that as president he saw Nazi Germany, not Japan, as the number one threat to civilization.

"In 1931, ten years ago," the President began, "Japan invaded Manchukuo — *without warning*. In 1935, Italy invaded Ethiopia — *without warning*. In 1938, Hitler invaded Austria — *without warning*. In 1939, Hitler invaded Czechoslovakia — *without warning*. Later in '39, Hitler invaded Poland — *without warning*. In 1940, Hitler invaded Norway, Denmark, the Netherlands, Belgium and Luxembourg — *without warning*. In 1940, Italy attacked France and later Greece — *without warning*. And this year, in 1941, the Axis Powers attacked Yugoslavia and Greece and they dominated the Balkans — *without warning*. In 1941, also, Hitler invaded Russia — *without warning*. And now Japan has attacked Malaya and Thailand — and the United States — *without warning*."

It was a pattern of deceit that illustrated the difference between democracy and totalitarian government; between good and evil. "I can say with utmost confidence that no Americans today or a thousand years hence, need feel anything but pride in our patience and in our efforts through all the years towards achieving a peace in the Pacific which would be fair and honorable to every nation, large or small. And no honest person, today or a thousand years hence, will be able to suppress a sense of indignation and horror at the treachery committed by the military dictators of Japan, under the very shadow of the flag of peace borne by their special envoys in our midst."

"We are now in this war," the President concluded. "We are all in it — all the way. Every single man, woman and child is a partner in the most tremendous undertaking in our American history. We must share together the bad news and the good news, the defeats and the victories — the changing fortunes of war.

"So far, the news has been all bad. We have suffered a serious setback in Hawaii. Our forces in the Philippines, which include the brave people of that Commonwealth, are taking punishment, but are defending themselves vigorously. The reports from Guam and Wake and Midway Islands are still confused, but we must be prepared for the announcement that all these three outposts have been seized . . ."

The President's honesty was as shocking as was his familial, homey tone, which was warm, even intimate. He warned against "rumors" and "ugly little hints of complete disaster" that "fly thick and fast in wartime." News would necessarily be delayed, lest it give valuable information to the enemy, but it would in time be released, and would not be doctored, he promised. He quoted, for example, a statement made on the night of Pearl Harbor that "a Japanese carrier had been located and sunk off the [Panama] Canal Zone," attributed to "an authoritative source." As the President pointed out, "you can be reasonably sure from now on that under these war circumstances the 'authoritative source' is not any person in authority."

If the news from the Pacific was bad, his prognosis for the war was somewhat better, the President maintained. "Precious months were gained by sending vast quantities of our war material to the nations of the world still able to resist Axis aggression. Our policy rested on the fundamental truth that the defense of any country resisting Hitler or Japan was in the long run the defense of our own country. That policy has been justified," he claimed. "It has given us time, invaluable time, to build our American assembly lines of production."

Those "assembly lines are now in operation," he stated. "Others are being rushed to completion. A steady stream of tanks and planes, of guns and ships and shells and equipment — that is what these eighteen months have given us. . . .

"It will not only be a long war," the President had warned, however, "it will be a hard war. That is the basis on which we now lay all our plans. That is the yardstick by which we measure what we shall need and demand; money, materials, doubled and quadrupled production — ever-increasing. The production must be not only for our own Army and Navy and air forces fighting the Nazis and the war lords of Japan throughout the Americas and throughout the world. I have been working today on the subject of production," he said, explaining his agenda: "to speed up all existing production by working on a seven-day-week basis in every war industry, including the production of essential raw materials," and the building of "more new plants, by adding to old plants, and by using the many smaller plants for war needs." The days of labor strife, "obstacles and difficulties, divisions and disputes, indifference and callousness" were "now all past — and, I am sure, forgotten."

The President had one final thing to add, however, which presaged not only American determination to avenge Pearl Harbor, but a far more historic resolve. "In my message to the Congress yesterday I said that we 'will make very certain that this form of treachery shall never endanger us again.' In order to achieve that certainty, we must begin the great task that is before us by abandoning once and for all the illusion that we can ever again isolate ourselves from the rest of humanity.

"In these past few years — and most violently, in the past three days — we have learned a terrible lesson.

"It is our obligation to our dead — it is our sacred obligation to their children and to our children — that we must never forget what we have learned.

"And what we have learned is this," he continued. "There is no such thing as security for any nation — or any individual — in a world ruled by the principles of gangsterism. . . . We have learned that our ocean-girt hemisphere is not immune from severe attack — that we cannot measure our safety in terms of miles on any map any more. We may acknowledge that our enemies have performed a brilliant feat of deception, perfectly timed and executed with great skill. It was a thoroughly dishonorable deed, but we must face the fact that modern warfare as conducted in the Nazi manner is a dirty business. We don't like it — we didn't want to get in it — but we are in it and we're going to fight it with everything we've got." He pointed again to the connection between the aggressions of Hitler's Third Reich and Hirohito's Japanese Empire, codified in the Tripartite Pact of September 1940, by whose terms the world would be divided between Axis and Japanese spoils of conquest and subjugation. It was a global strategy of evil that the United States could no longer tolerate. "I repeat that the United States can accept no result save victory, final and complete. Not only must the shame of Japanese treachery be wiped out, but the sources of international brutality, wherever they exist, must be absolutely and finally broken."

"The true goal we seek is far above and beyond the ugly field of battle," the President emphasized. "When we resort to force, as now we must, we are determined that this force shall be directed toward ultimate good as against immediate evil. We Americans are not destroyers — we are builders. We are now in the midst of a war, not for conquest, not for vengeance, but for a world in which this nation, and all that this nation represents, will be safe for our children." The United States was economically the most powerful nation on earth — and the time had come for America to exert that power, for good. "We expect to eliminate the danger from Japan, but it would serve us ill if we accomplished that and found that the rest of the world was dominated by Hitler and Mussolini."

"So we are going to win the war," the President declared — his broadcast heard by an estimated 92.4 percent of American families[25] — "and we are going to win the peace that follows."

The President's words were those of a new leader on the world stage: one whose rhetoric was backed by a vast military potential that was being unlocked, and could be unleashed against Nazi Germany, not just Japan, unless the Führer was careful not to provoke war with the United States. Without a German declaration of war, the President could give all the Fireside Chats he wished; the Constitution still forbade him to wage war against any nation without the assent of the Capitol.

Why did Hitler then court war with such an opponent, when only Congress could declare war — and would in all likelihood not do so against Germany, given the public fury that was currently directed against Japan?

Certainly Germany was not obliged to go to war with the United States, according to the Tripartite Pact of 1940, any more than Japan was obliged to go to war with Russia.

Neither then nor later could observers and historians of World War II quite explain Hitler's fatal decision. Aware in advance of Japanese intentions with respect to the United States — though not informed of the specific target or the date the Japanese military had decided upon — the Führer had been delighted by the prospect of a sneak attack. He had therefore telephoned from the Wolfsschanze, or Wolf's Lair, his field headquarters near Rastenburg, in East Prussia, to the Reichskanzlei in Berlin several days before Pearl Harbor, instructing his foreign minister, Joachim Ribbentrop, to begin redrafting the existing Tripartite Pact with Italy and Japan. On December 3, 1941, Count Ciano, the Italian foreign minister, had thus noted with alarm in his diary how Ribbentrop was demanding not only that Italy "sign a pact with Japan agreeing not to make a separate peace," but "that Italy declare war on the United States as soon as the conflict begins."[26]

Declare war on the *United States?* The interpreter who was taking down these requests, in Rome, was "shaking like a leaf," Ciano had recorded, as the poor man translated Ribbentrop's "requests." The Duce claimed to welcome the looming global struggle --"So now we come to the war between continents, which I have predicted since 1939," Mussolini boasted — but Count Ciano, despite being Mussolini's son-in law, was less convinced of its outcome. "Who will have the most stamina?" he'd asked himself — a question he wished the Duce and others would address *before* declaring war, rather than preening themselves over their current prowess in battle.[27]

Days later, when news of the Pearl Harbor attack came through, Ciano's heart had sunk. "One thing is now certain: America will enter the conflict, and the conflict itself will last long enough to allow all her potential strength to come into play," he'd noted — a prediction even the king of Italy, when Ciano discussed it with him that day, admitted "could be right."[28]

Hitler, however, had had other concerns. As leader of a Third Reich bogged down in a winter war with the Soviet Union that it had not envisaged, he saw the Japanese coup de main quite differently from the Italians. The latest attempt by the Wehrmacht to reach Moscow had gotten within a few miles of the city, causing the Russian capital to be largely evacuated.

Winter temperatures had then plummeted, however — and the much-vaunted Wehrmacht, which was meant to have swept over Russia "like a hailstorm,"[29] had failed, in the end, to reach its spectacular goal.

Worse still was what had followed. The Russians not only held the German armies before Moscow, but on December 5, 1941, a *hundred* Russian divisions suddenly appeared out of seeming nowhere, and launched a counteroffensive to throw the enemy back.

Hitler had been stunned as messages had flooded into his headquarters in East Prussia, begging permission to allow the German Army Group Center to retreat to more defensible lines — requests the Führer denied, eventually firing General Guderian, his top panzer commander.[30]

Japan's miraculous achievement in sinking the vaunted U.S. fleet at Pearl Harbor in a single morning, two days after the start of the massive Russian counteroffensive, had therefore given the embattled Führer new hope that, acting in concert with the Japanese, he might yet realize his dream. According to his staff, the Führer "slapped his thighs with delight as news of the report was brought to him. It was as if a heavy burden had been lifted, as with the greatest excitement he explained the new world situation to everyone around him."[31] His change of mood infected his whole headquarters at Rastenburg, which was "caught up in an ecstasy of rejoicing."[32] "We simply can't lose the war now," Hitler declared — "We have a partner who has never been beaten in three thousand years!"[33] Ribbentrop, calling Ciano from Berlin, was "jumping with joy about the Japanese attack on the United States," Ciano noted in Rome. "He is so happy that I can only congratulate him, even though I am not so sure about the advantage."[34]

Hitler was, however. He left the Wolfsschanze on December 8, 1941, and flew back to Berlin, where for several weeks he had been planning to give his own version of a State of the Union address: a speech he would deliver to the assembled deputies of the Reichstag on the progress of his war.

Meeting with Ribbentrop, the Führer there learned that the Japanese — exulting over their successful attack on Pearl Harbor — were pressing that the Third Reich, too, should declare war on the United States, as per Hitler's recent assurances and the gist, if not the letter, of the existing Tripartite Act.

Ribbentrop explained to Hitler that he had deflected the Japanese request. There was surely no need for Germany to engage the United States in open war; American naval forces would inevitably be sent to the Pacific to defend U.S. territories there and in the Far East, from the Philippines to Guam and Wake—thus making Britain even more isolated, and more vulnerable to invasion, once the Russian front had stabilized, or the war with Russia was won. In fact Ribbentrop had pointed out to the Japanese ambassador, as he reported to the Führer, that the Tripartite Pact in its extant form still did not commit signatories, unless themselves attacked, to wage war upon each other's enemies. The Japanese had not been attacked by the Soviet Union, so the Japanese had not felt obliged to declare war on Russia as a third party—to the disappointment of the German government. By the same token, Germany had not been attacked by the United States; Germany was thus not bound to fight America—at least, not now, when it had its hands full in Russia. According to Ribbentrop, Germany was required by the original pact only to supply aid—though a new draft addition was being drawn up, by which each signatory bound himself not to make peace with an enemy without the consent of all.

Hitler did not wait for Ribbentrop to finish. The Führer, Ribbentrop later recalled, cut him off midsentence. Hitler wanted, he said, an updated pact that he could announce in his forthcoming address to the Reichstag—a pact in which Germany would declare its solidarity with Japan by declaring war on the United States, with or without a Japanese declaration of war on Russia. "If we don't stand on the side of Japan, the pact is politically dead," Hitler stated, tellingly.[35]

He was the führer: the leader of a great movement in the world, a New Order. He wanted to appropriate the Japanese triumph in the Pacific as part of that New Order, to give the functionaries and population of the Third Reich, and its allies in Europe, a political message: that the Führer knew what he was doing, despite the reverses in Russia; that his world war was on track. Standing tall with Japan and Italy in a Three Musketeers trio would achieve that. Moreover, from a military standpoint, a German declaration of war on the United States would not impose a new burden on the Reich, for the United States would be locked in do-or-die combat in the Pacific and Southeast Asia. In other words, war with the U.S. would be *kostenlos*—free.

Herr Ribbentrop did not dare argue. He then left Hitler's four-hundred-square-meter marbled office, the Reichskanzlei, promising to get Italy and Japan to sign the latest protocols to the Tripartite Pact, committing them to the new agreement—one for all, and all for one—so that the Führer could include such an announcement in his forthcoming speech.

In his excitement, Hitler seemed completely oblivious to the possible repercussions. At a perilous moment in the Nazi attempt to destroy the Soviet Union — Russian Jews and commissars to be "liquidated" as the armies moved forward, "the intelligentsia" to be "exterminated," cities razed, the survivors returned to serfdom, but under German rulers[36] — the notion of a pact with military partners had taken on a new psychological importance for him, given the latest confidential report on public disaffection in the Reich: namely, warnings of a "1918 mentality" or weariness prevalent among German civilians. Pearl Harbor had galvanized the Axis at a critical moment — Germany no longer alone, with Mussolini's Italy somewhat by its side and a few minor central European satellites. Instead, the Third Reich would henceforth be fighting in a global military alliance with the great Empire of Japan: Japanese forces stretching Britain's diminishing resources to the breaking point in the Far East, and also diverting American naval and mercantile attention from the Atlantic to the defense of U.S. territories in the Pacific.

The die, then, was cast.

No one around the Führer could be in any doubt about his exultant mood. The "East-Asia conflict drops like a gift into our lap," Hitler assured his propaganda chief in Berlin. The revised pact would, he told Dr. Goebbels, fulfill the strategic war directive he'd issued some eight months earlier. In it he'd laid out, in advance, his global strategy for the victory of the Third Reich. "The aim of cooperation based on the Tripartite Pact," he'd explained, "has to be to bring Japan to active operations in the Far East as soon as possible. Strong English forces will be tied up as a result, and the main interest of the United States of America will be diverted to the Pacific."[37] Japan's attack at Pearl Harbor had now conformed to that strategic calculation to a T. As Hitler's adjutant recalled the Führer boasting to his entourage in Berlin on December 9, 1941: "Compelled by the conflict with Japan," America would "not be able to intervene in the European theater of war."[38]

But if America would not be able to intervene, by virtue of the Japanese triumph at Pearl Harbor, why the need for Germany to go to *war* with the United States? individuals like Ciano wondered.

Goebbels, however, did not dare question the Führer any more than Ribbentrop had. Instead, Dr. Goebbels attempted to see the new developments through the Führer's infallible eyes. "Thanks to the outbreak of war between Japan and the USA," he articulated in his diary that day, after speaking with Hitler, "a complete shift in the general world picture has taken place" — a fact that could soon be trumpeted by his propaganda ministry. Great benefits would accrue, aiding Germany's battles in the Atlantic, the Middle East, and Russia. "The United States will scarcely now be in a position to transport worthwhile material to England let alone the Soviet Union," Goebbels summarized the Führer's thinking.[39]

So certain was Hitler that America's attention would now "switch" to the Pacific, in fact, that he ordered unrestricted submarine warfare against American-flagged vessels in the Atlantic to begin that very day, December 9, 1941, even before he officially declared war on the United States. The "American flag will no longer be respected," Goebbels noted in his diary. "Anyone caught on the way to England must reckon with being torpedoed by our U-boats."[40]

Hitler's intention had been to address the Reichstag the next day, December 10, 1941 — but he didn't. Did he have second thoughts? Was he still hoping that the Japanese would sign up to declare war on Russia, simultaneously? Or was he simply psyching himself up to deliver a historic speech for the occasion, which he insisted on writing himself?

No one knew. As the clock ticked in the White House, considerable apprehension arose — as it did in London. Suppose the Führer thought better of his decision? Suppose he was advised there was no real need to go to war with the United States: that only Congress could approve war, and was loath to do so against Germany when U.S. defense forces were now desperately needed to fight Japan's predations in the Far East?

It was only the next day, at 8:00 a.m. on December 11, 1941, that the German chargé d'affaires in Washington appeared at the State Department, next to the White House, to deliver an important message. Since Secretary Hull would not receive him, Herr Thomsen was told to wait.

Eventually, at 9:30 a.m., Thomsen was able to hand over to the head of the European Division of the U.S. State Department his note, explaining that Germany's patience with the United States was at an end, and that a state of hostilities, of war, now existed between their two countries.

Simultaneously in Berlin, the U.S. chargé d'affaires was given the same message. Then, at 3:00 p.m. that day, Berlin time, after receiving confirmation that the Japanese had signed the new tripartite agreement — but without the Japanese having agreed, reciprocally, to declare war on Russia — the Führer went before his assembled, fawning "party comrades" in Berlin and ended speculation across the globe. His speech was an hour and a half long — and was soon in the President's hands. Reading it, Roosevelt was stunned by how personal it was: a speech primarily directed at him.

"Providence," the Führer announced, to the Reichstag's amazement — since Hitler had never shown signs of religious belief — had personally entrusted him "with the waging of a historic struggle which will decisively fashion not only our German history for the next thousand years, but also the history of Europe — even the history of the entire world."

Following a review of earlier world history, the Führer brought Reichstag deputies up to date on the progress of the war in Russia. He claimed that Stalin had fully intended to attack the Third Reich and conquer Europe, and thus Operation Barbarossa had been but a preemptive spoiling attack: a necessary act of German self-defense that had, however, succeeded in capturing no fewer than 3,806,865 imminent Russian invaders, for the loss of only 158,773 German lives.

Before the deputies could digest the sheer enormity of these numbers — 158,733 Germans *killed* (which understated German dead by four-fifths), and half a million German casualties since June — the Führer moved on to the president of the United States.

"The course of these two lives!" the Führer said, comparing their careers — and worldviews. Acknowledging that "the philosophy of life and the attitude of President Roosevelt and my own are worlds apart," Hitler proceeded to defame the U.S. president as the dupe of "members of the same people that we once fought in Germany as a parasitic phenomenon of mankind, and which we had begun to remove from public life": the Jews. Sneering at the New Deal, the Führer claimed that Roosevelt had "increased the national debt of his country to enormous proportions, devalued the dollar, continued to ruin the economy, and maintained unemployment" — thanks to "those elements which, as Jews, have always had an interest in ruin and never in order."

The Führer then pointed out that there were many isolationists in America who held similar racist views to his own. "Many distinguished Americans agree with this assessment, or rather, realization. A threatening opposition hangs over the head of this man," he claimed — and accused the President of "sabotage" of "all possibilities for a policy of European pacification," as he put it: possibilities of peace destroyed by Roosevelt's insistence on helping governments in exile, and supplying American weapons to those who were holding out against Nazi "pacification" efforts.

The December 7 attack on America was thus fully deserved, Hitler declared, getting to the point. "I think that all of you felt relieved that now finally one state has protested, as the first, against this historically unique and brazen abuse of truth and law," the Führer said, congratulating Germany's ally, Japan. "It fills all of us — the German Volk and, I think, all decent people of the world — with profound satisfaction that the Japanese government, after negotiating with this falsifier for years, has finally had enough of being derided in so dishonorable a manner. We know what force stands behind Roosevelt. It is the eternal Jew," a race whose international tribe had "destroyed people and property in the Soviet Union," where "millions of German soldiers" had witnessed for themselves what Jewry had wrought: Bolshevism. "Perhaps the president of the United States himself has failed to understand this," Hitler speculated. "This speaks for his mental limitations," he sneered. And with that, the Führer poured scorn on the Atlantic Charter principles for postwar peace — "a new social order" that was, in Hitler's view, "tantamount to a bald hairdresser recommending his unfailing hair restorer."

Reichstag deputies tittered at the simile. In contrast to the homilies of the Atlantic Charter, the Third Reich and its New Order represented the wave of the future, the Führer proudly claimed. "Thanks to the National Socialist movement," he declared, Germany had "never been as united and unified as it is today and as it will be in the future. Perhaps never before has it been so clear-sighted and rarely so aware of its honor."[41]

The Führer came then, at last, to the climax of his speech. "I have therefore had passports sent to the American Chargé d'Affaires," he confirmed — together with a copy of the four new articles of the Tripartite Pact, "signed today in Berlin," which he proceeded proudly to read out: "Article 1: Germany, Italy, and Japan will together fight this war, a war that was forced upon them by the United States of America and England, and bring it to a victorious end by employing all instruments of power at their disposal . . ."[42]

It was, then, global war — a war that Germany, Italy, and their noble ally, Japan, would win. "Today," the Führer boasted, "I head the strongest army in the world, the mightiest air force, and a proud navy." Anyone in the Third Reich or elsewhere who criticized the "front's sacrifices" or sought to "weaken the authority of this regime" would be executed, he warned — without mercy. "The Lord of the Worlds," he ended, "has done so many great things for us in the last years that we bow in gratitude before Providence, which has permitted us to be members of such a great

Volk. We thank Him that, in view of past and future generations of the German Volk, we were also allowed to enter our names honorably in the undying book of German history."[43]

Surprised by Hitler's affirmation of an Almighty, but puffed up by his references to the German Volk, and anxious not to be accused of criticizing the Führer, or "weakening" his authority, the Reichstag deputies gave him a great ovation.

Hitler's remarks about "many distinguished Americans" or isolationists were not entirely wrong.

"I was somewhat surprised at Germany and Italy declaring war upon us," admitted Hiram Johnson to his son in California — blaming his own country, rather than Hitler or Mussolini, since "we had been guilty of many breaches of peace, and have given the greatest causes for war that, under international law, can be given." Still and all, the U.S. senator confessed, "I did not think they would declare war" — in fact, "the day before, when I had made my objections" to a new American Expeditionary Force or AEF, he was confident he had up to "ten votes with me in the Senate," whereas the "day after when war was declared [by Hitler], I did not have a single damned vote."[44]

This, in truth, was the measure of the Führer's historic miscalculation. Without a German declaration of war, Congress would not have authorized the President to declare war on Germany, given the disaster at Hawaii and the worsening military situation in the Philippines and Pacific Islands. Hitler could thus have gotten America off his back, for free. Instead, by declaring war on the United States he now silenced America's isolationists like Senator Johnson — and just as importantly, provided the President with the power to act not simply as president, but as the world's most powerful commander in chief, sending American forces into combat on a global scale.

Shortly before 3:00 p.m. Eastern Standard Time on December 11, 1941, the President therefore sent over to Congress, in response to Hitler's declaration of war, his formal, written request that Congress "recognize a state of war between the United States and Germany," as well as "between the United States and Italy." Not he, but the dictators — the Japanese, and now the Germans and Mussolini's Italians — had chosen to wage war on the United States. In a unanimous voice-vote in the House of Representatives and a unanimous recorded vote in the Senate, the U.S. legislature gave its approval to the President's request. Senator Johnson even withdrew his opposition to an American Expeditionary Force — which would be under the President's sole direction.

"Those who know," the senator confided to his son, "claim that this will be a long war. . . . I doubt this. I think it will be fast and furious for a time, and then it will begin to crumble. . . . We may be certain of one thing, however," he added in one of the most celebrated mispredictions of a member of the august U.S. Senate. "It will last long enough to demolish our internal economy; and we'll find at its conclusion little value to our money and less to our properties."[45]

PART THREE

Churchill in the White House

4

The Victory Plan

UNTIL EARLY ON December 22, 1941, Eleanor Roosevelt had not even been told that Prime Minister Winston Churchill would be staying at the White House. The President had, however, recently spoken with Malvina Thomson, his wife's secretary, asking idly whom the First Lady had invited to stay over Christmas, Eleanor recalled, "as well as the people invited to dinner."

Who to dinner? "In all the years that we had been in the White House he had never paid much attention to such details," Mrs. Roosevelt reflected, "and this was the first time he had made such a request of Miss Thomson." Since the President "gave no explanation and no hint that anything unusual was going to happen," the First Lady and Miss Thomson could only conclude that the President "felt a sudden curiosity."[1]

Given Mrs. Roosevelt's work for civilian defense, the many causes she supported, as well as her efforts to keep the members of the large Roosevelt family connected with each other and with their paterfamilias, her lack of particular concern was understandable.[2] The nation, after all, was now at war. She'd ordered blackout curtains to be made for the White House. She had watched while antiaircraft guns were placed on the roof, gas masks were distributed, three-inch bulletproof glass was installed, and a tunnel was constructed to an air raid shelter beneath the building next door, on the orders of the Treasury secretary, Mr. Morgenthau, who was responsible for the President's physical security. (The President had not been amused. "Henry, I will not go down into the shelter," Roosevelt warned Morgenthau when refusing to have anything to do with such a scheme. Then, smiling, he added: "unless you allow me to play poker with all the gold in your vaults.")[3] But about a visitor from England, not only to dine but to stay with them, barely two days before Christmas, she had had no idea.

The British ambassador to the United States, by contrast, had known about Churchill's upcoming visit ever since the President issued the invitation. "After lunch I had twenty minutes with the President about plans for the talks this week," Lord Halifax had noted in his secret diary on December 21, the day before the Prime Minister's arrival. "The arrangements are all a bit fluid," he'd added, "depending on what time the people concerned can get here, and I foresee a good many last minute changes."[4]

There were. In the course of December 22, "we got news that the arrangements to meet Winston and co. had to be revised owing to a change of time of their arrival, and accordingly aeroplanes and special trains were improvised," the ambassador recorded. "Rather surprisingly, this all worked out pretty well, and they duly arrived at the airport about half past six, the President meeting them."[5]

Emerging from the U.S. Navy Lockheed Lodestar that had flown him from Norfolk, Virginia, once the Prime Minister's battleship, HMS *Duke of York,* had moored there, Winston Churchill espied the familiar figure of the President of the United States leaning against his car. He had come — in person! In the summer they had gotten together only as *potential* partners, meeting aboard their respective battleships. Now they were in the same, if metaphorical, boat.

The ten-day voyage across the North Atlantic had been brutal, the Prime Minister recounted to his host — storms so severe the vessel was reduced at times to six knots out of concern for its destroyer escort. In the end it had been compelled to shed its ocean antisubmarine lifeguards completely.

"Being in a ship in such weather as this is like being in prison, with the extra chance of being drowned,"[6] the Prime Minister paraphrased Dr. Johnson's famous quip in a letter he posted that night to his wife. For his part, Lord Beaverbrook, the Canadian-born British minister of supply who had accompanied Churchill on the voyage, declared he would have preferred traveling by submarine to being tossed about like balsa wood on the surface.

"They didn't enjoy their journey much," Lord Halifax confided to his diary. "Max Beaverbrook told me he wasn't sure whether their journey had been seven days or seven weeks at sea, but Winston seemed in good form, and we had quite a pleasant dinner at the White House — ourselves, Cordell Hull, Sumner Welles, Harry Hopkins, Winston and Max and one or two of their personal staff."[7]

Steaming alone and as fast as possible into the shallow waters of Chesapeake Bay to make up time, they had created so much swell that the Prime Minister's luggage had been inundated in the hold in the ship's stern. Fortunately, his clothes had stayed dry. After dinner at the White House the small group went upstairs to the Blue Room, "where we talked in the President's study about Vichy and North Africa, and various other matters on the Atlantic side of the world," as the British ambassador noted. "Complete unanimity of view and the atmosphere very good, Winston and the President getting on very well indeed together."[8]

In later years, following publication of Churchill's memoirs and the diaries of Churchill's doctor, Charles Wilson, a myth would spawn that the Prime Minister had somehow exercised strange magic on his Christmas visit to Washington: that he had somehow persuaded the legendary sorcerer of the White House into following a Churchillian rather than Rooseveltian strategy for winning the world war.

It is an absurd myth. Dr. Wilson, who became Lord Moran, was not even present at the White House dinner, nor at the long discussion in the President's study afterward. He had, it was true, been summoned from his hotel across the road by the Prime Minister. However, when he got to the upstairs bedroom where Churchill was staying, opposite that of Harry Hopkins, the Prime Minister was not there, he recalled. The White House Rose Room "smelt of cigar smoke and I tried to open the window. The crumpled bed-clothes were thrown back, and the floor was strewn with newspapers, English and American, just as the P.M. had thrown them away when he had glanced at the headlines," for "he always wants to know what the papers are saying about him."[9]

An hour and a half later, "the P.M. came out of the President's room. He looked at me blankly; he had forgotten he had sent for me."[10]

Churchill certainly seemed fired up, though. "I could see he was bottling up his excitement," Dr. Wilson described. Seeing the agitation in Churchill's whole being, he allowed the Prime Minister two "Reds," or barbiturate pills, to ensure he got a good night's sleep. In the elevator with Beaverbrook, thereafter, Churchill's minister of supply remarked to Wilson that he had never "seen that fellow [Churchill] in better form. He conducted the conversation for two hours with great skill" — claiming the "P.M. had been able to interest the President in a landing in North Africa."[11]

The PM had interested the President in a landing in North Africa, rather than the other way around? Either Beaverbrook expressed himself badly in front of Dr. Wilson, or Dr. Wilson (who reconstructed many of his wartime conversations later, under the guise of contemporary diary entries) misheard him. Wilson, on his first trip abroad with Churchill, was a sensitive man and a cautious doctor; he had no idea what he was writing about militarily, beyond what Churchill purportedly said to him. The Prime Minister's excitement that December night had certainly been palpable, but in reality it was owing to profound relief that, despite the disaster at Pearl Harbor and worsening situation in the Pacific and Far East — where Guam and Wake had been surrendered to the Japanese, Hong Kong was besieged, British forces were retreating to Singapore, and the Philippines looked next in line for Japanese conquest — the President was still determined upon a "Germany First" strategy.[12] And, moreover, that the two leaders were of like mind about how that offensive strategy should start: in North Africa.

The question in Churchill's mind the entire time he was onboard the *Duke of York,* crossing the Atlantic, had been: would Pearl Harbor force President Roosevelt to change his mind, and to direct American efforts to the Pacific, as Hitler was hoping? On finding that this was *not* the case, and that the President was still bent on following a "Germany First" policy, beginning with his "great pet scheme" (as Secretary Stimson dubbed it) for American landings in Northwest Africa, Churchill's excitement threatened to run wild.

As Churchill cabled the next day to the war cabinet and rump Chiefs of Staff Committee (whose members had accompanied the Prime Minister to Washington, with the exception of General Sir Alan Brooke, the new chief of the Imperial General Staff, or CIGS), there had been "general agreement" in his late-night discussion with the President about preempting a German occupation of Vichy-controlled Northwest Africa. Also about seizure of French battleships rather than allowing them to fall into German hands; and about invading, if necessary, the Atlantic islands of the Azores and Cape Verde. With regard to the North Africa enterprise, Churchill proudly reported, "it would be desirable to have all plans made for going into North Africa with or without invitation. I emphasised immense psychological effect likely to be produced in France and among French troops in North Africa by association of United States with the undertaking."[13]

Association with the undertaking? It was an odd yet characteristic circumlocution, typical of Churchill's often deliberately antique style of reportage. What he meant was, he was convinced the President was right to make landings in French Northwest Africa — Morocco and Algeria — an *American,* rather than British or Allied, enterprise: embarrassed to admit in writing that, given the unpopularity of the British among Vichy officials following his cruel orders for the sinking of the French fleet at Mers el-Kébir on the coast of French Algeria the year before, any hope of getting Vichy French commanders to welcome British troops alongside American soldiers might well doom the project.

What made Churchill's blood run so much faster, however, were the strategic advantages to the Allies of such an operation. As Churchill explained in detail in his cable to his war cabinet, the President "favored a plan to move into North Africa being prepared for either event, i.e. with or without [Vichy French] invitation. It was agreed to remit the study of the project to Staffs on assumption that it was vital to forestall the Germans in that area." The real meat of the plan was, however, its ramification: the assumption that the British Eighth Army, currently advancing from Egypt into Libya in Operation Crusader, "achieved complete success. I gave an account of the progress of the fighting in Libya, by which the President and other Americans were clearly much impressed and cheered."[14]

Between the two American and British armies, advancing from either end of the Mediterranean in a vast pincer movement, General Rommel's German-Italian Panzerarmee Afrika could thus be squeezed to extinction — if General Claude Auchinleck, commander in chief in the Middle East, fulfilled Churchill's proud expectations.

Given that this North African strategy would, ten months later, prove the very strategy that turned the tide against the Third Reich, leading inexorably to Hitler's downfall, it is extraordinary that its genesis and authorship would become so misunderstood, so misconstrued, and so fought over by historians in subsequent years[15] — especially those who mistrusted Winston Churchill and his tendency to bend the truth with "glittering phrases."

Among those who distrusted Churchill right from the time of his arrival at the White House on December 22, 1941, was General Joseph Stilwell, a fearless, feisty American commander slated to go to China as chief of staff to Generalissimo Chiang Kai-shek. "Vinegar Joe" Stilwell not only resented what he saw as Roosevelt's preference for the U.S. Navy over the U.S. Army, but — after conversing with Secretary Stimson and War Department planners who were convinced the President's French North African landings would fail, and serve no strategic purpose — he proceeded to trash the President in his diary as a "rank amateur in all things military," subject to "whims, fancy and sudden childish notions," a U.S. commander in chief who had been "completely hypnotized by the British" into supporting a "cockeyed" and "crazy gamble" in North Africa, when the better strategy was so obvious. "We should," he wrote in his diary, "clean the Pacific first and then face East" — exactly as Hitler had hoped when declaring war on the United States.[16]

Stilwell, unfortunately, was not alone in holding such views at the time. Colonel Edwin Schwien, of the U.S. Army's G-2 Intelligence Division, had already ridiculed the President's insistence on American landings in French Northwest Africa as "a patent absurdity" in comparison with the opportunity to embrace cross-Channel landings in northern France.[17] Colonel Albert Wedemeyer, a senior planning officer in the War Department who had been tasked with drawing up estimates of what would be required for whatever strategy was chosen, was also opposed to the idea of American landings in Morocco and Algeria — especially when Churchill arrived in the U.S. capital. As Wedemeyer warned his colleagues, Churchill was weaving an imperial "plot" that was against America's interests.

Whispers of such dissension within the War Department, moreover, were quick to circulate in rumor-ridden wartime Washington. Senator Hiram Johnson, the eighty-one-year-old isolationist, continued to believe America could avoid hostilities with the Third Reich, even after Hitler's declaration of war. "The war is getting worse all the time, and we're feeling it more and more. The President is trying to keep all matters within his hands," he would write to his son several weeks later, after Churchill's departure from Washington. Roosevelt "has been made a fool of by Winston Churchill, and in his innermost heart, I think he begins to realize it. We go merrily on spending money until we are pretty nearly over our debt limit, and it will be but a short time that we are. Another billion now for Russia. What a travesty this is! We are going to come out, everyone of moderate means, absolutely broke."[18]

• • •

Such criticism of the President, paraded at the time and in subsequent years, was not helped by Churchill himself.

After being voted out of office in 1945, Churchill was doubly anxious to paint himself, in his six-volume memoirs, *The Second World War,* as a successful wartime prime minister. Against a background of the British losing every single battle against the Nazis in the two years after he became prime minister, he naturally wished to portray himself as the coauthor, at least, of the eventual strategy that reversed this sorry saga. Describing his visit to Washington shortly before Christmas, 1941, he thus introduced the reader to the only extant, documented account of his first discussion with President Roosevelt, on the first night of his trip. This was his cabled message to the British war cabinet, a document Churchill was making public for the first time, eight years after the event — Churchill explaining in his memoirs how, straightway after his arrival at the White House, he had "immediately broached with the President, and those he had invited to join us, the scheme of Anglo-American intervention in North Africa. The President had not, of course at this time read the papers I had written on board ship, which I could not give him till the next day. But he had evidently thought much about my letter of October 20. Thus we all found ourselves pretty well on the same spot. My report home shows that we cut deeply into business on the night of our arrival."[19]

This was, unfortunately, to mislead readers and historians, since it implied that Churchill had suggested U.S. landings in Morocco and Algeria on October 20, and the President had "evidently thought much" about the idea.

The reverse, however, was the truth.

President Roosevelt's preferred strategy for U.S. landings in French Northwest Africa went way back to midsummer 1941, long before he even met Churchill off the coast of Newfoundland.

Recognizing, in the wake of the Nazi invasion of Russia on June 22, 1941, that Hitler could never be ultimately constrained save by force, Roosevelt had instructed the Joint Chiefs of Staff to research and then draw up an estimate of military production requirements — a program that would, of necessity, "make assumptions as to our probable friends and enemies and to the conceivable theatres of operation" in order "to defeat our potential enemies."[20] This secret Victory Plan — as it became known — was not to be too "detailed," the President had ordered in July;

rather, he'd urged, it was to be "general in scope," in order to ensure "the efficient utilization of our productive facilities." To meet the President's directive, the secretaries of war and navy and the chiefs of staff had then taken two months to carefully set out, in consultation with the President, a top-secret, twenty-three-page gauge of what it would require for America to win a probable war against Germany and Japan, both in strategy and production numbers. Their report, or "Joint Board Estimate," had been readied for the President on September 11, 1941, several weeks after he returned from Newfoundland.[21]

The Victory Plan's assumptions and predictions remain astonishing for their clarity and accuracy even seventy years after they were prepared for the President.

"Assumed enemies" were "Germany, and all German-occupied countries whose military forces cooperate with Germany; Japan and Manchuko; Italy; Vichy France; and possibly Spain and Portugal.

"Countries considered as friends or potential associates in warfare are the British Commonwealth, the Netherlands East Indies, China, Russia, Free France, people in German-occupied territory who may oppose Germany, and the countries of the Western Hemisphere."

The "national objectives of the United States" were given as "the preservation of the Western Hemisphere; prevention of the disruption of the British Empire; prevention of the further extension of Japanese territorial dominion; eventual establishment in Europe and Asia of balances of power which will most nearly ensure political stability in those regions and the future security of the United States; and, so far as practicable, the establishment of regimes favorable to economic freedom and individual liberty."

The U.S. document had then lain down the requirements necessary even if "the British Commonwealth collapsed" — necessitating a five-year struggle for the United States, which would last until 1946. With relentless realism, the report had considered "the overthrow of the Nazi regime by action of the people of Germany" to be unlikely — certainly not "until Germany is on the point of military defeat." Even were a new regime to be established in Germany, "it is not at all certain that such a regime would agree to peace terms acceptable to the United States" — necessitating, therefore, unconditional surrender. Since Hitler's Germany "can not be defeated by the European Powers now fighting against her," the report had thus concluded, and "if our European enemies are to be defeated, it will be necessary for the United States to enter the war and to employ a part of its armed forces offensively in the Eastern Atlantic and in Europe or Africa."

Or Africa.

It was this phrase that had, in truth, raised the hackles of the secretary of war and others working in the War Department. Nazi Germany, Secretary Stimson accepted, would be America's primary foe in the event of war. Even so, a simultaneous two-ocean war would probably have to be waged, to hold the Japanese forces at bay until Hitler's Germany surrendered, for the report did not envisage the British or the Free Dutch (whose government was in exile in London) would be able to "successfully withstand" a Japanese assault "against the British in Malaya and against the Dutch in the Dutch East Indies." Therefore it would be up to the United States to furnish the munitions and the troops, not only to deal with Hitler in Europe, but to hold off the Japanese, and eventually turn defeat in the Pacific into victory in Southeast Asia.

The report for the President had then addressed with great realism the thorniest question: how could such a simultaneous, two-ocean war be *fought,* with *Germany* as the primary foe? In accordance with the President's wishes, the report had laid down initial American offensive operations to be directed on those areas where Germany's "lines of communication" were most extended — Morocco, French West Africa, Senegal, and the Azores, if the Germans attempted to occupy those territories. In the case of Japan, likewise, it would mean striking where Japanese "lines of communication" were most extended: a strategy that would allow the United States to stretch the Japanese until Japan's pips squeaked "owing to a lack of adequate resources and industrial facilities." Meanwhile, by building up its own arsenal of trained combat troops and munitions, the U.S. would, over time, work its way into a position to win decisive victory, first over Germany, then over Japan.

With the exception of Russia, the great strength of America's assumed allies in such a war would be in naval and air forces — forces that "may prevent wars from being lost, and by weakening enemy strength may greatly contribute to victory," the Victory Plan acknowledged. "By themselves, however, naval and air forces seldom, if ever, win important wars," the report continued. "It should be recognized as an almost invariable rule that only land armies can finally win wars."

Those land armies would, with the exception of Russia, have to be pre-dominantly American.

The President's Victory Plan strategy, then, had already been clearly established in September 1941, months before the U.S. entered the war. In particular, Roosevelt's strong doubts about the feasibility of successfully landing American forces across the English Channel anytime soon had, at his insistence, been clearly addressed in the document. After all, had not Hitler, even at the height of his military conquests in 1940, balked at attempting a crossing of the Channel to defeat the remnants of British forces after Dunkirk? It was, in the words of the Victory Plan, "out of the question to expect the United States and its Associates to undertake in the near future a sustained and successful land offensive against the center of the German power" — something that was beyond even Soviet Russia, with its *millions* of troops fighting in the field.

How then was Germany to be ultimately defeated? "It being obvious that the Associated Powers can not defeat Germany by defensive operations, effective strategic offensive methods *other than an early land offensive in Europe* must be employed," the report had summarized.[22] A two-part strategy would have to be adopted — defensive at first. The Associated Powers, or Allies, would have initially to concentrate on cauterizing the ambitions of the dictators. This should be done by "a continuation of the economic blockade," and by "the prosecution of land offensives in distant regions where German troops can exert only a fraction of their total strength." In the case of Japan, a "strong defense of Malaysia," would be necessary, as well as an "economic offensive through blockade; a reduction of Japanese military power by raids; and Chinese offensive against the Japanese forces of occupation."

Cauterization would not bring victory, however. In the second stage of American strategy, American armies would have to go on the offensive: aiming first at Rome and Berlin, then at Tokyo.

The route of such offensive action in Europe was here the issue — since the planning and especially the production targets for eventual offensive action would be contingent upon that decision. In setting out the "major strategic objectives" in the ultimate defeat of Germany, the report had emphasized — at the President's specific direction — that an initial, indirect step in an American march on Rome and Berlin be rehearsed: *namely via Northwest Africa* — currently not occupied by German forces — which the President saw as the vital strategic first act in defeating Germany.

American occupation of French Northwest Africa — with or without Vichy help — would not only deny German access to the Atlantic Islands (a possible steppingstone to South America), the President was certain, but would provide the United States with "a potential base for a future land offensive," as the Victory Plan concluded. "In French North and West Africa, French troops exist which are potential enemies of Germany, provided they are re-equipped and satisfactory political conditions are established by the United States. Because the British Commonwealth has but few troops available and because of the unfriendly relations between the British and Weygand [Vichy] regime, it seems clear that a large proportion of the troops of the Associated Powers employed in this region must be United States troops."[23]

This, then, had been the President's blueprint, prepared over the summer of 1941, for prosecuting a future global war, both in the short term and the long term — once hostilities came. The typed report, with numerous appendices, had been dated September 11, 1941, and had borne the President's imprint and imprimatur on every page. Moreover, in the weeks after its preparation, the President's predilection for landings of U.S. forces in Vichy-controlled French Northwest Africa had only grown stronger.

On October 3, 1941, for example, the U.S. secretary of the navy, Frank Knox, had confided to Lord Halifax that "what he wanted to see happen" — as Ambassador Halifax immediately reported to Prime Minister Churchill — "was for the Americans to send 150,000 men to Casablanca and join hands through an assenting Weygand with us [the British] in North Africa. The President, according to him, was much interested in this idea. I should suppose we are some way off that yet but the fact that they should be thinking about it at all is interesting."[24]

Interesting it was! A giant pincer movement, using American naval, air, and ground forces that would, with British forces pressing from Libya, crush the German-Italian Panzer Army in Africa and provide a base and springboard on the very threshold of Europe — forcing Hitler to defend the continent from Norway to the Mediterranean! As Halifax had also learned, however, the President's enthusiasm for such an indirect strategy was by no means shared by the aging Republican secretary of war — or even by General Marshall, who saw North African landings as too dangerous to undertake, and in any event a distraction from the most direct route to Berlin. They had thus favored U.S. troops being sent directly to Britain in the event of war, thence to be put into combat on a more straightforward path to the capital of Hitler's Third Reich, beginning with cross-Channel landings, mounted from England's southern coast against the coast of mainland France.

A week later, on October 10, 1941, over lunch at his desk at the White House, the President had confided his Northwest Africa plan in person to the British ambassador,[25] informing Halifax he'd "told Stimson and Marshall to make a study of the proposal to send an American Expeditionary Force to West Africa. This had greatly excited Stimson and Marshall, who thought he was 'going off the deep end' and embarking on a dispersal of effort that they thought unwise," Halifax had secretly reported to Churchill in London the next day, October 11, 1941. "He had explained to them, however, that he did not contemplate anything immediate, but none the less wanted the question studied," Halifax had cabled the Prime Minister. The titular Vichy leader, Maréchal Pétain, "might die," and his understudy, General Weygand, "might feel himself released from his personal pledge of loyalty" to Pétain and to Hitler, "and things might move. I don't suppose that all this is to be taken very seriously at present, but it is a pointer," the ambassador had added in his letter to Churchill.[26] The long term, in other words, might well become the short term.

Given that America was not at war with Germany at the time, such a difference of opinion between the President and his War Department officials had remained academic — but potentially problematic, too, Halifax had wisely recognized. It would be unfortunate, he felt, if the President's coalition pincer-strategy were to be defeated, not by the Germans, but by the U.S. War Department.

To check out for himself, Halifax had therefore wisely gone to the Munitions Building to sound out the secretary of war in person that very evening — October 10, 1941, as he informed Churchill. Stimson was dead against U.S. landings in North Africa. "Stimson told me that he was inclined to hold the President off schemes that would dissipate United States effort, the possibilities of which were severely limited" — for Stimson, like General Stilwell (who was initially chosen to lead the Casablanca attack), feared such an operation of war could never succeed — indeed, as the war secretary told the British ambassador in somewhat defeatist language, he was now far from confident the United States could do more than send American troops to help defend Britain against a possible Nazi invasion if, as Stimson suspected, the Russians were defeated in Operation Barbarossa, or sued for peace.

Churchill, in contrast to Colonel Stimson, had been *delighted* to hear of the President's "great pet scheme" for North African landings — and had made it his personal task to help the President override Stimson's objections to it.

Nine days after receiving Halifax's cable, Churchill thus wired to tell the President that, if the United States chose to remain out of the war against Germany, and in the event of German pressure on the Vichy government to grant the Nazis "facilities in French North Africa," he himself was "holding a force equivalent to one armoured and three field divisions ready with shipping," that could "either enter Morocco by Casablanca upon French invitation or otherwise help to exploit in the Mediterranean a victory in Libya."[27]

The President had smiled at such well-meant Churchillian bravado. How the British, whose performance in amphibious landings since Norway in April 1940 had been uniformly disastrous, imagined that a unilateral British invasion of French Northwest Africa would succeed against hostile Vichy forces without U.S. help did not say much for the Prime Minister's realism. But the President had said nothing — admiring Churchill's offensive spirit, and his support for Roosevelt's strategy.

There the matter of potential American military operations in Europe had rested, up until December 4, 1941. For it was on that day, in the most egregious act of treachery, that Colonel McCormick had published many of the details of the President's Victory Plan — the entire report to the President having been deliberately leaked by an individual in Stimson's War Department. Printed by McCormick, it had inevitably found its way straight into Hitler's declaration of war on the United States, announced before the Reichstag on December 11, seven days later.

By then, however, events had swamped the scandal — the Japanese attack on Pearl Harbor making McCormick's isolationism risibly naïve. Indeed, in the days after the terrible news from the Far East, there was many a patriot in Washington who, reflecting on the *Chicago Tribune*'s recent revelations, thanked the Almighty that, despite the disaster in Hawaii, the United States at least *had* a plan for fighting the war — and in Britain, an ally willing to fight with the U.S. to win it.

• • •

In days of preparation for Churchill's arrival and "the strategic problems which are confronting us in the coming conferences,"[28] the President had convened meeting after meeting at the White House. The first had been on December 18, 1941, at 3:00 p.m., a conference at which Stimson, Knox, General Marshall, Admiral Stark, Admiral King, Harry Hopkins, and Admiral Nimitz — the new commander the President had appointed to replace Admiral Kimmel in the Pacific — were present.

"The President then told this conference exactly the nature of the conference which is coming next Monday [December 23, 1941] and who will be there, and he said that he desired us to attend it as his advisers. A paper was produced containing [a] suggested agenda which had been drawn up by the British," Stimson noted in his diary.[29] The President, however, had wanted an American version — and had therefore told his advisers to draw up a counteragenda. America, not Great Britain, was to run the war, the President made clear — not only because the United States would be providing the bulk of the necessary forces to defeat Nazi Germany and Japan, but because the performance of the British so far had been, in all frankness, miserable.

The Japanese invasion of Malaya looked increasingly ominous — aiming toward Singapore, Britain's primary naval base in the Far East. The Australians and New Zealanders were panicking — with very few British naval, air, or army forces to defend them. Stimson, for his part, was all for "safety first" — and therefore opposed any discussion of offensive action at this point. Defending the American West and East Coasts, helping to defend the British Isles, providing arms to help the British defend the Middle East and India, using American forces to defend Australia and New Zealand — these were the first priorities to be tabled, Stimson thus insisted. Beyond that, he forecast, there were "a number of things on which there will be sharp divergence" between the U.S. Army and the Navy — and between the United States and Great Britain.[30]

The President was disappointed in his war secretary. He felt it politic, however, not to risk dissension at such a critical moment. *Unity of purpose* was the foremost consideration, since the whole world was now looking to the United States to take the reins in a global war. The President's plan was therefore to focus not on the things that might divide his advisers, the armed forces, and the U.S. and British, but on those that bound them together. He therefore laid down his first priority: namely, the moral basis for a coalition war, involving as many allies as possible in the fight against Germany and Japan. His Atlantic Charter should, he told Secretary Hull, now be enshrined in a new declaration of principles that all of America's allies could sign up to.

Simultaneously, a good working relationship with America's closest new coalition partner, Great Britain, should be fostered. Allied military strategy should be concerted, he explained — but with Washington, not London, as the central headquarters of the Allies. If, in the next days over Christmas, 1941, he got agreement on these two priorities, the President felt, he would be doing very well, no matter how bad the immediate news "from the front" might be. All would fall into place.

Winston Churchill, for his part, had a very different modus operandi from the President. Where Roosevelt sought to achieve agreement with his wishes by charm and goodwill, Churchill simply relied on his commanding personality and sense of privilege — fueled by an intake of alcohol that made him relatively impervious to criticism or rebuke. Immediately upon his arrival in the White House, the Prime Minister had made himself at home. "We had to remember to have imported brandy after dinner," Eleanor complained — deeply aware of her own family's history of alcoholism. "This was something Franklin did not have as a rule."[31] "Never had the staid butlers, ushers, maids and other Executive Mansion workers seen anything like Winston before," recalled Roosevelt's Secret Service detail chief — the Prime Minister consuming "brandy and scotch with a grace and enthusiasm that left us all openmouthed in awe."[32]

Churchill's commandeering of the First Lady's office, the Monroe Room, for his portable maps and files did not endear the Prime Minister to Mrs. Roosevelt, either.

The President did not share his wife's shock, nor her barely concealed disapproval. He liked eccentricity, which made people the more interesting, he found. Observing the diminutive politician setting up shop in his, the President's, own residence, Roosevelt was amused — indeed, he wondered how he might turn the Prime Minister's premature arrival in America into a public relations winner — thus helping him override the concerns of his secretary of war and senior generals in the War and Navy Departments. Hitler's military success, after all, could not solely be ascribed to German tanks and air power. The Führer had spent years perfecting the art of propaganda, using the dark genius of his associate, Dr. Goebbels — and the sense of national unity they had created in the Third Reich was a fundamental component of German military morale.

Well then, the President recognized, the Associated Powers must do even better! In this respect, Churchill's presence in the U.S. capital might prove a perfect foil in concealing American disarray — as well as internal dissension over future operations. The Prime Minister's distinctive, pugnacious personality could be used to advantage — a perception the President put straight into action by asking, over lunch at his cluttered desk in the Oval Study, whether Winston would appear with him at his weekly press conference in the West Wing at 4:00 p.m. on December 23, 1941.

The Prime Minister said he would be delighted to do so. And thus, at one of the darkest moments of the war, before a barrage of cameras, microphones, and journalist's notepads, the first image of a truly Grand Alliance was created, at the White House, in Washington, D.C.

Gazing at the extraordinary scrimmage of a hundred White House reporters jamming the small room — each one having been screened for security purposes — Roosevelt began with an apology. "I am sorry to have taken so long for all of you to get in, but apparently — I was telling the Prime Minister — the object was to prevent a wolf from coming in here in sheep's clothing. (Laughter) But I was thereby mixing my metaphors, because I had suggested to him this morning that if he came to this conference he would have to be prepared to meet the American press, who, compared with the British press — as was my experience in the old days — are 'wolves' compared with the British press 'lambs.' However, he is quite willing to take on a conference, because we have one characteristic in common. We like new experiences in life."[33]

The President's genuine affection for the Prime Minister was instantly clear to all. "Mr. Roosevelt liked Churchill a great deal," wrote the AP reporter A. Merriman Smith, later; "disagreed with many of his ideas and suggestions, but nevertheless found his presence stimulating, often to the point of fatigue."[34]

Before Churchill stood to speak, however, the President said he wanted "to make it clear that this is a preliminary British-American conference, but that thereby no other Nations are excluded from the general objective of defeating Hitlerism in the world. Just for example, I think the Prime Minister this morning has been consulting with the Dominions. That is especially important, of course, in view of the fact that Australia and New Zealand are very definitely in the danger zone; and we are working out a complete unity of action in regard to the Southwest Pacific. In addition to that, there are a good many Nations besides our own that are at war. . . . I think it is all right to say that Mr. Mackenzie King [prime minister of Canada] will be here later on. In regard to the other Nations, such as the Russians, the Chinese, the Dutch, and a number of other Nations which are — shall I say — overrun by Germany, but which still maintain governments which are operating in the common cause, they also will be on the inside in what we are doing."

Churchill's country, then, was but one combatant in a great coalition of nations the President was assembling to stand against Hitler, Mussolini, and the Japanese. "In addition to that, there are various other Nations, for example a number of [South] American Republics which are actually in the war, and another number of American Republics which although not acting under a declaration of war are giving us very definite and much-needed assistance. It might be called on their part 'active non-belligerency.'

"At five o'clock we are having a staff meeting. We have already had a meeting with the State Department officials, and during the next few days decisions will materialize. We can't give you any more news about them at this time, except to say that the whole matter is progressing very satisfactorily.

"Steve [Early] and I first thought that I would introduce the Prime Minister, and let him say a few words to you good people, by banning questions. However, the Prime Minister did not go along with that idea, and I don't blame him. He said that he is perfectly willing to answer any reasonable questions for a reasonably short time, if you want to ask him. . . . And so I am going to introduce him, and you to him, and tell you that we are very, very happy to have him here. . . . And so I will introduce the Prime Minister.

"(To the Prime Minister) I wish you would just stand up for one minute and let them see you. They can't see you. (Applause greeted the Prime Minister when he stood up, but when he climbed onto his chair so that they could see him better, loud and spontaneous cheers and applause rang through the room.)

"THE PRESIDENT: (to the press) Go ahead and shoot."[35]

The reporters shot — though the first question ("What about Singapore, Mr. Prime Minister? The people of Australia are terribly anxious about it. Would you say to be of good cheer?") went so straight to the heart of the war crisis that the President almost fell off his wheelchair. "The President laughed so hard that he nearly choked on his cigarette holder," Smith recalled.[36]

Faced with "wolves" the like of whom he'd never encountered before, Churchill acquitted himself extremely well. Chubby-cheeked, wielding his trademark cigar, and wearing a dark jacket with a polka-dot bow tie and striped pants, he parried calls for predictions and delivered memorable phrases of moral uplift. However, there was never any question but that he was now an admired but junior partner in a new coalition — utterly dependent on the United States for the successful prosecution of the war.

"My feeling is that the military power and munitions power of the United States are going to develop on such a great scale that the problem will not so much be whether to choose between this and that," Churchill responded to questions of strategy, "but how to get what is available to all the theaters in which we have to wage this World War."

Churchill was telling the truth. However defeatist Secretary Stimson and other generals might be, the numbers spoke for themselves. From the President himself and from Harry Hopkins, Churchill had heard preliminary numbers of estimated U.S. war production that had made the blood in the Prime Minister's veins run faster — and did so even more when, at the first formal Anglo-American staff conference that followed, it was made clear the war would indeed be directed from Washington.

The writing was on the wall — and it read quite clearly: "United States of America First."

Convincing the press and public that the democracies were united in confronting the Axis powers was one thing. Convincing the British visitors that the American military was, under its commander in chief, ready for the big leagues was another.

Fresh from bombed-out London, Churchill's huge retinue of staff officers and clerks had expected a land of plenty, yet they found themselves awed by life in America. From thirty-six-page newspapers "an inch thick" to the huge cars in which they were taken to their hotels, Churchill's almost eighty attendants were mesmerized by the very scale of things — much like Gulliver's adventure in the "Voyage to Brobdingnag."

The traffic in Washington, for example, amazed Churchill's military assistant, Colonel Ian Jacob: "a flood of American saloon cars, all looking new, all almost alike, and most of them with only one or two people in them. There is a car to every 2½ people in the city. No-one walks a yard. Cars lie parked everywhere, and no-one bothers about having a garage. You simply leave the car on the side of the nearest street, if you can find a spare hole. The whole effect is as of an ant-heap, or a swarm of beetles."[37]

As at the Newfoundland summit in August, there appeared to him to be a vast difference between the American approach to high command, however, and the British version. "At 5.30," Jacob noted in his diary immediately after the President's press conference, "there took place the first meeting between the Prime Minister and the president and their Chiefs of Staff," held in the Cabinet Room, which was situated "in the West block, on the garden level," next to the Mansion. "It is a pleasant room, about the size of the Cabinet Room at No. 10 [Downing Street] but a little wider. It has four French windows each in an archway, and is devoid of furniture except for a table and a number of chairs including arm chairs disposed around the walls. Two or three pictures of former Presidents hang on the walls which are white." The long, almost coffin-shaped table was unexpectedly Arthurian, widest about halfway along one side, where Mr. Roosevelt presided. The table seated "16 in comfort, all of whom can see each other well." To the right of the President sat Prime Minister Churchill; to the President's left, the secretary of the navy, Mr. Knox, flanked by Admirals Stark, King, and Turner, the chief of naval planning; and to Churchill's right, Secretary Stimson and the other U.S. and British chiefs of staff, occupying the rest of the table, together with Harry Hopkins and Max Beaverbrook.[38]

"The President led off with a statement as to the talks which he already had during the day with Churchill," Secretary Stimson noted in his own diary — expressing surprise and delight as the President pulled out Stimson's somewhat feeble "Memorandum of Decisions Made at the White House on December 21," 1941, "and made it the basis of the entire conference."[39]

"He went over it point by point," Secretary Stimson noted, "telling the conference of their views on each point and then asked Churchill to follow and comment on it, which he did. There was then a little general discussion participated in by the American military and naval members and the British military and naval members, and it became very evident that there was a pretty general agreement upon the views of the grand strategy which we had held in the War Department and which were outlined in my paper. Churchill commented feelingly on the sentence of my summary where I described our first main principle as 'the preservation of our communications across the North Atlantic with our fortress in the British Isles covering the British fleet.'"⁴⁰

In truth Roosevelt was concealing from Stimson his own determination to proceed, as soon as practicable, with an American counterstroke: the invasion of Casablanca, Morocco, and Algeria with 150,000 troops. For the moment, however, the President expressed himself in complete agreement with the U.S. war secretary as to the importance of sticking to a "Germany First" strategy.

Roosevelt's charm and confident air certainly deceived Colonel Jacob. "The President is a most impressive man and seems on the best of terms with his advisers," Jacob described in his diary — evincing no idea of what was going on, in reality, namely an awkward dance between the Democratic president and his elderly Republican secretary of war, whose tone was one of fear and anxiety over the current situation in the Far East, and America's limited ability to do anything offensively. By the side of the Prime Minister, the President appeared to the innocent Jacob to be "a child in Military affairs, and evidently has little realization of what can and can't be done. He doesn't seem to grasp how backward his country is in its war preparations, and how ill-prepared his army is to get involved in large scale operations."⁴¹

The very opposite was, in verity, the case — the President all too aware of American disarray in the wake of Pearl Harbor and the time it would take, behind the scenes, to ready American forces of any size to be put into battle, yet determined to look beyond the current trials in the Pacific. "To our eyes," Jacob wrote, "the American machine of government seems hopelessly disorganized. The President, to start with, has no private office. He has no real Private Secretary, and no Secretariat for Cabinet or Military business. The Cabinet is of little account anyway, as the President is Commander-in-Chief. But he has no proper machinery through which to exercise command. . . . We found this complete lack of system extended throughout. . . . Their ideas of organization and ours are wide apart, and they have first to close the gap between their Army and Navy before they can work as a real team with us."

As a result, Jacob blamed American mismanagement and disorganization for what he saw as a disappointing military summit. As he put it, sailing back to England, "the Chiefs of Staff meetings which now took place almost daily for the next three weeks never really achieved anything. There was never any settled Agenda, and every kind of red herring was pursued. We thought we had achieved a considerable triumph when we got our general strategy paper agreed to," he lamented, "without amendment by the U.S. Chiefs of Staff. I am pretty sure however that it is regarded as an agreeable essay which all can pay lip service to, while each American Service follows its nose and does the job which seems to stick out at the moment."[42]

Poor Jacob — whose father had been a British field marshal in World War I — was completely bamboozled, unaware that the president's modus operandi was the product of decades of experience in marshaling American talent to serve his purpose and strategies. In this respect, Churchill's modus operandi and vivendi were the polar opposite. Churchill's methods, however, could boast only of having produced in two years the longest series of military disasters in British history. By contrast the President's methods, as U.S. commander in chief, had yet to be tested in war.

All too soon Jacob's ignorance of the American system, and his dedicated bureaucratic approach to high command in the service of the British prime minister/minister of defense, were to embroil Roosevelt in the near-resignation of one of the senior members of the President's own administration, his secretary of war. For what Jacob could not understand was that this was America, not India.

Jacob's faux pas would be telling. British imperial bureaucracy had incontestably served its empire well. Over the centuries, following conquest or annexation, the British had learned to administer vast indigenous populations by imposing a hierarchy of paper wallahs, or colonial bureaucrats, much as the Chinese had done over millennia in their own territories: a governor and, below him, a multitiered hierarchy of civil servants, with small but highly disciplined naval and army forces on hand to impose civil order when and where required.

For generations this British system of colonial administration had proven almost unimaginably successful — but it had also led, in such a huge and scattered global jurisdiction, to a white elitism disguising an almost fatal aversion to manual labor. It was simply assumed that Indians, or coolies, or foreign servants and mercenaries, would provide the necessary muscle to maintain an imperial system that guaranteed order, was generally not corrupt, preserved freedom of religion — and ensured British profits. Thus a tiny cadre of British civil servants, educated at elitist British "public" (actually private) schools, had managed the necessary administrative and clerical paperwork of an empire with admirable diligence — one that elicited even Hitler's admiration.[43]

In times of war, moreover, British Empire administrators and clerics had simply continued to do the same as they'd done in peace: giving orders in writing to those responsible for carrying them out. In recent decades, in the aftermath of World War I, with its terrible loss of life, there had been fewer and fewer competent British administrators — especially soldiers — willing or able to see these orders were executed. And once the fires of World War II had been kindled by Hitler in Europe and the French Republic collapsed, the heart had seemed to go out of the elderly British imperial motif. Against more disciplined, ideologically inspired, and well-armed Nazi troops in Norway, Belgium, France, Greece, Crete, Libya, and Egypt, Britain's valiant forces — its Royal Navy, RAF, and Army — had simply failed to operate together as a unified, cohesive, modern military force on the field of battle, even though the performance of individuals and individual units — as in the Battle of Britain — was often meritorious.

The results, when pitted against Hitler's Nazi legions in France, the Mediterranean, and North Africa, had shamed the island nation: campaigns studded by retreat, evacuation, and surrender. More worrying still, the current British performance in the Far East, following the Japanese declaration of war, held out little hope of being more fortunate. Hong Kong was expected, Churchill had assured the President, to hold out for several months, until reinforcements could be assembled and sent out; in fact, outnumbered four to one, the crown colony would surrender after seventeen days, on December 25, 1941. The same was to hold true of Singapore, the "Pearl Harbor" of the Far East — which Churchill had hoped would hold out for many months. Moreover, despite Churchill's assurances to the President, the case of Libya — where General Auchinleck had already found it necessary to fire the Eighth Army field commander he'd appointed, General Alan Cunningham — was not promising to be any better in terms of British military competence on the field of battle, whatever the Prime Minister might claim.

In a word, the British had perfected the bureaucratic arts, but had let slip the art of fighting — at least in terms of modern combat. And the President, better than anyone, knew it: not from his "advisers," but from his special sources.

However much his cabinet colleagues and subordinates deplored the habit, President Roosevelt liked to send for, see, and hear personal reports on what was going on around the world from those he trusted.

These reports to the President — both verbal and written — were necessarily anecdotal, but they ensured that a highly intelligent and above all curious U.S. commander in chief was able to gauge the reality of what was going on, rather than relying on the sanitized version from his various ambassadors and government officials, as Churchill did. The President's emissaries thus kept him well informed, at least anecdotally, about reality on the ground, acting as the President's "eyes and ears" outside the White House — at home and abroad. Where Churchill relied on his reading of history and his abiding, romanticized Victorian vision of British arms, the President liked to question every visitor, and every report. Moreover, the President's emissaries and informants reflected every area of government and society, high and low. His wife, Eleanor, might — and did — attract opprobrium for her dedication to progressive social causes, for example, but the President, restricted by his wheelchair and the discomfort of traveling, admired her for her openheartedness and willingness to journey forth to see things firsthand. "You know, my Missus gets around a lot," Roosevelt told Churchill's physician, Dr. Wilson. "She's got a great talent with *people*."[44]

As Dr. Wilson reflected later, "when the President was so immersed in the war that he was in danger of forgetting the hopes and aspirations of the ordinary people, Eleanor was at his elbow to jog his memory." This was in marked contrast to the doctor's formal patient, the Prime Minister of Great Britain, and *his* wife. "Mrs. Churchill played no such part in her husband's political life. They were a devoted pair," Dr. Wilson acknowledged, "but he paid little attention to her advice, and did not take it very seriously."[45]

Wilson may have overstated the case, but his perception was revealing. Winston Churchill might paint his trip to Washington, both at the time and later, as an example of his own great leadership at a moment of world crisis. In many respects it was, in terms of Allied unity and propaganda — certainly when contrasted with the visit by his deputy prime minister, Major Clement Attlee, leader of the Labour Party, only a month before. ("All quite useful for the Americans to hear," Lord Halifax had written in his diary on November 10, 1941, after listening to Mr. Attlee making a speech at the National Press Club in Washington, "but I don't think he is a very impressive personality.")[46] Churchill, by contrast, was out to impress — from the start.

Attempting to save the British Empire as Neville Chamberlain's successor, Churchill had sought to infuse Britain's military hierarchy with new energy from the top, even if this meant riding roughshod over his colleagues and staff. Like a natural, aggressive chess player, Churchill had a wonderful, instinctive grasp of grand strategy, backed by the ability to withdraw his mind from the current fray in order to achieve a transcending perspective across time and globe. This made him an inspiring speaker, and courageous leader in a great cause — giving heart to his staff and to his nation at a time of ever-worsening military defeats. It could not, unfortunately, substitute for good judgment.

Of all Wilson's perceptions about Churchill, it was his recognition of Churchill's poor judgment, in the context of a man so otherwise exceptional, that most testified to the doctor's honesty. Churchill's courage was genuine and exemplary, Dr. Wilson observed. On the other hand, in terms of people and decisions, Churchill was also endowed with desperately poor discernment. As Churchill's own wife put it, Winston had surrounded himself all his life with "charlatans and imposters," because his very genius — his ability to cast his mind across broad horizons, to play with ideas and invent "glittering phrases" — demanded a fawning rather than critical audience. Once asked by King George VI to become prime minister, in May 1940, Churchill had made himself minister of defense, thus licensing himself to become a quasi commander-in-chief. As the Prime Minister of Canada himself told Dr. Wilson, "Winston cowed his colleagues. He stifled discussion when it was critical and did not agree with his views."[47] Lord Hankey, who had for many years been secretary to the British cabinet and was the paymaster general, deplored Churchill's moody behavior and impulsive decisions, referring to the Prime Minister in his diaries and letters as "the dictator," a "Rogue Elephant" whose military disasters would have long since ended his career, had there been an alternative leader in Britain of any real timbre. "It was he who forced us into the Norwegian affair which failed; the Greek affair which failed; and the Cretan affair which is failing," Hankey had lamented in his diary earlier that summer — adding, in October 1941, that the British war cabinet had become a "crowd of silent men," enduring "the usual monologue by Churchill" — a British government of "utter incompetence,"[48] while another senior civil servant, Sir Norman Brook, described the Prime Minister's greatest failure as being "not much interested to hear what others had to say."[49] Leo Amery, the British secretary of state for India, declared that Churchill had reduced his country to "a one-man government, so far as the war is concerned."[50]

Had Churchill's military decisions been sounder, his dictatorial approach might have been forgivable; as it was, even the former British prime minister Arthur Balfour called him a "a genius without judgment."[51]

By comparison, the President — who appeared to lack a foolproof administrative machine to convey dictatorial orders, as Churchill possessed — was blessed by something far more important: the gift of good judgment. Lacking an imperial-style apparatus to assemble information on paper and then impart his decisions, and, moreover, a believer in the American system of checks and balances in making decisions that affected the nation, Roosevelt relied on his own sunny personality, not obedience, Dr. Wilson noted. Churchill "beat down opposition and struck men dumb who had come to the Cabinet to expostulate." By contrast, the President "was not a strong administrator," but "he got the work done by picking the right man for a particular job — he was a good judge of men — and trusting him to do it; he encouraged and inspired his man to get on with his job. If he didn't he got rid of him. And of course the man he trusted gave of his best. The plan worked."[52]

As he later looked back across the course of the war, Dr. Wilson — who knew Churchill probably better than anyone — found himself lost in admiration of Roosevelt. "To lead a nation in this fashion calls for unusual qualities," he wrote. "Roosevelt had them. Men came away from the White House feeling better." The President had not always solved their problems, "he had not even given them directions, but he sent them away determined to carry out their task . . . Roosevelt's detachment was always taking me by surprise; he kept his head above the sea of administrative problems; his task was not to straighten them out, it was to harness the nation to its work."[53]

Confident in his choice of subordinates, even when they failed to match his expectations, the President was thus not only a master politician, but a master of happy, confident delegation — whereas Churchill, who "unlike the President was not a good judge of men" and had "so often been let down when he entrusted to others the solution of anything," attempted to run everything, down to the last detail. "Winston tried to do the work of three men, he had his finger in every pie," Dr. Wilson reflected, recalling Foreign Secretary Eden's heartfelt protest, "I do wish he'd leave me to do my own job!"[54]

"Certainly it is not in that mood that men do their best work," the doctor chronicled. "Roosevelt knew this. The P.M. never did. Once I said to him, 'Hitler seems to tackle not only the strategy of his campaigns, but also the details.' Winston looked up at me with a mischievous smile spread over his face. 'That's exactly what I do,' he said."[55]

Churchill had said this with cheeky pride. Dr. Wilson — like so many of those serving the Prime Minister — found himself disappointed by this aspect of his genius-patient: a man who could see the larger picture so brilliantly, yet would interfere with, chide, overrule, and bring to ruin even his most professional subordinates. "He got caught up in a web of detail," Wilson wrote, "like a fly in a spider's web."[56]

How, then, was it possible for a national leader of such poor military judgment to get on with a U.S. commander in chief blessed with fine judgment, but a completely different approach to man management?

Dr. Wilson, watching the combination over the ensuing days, noted something strange — a key perhaps to how the miracle was effected. For the first time in his life, as Dr. Wilson observed, Churchill *listened*. And accepted his new position, not as the President's equal but as his honored vizier.

For his part, Colonel Jacob also watched Churchill's transformation or submission — though with incredulity. On Christmas Eve, 1941, at a meeting in the Monroe Room, temporarily serving as Churchill's Map Room, "at which the Prime Minister and our [British] Chiefs of Staff were discussing matters of domestic concern," a "peculiar incident" occurred, Jacob recorded in his diary.[57]

"In the middle of the meeting, the door opened and in came the President in the wheeled chair and joined us. He asked various questions, and then said he feared the news from the Philippines was not good, and that it looked as it would very soon be impossible to get any more air reinforcements into Manila as the aerodromes would be in the enemy's hands. He felt it would be for the Joint Chiefs of Staff to consider where, in the circumstances, the reinforcements could go. The Prime Minister agreed, and so did our [British] Chiefs of Staff."[58]

Once the President and Prime Minister had left to have dinner, Colonel Jacob, as a good staff officer, asked the British chiefs of staff — Field Marshal Dill, Admiral Pound, Air Marshal Portal — if he should draw up a record of the meeting for the U.S. chiefs of staff, so they could duly discuss the President and Prime Minister's haunting question about the reinforcements at their conference meeting the next day, Christmas Day, at 3:00 p.m. The British chiefs said yes.

The next day, Christmas Day, there was an explosion that rocked the new Grand Alliance.

"At 3 o'clock the meeting was just starting when an urgent call came for [Brigadier] Jo [Hollis] to go to the White House. Off he went," Jacob recorded. "Not long after that, I was called out to answer the telephone, and found Jo on the line. He said there was a regular flutter in the dovecote, and that we had dropped a brick, but he couldn't quite make out what we had done wrong. The Prime Minister had said that we had issued some Minutes containing statements, or a Directive, by the President, and that this had given offence. We must realize that the President had to be treated with ultra respect, and we had been guilty of some kind of lèse-majesté."[59]

"Lèse majesté" was an apt phrase for the realization, among dutiful British staff officers serving Mr. Churchill, that there was a new military monarch whose wishes and concerns must be treated as senior to those of their own, hitherto dictatorial, prime minister/minister of defense. Above all, they must never, ever embarrass the new monarch in terms of his U.S. war council and cabinet — which the President ran in a quite different way to that of Mr. Churchill.

The "dovecote" was, in fact, the U.S. War Department — where Jacob's neatly typed minutes of the British Map Room meeting had caused consternation.

In his own diary, a seething Henry Stimson recorded how, upon returning from a Christmas horseback ride that morning, he'd been bombarded by irate "Generals Arnold, Eisenhower [the new head of the army's Far Eastern Section of the War Plans Division, with a staff of one hundred], and Marshall" who "brought me a rather astonishing memorandum which they had received from the White House concerning a meeting between Churchill and the President and recorded by one of Churchill's assistants" — i.e., Jacob. "It reported the President as proposing to discuss the turning over to the British of our proposed reenforcements [destined] for MacArthur. This astonishing paper made me very angry," Stimson recorded, "and, as I went home for [Christmas] lunch and thought it over again, my anger grew until I finally called up Hopkins, told him of the paper and of my anger at it, and I said that if that was persisted in, the President would have to take my resignation; that I thought it was very improper to discuss such matters while the fighting was going on and to do it with another nation."[60]

Stimson's furious reaction went to the very heart of the new alliance being forged in the prosecution of a modern, global war. The resignation of the Republican secretary of war, in the wake of Pearl Harbor and the Japanese invasion of the Philippines, would certainly have done more than upset the dovecote. "This incident shows the danger of talking too freely in international matters of such keen importance without the President carefully having his military and naval advisers present," Stimson dictated on his tape recorder that night. "This paper, which was a record made by one of Churchill's assistants, would have raised any amount of trouble if it had gotten into the hands of an unfriendly press"[61] — as the Victory Plan had done. Stimson felt, in fact, that he had personally saved the President from personal disaster at the hands of his own leaky War Department staff.

Hopkins, sensing a dual threat — of resignation, and of a deliberate leak — made as if aghast. "He was naturally very surprised and shocked by what I said and very soon called me back telling me that he had recited what I had said to the President in the presence of Churchill," Stimson noted, "and they had denied that any such proposition had been made."[62]

"I think he felt he had pretty nearly burned his fingers," Stimson speculated about the President — causing Roosevelt, in fact, to summon Stimson, Knox, Marshall, Arnold, King, Stark, and Hopkins to a new meeting at the White House on Christmas Day at 5:30 p.m. The President "went over with us the reports up to date of the various matters and we discussed various things which were happening and the ways and means of carrying out the campaign in the Far East," the secretary of war noted. "Incidentally and as if by aside, he flung out the remark that a paper had been going around which was nonsense and which entirely misrepresented a conference between him and Churchill. I made no reply of course as he had given up, if he had ever entertained, the idea of discussing the surrender of MacArthur's reenforcements [to the British]."[63]

Stimson, who felt acutely the impotence of the U.S. Army as well as the Navy in confronting Japanese moves in the Far East, added that the episode had "pretty well mashed up" his Christmas.[64] The episode was, however, a painful illustration of how careful the President, in a democracy such as the United States, was obliged to be, if he was to avoid impeachment or press lynching.

Churchill, whose mother had been born an American and who had himself often traveled to the United States before the war, understood the danger only too well. Wisely he impressed upon his small army of note takers and imperial paper-wallahs that Britain would now have to accept a subordinate role in waging war against the Axis powers, and how important it would be for his staff to mind their p's and q's.

Behind Secretary Stimson's explosion at the War Department and his threat of resignation, of course, lay the awful truth of which both the President and his secretary of war were deeply aware: namely that, thanks largely to MacArthur's poor generalship, the Philippine Islands were now doomed, whatever reinforcements were sent out from U.S. shores.

MacArthur had lost his air force on the first day of war, and although he had insisted to the War Department since the summer that he would be able to hold the islands for six months against a Japanese invasion, there was never any real chance of resupplying him, let alone reinforcing him, once the Japanese sank the American fleet at Pearl Harbor. The distances were simply too immense, as Stimson, Eisenhower, and his team found when they marched their calipers across the Pacific Ocean: more than fifty-three hundred miles from Pearl Harbor to Manila, thirty-six hundred miles from Brisbane, Australia.

"I've been insisting Far East is critical and no other sideshows should be undertaken," Eisenhower would note in his diary a few days later. "Ships! Ships! All we need is ships!" Ike mourned some days after that. "Also ammunition, anti-aircraft guns, tanks, airplanes, what a headache!" The major general even briefly felt the President should reverse course — namely abandon the "Germany First" strategy that Stimson and the chiefs had laid down on December 23, 1941, and give in to Hitler's calculation. The United States should "drop everything else," Eisenhower penned, "and make the British retire in Libya," if necessary abandoning the Middle East. "Then scrape up everything everywhere and get it to the Dutch East Indies, Singapore, and Burma for a new Alamo."[65]

Christmas Eve and Christmas Day at the White House were, in the circumstances, somewhat mournful compared with the prewar Roosevelt family celebrations — the Roosevelts' four sons all in uniform now, and away from home.

Eleanor did her best as First Lady and hostess. "How hollow the words ["Merry Christmas!"] sounded that year!" she recalled. "On this visit of Mr. Churchill's, as on all his subsequent visits, my husband worked long hours every day." While the Prime Minister took a long nap each afternoon, the President caught up on his paperwork. Once Churchill was awake the President had again to play host to his guest — who, refreshed by his afternoon slumber, then kept the President up till all hours of the night. "Even after Franklin finally retired," Eleanor explained, "if impor- tant dispatches or messages came in, he was awakened no matter what hour, and nearly every meal he was called on the telephone for some ur- gent matter."[66]

The President's tradition of "mixing cocktails" at 6:00 p.m., or "chil- dren's hour," was one moment of Roosevelt's day that remained sacro- sanct no matter who the visitor might be. Confined to his wheelchair, the President had the opportunity to carry out an involved task himself, rather than instruct others to do it. "He would be wheeled in and then spin around to be at the drinks table, where he could reach everything," one visitor recorded. "There were the bottles, there was the shaker, there was the ice. . . . And you knew you were supposed to just hand him your glass, and not reach for anything else," lest this draw attention to the Pres- ident's disability.[67]

The President's signature creation was an FDR martini — although im- bibers were aware that his mix of gin, vermouth, and fruit juice followed no hard-and-fast ratio, and included on occasion rum from the Virgin Islands.

Churchill, however, hated the President's cocktail hour. Moreover, he found the President's favorite concoction foul, as another visitor noted — leading the Prime Minister to pretend to drink the martini, but in fact to take it with him to the bathroom after asking to be excused, and pour it down the sink — replacing it with water from the faucet![68]

The President, however, was the president. Told he should not light the traditional Christmas tree — which had been erected on the south side of the White House, rather than in Lafayette Square — for security reasons, Roosevelt dismissed such advice with a snort of ridicule. Instead he took the Prime Minister with him to witness the lighting, and participate in the prayers and carols on Christmas Eve; then on Christmas Day took his visitor to the Foundry United Methodist Church for an interfaith service, followed by lunch for the Joint Chiefs of Staff and their staffs, and the "biggest Christmas dinner we ever had — sixty people sat down at the table," Mrs. Roosevelt chronicled proudly. After dinner a movie — *Oliver Twist* — more Christmas carols, and "the men worked until well after one o'clock in the morning."[69]

Secretary Morgenthau had sat opposite the Prime Minister at the huge dinner. The next day the secretary told his Treasury staff how puzzled he'd been by the legendary British leader. "You know, he has a speech impediment," Morgenthau recounted (Churchill unable to pronounce the hard *r* sound). The Prime Minister had said very little, because "he just wasn't having a good time," Morgenthau surmised. The brilliant Treasury chief observed the faces of the British team closely. Max Beaverbrook's countenance, creased and lined like that of a lizard, presented "a map of his life." Churchill's skin, by contrast, seemed completely smooth, as if untroubled and unscarred. To Morgenthau, Churchill appeared — erroneously, as it was to turn out, only a day later, when the Prime Minister experienced heart trouble — "literally in the pink of health." Still and all, Churchill seemed preoccupied, Morgenthau was aware. He asked "three times to be excused after dinner so, he says, 'I can prepare these impromptu remarks for tomorrow.'" Sitting next to Morgenthau for the movie, nevertheless, followed by a documentary film on the war so far, the Prime Minister had seemed at least cheered by newsreel shots of the campaign in Libya, remarking: "Oh, that is good. We have got to show the people that we can win."[70]

Unlike the great financier, Churchill understood the huge political import of what the President had next asked him to do: to address not only Congress, but the people of America and the free world, from the rostrum of the U.S. Capitol.

For twenty-four hours the Prime Minister drafted and revised versions of his speech, even reading passages to the President, including the quotation from the 112th Psalm, "He shall not be afraid of evil tidings: his heart is fixed, trusting in the Lord."

Given that there were stirrings of revolt among a number of members of Parliament back home in London, there was good reason for Churchill to be anxious. "I saw Winston for a quarter of an hour before luncheon in the Map Room at the White House, complete in grey romper suit," the British ambassador had noted in his diary on Christmas Eve, "after which Stimson, whom I met as he came out from talking to him, must have reflected that he had never seen anything quite like it before."[71]

Stimson had not. Churchill "was still in dishabille, wearing a sort of zipper pajama suit and slippers," the secretary of war described the Prime Minister, whom he had come to brief on the worrying situation in the Philippines. "This has been a strange and distressful Christmas," Stimson noted the next day, after the "reenforcements" contretemps. "The news around us is pretty gloomy. Hong Kong has fallen; the Japanese have succeeded in making landings not only at Lingayen Gulf but two places south of Manila, and MacArthur has cabled that he was greatly outnumbered, would make the best fight he could, and retreat slowly down the Batan [*sic*] Peninsula and Corregidor," while evacuating the Philippine government and declaring Manila an open city.[72]

With bleak reports such as these, Churchill realized, his speech to Congress would have even more significance in terms of Allied morale. When Halifax visited him late on Christmas morning, he "found him in his coloured dressing gown in bed, preparing his speech for the Senate tomorrow, surrounded by cigars, whiskies and sodas and secretaries!"[73]

The President had tried his best to lighten the atmosphere, ribbing the Prime Minister and saying it had been good for him "to sing hymns with the Methodies" that day, at church. Churchill had attempted to smile, admitting it had been "the first time my mind has been at rest for a long time."[74] Yet in reality he could not relax, and the President eventually decided it would be best if he didn't accompany Churchill to the Capitol on the morning of December 26, lest he distract from the Prime Minister's reception on the Hill. Or worse still, in an atmosphere where all too many legislators still distrusted Churchill and the British for inveigling the U.S. into war with Germany, suggest unconstitutional collusion.

Where the President seemed to have no visible nerves, Churchill suddenly had too many. He worried about support in Parliament, back at home; he worried about the situation in the Far East; he worried about the situation in Libya — unable to sleep if he did not receive his nightly signal of good tidings from General Auchinleck, however bogus "the Auk's" claims.[75] Moreover, he worried about the relationship between Britain and the United States. For it was clear to him, if only haltingly to his staff, that the U.S., whose entry into the war he had so long prayed for, would now be *primus inter pares:* not simply, at last, a world power, but *the* world power. It would be important, Churchill recognized, to do everything he could to maintain good relations with the new imperium: supporting, aiding, advising, and, where necessary, flattering its emperor or pharaoh. At one point, he even wheeled the President into dinner at the White House — likening his act to that of Queen Elizabeth I's famous courtier, Sir Walter Raleigh, spreading his cloak before the sovereign, lest she get her shoes dirtied.[76]

Speaking before Congress was, however, a quite different challenge. "Do you realize we are making history?" Churchill remarked to Dr. Wilson shortly after midday, as he paced across the antechamber to the U.S. Senate chamber, still rehearsing his speech.[77]

For years the Führer had been the one to make history; even at this moment he saw himself being accompanied toward Valhalla by his accomplice, Emperor Hirohito, and his medieval warriors. Now, however, it would be the turn of the Associated Powers.

The "galleries were crowded, the Diplomatic Corps, the Supreme Court and others being accommodated on the floor," the British ambassador noted in his diary that night.[78] One listener, the son of Jewish immigrants, spoke for many Americans hearing the Prime Minister for the first time, describing it in his diary as a triumph — "the first sound of blood lust I have yet heard in the war." Churchill's rhetoric amazed him: "the color and the imagery of his style, the wonderful use of balance and alliteration and the way he used his voice to put emotions into his words. Why at one point he made a growling sound that sounded like the British lion!"[79]

"Winston spoke for about 35 minutes, and was much cheered," Lord Halifax recorded, for his part. "Everybody thought it very good, and he produced a great impression. Personally I did not think it so very good, but naturally I kept my opinion within a narrow circle."[80]

Churchill's doctor also had his doubts about the Prime Minister's speech. As rhetoric it was beautiful — beginning in humility and ending in dignity — but its length and content revealed both Churchill's brilliance and his flaws.

The Prime Minister could not admit to personal error, so was unable to resist lecturing senators and congressmen on their failure to stop Hitler "five or six years ago" when it "would have been easy" to do so. To make matters worse, however, he found himself unable to resist romanticizing British feats of arms to come, under his own military leadership. Buoyed by the newsreel film of fighting in Libya, he unwisely predicted imminent British victory in the desert, fighting a German-Italian army of 150,000 men.

"General Auchinleck set out to destroy totally that force," the Prime Minister announced to the august assembly. "I have every reason to believe that his aim will be fully accomplished. I am glad to be able to place before you, members of the Senate and of the House of Representatives, at this moment when you are entering the war, proof that with the proper weapons and proper organization we are able to beat the life out of the savage Nazi. What Hitler is suffering in Libya is only a sample of foretaste of what we must give him and his accomplices, wherever this war shall lead us, in every quarter of the globe."[81]

Given the drubbing Rommel was now about to administer to the British Eighth Army — a drubbing that Japanese forces were already administering to the British across the globe — this was simply asking for trouble. Yet the Prime Minister could not refrain from more boasting. Answering his own question "why is it" that Britain did not have "ample equipment of modern aircraft and Army weapons of all kinds in Malaya and the East Indies" to defend against the Japanese, he answered: "I can only point to the victories General Auchinleck has gained in the Libyan campaign. Had we diverted and dispersed our gradually growing resources between Libya and Malaya, we should have been found wanting in *both* theatres," he claimed. American generosity in arms shipped, under Lend-Lease, to British forces in North Africa, thus not only explained the weakness of Britain's Far Eastern defenses, he claimed, but "to no small extent" explained why American forces in the Pacific had been "found at a disadvantage" at Pearl Harbor and in the Philippines.[82]

Such exaggerated claims for current British prowess in Libya while salting the American wounds suffered in the Pacific in an effort to affirm his mastery as a British global strategist and commander in chief, were unfortunate, Halifax and others felt.

Such passages would, of course, be excluded from Churchill's memoirs, after the war — for by then Churchill had no wish to be reminded how he had crowed over Auchinleck's accomplishments against Rommel, only weeks prior to the longest British military retreat in the history of its empire.

Who, though, could penetrate the Prime Minister's wall of self-regard? Churchill was the sum of his strengths and weaknesses — and no one who ever met him could doubt the former, while even the latter could be tragicomic: eliciting compassion in a man so gifted, moreover so resolute in defending the values of decency and goodwill.

It was the Prime Minister's "aggressive" quality that most drew the President to him — even if he thought Churchill a figure from England's past rather than its future. "Winston is not Mid-Victorian — he is completely Victorian," the President was heard to remark,[83] while Dr. Wilson quoted the President as saying Churchill was not only "quite Victorian in his outlook," but a "real blimp."[84] Nevertheless, Churchill's *courage* moved Roosevelt — who knew a great deal about the quality, enabling him to differentiate between straightforward courage and principled, moral courage.

To the President the distinction was not academic. The legendary courage of a man like Charles Lindbergh, the pioneering aviator, was of a deeply tainted order, in the President's view. Lindbergh was brave but simple-minded — and more self-serving than was realized by most people. In this respect the President's instinct — as was the case with his perception of Hitler's demonic character — was instinctively sagacious. Lindbergh's acceptance of a Nazi medal, and his gullible, exaggerated reports on German Luftwaffe superiority before the shooting even began, had amounted to rank defeatism, tricked out in isolationist rhetoric, the President judged. Therefore when at Christmas the aviator applied to General Arnold, chief of staff of the U.S. Army Air Forces, to take up his former commission as a colonel in the U.S. Air Force, the President found himself on the spot.

The President asked not only the advice of the secretary of war, whose domain this was, but of the secretary of the interior, Harold Ickes — and of the director of the FBI, J. Edgar Hoover.

Ickes, after analyzing Lindbergh's speeches and articles, concluded that Lindbergh was "a ruthless and conscious fascist, motivated by a hatred for you personally and a contempt for democracy in general. His speeches show an astonishing identity with those of Berlin, and the similarity is not accidental." To achieve political power in the United States, Lindbergh would, Ickes reflected, require "a military service record" — which Secretary Ickes hoped the President would deny him.[85]

The President, as a political tactician of considerable renown, remained unsure. When he received a confirmed report, however, of what Lindbergh had said at a private meeting of America First members in New York ten days after Pearl Harbor, he felt his basic instinct about Lindbergh had been right. The former colonel was a blackguard.

"There is only one danger in the world," Lindbergh had reportedly said to the gathering in New York — that being "the yellow danger. China and Japan are really bound together against the white race. There could only have been one efficient weapon against this alliance, underneath the surface, Germany itself could have been this weapon," Lindbergh explained. "The ideal set-up would have been to have had Germany take over Poland and Russia, in collaboration with the British, as a bloc against the yellow people and bolshevism. But instead, the British and the fools in

Washington had to interfere. The British envied the Germans and wanted to rule the world forever. Britain is the real cause of all the trouble in the world today. Of course, America First cannot be active right now. But it should keep on the alert and when the large missing lists and losses are published the American people will realize how much they have been betrayed by the British and the Administration. Then America First can be a political force again. We must be quiet a while and await the time for active functioning. There may be a time soon when we can advocate a negotiated peace."[86]

Hitler would have ordered the execution of a purveyor of such treason against the Reich. The President, however, simply decided to deny Lindbergh's request to serve in American uniform. (About Lindbergh's self-serving lack of fundamental moral principle, the President would, moreover, be proven right — Lindbergh, a passionate eugenicist, conducted secret adulterous affairs with three German women two decades younger than himself, two of them disabled; he sired seven secret children by them in Germany and Switzerland, after the war.)[87]

In the meantime, however, the President had to decide how best to win the war — which was still going disastrously in the Far East, in the wake of Pearl Harbor. And would soon fare as badly in the Mediterranean, despite the Prime Minister's boasts.

Fueling Lindbergh's fire was the fact that the war in the Far East was going so badly. "Germany First" thus seemed to many, at this time, to be a mistake.

Certainly, by focusing America's primary war effort on the Pacific, the President would, had he been so willing, have been able to play to public opinion all across America — the majority of the nation clamoring to avenge the Japanese sneak attack, to save the Philippines, and to defend Australia and New Zealand if they were invaded by the Japanese.

In reality, however, the Philippine Islands could no longer be saved, Roosevelt knew. Their distance from the United States, the destruction of MacArthur's air force, and the emasculation of the American fleet made for a bleak outlook in the Southwest Pacific. At the same time, however, from his intelligence services and his emissaries, the President was convinced the Japanese had no intentions of invading Australia or New Zealand, despite the continuing panic consuming the Australian capital, Canberra. With sufficient U.S. naval, army, and air force reinforcement he had no doubt the Antipodes could easily be held — and would be, once

American forces were sent out. What was far more important, therefore, Roosevelt felt, was to deal with Hitler before the Führer could defeat the Soviet Union — following which he would undoubtedly turn back to Britain. In that case, the United States would truly become a second-rate nation on the world stage — with calls from Lindbergh-style "patriots" to abandon democracy altogether.

It was the recognition of this danger, as 1941 came to an end, that caused the President to review the question of an Allied Supreme War Council, which the secretary of state was recommending, and face up to the matter of how best to go forward. As commander in chief Roosevelt had a junior partner, vested with poor military judgment but supreme courage: Winston Churchill. With him, the President was certain, he could work. With others — especially a committee of others — he was less certain. Thus, where Secretary Hull had pressed for a politico-military Supreme War Council to represent all the Associated Powers, or Allies, as in World War I,[88] the idea of such a body now died. Instead, Hull was told by the President to concentrate exclusively on the new version of the Atlantic Charter, or war aims that *all* of America's partners in the conflict against Hitler and the Axis powers could sign. With regard to the waging of the war itself, however, Roosevelt made clear, he would take over this responsibility at the White House. In effect he would, with Winston Churchill as his chief lieutenant in London, become the supreme commander of the Associated Powers, or Allies, in Washington. There would naturally be differences of opinion and strategy, but he was now sure he had the skills to keep the Allied high command focused on eventual victory.

The Joint Chiefs of Staff in Washington would form a new military committee, with an officer present to represent the British chiefs of staff, that would henceforth be tasked with carrying out Roosevelt's orders and decisions — decisions he would make with Churchill as his junior partner. In that way the Prime Minister's capacity for poor judgment would for the most part be disabled, while his terrific moral strength could be applied to winning, not losing, the war.

It was an inspired intention. Whether it would work as 1941 came to a close was yet to be seen.

5

Supreme Command

ON DECEMBER 26, 1941, Winston Churchill suffered a minor heart attack while in the White House and was sent to Florida by the President to recuperate for a week. Roosevelt, whose patience had at times been sorely tried by the Prime Minister's visit, was relieved. "It always took him several days to catch up on sleep after Mr. Churchill left," Eleanor Roosevelt later wrote, concerned for her husband's rest.[1]

Churchill's stay in the White House certainly proved exhausting for the President, the First Lady, and for the White House staff. Plans for offensive action — especially the President's "great pet scheme" for U.S. landings in Northwest Africa — had had to be put on the back burner while the Japanese rampage in the Pacific dominated all military planning and operations. Many ideas were nevertheless advanced — perhaps the most important of which was the President's notion of a new declaration of principles by the Associated Powers.

The document's final maturation, indeed the President's whole method of bringing a project to fruition, amazed the Prime Minister's military assistant, Colonel Jacob — symbolized in the "mess" he saw in the President's study on the second floor of the White House. The President "leads a most simple life," Jacob described in his diary. "He moves about the White House in a wheeled chair. His study is a delightful oval room, looking South, and is one of the most untidy rooms I have ever seen. It is full of junk. Half-opened parcels, souvenirs, books, papers, knick-knacks, and all kinds of miscellaneous articles lie about everywhere, on tables, on chairs, and on the floor. His desk is piled with papers and alongside his chair he has a sort of bookcase also filled with books, papers and junk of all sorts piled just anyhow. It would drive an orderly-minded man, or a woman, mad. The pictures on the walls are fine, mostly prints or paintings of ships. There are also good bookcases round the walls, and the furniture is not bad. But the effect is ruined by the rubbish piled everywhere. It is rather typical of the general lack of organization in the American Government." As a proud English bureaucrat, Jacob found the "British Governmental machine" to be, by contrast, "like a motor car or even a train. Provided a reasonably efficient driver is in charge it will go. The American Government is not a machine at all. The various parts are not assembled into a working whole. The President is in the position of a patriarch, with a rather unruly flock, and much depends on the actual men who actuate or influence the various sections of that flock. The patriarch also relies to a great extent on sheep dogs, who are his stand-by, but are regarded with fear and suspicion by the sheep."[2]

One of the sheep dogs was Bill Donovan, a lawyer whom the President had put in charge of a "kind of super intelligence organization," the Office of the Coordinator of Information, forerunner of the OSS (and later the CIA). Another was Harry Hopkins, "a frail anaemic man of great honesty and courage, who lives permanently in the White House and is the President's constant companion. . . . Hopkins is usually to be seen in a magenta dressing gown and pyjamas. Other examples of the President's peculiar method of working are the personal representatives he sends about the place, such as [former ambassador William C.] Bullitt in the Middle East. These report to him direct, and to our way of thinking are irresponsible meddlers."[3]

When Lord Halifax went to the White House to discuss a draft of the revised Atlantic Charter with President Roosevelt and Harry Hopkins, he too was bewildered. "They are the most amazing people," he noted in his own diary, "in the way of what seems to us most disorderly and unbusinesslike methods of working. But somehow the result comes out not too badly and they seem quite happy working like that. It would drive me to drink," the ascetic Catholic reflected. "While the draft [charter] was being retyped Harry Hopkins took me to wait in his bedroom while he dressed, his bedroom serving as bedroom and office. It is the oddest menage I have ever seen."[4]

Equipped with his own silk Chinese-dragon dressing gown and beloved romper suit, Winston Churchill had fitted almost seamlessly into this strange ménage, however. He had certainly made himself at home. "Now, Fields," he had instructed the President's head butler, who at six feet three towered over the Prime Minister. "We want to leave here as friends, right?

So I need you to listen. One, I don't like talking outside my quarters; two, I hate whistling in the corridors; and three, I must have a tumbler of sherry in my room before breakfast, a couple glasses of scotch and soda before lunch and French champagne and 90 year old brandy before I go to sleep at night."[5]

In the end, Churchill stayed at the White House almost a month rather than his planned week. The First Lady might resent Churchill's heavy, all-day drinking and late hours, as well as his egoism, but the President seemed glad of his company, and never once complained — even when he and Churchill clashed over Roosevelt's desire to include India as a British Dominion in the proud list of nations subscribing to his declaration of the Associated Powers. "Being convinced that complete victory over their enemies is essential to defend life, liberty, independence and religious freedom," the draft text began, "and to preserve human rights and justice in their own lands as well as in other lands . . ."

Churchill would not, however agree to India as a signatory beside the Dominions of Canada, South Africa, Australia, and New Zealand — in fact, the Prime Minister refused even to agree to the inclusion of India as a colony. To the President's relief, though, the text of his joint declaration was accepted by the governments of some twenty-six nations in all, including the Soviet Union — despite, to the President's delight, his insistence upon the inclusion of religion as a freedom for which the signatories were fighting. "Let's get it out on Jan 1," Roosevelt penned with relief on December 30, 1941, in a note to Harry Hopkins. "That means speed. FDR."[6]

Awakening on the morning of New Year's Day, prior to a church service in Alexandria to which he was taking Churchill and the British ambassador, then to the laying of a symbolic wreath on President Washington's tomb at Mount Vernon, the President had a final brainwave, however.

Dressing quickly with the help of his valet, the President shifted to his wheelchair and rushed to the Rose Room, where Churchill was staying, to tell him: the revised Atlantic Charter, which currently had no formal name, should be called "A Declaration by the United Nations."[7]

Outside Churchill's door, however, stood W. R. Jones, an assistant to Colonel Jacob. Though an admirable clerk, Mr. Jones had, as Colonel Jacob noted with amusement in his diary, "a most peculiarly pompous and over-correct way of speaking. He never can get a perfectly straightforward sentence out. If you ask him where Brigadier Hollis [Jacob's immediate boss] has gone, instead of saying 'I'm afraid I don't know,' he will say 'I fear it is not within my knowledge where the Brigadier may be at the moment.'" Conveying a message from Colonel Jacob to the Prime Minister, Jones had been told that the Prime Minister was in the bath. Jones had therefore waited in "the central passage" on the second floor, "and stood looking about for a few moments, when what should he see coming towards him but the President in his wheeled chair, unaccompanied by anyone. Jones stood rooted to the spot, and the President addressed him saying:

"'Good morning. Is your Prime Minister up yet?'

"'Well, Sir,' said Jones, 'it is within my knowledge that the Prime Minister is at the present moment in his bath.'

"'Good,' said the President, 'then open the door.'

"Jones accordingly flung open the bathroom door to admit the President, and there was the Prime Minister standing completely naked on the bath mat.

"'Don't mind me,' said the President, as the Prime Minister grabbed a towel.

"Jones' day was made," Jacob recorded. "Not only had he seen the inside of the White House, but he had spoken to the President and seen a meeting between him and the Prime Minister in quite unique circumstances."[8]

Jones certainly had — the two leaders working in what Churchill would correctly call "closest intimacy" as they discussed the new name for the signatories to the upgraded Atlantic Charter: the United Nations.[9]

President Roosevelt's next great achievement during Churchill's time at the White House was his success in junking Secretary Hull's idea of a Supreme War Council and creating, instead, an official (yet never formally instituted, in writing or in law) military body to carry out his directions as commander in chief: the so-called Combined Chiefs of Staff. With its headquarters in Washington, the new body would translate the President's military policies into combined action by the forces of the United States and Britain, as well as subsidiary contingents. Moreover, to make the new system work, the President decided on General Marshall's advice that it would be best to appoint supreme commanders in each theater of combat fighting the Axis powers, to command the Allied air, naval, and ground forces.

This notion of supreme theater commanders had arisen at the meeting between the U.S. and British military chiefs of staff on Christmas Day. General Marshall had proposed the idea — a single commander directing not only the "air, ground and ships"[10] of his own nation in the region, but *all* the combatant forces of the nations contributing to the campaign. The President, still scarred by the dysfunctional, fragmented performance of the three armed services at Pearl Harbor, then leaped at the idea of such "unity of command" at a meeting at the White House on the morning of December 27, as Secretary Stimson recorded in his diary[11] — indeed, he had driven it through against the opposition not only of Admirals King, Stark, and Turner, but of Prime Minister Churchill, as Colonel Jacob noted in his diary.

"When the idea was first put forward there was almost universal opposition," Colonel Jacob wrote when he returned to England, "and the Prime Minister expressed his doubts about the wisdom of such a system as General Marshall proposed to set up. The U.S. Navy were also against it. General Marshall, however, had backing from the President, whom he had convinced that unity of command would be the only solution of the Far East troubles, and that nothing could be worse than having several independent commanders of different nationality, especially in a theater where interests are divergent."[12]

Churchill's opposition had initially threatened to derail the idea. General Marshall then put forward a suggestion the President thought inspired, politically: namely to appoint, as the first such supreme commander in the Far East, a *British* general! The President had therefore sent Marshall in person to convince Churchill — which Marshall did, proposing that the supreme commander should be General Sir Archibald Wavell, the current commander in chief in India. "This very naturally put a different complexion on the affair," Colonel Jacob noted, "as it was hard for the Prime Minister to refuse to back a principle which was undoubtedly attractive in theory and which was to be applied in a way which recognized the pre-eminence in the field of choice of a British general."[13]

The die was thus cast — even Colonel Jacob being amazed at his deeply conservative Prime Minister's apostasy. Churchill's acquiescence was, however, followed by an even more revolutionary innovation: namely that the Combined Chiefs of Staff would be headquartered not in London but in Washington, D.C. — a decision that the Prime Minister meekly accepted, but which Jacob, on his return to England, found had raised the hackles of every English patriot in the War Office. "Special body in Washington to control [military] operations under PM and USA president," General Sir Alan Brooke, the owl-faced new chief of staff of the British Army, sniffed in his diary on December 29, 1941.[14] The "special body" would doubtless comprise General Marshall, Admiral Stark, Admiral King, and General Arnold — leaving the British chiefs of staff with only "representation" at the Combined Headquarters in Washington, invested in a single British officer, yet to be appointed. "The whole scheme wild and half-baked," Brooke had snorted.[15] To Brooke's further chagrin the Prime Minister had then cabled Acting Prime Minister Attlee from the White House, saying it was, in effect, a done deal — with Allied supreme commanders for different theaters of war. Churchill, moreover, had made no attempt to conceal the origin of the idea. "Last night President urged upon me," Churchill explained, "appointment of a single officer to command Army, Navy, and Air Force of Britain, America and Dutch."[16] Since the "President has obtained the agreement of the American War and Navy Departments" to the scheme,[17] and since the first Allied supreme commander was to be General Sir Archibald Wavell, the British cabinet could do little else than wring their hands.

General Brooke had been mortified, having been promoted to be his nation's CIGS, only to discover his war-making powers would be entirely dependent on decisions made in Washington. "The more we looked at our task the less we liked it," he noted not only of the supreme commander business but of the very idea of a global command headquarters in the U.S. capital — recalling later that he "could see no reason why at this stage, with American forces totally unprepared to play a major part, we should agree to a central control in Washington."[18] There was nothing Brooke could say, at least aloud, however — the British cabinet "forced to accept PM's new scheme," as Brooke had lamented, "owing to the fact that it was almost a fait accompli!"[19]

It was — the more so, moreover, when reports had come in of the President's State of the Union address to Congress on January 5, 1942 — a speech in which the President had announced arms production goals that had made it clear the United States would win the war by industrial output alone.

"Plans have been laid here and in the other capitals for coordinated and cooperative action by all the United Nations — military action and economic action," the President had declared. "Already we have established, as you know, unified command of land, sea, and air forces in the southwestern Pacific theater of war. There will be a continuation of conferences and consultations among military staffs, so that the plans and operations of each will fit into the general strategy designed to crush the enemy. We shall not fight isolated wars — each Nation going its own way. These 26 Nations are united — not in spirit and determination alone, but in the broad conduct of the war in all its phases.

"For the first time since the Japanese and the Fascists and the Nazis started along their blood-stained course of conquest they now face the fact that superior forces are assembling against them. Gone forever are the days when the aggressors could attack and destroy their victims one by one without unity of resistance. We of the United Nations will so dispose our forces that we can strike at the common enemy wherever the greatest damage can be done him," the President had warned. "The militarists of Berlin and Tokyo started this war. But the massed, angered forces of common humanity will finish it."

"Victory," however, "requires the actual weapons of war and the means of transporting them to a dozen points of combat. It will not be sufficient for us and the other United Nations to produce a slightly superior supply of munitions to that of Germany, Japan, Italy, and the stolen industries in the countries which they have overrun," Roosevelt had pointed out. "The superiority of the United Nations in munitions and ships must be *overwhelming* — so overwhelming that the Axis Nations can never hope to catch up with it. And so, in order to attain this overwhelming superiority the United States must build planes and tanks and guns and ships to the utmost limit of our national capacity. We have the ability and capacity to produce arms not only for our own forces, but also for the armies, navies, and air forces fighting on our side."

Thereupon the President had openly announced astronomical figures for U.S. military output. "I have just sent a letter of directive to the appropriate departments and agencies of our Government, ordering that immediate steps be taken:

"First, to increase our production rate of airplanes so rapidly that in this year, 1942, we shall produce 60,000 planes, 10,000 more than the goal that we set a year and a half ago. This includes 45,000 combat planes — bombers, dive bombers, pursuit planes. The rate of increase will be maintained and continued so that next year, 1943, we shall produce 125,000 airplanes, including 100,000 combat planes.

"Second, to increase our production rate of tanks so rapidly that in this year, 1942, we shall produce 45,000 tanks; and to continue that increase so that next year, 1943, we shall produce 75,000 tanks.

"Third, to increase our production rate of anti-aircraft guns so rapidly that in this year, 1942, we shall produce 20,000 of them; and to continue that increase so that next year, 1943, we shall produce 35,000 anti-aircraft guns.

"And fourth, to increase our production rate of merchant ships so rapidly that in this year, 1942, we shall build 6,000,000 deadweight tons as compared with a 1941 completed production of 1,100,000. And finally, we shall continue that increase so that next year, 1943, we shall build 10,000,000 tons of shipping.

"These figures and similar figures for a multitude of other implements of war will give the Japanese and the Nazis a little idea of just what they accomplished in the attack at Pearl Harbor."[20]

Listening, the British ambassador, Lord Halifax, rubbed his eyes. Could the President be serious? "[C]ertainly if they can make the figures to which they have hitched their wagon on the supply side come out," he noted in his diary with a mix of incredulity and new confidence, "it will be prodigious."[21]

In London, however, General Brooke could only pray the British Empire would hold fast long enough for the United States, with its prodigious output of men and materiel, to save it.

As the veritable new Allied commander in chief in Washington, then, the President successfully imposed his will in the first days of January 1942, not only on his own staff but upon his new primary ally, and in an almost magical way: overcoming his dissenters by dint of his seemingly effortless goodwill, common sense, charm, and positive spirit.

With Churchill's departure on January 14, however, the President suddenly found himself alone in the White House—a relief, but the Prime Minister's absence also created a distinct vacuum. The President realized, in fact, that he missed his British counterpart. Short, squat, bald, chubby-cheeked, Churchill had exuded not only cigar smoke but a fierce, indomitable energy, whatever setbacks he faced. And with his retinue of personal and military staff, he had left, too, an unforgettable image of a traveling chieftain—especially the sight of his staff unrolling the Prime Minister's world maps and charts, marked up with the latest information on British and enemy forces.

In honor of his departing guest, the President, his aides learned, decided to set up in the White House his own Map Room, modeled on the Prime Minister's portable headquarters. It would not, however, be in the Monroe Room — to Eleanor's understandable relief. And definitely not in the underground headquarters or bunker that the President's advisers were urging be constructed in the White House, modeled on Churchill's War Rooms in London.

6

The President's Map Room

THE PRIME MINISTER'S War Rooms in London dated back to 1938, when the British government ordered the construction of a vast underground complex for the war cabinet, complete with military headquarters and communications. This was secretly installed below the "New Public Offices" on Great George Street, close to 10 Downing Street, the prime minister's residence and office. It was on a visit to the underground War Rooms that Churchill, on becoming prime minister in May 1940, had declared: "This is the room from which I'll direct the war."[1]

Known as "the Bunker" or "the Hole,"[2] the underground complex had been designed to allow the closest working (and living) proximity between the members of the war cabinet and the British chiefs of staff, as well as their ancillary civil and military staffs and clerks: a veritable rabbit warren of rooms to house the joint military planning, operations, intelligence, and civil defense departments of the government, complete with bedrooms for all. A further five-foot-thick concrete slab had wisely been inserted over the ever-expanding series of rooms during the London Blitz.

At the heart of the complex, however, lay the Map Room, staffed twenty-four hours a day by officers and ratings from the three services: men and women who not only maintained up-to-date wall maps of the war's progress, with the latest positions of British and enemy forces at sea and on land, but produced daily intelligence summaries for the chiefs of staff, the Prime Minister/Defense Minister, and the King.[3]

Such a secure bunker from which to conduct the war was eminently sensible, given the original RAF forecasts of potential bombing casualties of up to two hundred thousand victims per night. Actual casualties had been considerably lower — yet still daunting. During the Blitz, on October 10, 1940, a German bomb had in fact fallen only yards from 10 Downing Street, destroying the Prime Minister's kitchen, pantry, and offices, and forcing Churchill to move into an apartment immediately above the secret War Rooms, called the No. 10 Annex. Treasury Secretary Morgenthau had heard of the headquarters, and perhaps understandably — given that he was responsible for the Secret Service and President Roosevelt's safety — had been the first to push for something similar to be constructed in Washington, D.C., following the surprise Japanese attack on Pearl Harbor. Moreover, Morgenthau believed that he had, in the somewhat panic-stricken days that followed December 7, gotten the President's approval. But he'd been mistaken.

An entire half-block between Pennsylvania Avenue and H Street had already been acquired as a proposed extension for the State Department, west of Lafayette Park — with more that could be added later, Morgenthau was assured.

Was an underground bunker necessarily the best idea, though? Morgenthau had queried. Hitler's Berlin bunker (Vorbunker) had been constructed beneath the garden of the Reichskanzlei in 1936, and another at Wolf's Lair, his forward headquarters in the Masurian forest near Rastenburg in East Prussia in the winter of 1940–41. But new information from Britain indicated to Morgenthau — an inveterate believer in research — that bunkers below ground were even more susceptible to bomb damage than above-ground fortified premises, owing to the transmission of subterranean shock waves.

"The suggestion," General Fleming told the Treasury secretary as he unrolled a map of Pennsylvania Avenue, was therefore "to build about a five story building on that site, a complete blackout building. No windows at all. It can be made — it would have about two hundred seventy-five thousand square feet of floor space. We can make it so that there is living quarters and everything else there. It can go ahead and just stand a long siege, that building. It has a very heavy reinforced roof"[4] — in fact, at twelve feet thick it would be only eight feet less thick than the latest windowless Admiralty building in London, a veritable fortress near Churchill's War Rooms.

In actuality Churchill had declined to use the Admiralty Citadel, referring to it later as "a vast monstrosity which weighs upon the Horse Guards Parade."[5] Such a windowless, above-ground fortress had definite advantages over a below-ground complex, General Fleming assured the Treasury secretary, however. Within the building, the "farther down the safer it is, so the ground floor and basement are completely safe," he claimed, and extolled its virtues: an above-ground reinforced-concrete building, like a medieval castle, capable of housing "fifteen to twenty thousand people." The building would be "about a hundred and forty-four feet deep," and would accommodate "Treasury, State, and the Executive Offices," as well as the senior military personnel. "I think he [the President] probably wants some of the higher staff officers of the Army and Navy in there," General Fleming had explained to Morgenthau. The President would have his own access via a secret tunnel from the White House that would branch off the current zig-zag tunnel being dug to the basement shelter in the Treasury's gold vaults — avoiding trees.

"That will please the President. He and I both like trees," Morgenthau had commented. Claiming that "the President asked me to get together and have ready a building which would house the White House staff, State, and Treasury," Morgenthau had then telephoned General "Pa" Watson, the President's appointments secretary, on December 15, 1941, to say they had an architect's plan for the bunker, had already purchased virtually the complete site, and were "ready to go ahead. I'd like to show it to the President, with General Fleming, and it would take about five minutes." He even had the money — although, as Morgenthau wisely cautioned, "I don't want to go ahead and order a seven million dollar building without the President seeing it."

The monster complex was not the only fortification Morgenthau wanted in order to protect "the Boss," as the President was called. As in Alice's Wonderland, Morgenthau and his team of security advisers also planned a thirty-feet-deep interim bunker in the grounds of the White House itself, with eight-feet-thick walls and ceiling, inside of which was a second, interior box-like room with walls two feet thick, which "gives you a pretty good protection" — though not against a "four thousand pound bomb." It was to be dug in front of the White House, "for the President and for our communications center," and would protect against . . .

Here the Treasury secretary was unclear. General Fleming had explained that the U.S. Air Corps had told him to expect only "token raids," for the moment — planes that would "come in and terrify the population, show what they can do. They would have to come in from a carrier some place. That therefore limits the size of the bomb that can be carried to about two thousand pounds."

German or Japanese air raids were not the only danger envisaged, it appeared; there might also be enemy ground forces parachuted in and deployed against the President and even Congress, General Fleming had added.

The mention of Congress complicated the matter still further. While the bunker plans for the President were being prepared, there were now other, equally zealous proposals also put forward to protect the capital — and Capitol. There were to be machine-gun nests protected by sandbags everywhere, including on the roof of the White House; bulletproof glass in the President's office and study windows. Moreover, the White House itself would no longer be white. It would be repainted, Fleming had explained, in camouflage colors, with a fifteen-feet-high "sand-bag barricade" that would go "completely around the White House building and Executive Offices" or West Wing.[6]

Even Fleming expressed skepticism as to whether the President, who loved history and had been for some years planning a museum in the new East Wing in order to house the many artifacts and documents he and his predecessors had been given, would tolerate such draconian changes — especially given his love of trees and landscaping. "It is believed the President would not permit it," Fleming had warned Morgenthau about the great earthwork/barricade proposal — or indeed the other plans.

Such wariness as to the President's response was well founded. General Watson called Morgenthau back on the afternoon of December 15, 1941, to say that not only would the President not see the Treasury secretary, but he was not pleased. "He said you were crazy as hell. He's not going to build that building."[7]

"He asked me to!" Morgenthau had vainly protested.

General Watson, however, repudiated this claim, quoting the exact words the President had used and which he wanted Watson to convey to Secretary Morgenthau. "'Why,' he said, 'tell him he's crazy, what is he talking about?'"[8]

Putting the kibosh on Morgenthau's bunker idea had turned out to be but the tip of the President's derision. To Morgenthau's chagrin, Roosevelt had been equally disparaging about Morgenthau's idea to cancel the traditional lighting of the Christmas tree, in front of the White House, on Christmas Eve. General Albert Cox had warned how dangerous such a public illumination would be — a veritable invitation to the enemy — saying, "you might just as well put up an airplane beacon right in front of the White House." The President had remained adamant, however. Mor-

genthau was thus forced to drop this and any idea of a fortified govern-
ment control center or bunker. "We'll have to let it rest there until the
President changes his mind," Morgenthau had acknowledged wearily on
December 22.

The President hadn't changed his mind, however — even after the
Prime Minister's long stay over Christmas. The notion of a "token raid,"
launched from "a carrier some place," seemed too remote a possibility to take seriously — though the idea itself lodged in the Commander
in Chief's capacious mind as something the U.S. might well carry out
against the enemy.

Maps were a different matter. The President loved maps, just as he loved
stamps — a hobby that had become the more passionate the less he himself could travel, owing to his disability. It was no surprise, then, when the
President ordered that something similar to Churchill's portable map-
and-filing system be installed in the White House.

"I can't think how I'm going to get on when you take your Map Room
away," the President had said to Churchill before his departure. "I shall
feel quite lost."

"But Franklin, you must have a Map Room of your own. That shall
be my parting present," Churchill had responded. "And you shall have
my lieutenant to help make it and to run it for you. Lieutenant Cox, how
would you like to work for the President?"[9]

Sublieutenant Cox had been thrilled. When first introduced to Mr.
Roosevelt, he'd "found my hand taken in a warm, strong grasp and saw
two piercing eyes looking into mine with a kindly twinkle, and the wide
mouth was curved up in an understanding grin."[10] It had been clear to
Cox from the start how deeply Churchill admired the President — Cox
writing to his mother in England how the Prime Minister had said to
him, "What a wonderful man that is. It is a mercy for mankind he is
where he is at this moment."[11]

The Prime Minister, Cox recalled, was like a "miniature whirlwind,"
his mind forever racing, calculating, preparing. The President seemed
the opposite — as if no burden, however great, would ever dent his smile.
"He is an amazingly great man," Cox described his feelings to his mother,
"though not as fiery as the P.M. . . . He is a great admirer of Churchill's,
but the P.M.'s energy seems to have worn him out a bit during the past
few days, and I can well understand it!"[12] "Your man has worn me out so
I am taking the day in bed," the President had stated in a message to Cox,

when Churchill briefly flew to Canada. "I guess he's worn you out too, so I suggest you take the day off," he ordered — an order "I obeyed," noted the sublieutenant, gratefully.[13]

Cox's "temporary" commission was to train a U.S. officer in the mechanics of setting up and running a map room for the Commander in Chief. "Roosevelt wanted something comparable to the Map Room," explained Commander George Elsey seventy years later, and "asked his naval aide [Captain Beardall] to establish some form of communications center at the White House." However, the idea was never, Elsey was at pains to point out, intended to be a version of Churchill's London War Rooms — which soon led to yet another round of Alice-in-Washington misunderstanding when Captain Beardall "looked around and found this young Reserve officer," Lieutenant Robert Montgomery, a famous former Hollywood actor.[14]

"Montgomery had been on duty in London, as an aide to the U.S. naval attaché, and had become acquainted with Churchill's War Room," Elsey (who had been a naval ensign working for Lieutenant William C. Mott, who was transferred to the White House as an aide to Captain Beardall) explained. It was from Captain Mott that Elsey had obtained a firsthand account of how the President had put his *über*zealous military aides in their place.

Roosevelt had "responded positively right away, because Montgomery had quite a reputation as a movie actor." The movie actor, however, completely misunderstood the President's instructions. Whether Montgomery was "got at" by Secretary Morgenthau or other conniving figures such as General Fleming remains unclear, but the suggestions he began to make for a fortified bunker seemed eerily similar to Morgenthau's. "Robert Montgomery had the same sort of grandiose plans," Elsey explained with a laugh more than a half century later. "He had been on duty in London, he was familiar with the catacombs there, and he prepared the same sort of thing to be built on Constitution Avenue, across from where the War and Navy Departments were."

The President, when he heard Montgomery's latest scheme, was as appalled as he had been by Morgenthau's plans the month before. "All Roosevelt wanted," Elsey pointed out, "was simply one secure spot in the White House itself which he and only his immediate associates would have access to — not something for *the whole military* to use!" In particular the President had no wish to set up a "control room." Montgomery's proposition was "beyond anything FDR wanted," Elsey made clear, given the accretion of myths and misconceptions that had built up in subsequent years. "This was *in no sense* to be a command center, as Churchill's War Room was," the President's former aide emphasized, for that was simply not how the President operated — nor wished, instinctively, to operate in directing the war.

"*And that was it!*" Elsey remarked with finality. The idea of a presidential control room on the lines of Churchill's London bunker, or Hitler's bunkers in Berlin and Rastenburg, was irremediably nixed — indeed, its progenitor was soon fired. "[Robert] Montgomery was brought down to earth" and removed from the White House, Elsey recalled. Instead of a grand above- or below-ground bunker, the President merely wanted a small, secure room to house his secret signals to and from Allied leaders and his own military advisers. And with that in mind it was temporarily installed "right across a narrow corridor from the Oval Office in the West Wing," in the Fish Room.

"It was called the Fish Room because that was where Herbert Hoover had mounted his fish trophies," Elsey recounted, amused by the irony. "Roosevelt had replaced Hoover's fish with his own fish, and it became the Fish Room." Instead of fish stretching across its walls, however, there were soon global and campaign maps, just as Churchill had recently mounted in the Monroe Room. Even this setup proved unsatisfactory to the President, however — in fact within a few days Roosevelt decided it was no good. "It was too public, there was too much access to it — the room had been used by the President and senior White House staff members for all kinds of meetings, and there just wasn't adequate security," Elsey explained of the Map Room's demise in the West Wing. "Too many newspaper people and others pushing around! So it was moved."

The new location that the President chose was in the presidential mansion itself — installed, by even greater irony, in "the Museum," a small ladies' cloakroom, next to the Diplomatic Reception Room, where guests had traditionally hung their coats and freshened up. This room was on the ground floor of the White House, below the formal entrance vestibule of the mansion. Barely twenty-four feet by nineteen, the new Map Room would be closer to the President's elevator, so he could visit the secret communications sanctum in private, from his bedroom or study, without needing to go to the West Wing at all.

In due course, the cloakroom was easily converted. The door to the beautiful Diplomatic Reception Room was blocked off, the elegant wood-paneled walls were faced with soft wallboard, and maps of the world and of the various battlefronts were mounted at eye level. "The ground situation was marked with grease-coated pens on plastic sheets over the maps," recalled Elsey, who began working under Lieutenant Mott at the new Map Room in April 1942, after Montgomery's departure. In the middle of the room, filing cabinets were installed for the signals that came in and went out, brought by army and navy couriers in locked leather pouches, with the latest information and intelligence. Most important, Mott explained to Elsey, were the President's secret, direct communications with Churchill, Stalin, and Chiang Kai-shek, as well as top-secret messages and reports from the secretaries of war and navy and chiefs of staff for the President. But what struck Elsey later was not only Roosevelt's deliberate decision not to replicate Churchill's bunker or War Rooms, but the President's reasons for doing so.

"During the early days the President visited the growing room with keen interest," Cox explained, "remarking on the progress of construction and suggesting modifications about the fittings and the placing of the furniture. When the room was at last working, Mr. Roosevelt's visits tended to occur towards the end of his working day, usually just before 7 o'clock, but as the collection, evaluation and display of information increased in efficiency, he came to pay a regular routine visit at 10.45 a.m., immediately before his conference with his Chiefs of Staff."[15]

As time went on, however, the President's visits to the Map Room grew less frequent — the President possessing, as Cox recalled, an almost photographic memory for geography. By the time Elsey joined the staff in April, "the President rarely came into the Map Room," Elsey later recalled. Instead, Roosevelt asked that important communications from his global counterparts — Churchill, Stalin, Chiang Kai-shek — as well as other secret signals be brought to *him,* wherever he was. Even more intriguingly to the young ensign, the President insisted that outgoing presidential messages continue to be enciphered and sent by the Navy Department, while incoming messages be deciphered and sent over by the Army Department. In this way neither department had more than half the story. It was "characteristic of Roosevelt," reflected Elsey with a chuckle — "all *too* characteristic of Roosevelt! Wanting to be the only person who knew *everything.*"

The simple truth remained, however, that although manned eventually by a six-officer staff and guarded twenty-four hours a day, the President's new Map Room was only ever intended to be his own secret store of information or reference.[16] It was never meant to be a control center like Churchill's War Rooms — for by the time Ensign Elsey was posted to the Map Room in April 1942, Roosevelt clearly had developed his own distinctive vision of how he would direct the war as commander in chief.

First off, the President seemed to have no intention of rubbing shoulders continually with his military chiefs, as Churchill did; indeed, the army, air, and navy chiefs would not even have access to his new Map Room, unless the President or one of his immediate staff personally accompanied them into it. The Commander in Chief's "control center" would remain, by contrast, the same as it had always been, upstairs: his bedroom, or his beloved, cluttered, but welcoming Oval Study, next to his bedroom; or his larger, equally cluttered oval-shaped room, the Oval Office in the recently rebuilt West Wing, connected to the White House via a colonnade.

From those rooms, the Commander in Chief would exercise his unique approach to military command — hoping it would prove more effective than had Churchill's, thus far.

PART FOUR

Trouble with MacArthur

7

The Fighting General

THE PRESIDENT WOKE, as usual, around 8:30 a.m., and was served breakfast in bed.

"The President always had a tray in his room," recalled Alonzo Fields, the White House chief butler. "The coffee for the President was a deep black French roast, prepared in the kitchen. We roasted the green coffee beans to any degree we wanted. The President's coffee, however, was a much deeper roast than we used for the family, and it was freshly ground. A coffeemaker was placed on the tray so the President could control the brewing."[1]

As he drank his coffee Roosevelt read through the morning's newspapers, looking to see what new inanities were being published about his commanding general in the Far East, Douglas MacArthur, whose brave Army of the Philippines was fighting a doomed, rearguard battle against the Japanese. Among the absurdities: growing calls to have MacArthur brought back to Washington in order to make him U.S. commander in chief.

The President could only wince at such media madness, trumpeted by an increasing number of Republicans. Among them was the defeated contender for the 1940 presidential election, Wendell Willkie — who had the backing of newspaper magnates such as Ogden Reid of the *New York Herald Tribune,* Roy Howard of the Scripps-Howard newspaper chain, and John and Gardner Cowles, publishers of *Look* magazine, the *Minneapolis Star* and *Tribune,* and the *Des Moines Register.*

Some of the adulation being showered on the Far Eastern general took the President's breath away. The *Baltimore Sun,* for example, had recently proclaimed MacArthur a "military genius" — a general whose skills rose high above the "single field" of battle. "He has some conception of that high romance which lifts the soldiers' calling to a level where on occasions ethereal lights play upon it," the newspaper waxed lyrical.[2] The *New York Herald Tribune,* meanwhile, had run fully half a page of photographs of the general,[3] while towns across the United States were considering renaming their roads, even themselves, in his honor. The TVA's Douglas Dam should be called "Douglas MacArthur Dam," it was proposed in Congress; another congressman had called for MacArthur to be awarded the Congressional Medal of Honor, the nation's highest award for bravery in battle.[4] The U.S. Senate was equally, if not more, adulatory than the House of Representatives. Senator Elbert D. Thomas of Utah, a Democrat and former professor of history, had declared: "Seldom in all history has a military leader faced such insuperable odds. Never has a commander of his troops met such a situation with greater and cooler courage, never with more resourcefulness of brilliant action."[5]

The *Washington Post,* for its part, had declared that MacArthur, by his "last-ditch fight in the bamboo jungles of Bataan," had now shamed the ignorant "prophets of disaster" who had written off the Philippines as a hopeless cause.[6] The *Philadelphia Record* considered Bataan had proved "anew" that MacArthur "is one of the greatest fighting generals of this war or other war. This is the kind of history which your children will tell your grandchildren." Thanks to General MacArthur, Bataan "will go down in the schoolbooks alongside Valley Forge," the newspaper predicted, "Yorktown, Gettysburg and Chateau Thierry."[7]

The President could but shake his head. If the press only knew what a mess General MacArthur had made of the war thus far!

The President had known Douglas MacArthur since before the First World War — a war in which MacArthur had been awarded an unparalleled seven Silver Stars for courage and exemplary combat leadership, becoming the youngest brigadier general in the United States Army.

The relationship between the two men had been cordial, but never easy. Both came from somewhat "aristocratic" backgrounds: Roosevelt's "Dutch" lineage stretching back to the first settlers in America, while MacArthur's father had won fame and the Medal of Honor in the Civil War at age nineteen, and later, as a distinguished major general.

Both men were only-surviving sons born of strong, domineering mothers — mothers who had moved into nearby accommodation, for example, when their sons went to college. Both men were tall, handsome — and charismatic. Where Douglas MacArthur was a traditional Republican, however, Franklin Roosevelt was a compassionate Democrat — a difference that had come to a head in 1932, during the Great Depression.

As chief of staff of the U.S. Army in Washington at the time, General MacArthur had been charged by the president, Herbert Hoover, with the eviction of veterans who had marched on the capital to demand early payment of their promised war bonuses that summer. Despite President Hoover's express order to halt his thousand troops at the Anacostia River, MacArthur had insisted on taking personal charge of the brutal operation, involving tanks, cavalry, gas, and infantry with bayonets. The general had claimed the war veterans had no cause to claim their promised bonus early, indeed that the protest had been planned by the Communist Party, hoping to incite "revolutionary action" in America.[8] Casualties had reached three figures, and there were a number of deaths.

"You saw how he strutted down Pennsylvania Avenue," Governor Roosevelt had commented to Dr. Rexford Tugwell, a member of his famous Brain Trust. "You saw that picture of him in the *Times* after the troops chased all those vets out with tear gas and burned their shelters. Did you ever see anyone more self-satisfied? There's a potential Mussolini for you. Right here at home." And the presidential candidate had gone on to say: "I've known Doug for years. You've never heard him talk, but I have. He has the most pretentious style of anyone I know. He talks in a voice that might come from an oracle's cave. He never doubts and never argues or suggests; he makes pronouncements. What he thinks is final."[9]

Once Roosevelt was inaugurated as the thirty-second president of the United States, in March 1933, a confrontation between two such ambitious men had become inevitable. At a time of deteriorating international relations, MacArthur objected — with good reason — to proposed budget cuts involving more than 50 percent of the U.S. Army's budget appropriation for 1934. Summoning Major General MacArthur to the White House, the President — facing the worst economic crisis in American history — had "turned the full vials of his sarcasm" on the army chief of staff, who in "emotional exhaustion" had retorted "recklessly," as MacArthur himself later admitted, with "something to the effect that when we lost the next war, and an American boy, dying in the mud with an enemy bayonet through his belly and an enemy foot on his dying throat, spat out his last curse, I wanted the name not to be MacArthur, but Roosevelt."[10]

"You must not talk that way," Roosevelt had responded, "to the President."

"He was of course, right, and I knew it almost before the words had left my mouth," MacArthur recalled. The President was clearly furious. "I said that I was sorry and apologized. But I felt my Army career was at an end. I told him that he had my resignation as Chief of Staff. As I reached the door his voice came with that cool detachment which so reflected his extraordinary self-control, 'Don't be foolish, Douglas; you and the budget must get together on this.'"[11]

The bitter confrontation over army funding had in fact cleared the air between the two men: MacArthur respecting the President's amazing way with people, while the President respected MacArthur as a "brilliant soldier," as well as for his "intelligence" and leadership.

"We must tame these fellows and make them useful to us," Roosevelt had said of MacArthur and other prominent right-wing individuals — and he had.[12] Extending MacArthur's term of duty by a year — the first time ever in the history of the U.S. Army chief of staff's position — he had asked General MacArthur to implement his new Conservation Corps, which duly trained over a quarter million recruits, veterans and foresters, for civilian duties, putting them to work in some forty-seven states, at nominal federal expense.[13] When MacArthur's term was finally coming to a close in 1935, however, the President and MacArthur had had yet another falling-out — this time over the Philippines.

MacArthur had a long connection with the Philippine Islands, which in 1902 had become an American "insular area," or territory, at the conclusion of the Spanish-American and Philippine-American Wars. MacArthur's father, Brigadier General Arthur MacArthur, had fought as a brigade commander in the Philippine-American War; he had then become the first American military governor of the Philippines.

First as an army engineer, then in command of the Philippine Military District, then of the Philippine Division, and finally of the Philippine Department of the U.S. Army in the 1920s, Douglas MacArthur had followed in his father's footsteps. He had gotten to know not only the islands and their political leaders intimately, but a number of women — including a certain Isabel Rosario Cooper, half-Scottish, half-Filipino, who became his mistress in Washington, and unfortunate pawn in a failed high-profile libel lawsuit brought by General MacArthur for criticism of his egregious Bonus March operation.[14]

In spite of being humiliated by the Isabel Cooper scandal, Lieutenant General MacArthur had hoped that, on his mandatory retirement as U.S. Army chief of staff in 1935, President Roosevelt would appoint him U.S.

high commissioner to the Philippines — the islands having been granted interim semi-independence in 1935, and by an act of Congress assured full independence, to take place in 1946.

Roosevelt, however, had failed to give MacArthur the political appointment.

"Douglas, I think you are our best general," the President had said to the distraught soldier, "but I believe you would be our worst politician."[15] Instead, MacArthur had had to settle for a reduction in rank to brigadier general, and a posting to the Philippines as head of the small U.S. military mission in Manila.

MacArthur's exile had certainly been to President Roosevelt's political advantage.

Roosevelt had been well aware of the much-decorated general's appeal in the eyes of Republican political kingmakers at home. Although as an orator he required a prepared text, the general shone on paper and in one-on-one conversation, where he conveyed passion as well as incisive analysis. His World War I bravery was legendary; his reforms as commandant of West Point in the 1920s had demonstrated great military and educational vision. Like Roosevelt himself he had an astonishing ability to absorb complex information and pick out essentials. When MacArthur yet again applied for the job of U.S. high commissioner to the Philippines in 1937, the President had been torn. He did not trust, nor could he quite forgive, MacArthur, who was widely known to have backed the candidacy of Republican nominee Alf Landon in the 1936 presidential election, telling all who would listen — including President Manuel Quezon of the Philippines — that Landon would win by a landslide. Landon had lost by a landslide, however.

The President thus turned down MacArthur for a second time for the post of high commissioner. MacArthur's career seemed over.

In retrospect the President wondered if he had made the right decision. But at a time when the Japanese had invaded Manchukuo and were waging a major war of conquest in southern China, elevating Brigadier General MacArthur to the political post of high commissioner would have offered his potential Republican rival a free steppingstone to the Republican presidential nomination in 1940. On the other hand, however, blocking the career of such an outstanding American leadership-figure was, Roosevelt knew in his heart of hearts, unworthy. The political and diplomatic experience MacArthur would have gained as a U.S. high commissioner might well have tempered the general's somewhat lonely, intro-verted personality and broadened his mind.

Instead, the President had allowed MacArthur to "rot" in the Far East — permitting him to retire from the active list of the U.S. Army in 1937 and to become (at MacArthur's own quirky request) a Filipino "field marshal," replete with his own special uniform and gold braid–splattered hat, taking on the role of "civilian adviser" to the Philippine president on military matters in Manila. There, for four years, MacArthur — who remarried in 1937 — had drawn his U.S. military pension and his Philip-pine government salary, to become the highest-earning military officer in the world, with a generous expense account and magnificent penthouse apartment in the Manila Hotel.[16] If the war had not come, the President reflected, MacArthur might simply have remained there, in luxurious semiretirement.

But the war had come. In the spring of 1941 President Roosevelt had turned down the general for a *third* time as possible U.S. high commis-sioner — in spite of a fawning letter from MacArthur to the President's press secretary, lauding the President as "not only our greatest statesman," but "our greatest military strategist."[17] This time the President's rejection was no longer out of pique or political rivalry. As the war clouds over the Pacific darkened, Roosevelt had indicated via his military aide, General "Pa" Watson, that he wanted to use MacArthur in a "military capacity rather than any other." And sure enough, on July 28, 1941, having feder-alized the Army of the Philippines, Roosevelt had restored MacArthur to the U.S. Army's active list as a brigadier general and then lieutenant general. MacArthur had thus become commanding general of the United States Army Forces in the Far East — USAFFE.

Given their vast distance from the United States (ten thousand miles from Washington), the Philippine Islands could never be successfully defended against a Japanese invasion, the President knew. Nonetheless, the Army of the Philippines could be used as a lever: an interim threat in a last-ditch attempt to dissuade the Japanese from going to war with the colonial powers in the Far East. It was with this strategy in mind that the President embarked on a crash program of reinforcement of all U.S. bases in the Pacific. Assured of major shipments of weapons and air-planes, Lieutenant General MacArthur had mocked his naval counter-part, Admiral Tommy Hart. "Get yourself a *real* Fleet, Tommy, then you will belong!" he'd sneered — boasting that the War Department would be

The Plan of Escape

Worn down by cares at the White House, following Barbarossa, the German invasion of Russia, FDR claims he is leaving Washington on August 3, 1941, for a private fishing trip aboard the presidential yacht, the USS *Potomac*.

Instead of fishing, the President secretly transfers to the USS *Augusta,* flagship of the Atlantic Fleet. He then speeds to Argentia, the new U.S. military base in Placentia Bay, Newfoundland. There, on August 9, 1941, the former assistant secretary of the U.S. Navy invites the former First Lord of the British Admiralty, Winston Churchill, to board —and to dine with him and his "advisers."

Using the U.S. destroyer *McDougal* as a floating bridge, the President boards Churchill's battleship, HMS *Prince of Wales,* where he walks the length of the vessel, supported by his son Major Elliott Roosevelt for a binational Sunday worship.

Parrying Churchill's hopes of a promise to enter the war against Hitler, the President insists first on a declaration of anti-imperialist principles, or the Atlantic Charter.

Pearl Harbor

In his Oval Study at the White House at lunchtime, December 7, 1941, FDR and his assistant Harry Hopkins await the termination of Japanese diplomatic negotiations — unaware that five thousand miles away Japanese carrier-borne bombers are swooping over Pearl Harbor and will destroy the entire Pacific Fleet moored in Battleship Row.

A Date Which Will Live in Infamy

As crowds anxiously gather, the world waits for a reaction from the White House. On December 8, 1941, the President asks Congress for a declaration of war against Japan. Believing that the United States will be preoccupied by war in the Pacific, Hitler declares war on America on December 11, 1942.

At Christmas 1941, Churchill arrives at the White House to help concert direction of the war. In the Oval Office he is thrown to the wolves — the U.S. press. As the British Empire in the Far East collapses, FDR takes supreme command, broadcasting to the nation on February 23, 1942.

Modeled on Churchill's portable map and filing system, FDR's White House Map Room allows him to cable directly to commanders across the globe, including MacArthur and President Quezon in the Philippines—instructing them not to negotiate with the Japanese.

The Raid on Tokyo

On April 19, 1942, Colonel James Doolittle leads a flight of B-25 bombers off the deck of the USS *Hornet* to attack Tokyo, six hundred miles away — the first time in history such a carrier takeoff had been effected — with no possibility of return. For his valor, President Roosevelt personally awards him the Congressional Medal of Honor on his return from China.

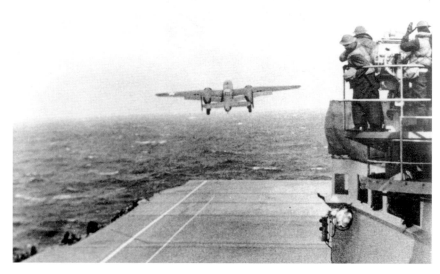

sending the bulk of its latest B-17 bombers to the Philippines under MacArthur's army command.[18] Moreover, MacArthur had unwisely assured President Quezon: "I don't *think* that the Philippines can defend themselves, I *know* they can."[19]

Roosevelt's diplomatic gamble — backed by a show of belated but growing American air power — had failed. Japan's military government, or junta, had simply made a careful assessment of the production, supply, and installation rate of proposed American reinforcements, and concluded that the United States would reach naval and air force parity by the spring of 1942, after which it would steadily surpass Japan's military production capacity. It was now or never, if the Empire of the Sun wished to expand its stalled war of conquest in the Far East, while the Western powers were so weak. Japan, their admirals reasoned, had but one sole chance of success if they wished to achieve their aims by force. And on December 7, 1941, they had taken it.

MacArthur's performance in the Philippines, beginning that same day, had been execrable, as President Roosevelt knew better than anyone in America, the decorated general having lost virtually his entire air force *on the ground* — despite nine hours of warning, both from Hawaii and from General Marshall himself in Washington.[20]

"MacArthur seems to have forgotten his losses in the Japanese surprise attack on Manila," the President would later tell his private secretary, Bill Hassett — "despite the fact that Admiral Kimmel and General Short face court-martial on charges of laxity at Pearl Harbor."[21]

Even after losing his air force on day one, MacArthur had performed miserably. As he had earlier told Admiral Hart, the commander of the U.S. Far Eastern Fleet, he refused "to follow, or be in any way bound by whatever war plans have been evolved, agreed upon and approved" by Washington[22] — and he didn't, simply failing to put into effect the plan that the War Department had laid down in the event of war. Instead, he'd ordered his Army of the Philippines to carry out an ill-rehearsed plan of "Beach Defense" without naval or air support — a scheme that failed to stop any of the Japanese landings that began at Lingayen (without Japanese air cover)[23] on December 22, 1941. All too quickly MacArthur's hastily assembled, ill-trained, and poorly armed Philippine troops had run, and within hours Manila, the capital, was threatened.

Belatedly recognizing his beach-defense scheme was a shambles and that the capital could not be defended, MacArthur had reported to the

President and War Department in Washington his decision to declare
Manila an open city, occupied only by civilians, while belatedly pulling
back his military forces, in conformity with War Department plan WPO-
3, to the thirty-mile-long Bataan Peninsula. His own headquarters would
move farther back still, to the island of Corregidor, a four-mile-long
fortress isle, replete with deep tunnels, guarding the entrance to Manila
Bay. In so doing, however — despite *months* to make contingency preparations, as the War Department had instructed him — MacArthur had
failed to ensure sufficient provisions were sent back to the Bataan Peninsula and Corregidor. One depot, for instance, at Cabanatuan, on the central plain of Luzon, had held enough rice to "feed U.S. and Filipino troops
for over four years,"[24] but was not relocated. Instead, MacArthur had air-
ily assured the War Department — and President Quezon, whom he took
with him by boat to Fort Mills, Corregidor, on Christmas Eve, 1941 — that
his Army of the Philippines could hold out against the Japanese for six
months in the difficult, jungle Bataan Peninsula territory, until reinforcements could be dispatched from Hawaii or the United States.

Not the lack of men or weapons but the lack of food had thereafter become the single most critical factor in the defense of Bataan — MacArthur
having completely underestimated the number of mouths he must feed.
In his cables to the President and War Department in Washington, he had
claimed his army numbered only forty thousand men, while the enemy
numbered eighty thousand.[25] In actuality it was the other way around.
With the Army of the Philippines bottled up on the Bataan Peninsula, the
Japanese could, by blockading it, simply starve out its opponents.

Moving their air force and one of their two divisions to prepare the invasion of the Dutch East Indies in preparation for their next major campaign, the Japanese had done exactly that. However hard they tried thereafter, neither the U.S. Army nor the Navy was able to break the blockade.
And without enough food, thanks to MacArthur's error, the garrison was
doomed.

None of this was known by the public in America, thanks largely to
MacArthur's publicity machine on Corregidor. At his underground headquarters in the Malinta Tunnel beneath the Corregidor "Rock," two miles
across the water from the Bataan Peninsula, MacArthur had reserved to
himself the sole right to issue press communiqués and press releases, telling each day more stories of heroic combat against the Japanese under his
sterling generalship — even though MacArthur only once ever crossed

the water to visit his army in the field.[26] He was writing pure propaganda. "General MacArthur personally checks all publicity reports, and writes many of them himself," his chief of staff afterward explained, "always with an eye on their effect on the MacArthur legend."[27]

MacArthur's subsequent air force commander, Brigadier General George Kenney, mockingly described the communiqués as having "painted the General with a halo and seated him on the highest pedestal in the universe."[28] Of almost 150 communiqués put out by the headquarters of the USAFFE in the weeks following Pearl Harbor, 109 mentioned only one individual: MacArthur.[29]

As a battlefield commander MacArthur was, Roosevelt reflected, a fraud — his January 15, 1942, message, "to be read out to all units," declaring that "help is on the way," being "criminal" in its mendacity and the raising "of false hopes," the President told his personal secretary, " — hopes that MacArthur knew could not be fulfilled."[30]

But what of the general's credentials to replace the President as U.S. commander in chief — a replacement that had never taken place in American history, given the Constitution's express condition that only the President of the United States should hold that title, rank, and responsibility?

Here the President was even more disappointed by MacArthur's histrionics — the only term that could describe the "flood of communications" (as Eisenhower called it in his diary)[31] the general had transmitted to Washington by wireless since Pearl Harbor. For in their miscalculations, wild exaggerations, grandiose recommendations, and doomsday warnings, MacArthur's cables had given cause for the President to question MacArthur's mental health.

Among many others, Admiral Tommy Hart had long despaired of MacArthur's contact with reality. "The truth of the matter is that Douglas is, I think, no longer altogether sane," Hart had confided to his wife even before the Japanese assault; in fact, Hart added thoughtfully, "he may not have been for a long time."[32]

In terms of army-navy cooperation, MacArthur had evinced a fatal lack of interest — adamantly refusing Hart's request to let the navy call upon the army's long-range B-17s for reconnaissance or protection purposes over the sea. Instead, the "field marshal" had simply gloried in his refusal to take orders from Washington, telling Hart it was his aim to create a "200,000-man army" and fight "a glorious land war" in defending the Philippines *without naval support*. The "Navy had its plans, the Army had its plans," MacArthur had declared with finality, "and we each had our own fields" — waving away Hart's proposals for combined defense.[33]

The loss of his air force on December 7, 1941 (Washington time), had rendered the U.S. fleet in the Far East sitting ducks. Such a disaster might have chastened a lesser man than MacArthur. Given his monumental ego it had not, at least to judge by his signals to Washington, which Marshall arranged to be messengered to the Commander in Chief in the White House immediately on receipt, given the crisis in the Pacific. "I do not know the present grand strategy," MacArthur had shamelessly cabled, for example, on December 13, 1941, a week after his air force had been destroyed — "but I do know what will follow here unless an immediate effort, conceived on a grand scale, is made to break the Jap blockade. If Japan ever seizes these islands the difficulty of recapture is impossible of conception. If the Western Pacific is to be saved, it will have to be saved here and now. If the Philippines and the Netherlands East Indies go, so will Singapore and the entire Asiatic continent," he warned. "The Philippines theatre of operations is the locus of victory or defeat," he claimed, "and I urge a strategic review of the entire situation lest a fatal mistake be made. The immediate necessity is to delay the hostile advance. This can be effectively accomplished by providing air support" for U.S. ground forces, as well as "bombardment to operate against [enemy] air bases, communications and installations" — the very things he had conspicuously failed to order on the day of Pearl Harbor. "The presence of air forces here would delay the enemy advance," the general summarized, and would moreover serve to protect the "Netherlands East Indies and Singapore, thus insuring the rapid defeat of the enemy. It justifies the diversion here of the entire output of air and other resources. Please advise me on the broadest lines possible. End. MacArthur."[34]

A week later, when the Japanese invasion of the Philippines began in earnest, MacArthur had sent his inexplicable estimate of his forces and those of the enemy he faced. He commanded only "about forty thousand men in units partially equipped," he had signaled on December 22, 1941, confronting "eighty to one hundred thousand" Japanese[35] — when in truth he had no fewer than eighty-five thousand of his own armed troops, facing less than half that number of Japanese. On January 2, 1942, he had then revised his numbers, claiming to have "only seven thousand American combat troops here, the balance of force being Filipino" — and had begged not only for U.S. planes to be urgently delivered, but "the landing of an expeditionary force" — emphasizing his firm belief "that the loss of the Philippines will mark the end of white prestige," and that U.S. forces must "move strongly and promptly," as he put the choice, "or withdraw in shame from Orient. Stop."[36]

Five days later, on January 7, 1942, the general had urged that, as in some pageant of miracles, "an Army corps should be landed in Mindanao" — the largest southern island of the Philippines — "at the earliest date possible." He begged also for "more aggressive and resourceful handling of naval forces in this area" — while reporting that, despite the War Department's long-laid plans for a staged withdrawal of U.S. forces to the Bataan Peninsula, he now had insufficient food to feed them, and had been compelled to place them on "half rations." He therefore demanded "steps must be taken immediately to get in supply ships no matter at what loss."[37]

How such steps could be taken ten thousand miles away was unclear, though the President had ordered everything possible to be done to get supplies through. Troop reinforcements — especially an entire "Army corps" — were not only impossible to prepare and transport to the battlefield, but strategically absurd. In his diary at his headquarters in Java, toward which Japanese forces were now steaming, Admiral Hart painted on January 11, 1942, a mocking image of the field marshal on Corregidor: "Douglas sitting in his tunnel dreaming up suggestions of how the Navy could help him win the war that he actually had lost in the first 24 hours."[38]

Undeterred, a week later, on January 15, 1942, MacArthur had issued his message to be "read and explained to all troops" on Bataan and Corregidor: "Help is on the way from the United States. Thousands of troops and hundreds of planes are being dispatched," the commanding general had assured them. "The exact time of arrival of reinforcements is unknown as they will have to fight through Japanese attempts against them. It is imperative that our troops hold until these reinforcements arrive. . . . If we fight we will win; if we retreat we will be destroyed."[39]

Two days after that, on January 17, 1942, however, MacArthur had appeared at his wit's end. The rations he needed, "measured in ships capacity," were "small indeed," he begged Washington. "Many medium sized or small ships should be loaded with rations and dispatched along various routes. Stop. The enemy bomber formations are no longer here but have moved south. Stop. Unquestionably ships can get through but no attempt yet seems to have been made along this line. Stop. This seems incredible to me and I am having increasing difficulty in appeasing Philippine thought along this line. Stop. They cannot understand the apparent lack of effort to bring something in. Stop. I cannot overemphasize the psychological reaction that will take place here," he warned, "and unless something tangible is done in this direction a revulsion of feeling of tremendous proportions against America can be expected. Stop. They can understand failures but cannot understand why no attempt is being made at relief through the forwarding of supplies. Stop. The repeated statements from the United States that Hitler is to be destroyed before an effort is made here is causing dismay. Stop. The Japanese forces — air, land and ground — are much overextended. Stop. His success to date does not measure his own strength," MacArthur claimed of the Japanese invasion, but rather "the weakness of his opposition" — despite even three-to-one superiority in troops on Bataan.[40] "A blow or even a threatened blow against him will almost certainly be attended with some success. Stop. I am professionally certain that his so-called blockade can easily be pierced. Stop. The only thing that can make it really effective is our own passive acceptance of it as a fact. Stop. If something is not done to meet the general situation which is developing the disastrous results will be monumental. Stop. The problems involved cannot be measured or solved by mere army and navy strategic formulas they involve comprehensiveness of the entire oriental problem. End. MacArthur."[41]

MacArthur's doomsday language had been ridiculed at the War Department — which nevertheless tried again and again to get blockade runners through to Mindanao, on the President's specific orders. Yet there was no one in the War Department willing to put the distinguished general in his place, let alone criticize him for losing his own air force on the first day of battle. Every message had therefore been replied to with courteous War Department assurances, signed by General Marshall himself, explaining that everything possible was being done to get supplies to him, as well as reinforcements to Australia and the Far East in order to assemble an eventual coordinated counterattack.[42] But with Malaya being overrun, Singapore within Japanese sights, the Dutch East Indies vulnerable, and Australians themselves rattled over imminent invasion, there was, undoubtedly, a tendency to see MacArthur and his eight or more thousand beleaguered American troops as "expendable." The view in the Munitions Building on Constitution Avenue — and even more so in the Navy Department next door — was that, having lost his air force and failed to provision his army on the Bataan Peninsula as he had been instructed to do in advance of Pearl Harbor — instructions he had labeled "defeatist" — MacArthur had made his own bed and must lie in it.

MacArthur's cables to Washington had understandably only grown more desperate in the days that followed — indeed MacArthur's wild pleas and warnings seemed to Eisenhower and others at the War Department to "indicate a refusal on his part to look facts in the face, an old trait of his." Highly emotional in their language, envisaging a "fatal" scenario for the Allies if his wishes were not met, his cables showed the hero, by January 29, 1942, to be "jittery!" as Eisenhower jotted in his diary.[43] "Looks like MacArthur is losing his nerve," Eisenhower wrote on February 3, 1942.[44]

Eisenhower — who had come to despise MacArthur, for all his "brilliance," after years working for him in Washington and the Philippines — had simply lost patience with the braggart, as had others in the War Department, despite all the sympathy they felt for their fellow servicemen, beleaguered on Bataan.

MacArthur's pleas were filed in the new ground-floor Map Room at the White House, once the President had read them. "The President has seen all of your messages," Marshall had assured MacArthur in late December 1941,[45] and the President continued to read them over the following days and weeks. "I welcome and appreciate your strategical views," Marshall signaled back to MacArthur in February, "and invariably submit them to the President."[46]

Was the Far Eastern general a "strategical" genius, as the press and Republicans increasingly seemed to believe? Or was he a charlatan — a Mad Hatter, ensconced in a rabbit hole of a tunnel — driven literally to distraction by his unenviable situation in the Philippines?

The President had his own views, knowing MacArthur over so many years. Yet it was part of Roosevelt's genius as a leader that he was able, for the most part, to take a more Olympian view than others, especially in times of stress and ill success. His long political battles and his struggle against polio had given him a stature among his colleagues and contemporaries unrivaled by any other figure in America. And at the heart of this robustness of character, tempered by so many reverses across the years, was his abiding optimism. MacArthur might well be mad — but as King George II had famously said when listening to his advisers' objections to the appointment of young Brigadier General James Wolfe to command an amphibious operation to seize Quebec: "Mad, is he? Then I hope he will bite some of my other generals!" MacArthur was a potentially great leader, whose flaws were as large as his strengths. He was *symbolically* important, as an inspiration to so many.

As Commander in Chief of the Armed Forces of the United States and *de facto* leader of the United Nations, the President thus had a wider perspective than those in the War or Navy Departments who derided MacArthur's histrionics, and who deplored MacArthur's failure to mind his own business in his endless "strategical" outpourings, instead of actually commanding his troops in battle on Bataan. At least MacArthur was determined to strike back against the Japanese!

It was all very well, the President reflected, to point to MacArthur's mistakes from day one of the war — indeed even before war began — but who in the Far East, or the West, was any better as a military commander? As the President noted in a cable to Manuel Quezon that he sent via MacArthur, "The deficiency which now exists in our offensive weapons are the natural results of the policies of peaceful nations such as the Philippines and the United States" — nations "who without warning are attacked by despotic nations which have spent years in preparing for such action. Early reverses, hardships and pain are the price that democracy must pay under such conditions." Roosevelt had assured Quezon that "every dollar and every material sinew of this nation" were being thrown into the fight, a fight whose objective was in part the restoration of "tranquility and peace to the Philippines and its return to such government as its people may themselves choose."[47] Yet patient realism of this kind, sincere as it was, would have no value, the President recognized, without military commanders able to convey confidence and a transcending belief in their own leadership.

"This war can't be won with men who are thinking only about retiring to farms somewhere and who won't take great and bold risks," the President had told Harry Hopkins at dinner on January 24, 1942 — Hopkins noting that Roosevelt "has got a whole hatful of them in the Army and Navy that will have to be liquidated before we really get on with our fighting."[48]

What a contrast MacArthur was, for example, to Admiral Tommy Hart, the four-star commander of the U.S. Navy's Far Eastern Fleet, as the President explained to Hopkins. The President had known Hart for many years. Like Admiral Stark, Hart was a highly professional officer — but one who exuded defeatism, however much he called it realism. From Admiral King and others in the Navy Department, the President was hearing how Hart was spreading little but weariness and resignation wherever he went — prompting the chief of naval operations to send messages from the Navy Department warning Hart of what was being said about him in Washington,[49] and Harry Hopkins to write in his diary, before he himself went into hospital for another prolonged bout of treatment, that the President was "going to have many of the same problems that Lincoln had with generals and admirals whose records look awfully good but who may turn out to be the McClellans of this war.[50] The only difference," Hopkins wrote, "is that I think Roosevelt will act much faster in replacing these fellows."[51] *Faute de mieux,* Hart had recently been appointed commander in chief of all American, British, Dutch, and Australian naval forces in the Southwest Pacific (the so-called ABDA area), under General Archibald Wavell, the new supreme commander in area — but was letting down the American flag. As Hopkins noted, the President felt Admiral Hart "is too old adequately to carry out the responsibilities that were given him and I fancy before long there will be a change in our naval command in the Far East."[52]

It was to ponder over Hart's command, among other matters, that on January 31, 1942, the President set off in his special train from Washington's University Station to spend a few days at his home in Hyde Park, north of New York.

Winston Churchill had urged him to get out of Washington whenever he could, in order to "think about" the war in quiet — Churchill often spending his weekends at Ditchley Park, an American-owned manor house outside London, where he could obtain respite from the German bombing and the cares of Parliament. Despite the inclement weather, which presaged snow, the President had finally taken Churchill's advice. He was "in rare form, full of wisecracks" on the journey, his secretary, Bill Hassett noted in his diary, the "perfect host" to the small staff he took with him. "He seemed a trifle tired to me," Hassett allowed, "but he was in excellent spirits."[53]

In truth the President was worn out. He had even taken, briefly, to wearing "quite a snappy gray-zippered siren suit," like Churchill's,[54] Hassett described, but seemed to enjoy the change of scenery — knowing he would have to return to Washington to face the press on February 6, and a battery of questions about his prosecution of the war.

Four inches of snow had indeed fallen by the time they arrived. The President had developed such a cold that his doctor, Ross McIntyre, had been summoned from New York. Although he seemed "in good shape and good spirits," according to Hassett, the President appeared "reluctant to go back" to Washington.[55] He therefore stayed put.

The days at his family home — so big and quiet and lonely without the presence of his mother, Sarah, who had passed away the previous fall (causing the President to wear a black armband for a full year to mark his grief) — now enabled the President to see what his own military team were missing — even those like Eisenhower and Colonel Handy, who were now urging that the Philippines be written off.[56]

Ike, as he was universally known in the War Department, could only scoff at MacArthur's melodramatic cables, especially the general's recent signal stating that "in the event of my death" he wanted his chief of staff, Richard Sutherland, to assume command in the Philippines — a man Eisenhower considered one of MacArthur's biggest "boot lickers."[57]

Only a handful of officers or men of the Army of the Philippines had seen MacArthur, their commanding general, on his one-and-only visit to the Bataan Peninsula, on January 10, 1942. They had become even less enchanted with MacArthur's generalship when, on January 24, he had given orders reducing the limited rations on Bataan by half — while ordering a doubling of food stocks for the eleven thousand men on Corregidor, who — apart from antiaircraft and long-range artillery units — were not even fighting.[58] It was this, primarily, that had led to the famous ballad, sung by the soldiers to the tune of "The Battle Hymn of the Republic," deriding their commanding general as "Dugout Doug":

> *Dugout Doug MacArthur lies ashaking on the Rock*
> *Safe from all the bombers and from any sudden shock*
> *Dugout Doug is eating of the best food on Bataan*
> *And his troops go starving on.*

> *Chorus*

> *Dugout Doug, come out from hiding*
> *Dugout Doug, come out from hiding*
> *Send to Franklin the glad tidings*
> *That his troops go starving on!*[59]

Whether or not the general was "hiding out" in the Malinta Tunnel while his valiant army was continuing the Battle of Bataan, FDR understood, however, a key fact: MacArthur had gotten the Filipinos to fight the Japanese, not welcome them. *This,* the President recognized, represented a potentially war-changing phenomenon in terms of Japan's moral basis for hostilities — and America's destiny in countering the Japanese rampage. Though the American press and Republican politicians might be wildly overstating his claims to fame — mythologizing MacArthur's prowess as a commander in the field and his fitness to be U.S. commander in chief in Washington in place of Roosevelt himself — MacArthur's *spirit,* like that of Churchill's in 1940, might turn out to be more important to American and Allied morale in prosecuting the war than all his errors as a general combined.

The parallel with Churchill fascinated the President. How alike were the two in many ways! Both men loved symbols to mark their individuality — Churchill his cigars, General MacArthur his corncob pipe and cane. Even their distinctive hats were designed to be memorable: Churchill's bowler, MacArthur's special "field marshal's" cap, with its intricate, spaghetti-splash of gold braid. Both men were positively dangerous in terms of their lack of realism, their tactical missteps, their mood swings. Churchill's performance during the fall of France — his wild orders for counterattack that bore no relation to what was possible after Guderian and Rommel's breakthrough, and his instructions to Lord Gort to surrender the British Expeditionary Force rearguard at Dunkirk when it was not necessary — had been as pitiful as MacArthur's defense of Lingayen and ill-provisioned retreat to Bataan. Even so, the performance of Churchill's ally, France, had been even *more* deplorable! What Churchill and MacArthur both exuded, the President acknowledged, were a pluck and defiance that made others seem small and minion. MacArthur's pie-in-the-sky calls for counteroffensive action took no account of what was actually possible in the Southwest Pacific at such an early stage in the war, and the general's own responsibility in failing to prepare for a prolonged siege, as the War Department had instructed him. For all his faults, however, MacArthur was at least expressing the spirit of a fighters, determined to strike back at the Japanese, if possible — not run from them.

Hopkins — who remained in hospital for ten days — thus soon proved correct. When the President returned to Washington, it was, as U.S. commander in chief, to order that Admiral Hart be fired — Hart having confided to his supreme commander, General Wavell, that at age sixty-four he was simply too weary for the stress of the job, had already passed his retirement age, and could not be expected to run the Japanese blockade encircling the Philippines, where his ships would be subjected to heavy attack by hostile land-based aircraft.[60] Instead, Hart had advised, they should concentrate only on trying to attack Japanese naval ships and transports as they approached the Netherlands East Indies and Java, and let MacArthur wither on his vine.

By contrast, the President remained rather proud of his Far Eastern general.

The President was aware, however, that MacArthur's nerves were increasingly on edge — as well they might be. In his almost daily cables of woe — as well as suggestions on how to vanquish the enemy — the general was, in a sense, letting off steam, the President knew: his language reflecting the torment he was going through.

On February 4, 1942, for example, the War Department had flown up to Hyde Park a new signal from MacArthur in which the general had referred to what was, in his view, "a fatal blunder on the part of the democratic allies. The Japanese are sweeping southward in a great offensive and the allies are attempting merely to stop them by building up forces in their front. This method," MacArthur had signaled, "as has always been the case in war, will fail. Such movements can only be negated by thrusts not at the enemy's strength but at his weakness. The lines of weakness from time immemorial have been the lines of communication. In this case they are stretched over two thousand miles of sea, with the whole line subject to American sea thrust. This line is not defended by enemy bombers but is held by scattered naval elements. A sea threat would immediately relieve the pressure on the south and is the only way that pressure can be relieved. A great naval victory on our part is not necessary to accomplish this mission; the threat alone would go far toward the desired end. The enemy would probably not engage his entire fleet in actual combat. If he did and lost, the war would be over. If he did and won, the losses he would sustain would still cripple his advance and take from him the initiative. You must be prepared to take heavy losses," MacArthur warned, "just as heavy losses are inflicted in return. I wish to reiterate that his bomber strength is entirely engaged on his southern front and represents no menace at all to such a naval thrust. With only minor menace from the fleets of Germany and Italy the American and British navies can assemble without serious jeopardy the force to make this thrust. I unhesitatingly predict that if this is not done the plan upon which we are now working, based upon the building up of air supremacy in the Southwest Pacific, will fail, the war will be indefinitely prolonged and its final outcome will be jeopardized. Counsels of timidity based upon theories of safety first will not win against such an aggressive and audacious adversary as Japan. No building program no matter of what proportions will be able to overtake the initial advantages the enemy with every chance of success is trying to gain. The only way to fight him is to fight him immediately. . . . From my present point of vantage I can see the whole strategy of the Pacific perhaps clearer than anyone else. End. MacArthur."[61]

It was easy enough, as Brigadier General Eisenhower did,[62] to ridicule such *pronunciamentos*. MacArthur was correct, strategically. The problem was simply a practical one: his advice could not be followed. But at least MacArthur was thinking *aggressively* as a commander — in fact, he was by the very force of his personality holding together a symbolic partnership between American and Filipino forces that had incalculable importance for the Western alliance. This, the President recognized, was a pearl beyond price — something that the President's advisers (and many later critics, also) simply failed to understand.

On New Year's Eve, already, the President had suggested that President Quezon be rescued from the Philippines and brought to Washington to lead a government in exile, like that of the Dutch government.[63] MacArthur had instinctively demurred, claiming Quezon — who was suffering from tuberculosis — would not survive the flight, and that his presence on Corregidor was vital for Filipino troops fighting alongside U.S. soldiers. Anxious lest Quezon be captured by the Japanese and made into a quisling, President Roosevelt had felt MacArthur's intransigence to be a mistake, but had concurred, leaving the decision as to the best moment for Quezon's evacuation up to MacArthur.

As the days had gone by, however, and it had become more and more obvious the Allies would not be able to mount a relief of the Philippines, MacArthur's insistence on keeping Quezon at Corregidor to fire up his Filipino troops had begun to backfire. It had become obvious to Quezon that, whatever promises President Roosevelt made and MacArthur assured him of, the United States was not going to be able to save the Philippines from Japanese conquest.

Quezon had already sent the President a despairing message on January 13, 1942,[64] which Roosevelt had not answered, but which had certainly disturbed him. Then on January 29, Quezon had written out a formal letter to MacArthur, intended for transmission to the President, pointing out again that the "war is not of our making. Those that dictated the policies of the United States could not have failed to see that this is the weakest point in American territory. . . . We decided to fight by your side and we have done the best we could and we are still doing as much as could be expected from us under the circumstances. But how long are we going to be left alone? I want to decide in my own mind whether there is any justification in allowing all these men to be killed, when for the final outcome of the war the shedding of their blood may be wholly unnecessary."[65]

The President had relied on MacArthur to keep up the spirits of the Philippine president, but Quezon's latest appeal he had had to answer — assuring Quezon that he recognized "the depth and sincerity of your sentiments" with respect to "your own people." He wanted Quezon to know that he himself would be "the last to demand of you and them any sacrifice which I considered hopeless in the furtherance of the cause for which we are all striving. I want, however, to state with all possible emphasis that the magnificent resistance of the defenders of Bataan is contributing definitely toward assuring the completeness of our final victory in the Far East. While I cannot now indicate the time at which succor and assistance can reach the Philippines, I do know that every ship at our disposal is bringing to the southwest Pacific the forces that will ultimately smash the invader and free your country. . . . I have no words in which to express to you my admiration and gratitude for the complete demonstration of loyalty, courage and readiness to sacrifice that your people, under your inspired leadership, have displayed. They are upholding the most magnificent traditions of a free democracy."[66]

MacArthur had been delighted by the response. As he had cabled back to General Marshall in Washington: "The President's message to Quezon was most effective. Stop. Quezon sends following reply for President Roosevelt. Colon. Quote. Your letter has moved me deeply. Stop. I wish to assure you that we shall do our part to the end. Signed Quezon. Unquote. MacArthur."[67] Quezon had even broadcast, on Voice of Freedom radio from Corregidor, that night, urging "every Filipino to be of good cheer, to have faith in the patriotism of valor of our soldiers in the field, but above all, to trust America. The United States will win this war, America is too great and powerful to be vanquished in this conflict. I know she will not fail us."[68]

· · ·

What, then, went wrong? Hardly had Quezon's cable arrived in Washington than, two days after the President's return from Hyde Park, a new cable from Quezon arrived, with a very different message. In transmitting President Quezon's text, General MacArthur prefaced it by saying that he himself would be sending a second part to the cable, in which he would give his own thoughts on the matter. That part, however, had not yet been deciphered.

It was the first part, however — the text from Quezon — that filled the President with trepidation as he went to sleep on February 8, 1942. As Secretary Stimson noted in his diary — having spent an hour and a half discussing the ramifications of the partial message with General Marshall that afternoon — the war in the Far East was coming to an inevitable crisis.

Quezon's cable had been blunt. "I feel at this moment that our military resistance here can no longer hold the enemy when he sees fit to launch a serious attack," Quezon had written. "I deem it my duty to propose my solution.

"That the United States immediately grant the Philippines complete and absolute independence;

"That the Philippines be at once neutralized;

"That all occupying troops, both American and Japanese, be withdrawn by mutual agreement with the Philippine government within a reasonable length of time;

"That neither country maintain bases in the Philippines . . .

"It is my proposal to make these suggestions publicly to you and to the Japanese authorities without delay and upon its acceptance in general principle by those two countries that an immediate armistice be entered into here pending the withdrawal of their respective garrisons."[69]

Reading this, Colonel Stimson could only shake his head. It was, in short, yet "another appeal from Quezon who has evidently made up his mind to make a surrender for his people in order to avoid useless sacrifice," as the secretary summarized in his diary. Which now raised the question "not only as to Quezon and the Philippines' future," he mused, "but what we should do with the devoted little garrison that has been holding out" — and "what we should do with MacArthur."[70]

The President, as commander in chief, would finally have to make a decision "ghastly in its responsibility and significance"[71] — but first they must wait for the second part of the cable to be decoded.

* * *

Henry Stimson, aged seventy-four, had good reason to be anxious, since the crisis over the Philippines put his own post as secretary of war on the line.

The U.S. War Plans Division had already produced on January 3, 1942, a "very gloomy study," stating "that it would be impossible for us to relieve MacArthur and we might as well make up our minds about it," as Stimson had noted in his diary.[72] Such a relief would require an unachievable task force to be assembled, overnight: not only 750 more warplanes but between six and nine more battleships or heavy cruisers, five to seven aircraft carriers, almost fifty destroyers, sixty submarines as well as their auxiliary vessels, and "several hundred thousand" troops.[73] As the secretary had noted in his diary two nights later, the truth was written on the wall, but no one was allowed to speak it. "Everybody knows the chances are against getting relief to him, but there is no use saying so beforehand," Stimson had confessed — having ordered the report to be kept secret.[74]

The simple truth was, the Philippines was doomed. The remnants of the U.S. Pacific Fleet could not be risked, so soon after Pearl Harbor, in such a wild adventure — leaving Pearl Harbor undefended. The surviving vessels of Admiral Hart's Far Eastern Fleet had wisely sailed south to Java. And with the U.S. Army Air Forces lacking sufficient available planes to get beyond Mindanao, the southernmost Philippine island, there was no hope of staging a relief mission — indeed, it was questionable whether the Allies could hold on to the Netherlands East Indies, with its crucial oil resources. MacArthur would have to fight it out to the bitter end, with the forces he had. "None of us is likely to make the mistake," Stimson had admitted, "of taking too much risk."[75]

As the inevitable surrender of the Bataan and Corregidor garrisons approached, however, cruel words were spoken in the press and in Washington about Secretary Stimson's performance — indeed, Stimson would be urged to retire by a member of Congress speaking on the floor of the House.[76] It was small wonder that, as the concluding part of General MacArthur's cable was received and successfully decoded early on the morning of February 9, 1942, the secretary of war blanched.

"When I reached the War Department," he recorded that night, "the telegram which had begun coming in yesterday had been finished." First, however, Stimson reread President Quezon's "somber" evaluation of the situation in the Philippines — "arraigning the United States for delinquency in helping the Philippines in many matters which were entirely false," and therefore proposing "that we should declare the independence of the Philippines and retire and that the Japanese should be appealed to on the basis of a recent speech by the Prime Minister of Japan" — a speech to the Japanese Diet in which Prime Minister Tojo had promised eventual independence to the Filipinos if they would stop fighting side-by-side with the Americans.

If Quezon's recommendation — namely a pact with the Japanese to withdraw all forces, Japanese and American, from the Philippine Islands in the midst of a critical battle — was not bad enough, MacArthur's accompanying telegram was even worse. "This telegram was most disappointing," Stimson dictated in his diary, for MacArthur "went more than half way towards supporting Quezon's position."[77]

Having talked over the telegram with Marshall and Eisenhower, "I then called up the President, told him of the [second part of the] message, and said I was on the point of sending it to him by messenger. I gave him an outline of it to break the news and he at once suggested that Marshall and I come over at half past ten."[78]

Stimson and Marshall were duly driven to the White House. In the President's study on the second floor they found not only the Commander in Chief but Assistant Secretary of State Sumner Welles — "Cordell Hull being sick."[79] Quezon's message might be disappointing, but it was MacArthur's telegram recommending "neutralization" of the Philippines in the middle of a battle that most amazed the President.

Japanese forces had already invaded Borneo and Celebes, prior to the seizure of Java and Timor; meanwhile, they had other forces preparing for the conquest of Sumatra. What earthly reason would the Japanese have to accept "neutralization" of the Philippines — the closest major islands to Japan — and the evacuation of American forces, when they already had the islands within their grasp, indeed had withdrawn one fighting division, with the intention of dealing with the Bataan business later, once they had reached Borneo?

It made no sense — yet MacArthur, in his cable, had supported President Quezon's appeal, and had quoted the high commissioner, Francis Sayre, as supporting it too. "I took the liberty of presenting this message to High Commissioner Sayre for a general expression of his views," MacArthur reported in the second part of his cable. "States as follows: 'If the premise of President Quezon is correct that American help cannot or will not arrive here in time to be availing I believe his proposal for immediate independence and neutralization of Philippines is sound course to follow."[80] To which MacArthur had appended his own estimate of the military situation.

MacArthur's report was as "gloomy," in Stimson's view, as that of Quezon — claiming "we are near done. . . . Since I have no air or sea protection you must be prepared at any time to figure on the complete destruction of this command. You must determine," MacArthur had addressed himself to General Marshall, "whether the mission of delay would be better furthered by the temporizing plan of Quezon or by my continued battle effort. The temper of the Filipinos is one of almost violent resentment against the United States. Every one of them expected help and when it has not been forthcoming they believe they have been betrayed in favor of others. It must be remembered they are hostile to Great Britain on account of the latter's colonial policy. In spite of my great prestige with them, I have had the utmost difficulty in keeping them in line. If help does not arrive shortly nothing, in my opinion, can prevent their utter collapse and their complete absorption by the enemy. The Japanese," he admitted, "made a powerful impression upon Philippine public imagination in promising independence." In the general's view, then, "the problem presents itself as to whether the plan of President Quezon might offer the best possible solution of what is about to be a disastrous debacle. . . . Please instruct me."[81]

If MacArthur's recommendation was anathema to the war secretary, it was even more so to Roosevelt.

It was, after all, a betrayal of MacArthur's aggressive spirit. On January 31, the President had asked Stimson to look into whether MacArthur could be awarded the Medal of Honor, the nation's highest medal for bravery in the field, in recognition of the general's fighting ardor. Now the general was proposing to parley with the enemy!

The President asked Marshall for his opinion, but it was Secretary Stimson who first responded, allowing that General Marshall "said that I could state our views better than he could." Stimson thus now "gave my views in full and as carefully as I could," as he subsequently explained his action — aware that this was perhaps the most critical moment of the war since Pearl Harbor.

"I arose from my seat and gave my views standing as if before the court"[82] — for Stimson was not only a highly successful prosecuting attorney, but had himself been governor-general of the Philippines, and felt that the notion of asking the Japanese to stop fighting in midconquest and vacate the Philippine Islands, halfway through their campaign to seize the entire Malay Barrier, was ridiculous.

However eloquent the secretary of war, and however much General Marshall agreed with him, the plain fact of the matter was that they were both afraid of MacArthur. In the circumstances, only the President had the moral as well as constitutional authority to respond to what was effectively "surrender."

All now looked at the President — who shook his head, negating any such idea.

"Roosevelt said we won't neutralize," Marshall later recalled the President's emphatic words — and his own relief. At that moment of world crisis, "I decided," he added, "he was a great man."[83]

The President having made his decision, Marshall and Stimson were instructed to go draft replies on the lines they then agreed — a cable over which both Stimson and Brigadier General Eisenhower labored "the entire day," as Eisenhower duly noted in his diary.[84]

The President was dissatisfied when the drafters returned around three o'clock that afternoon, however — Stimson's prose being mealy-mouthed and apologetic.[85] Recognizing the importance of the decision, the President had meantime called in Admiral King and Admiral Stark, as well as Sumner Welles, to assist in the business. The time had come, the President recognized, when he must not only take action as commander in chief, but be seen by his military staff to do so.

"My reply must emphatically deny," Roosevelt warned MacArthur straight off the bat, "the possibility of this Government's agreement to the political aspects of President Quezon's proposal." A full presidential response, to be handed to Quezon, would be contained in the "second section of this message."[86] First, however, the Commander in Chief had personal and confidential instructions for General MacArthur.

"I authorize you to arrange for the capitulation of the Filipino elements of the defending forces," the President's cable began, "when and if in your opinion that course appears necessary and always having in mind that the Filipino troops are in the service of the United States. For this purpose the Filipino troops could be placed by you under the command of a Filipino officer who would conduct actual negotiations with the enemy. Such negotiations must involve military matters exclusively. Details of all necessary arrangements will be left in your hands, including plans for segregation of forces and the withdrawal, if your judgment so dictates, of American elements to Fort Mills [Corregidor]. The timing also will be left to you," the President laid down.[87] With regard to American troops, however, the Commander in Chief minced no words.

"American forces will continue to keep our flag flying in the Philippines so long as there remains any possibility of resistance. I have made these decisions in complete understanding of your military estimate that accompanied President Quezon's message to me. The duty and necessity of resisting Japanese aggression to the last transcends in importance any other obligation now facing us in the Philippines."[88]

For almost thirteen weeks the Commander in Chief had tolerated MacArthur's increasingly melodramatic appeals for an American imaginative counteroffensive strategy in the Pacific — naval, air, and army operations that would have been hard for a nation at the very apex of its military power, let alone one whose forces were depleted in the first, halting weeks of a war it had not sought. Now it was Roosevelt's turn to educate his commander in the field — and he proceeded to do so, uncompromisingly.

"There has been gradually welded into a common front," he reminded MacArthur, a global coalition confronting "the predatory powers that are seeking the destruction of individual liberty and freedom of government. We cannot afford to have this line broken in any particular theater. As the most powerful member of this coalition we cannot display weakness in fact or in spirit anywhere. It is mandatory that there be established once and for all in the minds of all peoples complete evidence that the American determination and indomitable will to win carries on down to the last unit.

"I therefore give you this most difficult mission in full understanding of the desperate situation to which you may shortly be reduced. The service that you and the American members of your command can render to your country in the titanic struggle now developing is beyond all possibility of appraisement."[89]

It was, in short, time for General MacArthur to cease sending home schemes of grand strategy from his tunnel below Fort Mills, and to concentrate on his troops in Bataan and Corregidor. "I particularly request that you proceed rapidly to the organization of your forces and your defenses so as to make your resistance as effective as circumstances will permit," the Commander in Chief ordered, "and as prolonged as humanly possible."[90]

Perhaps no signal in history from a United States president, in his role as commander in chief, to his commanding general in the field had ever been as candid or coldly imperative. It was a directive calculated to pierce MacArthur's *amour propre:* to rouse him out of his temporary mental collapse, and to sting.

It did — transforming MacArthur from a near-wreck into his old self: a great commander.

The President's signal to President Quezon would, too, go down in history — though for another, perhaps even more significant, reason: articulating, at a critical juncture in the unfolding drama of World War II, the goals of an undaunted United States emerging from its long isolationist slumber and beginning its new role as the unchallenged leader of the democracies — not only in the Western world, but the East.

"I have just received your message sent through General MacArthur," Roosevelt began his reply to President Quezon. "From my message to you of January thirty, you must realize that I am not lacking in understanding of or sympathy with the situation of yourself and the Commonwealth Government today. The immediate crisis certainly seems desperate," he allowed, "but such cris[e]s and their treatment must be judged by a more accurate measure than the anxieties and sufferings of the present, however acute. For over forty years," he pointed out — his language carrying shades of Sumner Welles's contributions, reminiscent of the assistant secretary's work on the Atlantic Charter — "the American Government has been carrying out to the people of the Philippines a pledge to help them successfully, however long it might take, in their aspirations to become a self governing and independent people with the individual freedom and economic strength which that lofty aim makes requisite. You yourself have participated in and are familiar with the carefully planned steps by which that pledge of self-government has been carried out and also the steps by which the economic dependence of your islands is to be made effective.

"May I remind you now that in the loftiness of its aim and the fidelity with which it has been executed, this program of the United States towards another people has been unique in the history of the family of nations," the President pointed out. "In the Tydings McDuffy [*sic*] Act of 1934, to which you refer, the Congress of the United States finally fixed the year 1946 as the date in which the Commonwealth of the Philippine Islands established by that Act should finally reach the goal of its hopes for political and economic independence.

"By a malign conspiracy of a few depraved but powerful governments this hope is now being frustrated and delayed," the President went on — but only delayed. Moreover, the Commonwealth of the Philippines was not alone among the United Nations in its suffering. "An organized attack upon individual freedom and governmental independence throughout the entire world, beginning in Europe,[91] has now spread and been carried to the Southwestern Pacific by Japan. The basic principles which have guided the United States in its conduct towards the Philippines have been violated in the rape of Czechoslovakia, Poland, Holland, Belgium, Luxembourg, Denmark, Norway, Albania, Greece, Yugoslavia, Manchukuo, China, Thailand, and finally the Philippines. Could the people of any of these nations honestly look forward to a true restoration of their independent sovereignty under the dominance of Germany, Italy or Japan? You refer in your telegram to the announcement by the Japanese Prime Minister of Japan's willingness to grant to the Philippines her independence. I only have to refer you to the present condition of Korea, Manchukuo, North China, Indo-China, and all other countries which have fallen under the brutal sway of the Japanese government, to point out the hollow duplicity of such an announcement. The present sufferings of the Filipino people, cruel as they may be, are infinitely less than the sufferings and permanent enslavement which will inevitably follow acceptance of Japanese promises. In any event is it longer possible for any reasonable person to rely upon Japanese offer or promise?"

With this the President came to the crux of the matter. "The United States is engaged with all its resources and in company with the governments of 26 other nations in an effort to defeat the aggression of Japan and its Axis partners. This effort will never be abandoned until the complete and thorough overthrow of the entire Axis system and the governments which maintain it. We are engaged now in laying the foundations in the Southwest Pacific of a development in air, naval, and military power which shall become sufficient to meet and overthrow the widely extended and arrogant attempts of the Japanese. . . . By the terms of our pledge to the Philippines implicit in our forty years of conduct towards your people and expressly recognized in the terms of the Tydings McDuffie Act, we have undertaken to protect you to the uttermost of our power until the time of your ultimate independence had arrived. Our soldiers in the Philippines are now engaged in fulfilling that purpose. The honor of the United States is pledged to its fulfillment. We propose that it be carried out regardless of its cost. Those Americans who are fighting now will continue to fight until the bitter end," the Commander in Chief of the

United States made clear. In the meantime the Philippine president could be proud in the knowledge that "Filipino soldiers" were not mercenaries, but "have been rendering voluntary and gallant service in defense of their own homeland."

In sum, the President concluded, the war in the Southwest Pacific was only beginning; Japan had no idea what it had taken on. "So long as the flag of the United States flies on Filipino soil as a pledge of our duty to your people, it will be defended by our own men to the death," the President promised. "Whatever happens to the present American garrison we shall not relax our efforts until the forces which we are now marshaling outside the Philippine Islands return to the Philippines and drive the last remnant of the invaders from your soil. Signed Franklin D. Roosevelt."[92]

At 6:45 p.m. Brigadier General Eisenhower brought the final texts to the President for signature, prior to transmission. It had been a "Long, difficult, and irritating" day. "But now," Eisenhower noted in his diary, "we'll see what happens."[93]

Washington waited — the business of encryption and decryption seeming to take an eternity. At 9:51 a.m. on February 10, however, General MacArthur — who had still not received the President's cable — transmitted *yet another* message from Quezon to President Roosevelt, enclosing the text of the "letter I propose to address to you," Quezon stated, "and to the Emperor of Japan if my recent proposal meets with your approval."[94]

It didn't — indeed the President's response was tarter than the day before.

"1037. From the President to General MacArthur. Transmit the following message from me to President Quezon: 'Your message of February 10 evidently crossed mine to you of February 9. Under our constitutional authority the President of the United States is not empowered to cede or alienate any territory to another nation. Furthermore, the United States ha[s] just bound itself in agreement with 25 other nations to united action in dealing with the Axis powers and has specifically engaged itself not to enter into any negotiations for a separate peace. You have no authority to communicate with the Japanese Government without the express permission of the United States Government. I will make no further comments regarding your last message dated February 10 pending your acknowledgement of mine to you of February 9 through General MacArthur. Franklin D. Roosevelt."[95]

To MacArthur himself General Marshall sent his own, equally tart, message from the White House: "The President desires that no public statement of any kind bearing directly or indirectly on this subject be permitted to go out from any station or source under your control unless and until the President of the United States ha[s] had prior and specific notification and you have received his reply and further instructions." General Marshall added that, as the President had already made clear, Quezon was to be evacuated, if willing, as soon as possible "by submarine" for "a safe and speedy trip" via Australia "to the United States" — in which country he would, "because of the gallant struggle the Filipino soldiers have made under your command," receive "an extraordinary welcome and honors" in leading a Philippine government in exile.[96]

By the evening of February 10, 1942, then, there could no longer be any debate about who was the commander in chief of the United States Armed Forces. MacArthur's self-serving, self-lauding press communiqués were now to be submitted first to the President, if they related in any way to the subject of neutralization, surrender, independence, or relief. President Quezon was to be evacuated from the Philippines as soon as possible, lest he take any steps to parley with the enemy; MacArthur was to concentrate on defending Bataan and Corregidor — not grand strategy.

MacArthur's pride was more deeply dented than at any other time in his life — more so even than in his contretemps with the President in 1934, since his honor as a soldier had now been called into question in recommending parleying with the enemy.

Even MacArthur's secretary and stenographer, a young private first class who had damned "all politicians including roosevelt,"[97] now recorded in his secret, shorthand diary the reality that MacArthur had been struggling to avoid for eight weeks. "All help that can be given at the present time has been given," he summarized, having presented to the commanding general the decoded messages from the President. "If the present American force is destroyed," he noted, "another will be sent" to liberate the Philippines "in the future" — not the present. As for the Filipino leader, "Quezon reminded of America's faithfulness in the past and the deception of the Japanese promises of independence for the Philippines."[98]

So there it was. General MacArthur, in the cordoned-off portion of the Malinta Tunnel where he spent all day with his wife, Jean, and four-year-old son, Arthur, was understandably chastened. By "First Priority" on February 11, 1942, he wired back to assure the President he had "delivered your message to President Quezon," as well as to High Commissioner Sayre, who was also to be evacuated with his family by submarine. MacArthur's own plans, he claimed, "have been outlined in previous radios; they consist in fighting my present battle position in Bataan to destruction and then holding Corregidor in a similar manner."[99]

There was little doubt that the general had spoken with President Quezon, though, for he continued: "I have not the slightest intention in the world of surrendering or capitulating the Filipino elements of my command. Apparently my message gave a false impression or was garbled with reference to Filipinos. My statements regarding collapse applied only to the civilian population including Commonwealth officials the puppet government and the general populace. There has never been the slightest wavering of the troops. I count upon them equally with the Americans to hold steadfast to the end. End. MacArthur."[100]

To this response MacArthur then added a second telegram, assuring General Marshall that "President Quezon's suggested proposal was entirely contingent upon prior approval by President Roosevelt. Replying your 1031 he has no intention whatsoever so far as I know to do anything which does not meet with President Roosevelt's complete acquiescence. I will however take every precaution that nothing of this nature goes out."[101]

Swallowing his wounded self-esteem, MacArthur thus accepted Roosevelt's orders without demur — in fact refused the President's suggestion that his wife and his son should be evacuated by submarine with the Sayre and Quezon families. As he responded, somewhat bathetically, he was "deeply appreciative of the inclusion of my family in this list but they and I have decided that they will share the fate of the garrison."[102]

General MacArthur might be penitent — even resigned to die on Corregidor, as he told two war correspondents[103] — but for his part, President Quezon was not.

Quezon was incensed — at once ashamed of his naiveté and furious with President Roosevelt for pointing it out. Pride, humiliation, ill health, and horrible conditions in the cramped 835-foot-long tunnel at Corregidor, with its twenty-four 160-foot-long "laterals" where the MacArthur, Sayre, and Quezon families lived and slept, made President Quezon see red. Would Americans ultimately triumph over the Japanese, he asked himself? Did the United States really have the determination and the power?

According to James Eyre, a later adviser to Philippines vice president Sergio Osmeña, Quezon "flew into a violent rage" on receiving the copy of the President's signal that MacArthur gave to him. "His anger giving him new-born strength, Quezon got up from his wheelchair and walked back and forth within the narrow confines of the tent in which he was resting near the mouth of the Malinta tunnel. As if addressing an invisible audience he bitterly attacked Roosevelt's direction of policy with reference to the war." Calling for his secretary, he thereupon "resigned as President of the Commonwealth," saying he "would return to Manila. Repeating his verbal attacks upon Roosevelt and American policy, he stated that he wanted no further responsibility for the continued participation of the Filipinos in the war."[104]

Vice President Osmeña urged Quezon to reconsider. Even as a resigned president, Quezon might "bring permanent dishonor to himself and his country" by returning to Manila — the duty of Filipinos surely being to "defend their homeland against the invading armies" of Japan, the vice president argued.[105] Manuel Roxas, the senior liaison officer between the Commonwealth and MacArthur's headquarters, supported Osmeña[106] — as did Lieutenant Colonel Carlos Romulo, a Filipino newspaperman and broadcaster at MacArthur's headquarters.[107]

As Romulo later recalled, Roosevelt's message had, in essence, allowed Quezon the right to surrender his Filipino forces, but had stated that the U.S. Army, for its part, would go on fighting. "Since then I have thought often of this struggle between Roosevelt and Quezon," Romulo wrote — "of Quezon's willingness to yield and Roosevelt's telling him to go ahead, American soldiers would fight on. Would the Filipino soldiers," Romulo wondered, "have stayed with the American fighters or would they have given up?"[108]

According to Osmeña's chronicler, Quezon "remained adamant" all day and night that he would return to the Philippine capital, now under Japanese military occupation. "Because of Roosevelt's insulting message, it is no longer possible for me to serve as President of the Commonwealth," he told his entourage. "I have been deceived and I intend to return to Manila."[109]

A further day passed, and a small boat was actually readied for the President's journey across the bay to Manila.

Early on the morning of February 12, 1942, however, Vice President Osmeña spoke quietly with the Filipino president, pointing out that, if

Quezon returned to Manila, "history might record him as a gross coward and a traitor."[110]

Osmeña himself would have nothing to do with such a move; he would go to Washington as vice president, he made clear, and lead a government in exile on the part of proud Filipinos — not cowards.[111]

MacArthur waited patiently for Quezon to make his decision. So did the White House.

At last it came: MacArthur transmitting on February 12, 1942, the "following message from President Quezon." It was addressed to "The President of the United States: I wish to thank you for your prompt answer to the proposal which I submitted to you with the unanimous approval of my cabinet. We fully appreciate the reasons upon which your decision is based and we are abiding by it."[112]

The U.S. secretary of war and all the senior officers of the War Department, as well as the State Department, breathed a sigh of relief. President Roosevelt had certainly won a great moral battle — despite a pending military defeat. And he had gained the grudging obedience and respect of his theater commander, as well as the support of the elected president of the Philippines.

Quezon, in retrospect at least, was proud of Roosevelt, too. "I first knew President Roosevelt when he was Under-Secretary of the Navy," Quezon afterwards wrote, in exile, before his death in 1944. "From the first time that I had met him, his irresistibly winning smile had attracted me to him. I gave him from the beginning my personal affection. From my official dealings with him, I had come to the conclusion that he was a great statesman — with broad human sympathies and a world-wide knowledge of affairs; a leader of men, with physical and moral courage rarely seen in a human being."[113]

At the point of choice between throwing in his lot with the Japanese or with Washington, Quezon had chosen Washington — because of Roosevelt. "I had become convinced of his extreme regard for the welfare of the Filipino people and his abiding faith in liberty and freedom for the human race," Quezon explained. "When I realized that he was big enough to assume and place the burden of the defense of my country upon the sacrifice and heroism of his own people alone, I swore to God and to the God of my ancestors that as long as I lived I would stand by America regardless of the consequences to my people and to myself. We could not in decency be less generous or less determined than President Roosevelt. Without further discussion with anybody I called my Cabinet and read them my answer to President Roosevelt . . ."[114]

In truth, the process of digestion — or indigestion — had been fraught. There were other things that went missing from the record, too — one of them so egregious it would be covered up for forty years. For at the very moment when the President had shown his mettle as commander in chief, General MacArthur — who had been given a fourth star on December 20, 1941 — did something that would stun and disappoint even his most ardent admirers.

Forty years later, MacArthur's former wartime office secretary at Corregidor could only scratch his head in retrospect as to why MacArthur would do something so stupid — for on February 13, 1942, the day after President Quezon had agreed to turn down the Japanese offer of independence for the Philippines and for the Philippine government to stand by the United States, General MacArthur persuaded Quezon to award him a backdated bonus or bribe of half a million dollars — the sum to be wired into MacArthur's personal bank account in New York.[115] Not only that, but until the general received a cable from Chase National Bank in New York confirming that the money had been credited to his account, Quezon was to give MacArthur half a million dollars in cash (or bonds) as a surety. "God, would I like to be a General!" Private Rogers noted in amazement in his shorthand diary that night — so embarrassed by the transaction and the negotiations for it, in the midst of a significant battle in a world war, that he did not dare set down the true sum — changing it to $50,000.[116]

That MacArthur would take such a huge sum ($4.7 million in today's currency) for supposed "past services" to the president of the Philippines was not only illegal for a serving U.S. officer, but a tremendous risk for General MacArthur in terms of his stature as an officer and a gentleman. Such an urgent, cabled request, from a commanding general in a combat zone in the Far East, would obviously be seen by others — indeed, it would require the authorization of senior U.S. Army and cabinet officers, as well as directors of Chase National Bank. It could not be (and was not) hidden from the President (who kept a copy of MacArthur's secret wire in his files), the secretary of war, the secretary of the interior, the chief of staff of the U.S. Army, the adjutant general, or Brigadier General Eisenhower — who became head of the Far East section of the War Department on February 16, 1942, just as the strange money-transfer cable request was going through.[117]

The President could be forgiven for wondering why MacArthur and his closest staff (who also were offered and accepted lesser sums) should take such fortunes from the president of an American territory, at a critical juncture of the war, when tens of thousands of men were fighting for their lives — and would necessarily be abandoned — on Bataan. Was MacArthur, as Admiral Hart claimed, completely "mad"?

Under Article 94 of the Articles of War of 1920, "Frauds Against the Government" as well as "conduct unbecoming of an officer and a gentleman" could be punished "by fine or imprisonment, or by such other punishment as a court-martial may adjudge."

Rogers was ashamed of the risk MacArthur was taking, but took some comfort in the fact that the bribe, though kept secret, was known to the highest authorities in America. "If Roosevelt had not approved the transfer," as Rogers later wrote, "the entire affair would have been annulled."[118]

In the event, however, the question of corruption or insanity was set aside by the President, and by Secretary Stimson — both of whom had law degrees. For on February 15, 1942, the war in the Pacific turned a new and darker page. Singapore, the "Gibraltar of the East," was surrendered by the British without more than a token fight. More than forty thousand of their Indian troops went over to the enemy, offering to fight *with* the Japanese, against the British.

Like a house of cards, Britain's empire in the Far East collapsed, overnight. And General Douglas MacArthur, the man who had helped President Quezon and the Filipinos to continue fighting with the democracies, instead of becoming a felon became the U.S. Commander in Chief's "indispensable man" in the Pacific.

PART FIVE

End of an Empire

8

Singapore

"BRING DOUGLAS MACARTHUR HOME!" shouted Wendell Willkie, Roosevelt's Republican rival for the presidency in the 1940 election, to a big audience in Boston, Massachusetts, on February 12, 1942. "Place him at the very top. Keep bureaucratic and political hands off him. Give him the responsibility and the power of coordinating all the armed forces of the nation to their most effective use. Put him in supreme command of our armed forces under the President."[1]

"Ordinarily it might be hard, it might be impossible to find such a man," Willkie allowed. "But as the last two months have proved, we have the man," he declared " — the one man in all our forces who has learned from first hand, contemporary experience the value and the proper use of Army, Navy and air forces fighting together towards one end; the man who on Bataan Peninsula has accomplished what was regarded as impossible by his brilliant tactical sense; the man who almost alone has given his fellow countrymen confidence and hope in the conduct of this war — General Douglas MacArthur."[2]

Henry Stimson was appalled — having found the same suggestion circulating in his War Department. Secretary Stimson had, in fact, "just come from a series of discussions" with a group of men charged with the "reorganization of the [War] Department," in which the same question of a commander in chief of all, or at least all U.S. Army forces, had been raised. Stimson had been at pains to argue "just the opposite position — that in the United States there should be nobody between the President and the commanders of different task forces, and that the Chief of Staff should be a Chief of Staff," he noted in his diary. In other words, General Marshall's job was to run the War Department under the commander in chief, not take his place *as* commander in chief.[3]

When, the next day, Stimson "picked up the newspapers and saw that Willkie had come out for making MacArthur General-in-Chief of all forces of the United States under the President," he was appalled by such "Republican talk."[4]

The President, for his part, had heard much the same. In the aftermath of his contretemps with General MacArthur and Quezon, however, he was confident he could bat away such nonsense. "No," Roosevelt responded to the White House correspondents gathered at the 806th press conference of his presidency, he would not "comment on the agitation to have MacArthur ordered out of the Philippines and given over-all command." He had little time for such silly talk. "I think that is just one of 'them' things that people talk about without very much knowledge of the situation."[5]

And there the matter of Roosevelt's commander-in-chief-ship of the Armed Forces of the United States was laid to rest for the rest of the war.

Winston Churchill, in London, was also under fire as quasi commander-in-chief of British imperial armed forces. In his case this stemmed from the British Eighth Army's lamentable showing against General Rommel's forces in Libya, and even worse performance in the Far East. He was also being pilloried as a poor protector of Britain's preferential prewar trading rights, in view of President Roosevelt's latest Declaration of the United Nations, on January 1, 1942.

A month later, on February 2, 1942, a fierce new argument had erupted over the looming Master Lend-Lease Agreement. Article 7 stipulated there was to be an eventual termination, after the war's end, to trade tariffs, known as "imperial preference," which unfairly benefited Britain.[6] By February 7, 1942, Churchill had felt compelled to beg the President not to insist upon the article's inclusion in Lend-Lease, lest the United States be accused, he said, of "breaking up the British Empire and reducing us to the level of [a] territory of the Union."[7]

Economic concerns, with the prospect of postwar bankruptcy, were only the tip of the looming iceberg for Great Britain. The once-majestic British Empire, with its king-emperor as lord of a quarter of the world's population and landmass, was approaching a crisis of existence — something that now became vividly, tragically, symbolically, and militarily clear.

With a population of only 50 million in 1939, the notion of the British

Isles continuing to command the fortunes of such a vast Victorian imperial construct was inherently unlikely. Even as far back as 1883, the British
historian Sir John Seeley had forecast a day when the game would be up.
"Russia and the United States will surpass in power" Great Britain, he
had written, just as the emerging nation-states in the sixteenth century
had "surpassed Florence."[8] Compared with 140 million Americans and
180 million Russians, what chance did the little United Kingdom have in
administering and defending an ill-assorted global empire of 490 million
people, from the Faroe Isles to Hong Kong?

"Imperial tariffs" could not, Churchill realized, keep a failing economic
network of colonies and Dominions alive unless, as in the nineteenth
century, there was at its core a crusading *moral* zeal: exploratory, exploi-
tive, even extortionate, but benevolent, too. As had become obvious even
to Churchill, as a stalwart champion of colonial empire during the rise of
the dictators in the 1930s, the moral zeal had gone — a reality epitomized
in the appeasement policies of Neville Chamberlain and of the "Clivedon
set" of mainly aristocratic Britons.

For his part, Churchill would embrace no accord with Hitler merely
to preserve the fruits of the British Empire. By his own individual energy,
imagination, and military leadership, he was certain he could reverse
Britain's moral decline — but he needed American help. By declaring war
on the United States, the Axis powers had, to his abiding relief, brought
the United States into the war not only on Britain's side, but *at* Britain's
side. The British Empire would thus be saved by Professor Seeley's emerging empires: the United States on the one hand, and the Soviet Union on
the other. The British Empire would then act as a sort of middleman: rich
still in military bases, in mineral resources, and in colonial and Dominion management-manpower.

The heart of this network of military bases in the Far East was Britain's
supposedly impregnable naval and military base at Singapore. Holding
Singapore was, to Churchill, crucial: a symbol of British willingness to
stand up for its imperial assets, in a war that would determine the shape
of the rest of the twentieth century and beyond. "The honour of the British Empire and of the British Army is at stake," he had cabled the new
Allied supreme commander, General Sir Archibald Wavell, on February
10, 1942[9] — and he meant it.

To preserve that honor, Churchill had, in his own role as generalissimo,
employed U.S. transport ships to convoy the British Eighteenth Division

to Malaya via the Cape of Good Hope, as he'd informed the President with gratitude on December 12, 1941;[10] then, in his *tour d'horizon* of grand strategy on his way to Washington on December 17, the Prime Minister had assured the President that the island of Singapore and its "fortress will stand an attack for at least six months," since a "large Japanese army with its siege train and ample supplies of ammunition and engineering stores" would be required to take it.[11]

As the relatively small Japanese invasion army, comprising 33,000 troops, made its way down the Malayan peninsula in January 1942, however, Churchill's assurances of stout resistance by the 130,000 British, Australian, and Indian troops had become less convincing. On February 7, 1942, the Prime Minister modified his predictions. "Seventy per cent of our forces which fought in Malaya got back to the [Singapore] Island," he admitted, glossing over the helter-skelter British retreat toward Johore, in a new cable to the President. "Eleven convoys of stores and reinforcements including the whole 18th Division and other strong good A.A. and A/T [antiaircraft and antitank] units are now deployed making the equivalent of four divisions, a force very well proportioned to the area they have to defend. I look forward to severe battles on this front, where the Japanese have to cross a broad moat before attacking a strong fortified and still mobile force."[12]

Churchill prided himself, as a former cavalry officer, on his command of military detail. Decades had passed, however, since he had served in the line in World War I — and even more decades since he had served in Asia. In his underground London bunker, not having traveled to India or the Far East since 1889, he seemed completely unaware of what was going on in the farther reaches of the empire he so doggedly represented. What had begun as a phased withdrawal by British imperial troops from the frontier with Indochina became, in reality, a helpless rout. Now, as Churchill looked forward to a glorious, medieval-style defense at Singapore, even those around the Prime Minister failed to share his optimism.

"News bad on all sides," Churchill's new chief of the general staff in London, General Alan Brooke, had already noted in his diary on January 30, 1942 — for in Libya the German panzer commander, General Rommel, had replenished his forces and had struck back at General Auchinleck's British Eighth Army with venomous daring. "Benghazi has been lost again and Singapore is in a bad way," Brooke lamented. Churchill had told the President Singapore would hold out for six months; Brooke was dubious. "I doubt whether the island holds out very long," he scribbled in his slashing green handwriting.[13]

Brooke was right. Three days later he was mauled by members of the cabinet "in connection with defeat of our forces!" he recorded that night. "As we had retreated into Singapore Island and lost [control?], besides being pushed back in Libya, I had a good deal to account for,"[14] he noted — unaided by the head of the British Navy, Admiral Sir Dudley Pound, who — suffering from an undiagnosed brain tumor — was constantly falling asleep, in fact "looked like an old parrot on his perch!" the amateur ornithologist described.[15]

The British Chiefs of Staff Committee, chaired by Admiral Pound, certainly evinced little confidence among British cabinet members. Aware of this, but refusing outwardly to show signs of anxiety, the Prime Minister — having survived a vote of no confidence in the House of Commons by 464 votes to 1 — was becoming hysterical behind the scenes. "He came out continually with remarks such as: 'Have you not got a single general in that army who can win battles, have none of them any ideas, must we continually lose battles in this way?'" Brooke later recounted.[16] Singapore was to be "defended to the death," and the "Commander, Staffs and principal officers are expected to perish at their posts," Churchill had laid down on January 19, 1942: complete with a ten-point plan of defense.[17] It was crucial, he felt, to show the Japanese — and the world — that British imperial troops believed in the British Empire, and would die for it.

To his chagrin, however, they refused to do so.

For his part, Brooke blamed the United States. By agreeing to the Combined Chiefs of Staff system based in the U.S. capital, he felt that the British chiefs of staff — harried, bullied, disparaged, and constantly overruled by their own prime minister — had lost imperial prestige and authority over their own forces.

"Ever since [Air Marshal] Portal and [Admiral] Pound came back from the USA I have told them that they have 'sold the birthright for a plate of porridge' while in Washington," Brooke lamented on February 9, 1942. "They have, up to now, denied it flatly. However this morning they were at last beginning to realize that the Americans are rapidly snatching more and more power with the ultimate intention of running the war in Washington! I now have them on my side," he congratulated himself.

Brooke's satisfaction was short-lived. Several hours later he was summoned to face the wrath of his political masters. "An unpleasant Cabinet meeting," he jotted in his diary — for the news from the Far East was terrible. Churchill's "moat" — the Johore Strait, separating Malaya from Singapore — had been breached by the Japanese in a few hours.[18]

"The news had just arrived that the Japs had got onto Singapore Island," Brooke recorded that night. "As a result nothing but abuse for the army. The Auk's retreat in Cyrenaica is also making matters more sour! Finally this evening, at 10.45, I was sent for by PM to assist him in drafting a telegram to Wavell about the defense of Singapore, and the need," once again, "for Staffs and Commanders to perish at their posts."[19]

Churchill's assurances to President Roosevelt of British stoutheartedness had so far proven empty, despite Brooke's derision of the notion of a Combined Chiefs of Staff operating in Washington rather than London. "The news from Singapore goes from bad to worse," Brooke confided to his diary on February 11. "PM sent for me this evening to discuss with him last wire from Wavell about Singapore from where he [Wavell] had just returned" with somber tidings. The British commander in chief, Lieutenant General Percival, had failed to erect defenses along the "moat" — even barbed wire — lest he be accused of being defeatist. This had allowed the Japanese to cross virtually at will. Some of Wavell's subordinate commanders were already talking of surrender.

"It was a very gloomy wire and a depressing wire as regards the fighting efficiency of the troops on Singapore Island. It is hard to see why a better defence is not being put up, but I presume there must be some good reason," Brooke recorded, hopefully. "The losses on the island will be vast, not only in men but in material. I have during the last 10 years had an unpleasant feeling that the British Empire was decaying and that we were on a slippery decline! I wonder if I was right? I certainly never expected we should fall to pieces as fast as we are, and to see Hong Kong and Singapore go in less than three months plus failure in the Western Desert is far from reassuring!"[20]

Next day, as if the gods were out to further humiliate the Prime Minister and his military chiefs, there was a new disgrace. For early on February 12, 1942, the German Kriegsmarine astonished the world. The 32,100-ton battleships *Gneisenau* and *Scharnhorst* — which had sunk the aircraft carrier HMS *Illustrious* — accompanied by the 18,750-ton heavy cruiser *Prinz Eugen* — which had helped sink HMS *Hood* — succeeded "in running the gauntlet of the Channel yesterday without being destroyed," Brooke noted in his diary:[21] the three huge warships racing at almost thirty knots through the entirety of the English Channel from Brest to their naval base in Kiel without serious damage to any of them, despite hapless, even suicidal efforts by Royal Navy destroyers and torpedo boats, RAF bombers, and Swordfish torpedo planes (all of which were shot down), and even radar-directed coastal artillery, capable of covering the width of the Channel at Dover, unable even to "knock any paint" off them, as Sir Alexander Cadogan, the permanent secretary to the British foreign secretary, Anthony Eden, phrased the misfortune.[22] Even the solitary British submarine detailed to stand guard outside the harbor at Brest, it appeared, had left station to recharge its batteries, with no replacement! "We are nothing but failure and inefficiency everywhere," Cadogan noted in his diary on February 12, "and the Japs are murdering our men and raping our women in Hong Kong. . . . I am running out of whiskey and can get no more drink of any kind. But if things go on as they're going, that won't matter."[23]

"These are black days!" General Brooke noted.[24]

The blackest of all, however, came on February 15, 1942.

Hoping to circumvent the eyes of the Combined Chiefs of Staff in Washington, Churchill had sent more and more hectoring, do-or-die cablegrams direct to General Wavell. Thanks to the new Allied command system, however, the supreme commander was, for his own part, duty bound to report to the Combined Chiefs of Staff in Washington. This made it impossible for the Prime Minister to disguise from the President or the U.S. Joint Chiefs of Staff the impending British disaster at Singapore.

Wavell's reports to Washington had been all too candid. One of the supreme commander's staff officers later recorded how, on the way to the front, they had "passed groups of Australian troops streaming towards the harbor, shouting that the fighting was over and that they were clearing out."[25]

Clearing out? Churchill's orders to officers and men to fight and die where they stood seemed to fall on deaf ears. On February 14, 1942, Japanese forces, despite being heavily outnumbered and running out of ammunition, advanced across Singapore Island toward the city and harbor. The 130,000 defenders for the most part refused to fight; desertions were pandemic among Australian troops — even their commanding officer commandeering a boat and sailing away, leaving his men.

Among Indian troops, moreover, there was something more ominous still: a mass refusal to risk their lives for a British Empire that denied them self-government, independence, or even Dominion status, such as the Australians enjoyed.

Hushed up for decades and for the most part ignored by historians of the Malaya campaign and its ultimate debacle, the majority of Indian troops — some forty thousand out of forty-five thousand — captured by the Japanese at Singapore thus volunteered to join the Indian National Army (INA) and fight the British.[26] And still more would do so over the following year.

Churchill, hearing at midday on February 15, 1942, that General Percival had surrendered an army of over a hundred thousand armed men to the Japanese, without fighting, went into shock.

To the White House the Prime Minister had, on February 11, cabled: "We have one hundred six thousand men in Singapore Island, of which nearly sixty thousand are British or Australian," while forty thousand were Indian. "The battle must be fought to the bitter end," he'd assured the President, adding, "Regardless of consequences to the city or its inhabitants."[27]

Instead, four days later, they had surrendered to no more than a few thousand Japanese infantry troops. It was not only humiliating. It was a disgrace.

That night, the Prime Minister gave the saddest broadcast of his life, delivered from his official country residence, Chequers. In it the great orator of empire reached for every metaphor that might, by its brilliance, distract from his dismal sense of shame. Borrowing from the President's State of the Union address, he titled his broadcast "On the State of the War": beginning by spinning out the story of the entire conflict since 1939. How did matters now stand on February 15, 1942, the Prime Minister therefore asked his listeners? "Taking it all in all, are our chances of survival better or worse than in August, 1941? How is it with the British Empire, or Commonwealth of Nations — are we up or down?"[28]

"Commonwealth of Nations" sounded, to the President, as he listened to the speech in Washington, a great deal better than the "British Empire." The President was therefore pleased to hear the Prime Minister's alternative title for Britain's imperial domains — especially when Churchill pointed to Britain's alliance with the United States and repeated it, without mentioning "British Empire" at all, a minute later. "When I survey and compute the power of the United States, and its vast resources, and feel that they are now in it with us, the British Commonwealth of Nations, all together, however long it lasts, till death or victory, I cannot believe there is any other fact in the whole world which can compare with that," Churchill declared. "That is what I have dreamed of, aimed at, and worked for, and now it has come to pass."[29]

At this remark, sitting by the radiogram with Harry Hopkins in his study at the White House, the President shuddered — knowing immediately how it would be parsed and interpreted by former isolationists, anti-British citizens, and reluctant interventionists in America. Why, Hopkins wondered, did the Prime Minister have to mention his almost two-year campaign to entreat, and if necessary inveigle, the United States into entry into the war?

Worse still was to come, however. After a long explanation of how Britain's resources had been stretched to breaking point in holding its "Commonwealth" lines of communication open, the Prime Minister began his announcement of the fall of Singapore by blaming America. By an "act of sudden violent surprise, long calculated, balanced and prepared, and delivered under the crafty cloak of negotiation," the Japanese had "smashed the shield of sea power which protected the fair lands and islands of the Pacific Ocean," in fact "dashed" it "to the ground" — at Pearl Harbor. "Into the gap thus opened rushed the invading armies of Japan. We were exposed to the assault of a warrior race of nearly eighty millions with a large outfit of modern weapons, whose war-lords had been planning and scheming for this day, and looking forward to it perhaps for twenty years — while all the time our good people on both sides of the Atlantic were prating about perpetual peace and cutting down each other's navies in order to set a good example. The overthrow, for a while, of British and United States sea power in the Pacific was like the breaking of some mighty dam," the Prime Minister narrated in his bewitching, metaphorical style. "The long-gathered pent-up waters rushed down the peaceful valley," he continued, "carrying ruin and devastation on their foam and spreading their inundations far and wide."[30]

Only at the very end of his extended broadcast did the Prime Minister finally get to the point. Britain's great outpost in the Far East, its equivalent of Hawaii and Pearl Harbor, he at last confessed to the millions listening, had surrendered.

Churchill's voice dropped a whole register, as he continued his broadcast on a new note: one of sadness and misery. "Tonight I speak to you at home. I speak to you in Australia and New Zealand, for whose safety we will strain every nerve, to our loyal friends in India and Burma, to our gallant allies, the Dutch and the Chinese, and to our kith and kin in the United States. I speak to you all under the shadow of a heavy and far-reaching military defeat. It is a British and Imperial defeat," the Prime Minister acknowledged. "Singapore has fallen. All the Malay Peninsula has been overrun."

It was, Churchill nevertheless urged his British imperial listeners, "one of those moments" when the "British race and nation" could "show their quality and their genius": a moment when "they can draw from the heart of misfortune the vital impulses of victory."[31]

The President had good reason to take a deep breath. Blaming the fall of Singapore and the British Empire in the Far East on America's defeat at Pearl Harbor was decidedly impolitic in terms of American public opinion. As the President remarked to Hopkins, however, "Winston had to say *something*."[32]

The President's patient magnanimity was an endearing trait — certainly one that contrasted with the characters of the dictators wreaking mayhem and genocidal violence on the innocent. Churchill had called them, in his broadcast, "barbarous antagonists"[33] — and they were. At Singapore the Japanese promptly began murdering tens of thousands of Chinese civilians;[34] and in the Philippines MacArthur had already passed back to Washington reports of Japanese atrocities and mistreatment of prisoners in Manila so disturbing that he recommended the President take a number of Japanese immigrants in America hostage, as a surety against further barbarity[35] — a suggestion that in part persuaded Roosevelt to authorize the removal and internment of over one hundred thousand members of Japanese immigrant families from the California area. It would be one of the most controversial decisions the President ever made — licensing paranoia and xenophobia over the very virtues the President claimed as the moral basis of the democracies.[36]

Wars, in any event, could not be won by hostage taking. In ordering General MacArthur to stand and fight rather than negotiate with the Japanese, the President had rightly been concerned to put down a marker of American intent, both military and moral. The failure of the British imperial troops to fight at Singapore, however, would now compel the President to question his whole concept of the global struggle.

Britain's imperial forces were proving everywhere a broken reed, as even the British Army's CIGS — chief of the Imperial General Staff — recognized. Rommel was once again trouncing British imperial troops in Libya. And in the Far East it was now questionable whether British Empire forces would even fight for Burma: the vital causeway the President was counting on for American supplies to Chiang Kai-shek's army, currently fighting the Japanese in China.

Sitting with the President over dinner at the White House, after listening to Churchill's grim broadcast, Harry Hopkins took notes on how the President proposed to fight the war.

It was, in its way, a turning point, though largely ignored or papered over after the war. The British had failed to perform as competent coalition partners in the global conflict. Having embraced the President's insistence on a "Germany First" policy they had proceeded to lose their main pivot in the Far East, Singapore, without a fight — while blaming the United States for its failure to protect them, after Pearl Harbor. The British could not be depended upon, at least for now. This was the sad conclusion.

The war, as Hopkins wrote down the President's new "list of priorities" that night, would have to become an American undertaking, for the British Empire was proving a figment of Churchill's imagination. As an empire it was over. The fact was, the British Dominions, the still-free nations of the world, and even the occupied and threatened nations, now looked to the United States, not to Great Britain, to liberate and protect them. "The United States to take primary responsibility for reinforcing the Netherlands East Indies, Australia and New Zealand," the President's list began.[37]

It was in this respect that the example of the Philippines, at that precise moment in the war, was in the President's view a key factor. Not because the Philippines could be saved from Japanese occupation, but because the Filipinos were continuing to fight alongside American troops, rather than joining the Japanese — as Indian troops were doing in huge numbers in Malaya and Singapore. More than any other instance, the example of the Philippines would be the core of President Roosevelt's confidence in assuming the mantle of leadership of the United Nations: the Philippine troops fighting alongside U.S. soldiers and thereby presenting a symbolic demonstration of the trust that free governments had in the United States' direction of the war.

There would be consequences, the President knew — with difficult pills for the British to swallow in the days ahead. At a critical juncture of the war, with the Japanese rampage in the Pacific seeming to be irreversible, it was vital, Roosevelt felt, that the Allies should affirm their faith in the Atlantic Charter not as a "Magna Carta" for only the white nations of downtrodden Europe, as Churchill was interpreting it,[38] but as a document for humanity across the globe.

Under the terms of the Atlantic Charter, as attached to the Declaration of the United Nations, the British government, the President felt, *must* be persuaded to accept decolonization, both as an aim of the war and the postwar: an approach that would, at a stroke, delegitimize the propaganda of Japanese forces in their brutal campaign of conquest across Southeast Asia and the Pacific. Whether it was already too late remained to be seen, but Roosevelt would work on Churchill to that effect — much as Churchill had worked on him to wage war on Britain's side.

The ignominious fall of Singapore on February 15, 1942, thus became a pivotal moment in World War II, as the British Empire fell apart and the United States was forced to take over.

9

The Mockery of the World

SINGAPORE HAS WEAKENED his position enormously," the Führer remarked of Churchill — in fact, talking with his propaganda minister, Joseph Goebbels, Hitler thought Churchill's days as prime minister might now be numbered: the sorry chain of British failure in the field of battle inevitably leading "one day," he postulated, "to catastrophe."[1]

Such thoughts led, sickeningly, to ever-greater hubris on the part of the Führer. Satisfied that the British would never be able to interfere with his plans for the extermination of German and European Jewry, an emboldened Hitler was now encouraged by Britain's pusillanimous showing on the field of battle to be more murderous than ever toward the millions of "Hebrews" his henchmen were rounding up and incarcerating across the Third Reich and its occupied territories.

"Once again the Führer expressed his determination to cleanse Europe of its Jews, ruthlessly," Goebbels noted in his diary on the day of Churchill's broadcast announcing the fall of Singapore. "No room for squeamish sentimentality. The Jews have earned the catastrophe they are suffering today. They will be destroyed, at the same time as we destroy our enemies. We need to accelerate the process with utter ruthlessness, and will be doing humanity, for thousands of years tormented by the Jews, a priceless service. We have to make sure we spread this virulent anti-Semitic attitude throughout our own people, whatever the objections. The Führer puts great stress on this, repeating it afterwards to a group of officers, to get it into their thick heads. He is fully aware of the great opportunities the war is providing us. The Führer recognizes he is waging war on a vast canvass and that the fate of humanity depends on its outcome . . ."[2]

The two men then gleefully discussed how the pitiful performance of

British Empire forces could be used to insert a wedge between the trans-atlantic partners: Roosevelt and Churchill.

The "widespread political gloom and plummeting morale" that Dr. Goebbels perceived in reports from London were, in the early months of 1942, all too real — a British Empire without clothes, dangerously increasing the chance that Hitler would get away with mass murder in Europe and Russia on a scale so immense it would eventually be called "the Holocaust."

In Berlin — many hundreds of miles from the fighting — Goebbels began to describe the war against the Allies, in his own metaphor, as a boxing match. The Axis had, unfortunately, not quite "KO'd" its adversaries in the first round, he acknowledged eight months after the launch of Operation Barbarossa; it would require many more punches. The winter, in particular, had been tough going on the Eastern Front, but for the rest he was once again confident the Third Reich would prevail in battle. "As long as we go on fighting as we are, the day will come when England and America are flattened," he noted. "Once again," he prided himself after seeing the latest newsreels on the German Navy's daring seamanship in the English Channel, "we're on our feet, and the German people welcome the successes of the Axis powers with great pride and satisfaction."[3]

Alerted by his U.S. ambassador in London that the Prime Minister was lapsing into depression over recent events,[4] Roosevelt sympathized with his new partner — even though, in the President's eyes, Churchill seemed to have invited the latest battlefield disasters by his inability to pick effective subordinates, and his insistence on meddling in operational matters. Added to this, however, was Churchill's refusal to credit why British soldiers were refusing to *fight*.

The Prime Minister's cables to General Percival in Singapore had been meticulous in their detailed military instructions for defense against siege — instructions entirely worthy of Churchill's childhood fascination with soldiering, his love of military history, his training at Sandhurst military college, and the many savage wars in which he had personally fought, as subaltern on India's North-West Frontier and lieutenant colonel in the trenches in World War I.[5] But although the Prime Minister had every idea of what he was talking *about,* he seemed to have no idea *to whom* he was speaking. The nation he had dreamed his entire life of leading was no longer the Victorian society in which he had grown up as the grandson of a duke and son of a lord — indeed, the people of Britain were now more isolationist than those in the United States. Poorly led by "toffs" and

"Blimps," British soldiers were voting with their feet — for the most part simply no longer willing to lay down their lives in foreign fields on behalf of a colonialist empire in which they no longer believed.

Churchill's myopia in this regard never ceased to amaze President Roosevelt. Reeling from the vituperative criticism in the British press, the Prime Minister neither blamed himself as British quasi commander-in-chief nor even attributed the surrender of Singapore to the fortunes of war, but instead derided the troops — expressing to a friend "a dreadful fear that our soldiers were not as good fighters as their fathers were. 'In 1915 our men fought on when they had only one shell left and were under fierce barrage,'" Churchill confided to Violet Bonham-Carter. "'Now they cannot resist dive-bombers. We have so many men in Singapore, so many men — they should have done better.'"[6]

Churchill was far from alone in such reflections.

The Prime Minister's blindness reflected an older English generation, born in Queen Victoria's reign, unwilling to surrender the privileges of their class. "It is the same in Libya. Our men cannot stand up to punishment. And yet they are the same men as man the merchant ships and who won the Battle of Britain," Harold Nicolson — a member of Parliament, governor on the board of the BBC, and married to the daughter of the third Baron Sackville-West, living in Sissinghurst Castle — noted with equal puzzlement in his diary. "There is something deeply wrong with the whole morale of our Army."[7]

Sir Alec Cadogan, who had helped Sumner Welles draft the Atlantic Charter, felt the same concern — though he at least could see that without commanders able to inspire their troops, Britain was a spent power. "Our generals are no use," Cadogan wrote in his diary, as news came in that the Japanese were within striking distance of Singapore. "[D]o our men fight? We always seem to have 'Indian Brigades' or Colonials in the front line. . . . Our army is the mockery of the world."[8] After the battle was lost, the Prime Minister's Singapore speech certainly did nothing to reassure his senior civil servant in the Foreign Office. "His broadcast not very good — rather apologetic," Cadogan noted, "and I think Parliament will take it as an attempt to appeal over their heads to the country — to avoid parliamentary criticism."[9]

Woven through the anger and distress in the debate in the House of Commons on February 24 was a common, underlying thread: "the implication that our Army has not fought well," Nicolson recorded frankly —

and in shame. "How comes it that we were turned out of Malaya by only two Japanese divisions? How comes it that our casualties were so few and our surrenders so great? This is the most disturbing of all thoughts," he confessed in the quiet of the night. He added that he had wakened from a dream in which a hand on his shoulder had not been that of his wife, as he had thought. It was the hand, he recorded, of "Defeat." "This Singapore surrender has been a terrific blow to all of us. It is not merely the immediate dangers which threaten in the Indian Ocean and the menace to our communications with the Middle East. It is the dread that we are only half-hearted in fighting the whole-hearted. It is even more than that. We intellectuals must feel that in all these years we have derided the principles of force upon which our Empire is built. We undermined confidence in our own formula. The intellectuals of 1780 did the same."[10]

Nicolson, like Churchill, was only half-right. For sure, grand ideals of universal disarmament at the conclusion of the "war to end all wars" in 1918, as well as economic hardship in the Great Depression a decade later, had set the Western powers at a tragic disadvantage in relation to rising military dictatorships. Yet imagining that "principles of force," rather than a postcolonial *moral* vision, could have kept an ailing colonial empire alive did little credit to Nicolson as a historian of the Versailles Treaty. It was this tragic nearsightedness — reflecting an empire that had lost its way, and could find no alternative vision of the future — that threatened to doom Britain to defeat in its struggle against the Axis powers.

Ironically, it was Dr. Joseph Goebbels, analyzing Churchill's broadcast acknowledging the fall of Singapore, who recognized how much the Prime Minister was throwing himself at the mercy of the United States — utterly dependent as Churchill now was on the might of America, as the British will to fight abroad appeared effectively broken. "It had been his great and remorseless effort to get the U.S. into the war, and now he had achieved it,"[11] Goebbels paraphrased the Prime Minister's broadcast. All Churchill could offer Britons were more tears, the propaganda minister mocked — determined, for his own part in Berlin, to let Britain's continuing military disasters "water the plant" of conflict between the two transatlantic allies rather than devote extra Nazi propaganda to the mission.[12]

Buoyed like his führer by Japan's astonishing successes in the Far East, Rommel's rebound in North Africa, and preparations in Russia for a renewed German offensive as soon as the snow melted, Goebbels was once more convinced that German force of arms and military professionalism would prevail. Wherever an Englishman looked, he was faced by "retreat, humiliation, capitulation and white flags," the propaganda minister jeered. "To what depths has Churchill led his great English empire!"[13]

By February 19, 1942, Goebbels was noting in his diary that the fall of Singapore and the successful passage of the German battleships through the English Channel had given rise to a sense of victory among the public in Germany that "actually worries me more than the reverse."[14]

Anxious about reports of Churchill's sinking mood, the President telephoned from the Oval Office to speak with his U.S. ambassador in London, John Winant. He then cabled direct to Churchill at his War Rooms.

"I realize how the fall of Singapore has affected you and the British people," Roosevelt wrote, but it was, he urged, important that the British not lose heart. "It gives the well-known back seat drivers a field day but no matter how serious our setbacks have been, and I do not for a moment underrate them, we must constantly look forward to the next moves that need to be made to hit the enemy."[15]

From there the President went on to tell the despairing British leader — who admitted he was finding it difficult to "keep my eye on the ball"[16] — what the new strategy of the United Nations in the Far East should best be.

It was time, the President made clear, to face facts. America and the United Nations would have to begin again, pivoting not on their farthest outposts in the Orient, but on their backstops, in North and South Asia — i.e., at the extremities of Japan's rampage. In this way, the United States could stretch and disperse Japan's naval forces, while securing bases that could be supplied, expanded, and used as launching pads for later Allied counteroffensive action, as per his original Victory Program, once American war production ramped up.

The prospect was unappetizing in the short term, he allowed. General Wavell's supreme command in the South Asia region would have to be dissolved. Britain's great Dominions in the southern Pacific — Australia and New Zealand — would have to come under American, not British, military protection and control. The Pacific, in fact, would have to become an American theater of war, from Chiang Kai-shek's U.S.-funded and -supplied Chinese forces operating in the north (with an American general, Joseph Stilwell, acting as Chiang's chief of staff) down to the vast Australian continent in the South Pacific — where an American commander in chief would be installed.

In terms of the latter, the President already had in mind the man he wanted — however controversial the half-million dollars the general had just extracted from the president of the Philippines. For what would *win* the war for the United Nations, Roosevelt recognized, was not only the moral purpose and industrial might of America, but the determination of Americans to use that might offensively, under aggressive leaders. And General Douglas MacArthur, for all his faults and fantasies, was nothing if not aggressive.

MacArthur's military blunders in the Philippines had been appalling — even Dr. Goebbels noting that MacArthur's "successes" only existed "on paper"[17] — but in the United States they had been hushed up. In the battle for high morale — especially when compared to General Percival's performance in Singapore — General MacArthur had proven himself a potentially great wartime leader, whose Filipino troops were fighting as hard as his Americans.

Already on February 4, 1942, General Marshall had, on behalf of the President, warned MacArthur he would be needed for a higher command. "The most important question concerns your possible movements," Marshall had warned the general — once Bataan could no longer be held, and dissolved into guerilla warfare conducted behind the Japanese lines. "Under these conditions the need for your services [there] will be less pressing than [at] other points in the Far East."[18] Once spirited out of the Philippine Islands, MacArthur would, the President was certain, quickly put an end to the veritable panic sweeping through Australia — where the port and town of Darwin, on Australia's north coast, now suffered its own Pearl Harbor: an unprotected American convoy devastated in the harbor, as was the town itself, and its airfields heavily bombed, on February 19, 1942, despite ample advance warning.[19]

The air attack on Darwin would at least wake up the sleepyheads in Australia, the President consoled himself. No landings had taken place, at least. In taking full responsibility for the protection of Australia and New Zealand, however, the United States would now expect a quid pro quo. Roosevelt would insist that the British use the forces released by this new southern Pacific strategy to defend Burma, in the north — which offered the only overland supply route for U.S. munitions to Chiang Kai-shek.

Would the British prove any more robust in fighting for Burma than they had in Malaya, though? Roosevelt had cause to wonder. And beyond Burma, could Britain's forces stop the Japanese from invading the Indian

Subcontinent? If not, Japan would control too much of the Far East to be evicted.

In the President's eyes it was thus a thousand pities that Churchill had so set his heart and mind — year after year, month after month, week after week — against Indian self-government: self-government that could ensure the willing cooperation of India's own political leaders and population — as it had in the Philippines with respect to Quezon and his forces.

Somehow, the President reasoned, Churchill must be bucked up — and urged to embrace the future, not the past.

From London Averell Harriman, Roosevelt's Lend-Lease administrator and special envoy, reported confidentially that the "surrender of their troops at Singapore has shattered confidence to the core" in the English capital — so much so, in fact, that the British were losing confidence "even in themselves but, more particularly, in their leaders."

Churchill, according to Harriman, looked as if he had lost the thread. "Unfortunately Singapore shook the Prime Minister to such an extent that he has not been able to stand up to this adversity with his old vigor" — leading "astute people, both friends and opponents" to say it was "a question of only a few months before his Government falls."[20]

For President Roosevelt, attempting to lead the United Nations at a critical moment in the history of humanity, the collapse of British imperial armed forces on the field of battle presented a new and potentially fatal threat to the Allied effort.

Rarely in the history of war had the connection between moral and military goals been more vividly demonstrated than in the cascading collapse of the British Empire in the spring and summer of 1942. The British seemed finished as a martial race. They had no genuine map for the future, only the past. Yet somehow, with a centuries-old network of foreign bases and its island fortress off the coast of Northwest Europe, as well as its not inconsiderable industrial capacity, Britain *had* to be saved — not only from its enemies but from itself.

Churchill had looked to American military industrial production as a panacea that would rescue Britain. In reality it was American moral leadership that would ensure the survival of the democracies.

It was to this challenge, the President recognized in late February 1942, that America must now rise.

10

The Battleground for Civilization

IT IS A SMALL ROOM, as such rooms go — say, about the length of an ordinary Pullman car and four times as wide," Judge Samuel Rosenman recalled. A portrait of President Woodrow Wilson, Roosevelt's former boss, hung over the fireplace, and paintings of Presidents Jefferson and Jackson stared down from the otherwise bare white walls. Red damask drapes framed the French windows overlooking the Rose Garden and South Lawn. Andrew Jackson's huge but leafless magnolia tree still rose above the pillared, curving balcony of the presidential residence itself.

Sitting in the Cabinet Room in the West Wing of the White House, Judge Rosenman watched as the President suddenly came into view, careening "along the covered walk at a speed which made you fear he could not possibly continue to hold on to his armless little wheel chair. In his hand there was always some document he had been reading. In his mouth was his cigarette holder tilted at the usual jaunty angle. Fala, his Scottie dog, ran along his side. A Secret Service agent raced alongside also; and a messenger followed, holding a large basket containing the mail and memoranda on which the President had worked in his bedroom the night before or that morning. A bell had rung three times to alert the White House police that the President was on his way; and officers were stationed at several different points along the path."[1]

Clearly, the President meant business. Starting with his own thirteen-page copy of the address, they were on the fifth draft by the morning of February 21, 1942. For his part, Harry Hopkins had "stopped in the map room on the way over," and had reported that the news from the Pacific was "going to get worse instead of better," Rosenman recalled.[2]

The President had not spoken to the nation since Pearl Harbor. For several weeks he'd wanted to deliver another Fireside Chat, but the press of work had made it impossible — preparations for such an important broadcast requiring days of research and rhetorical iteration.

"I'm going to ask the American people to take out their maps," the President had told Rosenman when summoning him to help draft the talk. "I'm going to speak about strange places that many of them have never heard of — places that are now the battleground for civilization. I'm going to ask the newspapers to print maps of the whole world. I want to explain to the people something about geography — what our problem is and what the over-all strategy of this war has to be. I want to tell it to them in simple terms of A B C so that they will understand what is going on and how each battle fits into the picture. I want to explain this war in lay-men's language; if they understand the problem and what we are driving at, I am sure that they can take any kind of bad news right on the chin."[3]

The cascade of reverses in the Far East, climaxing with the fall of Singapore, had produced an increasing "atmosphere of defeat and despair," as Rosenman called it[4] — an atmosphere that Churchill's oratory, full of pain and suffering, had done little to dispel; in fact, other than appealing for a new display of British "genius," Churchill had made it clear in his February 15 broadcast that he was bereft of ideas beyond passing the buck for winning the war to the United States — financially, productively, and militarily.

The President's new Fireside Chat would thus be of critical import — not only his first since December 9, 1941, but his most significant since "the dark days of 1933 during the banking crisis," when as incoming president, Roosevelt had had to "inform the people of the complicated facts of finance and to reassure them that their government was taking any action," no matter how radical, "necessary to protect them."[5]

It would be a talk "encouraging Americans — and people all over the world — to the belief," as the President explained to Judge Rosenman, "that victory and liberation could be won."[6]

Churchill, in his Singapore speech, had lambasted the men who, in the 1930s, had failed to nip the Nazi menace in the bud, but Hopkins thought the President wrong to trash, in similar fashion, American isolationists like Senator Wheeler and Colonel Lindbergh. "That kind of vindictiveness about the old isolationists is out of place now," Hopkins warned[7] — and Roosevelt heeded his advice.

Out went the President's "I told you so" reference.

The President had also wanted to say something magnanimous about the British misfortune in the English Channel, hoping thereby to "stiffen the morale of the British people," he made clear.

Both Rosenman and his fellow speechwriter, Robert Sherwood, were dead set against the inclusion, however — not because they were in any way unsympathetic to the British, but because they felt it veered off message. As "we read what he had written, it seemed to us too apologetic; none of us liked it," Judge Rosenman recalled. "We spent some time that night rounding up our arguments — and our nerve — to go after him on it, although he had already told us several times that he wanted it in."[8]

Out, in the course of the next draft, went that reference, too.

The fact was, as the speechwriters spread their papers and drafts across the great Cabinet Room mahogany table and the old clock chimed every quarter of the hour, all were aware that this talk, given to the people of the free world, would make history, on Washington's Birthday.[9]

So concerned were the Japanese by President Roosevelt's widely announced forthcoming broadcast — which led to huge sales of maps and atlases across America — that a Japanese submarine was ordered to approach the coast of California and fire some shells ashore, in the hope of stealing the headlines in what was, after all, a war of public relations as well as military prowess.

The submarine's salvo did, indeed, garner attention — if not the kind the Japanese were hoping for.[10] More than a hundred thousand Japanese and Japanese American citizens had been taken into custody in California, in order to shield the huge aircraft and shipbuilding plants on the West Coast from potential sabotage or spying; these citizens were now moved out of state to special internment camps inland, and what remained of American sympathy toward individual Japanese Americans in their midst eroded still further.

The Japanese military had good cause to fear Roosevelt's oratory on February 23. Drawing an analogy with General Washington's winter of survival at Valley Forge, the President proceeded to sketch the lines of communication across the world by which the United States would take the war to the enemy — an enemy that had already passed its maximum war production, whereas the United States was only truly beginning to unveil its manufacturing potential. Axis hopes of isolating the constituent countries of the United Nations were thus doomed, the President maintained, not only because of America's war-making arsenal, but because the enemy's aims were nihilistic and despotic. "Conquered Nations in Europe know what the yoke of the Nazis is like. And the people of Korea and Manchuria know in their flesh the harsh despotism of Japan. All of the people of Asia know that if there is to be an honorable and decent future for any of them or any of us, that future depends on victory by the United Nations over the forces of Axis enslavement. If a just and durable peace is to be attained, or even if all of us are merely to save our own skins, there is one thought for us here at home to keep uppermost — the fulfillment of our special task of production." Existing plants were being extended, and new ones created. "We know that if we lose this war it will be generations or even centuries before our conception of democracy can live again. And we can lose this war only if we slow up our effort, or if we waste our ammunition sniping at each other."

"This generation of Americans has come to realize," the President declared, "that there is something larger and more important than the life of any individual or of any individual group — something for which a man will sacrifice, and gladly sacrifice, not only his pleasures, not only his goods, not only his associations with those he loves, but his life itself. In time of crisis when the future is in the balance, we come to understand, with full recognition and devotion, what this Nation is, and what we owe to it.

"The Axis propagandists have tried in various evil ways to destroy our determination and our morale. Failing in that, they are now trying to destroy our confidence in our own allies. They say that the British are finished — that the Russians and the Chinese are about to quit. Patriotic and sensible Americans will reject these absurdities" — as well as those directed at the United States. "From Berlin, Rome, and Tokyo we have been described as a Nation of weaklings — 'playboys' — who would hire British soldiers, or Russian soldiers, or Chinese soldiers to do our fighting for us.

"Let them repeat that now!

"Let them tell that to General MacArthur and his men.

"Let them tell that to sailors who today are hitting hard in the far waters of the Pacific.

"Let them tell that to the boys in the Flying Fortresses.

"Let them tell that to the Marines!"[11]

Simple, homey, and inspiring, the President took listeners on a tour of the world and the "battlefield for civilization" — a historic example of patient but firm presidential exposition. By the end nobody could doubt the President's confidence in the eventual outcome, or his mastery of the situation, however temporarily bleak. Pointing to the difference between the United Nations and the Axis powers, he again emphasized how the coalition or alliance of twenty-six constituent countries would inevitably prevail. "We have unified command and cooperation and comradeship," he reminded listeners. "We Americans will contribute unified production and unified acceptance of sacrifice and effort. That means a national unity that can know no limitations of race or creed or selfish politics. The American people expect that much from themselves. And the American people will find ways and means of expressing their determination to their enemies, including the Japanese Admiral who has said that he will dictate the terms of peace here in the White House.

"We of the United Nations are agreed on certain broad principles in the kind of peace we seek," he went on. "The Atlantic Charter applies not only to the parts of the world that border the Atlantic but to the whole world; disarmament of aggressors, self-determination of Nations and peoples, and the four freedoms — freedom of speech, freedom of religions, freedom from want, and freedom from fear." As a final flourish, the President quoted Thomas Paine's words that General Washington had ordered "to be read to the men of every regiment in the Continental Army," distinguishing between the "summer patriot" and the true patriot. "'Tyranny, like hell, is not easily conquered; yet we have this consolation with us, that the harder the sacrifice, the more glorious the triumph.'

"So spoke Americans in the year 1776.

"So speak Americans today!"

The President's 10:00 p.m. "Fireside Chat on Progress of the War" was listened to by sixty-one million Americans. The *New York Times* dubbed it "one of the greatest of Roosevelt's career."[12]

Ironically, of course, the homily General Washington had ordered to be read to his troops, two centuries before, concerned British tyranny. Nevertheless the broadcast elicited admiration even in Italy, where Mussolini's foreign minister, Count Ciano, noted the difference between his father-in-law, the Duce, and the American president. Mussolini had told him, sententiously, "Wars are necessary in order to see and appraise the true internal composition of a people, because during a war the various classes are revealed: the heroes, the profiteers, the indolent."[13]

Ciano worried that Italian heroes were now dead — leaving only the profiteers and the indolent. Roosevelt's speech, by contrast, impressed him. "A calm, measured, but nonetheless determined speech. It doesn't sound like the speech of a man who is thinking of suing for peace soon," despite popular Italian beliefs and Japanese claims to that effect. Given the failure of Barbarossa to defeat the Russians in 1941, President Roosevelt's predicted outcome of the war sounded, on reflection, all too likely. Certainly in Germany — in private at least — "they all believe that another winter of war would be unbearable. Everyone is convinced of this, from the supreme heads of the army to the men close to Hitler."[14]

Italy, Ciano confided to his diary (which would eventually lead to his execution by his former fellow Fascists several years later), ought really to begin to sue for peace, or at least offer to act as "peacemaker" between the combatant nations, before the conflagration got out of hand.

"But no one dares tell Hitler," Ciano added.[15] Moreover, it was too late — Italy a puppet partner of the Führer, who was hell-bent on a German fight to the death, if necessary; the Japanese likewise.

PART SIX

India

11

No Hand on the Wheel

PLEASE TREAT IT AS SOMETHING I would say to you if you and I were alone," the President wrote to Winston Churchill, two days after his widely praised Fireside Chat. He was struggling with the first draft of an urgent but rather delicate message he wanted to send the Prime Minister. Before encoding and dispatching it, however, he wanted Ambassador Winant and Averell Harriman in London to offer advice on his draft. "As you may guess," he signaled to Winant at 11:40 p.m., on February 25, 1942, "I am somewhat concerned over the situation in India, especially in view of the possibility of the necessity of a slow retirement through Burma itself."[1]

"From all I can gather the British defense will not have sufficiently enthusiastic support from the people of India themselves," the President confided. "In the greatest confidence could you or Harriman or both let me have a slant on what the Prime Minister thinks about new relationships between Britain and India? I hesitate to send him a direct message because, in a strict sense, it is not our business. It is, however, of great interest to us from the point of view of the war."[2]

The two American envoys did their best to press Churchill about Indian self-government, but the response was not encouraging. Still smarting over the abject surrender at Singapore and the prospects of another disaster in Burma, the Prime Minister was so livid at the mention of India, he would scarcely speak to them when they arrived in his office. For some days, therefore, there was little or no signals traffic between the White House and Churchill's War Rooms — the very alliance darkened by disagreement over Britain's colonial rights.

If Burma fell, Roosevelt reflected, the northern bastion of his whole

Pacific defense strategy would be compromised. Thus, as reports of the deteriorating situation in Burma continued to come in to the White House Map Room, the President became more and more concerned lest the defense of India, too, be at risk—Roosevelt certain that Indians, if only they were given self-government by the British, would fight for their country against the Japanese, as the Filipinos were doing.

Churchill continued to dig in his heels, however, and by March 2, 1942, five days later, the undersecretary at the Foreign Office, Sir Alexander Cadogan, was recording in his diary that his boss, Anthony Eden, the foreign secretary, "feels—as I do—that for the last fortnight there has been no direction of the war. War Cabinet doesn't function—there hasn't been a meeting of Defence Committee. There's no hand on the wheel. (Probably due to P.M.'s health). . . . News from everywhere—except Russia—bad. There's something wrong with *us,* I fear."[3]

Two days after that, Cadogan noted: "Poor old P.M. in a sour mood and a bad way. I don't think he's well and I fear he's played out."[4]

It was small wonder the Prime Minister was cast down. Not only were British and British Empire troops not fighting as stoutly as he hoped, but Churchill was being asked by Stalin to accept, as the Soviet Union's price for shouldering the burden of fighting the Nazis, a new treaty by which the Soviets would keep a slice of Poland as well as all the Baltic States after the war. And now, from across the Atlantic, he was being cajoled by the President of the United States: the head of state of a foreign country telling the British Prime Minister that he ought to grant self-government to India, leading to Dominion status or even complete independence after the war—the President quoting not only the current model of the U.S. relationship with the Philippines, but that of the American Revolution in 1776!

Seen in retrospect, Russia and the United States were thus laying down their own markers for a postwar world, at the expense of the dying British Empire—even as the world war itself reached its most critical point for the survival of the United Nations. Military intelligence revealed to Stalin that the German high command was preparing a vast new mechanized assault into the southern regions of Russia, giving access to the oil fields Hitler needed to fuel, literally, his Nazi rampage. Meanwhile, German-Italian forces in Libya, under the command of General Erwin Rommel, were pushing back the British Eighth Army through Libya—with the possibility that, if successful, Rommel could sweep the British out of the Middle East entirely, and threaten the region's oil resources from the south.

In the Far East the situation was even more menacing. Rangoon, the capital of British Burma, was in its death throes — the British beginning to set fire to the oil depots, and getting ready to abandon the city to the Japanese.

In these circumstances, under pressure from President Roosevelt, Churchill finally gave in. He who pays the piper, the Prime Minister reluctantly acknowledged, plays the tune.

On March 4, 1942, the Prime Minister finally signaled to the President that he and his cabinet were "earnestly considering whether a declaration of Dominion status after the war, carrying with it, if desired, the right to secede, should be made at this critical juncture."[5] Moreover, to try and effect this turnabout, Churchill was seeking enough support from the Conservative members of his cabinet to appoint Sir Stafford Cripps, the leader of the House of Commons, as the British government's express emissary to Delhi, bypassing the viceroy of India, Lord Linlithgow.

Cripps would be empowered to seek an immediate, if provisional, accommodation with Indian leaders, including Mahatma Gandhi and Jawaharlal Nehru, in order to win majority Indian support for what promised to be a last-ditch defense of the subcontinent against Japanese invasion from the north, once Burma was completely overrun.

There was also the possibility of an amphibious invasion by Japanese troops landing from their assault vessels in the Indian Ocean — an ocean that the Royal Navy was currently ordering its ships to abandon, in fear of approaching Japanese fleet carriers and their deadly attack-fighters and bombers. It was time — high time — to act.

Churchill's problem, however, lay in the very quality that had enabled him to stand up to Hitler in 1940, when France collapsed — his pride. And more than pride: namely, his complete unwillingness to embrace a vision of Britain as a postcolonial leader of a commonwealth of English-speaking nations.

"Trouble in Cabinet," Sir Alec Cadogan noted in his diary on March 5, 1942, lamenting the Prime Minister's attempts to sabotage the very policy he'd assured the President he was advancing. "Winston having agreed in War Cabinet to [President Roosevelt's] Indian plan, puts it to other Ministers with a strong bias *against,* and finds them unanimously of that way of thinking! Talk — only talk — of [Conservative] resignations from War Cabinet — who met again at 6. Poor old Winston, feeling deeply the present situation and the attacks on him, is losing his grip, I fear. The outlook is pretty bloody."[6]

Sir Stafford Cripps, the leader of the House of Commons, was one of those threatening to leave the coalition government in London. In Delhi, the viceroy, Lord Linlithgow, threatened, however, to resign his post over any usurpation of his imperial role. With Churchill's mishandling of the war as minister of defense — invoking renewed calls for him to relinquish the post, or at least take a deputy such as Anthony Eden in that position — the question now arose as to whether Winston could survive as coalition prime minister.

Since Churchill's doctor claimed the Prime Minister's very health was being adversely affected by the Anglo-American dispute over India, Ambassador Winant decided to return to Washington to brief the President in person. Averell Harriman, meanwhile, penned a long letter to Mr. Roosevelt on March 6, telling of his own worries about the Prime Minister — "both his political status and his own spirits." Churchill had, it was true, reshuffled his war cabinet, making Clement Attlee his formal deputy prime minister. Though "the British are keeping a stiff upper lip," he reported, "the surrender of their troops at Singapore" had been a terrible shock. As things stood, "they can't see an end to their defeats" — and in all frankness, nor could the Prime Minister, in his view.[7]

Harriman, at least, felt Churchill would survive, if only because there was no other figure on the English political scene who could supplant him. Sir Stafford Cripps vainly imagined he could lead the country — but without popular appeal or support. "Eden you know all about" — a lightweight. "[Sir John] Anderson [Lord President of Council] is an uninspired, competent technician. Bevin has never really risen above labor union politics. And then we have Max!" — Lord Beaverbrook, who had resigned as minister of production in a huff, hoping he could wait in the wings and then be called to lead Britain by acclamation, once Churchill collapsed, from his seat in the House of Lords. "There is no one else on the horizon," Harriman pointed out candidly.[8]

The prospect, for the United States, was discouraging.

In the circumstances, Roosevelt decided, he would have to make do: pressing the Prime Minister, yet not to the point of causing him to fall —

and in the abiding hope that, in terms of the current British panic in Burma, it was not too late.

The President's patient pressure seemed to pay off. Swallowing his pride, the Prime Minister at last did as the President bade him. Recognizing that his own history of fierce objection to Indian independence meant that he himself would never be accepted by Indian leaders as a credible broker if he traveled there in person to negotiate, Churchill now formally asked Sir Stafford Cripps, the former British ambassador to the Soviet Union, on March 10, 1942, to set off for India as the cabinet's chosen representative as soon as possible. "We have resigned ourselves to fighting our utmost to defend India in order, if successful," Churchill wrote mournfully to Mackenzie King, his fellow prime minister, "to be turned out."[9] Yet that was what American troops were doing in the Philippines, proudly.

How genuinely, though, did the Prime Minister intend the British to bow out after the war, Indian leaders asked themselves. And how much fighting would the British really *do* to defend India in the meantime, judging by their performance in Malaya and Burma — where dreadful cases of cowardice, military incompetence, and racial as well as imperial misconduct were reported? Was it really worth Indian Congress Party leaders throwing in their lot with "perfidious Albion," in such circumstances?

For President Roosevelt, there now unfolded the most difficult test of his career as commander in chief, not only of the United States Armed Forces, but of the United Nations in the struggle against the Axis powers.

12

Lessons from the Pacific

THE PRESIDENT DOESN'T KNOW me and besides, I'm no New Dealer," Captain John McCrea had protested his appointment to be Mr. Roosevelt's new naval aide. The secretary of the navy, Frank Knox, had laughed, telling McCrea that "FDR needs some of our kind" — Republicans — "to give him support!"[1]

The President's ability to draw people into his orbit was legendary — and effective. "Most cordial — offered me a cigarette and remarked: 'Up in Dutchess County I have a friend by the name of John McCrea Livingstone. By any chance are you related to him?'"

McCrea was "astounded that the Pres. of the U.S. has time to look up my name in register. Flattered a bit too," the captain confessed. "Invites me to his birthday party. I am completely charmed by him."[2]

The Commander in Chief appeared relaxed and confident, despite the worrying reports McCrea brought him each morning at breakfast — his coffee served in a "very large" cup that "must hold as much as four ordinary cups." He seemed to know "more naval officers by their nicknames," from his earlier days as assistant secretary of the navy and later as president, than McCrea knew as a serving officer.[3]

McCrea was also stunned by how astute the President was, behind his mask of easy affability. "Had luncheon with President at his desk," he recorded — "cream spinach soup, veal on toast, mushrooms, potatoes, asparagus tips, double ice cream and fresh raspberries. Told me some remarkable things about MacArthur — I feel flattered at the confidence!"[4]

Roosevelt's huge, handsome head seemed to McCrea to be like an intelligence-gathering machine — putting people at ease, then encouraging them to be frank with him. One example was the way he asked to see the recently fired Admiral Tommy Hart, MacArthur's former naval counterpart in the Philippines, on his return from Batavia, following his brief but tragic stint as Allied naval commander in chief in the Southwest Pacific, serving under the supreme commander, General Sir Archibald Wavell.

At Wavell's request, Hart had been relieved of his command on the grounds he was "a defeatist" — a view with which Hart had not demurred. "They don't like to hear anything which is not optimistic," Hart had noted in his diary. "I think their idea is that frank statements which openly express something which is unpalatable smacks too much of defeatism — and in that they may well be much nearer right than I."[5] His "blunt fashion" realism[6] had, however, proved all too accurate — his successor, the senior Dutch officer, Admiral Conrad Helfrich, subsequently lost virtually the entire Allied fleet in the South Pacific.[7]

On March 10, 1942, the "defeatist" was "convoyed" at the President's request into the Oval Office by Captain McCrea, accompanied by Navy Secretary Knox and Admiral Ernest King, commander in chief of the U.S. Navy. As Hart wrote in his diary that night, "F.D.R. greeted me as 'Tommy,' turned on all his charm, etc. He asked some searching questions, particularly as regards MacArthur's affairs and therein indicated that he was not sold on Douglas' 'masterful defense' to the extent the public is."[8]

"In the public eye," Hart jocularly noted, "MacA[rthur] now stands as the best soldier, say, since Napoleon!!" but at the White House, Roosevelt was having none of it — in fact, the President "simply astounded me by saying that Gen. Marshall had assured him" — thanks to MacArthur's overoptimistic signals from Manila to the War Department — "that the Army was ready in the Philippines *on 1 Dec* [1941]!! That otherwise he, F.D.R. could have held the Japs off, say, another three months" by spinning out negotiations. Hart was incredulous. "That is difficult to swallow," he noted, "but the President is the man who said it."[9]

In part the President was trying to console the admiral. Yet what most interested the Commander in Chief now, as he talked to Hart, were the lessons to be learned about the war in the Far East.

It was in this respect that the difference between Roosevelt and Churchill — indeed between Roosevelt and Hitler — was revealing, as the President *listened* to the admiral's analysis of the war in the East thus far.

Hart's report from the Pacific was sobering. The admiral had spent the several weeks it had taken him to return by sea and air to the United States pondering and analyzing recent military events.

"The man-in-the-street must have been tremendously surprised when the Japs attacked — probably could not possibly imagine that such a small and poor country would have the temerity to attack BIG US," he'd reflected in his diary, "to say nothing of taking on all of our Allies in the same breath. Moreover I wonder if our *Rulers,* in general, had anything like a true estimate of the danger of a war with Japan." For his part Hart had assumed that war with Japan "was entirely evident to responsible people in Washington. I wonder if it was? Well, what must not have been evident was that if said war did come, in the Pacific, we Allies would find ourselves in a war with a First Rate Power; 1st class in a military way, at least. I guess some of us realized *that;* we didn't guess that, even with the enormous advantage which an all-out surprise attack gives, we should find Mr. Jap anywhere near as high grade as he has been thus far. We Americans in general may have realized the imminence of this war," he'd summed up, "but thought that if it came it would be with a second or even third rate enemy."[10]

Listening to Hart's blunt American appraisal, given before Secretary Knox and Admiral King as well, the President could have taken offence — but he didn't. It was clear Hart was a professional and a realist. The war in the East was currently being lost because Allied military leaders — and their commanders in the field — had been unable to match the professionalism of a "First Rate" enemy. And here, Hart's analysis proved spellbinding to its witness.

"And now: lacking almost everything in the way of natural resources, hampered by so very many other disadvantages, after four years of an exhausting war in China, how *is* it that the Japs have set us so back on our heels in this theater of the war?" Hart had asked himself — "all in less than three months? The advantage of surprise of course but the fact remains that the Japs have done everything very well indeed and have repeatedly accomplished what we of the white race said it was impossible for them to do. How have they done it? Certain wise men have long been saying that the worth, strength and power of a country lies in the quality of its people. Well, in a military sense, the Japs are a strong people. Whatever the basis for it, the Jap's patriotism is first class. No race excels them in willingness to get killed or mutilated in war. Moreover, during all the grind of training for war, they have not had to be hired by high pay, good feeding, 'aids to morale,' etc. They have gone on, in peace and war, with a minimum of everything that we have to have to make life endurable. And they come to the 'push of pike' full of fight, hardy, tough, enduring, almost fanatical in courage and, thus far at least, equipped with the material they need for the task, with sufficient skill in its use and — seemingly — under adequate leadership. Now it has happened!"

"This war, in the western Pacific: it is an offensive war," the admiral reflected, "being the long talked about Southern Advance, or the solution of their national difficulties, which the Jap Navy has advocated for some years. It is the variety of war known as amphibious war — named thus I think by [the] British. My recent experience with the British Army didn't indicate that their generals ever use the term very much or that they understand that kind of war, as much as one would expect. I know that in our own Army there has been no understanding of it, and I have known a general or two who had never heard the term used. One, even though it was immediately confronting him," Hart added with sarcasm — a reference to General MacArthur in the first days of the Japanese invasion of Luzon.

"It is a risky variety — Amphibious War — but the advantage of surprise goes with it. And this war began as a surprise."

Hart correctly assumed that the "Jap Navy is in Supreme Command of this war," since it was "what nationalism would dictate — and the Southern Advance idea is theirs." But this was no old-fashioned independent Japanese navy, he noted — it was the very acme of *combined services* operating in the field, not simply at a distant headquarters. And the Japanese combination of those services began with air.

"We *know* that the control of the air, over the war theater, has been gained and exercised by the Jap Navy air. And that control is what has defeated all the defensive power which the Allies could get into the fight. The Japs know the value of the Ships-Plus-Planes combination, handled under one controlling command and without any of all those restrictive limitations which ham-strung the British Navy and so badly hampered ours. Moreover the Japs were prepared for an Amphibious War to the Enth [degree] because they had available a large population habituated to sea-going on all kinds of vessels. And a considerable part of those people knew the waters of the ABDA [American, British, Dutch, Australian] area, including all the harbors and surroundings, because of earning their living therein, as fishermen, small traders, etc." They had studied not only war, then, but the terrain and waters in which they would fight it. "Their expeditions could always be supplied with adequate pilots and guides, and their air service could always tell the Jap leaders what their enemies were doing."

Aspect by aspect, from advanced weaponry ("The Japs are copyists
... they codify and simplify") to war supplies, Hart had pondered the
extraordinary way the Japanese had developed their war machine — and
how they had applied it to the business of amphibious invasion. "It is to
be noted that the Japs have landed expedition after expedition from ships
directly on to open beaches and that these landings have included all the
equipment, munitions and supplies needed to win campaigns in Luzon
and Malaya at will," as well as "to seize many other points well scattered
over the ABDA area." Once ashore, Japanese Army troops could count
on naval supply and air support — but showed their own resourcefulness,
too. "In the Malaya campaign the expedition fought southward over 400
miles of rough country, during the rainy season. From what I have seen
of our own forces, I would estimate that expeditions having similar tasks
would require loading in improved harbors — and need a vast amount of
'Transport' to maintain supply lines as they advanced. So why the difference?" he asked pointedly.

Hart's answer was revealing. For one thing, the Japanese soldier was
able and willing to fight with only minimal resources: "he goes out, into
the field with his weapons and 5lbs of cooked rice, (he doesn't worry about
where the next meal after that is coming from — and no one worries for
him), treks, and then fights bravely. He also fights skillfully, whereas we
are to suppose that the troops which the Japs have been defeating were
really poor troops." For another, he was backed by applied air power of
amazing efficiency. The Japanese, he noted, had "gained quite full control
of the air, and have taken it by defeating some hundreds in all of British, American, and Dutch planes. Said defeat has been more or less in
detail, with the Japs producing superiority of numbers at different points
of contact but with all due allowances for everything — including the
fact that the Allied Air has comprised no less than six different organizations — it must be regretfully admitted that the white airmen and their
planes have not demonstrated superiority over the Japs. I repeat — most
evidence indicates that it is mostly Jap *Navy* air which we have been con-
tending against. The Jap observation, including photography, must have
been very good. Many of us have seen that their bombing has been very
high grade indeed; and their strafing has likewise been very good. As for
fighters: the 'Flying Fortresses' and the 'Catalina' have done very well in
carrying on in the presence of the Jap fighters. But the results gained by
the British and American fighters — of which there must have been 200–
300 in the area — have not demonstrated any superiority," he recorded

candidly, noting that "relatively few of the Jap pilots, or other airmen, are officers. Neither are they found to be of any particular education," being pilots largely selected "from the enlisted ranks. So much for one specialty as regards skill" — and he duly noted exactly "the same in Japanese land and seagoing forces."[11]

Hart's conclusion was thus uncompromisingly tart. The Allies had, as yet, "not defeated" or even turned the enemy back "at any point. At present," he'd noted, "it does not promise that we can prevent the Japs from taking the rest of the N.E.I. [Netherlands East Indies] or relieve Corregidor in time. Current danger is that they will also take Rangoon and cut the communication to Free China. Yes we got into a war with an eastern Asiatic power that is First Class in a military sense. It has now in its control, (or nearly so), riches sufficient to make it enduringly first class in an economic way," unless "interfered with and driven out from recent gains. That means a long war. Not a cheerful prospect but we must not forget that the enemy won't look so good when he in his turn is surprised, loses the initiative, and gets set back on his heels."[12]

Hart's prediction had proven all too accurate — in fact the Japanese "liberated" Rangoon the very day he met with the President.

Listening to Tommy Hart, it was easy for Roosevelt to see why Wavell had asked for him to be relieved — Hart himself expecting he would be demoted from a four-star admiral to a two star rear admiral for his alleged defeatism. Even Admiral Stark, the outgoing chief of naval operations, had told Hart on arrival in New York "that I was to go on up home and rest up," which "fitted my desires perfectly as I'm decidedly travel-worn," Hart had noted in his diary.

It was Hart's wife, Caroline, who had disagreed. "Not at all," she had declared. "She says the world then will think that I'm sick and senile. That whatever I've brought back with me is hot right now and that I should get to Washington with it forthwith" — in fact, the next day. "She shows me that I can well give head to the subject — and I shall," Hart had written.[13] Scenting a story, the *Washington Post* published a headline: "Let Hart Speak!" and there arose some concern in the administration that Hart, a die-hard anti–New Dealer and Republican with strong opinions on America's march to war, would prove an embarrassment to the President.

The reverse proved, however, to be the case. Roosevelt's insistence on hearing Hart's side of the story at the White House, unadorned and in person, became a turning point in Roosevelt's conception of the war.

The President's natural charm, his use of Hart's first name, Tommy, and his penetrating questions about the Pacific and about MacArthur in particular, not only won over Hart — who became one of the President's most loyal Republican supporters — but gave the President what he most needed at a critical juncture of the war: the truth.

Following this interview, the President ordered that Admiral Hart keep his four stars; arranged that the admiral appear the next day at the President's own press conference; and insisted Secretary Knox use the admiral to crisscross America, speaking to newspapers and professional organizations, in order to tell the American people the unvarnished verity.[14] It was not enough, the President recognized, for the United States simply to ramp up its output as the arsenal of democracy. Just as Hart had predicted in his diary, Rangoon *had* fallen, as would the Netherlands East Indies — Hart's successor, the bombastic Dutch naval commander Admiral Helfrich, wholly unable to compete with Japanese naval control of the air and Japan's seagoing skills.

Lack of cohesion between the U.S. Air Force, the U.S. Navy, and the U.S. Army, as well as the inevitable problems of inter-Allied coalition warfare, suggested that Hart was not only right about a long war in the Pacific, but that America *must* address the issues that the admiral had raised; issues that went to the core of modern warfare itself. The U.S. high command would have to examine, study, and learn the lessons of modern war against an indoctrinated, cohesive, professional, and skilled opponent. Those advocating that the U.S. Air Force be split apart from the U.S. Army, as had been the case with the RAF and the British Army, must be stopped, at least during the war, the President was adamant — for it was vital that growing potential U.S. air power be used to support U.S. ground forces effectively. Naval ones, too. And with better planes.

Admiral Harold Stark, the President had already decided the day before, would be sent to London to concert inter-Allied naval relations there, and would not be replaced as chief of naval operations, or CNO. Instead Admiral King would now take over Stark's responsibilities, as well as remaining commander in chief of the U.S. Navy. After lunch with the navy secretary, Hart gave a talk to a "jam-packed" meeting of the General Board of the U.S. Navy in New York — including Admirals King and Stark, and "all Bureau Chiefs and an Asst. Sec. or two. I talked about fifteen minutes along narrative lines and then twice as long on what I called the lessons which I had learned. In that I pulled no punches, was plenty critical and, as I said in the body of it, I set forth some quite revolutionary ideas" — ideas that would back the "general changes which King and his entourage would like to make, and may in general have helped toward some realism in certain respects wherein we have long been much too theoretical."

With Stark removed from the helm, it would be up to King's legendary "blowtorch" leadership, the President had decided, to kick the U.S. Navy into the mid-twentieth century. For the first time in American history, the head of the U.S. Navy would be answerable directly and only to his commander in chief, the President. He would be urged not only to ramp up naval aviation and order better interservice cooperation with U.S. Army and U.S. Army Air Forces, but to expand, develop, and employ the U.S. Marine Corps, a division of the U.S. Navy, in the same way as the Japanese were doing: as the spearhead of modern amphibious invasion forces.

It was not for nothing that the President had spent six years as assistant secretary of the navy — however much Hitler, who had been a messenger in the trenches of the Western Front in World War I, derided him. With Admiral King at his side, the President was determined as U.S. commander in chief to refashion the U.S. Navy into a force the Japanese would learn to fear.

13

Churchill Threatens to Resign

As ANOTHER NINETY-SIX thousand Allied troops surrendered to the Japanese in the Netherlands East Indies, Assistant Secretary of State Breckinridge Long wrote in his diary that he was now becoming "apprehensive lest we be left mostly alone to carry on this fight." If Russia made peace and the British lost the Middle East, America would be left to face a conflict "in two oceans against a combined navy superior to ours."[1]

Assistant Secretary Long had reason to feel anxious. Not only did British forces still appear unable to fight effectively overseas — whether on land, ocean, or in the air — but their political leaders seemed incapable of embracing a postwar vision that would give British soldiers, as well as soldiers of the British Empire, a reason to do so.

The consequences, for the United States, were thus serious. If Britain refused or failed to set out a postwar vision for the peoples of its former imperium, would Congress permit American sons to continue to give their lives for a crumbling colonial empire no longer capable of fighting, or willing to fight, for itself?

Breckinridge Long had recently reported "a serious undercurrent of anti-British feeling" among the members of the Foreign Relations Committee on Capitol Hill: senators expressing the concern that, unless given some form of self-government, Indians "would not have the desire to fight," once the Japanese reached the Burmese-Indian border, "just in order to prolong England's mastery over them."[2] Like the Burmese, Indians might well aid and abet a Japanese invasion, unless Prime Minister Churchill addressed the problem.

Long, who was advising President Roosevelt and the acting secretary of state, Sumner Welles, had agreed with the senators' view. "Concerning India," he reported from Senate hearings on the Hill on February 25, 1942, "the argument was that we are participating on such a large scale and had done so much for England in Lend-Lease that we had now arrived at a position of importance to justify our participation in Empire councils and such as to authorize us to require England to make adjustments of a political nature within the framework of her Empire."[3]

The senators were, in other words, losing patience with the British. "We should demand that India be given a status of autonomy. The only way to get the people of India to fight," they had concluded, "was to get them to fight for India."[4]

Bowing to appeals from the President, the Prime Minister had felt compelled to give in to pressure directly "from Roosevelt," as Leopold Amery, the British secretary of state for India, explained in a confidential letter to the viceroy in Delhi—the Prime Minister finally seeing the "American red light" that, together with the urgent prodding of Clement Attlee's Labour Party colleagues, had "opened the sluice gates" to Indian self-government. Churchill himself had cabled the viceroy that, thanks to "general American outlook," it would "be impossible to stand on a purely negative outlook"[5]—hence the decision to send out Sir Stafford Cripps to assure Indian leaders of postwar independence, and negotiate meanwhile Indian self-government.

Roosevelt had been delighted by Churchill's climb-down—as had been senators in Congress and newspaper editorial writers across America, who mistakenly welcomed the Prime Minister's decision to send out Cripps as a significant new demonstration, however reluctant, of the sincerity of the Atlantic Charter: putting into practice the moral aims of the United Nations.

None had quite reckoned, however, on the continuing obstinacy of Prime Minister Winston S. Churchill, even at the nadir of British military misfortunes in the Far East.

No sooner did Cripps arrive in India on March 23, 1942, than he met a duo of doubting Thomases: the British viceroy, Lord Linlithgow, and General Sir Archibald Wavell, the British commander in chief in India. Moreover, Churchill and the secretary of state for India, Leo Amery—whose son was an open Nazi sympathizer who hated Roosevelt and would later be hanged for treason—now proceeded to do their best, from London, to wreck the negotiations, in the subsequent view of President Roosevelt's personal emissaries. "Colonel Johnson and Colonel Herrington both reported, without using the word, that in their opinion the British Government had deliberately sabotaged the Cripps Mission and indicated that likewise in their opinion the Government in London had never desired that the mission be other than a failure."[6]

Roosevelt was at first disbelieving. Why, he wondered, were the British deliberately ignoring the Atlantic Charter? In his cable of March 10, the President had recommended "the setting up of what might be called a temporary government in India," a "group that might be recognized as a temporary Dominion Government," with executive and administrative responsibility for the civil government of India, "until a year after the end of the war," when a formal constitution could be settled. "Perhaps the analogy of the United States from 1783 to 1789 might give a new slant in India itself, and it might cause the people there to forget hard feelings, to become more loyal to the British Empire, and to stress the danger of Japanese domination, together with the advantage of peaceful evolution as against chaotic revolution. Such a move is strictly in line with the world changes of the past half century," the President had pointed out, "and the democratic processes of all who are fighting Nazism." Moreover, he had specifically warned against allowing the British colonial authorities in India — the viceroy and his acolytes — to kibosh the mission. "I hope that whatever you do the move will be made from London," he cabled Churchill — urging that the British viceroy of India, the pigheaded Marquess of Linlithgow, be discouraged from claiming that Indian self-government was being forced on him "by compulsion."[7]

Churchill, tragically, did the opposite — blaming American pressure. As his military assistant, Colonel Jacob, later reflected, Churchill was a thorough Victorian — his worldview "greatly coloured by his experiences in India, South Africa, and Egypt as a young man, and by his connection with the central direction of the First World War as a Minister. All these experiences tended to give him a great feeling for the British Empire as something, though diverse and growing, which could be directed from London, the great Imperial centre." Unfortunately, Churchill had "never been further East than India." Moreover, India itself was a country he had not seen since the end of the nineteenth century, four decades in the past. "By training and historical connection he was a European first, and then an American," thanks to his mother, Jennie, Jacob attempted to explain. "He did not seem to understand the Far East, nor was his feeling for Australia and New Zealand deep or discerning" — his assumption being that, once the Japanese forced the United States into the war, America would win the war for the British Empire and that American "power would in the end be decisive."[8]

For Roosevelt, this casual British "assumption" was galling; indeed, the saga over Indian self-government was doubly vexing, coming on top of Churchill's concurrent "duplicity" in dealing with Stalin: the Prime Minister agreeing to a draft treaty with the Russians that would, unless President Roosevelt stopped it, *also* vitiate the principles of the Atlantic Charter, by according Stalin the legal right to seize and rule the Baltic States and a large part of eastern Poland at the war's end. So much for the self-determination and self-government the Prime Minister had signed up to on the USS *Augusta*. Even Sir Alec Cadogan, the permanent undersecretary at the British Foreign Office who had helped Sumner Welles draft the final wording of the Atlantic Charter in the summer of 1941, was appalled—railing in his diary at the perfidy of Churchill's foreign secretary, Anthony Eden, who was "quite prepared to throw to the winds all principles (Atlantic Charter). . . . We shall make a mistake if we press the Americans to depart from principles, and a howler if we do it without them."[9]

In the event, President Roosevelt was able to stamp on such British appeasement of the Russians—for the moment at least. But getting the Prime Minister to back off from sabotaging the very Cripps mission he had authorized to negotiate Indian self-government proved a more difficult battle—threatening to ruin the President's entire strategy.

To ensure that Churchill held to the Cripps mission plan, the President had decided to upgrade his munitions envoy to Delhi, Colonel Louis Johnson. Johnson was now told to fly to India as quasi American ambassador to the Indian government, in the rank of minister, bearing the title "Personal Representative of the President of the United States."

Johnson duly arrived in Delhi on April 3, 1942. To his chagrin he found that the Prime Minister had pretty much destroyed any possibility of the Cripps mission succeeding—for Churchill had not only refused to recall the viceroy to London, as Deputy Prime Minister Attlee had urged him to do, but had deliberately encouraged the Marquess of Linlithgow to thwart Cripps's negotiations with the Indian leaders, once Cripps arrived in Delhi on March 23—and even as Japanese forces drew every day closer to the Indian border.

So effective was the Prime Minister's sabotage in this respect that, on

April 3, 1942, Cripps had wired London, through the viceroy's office, to give up. His "mission," had failed, he cabled: the Indian Congress Party having decided it could not accept the pathetically emasculated version of self-government ("collaboration," as Nehru called it) that was all Churchill, Amery, and Linlithgow would offer. Every mention Cripps made of a "National Government," or "Indian Cabinet," or "Indian Minister of Defense" to work with the British Commander in Chief in defending India had been immediately denied by the viceroy, Lord Linlithgow.[10]

The President was incredulous, given the deteriorating military situation—of which Churchill was either oblivious or willfully blind. On April 1, the Prime Minister had sent him a cable, claiming he was not in the least disturbed by the Japanese Army's rout of British forces in Burma, since he thought the Japanese would "press on through Burma northwards into China and try to make a job of that. They may disturb India, but I doubt its serious invasion," Churchill had added, complacently. "We are sending forty to fifty thousand men each month to the East. As they round the Cape we can divert them to Suez, Basra, Bombay, Ceylon or Australia."[11]

In view of the fact that similar British troops had failed to fight for Singapore, and were now failing to fight in Burma, Churchill's assurance seemed to the President to be optimistic at best. "In his military thinking," the Prime Minister's own military aide noted, "Churchill was a curious blend of old and new. He tended to think of 'sabres and bayonets,' the terms used by historians to measure the strength of the two forces engaged in battle in years gone by. Thus, when he considered Singapore," Colonel Jacob observed, "his mind seemed to picture an old fortification manned by many thousands of men who, because they possessed a rifle each, or could be issued with one, were capable of selling their lives dearly, if necessary in hand-to-hand fighting."[12]

Had Churchill interviewed a single veteran of fighting against the Japanese, he might have recognized how disastrously he was underestimating the enemy, and the sheer unwillingness of British troops to "sell their lives dearly" for a form of colonialism that was doomed. As a result, no one was more shocked than Churchill when the situation in Burma and in the Indian Ocean now spiraled out of control.

Ominously, U.S. and British intelligence had already reported on March 31, the night before Churchill's cable to the President, that the largest carrier fleet ever sent into combat by the Japanese—indeed the same force that had attacked Pearl Harbor — seemed to be heading through the Malay Barrier into the Indian Ocean.

In Churchill's underground headquarters in London, the Map Room became a scene of high alarm. Was the Japanese fleet moving to support the Japanese conquest of Burma? Or was it out to destroy British maritime shipping in the Indian Ocean, and annihilate remaining Royal Navy warships there? Did the Japanese intend to invade Ceylon as the steppingstone to an amphibious assault on southern India?

In the Map Room on the ground floor of the White House, there was equal concern. In the circumstances, it seemed incomprehensible to the President that the British government would seriously allow the Cripps mission to fail.

As the six Japanese aircraft carriers, five battleships, and seven cruisers were identified steaming into the Indian Ocean, shock turned to dismay. Virtually unmolested, Admiral Jisaburo Ozawa proceeded in the ensuing days to decimate Churchill's naval forces, sinking twenty-three British ships in the Bay of Bengal, while Japanese submarines sunk five more off the Indian coast, and Admiral Chuichi Nagumo attacked the British naval base at Colombo, Ceylon.

Then on April 5, 1942, Nagumo's forces not only found two British cruisers, HMS *Dorsetshire* and HMS *Cornwall,* and sent them to the bottom of the Indian Ocean, but went on to attack and sink the British aircraft carrier HMS *Hermes.*

It was a devastating blow.

"Poor American boys!" Radio Tokyo had recently broadcast a sneering challenge to U.S. troops and sailors in the Java area. "Why die to defend foreign soil which never belonged to the Dutch or British in the first place?"[13]

The President, proud of the way the U.S.-Filipino Army had held out against the Japanese in the Bataan Peninsula for so long, despite virtually no supplies or reinforcement, was deeply disappointed by Churchill's sabotage of self-government for Indians. It seemed to Roosevelt impossible that the British would cling to their colonial "rights of conquest" in India, rather than welcoming Indian participation in the war on the British side, when Gandhi himself had withdrawn from the Indian Congress Working Party to enable his "legal heir," Jawaharlal Nehru, to negotiate a deal with Sir Stafford Cripps and the British government. Nehru had promised in writing that Indians, if given self-government, would defend

India to the last hamlet; and Mohammed Jinnah, the Muslim League leader (and future founding governor-general of Pakistan), had also told Cripps he would go along with an Indian cabinet — yet *still* the viceroy and Churchill resisted.

In American eyes, Churchill's refusal to allow Cripps to make concessions amounted to fiddling while Rome burned. In a cable on April 4, Colonel Johnson begged Roosevelt to intervene personally, since unless the President "can intercede with Churchill, it would seem that Cripps' efforts are doomed to failure."[14] This prompted Welles to respond that he had "personally discussed with the President your telegram no. 145, April 4, 8p.m.," but that he did not "consider it desirable or expedient for him, at least at this juncture, to undertake any further personal participation in the discussion. You know how earnestly the President has already tried to be of help. . . . In view of the already increasingly critical military situation do you not believe that there is increasing likelihood of the responsible leaders adopting a more constructive attitude?"[15]

For his part, Colonel Johnson, in Delhi, did not blame the Indians. Like Cripps, the colonel thought it was the British who, in such a critical military situation, should have been more reasonable, if they wanted Indians to fight for their own territory.

Instead of offering the post of minister of defense to an Indian with genuine military responsibilities under a British war minister, however, Churchill and Amery would only agree to offer, on April 7, the possibility of appointing an Indian member on the viceroy's Executive Council with responsibility for "storage of petroleum products; welfare of troops; canteen organizations; stationery and printed forms for the Army . . ."[16]

How the British could be so stupid, at such a menacing time, seemed downright incomprehensible to the President. "I suppose this Empire has never been in such a precarious position in its history!" even Churchill's own army chief of staff, General Alan Brooke, acknowledged in his diary on April 7, 1942.[17]

As was inevitable, Churchill cabled the President in growing desperation that evening to ask if the United States Pacific Fleet in Hawaii could be ordered into action in order to "compel" the Japanese to "return to the Pacific."

The American fleet must save India and the British Empire — forcing the Japanese to retreat, "thus relinquishing or leaving unsupported any invasion enterprise which they have in mind or to which they are com-mitted. I cannot too urgently impress the importance of this."[18]

Churchill's *cri de coeur,* when it arrived, caused consternation. Instead of negotiating with Nehru, Churchill bombarded the President with disin-genuous claims about the exclusive fighting skills of Muslim rather than Hindu soldiers — despite the fact that neither Muslim nor Hindu nor Sikh soldiers were fighting the Japanese with anything but halfhearted-ness, as long as their home country was denied self-government.[19]

Despite Welles's formal response to his cable begging the President to intervene personally, Colonel Johnson was, therefore, quietly encouraged to act on the President's behalf. In a series of accelerando meetings on April 8 and 9, the colonel — who ran a top legal practice in America — knocked heads together and, after a meeting with General Wavell, got a "Cripps-Johnson Plan" unofficially accepted by the Indian Congress Party. "CRIPPS SAID TO HAVE ACCORD ON NATIONAL REGIME IN INDIA," the *New York Times* reported triumphantly on April 9, 1942.

Cripps was delighted — as was Colonel Johnson, who reported proudly to the President that "the magic name here is Roosevelt," and that "the land, the people would follow and love, [is] America."[20]

Colonel Johnson was speaking too soon. Churchill was still determined to counter the success of the Cripps mission, however dire the situation.[21]

Secretary Hull was still away from Washington, recuperating, but when he heard what had been done at this critical juncture, he too was disgusted — indeed, he deliberately titled the chapter of his memoirs covering the episode "Independence for India" — furious that Churchill had, after the signing of the original Atlantic Charter, "excluded India and Burma" from the principles and, as he put it, had already declared, in an address to Parliament in September 1941, that "Article 3 applied only to European nations under Nazi occupation and had no effect on British policy."[22]

For Roosevelt, Churchill's panic-stricken plea for the United States to rescue the Royal Navy marked the end of their military honeymoon. The President had authorized the surrender of all Filipino and American troops remaining on the Bataan Peninsula, after doggedly fighting the Japanese since December 10, 1941. Though Corregidor might hold out a further month, failure of the British to fight the Japanese, and their assumption that their colonial empire would merely be rescued by Americans who did fight, was unacceptable.

Roosevelt would not have been Roosevelt had he allowed his personal feelings of disappointment to affect his judgment, however. Coalition war, the President knew, meant allying oneself with partners who did not necessarily share the same political or moral principles, or vision — as, for example, America's military partnership with Stalin's Soviet Union. Collaborationist, imperialist Vichy France was another possible ally, or at least non-hostile government — a government whose military compliance might be of profound significance in launching a Second Front against the Nazis, either in North Africa or mainland France. Leading a coalition of United Nations, in other words, was bound to involve associations that were at best necessary, and at worst cynical.

Deliberately trivialized by Churchill in his memoirs,[23] and ignored by most historians in the decades following the war, the saga of the Cripps mission — and the President's role in it — marked in truth the end of Britain's colonial empire, as Churchill willfully surrendered Britain's moral leadership of the democracies in World War II.

Sir Ian Jacob, reflecting on the Anglo-American alliance, would later date the change that came over U.S.-British relations as taking place in 1943: the "change which came about when the Americans felt that they had developed enough power to conduct their own line of policy."[24] In reality, however, the change had taken place much, much earlier — as the White House records and diaries of those visiting with the President would show.

The President had absolutely no intention of risking the gathering strength of the U.S. fleet in the Pacific in an unprepared battle with the Japanese Navy. Instead, ignoring what he'd told Welles to say officially to Colonel Johnson, he wired Prime Minister Churchill on April 11, asking him please *not* to recall Cripps, but to make one last effort at accommodating Indian aspirations for a national government.

Why Churchill closed off this possibility will be debated by historians and biographers to the end of time — "one of the most disputed episodes in Britain's imperial ending in India," as Oxford historian Judith Brown would later call it.[25]

Did Churchill fear Sir Stafford Cripps returning to Britain in triumph — given broad British public support for a settlement — and supplanting him as prime minister? Or could Churchill simply not accept the idea of Indian leaders running their own country of four hundred million people, after all the years Churchill had fought to deny India self-government, let alone independence?

In any event, deliberately rejecting the President's advice as well as widespread British and American hopes for an act of statesmanship, Churchill now did the opposite — withdrawing all previous assurances he'd given Cripps, which had been the basis of the tentative agreement with Nehru. "I feel absolutely satisfied we have done our utmost," Churchill cabled the President with finality on April 11 — and instructed Cripps to return to London without any agreement.[26]

The President was dumbfounded. In a cable early that same day, Colonel Johnson had, by contrast, assured the President that, in regard to the impasse with Churchill, Sir Stafford Cripps and Nehru "could solve it in 5 minutes if Cripps had any authority" from Churchill. Johnson was at a loss to understand why the Prime Minister had become so intransigent. The Indian Ocean, after all, "is controlled by the enemy," the Japanese, he pointed out to the President. "British shipping from India has been suspended; according to plan determined many days ago, British are retiring from Burma going north while fighting Chinese go south; Wavell is worn out and defeated." In Colonel Johnson's view, the British were finished not only as an imperial, colonial power, but as a first-rate nation. "The hour has come when we should consider a replotting of our policy in this section of the world," he recommended. "Association with the British here is bound to adversely affect the morale of our own officers. . . . Nehru has been magnificent in his cooperation with me. The President would like him and on most things they agree. . . . I shall have his complete help; he is our best hope here. I trust him."[27] India, in other words, could become a great democratic partner to the United States.

Sir Stafford Cripps had complained that a patronizing speech by Lord Halifax in New York on April 7, broadcast on CBS, had "done the greatest harm at a most critical moment,"[28] and Johnson was of like mind, telling the President that the address had "added the finishing touches to the sabotaging of Cripps. It is believed here it was so intended and timed and I am told pleased Wavell and the Viceroy greatly" — with Churchill breaking into a victory dance in the Cabinet Room below Whitehall "on news the talks had failed," jubilantly declaring: "No tea with treason, no truck with American or British Labour sentimentality, but back to the solemn — and exciting — business of war."[29]

· · ·

Johnson was certainly right about the viceroy, the Marquess of Linlithgow, who was if anything more intransigent — and racist — than the Prime Minister. Linlithgow had earlier described the Japanese, before Pearl Harbor, as "Yellow Bellies" who would probably enter the war on Germany's side: "I don't see how they can help it, the silly little things!" he'd mocked them in a letter to Lord Halifax. Burma might be threatened, but the British would prevail, he'd been sure. American weaponry nevertheless remained important. In fact, in terms of the Indian Army, Linlithgow was "greatly dependent upon your constituents in North America," he'd admitted to Halifax, "for heavy gear. So don't tell them what I think of them," he warned.

What he thought was, in truth, mean, despicable, and almost unbelievably snooty. "What a country," he derided America, "and what savages who inhabit it! My wonder is that anyone with the money to pay for the fare to somewhere else condescends to stay in the country, even for a moment! What a nuisance they will be over this Lease-Lend sham before they have finished with it. I shan't be a bit surprised if we have to return some of their shells at them, through their own guns! I love some clever person's quip about Americans being the only people in recorded times who have passed from savagery to decadence without experiencing the intervening state of civilization!" Halifax, he was quite sure, shared his views, but would just have to be stoic and go on with his work in Washington to obtain more free military assistance, while "toadying to your pack of pole-squatting parvenus!"[30]

Why Churchill tolerated such an anti-American, bigoted buffoon as viceroy of India was hard both for Colonel Johnson and President Roosevelt to understand — especially since Linlithgow had begged Churchill for months to be allowed to retire, after almost six years in the post. Churchill had, however, insisted that, despite his unpopularity, Linlithgow should stay — with orders to abort Cripps's mission.

This the Scottish aristocrat did with enthusiasm. Colonel Johnson he described as "Franklin D.'s boy friend," whom Cripps had brought into "close sensual touch with Nehru, for whom J. has fallen." It was too bad — though Linlithgow hoped others could correct "in the President's mind, the distorted notion which I feel sure Johnson is now busy injecting into that very important organ."[31]

Distorted or not, the news from India mystified the President, who became more and more concerned lest the British use their crucial, American-provided weaponry not to combat the Japanese, but to put down the inhabitants of India, who might well revolt if denied at least a semblance of self-government.

In the circumstances the President decided he must try one more time to pressure Churchill into seeing sense. Harry Hopkins had recently set off for London with General Marshall to discuss prospects for a Second Front in Europe, and was staying with the Prime Minister at Chequers, his country residence. To Hopkins the President now sent an urgent cable, asking him to "give immediately the following message to the former naval person." As he added, "We must make every effort to prevent a breakdown."[32]

The President's signal — which Churchill later derided, after the President's death, as "an act of madness"[33] — was a simple request: namely for the Prime Minister to "postpone Cripps' departure from India until one more final effort has been made to prevent a breakdown in the negotiations."[34]

Roosevelt was, as he explained, "sorry to say that I cannot agree with the point of view set forth in your message to me that public opinion in the United States believes that the negotiations have failed on broad general issues. The general impression here is quite the contrary," the President corrected the Prime Minister. "The feeling is almost universally held that the deadlock has been caused by the unwillingness of the British to concede to the Indians the right of self-government, notwithstanding the willingness of the Indians to entrust technical, military and naval defense control to the competent British authorities" — as he had heard from Colonel Johnson himself. "American public opinion cannot understand why, if the British Government is willing to permit the component parts of India to secede from the British Empire after the war," as per the original Cripps mission's declaration, set out by the British government, "it is not willing to permit them to enjoy what is tantamount to self-government during the war."[35]

The President's cable might have been simple, but it was not, sadly, the sort of language the Prime Minister was prepared to tolerate; indeed, the more that the walls of Britain's empire appeared to be tumbling down in the Far East, the more the Prime Minister now dug in his heels. Reading the first lines of the message Hopkins handed him, Churchill's blood rose. Worse followed, however.

The President warned in the cable that if Churchill did not relent and India were invaded by the Japanese "with attendant serious military or naval defeats, the prejudicial reaction of American public opinion can hardly be over-estimated." He asked Churchill therefore to reconsider the Cripps mission, and "to have Cripps postpone his departure on the ground that you personally have sent him instructions to make a final effort to find a common ground of understanding." The President — who had been remarkably polite and helpful till now — had clearly given up pretending. "I read that an agreement seemed very near last Thursday night," he complained. Why had it been allowed to fail? If Cripps "could be authorized by you personally to resume negotiations at that point" — i.e., the position before Churchill had withdrawn the cabinet's approval of the terms Cripps had gotten — "it seems to me that an agreement might yet be found.

"I still feel, as I expressed to you in an earlier message," the President finished his cable, "that if the component groups in India could now be given the opportunity to set up a national government similar in essence to our own form of government under the Articles of Confederation" — on the "understanding that upon determination of a period of trial and error they would then be enabled to determine upon their own form of constitution and, as you have already promised them, to determine their future relationship with the British Empire" — then he was sure "a solution could probably be found."[36]

Poor Harry Hopkins, having handed over the rest of the President's cable, now witnessed Churchill's meltdown.

Hopkins, sickly but willing to do anything for his revered president, had traveled to London with General Marshall to ensure that U.S. planning to aid the Russians was not stymied by British bureaucracy and timidity. The spat over India, however, now banished European war plans to a back seat — Hopkins later telling Robert Sherwood that no "suggestions from the President to the Prime Minister in the entire war were so wrathfully received as those relating to solution of the Indian problem."[37] To the secretary of war, Colonel Stimson, Hopkins even confided, on his return to Washington, "how a string of cuss words lasted for two hours in the middle of the night" in London[38] — with Churchill adamant he would rather resign than permit an American president to dictate British imperial conduct. It was no idle threat.

The fact was, Churchill seemed exhausted, as all around him had noticed. He was drinking more, sleeping less, and busying himself in the minutiae of military operations across the world that he seemed unable or unwilling to delegate. The Australian prime minister had made it clear he had lost confidence in Churchill's leadership, and the Pacific War Council in London was entering its "death throes" — soon to be entirely replaced by the Pacific War Council in Washington. Japanese naval forces were roaming at will like sea monsters off the coast of India — and British forces were in helter-skelter retreat in northern Burma, abandoning their Indian units to be killed or captured. General Rommel was once again forcing British Empire troops to retreat in Libya.

However, as one of Churchill's own "closest and most affectionate associates" later confided to Hopkins's biographer, "the President might have known that India was one subject on which Winston would never move a yard."[39] Certainly Indian self-government, as Robert Sherwood recalled Hopkins telling him, was "one subject on which the normal, broad-minded, good-humored, give-and-take attitude which prevailed between the two statesmen was stopped cold" — indeed Churchill, rounding on the hapless Hopkins, told him he "would see the Empire in ruins and himself buried under them before he would concede the right of any American, however great and illustrious a friend, to make any suggestion as to what he should do about India."[40] Calling in his stenographer, the Prime Minister was determined to put his feelings in writing. To the President he therefore dictated a nasty rebuke.

"A Nationalist Government such as you indicate would almost certainly demand," he deceitfully claimed, "first, the recall of all Indian troops from the Middle East, and secondly, they might in my opinion make an armistice with Japan on the basis of free transit through India to Karachi of Japanese forces and supplies."[41]

For Churchill to send such unqualified "opinions" was sailing close to dishonesty. Both claims were specious, as Churchill and the viceroy (with whom Churchill was in secret correspondence, bypassing Sir Stafford Cripps) well knew — contradicting the assurances Nehru had given Cripps and the President's "Special Emissary," Colonel Johnson.[42] Nevertheless, Churchill argued in his draft response, "From their point of view this would be the easiest course, and the one entirely in accord with Gandhi's non-violence doctrines"[43] — despite Gandhi's express withdrawal from the matter, and public statement that Pandit Nehru would decide the Congress Party's conduct.

In Churchill's lurid forecast, the "Japanese would in return no doubt give the Hindus the military support necessary to impose their will upon the Moslems, the Native States and the Depressed classes." In conclusion, the Prime Minister made clear he would resign rather than permit this to happen — indeed, that he had "no objection at all to retiring into private life, and I have explained this to Harry just now" — a threat he larded with the prospect of a British parliamentary revolt by Conservatives in his favor. "Far from helping the defense of India, it would make our task impossible," he warned the President. And though as prime minister he would "do everything in my power to preserve our most sympathetic co-operation," he wanted the President to be aware that the U.S.-British alliance was now at stake. "Any serious public divergence between the British and United States Governments at this time might involve both of our countries in ruin."[44]

It was, in effect, blackmail.

In a subsequent telephone call to the President some hours later, Harry Hopkins relayed to Mr. Roosevelt the gist of Churchill's draft cable. It was a document that, in fear of the whole Western alliance now collapsing, Hopkins had begged the Prime Minister *not* to encode and dispatch[45] — in fact, so alarmed was Hopkins that he begged Churchill not even to raise the subject with the British cabinet, which was due to meet the following day, lest this become a test of the whole Atlantic coalition.

Roosevelt should simply back off, Hopkins therefore advised the President on the phone to the White House. He, Hopkins, would do his best to calm the Prime Minister down.

Mid-April 1942 now came to resemble, in terms of the Atlantic alliance, something of a French farce. Hopkins was begging Roosevelt, in the interests of Anglo-American cooperation, not to press for an Indian national government, but at the same time Colonel Johnson was cabling the President with the *opposite* plea: forwarding a personal appeal by Pandit Nehru, the Indian Congress Party leader, that contradicted Churchill's dire predictions. Nehru had absolutely no intention of negotiating with the Japanese, if they did invade India, he made clear in his letter — being himself all too aware of the likely consequences of Japanese invasion, if it happened, and the "horrors" that would follow, "as they have followed Japanese aggression in China."[46]

"To your great country, of which you are the honored head, we send greetings and good wishes for success," Nehru's message ended. "And to you, Mr. President, on whom so many all over the world look for leadership in the cause of freedom we would add our assurances of our high regard and esteem."[47]

Hearing the alarm in Hopkins's voice, the President, once again, could only sigh at Churchill's negative attitude—which seemed all the more racially demeaning and self-serving at a moment when the Japanese controlled the Indian Ocean and were nearing the Indian border in Assam.

Churchill's negative behavior at this juncture of the war seemed indefensible—moreover, shameful, given the mess into which the British had gotten themselves in the Far East. With the Japanese fleet causing mayhem off the Indian coast and threatening not only Ceylon and Calcutta with impunity (nine hundred thousand people had evacuated Calcutta, in fear of Japanese bombing and possible invasion), the Prime Minister could no longer fulfill his role in holding the northern flank or cornerstone of the President's two-point military strategy in the Far East. Not only had Churchill been forced to appeal for U.S. air forces to be sent urgently to India to protect the subcontinent, but for U.S. naval forces to be sent to the Indian Ocean to save the Royal Navy.

For Churchill the situation was deeply humiliating—a fact that, in part, explained his psychological resistance to reason. Twice already he had declined to show an act of statesmanship over Indian aspirations. Backed into a corner, he was declining for a third time to do so, threatening resignation as prime minister if the President insisted upon Cripps being told to continue negotiations with Nehru.

It was at this juncture that Harry Hopkins, in the interests of Allied unity, hit upon a solution.

Hopkins might have little understanding of military strategy or tactics or combat, but he was an indefatigable fixer. He was devoted to his president—and in thrall to Winston Churchill. These were the two greatest men of their time, at least in the West—and he, Harry Hopkins, had the privilege of serving them as intermediary. It was crucial, he felt, to find some way of defusing the mine threatening the Atlantic alliance. Hopkins had never been to India, and dumping Indian aspirations for self-government, even so that Indians would defend the subcontinent from the approaching Japanese, seemed a small price to pay for unity between the United States and Britain. Yet how could he bring the two leaders of the Western world back on course?

Rather than supporting President Roosevelt's doomed pressure on the Prime Minister to come to terms with Nehru, Hopkins hit upon an alternative: a new stratagem to persuade the President to rescue Britain's collapsing empire in India and its forces in the Indian Ocean without having to grant self-government to India. It would involve a gigantic pretense, by making the U.S. an offer it could not refuse. In the ensuing months it would bring not Churchill, but the President's military advisers, to the point of resignation, once they discovered how insincere it had all been. But at a critical moment in the war, when Allied unity seemed vital to the eventual victory of the democracies, it was all Hopkins could think of.

Churchill should, Hopkins suggested, simply ignore the President's plea regarding India completely. Instead he should, Hopkins advised, ditch the draft of his resignation letter and commence a new message: beginning on a positive note in terms of the Western alliance, by promising wholehearted British military cooperation in carrying out General Marshall's top-priority plan for a cross-Channel Second Front that very year.

Churchill's new cable — encoded and sent at 3:50 p.m. on April 12, 1942 — thus sidestepped the whole issue of India. It began, instead, by congratulating President Roosevelt on the truly "masterly document" that General Marshall had brought with him to London regarding U.S.-British strategy in Europe — adding that as prime minister and minister of defense Churchill was "in entire agreement in principle with all you propose, and so are the Chiefs of Staff."[48]

This was, in actuality, complete moonshine, as even Churchill's own senior military assistant, General Hastings Ismay, later admitted. Perhaps, Ismay confessed in shame, "it would have obviated future misunderstandings if the British had expressed their views more frankly"[49] — for the British chiefs of staff were *not* in "entire agreement" with General Marshall's "masterly document." In fact they were, from the very start, utterly *opposed* to American Second Front plans that would result in untold numbers of British deaths for no purpose. Even Churchill's most slavish chronicler would state that Churchill was being "at best disingenuous."[50]

At the time, however, the chiefs of staff were willing to practice such a deceit on behalf of their prime minister/minister of defense — Churchill calculating that, over time, the Americans would recognize the impracticability of a cross-Channel landing that year. And in the meantime, the charade would be enough to get the American president off the Prime Minister's back with regard to Indian self-government.

Hopkins's suggestion worked. Churchill's "masterly" signal did succeed in getting Roosevelt to back off. However, the problem of India would not go away so easily — indeed, the saga came to a head several days later, when Churchill was compelled to send a second, this time panic-stricken, plea to the President for help.

14

The Worst Case of Jitters

IN HIS MEMOIRS, Churchill would omit his desperate plea to the President on April 15, 1942, for it was simply too embarrassing to quote.

If the Prime Minister hoped there had been no witnesses to its reception in Washington, however, he was mistaken. For on that very day, the Canadian leader, Prime Minister William Lyon Mackenzie King, happened to be staying at the White House.

King, who had been invited to attend his first meeting of the new Pacific War Council in Washington, was suffering from bronchitis and a bad cold, but he found the President remarkably confident when he arrived. "Was conducted from the White House by the garden corridors to the President's Secretary's office, and from there into the Oval Office" in the West Wing, the Canadian prime minister noted in the detailed diary he kept. "The President was sitting working in his shirt sleeves, white shirt, no vest or coat. Gave me a very warm welcome. Laughed a little about his attire" — given King's own, rather formal clothing — "and we went in together into the Cabinet room."[1]

The President's naval aide, Captain McCrea, was there too — having been asked by the President to act as his liaison officer to the council. As McCrea noted in his own diary, Roosevelt told him privately: "Don't keep any minutes, but write out a memorandum afterwards."[2]

King, by contrast, had been in the habit of keeping copious, careful notes of all his meetings in a special account he dictated each day — and his description of Roosevelt's torment over India would provide historians with their most intimate glimpse of the President's reluctant assumption of overall Allied strategic command, as the British Empire collapsed in all but name.

• • •

The President was, in Mackenzie King's admiring eyes, a patrician — the Canadian prime minister proud to be asked "to be seated to his right." At 3:00 p.m. the President of the United States then "opened the proceedings," saying "that what was most upon the minds of all present was the news from France and the situation in India, and in the Indian Ocean."³

It looked, the President confided, as if the nefarious fascist Pierre Laval would soon become prime minister of the Vichy government, leading to yet "closer collaboration with Germany." Not only did this mean the Vichy French would now give voluntary aid to Nazi Germany, but "conditions" in France, the President noted, would continue to "become more serious through Laval's ascendancy."⁴ It was an ominous prospect. Laval — who was executed after the war — did indeed become Vichy prime minister a few days later and immediately agreed to dispatch three hundred thousand Frenchmen to work in German munitions factories. He also arranged to have all non-French Jews and their children rounded up and transported to German concentration camps, where they would be exterminated.

"With regard to India" the President showed even more concern — incredulous the British could be so obstinate over Indian self-government, yet not wishing to embarrass Sir Ronald Campbell, the representative from the British Embassy in the absence of Lord Halifax, as the council considered "the immense perils which confront us" in India and the Indian Ocean (in Churchill's phrase) — with no representative of India at the table.

The latest British Navy's "loss of the two ships 'Dorsetshire' and 'Cornwall,'" especially, aroused the President's incomprehension as U.S. commander in chief. "He mentioned," King recorded, "that this emphasized the need which the United States had asserted to the British of not allowing ships to get too far away from the coast, and the protection which land-based planes could afford."⁵

The more the President spoke, the more King saw how Roosevelt was quietly but confidently assuming the mantle of the war's overall direction, not just the provision of its weaponry. As the Canadian premier pointed out to the council, "since Japan's entry" it was no longer a European war, with "all plans" made "largely in consultation and co-operation with London" — a former time when "Britain was viewed as the centre of the Empire and the British Isles as the most important of the possible theatres of war." The global conflagration created a new "political" as well as "strategic" reality. Henceforth, in order to avoid "alienation of feeling between different parts of the British Commonwealth and any of the free countries," the old Dominions of the British Empire would look to leadership by the United States of America, not Britain — for the United States, not Britain, was now the glue holding together the antifascist alliance, the Canadian prime minister felt. "I pointed out how Australia's problem had created a problem in Canada such as had scarcely been dreamt of before. Just as the feeling had grown up suddenly in Australia which was causing Australians to look more to the United States than to Britain, so to the amusement of some of us, British Columbians" — on the Canadian Pacific seaboard — "were beginning to adopt a similar attitude toward the Government of Canada," with some of them "saying they would have to look to the United States rather than to Ottawa for an understanding of their problems."[6]

Mackenzie King was not alarmed by that. What struck him was how graciously and yet firmly Roosevelt was handling his enlarged role. Where Churchill had recently become somehow smaller, in both spirit as well as power, the President had seemed to grow larger. The President explained how he had secretly sent Marshall and Hopkins to London "to urge the necessity for offensive action which would help to relieve pressure on the Russians by creating another front" — but that this certainly did not mean he was willing to give in to the "Russian request regarding guaranteeing of [postwar] frontiers. He said any consideration of this meant an ignoring of the Atlantic Charter. The main difficulty was that beginning with one concession would only lead to concessions regarding boundaries of other countries. The Russians," Roosevelt said, "would keep pressing for all they were worth," but as president of the United States he would not alter his stance — leading King to consider "it inadvisable" to contest the matter at the meeting, no matter how much Churchill was imploring him to do so, in pursuit of a British treaty with the Soviet Union. The dispute was, as King noted, "a matter of rather delicate discussion at the moment between the United Kingdom and the United States." Canada, he said, would stay right out of it.

The Chinese, Netherlands, and Australian and New Zealand representatives on the council "all seemed to approve cordially of the President's action," King noted — Roosevelt promising at the meeting to dispatch not only U.S. planes to give backbone to the British in defending Ceylon, but American crews and even troops.[7]

All in all, however, it seemed a veritable tragedy that, with so many hundreds of thousands of British troops and personnel in India and

Burma, the British had so ignominiously surrendered the Allies' overland route via Burma to China — and now looked like they were being pushed back across the Burmese border into India itself.

The meeting of the Pacific War Council ended at 5:30 p.m. Later that evening the President gave a small, intimate dinner for Mackenzie King, who was staying in what was called Queen Elizabeth's Bedroom, or the Rose Room — beginning with cocktails in the President's Oval Study, next to his bedroom, at 7:10 p.m.

"The President himself mixed up the cocktails before going down to the small dining room, and we had a very happy little dinner party during which time the President recounted some of the events in connection with Churchill's visit and his stay in Florida" during his convalescence in January 1942[8] — including the British prime minister's embarrassment when telephoning Wendell Willkie, the 1940 Republican contender for the U.S. presidency, and getting, instead, President Roosevelt.[9]

Churchill, in other words, was admired as a great character, but not quite to be trusted. "We had a little talk with regard to some aspects of the war, but mostly a pleasant social evening during which the President and I talked a good deal across the table to each other and the younger people joined in with their observations," King wrote in his diary that night. "I confess I felt how much it adds to one's life to be surrounded by young people."[10]

The President seemed relaxed — and sanguine. Over dinner he had amused his guests by saying, in the event of an air attack, he would use the underground tunnel to the Treasury Building vaults, where he hoped "they would arrange to have some card tables and poker chips" set up, "so they could appropriately pass the time while concealed there." He had from the Army Air Forces the latest information on U.S. long-distance bombers — and expected that, over time, both the Japanese and the Germans would surely build similar ones that could reach the U.S. eastern and western coasts, and even bomb "the capital," Washington. "The news had just come before dinner of the very successful attack of MacArthur's men from Australia upon the Japs at the Philippines by bomber plane, taking a trip of 4,000 miles and return. Naturally every one was relieved and rejoiced at what had been done in that way," King noted.[11]

After dinner, "the young people withdrew and the President and I went to his circular library" — the President's upstairs Oval Study. There "the President seated himself in the corner of a large leather sofa to the left," King recorded, "and told me to sit on the sofa beside him."[12]

King at first declined, thinking it would be easier to converse facing his American counterpart, and took a chair instead. He quickly noticed, however, that this would cause the President "to be seated at a lower level," which seemed wrong. Moving to the place on the sofa that the President indicated, King was once again drawn into Roosevelt's affectionate orbit: his easy, intelligent charm and goodwill, despite his affliction — indeed the President's disability, as they sat there, seemed almost the opposite, investing Roosevelt, who was six feet, two inches tall, with a strangely powerful aura, at once humble and magnetic.

The President asked what King thought of the afternoon meeting. "I thought from the way he referred to the Pacific Council that he was a little uncertain himself as to its value" — given that it was originally to have had its location in London — "and really wanted to know what I thought of it. He then said to me he wanted to tell me about India, and made the significant remark that this would be of historic interest" in the future. "He then repeated what he had said at dinner, that he believed that the plan he had proposed" for an Indian national government "might have met the situation satisfactorily, and would have been accepted had the British Government been agreeable to it. He said: 'the idea was not my own but I communicated it to Churchill. He [Churchill] had this material before Cripps' interviews in India.'"

Churchill, clearly, had not been amused, the President confided. "'He, Churchill, sent me' (I am not using his exact words but tone) 'long accounts of the situation respecting India, going back to the days of [Governor-General] Warren Hastings and [General] Clive," in the eighteenth century. By contrast, "'What I proposed was along the lines of the way America proceeded at the time of the Revolution'" when American independence was declared. "'It was arranged that the delegates should be sent to an Assembly and an ad hoc provisional government set up which would carry on the government of the different states on matters of general concern, and later allowing a Constitution to be formed which would give full powers of government. What I proposed for India,'" the President explained, "'was to give the Indians complete right of government themselves at once with regard to such matters as tariffs, trade and commerce, post office, communications and external affairs or foreign policy, and also defense with the understanding, however, that for the actual military operations, General Wavell would have control of the strategy and direction of forces, etc. I pointed out that it was a great mistake in the British proposal to allow any part [of India] to secede, and spoke particularly of the civil war in our country which had been the result of an attempt at secession. All should have been prepared to work together for a time admitting there would be problems to be overcome, but that these should be worked out between themselves."[13]

King found himself astonished at how closely the President had been involved in the Cripps mission — and its reception in India. "The President went on to say," the Canadian premier stated, "that he had reason to know that his proposals would have been accepted by all of the different groups in India, and that they would have been satisfactory to Cripps."[14] Roosevelt had not, however, been able to get Churchill "to arrange for a plan on those lines" — this account verified by the Chinese foreign minister, Dr. Soon, the following day. (Dr. Soon confided to Mackenzie King "for my strictly personal information," that he had it "on the best of authority that a settlement could have been reached by Cripps, had the British Govt. allowed him to make the settlement on a basis which the Indians and he were prepared to agree on, but that the British Govt. would not give that extent of authority.")[15]

Clearly, the President was frustrated that the British would simply fiddle while Calcutta burned. It was, Roosevelt lamented, too bad. Yet not as bad as the next morning, when the President told King of the latest cable he had received from Churchill.

"It was midnight when I turned out the light. Slept soundly," King recorded in his diary.[16] When he awoke at 7.30 on April 16, 1942, in the Rose Room's four-poster bed, he had two visions, which deeply affected him. They both concerned, he thought, the President's plans for prosecuting the war against the Nazis in Europe — but before he could discuss them personally with Mr. Roosevelt, he met Admiral King (no relation) in the upstairs hallway. The admiral had been urgently summoned, together with General Joseph McNarney, the acting chief of staff of the U.S. Army in the absence of Generals Marshall and Arnold in London, to an early meeting with the President. Admitted into the Oval Study while the officers were asked to wait outside, Mackenzie King listened in amazement as the President told him the latest news.

The night before, Roosevelt had said he thought the British were falling apart — "that they had the worst case of jitters in Britain that he thought they had ever had," as King recorded in his diary. "That they were terribly concerned and fearful of the whole situation" in India and the Indian Ocean.[17] King had agreed — saying it was with good reason, given the British failure to handle the situation in India sensibly. Looking at the President on the morning of April 16, however, King was aware that the President's worst fears had now been realized, as Roosevelt "put his hand to his forehead." On the desk in front of him was a pile of telegrams. "I had a bad night last night," the President confided. "At 11:30, I received a war message from Winston. It is the worst message that I have received." Pointing to the cables, he said: "They are the most depressing of anything I have read."[18]

Calling in Admiral King and General McNarney, the President read aloud Churchill's tale of woe—a long cable "to the effect that he, Churchill, was greatly concerned about his position in the Indian Ocean. That he feared the Japanese were assembling a powerful fleet which might succeed in taking Ceylon and later Calcutta and lead to landing Japanese forces in India with internal situation arising there which might lead to any kind of consequences. That if Ceylon was taken, the getting of assistance to the Middle East, to Egypt, etc, might be cut off with consequent demoralizations of British position there. He [Churchill] did not think the British could hold the situation without some of the American fleet coming to their assistance and asked for a couple of battleships, mentioned one or two additional battleships which the British might be able to send."[19]

Churchill's panic was evident in every line. As the Canadian premier noted afterwards: "the passage that impressed me most in what came from Churchill was a statement to the effect that Madras and Ceylon might both be taken; also the steel industries of Calcutta. The possibility of internal trouble in India which might lead to anything there; also the Japanese might sweep on to the Persian Gulf, and that the whole Middle East might become demoralized. The message was a plea for urgent assistance by the American fleet."[20]

It was understandable that Churchill would later excise this entire saga from his six-volume war memoirs. It was far from his finest hour.

The "situation in India, and in the Indian ocean" marked the turning point in World War II, in the President's eyes: the moment when the collapse of the British as a primary global power became manifest.

"China and the U.S. together would have to settle the affairs in the Far East," Mackenzie King had noted Roosevelt's view the night before. "He did not see how Britain could be expected to do much in that area."[21] If the British fell apart, the United States would have to take over responsibility for the defense of the hemisphere. With "about 100,000" American troops already stationed in Australia and New Zealand[22] — men who would actually fight, rather than running away — the President had no real concern that this transfer of power in the Orient could be achieved — anchoring U.S. power in Hawaii and the Antipodes. Nevertheless, Roosevelt clearly felt the British had made a historic mess of their empire in the Far East.

"He could not understand that there was no reference," in Churchill's latest entreaty, to Roosevelt's "previous communication by which he had offered to supply large quantities of bombing planes to Ceylon which could be sent from Montreal and which were ready to start, just awaiting the press of a button. . . . He then said that he had repeated to Churchill that they should not let their ships get beyond air protection. The loss of the last two ships was like the loss of the *Repulse* and the *Prince of Wales,* getting far enough from land to be unable to take care of themselves. He felt the British were thinking too much of a fleet battle in the Indian Ocean"[23] — for, in his latest panic-stricken telegram, Churchill had informed the President that he was not only immediately dispatching his First Sea Lord, Admiral Sir Dudley Pound, to Washington to "discuss with you and Admiral King the whole position and make long term plans" but expressed the hope that, if the President agreed to use the U.S. Pacific Fleet as he, the Prime Minister, had suggested, in the Indian Ocean, "you will be able to have the necessary orders given without waiting for his arrival. We cannot afford to lose any time."[24]

A "fleet battle" by the U.S. Navy in the Indian Ocean, *at the British prime minister's suggestion?* Roosevelt was, once again, incredulous. "Until we are able to fight a fleet action," Churchill's cable ran, "there is no reason why the Japanese should not become the dominating factor in the Western Indian Ocean. This would result in the collapse of our whole position in the Middle East, not only because of the interruption to our convoys to the Middle East and India, but also because of the interruptions to the oil supplies from Abadan, without which we cannot maintain our position at sea or on land in the Indian Ocean Area. Supplies to Russia via the Persian Gulf would also be cut . . ."[25]

It was an absurd request. Not only had Roosevelt, as U.S. commander in chief, no intention whatsoever of sending an American fleet into the Indian Ocean, he had no intention of allowing the British tail to wag the

American dog. Coming on top of the Prime Minister's earlier threat to resign, Churchill appeared to have lost his mind.

To Admiral King's relief, the President explained he had no intention, nor had he had at any time any intention, of fighting a "fleet action" in the Indian Ocean — particularly in conjunction with a Royal Navy that had no idea how to cooperate with modern air force units. Even the British Army's chief of staff, General Brooke, was in despair at the refusal of the RAF to see its role as supporting British Army or Navy forces — dooming the British to defeat in battle. Why, then, would the President of the United States replicate the antiquated approach of the "Former Naval Person" — as Churchill called himself in his cables to the White House — to modern warfare?

Moreover, to imagine that the dimwitted, brave but ailing First Sea Lord would be able on arrival to sway the President and his chiefs of staff, especially Admiral King, to accept strategic direction from the Prime Minister, was, in this regard, yet another demonstration of Churchill's almost infallible instinct for choosing the wrong commanders of his military forces.

In the presence of the Canadian prime minister, the President told Admiral King and General McNarney to draft a blanket no to Churchill's cable — but to add a brief but guarded mention of American plans that were already in hand in the Pacific.

"Luncheon was served at his desk" in the downstairs Oval Office, Mackenzie King recorded — "which like the one in his library upstairs was literally covered with a lot of political souvenirs. Cloth dunkeys and other fantastic figures" — bric-a-brac from past political campaigns depicting Democrats as donkeys — seemed to the ascetic Canadian to be "incongruous. The President clearly enjoys nothing more than political campaigning and its associations. The game of politics is a great stimulus to him" — affording him "as many personal contacts as possible," despite his disability.[26]

The Canadian premier had been amazed, earlier that morning, to have been invited into the President's study while the chiefs of staff were kept waiting: a deliberate gesture designed, he realized, to remind the President's military advisers of their lower place in his sun — and a warning not to exceed it. Similarly, he would never allow a cable to go out over his signature that did not reflect his genuine views or feelings. "After lunch

General McNarney and Admiral King came in with a telegram prepared for Churchill which the President read over and" — to Mackenzie King's fascination — "revised and softened a bit here and there," as King noted.[27] Roosevelt was clear that, whatever Admiral King or General McNarney might draft, he was not going to humiliate his great ally in the war, despite Churchill's missteps.

The Prime Minister's stature as the embodiment of defiance was, Roosevelt thereby indicated to Mackenzie King, an essential part of the Allied cause. Using the USS *Ranger* aircraft carrier as a fast plane-transport, the President advised Churchill he would send planes immediately to reinforce British forces in India — not only to ensure the defense of Ceylon, Madras, and Calcutta from Japanese naval attack, but to "compel you to keep your fleet under their coverage," as the President added, pointedly. As for sending an American fleet to the Indian Ocean, though, Roosevelt was polite, but firm: "I hope you will agree with me that because of operational differences between the two services there is a grave question as to whether a main fleet concentration should be made in Ceylon with mixed forces." To follow such a course would be to play the Japanese game. Instead, the President had in mind a quite different strategem: to make the Japanese Navy withdraw from the Indian Ocean without the President having to compromise his ever-growing U.S. Pacific Fleet in Hawaii. This plan was something he was not, however, willing to confide to Churchill, as his second paragraph made clear.

"Measures now in hand by Pacific Fleet have not been conveyed to you in detail because of secrecy requirements," the President explained, "but we hope you will find them effective when they can be made known to you."[28]

More, on that score, the President would not say.

Listening to Roosevelt as he read aloud the telegram he was about to dispatch, Mackenzie King found himself intrigued, as he also imagined Churchill would be — "some venture by the Americans" that must be kept secret, the Canadian premier noted in his diary, for reasons that "would be apparent later and which could not be mentioned even to Churchill at this time. It seemed to me," he reflected, "this had reference to some attack the American fleet intended to make, or action to keep the Japanese away from the Indian Ocean."[29]

In a sign of how the balance of power among the Western allies was now changing, the Canadian prime minister arranged with President

Roosevelt to hold a military conference on allocation of Lend-Lease planes to take place in Ottawa the next month — without even bothering to first obtain Churchill's agreement. His work done, King bade farewell to the President and spent the night of April 17, 1942, in the special sleeping car of his train, traveling to New York and arriving in the early hours of April 18.

There, in the afternoon, the Canadian premier visited a spiritualist friend, Mrs. Coumbe — who had her own visions. "She spoke of not being alarmed about either France or India. She had a vision about large fleets and little fleets." Quite what it meant was unclear. "It seemed to her to signify unrest in France, which would, ultimately, be all to the good," he noted.

Back in Car 100 on his special train, King had dinner with a friend. "After dinner, I read the papers," he recorded, "including" — to his utter surprise — "an account of the bombing of Tokyo."[30]

The first of the President's secret "measures," it was clear, had begun. America was on the offensive.

PART SEVEN

Midway

15

Doolittle's Raid

AT 12:45 P.M. ON MAY 19, 1942, Brigadier General James Doolittle — recently promoted from the rank of colonel — was ushered into the Oval Office to meet President Roosevelt.

Doolittle was there to receive the coveted Medal of Honor, escorted by Generals Marshall and Arnold — and pretty Mrs. Doolittle, whom the officer had not seen for more than a month, when he set off from California on his epic mission: to bomb the capital of Japan for the first time in World War II.

Doolittle had stated in the car on the way to the White House that he didn't feel he deserved the Medal of Honor. "General, that award should be awarded for those who risk their lives trying to save someone else," he'd protested.

Marshall had silenced him in six words: "I happen to think you do."[1]

So did the President, as the originator of the April 18 "Doolittle Raid."

Ever since the fateful day of the Pearl Harbor attack, and in the succeeding weeks as Japanese forces cut their swath down the Malay Barrier toward Australia, the President had urged his chiefs of staff to find a way to retaliate; some operation that would shake Japan's sense of its own invincibility and show the rest of the world that the United States would retaliate against aggression — with a vengeance.

The Tokyo raid was "a pet project of the President's," in Secretary Stimson's words.[2] Since Stimson himself had opposed it from the start — considering it a dispersion of effort in the Pacific, and a beacon for "sharp reprisals" by the Japanese — he was not invited to the little Oval Office ceremony, held before newsmen and press photographers. Admiral King was late and missed the photo opportunity, yet in truth he had been as intimately involved in the undertaking as Doolittle, Marshall, and Arnold — and would be significantly more affected by its consequences.

Fleet Admiral Ernie King was the only senior admiral in the U.S. Navy with a pilot's license, as well as command experience in submarines, aircraft carriers, battleships, and cruisers. It was King who had, early in January 1942, first suggested U.S. Navy carriers could be used to launch U.S. Army bombers in invasion operations — the planes then able to land on airfields seized or established by amphibious troops. On January 10, 1942, King had proceeded to give the go-ahead, with General Arnold, for a medium bomber B-25 group of the USAAF to start training, under U.S. Navy supervision, for abbreviated carrier-takeoff. In this instance it was not to support an invasion but to fulfill the President's call for a bombing raid on the capital of the Japanese Empire, launched from the sea.

General Arnold had pleaded for pressure, rather, to be put on the Soviet Union to permit a Russian airbase to be used for the takeoff and landing of the planes. The President had ruled that out as naïve. With German forces massing for a repeat of Operation Barbarossa — code-named Blue, this time — Stalin would not dare incite a Japanese declaration of war that would then force the Russians to fight not just on one but two fronts. Equally, there were no U.S. bombers currently in China for the task — indeed, those that had been sent to India on their way to support China were inevitably reassigned to defend India, once British forces fell apart in Burma and the Indian Ocean.

Only by using U.S. carriers as mobile airfields could the President's directive be carried out — just as the Japanese were doing in the Indian Ocean, spreading mayhem and panic. But with this difference: that American carriers, wisely, would not risk being attacked by enemy land-based aircraft. They would launch their B-25s secretly, from outside the range of Japanese land-based planes — and it had been this operation to which the President, in his cable to Winston Churchill on April 16, 1942, had mysteriously referred.

At the very moment Prime Minister Mackenzie King was staying at the White House, a secret U.S. Navy carrier task force comprising sixteen ships, submarines, and ten thousand sailors had been sailing toward the Japanese mainland in the strictest secrecy. Once airborne, their sixteen long-distance, heavily loaded B-25 army bombers would blitz military targets in the Tokyo area, then fly on and land in western China, and there become, if all went well, the first contingent in Chiang Kai-shek's air force, counterattacking the Japanese.

The President had been thrilled with reports of the plan's progress since inception. Using painted outlines on airfields to resemble mock carrier decks, the pioneering speed-aviator Colonel James Doolittle had not only adapted B-25s for the task, but had trained his crews to take off in a matter of four hundred yards, then find their targets six hundred miles away across the Pacific, avoid anticipated antiaircraft and enemy fighter fire by flying absurdly close to the ground, aim their bombs on specified, strictly military targets — and then fly another thousand miles to reach relative safety in China — the first time land-based air force bombers had ever been so launched in human history.

Bombing their capital, Tokyo, would serve as an unmistakable warning to the Japanese public at home as well as in the front lines, the President calculated, even as their forces shelled and bombed the U.S.-Filipino defenders in the Philippines. More importantly, an air raid on Tokyo would, if successful, draw Japanese naval attention back from the Indian Ocean by demonstrating to the Japanese their failure to defend their own capital and homeland. At the very least it would force the Japanese high command to hold the major part of its navy in the Pacific, instead of sending it back to the Indian Ocean, after refueling.

Above all it was in the Pacific, not the Indian Ocean, that the President believed the U.S. Navy could best deal with the Japanese. Under the command of Admiral Chester W. Nimitz — who had been appointed the supreme Allied commander for all waters of the Pacific east of the Solomon Islands — the U.S. Pacific Fleet could confront the Japanese juggernaut in American-controlled waters. Flying from land bases in the Hawaiian Islands and American atolls such as Midway, U.S. Army Air Force bombers and fighters could, in intimate new cooperation with U.S. Navy aircraft, then deal with the Japanese *Kido Butai* (literally, "mobile force") carrier fleet on its own, American, terms.

Strict radio silence kept by the American task force, until it had withdrawn safely from the reach of Japanese land-based aircraft, meant that no report of the success or failure of the Doolittle Raid could be sent to Washington on April 18, 1942.

Roosevelt had been spending the weekend at Hyde Park, in any case. When Captain McCrea, his naval aide, finally called the President from the White House to tell him that hysterical announcements had been monitored on Tokyo radio about an enemy air raid on the city, Roosevelt was coy.

"My telephone conversation with him (about 10 a.m.) went something like this," Captain McCrea later recalled:

> *McCrea:* The most important item of the morning's report, Mr. President, is that Tokyo has experienced an air raid from U.S. planes.
> *The President:* Really (with a laugh) — How? Where do you suppose those planes came from?
> *McCrea:* That, Mr. President, is what the Japanese want to know. Our intelligence sources say that is the question in Tokyo everyone wishes an answer to — where did those planes come from?

Roosevelt had said no more until later that afternoon, when he called McCrea, "remarking about as follows: 'I think I can answer the question.'" The President continued, "Ask 'Ernie' King if he doesn't think it a good idea to say that the raid came from Shangri-la. If so, when the word reaches Japan, every Japanese will be busy looking at his or her equivalent of a Rand McNally atlas!"[3]

Captain McCrea had done as instructed. "I called Admiral King and told him what the President had said. Admiral King laughed softly, and thought well of the idea."

"Shangri-la" — the fictional valley in James Hilton's 1933 novel *Lost Horizon,* where a group of downed airplane passengers landed — thus became the President's response when questioned by the press, asking for details, on his return to Washington on April 21, 1942.

The Japanese military, by contrast, were incensed, once they figured out the mystery. An entire U.S. naval task force had approached Japan without being identified! Japanese air defenses had been either nonexistent or deplorable where they did exist — not a single B-25 had been shot down or even hit.

The triumph of the Japanese sneak attack on Pearl Harbor had thus been avenged, leading the Japanese military to embark on reprisals against the populace in China, reprisals of almost unimaginable atrocity: a fury of executions, butchery, and slaughter of civilians accused of harboring the American fliers responsible for bombing their capital city — Chiang Kai-shek cabling in a panic to say the Japanese were murdering as many as *a quarter million* Chinese civilians for harboring and aiding Doolittle's fliers, after they crash-landed or bailed out of their planes at night over western China. "The Japanese troops slaughtered every man, woman, and child in those areas — let me repeat — these Japanese troops slaughtered every man, woman, and child in those areas," the generalissimo wired.[4]

Murdering tens — even hundreds — of thousands of Chinese civilians was not going to win the war against the United States for Japan, however. In the headquarters of the Japanese high command there was consternation that the protective screen around Tokyo had proven as assailable as the American defenses at Pearl Harbor. Thus, failing to catch a task force under Admiral William Halsey's command before it could withdraw, the Japanese Combined Fleet staff argued over how best to respond to what amounted to an embarrassing, even shaming, defeat: one that was seen as a direct insult to their revered Emperor, since the American planes had flown right over the imperial palace, as if mocking its vulnerability. A distraught woman had broken in to Radio Tokyo's broadcast, shouting: "Your lives are in danger. Your country is in danger. Tomorrow — even tonight — your children may be blown to bits. Give your blood. Save them. Save yourselves. Save Japan."[5]

Even Secretary Stimson was astonished by the hysterical Japanese reaction to the Tokyo raid.

The Japanese, Stimson noted in his diary, "have been taken wholly by surprise and were very much agitated by it, and it is quite interesting to see their conduct under such conditions. It has not been at all well self-controlled. I have always been a little doubtful about this project, which has been a pet project of the President's, because I fear that it will only result in sharp reprisals from the Japanese without doing them very much harm. But I will say that it has had a very good psychological effect on the country, both here and abroad and it has had also a very wholesome effect on Japan's public sentiment."[6]

Stimson was right. The raid on Tokyo was taken by many in Japan's homeland as an evil omen: a harbinger of how the nation would one day be punished for its devotion to the god of total war. A Samurai nation that had not itself been invaded for thousands of years had embarked on a rash war of conquest across the entire Pacific and Southeast Asia — and only four months after its triumph at Pearl Harbor was rudely reminded what the cost might be. As one woman wrote her cousin, a Japanese pilot in the South Pacific, the "knowledge that the enemy was strong enough to smash our homeland, even in what might be a punitive raid, was cause for serious apprehension of future and heavier attacks."[7]

The effect was to be far more consequential than public sentiment, however. An April editorial in Japan's *New Order in Greater East Asia* had forecast that the United States and Britain would soon decline into "second-rate or third-rate powers, or even to total disintegration and collapse."[8] The Tokyo raid seemed to contradict that prediction.

Such an unanticipated, successful American air attack demonstrated to the Japanese high command the need to finish what the Japanese attack on Pearl Harbor had started: the destruction of America's remaining naval power in the central Pacific.

For some time Admiral Yamamoto, the commander in chief of the Japanese Imperial Fleet, had been arguing that the U.S. Pacific Fleet should be lured from its base at Pearl Harbor and dealt with, once and for all. His recommendation had been ignored, since Japanese invasion forces had been advancing farther and farther in the South Pacific, virtually without opposition. Why risk that success — which required constant naval carrier and warship support — to embark on an old-fashioned fleet naval battle? Japanese forces were, after all, almost at the southern end of the Malay Barrier, in Borneo. An amphibious invasion of the south coast of Borneo around Port Moresby, only three hundred miles north of Australia, would, if backed by a Japanese naval carrier force, enable Japan to cauterize Australia as an Allied military base, and allow Japanese forces then to take New Caledonia, Fiji, and the Samoan Islands — thus severing Australia's tenuous maritime communications with America. This seemed a far more effective strategy than risking a fleet battle in open seas.

The Doolittle Raid, however, had upset such calculations. Admiral Yamamoto, it now appeared, was right: the U.S. Pacific Fleet was too powerful to be left untouched. The humiliating American air attack on Japan's capital now gave Yamamoto the ammunition he needed — claiming that he must, at all costs, cauterize Pearl Harbor as the base of the carrier fleet from which Doolittle's bombers had sprung.

Given the number of bombers and fighter planes that the U.S. Army had since Pearl Harbor sent out to the Hawaiian Islands, another Japanese air attack on Pearl Harbor would now be suicidal, as would an attempted invasion, Yamamoto accepted. But seizure of the atoll of Midway, an

American military and air base 1,325 miles west of Hawaii, would give the Japanese an airfield for land-based planes with which to keep the American fleet locked up at Hawaii, while the Japanese *Kido Butai* carried out its operations in the South Pacific — or Indian Ocean. If the U.S. Pacific Fleet allowed itself to be lured out to contest the Midway landings, so much the better! The carriers that escaped destruction at Pearl Harbor could in that case finally be attacked by superior Japanese fliers' skills, and sunk.

Thus on April 20, 1942, the day after Doolittle's raid, the Japanese plan to seize New Caledonia, Samoa, and Fiji in order to cut America's sea communications with Australia was put on hold. Instead, a massive Japanese air, naval, and amphibious assault on Midway would be undertaken by the Japanese Imperial Navy, with ten thousand troops loaded on transports, just as soon as naval forces assigned to the imminent capture of Port Moresby, the Australian base in New Guinea, had completed their task and could be withdrawn.

And with that fateful decision, in the wake of the President's latest "pet project," the great Japanese march of victories in the Pacific came to its peak.

16

The Battle of Midway

IF THE PRESIDENT WAS NERVOUS about a major Japanese naval reaction to the Doolittle Raid, he refused to let his concerns show. A leader must exhibit confidence, he felt, since the slightest hint of anxiety or dejection would spread like ripples in a pond. It was for others — Stimson, Knox, Marshall, Arnold, King — to worry and second-guess; for him to solicit information, views, and observations before making his ultimate decisions as commander in chief.

Despite being (or in part because of being) surrounded by men and women who revered him, the President was lonely for the kind of relationships in which he could let down his guard — as Daisy Suckley, FDR's cousin and close friend, noted in her diary. His longtime secretary, office manager, and daily companion, Marguerite "Missy" LeHand, had been paralyzed by a stroke in June 1941. Sara Roosevelt, the President's mother, had died in September of that year. He missed their company. Eleanor had her own cottage on the Hyde Park estate, Val-kill (valley stream) — two miles away from the "Big House," which stood empty most of the time now. (In 1938 Roosevelt had built his own cottage, "Top Cottage," on the hill above the Big House, but Sara had forbidden him to spend the night away from the mansion — and her — while she was alive.) "The house has no hostess most of the time," Daisy recorded matter-of-factly, "as his wife is here so rarely — always off on a speaking tour, etc."[1]

Instead of retreating into wheelchair-bound isolation, however, the President had sought to allay it by leading a life of constant activity, meetings, and personal interaction when staying the weekend at Hyde Park. Despite his exalted status, he deliberately treated each person he encountered as an existing or potential personal friend. With each one — whether cabinet member or valet — he would make a swift determination as to their character and interests, and use it to interpret the information he elicited. With his personal secretary Bill Hassett he discussed genealogy and rare books; with Harry Hopkins he rehearsed past and possible power plays of senators and congressmen; with Daisy Suckley, their shared family history, New York society, and filing systems; with Crown Princess Martha of Norway — who had three small children — the business of parenting; with ornithologist and author Ludlow Griscom, the identification of North American birds — even rising at 2:00 a.m. on May 10, 1942, to go birding with him, Daisy, and others at Thompson's Pond, to hear the dawn chorus.

The President was elated — "Total for day 108 species," he noted with satisfaction, signing the checklist "Franklin D. Roosevelt."[2] "It is the kind of thing he has probably given up any idea of ever doing again," Daisy reflected, "so it did him lots of good. In that far-off place, with myriads of birds waking up, it was quite impossible to think much of the horrors of war."[3]

To keep such widely different relationships fresh, genuine, and vital in the complex clockwork of his daily presidency — at least without resorting to cold discipline and intimidation — the President employed both his charm and his sense of humor: at once ironical and teasing, balancing the deadly seriousness of his responsibilities with levity, even occasional mischief. Also: refusing to let anyone in his presence act pompously, or imagine he or she possessed more power than that which the President permitted in his presence.

Such had been the nature of Roosevelt's leadership style for many years — and in assuming the reins of global military leadership on behalf of the United Nations, Roosevelt appeared, as noted by his aides, to apply the selfsame principles now as war leader: dominating his colleagues and subordinates through his status, his high intelligence, and his abiding confidence in himself and his own authority. It was a domination he also maintained, as he had since 1933, by a process of often maddening divide and rule: appointing gifted people to key positions, delegating day-to-day responsibility to them, but ensuring they remained ultimately subordinate to him as chief executive of the nation.

Such delegation, at this time of Roosevelt's life and health, never allowed any question but that he, and he alone, was "the Boss." Around him kings abounded: Admiral King; Prime Minister King; General King; King Peter of Yugoslavia; Queen Wilhelmina of the Netherlands; Crown

Prince Olaf of Norway; the former King Edward VIII of England, now the Duke of Windsor. The President, however, remained the ultimate global monarch, as all around him were aware: charming, well-mannered, and above all, naturally seigneurial.

This was, Daisy Suckley noticed, the difference between the President and his adviser, Harry Hopkins, who was fawning in the presence of Winston Churchill, and was "almost familiar with the Cr. Princess Martha. That's the difference between him and the P.[resident], who doesn't have to show anyone he is not impressed by greatness of any kind. He is one of them," she noted perceptively[4] — a self-assurance, at an otherwise dark moment in the war, that struck those around him as much as it did monarchs in exile.

"He had been President for several years before the war came along," recalled George Elsey, who joined the Map Room staff in April 1942. "He had been Boss for several years. Congress had generally — not always, but generally — done what he wanted. The American public had supported him. He simply felt that he knew what the country needed, what it ought to have, and that he could get his way with what he wanted. Had he not been in his third term, his attitude would have been very different. Had he been a first-termer, or second-termer . . . But here he was: an unprecedented third-term President — and of course he knew better than anyone else what was good for the United States. *That was the attitude at that point!* He was supreme in every respect. And he was in a better position than was Churchill, who had to explain himself to Parliament; he was better than Chiang Kai-shek, who couldn't control his own country, that was riven with civil war," as well as war with a Japanese invader. "'I'm in control; this is the way it's going to be — it's going to be the way *I* want it!'" was the President's frame of mind.

"Now, that may be a false reading, but this is the sense I had of his perception of himself as the war went on," Elsey recalled. "It was accepted by *everyone* that he was the Boss — Stimson, Knox, Marshall, King, Arnold — everyone. *Absolutely!* After all, think how many years he had been President! All those officers had been relatively junior officers, and they had risen with his support and under his command to their present 'lofty' — relatively speaking — positions. And they had no reason to doubt or question his authority. What was Marshall? Marshall was a colonel, I guess, when FDR was elected president. What was King? Probably a captain in the Navy. And they'd all risen to where they were under FDR. They had no reason to challenge or contradict or believe otherwise than to accept his leadership. Except MacArthur — who of course was God, and superior to everybody — as taught him by his mother!"[5]

Elsey laughed at the memory. "In that sense," the commander reflected some seventy years later, "MacArthur and FDR were very much alike: they were 'Mama's boys,' who'd been raised by their mothers to believe they were supreme, superior to the ordinary human being. And by God, their life was going to prove it!"[6]

As, now, they proceeded to do: each in his own way.

Aware of MacArthur's failings as a commander in the field of modern battle, especially in terms of his relations with air and navy colleagues, Roosevelt had wisely turned down Marshall's insistent recommendation that MacArthur, operating in Australia, be made supreme commander in the entire Pacific, with authority over all U.S. and Allied forces operating in the theater. Certainly the campaign to oust the Japanese from their ill-gotten gains would be tough and unrelenting: something MacArthur would have to undertake from secure positions in Australia once sufficient forces were sent his way. In the meantime, however, the Japanese Imperial Navy, with its all-conquering, high-speed carriers, had to be dealt with — and for that, the President decided, Admiral Chester W. Nimitz, whom he had personally appointed to command the U.S. Pacific Fleet, was named supreme commander in the Pacific — commander in chief of all naval, army, and air forces in the north, central, and southern Pacific east of the 159th meridian: his operations monitored and checked on a daily basis by the President. MacArthur, by contrast, would command only the Southwest Pacific Area.

Just how much the President was in personal control of the war astonished even the secretary of war, Colonel Stimson — who had only been invited to go inside the President's Map Room on April 12, 1942, for the first time since the war began. "I had an interesting time with him in his map room which I had not seen before. Captain McCrea was there and acted as expositor," the war secretary had confided to his diary. "We went over all the areas of the globe where we are interested, and I was interested by the fact that the President had here what we are unable to have at the War Department — the naval movements."[7]

The President was clearly way ahead of Stimson, even the Joint Chiefs of Staff — men he deliberately kept firmly under his thumb, charging them to develop and carry out his overall policies as a military high command headquarters, yet making sure each of the committee members reported also to him *individually*—thus depriving them of any hint of collective power. It was in this way that his decision to appoint Admiral Nimitz to command the whole of the Pacific, despite Marshall's opposition, was final—but was now to be tested, as the Japanese Imperial Navy went into silent mode, permitting virtually no communications signals that American cryptographers could decipher. All eyes turned to their impending but surely devastatingly concentrated punitive response to Doolittle's daring raid on Tokyo.

Reading the ambiguous reports of his Washington cryptographic team, Admiral King cautioned that the Japanese might well attack Alaska, the West Coast, even South America.

Admiral Nimitz, fortunately, now had his own Magic unit in Hawaii. Nimitz's team correctly deciphered Japanese signals indicating an imminent amphibious invasion of Port Moresby by a mixed fleet of Japanese troop ships, supply vessels, carriers, cruisers, destroyers, and submarines. Six days after Doolittle's raid, on April 24, 1942, Nimitz flew to San Francisco to meet in person with Admiral King—who belatedly agreed not only to Nimitz's reading of Japanese intentions, but to Nimitz's plan: namely to engage in a sea battle with the Japanese invasion fleet in the Borneo area with the only two U.S. aircraft carriers he could bring to bear in the region, given that USS *Hornet* and *Enterprise* were still returning to Hawaii from Japanese waters, following the Tokyo raid.

To the President's joy, in the final days of April 1942, Nimitz's task force commander, Admiral Jack Fletcher, duly set upon the Japanese armada — and in the first carrier-to-carrier battle of World War II, as well as first naval battle ever conducted in which the combatant ships were out of sight of each other for the entire engagement, Fletcher's planes fought the Japanese invasion to a standstill: the Battle of the Coral Sea, fought between May 1 and 8, 1942.

A huge American carrier, the venerable thirty-six-thousand-ton USS *Lexington* (known as "Lady Lex") was sunk, and the USS *Yorktown* badly damaged, while only the small Japanese carrier *Shohu* was blown apart on May 7, 1942, by American torpedo and dive-bomber planes. Yet that was the first major Japanese warship to be sunk in World War II — and more importantly, its loss persuaded Admiral Inoue, at his headquarters at Rabaul, to abandon the entire Japanese Coral Sea operation.

Back in Japan, Admiral Yamamoto, the fleet commander, countermanded the pull-back order, but it was too late: the invasion vessels had turned back to Truk — and by nightfall, though both big Japanese carriers, the *Shokaku* and *Zuikaku,* were still afloat, they were down to only thirty-nine planes, and running low on fuel.[8] Besides, Yamamoto was reminded, the *Zuikaku* would be urgently needed for the impending Midway operation. Instead of another amphibious attack on Port Moresby, it was decided, an overland campaign by Japanese Army forces would be conducted across the Owen Stanley Ridge — an impenetrable jungle that was, in due course, to prove beyond even their fabled abilities.

Round one had therefore gone to Roosevelt: ensuring the security of Australia from invasion — indeed permitting it to become the springboard for a counteroffensive that could, in time, take back all the territories the Japanese had stormed since December 1941.

"Delighted to hear your good news," Churchill cabled the White House[9] — aware how wise the President had been to ignore his request for help in the Indian Ocean, only days before.

However, as the *Zuikaku* withdrew to Japanese waters to rendezvous with the gathering Imperial Fleet, there was a far bigger naval battle to be fought — over Midway.

Watching Japanese reactions to the Doolittle Raid, the President held his breath, scarcely able to believe the Japanese Navy would risk the virtually complete ascendancy they had hitherto gained in the Pacific and Indian Oceans in a do-or-die sea battle — especially if its object was little Midway, an atoll in the middle of the Pacific with a simple landing strip. Yet this was what American intelligence in Hawaii was predicting.

Secretary Stimson, ashamed he had not installed a similar Map Room to that of the President, had set about rectifying the War Department's myopia. It was, he realized belatedly, small wonder the President had refused to put Nimitz under MacArthur's supreme command, for the President was able to see not only the global picture, but naval and army perspectives of the picture that were hitherto a closed book to Stimson's team. "It was a great help to go over them tonight with him," Stimson had recorded, noting the movements on the President's maps of U.S. naval forces in the Pacific as well as the Atlantic, after leaving him. "Every task force, every convoy, virtually every ship is traced and followed in its course on this map as well as the position of the enemy ships and the enemy submarines so far as they can be located."[10]

The President, moreover, had "talked very frankly" to Stimson about the inability of the British to marry their naval and RAF forces in India.

However hard Prime Minister Churchill begged for U.S. naval rescue in the Indian Ocean, he'd told Stimson, the U.S. Navy would only engage the Japanese Imperial Navy *on its own terms,* and in its own waters — where U.S. air power, army air force as well as naval, could be husbanded and put into battle *together,* to maximum effect.

Admiral King's intelligence team had initially been unable to fathom where the secret Japanese invasion fleet was heading, following the Doolittle Raid — causing Colonel Stimson to ask General Marshall to fly out to California to make sure, in person, that U.S. coastal forces were prepared for an onslaught, if Yamamoto's forces were heading for America.

The President had been unconvinced, though happy to see California's air and coastal defenses put on a more warlike footing. What would a raid against the West Coast achieve? Why would the Japanese *Kido Butai* fleet take the risk?

Nimitz's team was convinced Midway was the designated target — and in order to overcome the skepticism of Admiral King's cryptographers in Washington, they came up with a simple but brilliant idea. Operating under the foremost cryptanalyst of his time, Commander Joe Rochefort, Nimitz's intelligence analysts ordered a hoax American radio transmission to be sent out from U.S. forces on Midway, requesting water. The Japanese intercepted the signal — and in dutifully forwarding a copy of the message to their headquarters in their own secret naval cypher, they inadvertently gave away the code name they had been using for target Midway, since before their fleet set out. Thenceforth Nimitz had, at his headquarters, an advance copy of Yamamoto's plan, complete with dates, times — and its true destination.[11]

By May 20, 1942, with more than 85 percent of Japanese orders successfully deciphered, it was agreed between King and Nimitz that an intended Japanese feint or diversion toward the far-north Aleutian Islands would be left to local U.S. Army, Army Air Force, and naval units to repel. Instead, the United States would focus on repelling the attack on Midway. The airfield defenses and U.S. Air Force contingent would be substantially reinforced from Hawaii, together with submarines. Meanwhile, the three remaining carriers of Nimitz's Pacific fleet (the fourth having been sunk in the Coral Sea) would be sent out ahead of time from Hawaii, under strict radio silence and hopefully undetected by Japanese long-range patrol aircraft. They were ordered to lie concealed in waters several hundred miles from the atoll, out of Japanese view: an ambush to ambush the ambushers. Only after the Japanese invasion of the island began would they be put into battle, when the four huge Japanese carriers would be awaiting the return of their bomber planes.

Thus was the Midway counterstrike prepared, less than six months after Pearl Harbor.

Like Admirals Nimitz in Hawaii and King at the Navy Department in Washington, the President followed the build-up to the great sea battle at the end of May with mounting anticipation.

"Called me up last night from Wash[ington] about the weekend," Daisy Suckley noted, disappointed, in her diary on May 26, 1942, when Roosevelt canceled his weekend plans to come to Hyde Park. "He can't get away until next Monday or Tuesday."[12] He was, he explained, expecting the Russian foreign minister, Vyacheslav Molotov, who would be pleading for an immediate American invasion of France to draw off German divisions in Russia. He also had a bevy of foreign royals visiting, including the Duke and Duchess of Windsor — "who are in Washington on their own invitation and about as welcome as a pair of pickpockets," the President's secretary, Bill Hassett, noted caustically in his own diary.[13] "He said he was very tired & all alone & was going to bed at 10," Daisy meanwhile recorded. "He said Fala," his faithful Scottie, "was very sweet — jumped into the front seat of the car beside him & went to sleep."[14]

As former assistant secretary of the navy in World War I, and now U.S. commander in chief in World War II, the President was all too aware of the critical importance of Nimitz's plan for the impending naval battle — details of which he did not even share with Churchill. Against Japan's eight aircraft carriers, ten battleships, and twenty-four heavy and light cruisers, seventy destroyers, and fifteen submarines, as the Imperial armada set out from Palau and Japanese waters on May 27, 1942, Nimitz could only furnish three carriers, seven heavy cruisers and one light cruiser, fourteen destroyers, and twenty-five submarines.

On April 9, MacArthur's former U.S-Filipino forces on Bataan had finally been forced to surrender,[15] and a month later, on May 6, 1942, after full-scale Japanese landings across the strait, General Wainwright was forced to surrender his thirteen thousand remaining forces on Corregidor Island to the seventy-five-thousand-strong Fourteenth Japanese Imperial Army under General Masaharu Homma (who was subsequently executed for his role in the infamous Bataan Death March). For weeks thereafter, General MacArthur had been bombarding the President and Combined Chiefs of Staff from his headquarters in Melbourne with new warnings of "catastrophe" unless the President sent him aircraft carriers and more aircraft. "The Atlantic and the Indian Ocean should temporarily be stripped" to provide security for Australia, he cabled to instruct General Marshall. "If this is not done, much more than the fate of Australia will be jeopardized. The United States itself will face a series of such disasters and a crisis of such proportions as she never faced in her whole existence."[16]

The President — aware that crying wolf was par for MacArthur's course — patiently explained to the general that his fears were unfounded. A huge Japanese fleet — the largest amphibious invasion fleet it had ever sent into combat — was currently at sea, invisible thanks to dense fog, but "it looks, at this moment," he cabled MacArthur on June 2, "as if the Japanese fleet is heading toward the Aleutian Islands or Midway and Hawaii, with a remote possibility it may attack Southern California or Seattle by air" — i.e., *not* Australia.[17]

The President's message shut MacArthur up — the general victim of his inveterate localitis. Admiral Yamamoto, as forecast by Nimitz's code breakers, meanwhile split his armada; directing one-third to the Aleutians and Dutch Harbor, the rest to Midway to support his ten-thousand-man invasion of the island, backed by four aircraft carriers and a formidable amount of naval artillery. Assuming the Japanese proved successful, there was no end to what they could next undertake — indeed, in the absence of General Arnold, who had flown to England, General Marshall had sent all currently available Lend-Lease bombers still in the United States to the West Coast rather than to Britain.

As the President politely dealt first with the Russian foreign minister in Washington, then with the visiting royals at Hyde Park, anticipation became torment.

Before lunch on June 3, the President took his guest Princess Martha, and her companion Madame Ostgaard, to the Library, where his personal and presidential papers were to be housed. The midday meal was taken early, however, as his personal secretary recorded that day — for the President had agreed to seek alternative summer accommodation for still other "royal exiles."[18]

That the President of the United States, directing critical military efforts across the entire globe, should be tasked with finding a summer residence for the Dutch royal family in exile struck Hassett as extraordinary. "Roosevelt, Inc, gentlemen's estates and summer homes," he added sarcastically in his diary. "Needs of royalty carefully attended to."[19]

Roosevelt enjoyed driving, though, given his immobility, and was happy to check out locations for the royals. Besides, there was nothing better the President could do while waiting for news from Midway. He had the utmost confidence in Admiral Nimitz, commander in chief of the Pacific Fleet, whom he liked and admired for his cool judgment. On the basis of Nimitz's brilliant intelligence breakthrough, the President had authorized the admiral's ambush. It would be the greatest sea battle of the war thus far — employing America's entire Pacific force of aircraft carriers. It was, in sum, all or nothing — and unlike Winston Churchill, he had no intention of interfering in the operations of his commanders in the field, or ocean.

"Some day," Nimitz had already written to his wife on May 31, 1942, "the story of our activities will be written and it will be interesting."[20]

Interesting it certainly was. On the morning of June 3, 1942, word came through both to Nimitz at his headquarters in Hawaii, and to the President in Washington, that two Japanese light carriers had begun their feint attack on Dutch Harbor. A thousand miles farther south, however, Yamamoto's primary fleet was approaching Midway.

USAAF bombers, operating from the Midway airfield, did their best to hit the approaching vessels of the Japanese landing force from eight to twelve thousand feet. Their aim was appalling — some bombs missing by more than half a mile. The great Japanese armada merely continued toward the atoll — and early on the morning of June 4, 1942, launched their expected attack — using some 108 Japanese naval bombers.[21]

There followed a day of intense drama — the airwaves crackling with claims and counterclaims.

That evening, near Hyde Park, the President's train was made ready, and at 11:00 p.m. it left Highland Station for Washington, complete with royals, Harry Hopkins, "and the rest of us," Bill Hassett recorded.

Waking the next morning, the President left the train at Arlington at 9:00 a.m. and made his way by car to the White House. There, in the Map Room and the Oval Office, tantalizing fresh news began to come through. First three, then *all four* Japanese aircraft carriers in the attack on Midway had been successfully ambushed. They were burning fiercely — indeed, in the course of the day they were ordered to be torpedoed and sunk by their own colleagues, lest they fall into American hands and be towed back to Pearl Harbor in quasi-Roman triumph. The entire carrier contingent of the Japanese *Kido Butai* fleet, under Admiral Nagumo — commander of the attack on Pearl Harbor — had been obliterated.

As Admiral Nimitz proudly declared in the official communiqué he issued on June 6, 1942: "Pearl Harbor has now been partially avenged. Vengeance will not be complete until Japanese sea power is reduced to impotence. . . . Perhaps we will be forgiven if we claim that we are about midway to that objective."[22]

As it transpired, the American ambushers had been extraordinarily lucky. The discipline, professionalism, and bravery of the Japanese aviators and seamen were beyond compare — indeed, at 10:00 a.m. on June 4, 1942, the great naval battle could well have gone the other way. Not a single American plane operating from the U.S. Army airbase on Midway, despite heroic attacks in which most were shot down, even scratched one of Admiral Nagumo's carriers. Nor did a single U.S. torpedo plane, operating from Admiral Raymond Spruance's Task Force 16, under Fletcher's overall tactical command, succeed in hitting the Japanese carriers, despite equal heroism — in fact, the Japanese carriers survived no less than *eight* waves of American attacks without suffering the slightest damage. U.S. Army Air Force bombers simply proved incapable of hitting the nimble Japanese carriers from high altitude, while the heavily laden, trundling TBD Devastator torpedo bombers, flying at fifteen hundred feet from their carriers with their mostly ineffective torpedoes, were sacrificial lambs when pounced upon by Japanese Zero fighters, as the President was informed by three Midway fliers invited afterward to visit him at the White House and tell him in person their version of the battle. What was needed, they said, was "something that will go upstairs faster."[23]

Yet the sacrifice of so many American fliers had not been in vain. With the Japanese Zeros rendered helpless at mounting a defense while flying at low altitude to deal with the Devastator torpedo bombers, a veritable storm of American SBD Dauntless dive-bombers suddenly swooped on the Japanese carriers from nineteen thousand feet. With their thousand-pound bombs they had hit each one of the three Japanese flattops in the main Japanese formation on its pale yellow flight deck, marked with a red "Rising Sun" disk — penetrating the vessel's wood and steel topskin and setting the warship ablaze.

One accompanying destroyer captain, Tameichi Hara, could not at first credit news that all three Japanese carriers were ablaze. "Was I dreaming? I shook my head. No, I was wide awake! . . . The horrifying reports continued until there was no room for doubting their accuracy."[24] Aboard the largest battleship in the world, the Japanese flagship *Yamoto,* hundreds of miles in the rear, Admiral Yamamoto "groaned" as he read the latest dispatch from the commander of the screening force at Midway: "Fires raging aboard *Kaga, Soryu,* and *Akagi* resulting from attacks by enemy carrier and land-based planes. . . . We are temporarily withdrawing to the north to assemble our forces."[25] Admiral Nagumo, victor of the Pearl Harbor sneak attack, was compelled to evacuate his flagship, the *Akagi,* as it burned — only dissuaded from suicide by a subordinate. Then the fourth and last Japanese carrier, the *Hiryu,* was attacked by still *more* SBD Dauntless planes — and though its pilots managed to reach and disable the USS *Yorktown* carrier, it, too, became an inferno, and had to be sunk by its own compatriots.

Four Japanese carriers sunk in a single day?

It was a victory on a scale not even Nimitz had dreamed possible. Moreover, though Admiral Yamamoto attempted to snatch a consolation victory by summoning his remaining cruisers and lighter vessels from support of his Aleutian expedition, he was out of luck. Admiral Fletcher prudently kept his remaining ships out of nighttime range. Instead he called upon U.S. Air Force B-17s and Marine Corps aircraft from Midway to attack and severely damage Yamamoto's luckless, retreating Japanese heavy cruisers in daylight the next day — one of which was finished off by more dive-bombers from Spruance's Task Force 16 on June 6, 1942.

The greatest sea battle of the Second World War was then finally over — its conclusion marked in the early hours of that morning when Admiral Yamamoto reluctantly issued his signal of defeat: Order #161, beginning with the words, "The Midway Operation is canceled."[26]

For Yamamoto, the naval confrontation in the central Pacific had turned into a calamity. Even his hopes that Japanese planes from the *Hiryu,* his last, burning carrier, could instead land on Midway's runway had gone up in smoke, literally.[27] Every single Japanese plane that had set out on the fateful, punitive expedition was therefore lost, together with more than a quarter of the Imperial Navy's best pilots.[28]

Admiral Yamamoto's chief of staff, Matome Ugaki, noted in his diary that those responsible "ought to have known the absurdity of attacking a fortress with a fleet!"[29] Yet it was Ugaki's own commander who had persuaded the Japanese Combined Headquarters to back the plan — dooming Japan to defeat in the Pacific if it failed.

At the White House, by contrast, there was jubilation — followed by alarm when a reporter from the *Chicago Tribune*, Robert McCormick's isolationist newspaper that had earlier leaked the President's Victory Program before Pearl Harbor, wrote a new dispatch detailing exactly what American intelligence had known of the Japanese plan, in advance of the battle. "NAVY HAD WORD OF JAP PLAN TO STRIKE AT SEA," ran the nefarious *Tribune* banner. "UNITED STATES NAVY KNEW IN ADVANCE OF JAP FLEET: Guessed There Would Be Feint at One Base, Real Attack at Another," was the headline as McCormick's exclusive was then repeated in the *Washington Times-Herald* on June 7, 1942 — together with exact details of the Japanese order of battle and three echelons.

The President was so angry, he first considered sending Marines to close down McCormick's building in Chicago, and having McCormick tried for treason — which carried the death penalty. A few days later, however, Secretary Knox talked him out of that — substituting a grand jury investigation of McCormick for violation of the Espionage Act.[30]

Fortunately, the Japanese were too shocked to take note of McCormick's publication of the leak. They had, in any case, already changed their JN25 code a week before the battle, which henceforth proved formidably difficult to break. Besides, nothing good would come from drawing further attention to McCormick's story, any more than it would have after his Victory Program revelation. McCormick would only hate the President more deeply, given the subsequent national rejoicing over the triumphant feat of American arms. Even General MacArthur was reluctantly compelled to signal his personal congratulations to Admiral Nimitz, his fellow supreme commander, on his "splendid" naval victory.[31]

In Washington, the President breathed a sigh of relief. And apprehension — knowing the United States must now turn its full attention to Europe and the defeat of Adolf Hitler, who was hell-bent on conquering Soviet Russia in a second, titanic version of Barbarossa that year.

PART EIGHT

Tobruk

17

Churchill's Second Coming

SHORTLY AFTER THE TRIUMPH of Midway, while on the floor of the House of Commons in Ottawa, the Canadian prime minister, Mr. Mackenzie King, received word that "President Roosevelt wished to speak to me over the 'phone. I left at once," he noted in his diary on June 11, 1942.

After exchanging greetings, King asked the President: "How are you? To which he, the President, replied: I am terribly 'upshot.'"[1]

Upset?

King waited to hear what about.

The President "then asked me if I had any information about a certain lady who was crossing the Atlantic to pay a visit to this side."

If enemy agents were eavesdropping — and subsequent evidence would prove that they were — they would have been puzzled. The President was unable to refer to anyone by name, it being an open line, but King "said that I thought I knew who he meant." In fact the premier had, "this morning, received word that the person mentioned would be leaving almost immediately."

The President corrected him. The "certain lady's" flight from England had been postponed by a day, Roosevelt informed his Canadian counterpart — and "then asked: 'Do you know where she is to land?'"

"I replied: I do not know. He said: 'I do not know either.'"

The President tried, elliptically, to explain. He was referring, he said, to "the lady [who] was coming to stay with her daughter at a house which had been engaged for the summer at Stockbridge, Mass[achusetts]." The house wasn't ready for the lady in question — yet the President had found himself simply unable to get her to postpone her trip. As the President complained, he had personally been charged with "the job of getting the house," which had entailed quite some searching, "and in addition, he had done pretty well everything else including obtaining the servants," in fact everything "short of supplying the silver." "He said to me," King recorded the President's expostulation, "Don't you love it?"

"Well," responded the premier with a chuckle, "that comes from your making such a favourable impression" on the daughter of the "certain lady."

And at that the two political leaders burst into laughter.[2]

It was true. The President had a soft spot for Princess Juliana of the Netherlands, her husband, and their children.

To help the President out, the Canadian premier duly agreed to house the princess's mother, Queen Wilhelmina, and her family on their arrival in North America, at least until the Massachusetts summerhouse was ready — the two men shaking their heads at such responsibilities in the very midst of a world war for civilization. "The President was quite amusing about the whole affair," Mackenzie King summarized in his diary that night, "saying that it was pretty much the limit in the way of imposition."[3]

Worse would surely follow, the President added. Once Queen Wilhelmina — a notoriously demanding lady — arrived in the United States, he would, as President, have to invite her over to Hyde Park, for the summer home he'd found for her was not far from his own home. He was "afraid the lady might be shocked by his informality around Hyde Park in the summer," he confided to King. Fortunately, "the Legation had told him she did not wish anything in the nature of ceremonies," he added with relief: "no salute or guard of honour or anything of the kind. . . ."[4]

Again, the two men chuckled at the irony: Mackenzie King hauled out of a crucial debate on military conscription — a knife-edge issue in Canada, given the country's French-speaking population with mixed cultural loyalties to Canada, Vichy France, and General Charles de Gaulle's Free French movement — to speak with the President. Reflecting on the mix of wartime crisis and the accommodation expectations of the royals, King noted that the situation was approaching "opera bouffe."[5]

It seemed unlikely, however, that the President of the United States would be calling the Canadian premier only about a matter so trivial. Aware still of the security issue of an open telephone line, King went on to congratulate his interlocutor on news of the American victory at Midway.

"Was it not splendid?" he recorded Roosevelt's response. "It made a complete difference in regard to the whole situation in the Far East and throughout the Pacific as well." The President didn't have "all the information yet," but was able to tell King cautiously that the situation was "very good."[6]

Only then, finally, did the President get to the point.

Prime Minister King should be ready for a phone call summoning him to Washington "on pretty short notice some day soon."[7]

The President was expecting a yet more important VIP than "a certain lady."

Two days later the anticipated cable came from London.

"In view of the impossibility of dealing by correspondence with all the many difficult points outstanding," Winston Churchill signaled the President, "I feel it is my duty to come to see you."[8]

The President knew what this meant. Since he had personally promised Mr. Molotov, the Russian foreign minister, that the Allies would launch an Allied landing in France that year in order to draw German divisions away from the Eastern Front — German divisions that would otherwise be thrown into Hitler's renewed offensive in Russia — and since the British would have to furnish the majority of troops for such landings in France, the President was pretty sure what the Prime Minister was coming to say.

Whatever he had promised in the spring, when India looked vulnerable to Japanese invasion and he desperately needed American help, he was going to go back on his word. The British wouldn't do it.

Churchill's second visit to Washington would certainly put the cat among the pigeons — and given the feelings of the U.S. War Department on the subject, would require even more finessing than dealing with the Dutch battle-ax, Queen Wilhelmina.

In preparation for the inevitable uproar that the Prime Minister's arrival would cause, the President called a meeting of his old war cabinet at the White House at 2:00 p.m. on June 17, 1942, before heading to Hyde Park for a last weekend of peace and quiet.

It was in the war cabinet meeting that the President "sprung on us a proposition which worried me very much," as Secretary Stimson recorded in his diary that night — full of foreboding.

The President's "proposition" was the one Stimson had feared for over a year, since Roosevelt first ordered the Victory Program to be prepared:

namely, Roosevelt's personal preference for American landings in French Northwest Africa, where there were currently no German forces.

Stimson had always hated the Northwest Africa plan — preferring the idea of a single Anglo-American thrust across the English Channel. So too did General Marshall — who had hoped that his recent appointment of young Major General Dwight Eisenhower to head up U.S. military forces in Britain would bring a sense of urgency to Allied plans for landings on the coast of mainland France: plans that, on a prior trip as an "observer," Eisenhower had thought lamentably unfocused.[9] "I'm going to command the whole shebang," Eisenhower had proudly told his wife, Mamie, as he got ready for his departure to London, slated for June 24, 1942, to stiffen British resolve.[10]

Thanks to Churchill, the "shebang" suddenly seemed in grave jeopardy. "It looked as if he [the President] was going to jump the traces over all that we have been doing in regard to BOLERO [code name for the build-up of U.S. forces in Britain leading to an invasion of France] and to imperil really our strategy of the whole situation," Stimson recorded in his diary. "He wants to take up the case of GYMNAST [the U.S. invasion of French Northwest Africa] again, thinking that he can [thereby] bring additional pressure to save Russia. The only hope I have about it at all is that I think he may be doing it in his foxy way to forestall trouble that is now on the ocean coming towards us in the shape of a new British visitor."[11]

The "British visitor" was not on the ocean, however, but in the air — and already almost over Washington.

Forewarned was, at least, forearmed, Stimson comforted himself. General Marshall, at the meeting with the President, thus had "a paper already prepared against" Gymnast, "for he had a premonition of what was coming," Stimson noted with satisfaction. "I spoke very vigorously against it [Gymnast]. [Admiral] King wobbled around in a way that made me rather sick with him. He is firm and brave outside of the White House," Stimson derided the "blowtorch" sailor, "but as soon as he gets in the presence of the President he crumples up. . . . Altogether it was a disappointing afternoon."[12]

The President insisted — insisted — he wanted a renewed study of what it would require to mount landings in French Northwest Africa.

There was little the secretary of war or the chiefs of staff could therefore do, other than to comply. "The President asked us to get to work on this proposition," Stimson noted in anguish, "and see whether it could be done."[13]

In their collective view, it couldn't.

At the British Embassy on Massachusetts Avenue, meantime, there had been "every sort of minor turmoil" over Churchill's imminent arrival — and how to explain to the American press the reason for the Prime Minister's Second Coming.

For his part, Winston Churchill could not wait to see the President, not the press — and having landed in a Boeing seaplane on the Potomac River on June 18, 1942, after flying direct from Scotland in twenty-six and a half hours, he declared he was ready to fly straight up to meet with Roosevelt at Hyde Park.

The President, to his chagrin, was not ready to see him.

"Winston arrived at 8 p.m.," Lord Halifax noted that night in his diary, "and I brought him to dine and sleep at the Embassy. He was rather put out at the President being away, and inclined to be annoyed that he hadn't been diverted to New York, from where he could have flown on more easily" to Hyde Park. "He got into a better temper when he had had some champagne, and we sat and talked, he doing as usual most of it, until 1.30 a.m."[14] Even General Sir Alan Brooke, and Major General Ismay, Churchill's chief of staff, "took advantage of the darkness on the porch to snatch bits of sleep," Halifax described, "while Winston talked."[15]

Halifax — who had good reason to resent that Churchill, not he, Edmund Halifax, had become prime minister in May 1940 — was now strangely passive, recognizing he himself would never have had the stamina or the determination to lead Britain in war. "He certainly is an extraordinary man," the ambassador described Churchill in his diary; "immensely great qualities, with some of the defects that sometimes attach to them. I couldn't live that life for long!"[16]

The Prime Minister seemed full of beans. The Battle of Midway had removed his fears of a Japanese invasion of India, as well as any possible Japanese threat to the Middle East from the Orient — so much so that Churchill appeared utterly indifferent to the mounting negative reaction to his refusal to grant self-government to the British colony. In a moment of vexation a few days before, he had even cabled to instruct the viceroy of India to arrest Mahatma Gandhi if he "tries to start a really hostile movement against us in this crisis"[17] — claiming that "both British and United States opinion would support such a step. If he starves himself to death we cannot help that."[18]

Even Halifax found that difficult to swallow. But what of German moves in the opposite direction — the threat of German armies blitzing their way through southern Russia and the Caucasus, and Rommel's Pan-zerarmee Afrika, aiming toward Egypt and the Suez Canal?

The "news from Libya doesn't look good," Halifax confided in his diary, with the British Eighth Army being forced to retreat toward the Egyptian frontier. This had left the big garrison at the port of Tobruk to be surrounded and to have to hold out, as it had the previous year, on Churchill's express, if meddling, orders. Surely, Halifax mused, "Rommel must be getting a bit strung out himself." He'd quizzed the Prime Minister on the subject. "Winston on the whole, though disappointed with Libya, was in good heart about the general situation."[19]

With British complacency born of American naval victory, the real Allied opera began.

Meeting briefly with Mr. Churchill at the British Embassy before the Prime Minister's departure by air to Hyde Park on the morning of June 19, 1942, General Marshall, for his part, became deeply worried. Not only did Rommel's panzer forces seem dangerously effective in North Africa, but the situation in Russia looked potentially worse than the previous year — with vast numbers of German tank and motorized troops assembling for a breakthrough.

In April that year, Churchill had sworn in person to him that the British government was one hundred percent behind American plans for a joint U.S.-British cross-Channel operation that summer or fall, if at all possible, to help the Russians, and begin at least the march on Berlin. Now, at the embassy on Massachusetts Avenue two months later, the Prime Minister sounded quite different — thanks to Midway.

The U.S. Navy had routed the Japanese — and thereby saved the British position in India. With India externally secure, Churchill's primary concern now seemed to be the defense of the Middle East as the lifeline of the British Empire — not the question of how best to mount an offensive in Europe that would help keep the Russians in the war, and bring down Hitler's odious Nazi regime.

Stimson, when he met with General Marshall later that morning, was as furious as Marshall over the Prime Minister's broken promises. Marshall explained he'd "seen Churchill this morning up at the Embassy," as Stimson confided to his diary, and had described Churchill as being "full of discouragement" about a Second Front, while sounding off with "new proposals for diversions. Therefore the importance of a firm and united stand on our part is very important," Stimson concluded.[20]

Frantic lest the Prime Minister, by flying up to Hyde Park to stay with the President, now ruin the plans which the War Department had been making for a cross-Channel invasion of France, Stimson and Marshall discussed their options. They were adamant they wanted no "diversions" — especially ones that would simply bolster the British position or empire in the Middle East. Sitting down, Stimson thereafter drew up a new strategy paper, or Memorandum to the President. General Marshall thought it brilliant. "Mr. Secretary," Marshall declared, "I want to tell you that I have read your proposed letter to the President [aloud] to these officers" — indicating Generals Arnold, McNarney, Eisenhower, Clark, Hull, and one or two others, who were present at the War Department meeting — "and they unanimously think it is a masterpiece and should go to the President at once."[21]

Stimson thereupon sent his Memorandum to the President by personal messenger, together with a letter saying it also represented the views of Marshall "and other generals" in the War Department. As if this were not enough, Marshall and King drew one up, too, which they also dispatched by courier. Marshall even telephoned the President at Hyde Park personally, asking Mr. Roosevelt to please, please read it, once it arrived — begging him to make no decisions with Mr. Churchill until there had been time for the President to meet with his military advisers in Washington, on Mr. Roosevelt's return to Pennsylvania Avenue.

Thus began Act 2.

Secretary Stimson's letter to the President certainly pulled no punches.

Not only was Bolero, the plan to build up massive American forces in the British Isles, a definitive way of dissuading Hitler from any thoughts of invading Britain, Stimson lectured the Commander in Chief in writing, it promised to be a potent launch pad for the U.S.-British invasion of France — an invasion that would "shake" Hitler's renewed invasion of Russia that year and eventually lead, in 1943, to "the ultimate defeat of his armies and the victorious determination of the war" for the United Nations.

"Geographically and historically," Stimson noted in his diary that night, "Bolero was the easiest road to the center of our chief enemy's heart. The base," in the British Isles, "was sure. The water barrier of the Channel under the support of Britain-based air power is far easier than the Mediterranean or the Atlantic. The subsequent over-land route into Germany is easier than any alternate. Over the Low Countries has run the historic path of armies between Germany and France."[22]

The recent "victory in mid-Pacific" at Midway had now ruled out any possibility of Japanese raids affecting U.S. aircraft manufacturing on the West Coast, Stimson was glad to record. "Our rear in the west is now at least temporarily safe. The psychological pressure of our preparation for Bolero is already becoming manifest. There are unmistakable signs of uneasiness in Germany as well as increasing unrest in the subject population of France, Holland, Czechoslovakia, Yugoslavia, Poland and Norway," he asserted — with rather less evidence. "This restlessness," he claimed, "patently is encouraged by the growing American threat to Germany. Under these circumstances an immense burden of proof rests upon any proposition which may impose the slightest risk of weakening Bolero," he added — fearing that the Prime Minister was going to suggest alternative schemes: schemes that would do nothing to expedite victory beyond frittering away America's huge but overstretched arsenal of men and materiel.

"When one is engaged in a tug of war," the secretary of war warned the President in his letter, "it is highly risky to spit on one's hands even for the purpose of getting a better grip." No "new plan should be whispered to a friend or enemy unless it was so sure of immediate success and so manifestly helpful to Bolero," he noted, "that it could not possibly be taken as evidence of doubt or vacillation in the prosecution of Bolero."

The problem, in Stimson's view, was Winston Churchill — and his predilection for fatuous diversions. The Prime Minister had even told Marshall at the British Embassy that he favored an Allied landing in *Norway*, instead of France, that year — a proposition Stimson could only shake his head over. Yet it was not Churchill's Scandinavian fantasy (Churchill having been responsible as First Lord of the Admiralty for utter disaster when ordering an Anglo-French invasion of Norway in the spring of 1940) that made the U.S. war secretary anxious. Rather, it was the President's own bright idea that *really* worried him: the "President's great secret baby," as Stimson would sneeringly call it: "Gymnast."[23]

Against the President's preference for a U.S. invasion of French Northwest Africa the secretary inveighed, in his letter to the President, with a kind of elderly man's fervor. Gymnast, Stimson claimed, would tie up "a large proportion of allied commercial shipping," thus making the American "reinforcement of Britain" in the Bolero build-up to an eventual cross-Channel landing "impossible."[24]

The Allies were coming, as Stimson saw it, to a real "crisis" in the direction of the global war[25] — with Prime Minister Winston Churchill more interested in saving British interests in Egypt and the Middle East, just as he had done in India, than in attacking Nazi Germany.

Stimson's talks with Marshall "over the crisis which has arisen owing to Churchill's visit" had in fact continued all morning on June 20, 1942, even after dispatching his "masterpiece" letter to the President.[26]

To add insult to injury, Stimson learned, a frank letter to Marshall had been received from Vice Admiral Lord Louis Mountbatten, in London. This indicated that the British chiefs of staff (in whose meetings Mountbatten, as chief of British Combined Operations, participated as an "observer") were not only unanimously opposed to a cross-Channel Second Front in 1942, but hoped to persuade the President of the United States, via Mr. Churchill, to abandon a further Bolero build-up of U.S. troops and eventual assault landing in France. Instead, they hoped the President could be persuaded to send American reinforcements to help the British in holding Egypt.[27]

Stimson was furious — seeing in all this a British conspiracy to turn the war against Hitler into a war to preserve, or even expand, the British Empire. All-out "American support of the Mideast"[28] — Britain's shortest lifeline to its empire — would thus be the British chiefs' game plan in accompanying the Prime Minister, according to Mountbatten's somewhat duplicitous warning — Mountbatten claiming, as chief of Combined Operations, that he personally was all in favor of an Allied assault on the French coast, in which he might be given a starring role.

All thus rested now upon the Commander in Chief of the United States, in Hyde Park — and how Mr. Roosevelt would respond to Churchill's artful arguments *against* a Second Front landing across the English Channel that year.

Stimson feared the worst. "I can't help feeling a little bit uneasy about the influence of the Prime Minister on him at this time," the war secretary noted in his diary that evening. "The trouble is Churchill and Roosevelt are too much alike in their strong points and in their weak points. They are both brilliant. They are both penetrating in their thoughts," the secretary dictated, "but they lack the steadiness of balance that has got to go along with warfare."²⁹

Roosevelt was certainly bombarded by arguments that weekend.

Responding to the President's latest June 17 request for an immediate, up-to-date study of U.S. landings in Morocco and Algeria, General Marshall's own couriered letter was emphatic. It informed the President that Marshall, Admiral King, and their army, air, and naval staffs had duly reexamined the "Gymnast project as a possible plan for the employment of U.S. forces against the Axis powers in the summer and fall of 1942, following our conversation with you Wednesday." Their conclusion was devastatingly negative. "The advantages and disadvantages of implementing the Gymnast plan as compared to other operations, particularly 1942 emergency Bolero operations, lead to the conclusion that the occupation of Northwest Africa this summer should not be attempted," they bluntly reported.³⁰

To explain their opposition to the President's plan, the U.S. Army chief and U.S. Navy commander in chief enclosed, with their letter, a three-page official army and navy analysis for the President. Gymnast would not work, they claimed, because the Luftwaffe would be able, they asserted, to move aircraft into "Spanish and North African bases, from which they could operate against Casablanca" — air operations that would threaten the U.S. aircraft carriers vital to provide the necessary air support for the invasion. If Gymnast was seriously being advanced as a major undertaking by the President, they argued, necessitating an inevitable diversion of U.S. forces from other projects, why on earth not invade Brittany or the Brest Peninsula — Operation "Sledgehammer" — instead? These would at least bring U.S. forces closer to an eventual Allied path to Berlin.

Gymnast's naval requirements, moreover, promised "disaster in the North Atlantic," the chiefs claimed, owing to the "thinning out" necessary to provide naval support to a Northwest African campaign as it unfolded. Moreover, Vichy French cooperation was essential, yet unlikely — the American vice consul at Casablanca having reported that the Nazis "have already made plans to meet a U.S. invasion of Northwest Africa." The Germans, according to the vice consul, had available three armored divisions, boasting three hundred tanks, on top of the "700 tanks there" and

"200–300 Stukas" and "58 Messerschmitts." There were even, the chiefs claimed, "250 to 300 fast launches collected on the coast of Spain" that Hitler might use . . .[31]

Polite as always, the President duly met Churchill's U.S. Navy plane when it landed at New Hackensack airfield on the evening of June 19, 1942. He was annoyed, however, at Churchill's presumption — the Prime Minister emerging from the aircraft with no fewer than five other people, including Major General Ismay, his military assistant or chief of staff. Faced with the unexpected retinue the normally stoic President said testily to his private secretary, "Haven't room for them" — and gave instructions some would have to be housed nearby.[32]

The President was yet more irritated when Churchill began to use the President's exclusive, personal telephone line to the White House as if it were his own. Churchill had, the President's secretary Bill Hassett recorded, "seated himself in the President's study and had entered upon an extended conversation with the British Embassy in Washington," until it was terminated by the President's chief switchboard operator, Louise Hachmeister.[33]

Churchill, though, was Churchill.

"You cannot judge the P.M. by ordinary standards," General Ismay had written to General Claude Auchinleck, commanding British forces in the Middle East, earlier that year. "He is not in the least like anyone that you or I have ever met. He is a mass of contradictions. He is either on the crest of the wave, or in the trough, either highly laudatory or bitterly condemnatory; either in an angelic temper, or a hell of a rage. When he isn't fast asleep he's a volcano. There are no half-measures in his make-up. He is a child of nature with moods as variable as an April day."[34]

The President could be forgiven for comparing the situation to that of August 1941, when meeting Churchill aboard their battleships off the coast of Newfoundland. Then, too, the President had known Churchill was approaching with a purpose — to get the United States to declare war on Germany — and had his own counterstrategy: to make the British sign up first to a statement of principles, before any idea of a wartime alliance could be discussed. But then, at least, the President had had his own chiefs of staff by his side. Now he was on his own, without even Harry Hopkins.[35] His chiefs were in Washington, imploring him by courier and phone not to make any premature "deal."

In the circumstances, the President resorted to his usual strategy in such matters: charm. Taking Churchill in his specially converted convertible, equipped with only hand controls, he drove the Prime Minister "all over the estate, showing me its splendid views," as Churchill later related — but with some close calls. "In this drive I had some thoughtful moments. Mr. Roosevelt's infirmity prevented him from using his feet on the break, clutch or accelerator. An ingenious arrangement" — designed by the President — "enabled him to do everything with his arms, which were amazingly strong and muscular. He invited me to feel his biceps, saying that a famous prize-fighter had envied them. This was reassuring; but I confess that when on several occasions the car poised and backed on the grass verges of the precipices over the Hudson I hoped the mechanical devices and brakes would show no defects."[36]

The President's performance was clearly intended to keep the Prime Minister quiet, rather than allow him to "talk business" without their advisers present — indeed, the picture of the two men was all too symbolic, careering around Hyde Park in the President's open-topped, dark-blue 1936 Ford Phaeton with Churchill attempting to tell the President that the Allies should invade either Norway, in the far north of Europe, or French Northwest Africa, to the south of Europe, or indeed anywhere but mainland France.

More ominously, Winston Churchill was bearing with him his own memorandum for the President, which he'd dictated to his secretary at the British Embassy that very morning — a document he had in his pocket and was intent on handing in person to Roosevelt, if he could, without any of Roosevelt's military advisers being present. And Churchill was no mean writer, the President knew.

The President promised to read it — side by side with General Marshall and Admiral King's three-page memorandum that night.

Once he'd read the two competing memoranda carefully, the President recognized there would be a tough session on his return to Washington.

"The President wanted to see secretaries of War and Navy, Admiral King, and General Marshall tomorrow afternoon," Hassett noted in his diary. "Said later he might not see them till evening and would notify them after reaching the White House. Does, however, want to see General Marshall at 11 o'clock tomorrow morning — all appointments off the record," Hassett added.[37]

• • •

Had Stimson written a better memorandum, he too might have been invited to attend the "crisis" meeting at the White House the next day. But the war secretary's prose was far from masterful, it was dour.

Stimson's argument for an immediate and exclusive Bolero build-up and cross-Channel invasion of France seemed not only doctrinaire, but his justifications for building up forces in Britain rather than sending them into battle in French Northwest Africa were jejune: among others he now asserted that Britain faced a possible, even imminently "probable," invasion by German paratroopers, "producing a confusion in Britain which would be immediately followed by an invasion by sea."[38]

The President shook his head over that.

Churchill's memorandum, by contrast, addressed squarely and without fear the real question the President had in mind: if a Second Front could not be mounted in 1942, where could the Allies actually *strike?* "Arrangements are being made for a landing of six or eight Divisions on the coast of Northern France early in September," Churchill began his critique. However, he declared, "the British Government would not favour an operation that was certain to lead to disaster," since this would "not help the Russians whatever in their plight, would compromise and expose to Nazi vengeance the French population involved and would gravely delay the main operation in 1943. We hold strongly to the view," he summed up, "that there should be no substantial landing in France this year unless we are going to stay."[39]

The fact was, neither Churchill nor his advisers could see any hope of such a successful "substantial" operation in France in 1942 — whatever the U.S. chiefs of staff might argue. "No responsible British military authority has so far been able to make a plan for September 1942 which had any chance of success unless the Germans become utterly demoralized, of which there is no likelihood," Churchill stated categorically. "Have the American Staffs a plan? If so, what is it? What forces would be employed? At what points would they strike? What landing-craft and shipping are available? Who is the officer prepared to command the enterprise? What British forces and assistance are required?"[40]

Churchill was famous for his Macaulayan eloquence, rich in metaphor and tart phrasing; this time, however, he simply ended with what he knew would resonate with the President. If an immediate Second Front landing was impossible in September 1942, "what else are we going to do?" he asked. "Can we afford to stand idle in the Atlantic theatre during the whole of 1942? Ought we not to be preparing within the general structure of BOLERO some other operation by which we may gain positions of advantage and also directly or indirectly to take some weight off Russia? It is in this setting and on this background that the Operation GYMNAST should be studied"[41] — unaware that General Marshall and Admiral King had just studied it yet again, on the President's orders, and had concluded it "should not be undertaken"!

Shortly before 11:00 p.m. on Saturday, June 20, 1942, the President's party left Hyde Park and drove to the local railway station. Churchill got out first, in his black topcoat, and walked up the ramp toward the train. In his diary Bill Hassett recorded the sight of the venerable little Englishman standing at the top, "at just a sufficient height to accentuate his high-water pants — typically English — Magna Charta, Tom Jones, Doctor Johnson, hawthorn, the Sussex Downs, and roast beef all rolled into one. Nothing that's American in this brilliant son of an American mother. The President went at once into his [railway] car and Winnie followed."[42]

The train then moved off, traveling slowly in order not to shake the President, who slept well.

"We all went to the White House together," Hassett recorded, once they had arrived at Arlington Cantonment, just before 9:00 a.m. on June 21, 1942, for what was to prove an historic, calamitous day.[43]

18

The Fall of Tobruk

LORD HALIFAX, a Roman Catholic, had gone to church at St. Thomas — "where everybody was provided with fans" to combat the heat — having been assured that "the party had got back all right" from Hyde Park.[1] He was relieved to know Churchill wouldn't be returning to the embassy — the Prime Minister having been invited by the President to stay at the White House for the remainder of his visit.

Once Churchill was reestablished in his old bedroom on the second floor, he and Major General "Pug" Ismay joined the President and General Marshall in the Oval Study to debate the pros and cons of Bolero and Gymnast. They had barely begun, however, when the whole issue of a Second Front in 1942 was exploded by a bombshell. It came in the form of a piece of pink paper: the copy of an urgent telegram, brought up from the Map Room and handed to the President.

The President read it, then handed it to Churchill.

It came from the war cabinet in London.

"Tobruk has surrendered," the message ran — "with twenty-five thousand men taken prisoners."[2]

Twenty-five thousand British troops? Without fighting?

"The year before," recalled the President's speechwriter, Robert Sherwood, "Tobruk had withstood siege for thirty-three weeks. Now it had crumpled within a day before the first assault. This was a body blow for Churchill. It was another Singapore. It might well be far worse even than that catastrophe in its total effect — for with Tobruk gone, there was little left with which to stop Rommel from pushing on to Alexandria, Cairo — and beyond."[3]

In his diary, Breckenridge Long, the assistant secretary of state, noted that the British "lost 1009 tanks" — largely to Rommel's secret weapon, his dreaded "88" (millimeter) antiaircraft gun, used as a long-range anti-tank weapon — "and just smashed the British. They have had six months to prepare — and are now licked. It is serious now. They have no real for-tifications between Rommel and Cairo or Suez — and a broken army. It may easily mean the loss of Egypt — unless we can stop it."[4]

As Churchill himself later wrote, it was "a bitter moment. Defeat is one thing; disgrace is another."[5]

Lord Halifax heard the same news. Meeting Churchill's doctor, Sir Charles Wilson, the ambassador "discussed probable reactions in England" to the catastrophe, "and how it is likely to affect the Prime Minister's plans here." The Prime Minister had "never meant to stay long this time," Halifax re-flected, "and he certainly will not make the mistake he made in January of overlooking feeling at home" — critical outcries that might well lead now to a vote of censure in the House of Commons.[6] He would surely have to fly home, instanter.

Back in England there was, indeed, consternation and calls for Churchill to stand down as prime minister. At the Foreign Office, Sir Alec Cadogan had just acknowledged in his diary that "Libya is a complete disaster"[7] when he learned "that Tobruk had fallen." It seemed impossible to believe. The heavily fortified port, with ample munitions, water, and troops, had "held out for 8 months last time, and for about as many hours this. I wonder what is most wrong with our army. Without any knowl-edge, I should say our Generals. *Most* depressing."[8]

Averell Harriman, who had returned to the United States with Churchill for talks about munitions and Lend-Lease consignments, called it "a stag-gering blow" to the Prime Minister, which Churchill at first refused to believe. "But when it was confirmed, by telephone from London, he made no attempt to hide his pain from Roosevelt."[9]

General Ismay recalled the same. Churchill had "scarcely entered" the President's study when the news was delivered. "This was a hideous and totally unexpected shock, and for the first time in my life I saw the Prime Minister wince."[10] Before Ismay could get official confirmation, on Churchill's disbelieving orders, he met Churchill's secretary, John Martin, in the corridor bearing a new telegram. This one was from the British naval commander in chief in the Mediterranean, Admiral Harwood. It confirmed not only that Tobruk had surrendered but went on to explain to the Prime Minister that, in the circumstances, Harwood was sending the Royal Navy's Eastern Mediterranean Fleet south of the Suez Canal, toward the Indian Ocean.

General Alan Brooke, the next day, recorded the timing differently — noting news of the disaster had come through only in the afternoon of June 21, after he'd lunched with the President. "Harry Hopkins and Marshall also turned up," and it was only in the midst of a "long conference" that "the tragic news of Tobruk came in!" he scribbled. "Churchill and I were standing beside the President's desk talking to him when Marshall walked in with a pink piece of paper containing a message of the fall of Tobruk!"[11]

Whatever the actual timing, the British team seemed distraught, even lost. As Brooke subsequently admitted, in his annotations to his diary, "Neither Winston nor I had contemplated such an eventuality and it was a staggering blow"[12] — with neither man having any idea what to do.

Certainly, when Sir Charles Wilson was finally summoned and went over to the White House to see the Prime Minister, later in the afternoon of June 21, 1942, around 3.00 p.m., he found Churchill "pacing his room. He turned on me," Moran recorded in his diary notes. "Tobruk has fallen."[13]

"He said this as if I were responsible. With that, he began again striding up and down the room, glowering at the carpet." "What matters is that it should happen when I am here," Churchill confessed — stung by the humiliation in front of his American hosts.[14]

Churchill went to the window. "I am ashamed. I cannot understand why Tobruk gave in. More than 30,000 of our men put their hands up. If they won't fight —"[15]

Churchill paused, midsentence — bitterly aware of the effect abroad of such an abject British surrender, following the disastrous showing of British imperial forces in Malaya, Burma, and the Indian Ocean. Not only might people in the occupied nations lose heart, but the surrender could even drive neutral countries like Turkey, Portugal, or Spain to parley with Hitler . . .

Directing all Third Reich propaganda, Joseph Goebbels reveled in the news from North Africa.[16] The Spanish press agency EFE, he noted, was describing "an atmosphere of catastrophe in Washington."[17]

Even Goebbels had not expected Rommel to be so successful, given the general's skimpy reports to Berlin since the beginning of Operation Theseus, his plan to drive the British out of Libya and Egypt, on May 26, 1942.

Not only had the great port of Tobruk now been captured by Rommel, but it contained enough food, oil, and weapons to keep the Panzerarmee Afrika going for three months. Churchill must have knowingly flown the coop in order to be out of London, Goebbels conjectured cynically — the Prime Minister knowing he'd be blamed for misleading the public into thinking the British were winning the desert war. The British press were now in an uproar, making mincemeat of Churchill's lamentable military leadership and personal "responsibility for the catastrophe."[18]

Goebbels thus gloried in Britain's shame. The British did not possess a "single general who has shown himself a real commander, on any current field of battle. After Wavell, Auchinleck; after Auchinleck, Ritchie" — the Eighth Army commander, appointed by Auchinleck after he'd had to fire General Alan Cunningham, his first commander. "And every one a failure," Goebbels sneered.[19] The latest German 88mm antitank guns and their armor-piercing shells had made a killing of British armored vehicles in the desert — even decimating the American M-3 "Grant tanks" the British had been given.[20] Rommel, who had invented a new tactic — luring the British armor onto his concealed 88mm gun positions, to be "shot like hares" — was "the hero of the hour"[21] and was instantly promoted by the Führer to the rank of field marshal, on the field of battle.

In such circumstances "talk in the U.S. of a Second Front can only be considered a joke," Goebbels sniffed.[22] "Churchill is no longer the leader of the most powerful empire on earth," the propaganda minister dictated in his office diary. "On the contrary, he has had to go to Washington like a pilgrim, seeking help, and Roosevelt has now taken over many of the functions that were once the Prime Minister's. Doubtless the President intends to inherit Britain's empire one day. But that is of no significance to us. We aren't interested in that. We'll be quite content to be allowed a free hand in Europe" — a free hand that would exterminate all Jews and reduce all non-Germans to accomplices, servants, slaves — or ashes. "That," he concluded, "is what we have to achieve in this war."[23]

How much Hitler's mind was focused on the territories to the east of Germany, rather than to the west, had again been made clear to Goebbels the previous month, as Hitler gave the orders for his legions to recommence their armored drive deeper into Russia. The Führer had already gotten a formal resolution from the Reichstag granting him absolute judicial powers as dictator, "without being bound by existing legal precepts." Thus empowered, Hitler had briefly returned from his East Prussian headquarters to Berlin again in May, certain he would overwhelm Russian forces by the end of the summer; if not, his armies would be better prepared for winter, he promised the country's assembled Nazi Party Gauleiters in a two-hour peroration.[24] To Goebbels's surprise, the Führer then confided to the assembled administrators just how critical the previous winter had been — admitting that by the time Japan attacked Pearl Harbor the Third Reich had been facing retreat and possible defeat on the field of battle. The Japanese had saved the Third Reich.[25] Now, thankfully, the situation was reversed — with the Soviet armies facing collapse before German might. Nothing could now stand in his way.[26]

The Führer had respect neither for Roosevelt nor untested American troops.[27] He had blindly forecast — thirteen days before Midway — that the Japanese Navy would destroy the U.S.-British fleet if it came to a major sea battle.[28] American preparations for a Second Front in the West were not worth taking seriously, either, he had mocked, given the current success of Germany's U-boat war. He'd positioned enough German troops in Norway to repel any invasion attempt, as was rumored to be planned by the British; moreover, with some twenty-five German divisions on call in the West, and no less than four first-class German panzer divisions and even a parachute division ready to meet an Allied landing,[29] he predicted a drubbing if the Americans and British attempted to create a Second Front anywhere on the French coast.

"Of course the Führer doesn't believe for a moment that, were there to be a British invasion even lasting ten or fourteen days, it would end with anything but an absolute catastrophe for the British. That might alter the whole course of the war, perhaps even end it," Goebbels recorded the Führer's words.[30] The Allies would hardly be so stupid, surely. In the meantime, German's destiny lay in the East, the Führer had emphasized. It was there that Germany needed room to expand — Hitler's perennial mantra since the 1920s — establishing as it did a sort of Chinese wall that would separate the West from Asia.[31]

"Never," Goebbels had recorded the Führer's strategic imperative in May, "must Germany allow itself to be sandwiched between two military powers, for then the Reich would always be threatened." Thankfully, the Führer had claimed, Germany had "succeeded in destroying the military power on its western front. Over the summer it would now proceed to destroy the military power on its eastern front. Then we'll be able to begin the process of reconstruction," he noted the gist of the Führer's address. "In the East we want, above all, to use our soldiers as frontier settlers. In that way German resettlement will proceed as it had in the greatest days of Germany's first empire. The German diaspora should be brought back from foreign countries, even from America, its men applied to the Reich's skills in colonization. We won't need to be cultural fertilizers for foreign countries any more, we'll be able to develop our own territories culturally, intellectually, and spiritually. . . . *This* was the point of the war," he sketched the Führer's *tour d'horizon,* "for the spilling of so much blood will only be justified by future generations on the basis of swaying cornfields. Of course it would be nice to inherit a few colonies, where we could plant coffee or rubber trees. But our colonial future lies in the East. That is where rich black earth and iron lie, the foundation of our national wealth. By smart demographic measures, above all using Germans returning from abroad, it would be easy to increase the German population to 250 million . . ."[32]

The future — "the next stages straightforward. Our punitive air raids on English cities ["Baedeker" raids on Exeter, Bath, Norwich, and York, following massive RAF bomber raids on Lübeck and Rostock] have already taught them a lesson. Once we have established our eastern frontiers, the British will reflect on whether to pursue such air attacks on German territory, because our Luftwaffe will once again be free for action . . . Once matters are settled in the East — and we all hope that will be done this summer — then Europe can, as the Führer says, get stuffed. For the war will be won for us. We'll be able to indulge in piracy on the high seas against the Anglo-Saxon powers, who won't be able to withstand it. The United States will lose all enthusiasm for the war, once they see the British empire plundered and disemboweled . . ."[33]

On and on in this vein the Führer had shared his apocalyptic vision with his Nazi functionaries — none of whom dissented. "He doesn't take American declarations of intent too seriously. Against their boast of their 120 million people at war with us, we can counter with about 600 million on our side. For now that Japan has entered the war, we are not talking just of a few continental powers, but we shall soon be able to turn it into a global struggle, spreading it across all continents. The United States are still thinking in terms of world war; but world war terms don't begin to describe this war."[34] All that was required to fulfill his demonic dream, Hitler repeated, were Nazis with nerves of steel; also Hitler's own personal survival "to the end of the war," in order that all actually happened as he willed, despite the inevitable trials and setbacks that would occur.

Spring had come, thankfully; the Führer seemed to be in the "best of spirits," Goebbels had noted. *"In glänzendster Form."*[35]

Four weeks later, as spring had turned to summer and the German armies had driven deeper into southern Russia, and in Libya Rommel turned the tables on General Ritchie's British Eighth Army, Hitler's dream had seemed eminently achievable to Goebbels. In late June 1942, it was simply marvelous, he felt, to be alive.

Gloom had meanwhile descended on Washington in the aftermath of the British surrender of Tobruk.

In the sticky heat, sixteen of the most senior British and American military staff officers met on June 21, 1942. They had intended to discuss offensive strategy, but they now switched to defense: addressing the ramifications of the collapse of the British in North Africa, and the possible fall of Churchill as prime minister.

The President's response, however, was different — indeed, would go down in world history. At the British Empire's nadir of shame, with British Empire soldiers refusing to fight — the number of those surrendering at Tobruk increasing to thirty-three thousand in subsequent hours — the President turned to Churchill and said: "What can we do to help?"[36]

General Marshall was consulted, and to the consternation of Secretary Stimson — who was not summoned — the President offered, with Marshall's approval, to take the Second U.S. Armored Division, currently being equipped with the latest M-4 Sherman tanks with swiveling turrets, and dispatch it immediately to Egypt, with its men and artillery, to defend Alexandria, Cairo, and the Suez Canal.

Churchill, shocked, chastened, and grateful, accepted. Americans and Britons would thus fight side by side.

It was in this way that the strategic Second Front "crisis" of June 1942 was temporarily averted — not by argument but by British disaster.

What earthly hope, after all, could there be of a successful Second Front that fall, at a moment when the British were collapsing in the Middle East? "Nobody seriously believes in the feasibility of a Second Front," even Goebbels noted in his diary on June 25.[37] After all, the majority of the forces for such an invasion would have to be British, given the time it would still take to ship significant numbers of U.S. troops to England. And in the wake of Tobruk's disgraceful surrender, what possible victory could be won on the fields of Europe, if the British lacked generals who could win offensive battles, or soldiers willing even to fight them?

19

No Second Dunquerque

ON TUESDAY, JUNE 23, 1942, three days after the fall of Tobruk — and the day that Major General Eisenhower set off to London to take command of the still-meager U.S. forces rehearsing for the Second Front[1] — the Canadian prime minister received the long-awaited call from Washington.

"[T]he President said: Hello Mackenzie. How are you? I expressed the hope that he was well. He said, Yes, very well. He then said: Winston and I are sitting together here. We want you to come down to Washington for a meeting of the Pacific Council on Thursday."[2]

"We drove to the White House through the private entrance to the grounds, at the rear," Mackenzie King noted in his diary entry for June 25. "We were shown into what I imagine judging from pictures, etc. would be Mrs. Roosevelt's sitting room" — for there was to be held, prior to the Pacific Council meeting, a conference of representatives of all the British Dominions, addressed in person by Mr. Churchill.

As he waited, King found a chance to speak with Field Marshal Sir John Dill, the British representative on the Combined Chiefs of Staff Committee in Washington.

Dill — who had been chief of the Imperial General Staff (CIGS) before General Alan Brooke, but had been fired by the Prime Minister for constantly contesting Churchill's interference in the operations conducted in the field — was gloomy. "He said to me that he regarded the reverse at Tobruk as very serious; from the quiet impressive way he spoke to me, it was clear that he felt this equally. He spoke of the difficulty of a campaign in the desert and of Egypt, and gave me the impression that he felt the whole situation was very grave. While he did not say it, I felt he realized it might be impossible to save the situation so far as the Suez was concerned."[3]

Captain McCrea, Roosevelt's naval aide, then ushered them into the next-door conference room, where the Dominion representatives of the British Empire took their places. Standing to address them in secret session, Churchill was, if anything, more pessimistic than his listeners, according to King: "When he came to speak on the Middle East, Churchill said that as far as he was concerned, he was prepared to lose the Middle East rather than sacrifice Australia's position if it had to come to that."

This was bleak — strangely contradicted, however, by Churchill's appearance. The Prime Minister looked "remarkably fresh," King noted, "almost like a cherub, scarcely a line in his face, and completely rested though up to one or two the night before," as he gave the assembled representatives a "review of the whole situation."

"He started at once with Libya and the fall of Tobruk," King recounted. "Said that we must not conceal the fact that it was a very serious reverse to him; it had been quite unexpected. The reports he had received from [General] Auchinleck had led him to feel that the British forces would be able to hold situations [positions] successfully and to win out, but there it was, and now the next concern was over Egypt. He said he had no doubt in his own mind about the British being able to hold Egypt. The enemy would find fighting over the desert, many miles [distant] of each other, no water, a very arduous business . . ."

The Prime Minister's mixture of brutal frankness and yet confident hope was bewitching to the Canadian prime minister, seated among senior fellow Dominion leaders and representatives — especially when Churchill went on to admit "that the present situation, bad as it appeared, was nothing to what it had been in April last at the time the Japanese fleet were assembled in the Indian Ocean. . . . Pointed out that it looked at one time as though India might readily have fallen to the enemy. There was very little in the way of protection in Ceylon or in India." The United States, however, had saved England's imperial bacon. "Happily since then, the Japanese fleet had encountered the attacks it had" — first in the Tokyo raid, then the Coral Sea and Midway — "and he now felt that India was in a better position than she had been in at any time from [point of view of] the number of soldiers there. She was better protected" — especially by Americans — "than she had ever been. As to the internal situation" — where Gandhi was putting together what would become his historic "Quit India" protest movement — Churchill was indifferent: "the British had made the best offer they could," he declared, claiming that "India was not a country," as King quoted him. "It was a continent, full of different races, etc. and had to be so regarded."

This was not a view that the Canadian premier shared. "I felt, however, that Churchill did not really appreciate the position in India." The Prime Minister spoke about never having changed his views—but claimed he had not allowed them "to interfere with the utmost effort being made at this time to meet the situation through Cripps."[4]

Given Churchill's "sabotage" of Cripps's mission, this was untruthful; yet there was something almost hypnotic about Churchill's oratory even to the Indian representative at the meeting, Sir Girja S. Bajpai. Churchill spoke of Russia, China, Australia. "Explaining the difficult situation generally," King recounted, "Churchill said it was the wide space that had to be covered with only limited numbers of men and supplies. He said it was like a man in bed trying to cover himself with a blanket which is not large enough. When his right shoulder was cold and he pulled it over to cover it, the left became uncovered and cold. When he pulled it back, the situation was reversed. Similarly when he hauled the blanket up to put around his neck and chest, his feet became cold and exposed and got cold. When he went to cover them up, his chest became exposed and he got pneumonia or something of the kind."

The Dominion representatives, spellbound, waited for the British prime minister to tell them how he proposed to deal with this "grave" situation.

Churchill was, however, aware he had his audience in thrall—and deferred the capstone of his talk. "He then suddenly stopped," King wrote, "and in a dramatic way, began to go over the situation compared as it was at the beginning of the war." Russia and now the United States were in the fight, he reminded them, on Britain's side, "and he referred to the heroism of the Russians and the magnificent work which the Americans were doing on their production etc."

Finally, however, the Prime Minister came to the climax of his peroration.

"He then said: but we have an ally which is greater than Russia, greater than the U.S."

The assembled Dominion representatives were agog.

Churchill was nothing if not an actor, when faced by an attentive audience. The Prime Minister, the Canadian premier recorded, "paused for a moment, and said: it is air power."[5]

• • •

Air power?

The Dominion representatives were at first disbelieving.

Troops of the British Empire had in the past two years lost Norway, France, Greece, Hong Kong, Malaya, Burma, and only four days before had surrendered Tobruk without a fight. They now looked to be losing Egypt, the gateway to the Levant. Did the Prime Minister really believe Britain's new "ally," far from any war front, would magically reverse the tide of war and defeat Germany and Japan any time soon?

It seemed ludicrous, given the failure of Germany's vaunted air power, the Luftwaffe, to bring Britain to its knees in 1940 and 1941.

It was all that Mr. Churchill could produce for his Dominion listeners at that moment, however — the Prime Minister extolling the recent, highly controversial RAF thousand-plane "bombing of Cologne and Essen," which had produced an uproar in the House of Commons, as the death toll among German civilians threatened to vitiate the moral principles upon which the Allies were defending "human civilization." "Told of the destruction there," Mackenzie King noted the Prime Minister's response: "He said our objective would continue to be military targets, though, some times, the airmen might go a little wide of the target. That the destruction of Cologne" — one of the glories of European medieval architecture — "had given the Germans great trouble in moving populations, taking care of those moved, trying to rebuild roads, etc., and intimated that there would be more of it, and it would be most demoralizing."[6]

Demoralizing? This was debatable — indeed, the deliberate killing of so many civilians might be counterproductive, *strengthening* rather than diminishing the resolve of ordinary Germans, as the Canadian prime minister — who read the Bible before rising each day — was uncomfortably aware. That morning King had read a passage that had given him guidance "throughout the day": "Chapter VII of Jeremiah with its words: 'Obey my voice and I will be your God and He shall be my keeper. Walk ye in all the ways that I have commanded you that it may be well unto you.'"[7]

"Terror bombing," as the Germans called it, did not sit well with such walking. Even Lord Halifax, a deeply religious man, had blanched when recently told by a British pilot what he had done — "a red-headed young Scottish sergeant-pilot from Motherwell who had been on nearly every trip to Germany including Rostock, but had missed Cologne as he was getting ready to come over here. About Rostock he said the fires were tremendous; 'I'm afraid we not only killed them but cremated them.'"[8]

The Prime Minister's much debatable paean to his new "ally," however, now led him to his ultimate revelation — a confidential admission in the White House that was far, far more welcome to the Dominion representatives.

As Mackenzie King recorded that night, "Churchill reserved to the last part of his talk the reference to the European front; here he spoke very positively" — or negatively.[9] A Second Front, he confided in absolute candor, was simply not on the cards for that year.

"He said, using the expression 'By God,' nothing would ever induce him to have an attack made upon Europe without sufficient strength and being positively certain that they could win. He said that to go there without a sufficient force would be to incur another Dunkirk, and what would be worse than that, they would have of course to supply the French with arms and cause them to rise when any invasion was made, and that to have to leave them to the Huns [in a subsequent evacuation] would be to have the whole of the French massacred, and none of them left."[10]

Churchill's only answer, beyond RAF terror raids on German cities, was therefore more minor raids on the French coast to force the Germans at least to keep their defense forces stationed there, rather than in Russia; but "he did not think they could afford to contemplate the invasion of the continent before the spring of 1943, despite the number of troops that the Americans might be able to send across . . . Perhaps in the spring, shipping facilities will be better and the attack could take place then."[11]

Stopping there, Churchill asked for questions or comments, "and turned to me."[12]

Mackenzie King's testimony would be important to historians, because the Canadian premier's relationship to the President was a sort of marker in the war's changing dynamic. Canada was producing huge amounts of war materiel, food, and shipping; it was also providing a considerable number of volunteer troops to the global struggle against the Axis powers. Canada, in fact, was now as important to the war effort as Great Britain — and King, as Canadian prime minister, was as opposed to a cross-Channel Second Front as was Winston Churchill — a fact the President had been aware of ever since King had stayed with him at the White House, earlier that year, when King had experienced a strange vision relating to Mr. Roosevelt.

"Had a very distinct vision during the night," the Premier had noted in his diary in April. "It seemed as though some being was seeking rest; alongside were forces in the nature of flames, not of a fire but of passion or an animal instinct like fighting, etc. were continually banging at the side of this individual and in a way seeking to compel a yielding to its influence." The person "who came to mind" with respect to this dream "was the President and the influence of those" of his senior military staff "who were forcing him into a line of warfare without sufficiently surveying the whole field. The more I think of the vision," King recorded, "the more I feel it was to let me see that there was a spiritual significance behind the attitude which I took yesterday at the Pacific Council and again with the President last night in discussing the plan of campaign in Europe for this year."[13]

At that time — April 16, 1942 — it had become clear to the Canadian prime minister that the President had no idea how few divisions there were, in reality, in Britain, with Roosevelt imagining there were a hundred. Nor had the U.S. president quite recognized, in King's view, the *magnitude* of military effort required to mount a successful cross-Channel assault. King had therefore warned the President at the April Pacific War Council that a failed assault would make Britain itself vulnerable to attack. There had been "no dissent" from the council members — the Australian representative supporting King, and speaking "very emphatically about the necessity of avoiding the possibility of a second Dunquerque, and how disastrous anything of the kind would be. He said he wished to support very strongly what I had said." The New Zealand representative had spoken "in an equal strain, saying that while everyone believed in a second front, and the need for offensive action, up to the present there had been no one who could say how it could be done."[14]

That was two months ago; now, in the wake of the disaster being suffered by the British Eighth Army in Libya and Egypt, a cross-Channel invasion seemed *even less* mountable that year — especially, Mackenzie King reflected, when the lives of volunteer Canadian troops, training in Britain, were at risk.

It was, in this respect, a tragic moment: Prime Minister King as straightforward as Churchill in responding to the British prime minister's appeal for questions or comments. Addressing the Dominion assembly on June 25, 1942, King warned "that the subject he had dealt with was one about which we [Canadians] were most concerned. That we felt very strongly he was right in what he had said about the necessity of overwhelming forces, and not taking unnecessary risks."[15]

It was abundantly clear, then, that in late June 1942 it was not simply the British who were balking at the implications of a cross-Channel Second Front, but America's crucial ally, the Canadians — whose premier felt no shame or inhibition in sharing with the President his concerns. None of the Dominions, in fact, were willing to risk another military debacle, whatever the U.S. chiefs might favor — especially after the surrender of Tobruk and the flight of the British Empire forces of the British Eighth Army toward Suez and Cairo.

20

Avoiding Utter Catastrophe

IRONICALLY, CHURCHILL AND HITLER agreed on one thing: a cross-Channel attack in 1942 would fail. Hitler and Goebbels naturally prayed that it would be attempted.

After reading secret intelligence reports from Moscow, Goebbels recorded on July 4 that the Kremlin was calling for a Second Front, "but Churchill and Roosevelt are in no position to comply." The situation was giving rise, to Goebbels's delight, to idle talk of the Soviets taking the "most extreme measures unless the English and Americans actually mount a Second Front. But how can Churchill and Roosevelt launch a Second Front in reality," he asked himself, "when they don't have the necessary shipping and are having such difficulties on existing fronts and suffering such fatal defeats?"[1]

Two weeks later Goebbels was noting the British "have no intention of rushing into any invasion adventure. Even they will have learned that we've now stationed, in the West, the quality of first-class German troops, well-trained and hardened by battle on the Eastern Front, who would *welcome* such a confrontation with pure joy."[2]

Scanning the British and American press, as well as reports from German agents, Goebbels noted the continuing pressure on Roosevelt and Churchill to launch just such an invasion. "The man in the street screams for a Second Front, and it remains an open question whether Churchill and Roosevelt might, in certain circumstances, together with the deteriorating military situation for the Russians, have to give in to such pressure. It's one of the disadvantages of democracy that it can't conduct politics or war according to logic and intelligence, but has to respond to the up-and-down swings of public opinion. In such circumstances," he mused, "a concession to public pressure for a Second Front could lead Churchill and Roosevelt to utter catastrophe."[3]

Ironically, it was not only the proverbial man in the street who was driving the President toward "catastrophe," but his most senior military officers in Washington.

General Marshall was becoming the most evangelical of Second Fronters — determined to avoid unnecessary dispersion of effort. Even the President's offer to send the Second U.S. Armored Division to reinforce and revitalize the British Eighth Army in Egypt had been revised on Marshall's instructions, since it would take, it was calculated by his staff at the War Department, three to four *months* to get such a fully armed division to Suez — by which time the war in Egypt would have been decided. Only the tanks themselves, and a cadre of technicians, were thus sent, by fast convoy. On limiting the forces to that, the general would not bend — in fact he actually walked out of the President's study rather than contemplate dispatching yet more American forces to the Middle East beyond the Second Armored Division's tanks — forces that would then not be available for the planned build-up in Britain prior to a Second Front attack.

The President was surprised, and disappointed. But then, as quasi Allied commander in chief, he saw the situation differently from his U.S. Army chief of staff and war secretary. The collapse of the British at Tobruk was disheartening, but might yet offer the Allies a great strategic opportunity for a counterstroke. Rommel had lured the tanks and vehicles of the British Eighth Army into the range of his deadly 88mm antitank guns, winning a historic victory in the desert at Gazala and causing the British to flee eastward across the deserts of Libya for their very lives. But driving his Panzerarmee Afrika onward toward Cairo, Rommel was leaving himself open to a possible strategic counterstrike — a huge American army landing in his rear, in French Northwest Africa, after which the new *Feldmarschall* could, if all went well, be crushed inexorably between the two Allied pincers.

Why Marshall, King, Stimson, and others held so firmly to their idea of a cross-Channel Second Front in 1942, and seemed so naïve about the reception they would be given by Hitler's waiting forces, never ceased to amaze the President. For almost an entire year, ever since July 1941 — long before Pearl Harbor — the President had favored as an alternative a U.S.

landing in French Northwest Africa, in the event of war, to forestall the Germans — yet every time he had pressed for serious operational study of the scheme he had met with opposition from the War Department.

At the very least, Operation Gymnast promised to allow the United States to control the whole Atlantic seaboard of French West Africa, including the vital port of Dakar — thus ensuring German forces would be denied the closest jumping-off point to a potential attack or invasion of South America. Better than that, though, it would give the Allies the chance to jam and crush German and Italian forces in North Africa between the west and eastern ends of the Mediterranean.[4]

Hitler would not be able to ignore such a threat to his Italian Axis partners and to his southern flank. He would *have* to join battle — but on the periphery of Europe, at the very farthest point from his own bases and supplies — while all the time having to hold significant German forces in France to meet a possible cross-Channel invasion from Britain. This would aid the hard-pressed Russians substantially, without risking a devastating reverse in a cross-Channel landing that year. Against nominal Vichy French resistance in North Africa, moreover, U.S. forces would get to rehearse the business of amphibious warfare. Then, in the relative "safety" of an American-occupied Northwest Africa, they would be able to put into practice in real time the command and combat techniques they would later need for an ultimate "Bolero" cross-Channel invasion, using preponderant force.

By contrast, the challenge of Bolero — facing at least twenty-five German divisions charged by Hitler with defending against Allied landings on mainland France — would be a far harder proposition. Allied formations would have to land on hostile shores that were within easy air, road, and rail reinforcement from Germany. And face a far, far tougher prospective enemy there than Vichy French troops in Morocco or Algeria.

In short, Churchill and the British chiefs of staff were right in being disinclined to carry out Bolero. Breaching Hitler's so-called Atlantic Wall and smashing down the gateway to Hitler's Third Reich was, in mid-1942, an almost impossible task — as Hitler and Goebbels knew better than anyone. Whereas U.S. landings in French Northwest Africa would give the Allies the initiative they needed in steadily pursuing a "Germany First" strategy. Shorn of its North African territories, and with Sicily and southern Italy within striking distance, Mussolini's Italy would very likely capitulate — leaving Hitler's Germany alone, battered from all sides.

In the President's eyes the United Nations were looking a gift horse in the mouth — for the Germans had *still* not occupied French Northwest Africa, even two years after their conquest of Western Europe! Morocco and Algeria were there for the taking — with Hitler still obsessively focused on defending the Atlantic Wall.

Yet how to get Stimson and the U.S. chiefs of staff to fall in line with such reasoning, without turning them against him as commander in chief?

Quietly the President began to cast around for a way to bring his reluctant sheep back into the fold, and support — instead of sabotage — Gymnast. It was at this point that he called on Bill Leahy.

The tall, balding, stern-looking Admiral William Leahy was well known to the President — Leahy having preceded Admirals Stark and King as chief of naval operations. Before his mandatory retirement as CNO, Admiral Leahy had even served on the newly minted Joint Chiefs of Staff board that the President had set up in 1939.

The President had come to admire Leahy's calmness of judgment — respect that had prompted him to make the admiral the U.S. ambassador to the French government in Vichy, after the 1940 French capitulation, and to press Leahy to gain and keep the trust of Vichy's military leaders.

Leahy had done well. Almost two years later the United States and Vichy French governments were still at peace with each other; indeed, even in the face of Premier Laval's active cooperation with the Nazis, Roosevelt had insisted that U.S. diplomatic relations with the Vichy government *not* be broken off, disregarding the pleas of the Free French leader, General Charles de Gaulle — who had almost zero influence or authority in Northwest Africa.

As Leahy had reported to the President, the commander in chief of all French Vichy forces, Admiral François Darlan, had told him confidentially that if the Americans landed "with sufficient force in North Africa to be successful against the Nazis, he would not oppose us."[5] It was this prospect, not specious public calls for a Second Front, that had remained the abiding lure of Gymnast for the President. As an extra incentive to French goodwill, Roosevelt had even insisted American food aid must continue to be sent to Vichy France and North Africa.

These had proved wise decisions, despite the political outcry that arose in the United States over appeasement of appeasers. Yet for all that Gymnast could achieve for the Allies in 1942, it had received only derisory responses from General Marshall and Admiral King — trained and experienced officers who claimed to see no point in such an invasion, and all too many military reasons why it was too daunting, and would founder.

The President disagreed. In fact he found their reasoning for the most part fallacious, and in some respects nonsensical, especially the claims in their memorandum of vast numbers of forces the Germans could bring to bear to smash a U.S. assault on Northwest Africa. Far from being in a numerically superior position to defeat such landings, the Germans were in no position to interfere with a U.S. invasion. In fact Admiral Leahy had assured Roosevelt, on June 5, 1942, when he returned to Washington from France for "consultations" with the President and Secretary Hull, that there were not 180 Germans in the whole of French Morocco.

Fewer than 180 Germans in Morocco?

It was in the context of Ambassador Leahy's revelation that, two weeks later, when the British surrendered at Tobruk and Churchill could only clutch at RAF bombing straws, the President's mind was largely made up. Bolero in 1942 was a pipe dream. The British disaster at Tobruk was simply the final straw. The British could no longer be depended upon to fight for their empire in the Far East, perhaps even the Middle East. How, then, could they be seriously expected to fight for the immediate liberation of mainland France, their ancient enemy in Europe, let alone for Europe?

Chances of Allied success in a cross-Channel invasion in 1942 were nil; a Second Front there would be suicidal. Instead, the President was now adamant, if the Western Allies were truly committed to a "Germany First" strategy, then the United States must land forces in French Northwest Africa *before the Germans did* — if he could overcome the skepticism of his own War and Navy Departments. It was they, after all, who would have to assemble and launch such an American invasion force.

As Churchill departed to face the music in the House of Commons (including a vote of no confidence in his government),[6] the stage was set in Washington for a monumental confrontation between the Commander in Chief and his own military staff, which had not taken place since Lincoln and the Civil War.

Hawaii Is Avenged

In a sea ambush at Midway, the U.S. fleet avenges Pearl Harbor, sinking all four Japanese carriers. Thus ends Japan's brief domination of the Pacific. At the White House, FDR is overjoyed — and proud of his supreme commander, Admiral Nimitz. Here Marine General Thomas Holcombe shows FDR a Japanese flag his son Marine Major James Roosevelt helped capture during a raid on Makin Island.

The Fall of Tobruk

On June 19, 1942, Churchill flies to Hyde Park to warn the President that the U.S. generals' plan for a Second Front in France that year is too difficult. Two days later, more than thirty thousand British troops surrender the vital port of Tobruk to Rommel without a fight. It becomes clear to FDR at the Pacific War Council in Washington that the United States will have to intercede in North Africa to save the British, while the Russians must save themselves.

Dieppe

The secretary of state for war, Henry Stimson, and General Marshall, the army chief of staff, do not agree. They threaten to switch to the Pacific unless the British go along with a Second Front invasion in 1942. The result, when Churchill feels compelled to mount a miniversion, is the British "fiasco" of Dieppe on August 19, 1942—where more than three thousand brave Canadians are killed, wounded, or captured in a few hours without getting off the beaches.

The President is mortified. He appoints retired Admiral Bill Leahy as his military chief of staff at the White House to put down the Stimson-Marshall insurrection and help enact his "great pet scheme": U.S. landings in French Northwest Africa, which the Germans have failed to occupy.

FDR Inspects the Nation

Boarding his presidential train, FDR sets off on September 17, 1942, on a fourteen-day inspection tour of U.S. production plants and military training facilities, prior to American landings in North Africa.

Gearing Up for Victory

From East Coast to West Coast, from the Gulf to South Carolina, the President inspects and inspires the "arsenal of democracy" he has fathered. The miracle of mass production — of ships, planes, tanks, guns, and munitions — is stunning: a new ship in ten days, the promise of a plane an hour . . . Together with rigorous training and rehearsal in amphibious operations, the tour confirms the President's faith in Allied victory — under American arms and leadership.

At Shangri-la, the President's secret camp in the Maryland mountains, FDR awaits news of the Torch invasion of Morocco and Algeria. The war secretary has bet him the invasion will fail, but FDR remains optimistic his "great pet scheme" will succeed.

Torch

Generals Eisenhower and Patton are FDR's favorite protégés — the one appointed by him to be supreme commander of the Torch invasion, the other his star performer as a saber-rattling armored corps commander at Casablanca.

With the surrender of all Vichy French forces in Northwest Africa to Eisenhower on November 11, 1942, the huge U.S. invasion is heralded around the world as the turning of the tide of World War II. In Washington that day, the President, accompanied by General Pershing of World War I fame, gives thanks at Arlington National Cemetery. "May He keep us strong in the courage that will win the war," he prays, "and may He impart to us the wisdom and the vision that we shall need for true victory in the peace which is to come."

PART NINE

Japan First

21

Citizen Warriors

BY JULY, WASHINGTON, D.C., WAS sweltering in all respects.

If only he could get away, the President sighed to his staff. Fortunately, he did not have long to wait. A "getaway" had been selected several months before, as a presidential retreat—and it was almost ready.

"Early in the spring of 1942, possibly late March or early April while having his sinuses packed one evening in [Dr.] Ross McIntire's office, President Roosevelt remarked about as follows," Roosevelt's naval aide, Captain McCrea, later related—attempting in his somewhat stilted English to recall the President's request.

"'Both of you'—referring to Ross McIntire and me—'know how very much I like to go to Hyde Park for weekend breaks. With the war on, I am conscious of the fact that I cannot go to Hyde Park as often as I have in the past'"—for the overnight journey from Washington to the Hudson Valley and then back was too time-consuming. Nevertheless, the President had said, "'I would like very much to dodge, as far as possible, the heat and humidity of the Washington summer: additional air conditioning is not for me, as you well know. As I have often told you, Ross, I never had sinus trouble until I became shipmates with air conditioning. The two may not be related but nevertheless I associate this condition'"—at which he tapped his sinus area with a forefinger—"'with air conditioning. Now, cannot we locate an area within easy access of Washington where it would be possible to set up a modest rustic camp, to which I could go from time to time on weekends or even overnight and thus escape for a few hours at least the oppressiveness of the Washington summer? I suggest this as an alternative to the Potomac'"—referring to the USS *Potomac*, the presidential yacht—"'since the Secret Service people are adamant against my using it, except on selected occasions.'"

"'Now I know that President Hoover had a camp on the Rapidau in the Catoctin mountains,'" the President had gone on to explain his idea. "'I know nothing about it but that might be a good area to investigate, anyway. Ross, I want John and you and Steve Early [FDR's press secretary] to find some place which will fit not alone my needs, but provide for the housing of the clerical staff which usually accompany me to Hyde Park. Remember now: nothing elaborate — something most modest, functional and within easy distance of the White House. This last requirement is important, so no doubt the choice of location will be limited to nearby Virginia and Maryland. Since the summer is approaching you should get after this as soon as possible.'"[1]

McCrea, McIntire, and Early had diligently begun their search.

"The Hoover camp was quickly eliminated," McCrea later recollected. The thirty-first president's camp had been built "alongside a nearby stream and had very little view of the surrounding countryside. President Hoover was interested in stream fishing and the camp, while ideal for that, did not fill the needs of President Roosevelt."

The general area, however, seemed ideal. "Nearby, atop the Catoctin Mountains at some 1800 feet elevation, was located a modest model recreation camp which had been built by the Civilian Conservation Corps and Works Progress Administration," as part of the New Deal economic-stimulus program in the early days of the Depression. "The exact number of the buildings involved escapes me at the moment but it could not have been more than eight or ten. The buildings were small save for one somewhat larger building which had a mess hall and kitchen. The larger of the cottages could, we thought, with a few alterations be adapted for the President's needs and the needs of his staff."[2]

The chief of the Bureau of Yards and Docks had then been brought in — a man who was no "stranger to action," as McCrea neatly put it. "In a few short days this building was altered by the Seabees to provide for a combination dining and living room, the President's bedroom, and three small bedrooms. All the small bedrooms had a common bath[room], which had no key! The living room area was, by usual standards, small, no larger in size than a modest living room. At one end was a stone fireplace which contributed greatly to the comfort of the place. The President's bedroom was the largest of the four bedrooms, but it too could be said to be of modest size. One side of the President's bedroom was equipped with a large hinged panel which, when tripped, would fall outward, and serve in an emergency as a ramp and escape route for the President's wheelchair. A combination kitchen and pantry adjoined the dining room. A screened in porch — entrance to which was via the dining room, providing a spectacular view of the surrounding countryside — completed the structure."

The man responsible for the camp, the President had decided, should be his naval aide. "'John,' said he, 'since I shan't be using the *Potomac* except on rare occasions you, in addition to your other duties, are hereby appointed the proprietor and landlord of the camp. And by the way, all camps should have a name. Let's see. I think it quite appropriate that we call this camp Shangri-la' — referring of course to the mythical area. . . . 'What do you say to this?'"[3]

McCrea had said he would be honored — the camp accommodations of "USS Shangri-la" somewhat primitive, but the views stunning, and the air mercifully cool compared with Washington. On Sunday, July 5, 1942, the President drove with Harry Hopkins, McCrea, and a party of friends including Daisy Suckley to "what the papers are calling Shangri-La, 'a cottage in the country'!" as Daisy noted. "No one is supposed to know, in order to give the President some privacy, and also for safety. But I am sure alien spies can find it out somehow without the slightest trouble."[4]

Walking with Hopkins to see the swimming pool, Daisy now found the President "cheerful & delighted & rested" — and reading *Jane's Fighting Ships*, the famous encyclopedia of the world's warships.[5]

Back in Washington the next day, refreshed by his trip to Shangri-la, the President took the first step in bending the chiefs of staff to his will over Gymnast. With the War Department still parrying his wishes, the President needed a new stratagem.

In all confidence, the President had admitted to Daisy, he was more "depressed by the situation" than he was letting on. "If Egypt is taken, it means Arabia, Afghanistan, etc., i.e. the Japs & Germans control everything from the Atlantic to the Pacific — that means all the oil wells, etc. of those regions — a bleak prospect for the United Nations."

"I asked where the blame lies for the present situation in Egypt," the President's confidante noted in her diary after speaking with him. The President thought about her question, then answered with surprising candor. "He said partly Churchill, mostly the bad generals."[6]

Was he, the President, any better than Churchill, though? Were American generals any better than their British counterparts?

Roosevelt found it difficult to understand why Marshall remained so intransigent in pressing for a cross-Channel attack, while objecting to an American invasion of French Northwest Africa. Yes, Russia needed help — but so, too, did the British in Egypt. And urgently. The British Eighth Army seemed to be in its death throes in North Africa, as Rommel drove its remnant forces back almost a thousand miles to Alamein, the last defensive position before Cairo and Alexandria. Was this, then, the best moment to launch a supremely risky cross-Channel Second Front assault that had almost no chance of success, given the number of German divisions defending the French coast and interior? Would not an American landing in Northwest Africa — in Rommel's rear — be the saving of the British in the Middle East, as well as a safe area in which U.S. forces could learn the art of modern war?

Field Marshal Dill, the British representative on the Combined Chiefs of Staff Committee, had been even more pessimistic than Churchill — prompting the President to say to him "that the trouble with the British is that they think they can beat the Germans if they have an equal number of men, tanks, etc." As the President pointed out to Dill, this was a serious error. It was simply "not so — the Germans are better trained, better generaled."[7]

It was, the President reflected, a fact of life — "You can never discipline an Englishman or an American as you can a German," he told Daisy what he'd shared with Dill.[8]

Daisy was charmed by the observation, noting it in her diary. Yet its significance in the President's growing realism went deeper than even she realized. For in that casual, consoling remark to Dill, the President of the United States had put his finger on the problem that his own U.S. generals were still not confronting.

Americans might scoff at the British failure to fight the Germans effectively, despite two years' experience of German tactics and interservice skills in action. *Would Americans fare better in battle, though, straight off the mound?* And was it fair to put them into battle in the supposedly right place but at the wrong time — when they would only get slaughtered? American troops, like most English soldiers, were for the most part *citizen* warriors, the President reflected — not professionals. They lacked the sort of self-sacrificing discipline that seemed second nature to German and Japanese troops.

American and British individualism was, in effect, their undoing against such an enemy. Yet it was also, Roosevelt felt, their ultimate strength — *if* they could be encouraged to work together toward a realistic, common cause in which they believed, and were put into battle in operations that had a reasonable chance of success.

This, then, was the insight that came to the President after Tobruk — and marked a profound shift in his thinking as his nation's commander in chief. Millions of American troops were being called to serve their country. They would do fine, he was sure, if they could be given the chance to learn the arts of modern warfare against German or Japanese troops, on ground of their own choosing, *not the enemy's*. The hostile beaches of mainland France, the President emphatically recognized, were not the place to do it, not yet — whatever General Marshall and his cohort of War Department staffers maintained.

Emboldened by his insight, the President formally asked Bill Leahy to resign on July 6, 1942, as ambassador to Vichy France. He was, the President requested, to leave the State Department, go back on the "active" list as a four-star admiral, and become the President's first-ever "military assistant."

The President had, it seemed, hit upon a solution to his Second Front problem. As Roosevelt explained over lunch with the admiral, at his desk in the Oval Study, Leahy would have his own office at the White House, once reconstruction of the East Wing was completed. As to the responsibilities of his new job, Roosevelt was deliberately vague — but Leahy knew the President well enough to know what he was plotting.

Besides, the admiral — whose wife had died unexpectedly after surgery at a hospital in France that spring — was lonely in Washington. He was thus happy to accept the position: bracing himself for what was, undoubtedly, in store.

22

A Staggering Crisis

Two days after appointing Admiral Leahy to be his new military assistant came the cable Roosevelt had been expecting. Captain McCrea brought it from the Map Room to the President in his bedroom: a personal signal from the Prime Minister of Great Britain, in uncompromising language.

"No responsible British General, Admiral or Air Marshal is prepared to recommend SLEDGEHAMMER" — code name for a cross-Channel invasion of France in the Brittany or Cotentin area that year — "as a practicable operation,"[1] Mr. Churchill commenced his broadside, explaining that the British chiefs of staff would be sending their collective, formal decision to the U.S. Combined Chiefs of Staff that very evening.

The cross-Channel idea was plainly madness in 1942 — as it had always been.

"In the event of a lodgement being effected and maintained it would have to be nourished and the bomber effort on Germany would have to be greatly curtailed," Churchill explained the view of his British chiefs of staff. "All our energies would be involved in defending the Bridgehead. The possibility of mounting a large scale operation in 1943 would be marred if not ruined. All our resources would be absorbed piecemeal on the very narrow front which alone is open. It may therefore be said that premature action in 1942 while probably ending in disaster would decisively injure the prospect of well organized large scale action in 1943."[2] The Prime Minister therefore turned to the alternative.

"I am sure myself that GYMNAST" — the American invasion of French Northwest Africa — "is by far the best chance for effective relief to the Russian front in 1942. This has all along been in harmony with your ideas," Churchill acknowledged. "In fact it is your commanding idea."[3]

The relief the President felt was palpable. The Prime Minister might be an exhausting companion — a meddling commander in chief in dealing with his field officers, and a very, very poor selector of army commanders. His chiseled English prose, however, put most of the paperwork the President received to shame. The telegram was not only splendidly worded in its refusal to carry out a currently impossible military undertaking, it brought the evidence the President had been praying for: that Churchill had overridden his own generals in London in order to back the President's "great secret baby." Since his return to England, the Prime Minister had clearly gotten the British chiefs and the rest of his government to support Gymnast — abandoning their preference for large numbers of U.S. troops to be dispatched to Egypt and the Middle East to give more backbone to existing British imperial forces. "I have consulted cabinet and defence committee and we all agree," Churchill's telegram read. Gymnast it was. "Here is the safest and most fruitful stroke that can be delivered this autumn"[4] — with several summer months now to prepare and launch the invasion of French Northwest Africa, before the Germans could stop it.

But if Churchill could override his generals, could he, the President, override *his* — American generals who were still clamoring for a cross-Channel attack that year, more and more loudly, while opposing Gymnast ever more venomously?

There now arose, in Washington, a veritable uprising or quasi mutiny, as General Marshall declared open hostilities on the British.

Marshall had never liked the President's "great pet scheme," and had done his best over the past year to wean the Commander in Chief from it — culminating in his and Admiral King's uncompromisingly negative memorandum on June 19, 1942. Though the President had been unimpressed by their argument — especially their assertion as to the forces Hitler could deploy against a U.S. invasion of French Northwest Africa — the chiefs had held to their insistence on Bolero, the build-up to a cross-Channel attack, and to Sledgehammer, in particular, to be mounted if possible in 1942.

British deceit in the spring — pretending to be in support of a 1942 cross-Channel assault but in truth opposing it from the start — had not helped. To Marshall — and to Secretary Stimson — the fight against Mr. Roosevelt's Gymnast idea had thus been acerbic and exhausting, filling them with suspicion not only of Churchill but of their own revered President. Refusing to countenance the President's Gymnast plan — which Marshall rightly feared would make a cross-Channel invasion impossible even in 1943, owing to the subsequent demands on U.S. reinforcement and supply, especially in shipping — Marshall had returned from his visit to London in April under the illusion that the British supported, albeit reluctantly, his 1942 cross-Channel plan. Churchill's appearance in Washington had disabused him of that notion. Despite the President's caustic remarks about his and Admiral King's memorandum, however, Marshall had thought he had gotten both the President's and Churchill's consent to hold off any decision on such a 1942 cross-Channel invasion until September 1942. Now, only two weeks after Churchill's departure from Washington, the Prime Minister's new cable on the night of July 8, followed by a similar one from the British chiefs of staff to their U.S. colleagues on the Combined Chiefs of Staff, left no room for misunderstanding. The British were *formally* refusing to carry out a cross-Channel operation that year, despite the generosity of the President in sending so much military help to Egypt.

Marshall, as well as his colleagues and staff, and the secretary of war, were incensed.

For his own part, General Marshall felt doubly betrayed. That the British had lied in pretending they were prepared to mount a cross-Channel attack he was willing to swallow. But why were they now rolling over and supporting the President's preferred course, Gymnast? The British chiefs of staff — especially General Brooke — had, after all, assured Marshall in June, only two weeks before, that they were just as opposed to Gymnast as he and Admiral King were, since they wanted all American help to go to Cairo, not to French Northwest Africa.

In disgust Marshall now exploded. Typically, Winston Churchill, in Marshall's view, wanted to use an American assault on French Northwest Africa as a distraction: a clever way of avoiding the challenge to Britain of a Second Front even in 1943 — but risking only American lives, since Gymnast would be a U.S. undertaking. And, in his view, a very dangerous one.

Ergo, the American response should be, Marshall decided, a switch of American military effort in the war. From "Europe First" to "Japan First."

Japan First?

George Catlett Marshall was admired by all as the very soul of integrity and loyalty — an officer unimpressed by flimflam, always deeply serious, and a first-class administrator. Tall, trim, calm, and direct, he had served as General Pershing's chief of staff in World War I, and was credited with excellent judgment, no matter what pressure he was under. He had never commanded in combat, but had a good eye for talented younger commanders and potential commanders. The President had come to rely on his administrative ability, working together with Secretary Stimson to transform a tiny professional army — seventeenth in world rankings in 1939, behind Romania — into the world's most powerful potential army-air force in 1942: its numbers slated to reach 7,500,000 by the end of the year.

Marshall was not joking, however. He was convinced that America's expanding army should not be frittered away in diversions from the country's main effort in World War II — and the fact that a British prime minister was refusing to assist in mounting a Second Front in 1942 but was now backing the President's deplorable plan reduced the otherwise wise, loyal, and imperturbable chief of staff of the U.S. Army to apparent apoplexy.

At the weekly meeting of the Joint Chiefs of Staff held on July 10, 1942, General Marshall once again excoriated the President's plan for landings in French Northwest Africa as "expensive and ineffectual." The British veto on a cross-Channel attack that year was, he declared, a mark of British pusillanimity, even cowardice. "If the British position must be accepted," he formally proposed to his colleagues, "the U.S. should turn to the Pacific for decisive action against Japan."[5]

Admiral King agreed — knowing the switch would please Admiral Nimitz in his preparations to contest the Japanese operations at Guadalcanal in the Solomon Islands, which the President had authorized.

General MacArthur, too, would be ecstatic. MacArthur had foretold only doom in Europe, whereas in the Pacific there was a chance for the United States to assert its burgeoning air, sea, and military power to good purpose.[6] Switching America's main effort to the war in the Pacific, Marshall thus asserted to his fellow chiefs, "would tend to concentrate rather than scatter U.S. forces." Moreover, such a move would "be highly popular on the West Coast," where there was still great concern about Japanese raids. The general even claimed that "the Pacific War Council, the Chinese, and the personnel of the Pacific Fleet would all be in hearty accord"; and from a strategic point of view in conducting the global war, switching to the Pacific was "second only to BOLERO" — in its potential. Going flat out in the Pacific, in other words, "would be the operation which would have the greatest effect towards relieving the pressure on Russia."[7]

Admiral King heartily agreed. He had never liked Gymnast. The transfer of aircraft carriers from the Pacific to support the invasion of French Northwest Africa would, he claimed, wreck U.S. naval domination of the central and southern Pacific—indeed, he even stated, "in his opinion, the British had never been in wholehearted accord with operations on the continent as proposed by the U.S. He said that, in the European theater, we must fight the Germans effectively to win, and that any departure from full BOLERO plans would result in failure to accomplish this purpose."[8] General Arnold, still only a lieutenant general and subordinate to General Marshall, kept silent.

The chiefs thus concurred, and in the first outright confrontation with their own commander in chief in World War II, they agreed that afternoon to send a new chiefs of staff "Memorandum for the President" drawn up by General Marshall, and signed by both King and Marshall.

Not content with this formal new July 10 memorandum by the Joint Chiefs of Staff, Marshall felt compelled to send an even more personal *third* memorandum, on his own individual account, explaining the Joint Chiefs' second memorandum: again decrying the President's Northwest Africa alternative as "indecisive" and leading to an "ineffective" Second Front in the spring of 1943, if such an invasion were actually mounted. The United States, he maintained, would "nowhere be pressing decisively against the enemy." Therefore, "it is our opinion that we should turn to the Pacific, and use all existing and available dispositions and installations, strike decisively against Japan."[9]

Marshall's advice to the Commander in Chief, then, was simple: that the President should give the British an ultimatum. Full, exclusive cooperation over a cross-Channel Second Front that fall, or latest by the spring of 1943. Otherwise the United States would switch its forces to the Pacific, and leave only token forces in Britain for defense, together with a few U.S. air missions. "Admiral King and I have signed a joint memorandum to you regarding the foregoing," Marshall ended, ominously, enclosing the somewhat sensational document and giving it to a dispatch rider.[10]

The President had already left for Hyde Park the night before. He'd reluctantly undertaken to spend the weekend entertaining Queen Wilhelmina of the Netherlands—the head of state of a main ally in the war against

Hitler and Japan. "The President rather dreads the coming of Queen Wilhelmina because of the stories of her stiff and stern ways that have preceded her," the President's personal secretary noted in his diary—one story being "that she is a teetotaler and once left the room when drinks were brought in."[11]

The Queen's visit proved not nearly as bad as feared—but the arrival of General Marshall and Admiral King's new memorandum was. Delivered by courier on the evening of July 10, it ruined any semblance of peace or relaxation for the President. The new memorandum, he was told, was once again supported by the secretary of war.

It was—Secretary Stimson having become deeply involved. "In the afternoon," the secretary noted in his diary on July 10, "Marshall told me of a new and rather staggering crisis that is coming up in our war strategy. A telegram has come from Great Britain indicating that the British war cabinet are weakening and going back on Bolero and are seeking to revive Gymnast—in other words, they are seeking now to reverse the decision that was so laboriously accomplished when Mr. Churchill was here a short time ago. This would simply be another way of diverting our strength into a channel in which we cannot effectively use it, namely the Middle East. I found Marshall very stirred up and emphatic over it. He is naturally tired of these constant decisions which do not stay made. This is the third time this question will have been brought up by the persistent British and he proposed a solution which I cordially endorsed. As the British won't go through with what they have agreed to, we will turn our backs on them and take up the war with Japan. That was the substance of a memorandum which he wrote and sent to the President this afternoon. It was fully concurred in by the Navy and secretly concurred in by Sir John Dill and the British staff here. I hope it will be successful in preventing a new series of painful negotiations. But there is no use in trying to go ahead with Bolero unless the British are willing to back up their agreements. I rather think this will serve as an effective block."[12]

Stimson, in other words, saw the ultimatum as a bargaining ploy—which, in effect, it was. The secretary and General Marshall had had enough of the President's niceness to the British—indeed, they were so confident their "showdown" would stun the President and compel him as commander in chief to back them that Marshall took the next day off "for rest and recreation at Leesburg," while Stimson went riding with a friend at Woodley, his estate outside Washington.

• • •

Receiving Marshall and King's memorandum at Hyde Park, the President shook his huge head. Not only was the document a renewed repudiation of his "great secret baby," but the document was filled with unsupported assertions and dictatorial absolutes unworthy of the chiefs of staff of the U.S. Army and U.S. Navy.

The memorandum, once again, ridiculed the President's Gymnast plan as "both indecisive and a heavy drain on our resources." It claimed, moreover, "that if we undertake it, we would nowhere be acting decisively against the enemy and would definitely jeopardize our naval position in the Pacific." The two chiefs acknowledged that the United States could not mount a Second Front on its own, however. For a Second Front to succeed, it needed "full and whole-hearted British support," since the British "must of necessity furnish a large part of the forces." Giving up all possibility of an immediate cross-Channel attack in 1942 "not only voids our commitments to Russia," but neither one of the proposed alternatives or "diversions" for that year — Churchill's idea of an invasion of northern Norway or the President's Gymnast plan — would achieve anything, in their unhumble view. Instead, those diversions "will definitely operate to delay and weaken readiness for Roundup [the actual liberation of France] in 1943." The chiefs' recommendation of a switch to operations in the Pacific would, they claimed, not only "be definite and decisive against one of our principal enemies, but would bring concrete aid to the Russians in case Japan attacks them."[13]

It was perhaps the worst-argued strategic document ever produced by America's highest military officers — as studded with ill-defined "definitely," "decisive," and "definitive" claims as MacArthur's most outspoken missives from the Pacific. The President was disappointed in them.

On Sunday, July 12, 1942, having pondered the best tactics to employ, Roosevelt telephoned the secretary of the General Staff, Brigadier General Walter Bedell Smith.[14] To Smith's consternation it was not, however, to ask for a meeting, but for something far more ominous.

23

A Rough Day

INSTEAD OF RESPONDING with anger or invective to his chiefs' defiance, as Churchill would have done, Roosevelt simply turned the tables on General Marshall and Admiral King. They had recommended switching American priorities to the Pacific. Well, then, what exactly *was* their plan for a "decisive and definitive" campaign in that hemisphere?

As Stimson found when he reached the War Department, a "telephone request had come in from the President for a memorandum in detail outlining the steps that would be necessary to make the alternative change over to the Pacific which General Marshall suggested in his memorandum on Friday that he and King would recommend if the British insisted on sabotaging Bolero," the secretary noted in his diary.

Roosevelt was calling their bluff. "This was important and required very immediate and prompt action, for the President wished to have such a memorandum flown up to him this afternoon."[1]

That afternoon? Marshall was not even in Washington that day. Moreover, as became instantly clear to Stimson as a first-class attorney, neither Marshall nor King had actually considered how a "decisive and definitive campaign" switch to the Pacific could be mounted.

As Stimson confided to his diary in embarrassment that night, it was clearly "impossible to have a careful study" of a new Pacific campaign manufactured in a few hours, without prior preparation; in fact it was unwise, even stupid, of Marshall and King to have proposed such a "decisive" switch without first bothering to rehearse its ramifications — and then disappearing for the weekend!

Panic ensued. General Marshall's senior planner, General Handy, was summoned urgently, and "he and his fellows in the General Staff plunged into work on it and I went down to the Department at three o'clock to be ready for consultation on the subject," Stimson noted — the trial lawyer in him reeling at the situation in which Marshall and King's empty threat had placed him and the whole War Office team. "Marshall was called back from his rest at Leesburg and came into the office at the same moment that I came in. By that time General Handy had a rough memorandum ready and Marshall went over to the Navy Department to consult over it with King."[2]

Had the moment in World War II been less serious — Hitler having moved his advance headquarters from East Prussia on July 6 to the Ukraine, near Vinnitsa, to be closer to his armored forces as they raced beyond Voronezh to the Caucasus — the scramble in Washington might have been comical. At the War Department on Constitution Avenue, Secretary Stimson read over Marshall's proposed reply, together with his assistant secretary of war, John McCloy. McCloy had been a captain in World War I like Stimson, but could hardly be expected to come up with a detailed "definitive" military strategy for the Pacific on his own, let alone in five minutes.

McCloy was quiet — sensing his bosses had been exposed. "He has always been somewhat of a 'Middle-East-ner' but I think my arguments before Marshall came in had pretty well knocked that out of him," Stimson claimed[3] — erroneously.

"Marshall came back and told us that he and King had revised it [the Handy memorandum] rather drastically and tried to put a little more punch into it. As soon as it was written out he brought me the revised draft, a copy of which I attach," Stimson wrote in his diary[4] — the document signed by Marshall, King, and Arnold.

"I told him and Marshall that I approved of the [new] memorandum as the only thing to do in such a crisis. I hope that the threat to the British will work and that Bolero will be revived. If it is not revived, if they persist in their fatuous defeatist position as to it, the Pacific operation while not so good as Bolero will be a great deal better and have a much stronger chance of ultimate effective victory than a tepidly operated Bolero in which the British do not put their whole heart."[5]

Still, George Marshall remained uneasy.

Marshall hated to be challenged in such a way — a general "as cold as a fish," in the words of the secretary of the Joint Chiefs of Staff.[6] As chief of staff of the U.S. Army, Marshall was the first to point out holes in subordinates' logic and to question unsubstantiated claims. He also hated to be contradicted over his decisions. When Major General George S. Patton protested in June over Marshall's decision to send only one U.S. division to Egypt to help fortify the British line at Alamein, rather than the two that Patton had said would be essential for such a mercy mission to be effective, Marshall had responded like a viper. Patton, he ordered, was to be put on the first plane from Washington to California "that morning"[7] for insubordination. "You see, McNarney, that's the way to handle Patton," Marshall had boasted[8] — even claiming later he had "scared him half to death."[9]

Now it was Marshall who was sweating for his career — yet unwilling to admit he might be wrong. He was for the most part an imperturbable officer, but he could be obstinate where his pride was concerned. His dander was up — unwilling to accept he had made a stupid mistake in proposing a course of action he had not thought through: a mistake he would have lashed a subordinate for making, but which he only made worse as, challenged by the President, he now faced the secretary of war — and argued for the seriousness of his overnight Pacific ultimatum.

"Marshall was eloquent and forceful in his advocacy of the plan," Stimson dictated that night. "He is a little more optimistic as to the speed with which he thinks Japan can be knocked out in the Pacific than I am. But he has thought it out more carefully than I and has more facts at his disposal. He told me that Sir John Dill, who is very loyal to Bolero and has been very helpful to us, has sent a telegram to Churchill warning him that, if the British government persisted in their defeatism as to Bolero, we would turn our backs and go to the Pacific. Such a telegram ought to have great force with the British government."[10]

This was to dig themselves only deeper — the U.S. Joint Chiefs of Staff, via General Dill, going behind the President's back to the British government.

As Marshall, King, and Arnold admitted in the new memorandum they now sent by air to the President, "There is no completed detailed plan for major offensive operations in the Pacific. Such plans are in process of being developed," they claimed — untruthfully. "Our current strategy contemplates the strategic defensive in the Pacific and offensive in the Atlantic," they acknowledged; therefore to switch to offensive in the

Pacific and withdraw from Europe, or merely remain on the defensive in the British Isles and Iceland, would, they confessed, be a mammoth planning task. "A change therein would require a great deal of detailed planning which will take considerable time."[11]

The lameness of this excuse was embarrassing even to Stimson. If the heads of the U.S. Army, Navy, and Air Force had no idea how such a switch could be done, why had the chiefs of staff gone out on a limb to propose such a supposedly "decisive" campaign in the Pacific?

Aware the issue was dynamite, Stimson held a war council with all senior army and air officers at the War Department on July 13, 1942, and "cautioned all present that this matter must not be spoken of to anyone whatever."[12] If word should get out to the press that the chiefs of staff were in revolt against their own commander in chief, the entire direction of the war could be compromised. Moreover, if word of Marshall's recommendation of a switch to the Pacific reached MacArthur, there would be no end of pressure from that source to make good on the threat.

The fact was, Colonel Stimson knew, to switch all U.S. military attention to the Pacific was something that had never been seriously studied. ("This shows how little we had really thought of the Pacific," Stimson admitted when annotating the account in his diary, after the war.)[13]

Hastily contrived, Marshall's arguments for such a major change in strategy defied common sense, Stimson recognized. Their argument that such a diversion would dissuade the Japanese from declaring war on the Soviet Union was utterly without merit, since there was no evidence whatever that the Japanese were currently intending to attack the Soviet Union — Japan far too heavily invested in China and across half of Asia and the Pacific. American operations to clear the Japanese from their conquests in the Malay Barrier would take *years*, even if such a Marshall-proposed switch to the Pacific took place — without having any appreciable effect on Hitler's war, or helping the Russians. Moreover, in terms of a reinforced Pacific counteroffensive, American soldiers would be fighting and dying to restore the Netherlands East Indies to a colonialist European power; Malaya and Burma to another colonialist power; and the Philippines to its mandated independence as a sovereign country. What was the urgency for this? And where was the "decisiveness," that such a campaign would offer?

While Marshall oversaw the dispatch to the President of his explanation of what he and Admiral King proposed to do in the Pacific, Stimson went to dinner at the Chevy Chase Club, somewhat perturbed.

It was now the President's move.

At Hyde Park, the President continued with his duties of hospitality toward Queen Wilhelmina — showing her his new presidential library and his estate, holding a picnic, then inviting her to dinner at the Big House, without ever intimating to her that one of the great crises of the war was now taking place: a crisis that would affect her country, the Netherlands, more directly than any other, since a cross-Channel Second Front promised to liberate Holland, while a switch to the war in the Pacific promised to oust the Japanese from the Netherlands East Indies — neither of which he was intending to do that year!

Receiving the new memorandum from Marshall and King, the President chose at first to ignore it — not even summoning his new military assistant, Admiral Leahy, who was in hospital at the Naval Medical Center at Bethesda, outside Washington, having emergency treatment for an abscessed tooth. Messrs. Stimson, Marshall, and King could wait, the President decided, until he returned to the White House to discuss the matter in detail. In the meantime, however, he let them know he was utterly unimpressed by their paper on Pacific strategy.

"My first impression," he notified them in a warning telegram July 14, "is that it is exactly what Germany hoped the United States would do following Pearl Harbor."

As if this was not enough, he added another paragraph.

"Secondly, it does not in fact provide use of American troops in fighting," as he pointed out tartly, "except in a lot of islands whose occupation will not affect the world situation this year or next.

"Third: it does not help Russia or the Near East. Therefore it is disapproved of at present."

He signed himself "Roosevelt C-in-C."[14]

In the entire war President Roosevelt would never express his contempt so forcefully. In addition to this rejoinder the President then added a further message, saying he wanted to see General Marshall at the White House first thing upon his arrival in Washington the next morning; he would then see all three Joint Chiefs in the afternoon. He had meanwhile "definitely" decided, he alerted them in the cable, to send General Marshall with Admiral King along with Harry Hopkins to London "immediately." There they could thrash out the matter of the next steps to be taken in Europe, North Africa, or the Middle East — but they were not to make mention of any empty Pacific threats; they should arrange to fly "if possible on Thursday, 16 July."[15]

The President's devastating response to the Marshall-King memorandum was perhaps the tersest rejection Marshall had ever experienced — or would experience — in his life. He read it aloud to his fellow chiefs of staff at a Joint Chiefs of Staff meeting on the afternoon of Tuesday, July 14. Colonel Albert Wedemeyer of the War Department — the officer reputed (though without proof) to have leaked the Victory Program before Pearl Harbor to the McCormick press — kept notes.

However humiliating, the chiefs would have to take the President's telegram seriously, Wedemeyer recorded, since "unquestionably the President would require military operations in Africa."[16]

The question was, therefore: *where in Africa?*

Once again the "relative merits of operations in Africa and in the Middle East" were discussed — none of the chiefs happy about the President's pressure on them. Despite the tart language of the President's telegram, none showed embarrassment or willingness to rethink their stance over switching to a "Japan First" strategy.

"All agreed to the many arguments previously advanced among the military men in the Army and Navy that operations in the Pacific would be the alternative if Sledgehammer or Bolero were not accepted wholeheartedly by the British. However, there was an acceptance that apparently our political system would require major operations this year in Africa."[17]

"Our political system" meant the United States Constitution, which stipulated that the President of the United States be commander in chief of the nation's armed forces.

The refusal of the U.S. chiefs of staff to consider the folly of a premature cross-Channel invasion was breathtaking in its lack of professional military realism — yet their response, when challenged, had only been to blame the democratic "political system." This did not reflect well on them.

For his part, Secretary Stimson preferred to blame "the other" politician, Winston Churchill. The President had asked to see Marshall, Arnold, and King on his return to Washington, before they left for England, but Stimson decided he should perhaps see the President first, and attempt a plea bargain: explaining perhaps that the chiefs were not *really* pressing for a turn to the Pacific, just trying to put further pressure on the British to be serious about a Second Front that year.

Landing at Bolling Field at 9:15 a.m. on July 15, 1942, Stimson thus went "directly to the White House where the President had just returned from his absence at Hyde Park. I had no appointment but he very kindly saw me and I had a long talk with him about the crisis which is happening in regard to Bolero."[18]

For Stimson, his July 15 interview with the Commander in Chief in the Oval Office was painful. The secretary brought with him a book he had recently been rereading, first at Fort Devens, then at his one-hundred-acre estate on Long Island: Field Marshal William Robertson's *Soldiers and Statesmen,* with its vivid account of Churchill's Dardanelles fiasco in World War I.

The decision "to go half-baked to the Dardanelles is being repeated now as to the proposed expeditions to North Africa and the Middle East which Churchill twenty-five years afterwards is trying to entangle us into," Stimson had noted in his diary two days before. "The trouble is neither he nor the President has a methodical and careful mind. They do not implement their proposal with any careful study of the supporting facts upon which the success of such expeditions must ultimately rest."[19]

Handing over the Robertson book, Stimson "begged" the President "to read the chapter on the Dardanelles in which I had carefully marked important passages," the secretary noted that night. "The President asserted that he himself was absolutely sound on Bolero which must go ahead unremittingly, but he did not like the manner of the memorandum in regard to the Pacific, saying it was a little like 'taking up your dishes and going away.'"[20]

Stimson, as a lawyer, was cut to the quick by the accusation of childish pique. "I told him I appreciated the truth in that but it was absolutely essential to use it as a threat of our sincerity in regard to Bolero if we expected to get through the hides of the British and he agreed to that. He said he was going to send Marshall and King abroad to thrash the matter out in London. I don't know how much effect I had on him although he was very clear in his support of Bolero. I think he has lingering thoughts of doing something in the Middle East in spite of my thumping assertions of the geographical impossibilities of doing anything effective."[21]

Clearly, Stimson was embarrassed by his own threat of a switch to the Pacific — indeed, he later noted that "the Pacific argument from me was mainly a bluff."[22]

A bluff that had been called.

Shaming the secretary of war and the Joint Chiefs of Staff into dropping their recommendation of a diversion to the Pacific was one thing. Getting Marshall and Stimson to back Gymnast, Roosevelt's "great secret baby," was another.

It became even harder once General Marshall, following Stimson's visit, arrived in the Oval Office.

Harsh words were exchanged.

Stimson noted the outcome later that night. "I had a talk with Marshall over our respective conferences in the White House, he having seen the President immediately after my early morning interview. He evidently had a thumping argument with the President and thought he had knocked out the President's lingering affection for Gymnast," the American invasion of Northwest Africa, "and then Middle East. Between us the President must have had a rough day on those subjects. I had told him that when you are trying to hold a wild horse the way to do it was to get him by the head and not by the heels, and that was the trouble with the British method of trying to hold Hitler in the Mediterranean and the Middle East. The better way would be to get a grip on his head."[23]

Marshall had, he said, "pointed out to the President that by going into the Middle East we lost Sledgehammer and Bolero '43 and got nowhere, being everywhere on the defensive, for the Middle Eastern operation at best was a defensive operation even if successful. At the same time by so doing, we put ourselves in great peril on the Pacific. Such a situation therefore cost us a year's delay in which Germany would recuperate herself while we simply imperiled ourselves."

For his part, Marshall was clearly not surrendering his notion of a switch to the Pacific lightly — whether out of pride or genuine strategic belief was unclear. The President had insisted on a campaign to hold Guadalcanal, in the Solomon Islands, as the ultimate stop line in confronting the Japanese. Well, then, switching to the Pacific, Marshall maintained, would permit the United States to build upon that, take the offensive, and win a victory there that "would have a tremendous beneficial effect on the general fortunes of the war. It would clear our Pacific area," halt Japanese thrust in the Indian Ocean, and "thereby make it impossible for Germany and Japan to clasp hands."[24]

The sheer silliness of this argument had, however, left the President speechless.

As Stimson noted, the President had had a rough day—he and the War Department clearly still at loggerheads.

Marshall's "thumping argument" with the Commander in Chief did his cause no good. Nor did it improve Marshall's chances of being chosen to command the Bolero landings, once they took place — indeed, Marshall's obstinacy and his outburst in the White House would ultimately wreck his chances of military fame.

Even in retrospect Marshall could not admit his error — blaming the "politicians" for a decision he deplored. "Churchill was rabid for Africa. Roosevelt was for Africa," Marshall recalled. "Both men were aware of the political necessities. It is something we [in the military] fail to take into consideration," he later said. "We failed to see that the leader in a democracy must keep the people entertained. That may sound like the wrong word, but it conveys the thought. . . . People demand action."[25]

This remark was unworthy of Marshall, who in other respects was an entirely honorable man. The "people" of America and the free world certainly demanded action, as newspapers in the United States and Britain trumpeted in 1942 — but in terms of political pressure, the action they wanted, by an overwhelming majority, was Marshall's Second Front.

Far from responding to political, and popular, pressure, the President was, however, doing the opposite: patiently preferring, as U.S. commander in chief, a military operation that had a reasonable chance of success. Moreover, one that might change the course of World War II if it succeeded.

PART TEN

The Mutiny

24

Stimson's Bet

NEITHER THEN NOR LATER did Marshall concede that the President, in his role as U.S. commander in chief, was demonstrating a greater military realism in devising Allied strategy in 1942 than his U.S. Army chief of staff.

In the meantime, however, the President wished to make sure there would be no misunderstanding — or ill will. Gymnast would not succeed unless the War Department got behind the plan wholeheartedly. He therefore wanted Marshall and King to see for themselves, in person, how impossible an imminent Bolero operation was — not because the British were cowards, but because Hitler's forces were waiting, and the Allies could not, that year, assemble preponderant force to ensure its success. Drawing up in his own handwriting General Marshall's and Admiral King's instructions for their mission to London on July 16, Roosevelt gave the document to Harry Hopkins, who was to fly with them — and make certain they stayed to the script.

Paragraph nine was direct and to the point. "I am opposed to an American all-out effort in the Pacific against Japan with the view to her defeat as quickly as possible," the President made clear. Yet some form of Second Front was desirable that year, since Hitler — whose troops were smashing their way deep into the Caucasus, as well as toward the gates of Cairo, at Alamein — would otherwise be given time to achieve total control of Europe. "It is of the utmost importance that we appreciate that the defeat of Japan does not defeat Germany and that American concentration against Japan this year or in 1943 increases the chance of complete [Nazi] domination of Europe and Africa." On the other hand, "Defeat of Germany means the defeat of Japan, probably without firing a shot or losing a life."[1]

There was to be no switch to the Pacific.

Successive military historians would extol General Marshall as the great architect and "organizer" of American military operations in World War II: a "titan"[2] whose strategic grasp and patient handling of his commander in chief would, like Marshall's opposite number in London, General Alan Brooke, entitle him to the highest pantheon in military history.

Such accolades were understandable with regard to a man of noble character — especially in countering the excessive admiration, even adulation, garnered by World War II field generals such as Eisenhower, Patton, Montgomery, and MacArthur. Certainly with regard to Marshall's administrative achievement there would be every reason to laud his record in World War II. But as to his strategic and tactical ability, such tributes were way off the mark.

As commander in chief, the challenge for Roosevelt was thus how to marshal Marshall: how to direct, encourage, and support his work at the War Department, while stopping him from losing the war for America. While Marshall and King journeyed to London on their presidential mission, therefore, the Commander in Chief decided now to put his coup de main into action — in their absence.

Ambassador Leahy, emerging from dental hospital, was summoned to see the President on July 18, 1942. The admiral would not only be his military assistant, the Commander in Chief announced, but his new chief of staff, or deputy. As the sole senior military officer supporting the American invasion of French Northwest Africa, Leahy was critical to the President's success in avoiding American defeat on the beaches of mainland France that year, and instead adopting the President's preferred course: U.S. landings in Vichy-held Northwest Africa, before the Germans could occupy the area. Leahy was therefore instructed by the President to become a member of the Joint Chiefs of Staff Committee, and the Combined Chiefs of Staff. Not only a member, in fact. He was, the President laid down, to be the chairman of the Combined Chiefs of Staff — speaking for the Commander in Chief.

Before submitting his formal resignation as U.S. ambassador to Vichy France, Leahy was asked first, however, to do everything in his power at the State Department, where Leahy still had an office, to ensure the

United States did not side with General de Gaulle, leader of the Free French, lest this lead to a hostile Vichy response to an American landing in Morocco and Algeria, as it had done when de Gaulle's Free French forces had attempted to assault Dakar, in 1940. This, in a meeting with the secretary of state, Cordell Hull, Leahy promptly did. ("Conferred with Secretary of State Hull regarding the advisability of maintaining diplomatic relations with the French Government in Vichy," Leahy noted in his diary).[3]

Four days later, on July 22, Leahy then transferred his papers from the State Department to the Combined Chiefs of Staff Building, at 1901 Constitution Avenue, and "took up my duties as Chief of Staff to the Commander in Chief of the Army and Navy of the United States," as Leahy proudly wrote in his daily diary, "which duties included presiding over the Joint Chiefs of Staff and the Combined Chiefs of Staff."[4]

By the time Marshall and King returned from England, the coup would be complete: the Commander in Chief's own man in control of the Combined Chiefs.

In the meantime, the Marshall-King mission fared badly at the hands of the British. The officers were forbidden by the President to use bluff or blackmail by threatening an American switch to a "Pacific First" strategy. Without the threat, they found, as the President knew would happen, that the British were wholly opposed to a cross-Channel invasion that year for the soundest of military reasons: namely, that it would fail.

In Washington, Secretary Stimson, on July 23, was stunned. Initial cables from Marshall had seemed as if the American chiefs were making headway, he had thought.[5] "A very bad jolt came this morning at nine thirty in the shape of a telegram from Marshall," he recorded in his diary, however — a cable "saying the British War Cabinet had definitely refused to go on with Sledgehammer and that perforce negotiations were going on along other lines."[6]

Stimson knew exactly what "other lines" signified.

"I went at once over to the White House," Stimson recorded, "and got into the President's room before he was up" — only to find he was too late. The President "had received his telegrams to the same effect last night and had replied to them."[7]

There was little that the war secretary could say or do. "Apparently

Marshall tried hard to carry his point," dropping all pretense of switching U.S. priority to the Pacific, while "offering to give up an attempt on the Pas de Calais," which the British said would be suicidal, "and to take instead another place" on the French coast, such as Brittany, using it as a quasi-permanent cross-Channel bridgehead through the winter — Sledgehammer. "But the British were obdurate and Marshall had informed the President that we would be unable to go with any Sledgehammer attack without their cordial cooperation."

This was exactly as President Roosevelt had anticipated. "The President had telegraphed expressing his regrets but saying American troops must get into action somewhere in 1942. He then suggested in order of their priority a number of places to the south, each of which seemed to me to be a dangerous diversion," Stimson lamented, "impossible of execution within the time we have."[8]

Stimson was now hopelessly outfoxed. He had been living, he began to realize, under a delusion in thinking Marshall was making headway with the British over a cross-Channel assault — an initial landing to be made in the fall of 1942, then reinforced in 1943, followed by a drive on Berlin.

Stimson had even met up with Frank Knox, to see if he could obtain *his* support and extend the strategic struggle to members of the cabinet. With the navy secretary by his side he had then approached the U.S. secretary of state, the most senior member of the administration, and had given Mr. Hull a grand *tour d'horizon militaire,* telling him the United States had enough forces to launch a cross-Channel attack *and* continue fighting in the Pacific, but not enough to chase their own President's red herrings. A "diversion of strength to an African expeditionary force would be fatal to both," he told the secretary of state, who seemed to have little or no idea what Stimson was talking about. Nor did Secretary Knox — who looked bemused by Stimson's "rather long-winded explanation," of current army and navy plans — Bolero, Sledgehammer, Roundup, et al. — which the navy secretary "has thus far been unable to assimilate," Stimson noted with irritation.

Stimson had been "amazed again at how little he [Secretary Knox] knows about the plans of his own people. This time I hope I got it across," he added, "and, when I parted with Knox on the street after we had left Hull's office, he expressed his warm appreciation of the entire situation and said he would back us up. We shall need him for we never can tell what is going to happen in the White House, although I hope that the President will this time stick to his confession of faith as to Bolero."[9]

With the arrival of Marshall and King's cable reporting the British war cabinet's latest rejection of a cross-Channel invasion that year, however, the bottom fell out of Stimson's strategic world. Given his open attempts to turn members of the cabinet against the President, he was deeply embarrassed — in fact, after several hours trying to calm down, on his return to the War Department, Stimson dictated a formal letter to the President, deploring the "fatigued and defeatist mental outlook of the British government," and had it couriered to the White House.[10]

The letter was as ill conceived as it was jejune. In a last-ditch effort to save Marshall's preferred strategy, he now urged the President to authorize Marshall and King to insist the Allies put all their eggs in one basket: discard the idea of a cross-Channel attack in 1942, but concentrate all efforts on preparing at least for a 1943 invasion of France — with no question of any "diversions" to Africa. American forces — "young vigorous, forward-looking Americans" — would, he claimed, have "a revolutionary effect" on the British. He even cabled General Marshall to tell him what he had written the President.

Stimson's appeal fared as badly as the chiefs' argument in London, however — as Stimson recognized when there was a knock on his door the next morning, July 24, 1942.

In came four-star Admiral Bill Leahy, the new military chief of staff to the Commander in Chief of the Army and Navy of the United States, who had arrived to talk to him — on the instructions of the President.

Stimson, a first-class prosecutor, did not propose to go down without a fight. He attempted to give Leahy, before the admiral could tell the secretary to get in line with the President's wishes, a brief history of the cross-Channel project since the previous December, hoping to turn Leahy against the Commander in Chief.

As Stimson claimed to Leahy, Marshall had gotten apparent British acceptance of the scheme on his last trip to London, in April, but then "Churchill had come over and tried to break it in June; and how we had rounded him up and again gotten his acceptance; and how he had jumped the boundary for the third time."[11]

Stimson's ranch metaphors had little effect on the new chief of staff, however — a full admiral, a former U.S. ambassador to Vichy France, and a supporter of Roosevelt's plan to invade Vichy French Northwest Africa, *not* German-occupied France. "I also gave him a copy of my last letter to the President about continuing the influx of men and munitions into Britain and he read it. But he dropped remarks which confirmed my fears that the President was only giving lip service to Bolero," Stimson confessed in his diary that night, "and that he really was thinking of Gymnast."

Stimson was at last correct — Leahy noting in his own diary that he returned from Stimson's office to the White House for an interview with the President "in which we discussed the practicability of 'Gymnast' in 1942."[12]

Matters were now moving fast. As Stimson dined quietly with his wife at his Woodley Mansion home, there came the "long awaited message from London giving the arrangement arrived at by the conference": Gymnast.

To me "it was most disappointing, not to say appalling," Stimson confided, "for Marshall and Hopkins had apparently been compelled, in order to get an agreement, to agree to a most serious diversion of American troops."[13] Not only were United States forces to embark on landings in French Northwest Africa, but the plan was to be enlarged! Instead of being just the President's plan for U.S. landings in Morocco and Algeria, the British — the very people who would not land troops across the English Channel — would contribute twenty thousand troops to back up the American landing at Algiers.

Stimson's heart sank. With a sickening sense of doom, he went over the cable with Marshall's deputy, General McNarney, who was with him, and "analyzed it, he agreeing with my analysis, and then after he had gone I got the President on the telephone and gave him my views."

It was fruitless to object. The President was at least compassionate in victory. "He said that he was strongly opposed to the giving up of Bolero but I could see," Stimson noted, "that nevertheless he was anxious to go on with Gymnast. And I felt in my soul that the going on with Gymnast would necessarily destroy Bolero even in 1943 and throw us on the defensive."[14]

The President, by contrast, was clearly delighted. Far from fearing it would put the United States on the "defensive," he thought his plan would put America on the *offensive* — a shot that would be heard round the world in the next few weeks.

"The President asked me to come to the White House bringing Arnold and McNarney to meet him and Admiral Leahy at 11:30 tomorrow Saturday," Stimson recorded.[15]

The President, it appeared, had truly taken over as commander in chief.

Henry Louis Stimson was nothing if not obstinate — a trait that had made him a fortune as a trial lawyer, but something of a millstone as secretary of war. He still thought he could, at the last hour, deflect the President from his preferred course, and therefore now "hurried down to the Department" early on July 25, where he "dictated an analysis of my views," as he called it[16] — driving with Generals McNarney and Arnold to the White House and handing his latest memorandum to the President, who received him with his new chief of staff, Admiral Leahy, standing behind him.

The President did not even look at it. He had, he announced, "decided that the going on with Sledgehammer this autumn was definitely out of the question," Stimson recorded.[17] The President had already telegraphed to Marshall, King, and Hopkins "that he accepted the terms of the agreement they had negotiated with Churchill except that he wished a landing made in Gymnast not later than October 30" — i.e., before the November congressional elections.[18] Hopkins was instructed to tell the British prime minister it was now "full speed ahead" on Gymnast — which was renamed "Torch" that day.[19]

It appeared to be a done deal — yet *still* Stimson objected to the idea, as did the senior air and army officers who had accompanied him to the President's office. "McNarney, Arnold, and I pointed out to him the dangers of the situation produced by this operation as contrasted with an operation in the Pacific."[20]

The Pacific? This was, given the weakness of King and Marshall's amateurish paper on the merits of a "Pacific First" strategy, a mistake. In any event it was of no avail. "I cross-examined him as to his realization that his decision on Gymnast would certainly curtail and hold up Bolero," Stimson added — and with complete frankness the President "admitted that it would," thus delaying, therefore, an eventual cross-Channel operation until 1944.[21]

Stimson was mortified. Pointing to his memorandum, he said he wanted it to be placed on record that he, the secretary of war of the United States, completely opposed the U.S. landings in Northwest Africa — indeed, in perhaps the single most dramatic gesture of the war's direction since Pearl Harbor, Stimson took up the President's offer to wager on the outcome of the landings: Stimson betting, in effect, against the success of his fellow Americans.

"I told him," Stimson recorded in his diary, "I wanted this paper read at the time when the bets were decided" — i.e., when the landings were made, that fall. "The decision," Stimson recorded, "marks what I feel to be a very serious parting of the ways." The secretary of war was distraught. "We have turned our back on the path of what I consider sound and correct strategy," he lamented, "and are taking a course which I feel will lead to a dangerous diversion and a possible disaster."[22]

Stimson's bleak "prophecy," as he referred to it afterward, was dire: that Russia would likely be conquered by the Germans that very year. As a result, if the United States went ahead with the invasion of Northwest Africa, a "large portion" of American troops would be left "isolated in Great Britain, Africa and Australia" — leaving "a Germany victorious over Russia" and "free to turn its forces on us."[23]

In the light of history, Stimson's prediction said little for his acumen. The war secretary's own preferred strategy for America was, if anything, even more fanciful. If the British would not mount a Sledgehammer version of a Second Front that year, he now felt the United States should switch all its forces to the West Coast of America, leaving only enough U.S. forces "consolidated" in Britain to be able to launch an "overwhelming attack on Germany if and when that time finally arrives" — while in the Pacific, Indian Ocean, and Far East the United States should seek "check-mating Japan's attack against Iran and India; falling on Japan's back in Siberia; and opening access to China through Burma."[24]

Japan's attack against Iran and India? Like the President, Admiral Leahy could only rub his eyes in disbelief when he read the war secretary's memorandum.

The Japanese, the admiral knew, had withdrawn their navy to home waters after their devastating defeat at Midway in June 1942; they would not be able to replace their sunken aircraft carriers for *years*. A successful invasion of India from the Burmese border or in the Indian Ocean was now unlikely, given the amount of air power the United States had diverted to protect the British. Moreover, how Stimson hoped to get Stalin to permit U.S. forces to move into *Siberia* and thereby risk Russian forces having to divert their efforts into a war with Japan, at a time when Soviet forces were only holding the German armies by the skin of their teeth, or how they might miraculously reopen the road to China through Japanese-held Burma, was beyond Leahy's comprehension. As Leahy noted laconically in his own diary that evening, the two-hour meeting that was held "with regard to a second front in 1942" had been lamentable. Secretary Stimson and his War Department team had been utterly and wholly negative. The President demanded, as Leahy noted, not pique but action: "an effort in the 'Gymnast' plan this Fall." But "the Army was not favorably disposed."[25]

Adamantly *opposed* would have been a better description. Marshall and Stimson seemed to have infected the entire senior staff of the War Department. General Eisenhower, who had arrived ahead of Marshall in London to take command of U.S. troops in Britain in preparation for a cross-Channel Bolero attack, even went as far as to call the July 22 cancellation of Sledgehammer "the blackest day in history."[26]

Stymied in their efforts at the White House, Secretary Stimson and Generals McNarney and Arnold returned to the War Department on July 25 to lick their wounds.

The next day, July 26, found the war secretary "very depressed." To his shame, he would never admit to the President that he, Roosevelt, had been right. Nor would he apologize, or make good on his bet. In his memoirs, written after the President's death, he glided over the saga,[27] unwilling to be reminded of his great protest in July 1942, in which he had thought of himself as a sort of Revolutionary orator, adopting the language and nobility of the Declaration of Independence. "They have been deaf to the voice of justice and consanguinity," the famous text had described the British under King George III. "We must, therefore, acquiesce in the necessity, which denounces our Separation, and hold them, as we hold the rest of mankind, Enemies in War, in Peace Friends."

Stimson had certainly felt the same way.

Even when reading over his diary, in private, after the war's end, Stimson remained surprisingly churlish. "As I look back on this paper," he wrote of his infamous bet and memorandum, "it seems clear that the one thing which saved us from the disaster" that he'd forecast "was:

1. the unexpected victory of Russia at Stalingrad
2. enormous luck in landing in Africa
3. success over submarines."[28]

Given that the Russian success at Stalingrad took place months *after* Operation Torch, as did Allied success against the U-boat menace, this was ungracious.

At Woodley Mansion, meantime, Stimson confided to his diary his sense of foreboding at "the evil of the President's decision. It may not ripen into immediate disaster. What I foresee is difficult and hazardous and very likely successful attempts made to attempt a landing in north-western Africa" — to be followed, however, by an American failure, since "even when obtained, it will be a lodgement more or less like that of the British at Gallipoli in 1915 — troops suffering constant attacks from the German air force and possibly German and Spanish land troops."

Stimson's mix of bravado, pessimism, and abject fear had reduced him to a wreck. He now worried for the safety of General Marshall, who was returning by air to Washington in poor flying weather. "On the whole this is written on a blue Monday morning," he confessed on July 27, 1942 — and his mood only got bluer the following afternoon, when Marshall's Stratoliner arrived from London and the secretary of war was given the "full story of what happened" — "a somber tale and I see very little light in it," the war secretary noted.[29]

Knowing that Stimson had spoken not only for General Arnold but for General Marshall, General McNarney, and most senior staff officers at the War Department, the President was acutely aware, in the White House, that he needed to change not only their minds but their hearts: to rally them to his Northwest Africa cause if the landings were to succeed.

25

A Definite Decision

THE PRESIDENT WAS INCREASINGLY disappointed in his aging war secretary — and furious when leaks began to filter into the American press
that the Commander in Chief was ignoring the advice of his senior military advisers.[1]

Fortunately, one of the President's qualities as a leader was to focus
on the positive aspects of an individual's character. Stimson's behavior
seemed uncharacteristic of the secretary, who despite his party affiliation
had hitherto been a loyal colleague in cabinet, and an effective administrator of the War Department alongside General Marshall. He had handled
the awkward business of internment of Japanese Americans on the West
Coast, and the noninternment of German Americans and Italian Americans on the East Coast, with tact and skill, even if the Japanese "relocation" was, in many ways, a tragedy. As reports of Japanese atrocities multiplied and anti-Japanese feeling grew, any hope of being able to release
the internees early was dashed. It was, Stimson had found, simply easier
to leave them in camps well away from the West Coast, where they would
be out of public sight and out of mind.[2] Stimson had also taken quiet
responsibility for development of the top-secret "diabolical weapon"[3] that
the President had ordered to be developed before the Germans could do
so, and was handling that efficiently, too. Above all, though, Stimson was
a Republican, and thus represented crucial bipartisanship in the Roosevelt administration in its conduct of the war — especially with midterm
elections approaching in November that could affect the passage of all
future legislation.

If Stimson's leaks were in part designed to stop Roosevelt from firing
him, they worked. They did not, however, change the President's mind —
Roosevelt simply bottling up his irritation rather than seeking a further

fight with his war secretary. Having initially ignored Stimson's memorandum when the secretary brought it to the White House in person, he now refused to respond to Stimson in writing. He did, however, set down his written response for posterity. Ever the antiquarian and history buff, Roosevelt wanted historians, at least, to have the truth. "Memorandum to go with Memorandum from the Secretary of War dated July 25, 1942," the President therefore dictated a response to his secretary, which he ordered should be filed with the rest of his secret papers at his presidential library in Hyde Park.[4]

"This memorandum from the Secretary of War is not worth replying to in detail," the President wrote bluntly, "because it is contradictory in terms and fails to meet the objective as of the Summer of 1942." The threat of further expansion of Japanese conquest in the Pacific was now almost nil — "They seem to be making little progress westward or southward," the President noted, thanks to the Battle of Midway. His decision to contest Japanese occupation of Guadalcanal in the Solomon Islands would, he was certain, seal off the Japanese rampage in the South Pacific. To mount an American amphibious offensive in the Pacific would, however, take "one to two years — and the total lack of effect on Germany of such a major offensive" would be unconscionable, in his view. It would not "win the war," particularly if "Germany puts Russia completely out of action, occupies the Near East and the Persian Gulf and starts down the west coast of Africa."

Europe or its doorstep, by contrast, was different. "On the other hand," as he pointed out, "helping Russia and Britain to contain Germany this Autumn and undertake an offensive in 1943 has a good chance of forcing Germany out of the war, in which case Japan could not conduct war in the Pacific alone for more than a few months."

In that, at least, the President and Colonel Stimson were as one. "The Secretary of War fails to realize," however, the Commander in Chief went on, "the situation which prompted me to send Hopkins, Marshall and King [to London] to urge 'Sledgehammer' or, failing that, some definite offensive, using American ground troops in 1942." The result had been a foregone — and in his view — correct conclusion. "They find 'Sledgehammer' is impracticable and, therefore, make the other proposal," the President's plan for U.S. landings in French Northwest Africa — a plan "with which the British," having initially objected to it, now "agree."

In the President's eyes the strategic situation was as clear as crystal —

and Stimson's wild alternatives quite unworthy of an American secretary of war. "The Secretary of War says in effect:

(a) Sledgehammer should not be abandoned.
(b) He offers no alternative for 1942.
(c) He agrees to further preparations for 'Bolero' which is, however, one year off.
(d) He speaks vaguely of some kind of major operation in the Pacific area."[5]

With devastating logic the President thereby punctured Stimson's warnings of "disaster" unless his strategy was followed; indeed, he found himself incredulous at how foolish his secretary of war was being — much as Lincoln, as commander in chief, had despaired of some of his colleagues during the Civil War.

In the following days the President did his best, along with his new chief of staff, to get his team to pull together and get behind Torch, as the Northwest Africa invasion was now code-named. On July 28 — having instructed Stimson to leave Washington and take a week's holiday in Maine[6] — he had Leahy, Marshall, King, and Hopkins come to his Oval Study and sign up with good hearts to Torch, wisely telling Leahy to get still "more relief supplies to French North West Africa and infant relief to unoccupied [Vichy] France" to help soften the blow that would be coming for the Germans would be sure to overrun metropolitan Vichy France, once American troops invaded French North Africa.[7]

Then, after lunch that very day, he ordered Admiral Leahy, his own chief of staff, not only to attend but to chair the weekly conference of the U.S. Joint Chiefs of Staff as the senior officer present.

Leahy was delighted to do so. "At 2:30 p.m. presided for the first time at a meeting of the Joint Chiefs of Staff committee," the admiral noted in his diary.[8]

Still, however, Marshall and King resisted — refusing to postpone cross-Channel attack preparations in Britain, arguing that the "agreement" made during Churchill's trip to Washington in June to leave open any decisions on Bolero was still in force until September! If Torch was to go ahead, it had to be ordered by the Commander in Chief himself, they said.

Admiral Leahy sighed, and scratched his balding widower head. He was, once again, disbelieving — incredulous that the heads of America's army, air, and navy could seek to delay the Commander in Chief's directive with such specious reasoning. As the minutes recorded, however, "he would now tell the President that a definite decision was yet to be made" by his colleagues.[9]

Roosevelt was now losing patience. At 8:30 p.m. on July 28, 1942, he decided to convene a conference at the White House, in his Oval Study. It was time, he felt, to issue a direct order, not hope for collegiate resolution.

"The PRESIDENT stated very definitely that he, as Commander-in-Chief, had made the decision that TORCH would be undertaken at the earliest possible date," the secretary of the Combined Chiefs of Staff, Brigadier General Bedell Smith, recorded. "He considered that this operation was now our principal objective and the assembling of means to carry it out should take precedence over other operations as, for instance, BOLERO."[10]

There was no time to lose. "He mentioned the desirability of sending a message immediately to the Prime Minister advising him that he (the President), as Commander-in-Chief, had made this decision and requested his agreement."[11]

The bickering was over; the doubters were, in the President's view as he said goodnight to his generals, vanquished. The race to mount a successful invasion of the threshold of Europe, before winter came, was on.

26

A Failed Mutiny

TORCH "WAS ONE OF THE VERY few major military decisions of the war which Roosevelt made entirely on his own and over the protests of his highest-ranking advisers," the President's speechwriter, Robert Sherwood, later wrote. The President "insisted that the decision had been made and must be carried through with expedition and vigor."[1]

Sadly, it was not — for though the Commander in Chief might insist, the War Department could desist.

"On no other issue of the war," reflected Forrest Pogue, the doyen of American World War II military historians, "did the Secretary of State and the Chief of Staff so completely differ with the Commander-in-Chief. Their distrust of his military judgment, their doubts about the Prime Minister's advice, and their deep conviction that the TORCH operation was fundamentally unsound persisted," Dr. Pogue admitted candidly, "throughout August" of 1942.[2]

Harry Hopkins's biographer noted the same. "It is evident," Sherwood chronicled after the war, "that even after Hopkins, Marshall and King returned from London on July 27, there were further attempts to change the President's mind about the North African operation."

That Secretary Henry Stimson, General George Marshall, and so many of the "top brass" in Washington would continue to press for the potential fiasco of a cross-Channel venture in 1942, while at the same time exaggerating the danger of failure in terms of the President's French Northwest Africa project, did not say a great deal for their military judgment at this stage of the war. Instead of knuckling down to the Commander in Chief's "full steam ahead"[3] order at the end of July, Secretary Stimson and General Marshall continued, as Marshall's biographer recorded, "by a fine splitting of hairs to insist that the final decision had yet to be made and that preparations for SLEDGEHAMMER," an immediate cross-Channel attack, "must be continued."[4]

This was, in the circumstances, disgraceful. In London the Prime Minister even attempted a ploy to buy General Marshall off, at long distance; in a cable to the President, Churchill suggested that General Marshall be appointed to command the eventual cross-Channel attack, while Lieutenant General Eisenhower — who seemed more amenable — should take command of Torch, the impending North Africa operation.

The President, having confided to Stimson that Bolero would probably not be mounted in 1943, given the paucity of naval vessels, did not even raise the matter with Marshall — who was far too important to him as U.S. Army chief of staff at home.

Roosevelt's dismissal of Churchill's suggestion masked, however, a deeper concern. In truth the Commander in Chief had lost faith in Marshall's judgment and objectivity as a military commander, however much he admired him as an individual and administrator. Appointing him to command, even from his perch in Washington, the planning for the Second Front landings might only encourage Marshall to pursue a course which, in 1942, the President had come to view as unrealistic. With rumors rife in Washington of a staff revolt at the War Department, and reports of a grave disagreement between the President and his military advisers leaking into the press, Roosevelt began to have real concerns about Marshall's loyalty and willingness to subordinate himself to civilian leadership. Relations between the two men became frosty, despite the summer heat — the President worried that Marshall, like Secretary Stimson, was turning the entire War Department against him and thus sabotaging the success of the Torch undertaking. In truth, Marshall declined for two entire weeks in August to give Lieutenant General Eisenhower, in London, an official directive to plan and carry out the Torch invasion of French Northwest Africa.

Time was wasting — the second wave of Hitler's renewed panzer attack in Russia, *Fall Blau*, having reached the Don on July 5, and Operation Edelweiss, to seize the all-important oil wells of the Caucasus, had begun on July 23 with 167,00 men, a thousand aircraft, over a thousand tanks — and 15,000 oil workers in tow.

Somehow the President had to show his armed forces and the world that he was not only in command but confident of American victory. A suicidal Second Front mission was not going to achieve it, whatever Marshall or Stimson maintained. Firing either or both of them might send a message of presidential determination. Given the "distrust" of his Torch plan throughout the War Department, however, this would not have aided preparations for the North Africa venture; nor, to be sure, was it the President's preferred modus operandi.

Once again, Roosevelt swallowed deeply and ignored the rumblings of discontent on the Mall. By remaining absolutely and irrevocably intent upon seeing through Torch, Roosevelt felt certain the gathering *momentum* of operational planning, preparations, and necessary training would gradually overcome his doubting Thomases, steering them toward his goal: American combat in or on the threshold of Europe, in a secure area, one where green U.S. troops and their commanders could be blooded and learn the business of modern combat without inviting catastrophe or risking a major setback to the expectations of freedom-loving people across the globe.

If General Marshall was less than supportive of his Commander in Chief in August, Secretary Stimson, for his part, was reaching a point of despair. Returning from his vacation on August 7 he found the War Department "hard at work on plans for Gymnast [as he still called it] and, as they go into them more and more, the preparations which we have been so carefully making for Bolero and Sledgehammer are being cut and delayed, the shipping reduced and the shipments [to Britain] of men put off or diminished. In fact, if Gymnast goes through, Bolero is out of the window at least until 1944," he noted in his diary, "and that seems to me a dreadful thing."[5]

To the Commander in Chief it did not. At a cabinet meeting in the White House the President attempted to convey a sense of unity in the administration. The United States had taken over direction of the war and was preparing to deliver a first great blow upon the enemy that would reinvigorate the free—and occupied—world. "During the meeting," however, "the President said that he was much troubled by charges which had appeared in some of the papers that he and Churchill were running the war plans of the war without regard to the advice of their military advisers."[6]

This was not far short of the truth—but the President was not to going to admit to such an assertion in front of his full cabinet. Rather, he intended his next remark to be a shot across Stimson's—and Knox's—

bows. "It was a matter evidently on his mind and he put it up before [Navy Secretary] Knox and myself apparently to silence us," Stimson recorded in his diary that night — the President claiming, as Stimson recorded, that he was in complete accord with his war and navy people, and that he never, ever intruded as commander in chief, except to arbitrate "when the Army and Navy differed and it was necessary for someone to decide between them."[7]

There was little the secretary could do about such lies — amazed at the President's ability to say such things with a straight face. Yet it worked: the President able to manipulate the members of his administration into doing what he wanted, even against their will or better judgment, and then sweep everyone along on a tide of goodwill and common purpose. Franklin D. Roosevelt had, in Stimson's thoughtful account that night, "the happy faculty of feeling [at one with] himself and this was one of the most extreme cases of it that I have ever seen because he must know that we are all against him on Gymnast," the secretary sighed, "and yet now that is going to be the first thing probably which is done, and we are all very blue about it."[8]

Far from being rested by his vacation, Stimson began to panic.

Sinkings of Allied merchant ships by German U-boats were reaching record numbers. News from the Pacific was no better: a battle royal taking place at Guadalcanal, in the southern Solomon Islands, where American Marines had seized the newly cleared Japanese airfield, daring the Japanese to retaliate in force — which they did.

Turning seventy-five that fall, Henry Stimson, despite being a first-rate lawyer, had not the flexibility and energy of a younger man. Once again, in his diary, he recounted for his own edification the sorry history of Torch, the "President's great secret baby" — charting yet again the way the President had "hankered and hunkered" to revive the "evil" plan each time General Marshall and the War Department had knocked it down. "Today the whole thing came into my conversations with [Generals] Marshall, Lovett and Handy and all of them feel strongly against Gymnast," Stimson noted with a sort of perverse satisfaction on August 7.[9]

Given that Averell Harriman, the President's personal emissary, was already on his way with Prime Minister Churchill to brief Joseph Stalin personally on the impending Torch operation, Stimson's efforts to find a way to stop the operation were becoming seriously dysfunctional. And detrimental to America's war effort.

The scene was, in fact, little short of tragic at such a critical moment of the war. In Stimson's tortured mind, however, the fact that the decision to mount Torch had "decisively" been taken on July 28 and that the British prime minister — approaching sixty-eight years of age and having already suffered a mild heart attack — was flying halfway across the world to explain the Torch operation to Stalin, was of no consequence. As Stimson saw it, Churchill had become the éminence grise behind America's president, and thus America's Public Enemy Number One.

The President's silencing words in cabinet also rankled. On his return from the cabinet meeting in the White House Stimson thus began, in the quiet of his office on Constitution Avenue, to mull over *yet another* official letter of protest to Roosevelt: one that would either stop the President in his tracks, or at least prove to the world, later, that the President had refused to take his chief military advisers' advice.

If the war secretary was to come out and openly oppose the President, he wanted "to be sure I am on solid ground." Taking the army chief of staff aside, Stimson had a "careful talk with Marshall over the strategic situation, getting our teeth right into it and into each other — a very frank talk and a rather useful one," the secretary confided to his diary that night. As Churchill prepared to fly on from Cairo to Moscow to tell Stalin in confidence about Torch, Stimson thus asked General Marshall point blank if he, Marshall, "was President or Dictator" of America, "whether he would go on with Gymnast and he told me frankly no."[10]

Marshall as president or dictator? Such language, exchanged between the country's most senior military officials on August 9, 1942, was sailing close to sedition — as even Marshall began to recognize the following day, when the war secretary showed him exactly what he had in mind.

Colonel Stimson's draft "Letter to the President" as U.S. secretary of war on August 10, 1942, took Marshall's breath away — for Stimson, having for months insisted on the most perilous American invasion of mainland France, across the English Channel, was now suggesting that Torch, the U.S. invasion of French Northwest Africa, was even *more* perilous.

Beginning "Dear Mr. President," Stimson acknowledged that, thanks to "the refusal of the British to join us in going forward" with a cross-

Channel attack in 1942, the chiefs of staff of the U.S. Army had agreed to substitute an invasion of French Northwest Africa. However, "intensive studies of the conditions and effects involved in the Torch proposal" by the War Department had led the secretary to take the same stance toward Torch as the British had done to the idea of a cross-Channel attack: to say no.

"I am now credibly informed that, in the light of these studies and of the rapidly unrolling world situation now before us, both the Chief of Staff and the General Staff believe that this operation should not be undertaken. I believe it to be now their opinion that under present conditions the Torch undertaking would not only involve serious danger of our troops meeting an initial defeat, but that it could not be carried out without emasculating any air attack this autumn on Germany from the British Isles and would postpone the operation known as Roundup [the invasion and conquest of France] until 1944. Furthermore, being an essentially defensive operation by the Allied Force, it [Torch] would not in any material way assist Russia."

These were bold assertions. Again Stimson urged the President to cancel the Torch landings — indeed any landings in Europe or in Africa. Instead he called for an application of all U.S. energies on concentrated *air* attacks on Germany, "with sufficient effectiveness to affect the morale of Germany more effectively than any of the other proposals which could be carried out this year. I earnestly recommend that before an irrevocable decision is made upon the Torch operation you should make yourself familiar with the present views of these your military advisers and the facts and reasons that underlie them."[11]

Throughout June and July Stimson had decried the British for being "defeatist" and lily-livered for not daring to mount a cross-Channel Second Front that year, relying merely on their RAF thousand-bomber "terror" raids — which shocked the world but showed no sign of denting German civilian or military morale, in fact only seemed to make the Germans more determined to support the Führer. Now Stimson was not only talking up the sole strategy of Allied bombing efforts, but recoiling at the prospect of "initial defeat" if U.S. troops attacked a region on the threshold of Europe where there were virtually no German troops!

A more defeatist protest to the President, two weeks after the "definitive" decision over Torch had been made, could not have been drafted.

General Marshall was embarrassed by it — especially given the manner in which Secretary Stimson was intending to speak for Marshall and his colleagues. "He takes an even severer attitude towards the President than I do," Stimson noted in his diary, "but he pleaded with me not to send it," the secretary admitted, as "he thought it would put him (Marshall) in the position of not being manly enough to do it himself."[12]

In the whole of World War II the United States would never come closer to a military mutiny — which had certainly not been General Marshall's intention. The President was the U.S. commander in chief. Marshall was a serving officer — a soldier. He had been given an order by the Commander in Chief, and it behooved him to carry it out, however much he might disagree with it, as the President well knew. Or resign. Marshall therefore begged the secretary not to send the letter. Stimson retorted by accusing him of "welching" on their opposition to the President's "evil" plan. Marshall was incensed. To Stimson's chagrin, Marshall now made clear he had no intention of making such a protest in his role as U.S. Army chief of staff — neither in writing nor in person. He would have no truck with talk of being president or dictator of the United States.

Seeing Stimson's crestfallen face, however, Marshall took pity on the secretary — who meant well, and had been devoted to the best interests of the U.S. Army since his appointment in July 1940. Marshall therefore assured the secretary "that I could rest confident that he and the Staff would not permit Gymnast to become actually effective if it seemed clearly headed to a disaster."[13]

General Marshall was not alone in stepping away from Stimson's revolt. To Stimson's added chagrin, Secretary Knox, the following day, also withdrew any presumed support for an official protest, mutiny, or further machinations against the President. The doughty Colonel Knox, who had served with courage in Cuba in 1898 with Theodore Roosevelt's Rough Riders, and again as an artillery major in World War I in Europe, was "less worried about Torch than I was," Stimson noted — admitting that, as secretary of the navy, Frank Knox was, by contrast, "more worried about Sledgehammer than I was."[14]

With this evaporation of support, Stimson decided he had best shelve his "Letter to the President."

The possible mutiny was over, for the moment at least. In high dudgeon the secretary went away for another two weeks' vacation.

Given what was awaiting the five thousand brave but inexperienced Canadians who had been assigned to Operation Jubilee, the mini-version of Sledgehammer that Churchill had felt compelled to authorize nine days later in order to silence men like Secretary Stimson, General Marshall, and the senior officers of the War Department, Colonel Knox had had every reason, however, to be worried.

PART ELEVEN

Reaction in Moscow

27

Stalin's Prayer

PERHAPS THE GREATEST IRONY of the 1942 Second Front/Torch im-
broglio was Stalin's reaction.

Secretary Stimson, the U.S. chiefs of staff, and the senior generals in
the War Department had all claimed that Torch would not aid the Russians. Winston Churchill, flying to Moscow to tell the Russian leader the
news that no Second Front would be mounted in France that year, but
that instead, U.S. landings would be substituted in Northwest Africa, was
understandably apprehensive. Bravely he ventured, on August 12, 1942,
to the heart of the Soviet Union — a country whose Communist forces
he had himself tried to destroy in 1920, after World War I. With Russian
backs to the wall in the Caucasus — Hitler's legions having crossed the
Don and now aiming to take Stalingrad — it felt as if he was "carrying
a large lump of ice to the North Pole," in the Prime Minister's immortal
later phrase.[1] "We were going into the lion's den," one general recalled,
"and we weren't going to feed him."[2] Fortunately, however, Churchill was
traveling to the Kremlin with the personal representative of the president
of the United States, Averell Harriman.

Reading the cables Harriman sent him from Russia, the President con
sidered Churchill's mission to have been nothing short of heroic. As soon
as Harriman returned to the United States, the President said he wanted
to see him and hear his firsthand account, in person.

Two weeks later, on August 30, 1942, Averell Harriman duly drove to
lunch with the President, together with the President's two speechwriters, Robert Sherwood and Sam Rosenman. The President was at his new
summerhouse retreat: the USS *Shangri-la,* as Roosevelt called it.

The rustic mountain camp consisted of "a number of rudely constructed, small pine cabins, each of two or three rooms," which did not impress Judge Rosenman—especially the President's hut. "It was furnished with the most rudimentary kind of secondhand furniture, most of which had come from a navy storehouse where unwanted and well-used furniture had been accumulated over the years,"[3] he sniffed.

The President didn't mind; the cabin was as Spartan as the rooms of his beloved presidential yacht, the USS *Potomac,* but possessed something forbidden on the steamer (a converted coast guard cutter): rugs. "The rugs," Rosenman recorded, however, "had come from the same place and were in a bad state of repair."

The view, Judge Rosenman allowed, was magnificent. "The President occupied a bedroom looking out through the woods over a beautiful valley. To it was attached one of the two bathrooms. The other three bedrooms were double bedrooms but none of them had space for more than two simple metal beds, a dresser, and a chair. These three bedrooms were all served by one bathroom. The door to the bathroom never quite closed quite securely, and the President laughingly used to warn each of his guests of that fact; but the door was never repaired."[4]

Most of all Rosenman was amazed at the President's buoyant mood, when the war seemed to be going so badly. The Germans, Rosenman had been informed, had by now advanced more than five hundred miles on the Eastern Front, capturing half a million Russian troops. They had already reached the peaks of the Urals: poised, it seemed, to race to the Caspian Sea, seize the crucial Caucasus oil wells, and threaten northern Iran. In North Africa Erwin Rommel, promoted to field marshal by the Führer following his capture of Tobruk, was bringing up hundreds of new and improved long-barreled Mark IV panzers as well as lethal 88mm antitank guns for his final assault on Alexandria, Cairo, the Suez Canal—and then on, if successful, to Palestine.

In the Pacific, Americans were fighting fiercely for a toehold on Guadalcanal, where on August 8–9 they had suffered a naval defeat so great it had had to be kept from the public: no fewer than four Allied cruisers—three American and one Australian—being sunk in the Savo Sea by the Japanese, who suffered no losses at all . . .

Questioned at Shangri-la by the President, Harriman assured him the Germans had still a huge task on their hands—contradicting reports of the War Department's head of intelligence, who was currently predicting the imminent fall of Stalingrad to the Germans.[5] The Russians *would* hold, Harriman assured the President—whatever Secretary Stimson and the men in the War Department might say to the contrary. "Averell gave a lucid analysis of the situation," Sherwood recalled Harriman's verbal report, "and then firmly predicted that Stalingrad would not fall, and that the battle could conceivably end in a major military disaster for the Germans." As far as the Ural Mountains were concerned, "He thought the Russians could prevent the breakthrough which would have cut them off from the Caucasian oil fields and given the Germans a clear road into Iran and the Middle East" — for Stalin had assured Harriman and Churchill he could hold both Baku on the Caspian Sea, and Batum on the Black Sea, for the next few months, when the approaching winter snow would "greatly improve their position."[6] Better still, Mr. Stalin had even confided to Harriman that he was planning a huge counteroffensive that would stun the Germans.

This was greatly encouraging to the President, who listened to his personal emissary's blow-by-blow account of the three-day series of summit meetings in the Kremlin with intense fascination — and sly amusement. Churchill had first off "announced the decision to give up Sledgehammer without mincing words." Stalin, in response, had been rude to the point of deliberate insult, Harriman related — "Stalin gave him hell," and "without mincing words" derided "the timidity of the democracies in comparison to Russia's sacrifices."[7] A tyrant by nature and struggle, Stalin could not resist denigrating the pathetic British military performance in the war so far — sneering at the Royal Navy's failure to protect its convoys to Murmansk, scorning the failure of the British Army to beat the Wehrmacht in open battle. War was war, he had grimly pronounced; to win a battle, one must be willing to accept huge casualties.

It was then that Churchill, according to Harriman, had delivered his tersest riposte.

"War is war," the Prime Minister acknowledged, "but not folly."[8]

The President, at Shangri-la, was utterly delighted by the phrase — and by Winston's refusal to be bowed by the Russian's ill-mannered rebuke. Or to be tempted to pack his bags, once Harriman put his mind at rest by passing him a note, in which he pointed out that this was merely par for the psychopath's bullying course. The next day, Harriman had promised the Prime Minister, the Russian monster would be all sweetness and roses.

The President "appeared to enjoy hearing about Churchill's discomfiture in those long reproach-filled sessions," Harriman later told his ghostwriter, Elie Abel[9] — for there, but for the grace of God, the President might well have been: attempting to explain in person to the Soviet dictator why neither the United States nor Great Britain were willing to make good on their promise of a Second Front in France that fall.

About the President's substitute invasion plan — Torch — however, the Russian leader had been, to even Churchill's astonishment, almost ecstatic.

Churchill, according to Harriman, had gone on to explain, after delivering the bad news, that there was good news, too. The Americans were, indeed, coming — within weeks!

At this the dictator had changed his tune entirely. By way of metaphor, the Prime Minister had described the President's substitute strategy as akin to dealing with a crocodile: instead of hitting the critter on its hard snout, it was best to cut into its "soft underbelly." Moreover, this would be far more than a mere slash: for the invasion that would be mounted by American and British forces would number a quarter of a million men: more troops than Hitler had sent into the Caucasus — dispatched separately from the British Isles and the United States with massive air and naval cover.

Secretary Stimson, General Marshall, General Arnold, Admiral King, General McNarney, General Handy, General Wedemeyer — all had sought to persuade the U.S. commander in chief that Torch was a mistake and would not help the Russians in any way in their hour of need. Instead, according to Harriman, the Russian dictator had *instantly* grasped how the U.S.-led invasion could change the whole dynamic of the war against Hitler.

As Prime Minister Mackenzie King subsequently heard the story, via the Canadian defense minister who'd met with Winston Churchill in London, "Stalin had approved strongly" of Torch. "He had thought for 10 minutes after Churchill had proposed it, and then was greatly pleased. This of course is to be the second front that will be opened this year."[10]

The description of Stalin's response given to Mackenzie King, though given to the President weeks later, was certainly in line with the detailed minutes of the summit meeting, taken down at the time by a stenographer and used by Churchill in his own cables from Moscow to the President in Washington. According to the typed minutes of the meeting, which Harriman then showed the President at Shangri-la, "Mr. Stalin appeared suddenly to grasp the strategic advantages of 'Torch.' He saw four out-standing advantages" of the operation:

1. It would take the enemy in the rear.
2. It would make the Germans and the French fight
   each other.
3. It would put Italy out of action.
4. It would keep the Spaniards neutral.[11]

Reflecting on this extraordinarily positive response, the President had shaken his head at the irony. Stalin had required but *ten minutes* to recognize the way Torch would turn the tide of World War II, whereas it had taken the War Department more than a year! Moreover, the most senior U.S. generals were reputedly *still* trying to sabotage the operation, by ordering preparations for Bolero to continue in England without interruption, even at the risk of compromising the success of the Torch operation.

However, Stalin's next remark had been, if anything, even more astonishing.

Turning to the President's personal representative, Stalin had said to Churchill and Harriman — as Harriman now told Roosevelt — "May God help this enterprise to succeed."[12]

PART TWELVE

An Industrial Miracle

28

A Trip Across America

RETURNING FROM SHANGRI-LA on August 30, 1942, the President summoned General Marshall to dinner at the White House. He wanted to see whether, with Hopkins and Harriman present, he could use Stalin's positive reaction to the news of Torch to reinvigorate the general, and get him to now put his whole authority at the War Department behind preparations for the U.S. landings. To the President's dismay, however, General Marshall presented him, instead, with a draft cable to Churchill, reducing Eisenhower's plans for a three-pronged invasion of French Northwest Africa to two: one outside the Mediterranean, one within. At Casablanca and Oran only.

"This matter has been most carefully considered by me and by my naval and military advisers," Marshall's draft cable ran, for the President to sign. "I feel strongly that my conception of the operation as outlined herein must be accepted and that such a solution promises the greatest chance of success in this particular theatre."[1]

The President could only laugh — suspecting that Secretary Stimson and Admiral King were behind the maneuver: the War Department still hoping that by limiting the landings to the Atlantic seaboard of Morocco and the westernmost part of Algeria, the United States could continue to pursue plans for a cross-Channel landing in the spring of 1943 — or even a switch to the Pacific, if the battle for Guadalcanal and the Solomon Islands became more and more menacing.

Shaking his head, the President told Marshall the cable was unacceptable. Landings only in Morocco and at Oran would not persuade the Vichy French that America was serious — indeed, facing such meager landings, Vichy French forces in the rest of Morocco, Algeria, and Tunisia would be encouraged to resist invasion by America as an outside power. Worse still, recognizing the weakness of such a force, Hitler would undoubtedly seize the chance to ship troops across the Mediterranean and order them to occupy the Vichy territories — threatening to create the very scenario Secretary Stimson had always feared: a sort of Custer's Last Stand by American troops, or second Gallipoli. Instead of a mighty American operation on the threshold of Europe that would give heart to all those praying for Hitler's defeat, Torch would be a flickering candle.

The President was deeply disappointed in Marshall. Somehow, Roosevelt insisted, enough naval forces must be found for *all three* landing areas to be simultaneously assaulted, however hard this might be. Redrafting Marshall's proposed cable, he turned it on its head.

Torch must succeed, by its very preponderance of men and munitions, convoyed and landed in overwhelming strength. "To this end I think we should re-examine our resources and strip everything down to the bone to make a third landing possible," Roosevelt reworded the cable to Churchill and the British Admiralty.[2] All three initial landings *must* be made by purely American forces, he also laid down in the telegram he eventually sent to Churchill that night, lest the Vichy French be inspired to defend their colonial territories the more determinately, given their hatred of the British. "I would go so far as to say," he wrote, "I am reasonably sure a simultaneous landing by British and Americans would result in full resistance by all French in Africa whereas an initial landing without British ground forces offers a real chance that there would be no French resistance or only token resistance."[3]

Poor Eisenhower, the designated supreme commander for Torch, now found himself torn between instructions from the Commander in Chief of the United States and his U.S. Army chief of staff to whom he owed his meteoric promotion since 1939. "I feel like the lady in the circus that has to ride three horses with no very good idea of exactly where any one of the three is going," he laughingly told General Patton, who'd been chosen to command the Western Task Force's assault landings in the Casablanca area, setting out directly from the United States.[4]

Receiving the President's cable, Churchill was understandably disappointed that no British troops would be landing in the first wave of Torch. He bravely accepted Roosevelt's logic, however — and urgency.

Time was running out, if the invasion was to be mounted that fall — the leaves at Shangri-la already beginning to turn. Over the following days the three-pronged Torch operation, despite Marshall and Stimson's objections, was finally set in stone. The Western Task Force's Casablanca operation was trimmed, the Eastern Task Force's Algiers landings increased. "We are getting very close together," the President cabled Churchill from Washington on September 4, 1942 — adding: "I am directing all preparations to proceed" — meaning that General Marshall and the War Department would now be told to obey, or resign. "We should settle this whole thing with finality at once."[5]

Trying to put together the largest Allied amphibious operation of the war from a headquarters in London, over three thousand miles from the troops that would be embarked in America, Lieutenant General Eisenhower was understandably nervous. For his own part he remained unconvinced that Torch was a better option than Sledgehammer, or Bolero staged in 1943, and gave it only a fifty-fifty chance of success.[6] He was, however, relieved that a final decision had been made — indeed, he was already proving a remarkably patient and intelligent coalition commander. The "Transatlantic essay contest," as he put it, was at least over.[7]

The next day, Churchill cabled his agreement. "It is imperative now to drive straight ahead and save every hour. In this way alone shall we realize your strategic design," he telegraphed the President in cipher, "and the only hope of doing anything that really counts this year."[8]

The President's simple comment was one word: "Hurrah!"[9]

On September 3, 1942, meanwhile, the President had agreed to give, in the White House, a talk to representatives of the International Student Assembly — a speech that was sent out across the world and gave perhaps a better idea of his growing sense of America's destiny in the modern world than any he had previously broadcast.

The talk was, the President explained to listeners, "being heard by several million American soldiers, sailors, and marines, not only within the continental limits of the United States, but in far distant points — in Central and South America, in the islands of the Atlantic, in Britain and Ireland, on the coasts of Africa, in Egypt, in Iraq and Iran, in Russia, in India, in China, in Australia, in New Zealand, in many parts of the Pacific, and on all the seas of the world. There — in those distant places — are our fighting men. And to them," Roosevelt declared in a voice not only of authority but of absolute conviction and confidence, "I should like to deliver a special message, from their Commander in Chief, and from the very hearts of their countrymen."

The speech touched on familiar themes. "Victory is essential," Roosevelt stated, "but victory is not enough for you — or for us. We must be sure that when you have won victory, you will not have to tell your children that you fought in vain — that you were betrayed. We must be sure that in your homes there will not be want — that in your schools only the living truth will be taught — that in your churches there may be preached without fear a faith in which men may deeply believe.

"The better world for which you fight — and for which some of you give your lives — will not come merely because we shall have won the war. It will not come merely because we wish very hard that it would come. It will be made possible only by bold vision, intelligent planning, and hard work. It cannot be brought about overnight; but only by years of effort and perseverance and unfaltering faith.

"You young soldiers and sailors, farmers and factory workers, artists and scholars, who are fighting our way to victory now, all of you will have to take part in shaping that world. You will earn it by what you do now; but you will not attain it if you leave the job for others to do alone. When you lay aside your gun at the end of the war, you cannot at the same time lay aside your duty to the future.

"What I have said to our American soldiers and sailors applies to all the young men and women of the United Nations who are facing our common enemies. There is a complete unanimity of spirit among all the youth of all kinds and kindreds who fight to preserve or gain their freedom."

"This," the President declared, "is a development of historic importance. It means the old term, 'Western civilization,' no longer applies. *World* events and the common needs of all humanity are joining the culture of Asia with the culture of Europe and the culture of the Americas to form, for the first time, a real world civilization. In the concept of the four freedoms, in the basic principles of the Atlantic Charter, we have set for ourselves high goals, unlimited objectives. These concepts, and these principles, are designed to form a world in which men, women, and children can live in freedom and in equity and, above all, without fear of the horrors of war.

"For no soldiers or sailors, in any of our forces today, would so willingly endure the rigors of battle if they thought that in another twenty years their own sons would be fighting still another war on distant deserts or seas or in faraway jungles or in the skies.

"We have profited by our past mistakes. This time we shall know how to make full use of victory. This time the achievements of our fighting forces will not be thrown away by political cynicism and timidity and incompetence."

It would not be straight sailing. "We are deeply aware that we cannot achieve our goals easily. We cannot attain the fullness of all of our ideals overnight. We know that this is to be a long and hard and bitter fight — and that there will still be an enormous job for us to do long after the last German, Japanese, and Italian bombing planes have been shot to earth.

"But we do believe that, with divine guidance, we can make in this dark world of today, and in the new postwar world of tomorrow — a steady progress toward the highest goals that men have ever imagined.

"We of the United Nations have the technical means, the physical resources, and, most of all, the adventurous courage and the vision and the will that are needed to build and sustain the kind of world order which alone can justify the tremendous sacrifices now being made by our youth.

"But we must keep at it — we must never relax, never falter, never fear — and we must keep at it together.

"We must maintain the offensive against evil in all its forms. We must work, and we must fight to insure that our children shall have and shall enjoy in peace their inalienable rights to freedom of speech, freedom of religion, freedom from want, and freedom from fear.

"Only on those bold terms can this total war result in total victory."[10]

Roosevelt was seeking not only to raise national morale in the weeks before the Torch invasion, but to prepare Americans for a far greater challenge: asking young Americans, especially, to step up to the plate in embracing America's moral role in a postwar world.

Along with more proselytizing, though, the President was anxious to make sure American industrial output and its expansion of the military were matching his high expectations. In his State of the Union address in January 1942, he had announced production targets that were ridiculed by Hitler and Goebbels. Not only were the majority of them being reached, however, but many of them were being exceeded, the President was informed, by dint of mass production on a scale never seen before in human history. To check on this, and to spread something of the gospel of inspiration that his personal presence would engender, Roosevelt now set off on what was for him an epic, 8,754-mile train journey across America — and was amazed.

Mrs. Roosevelt accompanied the President only as far as Milwaukee, but FDR's daughter Anna, his secretary, Grace Tully, and his stenographer, Dorothy Brady, as well as his first cousin, Laura Delano, continued on with him. Daisy Suckley was also a member of the party, together with the President's former law partner, Harry Hooker, as her escort, in order that there be no gossip. Steve Early, the White House press secretary, went along to ensure no word of the trip be reported in the press before the President's return;[11] also Ross McIntire, the President's doctor, and Captain McCrea manned the communications car.

"I can't quite believe it even," Daisy scribbled in her diary, ensconced in Stateroom B on Car No. 3, as it left Silver Spring, Maryland, "yet, here I am — on board — to tour the country with the P. of the U.S.!" Donald Nelson, head of the War Production Board, had briefed the President on "munition plants, the new airplanes, etc." that would be viewed on the President's tour.[12] It was only at the Chrysler Tank Arsenal in Detroit, however, that the true magnitude of what was being achieved industrially hit home.

At the tank plant in Detroit, "a boy with a yard-long Polish name plowed through water & mud" in his new M-4 Sherman, "straight up to the President's car, stopped and pushed his head through the hole with a smile. People standing around looked rather alarmed as the tank plowed forward, but the P. had a good laugh."[13]

"Good drive!" the President shouted.[14] "It was a monster performing his tricks & lacked only the final bowing of the front legs, like the elephant in the circus!" Daisy noted on September 18. "30 tanks a day —"[15]

A day? Two hundred a week? Sure enough, by year's end tank production had increased from under four thousand in 1941 to twenty-five thousand in 1942 — hoisted "like ducks on a spit" by thirty-ton jigs as they were assembled.[16]

It was the same story at Ford's new plant at Willow Run on September 18, 1942. Where in March that year there had been but trees there now stood a new aircraft factory a mile and a half long, containing the world's first mass-production assembly line for airplanes, which that month produced its first B-24 Liberator bomber for the President to see. Over succeeding months it would churn out planes at a phenomenal rate that would eventually top one B-24 *every sixty-three minutes* — the plant's contribution to some forty-nine thousand U.S. planes produced that year.[17]

At North Chicago some sixty-eight thousand naval officers and men were training; at Milwaukee a huge turbine manufacturing plant was visited. At Lake Pend Oreille in Idaho there had been nothing in March 1942. A naval training station opened only five days before the President's arrival. It would train almost three hundred thousand sailors over the following thirty months, becoming the second-largest training center in the world.

In Seattle the President drove beneath the wing and fuselage of a B-17F Flying Fortress at the new Boeing Plant 2 — the factory buildings camouflaged with burlap and fake trees to resemble a quiet American suburb. Produced both by men and women ("Rosie the Riveters"), production of the four-engine bomber rose from 60 that fall to almost 100 per week, or 362 per month, as the war progressed.

Factory workers "evidently knew nothing of the P.'s coming & looked up vaguely from their work as we drove between the machines," Daisy recorded. "It seemed incredibly crowded, though in perfect order. When we came out, the word had spread & workers were running to get a view of the P., clapping & smiling. We see many women in these plants, & they tell us more & more are being taken in. Here they are even welding, with masks on."[18]

From there they traveled to the aluminum smelting works at Vancouver, Washington — "Long sheds filled with electrolytic cell furnaces burning 24 hours a day and 7 days a week—No stop is possible."[19] Later that morning they inspected the Kaiser shipbuilding yard on the Willamette River, in Oregon. The country's biggest housing project had been undertaken to provide labor, and it was there that the President witnessed a true miracle of mass production: the launching of a ten-thousand-ton freighter, the USS *Joseph N. Teal*, built in only ten days.

"The work men were all lined up," Daisy noted as the President's car drove up a special ramp to face the bow of the ship. Roosevelt's daughter Anna was given a "bouquet" of Defense Stamps, tied with a "red white & blue ribbon. The ceremony began with a prayer by a priest." Then, as the last of the eight rivets holding the vessel were knocked out, the champagne bottle swung against the bow "showering Anna to the skin, & down the ways went the Ship — it is a most moving scene, specially now, when you realize that that ship may be sunk by a submarine on her very first trip."[20]

How was it possible to build and launch a vessel of that size in mere *days*—an almost biblical achievement? As the President was driven "around the shops where they are making the various parts & assembling them as far as possible," the genesis of Roosevelt's confidence in American industry became clear to Daisy. "Large portions of the ships were loaded on huge trucks with rubber tires ready to be taken to the 'ways,'" Daisy noted. "This is Mr. Kaiser's 'secret' for getting a ship built in 14 days!! The P. likes both Mr K. & his son Edgar who was there with him, said Mr. K is a 'dynamo.'"[21]

Henry Kaiser was. Notable too was the morale of the workforce, and the managerial and engineering masterminding that went into a process in which, like the assembling of a model from a kit, the constituent parts of a vessel were first manufactured, then merged at the appropriate moment with the nascent vessel, from the keel up.

This miracle of mass production was awe-inspiring for the President to witness with his own eyes, barely two years after he himself had secretly begun assembling the team that would cause it to happen: a marvel that had begun on May 28, 1940, when Roosevelt had put in a phone call to the CEO of General Motors, a Danish immigrant by the name of William Knudsen. "Knudsen? I want to see you in Washington. I want you to work on some production matters. When can you come down?"[22]

Knudsen had taken leave from General Motors and become a "dollar-a-year man" in Washington — first as leader of the Advisory Commission to the Council of National Defense, then as director general of the Office of Production Management. When Donald Nelson was made chairman of the War Production Board in January 1942, Knudson became a lieutenant general in the U.S. Army and director of production in the Office of the Under Secretary of War: Knudson and Nelson the equivalent of Hitler's production tsars, Fritz Todt and Albert Speer.

*Pre*fabrication, then, was the key to American military mass production, as the President explained to Daisy Suckley and his other guests — whole sections of a ship, such as deckhouses, built elsewhere, then transported and welded into place on the slipway — the shipyard becoming a literal as well as metaphorical assembly line. To achieve such output, Kaiser's Oregon complex would employ thirty thousand people — 30 percent of whom were women.

America's transformation from potential into actual industrial superpower dwarfed in swiftness, scale, and quality anything comparable in the world. It was small wonder the President felt proud; by the end of the year the United States would be producing more war material than all three Axis powers, Germany, Italy, and Japan, put together.[23]

From the Boeing plant the President traveled the next day to Mare Island Naval Shipyard, where fifty thousand workers tested, built, and repaired submarines. From there to Oakland Naval Station, where dozens more submarines and subchaser vessels were under construction and repair. At Long Beach, Los Angeles, he visited the huge Douglas Aircraft plant, which would manufacture upwards of thirty-one thousand aircraft during the war; at Camp Pendleton he inspected more naval training units and visited the San Diego naval hospital — caring for wounded men from the fighting in the Pacific, as well as some still recuperating from Pearl Harbor. Then to the Consolidated Vultee plant at Fort Worth, Texas, where not hundreds but thousands of B-24 Liberators were being mass-produced. And on to Louisiana — where the President visited the Higgins boatbuilding yard.

Employing twenty thousand people, Andrew Higgins had overcome initial U.S. Navy hostility and revolutionized landing-craft production. His accumulated knowledge of shallow-draft vessels required for the marshes and bayous of Louisiana had given him a fierce faith in his own product — enabling him, once contracted, to begin building landing craft for the U.S. Navy on a bewitching scale: more than twenty thousand craft being produced in the months after Pearl Harbor. "He is the same type as Mr. Kaiser, a genius at getting things done," Daisy Suckley wrote in her diary, "constantly inventing new gadgets. His trouble is that he is too blunt & fights with everyone, so that the maritime commission hates him and won't play ball with him — But, he turns out the goods!"[24]

And so the journey had continued: everywhere the same story, that of a nation not only at war, but operating at almost manic speed to provide itself with the means to win it. At Camp Jackson, in South Carolina, thousands of soldiers "marched before the P. and disappeared over the hill, raising a mist of dust, their guns and helmets showing against the sky," Daisy described. "It is our last evening on board. But the P. said the trip had worked so well with us four that he will take us on another! No complexes — no quarrels — etc.!"[25]

29

The President's Loyal Lieutenant

IF ANYONE QUESTIONED, LATER, just how it was that Roosevelt remained so deeply confident of victory in the fall of 1942, after such a summer of reverses for the United Nations, they need only have looked to the President's trip across America that September.

"So I think he has had a real mental rest, & is now ready to go back & 'talk turkey' to a good many people — He can talk from what he has seen with his own eyes," Daisy Suckley noted[1] — for the President knew now, beyond all doubt, that the United States was ready to win the war, whatever it took. He did not want Torch to be "delayed by a single day," as he wrote in a cable to Churchill from his train — and certainly not by diverting troops to a landing in Norway, as Churchill was suggesting once again, to mollify Stalin over the cancellation of further convoys to Murmansk, in view of the heavy casualties. Nor did he see a need to tell Stalin in advance that the latest convoy, PQ 19, would not sail. "I can see nothing to be gained by notifying Stalin sooner than is necessary and, indeed, much to be lost," he cabled. Torch, he was more and more certain, would change the whole dynamic of the war: would give the United States and United Nations the global initiative. "We are going to put everything in that enterprise and I have great hopes for it. . . . I am having a great trip. The training of our forces is far advanced and their morale excellent. Production is good but must be better. Roosevelt."[2]

Dimly, even Winston Churchill began to face up to what was obvious to the rest of the world: that the United States would not only win the war for the Western Allies, but was set to become the dominant world power thereafter.

No sooner had the President returned from his inspection trip than

Churchill cabled Roosevelt to question the incredible numbers that the American Production and Resources Board had given the British for U.S. military production — output amounting to some seventy-six thousand tanks by 1943, enough to equip two hundred U.S. divisions.

"This appears to me to be a provision on a scale out of all proportion to anything that might be brought to bear on the enemy in 1943," Churchill telegraphed in alarm. It was clear to him that if Great Britain was intending merely to cauterize Hitler's Europe by more ad hoc raids — operations like Mountbatten's "Operation Plough" mini-landings in snowbound Norway, or Rumania, or Northern Italy[3] — the President was not. Nazi Germany, Roosevelt was certain, would not be felled by pinpricks but by a sequence of ever-greater amphibious landings that would unroll the true military potential of the United States.

Churchill, having predicated his whole strategy for British survival in World War II upon his alliance with the United States, could hardly complain — and to his credit, beyond his mild protest over American über-production and Roosevelt's insistence on Torch being, in its initial phases, a completely U.S. operation of war, he didn't. When General Brooke, the British Army CIGS, protested against Averell Harriman's recommendation that U.S. teams take over the Persian port and railroad system, which would result in British forces in Iran becoming wholly dependent on America, Churchill had rounded on Brooke with the words: "In whose hands could we be better dependent?"[4]

The fall of 1942 thus marked, in effect, the turning point in the evolution of the modern world, as the British Empire wound down. Though Churchill might shortly declare in public his refusal to preside over its liquidation, the fact was, Great Britain was now to become, to all intents and purposes, the staging post of American power in Europe.

Reluctantly but with dignity, the Prime Minister — who had shown no mercy in putting down protest riots in India, where it was estimated that some 2,500 Indians were killed, 958 were recorded as having been flogged, and 750 government buildings destroyed[5] — accepted his new role. When the President instructed Harriman to return to London in mid-September to make clear to Churchill he wanted no further changes to Torch, and to insist it remain an American, not binational, operation, the Prime Minister gave way with little more than a murmur of protest.

"I am the President's loyal lieutenant," Churchill said to Harriman in person[6] — and in a cable direct to the President on September 14, 1942, the Prime Minister repeated his expression of fealty in writing. "In the whole of TORCH, military and political, I consider myself your Lieutenant," he wrote, "asking only to put my viewpoint plainly before you. . . . We British will come in only as and when you judge expedient. This is an American enterprise in which we are your help mates."[7]

As Harriman cabled the President that same day, the Prime Minister "understands fully that he is to play second fiddle in all scores and then only as you direct."[8]

Great Britain, which had once ruled more than half the earth, was now fated to play a subordinate role to the United States — a momentous comedown, but better than becoming junior partner, puppet, or quisling of Hitler's Third Reich, as the Vichy French had done. Besides, there was the very thrill of imminent battle, which could not fail to excite the warrior in Winston Churchill.

Ultra intelligence — decrypts of top-secret German military signals that Churchill loved to see raw and uninterpreted by his staff — was revealing the Nazis had no conception of what was about to hit them. Exultant, Churchill cabled Roosevelt on September 14, 1942, saying he was counting "the days" to "Torch"[9] — the more so since his own recent British landing, Operation Jubilee, had proven yet again an utter and bloody disaster.

PART THIRTEEN

The Tragedy of Dieppe

30

A Canadian Bloodbath

PRESSED BY GENERAL MARSHALL and Admiral King on their visit to London in July to mount Sledgehammer that year, Churchill had wisely refused. Yet he had also bristled at the accusations of British faint-heartedness — an accusation that in part explained why he allowed himself to be persuaded by his chief of Combined Operations, Vice Admiral Mountbatten, to go ahead with an operation that had already been canceled once evidence revealed the Germans were aware of it: a landing by an entire Canadian infantry brigade, with tanks, on the beaches of Dieppe, a small French fishing port south of the Pas-de-Calais, where Winston had once courted his wife, Clementine.

Churchill had hoped the "reconnaissance in force," as it was termed, would help convince not only Marshall and King but Stalin, too, that the British — which was to say, Canadians — were not lacking in courage. In a few days, Churchill had told the Russian leader, the operation — a sort of exploratory, miniature version of the full-scale Second Front landings planned for 1943 — would be mounted across the Channel on a selected target with "8,000 men with 50 tanks." They would "stay a night and a day, kill as many Germans as possible and take prisoners." The landing, as Churchill had described, could "be compared to a bath which you feel with your hand to see if the water is hot."[1]

Stalin had shaken his head at such military and political naiveté. Whatever happened on the day — whether successful or not — once the troops were withdrawn the Nazis would simply trumpet their withdrawal as "the failure of a British attempt at an invasion" or retreat — which would help no one, he sniffed.[2]

Launched on the early morning of August 19, 1942, the "Dieppe Raid" had proven Stalin's prediction tragically correct. The water had been scalding, the raid a "fiasco," as even Churchill acknowledged.[3] The Germans, whose troops occupied the entire Atlantic coastline of Europe as far as the Pyrenees, were not only waiting, but had even been conducting an exercise the day before to rehearse repelling just such an assault.[4]

As Stalin had predicted, the master of Nazi propaganda was over the moon when hearing of the operation. Goebbels had just landed in the Ukraine and been driven to the Führer's "idyllically concealed" new advance headquarters at Vinnitsa on August 19 when the news was given to him that at "6.05 in the morning a major invasion attempt had been made at Dieppe."[5] The Allies had landed "more than a division, and had established in one place a small bridgehead. The RAF had thrown large forces into the battle. The English had brought 20 panzers"; moreover, a huge number of vessels were reported to be waiting at Portsmouth to "reinforce the landings if successful." In other words, as Goebbels dictated for his diary, "under pressure from Stalin the British have clearly undertaken the attempt to establish a Second Front."

The Reich minister of propaganda had been contemptuous. "Not for a single second does anyone in the Führer's headquarters doubt that the British will be given a resounding whack and sent home."[6]

Goebbels was proved right. In an eight-hour interview with the Führer, the propaganda minister recorded Hitler's complete unconcern about Dieppe. In March that year the Führer had already stationed a top panzer division in the Pas-de-Calais area, with two further motorized divisions in reserve. They were not even needed — for by 2:00 p.m. on August 19 the invasion attempt had been "liquidated."[7] Sepp Dietrich, commanding the Führer's SS Life Guard motorized division, would surely be swearing blue murder, the Führer chuckled, that he hadn't even had the chance "to enter the fray."[8] Churchill must have ordered the landing as a sop to Stalin — the Russian leader a veritable giant in comparison to little Churchill, who could only boast a "few books he'd written, and speeches in Parliament,"[9] while Stalin had re-created a nation of 170 million and prepared it for a huge military challenge, as Hitler conceded. In fact, if ever Stalin fell into German hands, Hitler told his propaganda genius, as Führer he would out of respect spare the Russian premier, perhaps banishing him to some beach resort. Churchill and Roosevelt, by contrast, would be hanged for having started the war "without showing the least statesmanship or military ability."[10]

Flying back to Berlin to direct the Nazi propaganda response to the Dieppe invasion, Goebbels could only mock at how Churchill then sought to cover up the "true catastrophe," censoring and concealing in the press the huge casualties the Canadians had suffered. The Prime Minister had tried to parlay the attack into an "experiment" — but if it was such, it had achieved the opposite effect, Goebbels crowed. Not only had it shown how devastatingly effective were German defenses in the Pas-de-Calais and nearby region, but it had made the Führer decide to *further* fortify the entire Atlantic coast against invasion: a "full-blown defensive line in the same manner as the Atlantic Wall." "If the British mount a real invasion next spring, where they're planning, they are going to be battering against reinforced castle gates," the Führer had assured him. "They'll never set foot again on European soil. The Atlantic coast and the Norwegian coast will then be one hundred percent in our possession, and we will no longer be threatened by invasion, even if mounted on the most massive scale."[11]

The Führer had then turned to other, more important matters: his decision to seize Leningrad that very year, but to spare Moscow until the next year — though both cities were in due course to be completely "erased"[12] as part of the complete destruction of any kind of Russian national heritage or pride. Plus the thorny problem of the German churches, which were to be threatened with the same solution as was being meted out to the Jews, given their Christian leanings toward Bolshevism and their failure to support Nazism wholeheartedly . . .[13]

Churchill might ask the British and Allied press not to reveal the true extent of the Dieppe fiasco, but it proved impossible to conceal it from the Canadian prime minister, a thousand of whose soldiers had been killed in cold blood on the beaches of the harbor town, with further thousands wounded and taken into German captivity for the duration of the war — their feet even manacled, after an Allied operational order was intercepted and translated, detailing how manacling of captured German troops was to be carried out by the assault troops.

Mackenzie King had opposed the idea of a major cross-Channel landing that year, as long as the Allies lacked preponderant naval and air forces, as well as experienced soldiers. Nevertheless, his defense minister had gone along with the revived operation — and was the first to hear reports that night of the catastrophe. "While [War] Council was sitting," King recorded, "the first authentic word of its extent and probable extent of our losses" — completely contradicting a mendacious press release put out by Lord Mountbatten. In truth, the Canadian premier noted, "casualties were heavy. Number of Canadians taken prisoners but also many killed and wounded. One felt inclined to question," he added, "the wisdom of the raid unless it were part of the agreement reached when Churchill was with Stalin."[14]

Stalin, to be sure, was blameless — having argued against such an operation. Well over half of the sixty-one hundred troops who had taken part in the fiasco had been killed, wounded, or captured.

Two days later King's heart sank still further, as more news of the fatalities came in. "Reports received of raid make one very sad at heart for losses, which have been considerable," he noted again in his diary — German newsreel footage, bruited across neutral countries by Goebbels's propaganda team, making it impossible to maintain Mountbatten's fiction. How much better, Prime Minister King reflected, would it have been "to conserve that especially trained life for the decisive moment. . . . It makes me sad at heart."[15]

And on August 24, 1942, King lamented: "I keep asking myself was this venture justified, just at this time?"[16]

In Washington, the President felt deeply for his Canadian ally: aware that, had Stimson, Marshall, and King gotten their way and launched Bolero that year, it would have been Americans who perished at the hands of the waiting Germans.

PART FOURTEEN

The Torch Is Lit

31

Something in West Africa

WITH HUGE NUMBERS OF AMERICAN troops preparing to embark from ports in Britain and the United States for the invasion of Northwest Africa, how was it possible that neither Hitler, the commander in chief of the forces of the Third Reich, nor his Oberkommando der Wehrmacht (OKW), or German high command, saw the American invasion coming?

Historians could never quite decide. It was not, after all, as if there were no indications of an American surprise attack. On Columbus Day, October 12, 1942, for example, the President had given a special Fireside Chat from the White House. Encouraged by what he had seen of American industrial output, he explained to listeners across the nation — and abroad — that the worst times were now over for the United Nations. The Axis powers had already reached their full strength, the President described; "their steadily mounting losses in men and material cannot be fully replaced. Germany and Japan are already realizing what the inevitable result will be when the total strength of the United Nations hits them" — moreover hits them "at additional places on the earth's surface."[1]

Where, though? Reading British and American newspapers, Goebbels was less sure than the Führer that the Allies would now risk a Second Front, especially after the pasting the Canadians had received at Dieppe. "The Second Front seems to be definitively shelved," the propaganda minister recorded in his diary on September 8, 1942 — noting how even Russians were now contenting themselves with calls for the RAF to do heavier bombing rather than harping on an impossible cross-Channel invasion.[2] But if not a cross-Channel Second Front, might the Americans invade elsewhere? The south of France, perhaps?

Secret plans for military occupation of the remaining Vichy-controlled inland and southern regions of mainland France had long been drawn up

402 | THE TORCH IS LIT

by the German high command, code-named Case Anton, even though this would abrogate the terms of the Franco-German armistice, signed by Maréchal Pétain in 1940, following the French surrender. Case Anton would ensure the whole of the Mediterranean coast of France would be secured by German and Italian forces, if there were impending signs of an Allied invasion. But what of French Northwest Africa, where there were still only a handful of German officials?

Goebbels, like Hitler, discounted the notion. In the United States, in the October run-up to the November 3 congressional elections, press hostility to the President was rising — "a pretty tough and massive critical mass," Goebbels recorded with satisfaction.[3] All the President seemed to have to offer were words. Not only were the Germans "stealing food from the rest of Europe," the President had warned listeners in his Fireside Chat, but there had been an increase in the "fury" of German "atrocities" in Europe that would not be overlooked — or forgiven, he'd stated. The United Nations, the President declared, "have decided to establish the identity of those Nazi leaders who are responsible for the innumerable acts of savagery. As each of these criminal deeds is committed," he'd emphasized, "it is being carefully investigated; and the evidence is being relentlessly piled up for the future purposes of justice. We have made it entirely clear that the United Nations seek no mass reprisals against the populations of Germany or Italy or Japan. But the ringleaders and their brutal henchmen must be named, and apprehended, and tried in accordance with the judicial processes of criminal law."[4]

Reading the transcript in Berlin, Dr. Goebbels had known far better than the President what "atrocities" were being perpetrated, and on what a sickening scale. He'd put little credence in the President's warnings, however: neither the "additional places" where the Allies would strike, nor the justice that would be meted out for German — and Japanese — "criminal deeds." A Second Front in France that year, or the next, would never succeed, Goebbels reckoned — the British failure at Dieppe having demonstrated the impregnable nature of the Westwall defensive line from Norway to the Spanish border. "The English know as well as we do that they are in no position to launch even a modest start in that direction," he noted contemptuously a few days after the President spoke.[5]

The threat of postwar American justice tribunals Goebbels treated with the same contempt. "One can just dismiss such things with a shrug of one's shoulders," he'd added to his daily diary[6] — secure in his conviction that German victory in the war would make the notion of criminal trials thereafter ridiculous. Even if the renewed German assault on the Eastern Front were to grind to a halt at Stalingrad and in the Urals, forcing the Wehrmacht onto the defensive for another winter, German forces had seized a prodigious amount of Russian territory, which could be used to feed the Third Reich rather than its own people. "We have a swath in our possession that will allow us to develop our potential in undreamed of ways," he encouraged himself to believe,[7] recalling Hitler's grand design: German warrior-farmers, controlling a vast eastern border of the Reich in which those Slavs who were allowed to survive (half of all Russian captives were, in reality, killed or starved to death) would be kept as illiterate slaves of their German masters.

The propaganda minister, whose genius had been to manipulate and orchestrate the entire output of German newspapers, radio, film, theater, and publishing, thus dismissed the President's broadcast as hot air, glorying in Roosevelt's "democratic" difficulties with Congress, his embarrassment at Wendell Willkie's almost hysterical calls for a Second Front during a recent visit to Moscow, and declining support for the President in American public opinion polls — with anxious voices saying "We could lose the war!" or "We will lose the war!" Goebbels noted.[8]

But if so, how was it the President sounded so confident in his Fireside Chats, Goebbels wondered[9] — as did Churchill in the English Parliament, too? What were they up to?[10]

On October 6, 1942, Goebbels admitted that, in terms of a possible American or Allied offensive in or around the periphery of Europe, "absolutely nothing is known."[11]

With the Russians continuing their "infernal resistance" at Stalingrad, all eyes were on the Eastern Front, where snow would soon fall. Weather in the English Channel would, by the same token, surely make a cross-Channel attack impossible, whatever reports Wendell Willkie might be taking back to the President from Stalin in Moscow. On October 17, 1942, however, Goebbels noted there were "rumors that the Allies are preparing for something in West Africa. Apparently such plans are quite advanced. It's possible that the British and the Americans are trying to get clear of their commitment [to the Russians], and pretending to Stalin this would be a second front."[12]

No countermeasures were taken by Hitler's headquarters, however, and by October 20, Goebbels was noting that the French — a nation on the down and out, in his view — were getting worried about their hitherto undisturbed colonial territories in North Africa. "Sooner or later the British and above all the Americans will appear there," Goebbels accepted — not as a springboard to attack Italy and Germany so much as for reasons of imperial design, he thought. "The Americans without doubt intend one way or another to inveigle themselves into this war and do everything they can to pick up what's going free, so to speak" — colonies. He and the Führer therefore contented themselves with the assumption that the French could be relied upon to defend their colonial territories with the substantial naval, air, and land forces they had in Morocco, Algeria, Tunisia, and Dakar.

At the White House, meanwhile, the President, reading Ultra decrypts of German signals and hearing from his OSS chief, "Wild Bill" Donovan, could hardly believe the reports from Germany and North Africa. Could the Führer *really* have no idea of the magnitude of what was going to hit him?

That a thousand things could go wrong with the Torch invasion, Roosevelt was well aware, from the notorious autumnal surf off Casablanca to Axis identification of the approaching fleets from America and the British Isles. The Vichy French, too, might react as they were doing on the island of Madagascar still — defending their colonies with everything they had. Would the fact that the "invaders" were American not make a big difference, though? To make absolutely sure, the President prepared special printed leaflets addressed to the people of French North Africa, to be distributed and dropped from the air once the landings took place. He also made a specially recorded audio message to be broadcast on radio — in the President's best French.[13]

How the French would respond thus remained for Roosevelt the biggest question. General Weygand, the pro-American commander in chief of French forces in Africa, had been fired by Marshal Pétain, under pressure of the Nazis, and his successor, General Darlan, was fiercely anti-British and not necessarily pro-American — though he had assured Admiral Leahy that an American landing in overwhelming force would be enough to get the French to agree to a cease-fire, after perhaps token resistance *"pour l'histoire."* There was also the possibility being explored by Robert Murphy, the former chargé d'affaires at the U.S. Embassy to Vichy France and currently the President's special emissary in Vichy-administered North Africa, that General Henri Giraud, a brave and popular warrior who had escaped to France from a prisoner-of-war camp in

Germany, where he'd been held since 1940, could be used to rally French forces in North Africa to the American cause. For this to happen, however, he would have to be sprung from Vichy France by submarine, and attached to General Eisenhower's headquarters.

At the end of the day, however, the President had as little confidence that the Vichy French wished to be "liberated" as Hitler did. Or Churchill. Life in French Northwest Africa — save for French Jews — had been remarkably easy, and made all the easier by Roosevelt's decision to continue sending food. Resistance to an American invasion might therefore be weak — but the President doubted whether the French would resist a German invasion, either, if Hitler chose to contest the Allied campaign. It wouldn't matter, however. In fact the President was *counting* on German opposition, which would ensure that American troops learn on the field of battle the same military skills that the Russians had had to learn on the Eastern Front — but on ground of America's choosing, at the very limit of German communications, and with the strategic goal of gaining a secure steppingstone, on the threshold of Europe, that could be relentlessly reinforced from the United States, and lead to the elimination of Italy as an Axis belligerent — as Stalin had so swiftly understood. Roosevelt thus remained quietly optimistic, even as his secretary of war slipped into an ever deepening funk.

The Dieppe fiasco, paradoxically, frightened Stimson more as an example of what might befall Torch than it did in relation to his support for a premature cross-Channel invasion. No matter how much the President pointed out the difference — especially the fact that there were still only a handful of Germans in Morocco and Algeria — Stimson continued to argue and conspire to cancel the project. Dimly, though, he became aware that he was testing the President's legendary patience. When he insisted on lowering the age for the draft, or Selective Service, claiming it was immediately necessary for manpower reasons, *before* the congressional elections in November, the President was furious — but agreed to ask Congress for the bill — knowing it would dent his Democratic majority in the House and in the Senate. It did not endear Stimson to the Boss, however — the President refusing to invite Stimson to the White House.

"I have not been seeing as much of the President lately as I used to," Stimson acknowledged in his diary, but ascribed it erroneously to the President's increasing trust in General Marshall's judgment and advice. "That is a good result," he wrote, pretending to welcome the change, "but

I shall have to look out to be sure that it does not cut me out of situations where I have duties and responsibilities as constitutional adviser of the President and will be criticized if I do not present my views to him. I have been much worried lately over the African situation and our variances of views there, but I have presented my own views very clearly to him both verbally and in writing."[14] Reflecting on where it had gotten him, the aging war secretary at last faced up to his failure, however. "I have decided thus far," he noted, "that it would be unwise to do it again."[15]

Stimson, ever the lawyer, wanted a paper trail of protest if the Torch invasion proved a disaster, but steered away from dismissal for being defeatist. On September 17, 1942, only seven weeks before the projected invasion, he finally abandoned his incessant carping — having been told by Marshall to cut it out: by trying to stop the switch of U.S. bomber forces from Bolero to Torch he was only sabotaging General Eisenhower's chances of success.[16] "We are embarked on a risky undertaking but it is not at all hopeless," he acknowledged, "and, the Commander in Chief having made the decision, we must make it a success."[17]

Stimson's reluctant acquiescence in the Torch operation was a relief to the President, but it did not make the path toward victory certain by any means. The speed with which the army and navy operations staffs had to work was phenomenal — and interservice rivalry and disagreement became rife.

For his part General Patton, commanding the Western Task Force that would be setting out on its epic venture from the Chesapeake Bay, became more and more determined to smash Vichy French opposition if it came — but less and less inclined to work with his naval counterpart, Admiral H. Kent Hewitt.

Refusing to micromanage, Roosevelt declined to meddle in operational matters, once his strategy had been laid down and accepted: a confidence in his chosen theater and field commanders that was beginning to mark his leadership style as U.S. commander in chief. On occasion, however, he had no option but to intervene — as he did on hearing of the Patton-Hewitt feud. Learning from Admiral King that Hewitt and Patton had almost come to blows (Patton reported to have unleashed a "torrent of his most Rabelaisian abuse" that had made Hewitt's staff flee in "virtual panic, convinced they could never work with a general so crude and rude as Patton"),[18] the President flatly turned down Admiral King's recommendation that Patton be fired from the invasion lineup. Instead, both officers were summoned to the White House at 2:00 p.m. on October 21, 1942.

"Come in, Skipper, and Old Cavalryman," the President welcomed his two field commanders, "and give me the good news."[19]

Patton entered the Oval Office wearing his ivory-handled pistols, and holding under his arm his helmet with his two oversize major general's stars. Roosevelt had taken a personal interest in the swashbuckling tank commander as far back as 1933, when Patton commanded the cavalry at Fort Meyer, and seemed genuinely delighted by his swagger and pugnacious attitude — which contrasted greatly with so many of the War Department personnel he saw. "He was one of the earliest Cavalry officers to shift to tanks," the President later wrote of Patton. "He came to see me two weeks before the American expedition started for Casablanca and I asked him whether he had his old Cavalry saddle to mount on the turret of a tank and if he went into action, with his saber drawn," he recalled with a chuckle. "Patton is a joy."[20]

For his part, now that Torch was definitely "on," the cavalry general was determined to make the American landings a success. But if Admiral Hewitt had hoped the President would intercede over complications with the British over destroyers, and if Patton hoped he would intercede by giving an order to Hewitt that the landings must take place whatever the weather conditions, they were disappointed. The Commander in Chief refused to get involved. "Of course you must," he responded to Patton, declining to be drawn over the matter of touchdown conditions; meanwhile to Hewitt he advised temporizing with the British Admiralty, whose suggestion of switching around British destroyers with American warships threatened to compromise clear American fire control in support of their troops. "I never say no [to the British]," the President confided mischievously to Admiral Hewitt, "but we can stall until it is too late."[21]

"A great politician is not of necessity a great military leader," Patton left the White House thinking[22] — unaware that the very operation he was tasked with was "the President's great secret baby." Unaware, moreover, that to get the landings mounted at all the Commander in Chief had had to fight a far, far more prolonged and arduous battle than the brave tanker was having with his naval counterpart.

From the President's point of view, though, the White House meeting on October 21, two weeks before Torch, was exhilarating. In his characteristic manner Roosevelt had with charm and goodwill gotten his two commanders to stop squabbling and recognize they were on the same side, in a momentous enterprise that would alter the course of the war.

Patton's parting words, spoken in his high falsetto voice as he left the President's office, said it all:

"Sir, all I want to tell you is this. I will leave the beaches either a conqueror or a corpse."[23]

32

Alamein

THE PRESIDENT, TRAVELING to spend the last days of October at Hyde Park, had to pretend to reporters that nothing was afoot. This was so even as the White House Map Room became the focal point for a veritable fusillade of secret communications — and even as, in the midst of a world war, Americans went to the polls on November 3, 1942, to elect a new Congress.

The results were dismal — the Democrats retaining control over both chambers, the Senate and the House, though with sorely diminished majorities.[1]

How different might have been the outcome, the President reflected, if the Torch invasion had been mounted, as he had hoped, on October 30. But war was war, and the lives of the assault troops were too important to be risked without the extra week's training and issue of armaments that General Marshall had deemed necessary, when he asked for — and got — a week's extension of D-day.

Besides, the omens for Torch looked good. On his way to Moscow in August, Churchill had felt compelled to fire General Auchinleck, and appoint a new British Eighth Army commander. The man he'd chosen, Lieutenant General Richard Gott, was yet another of Churchill's poor selections, and would, in the view of almost all Eighth Army veterans, have lost the battle for Egypt. But Gott had been shot down by a flight of Messerschmitts while flying back to Cairo for a bath, and had been burned to death.[2] His replacement, General Bernard Montgomery, had dealt with Rommel's August 31 panzer offensive without turning a hair, and had then set about remaking the Eighth Army into a professional modern force of all arms, working together, in preparation for what he described, in a "Personal Message to be read out to the troops on the morning of D-day" as "one of the decisive battles of history."[3] On the night of October 23, 1942, over a thousand artillery guns of the British Eighth Army opened fire at El Alamein, and an all-out assault had begun in the Egyptian desert — Montgomery hoping to smash the German-Italian African Panzer Army at the very moment when Rommel was away in Berlin, officially receiving his baton as a field marshal in person from the Führer, as well as a standing ovation from his fellow Nazis at the Sportpalast.

Rushing back to Egypt on October 25, Rommel had found his vaunted Panzerarmee Afrika facing disaster — the British not only having attacked in the middle of the night, but having breached the minefields he had ordered to be sewn with half a million land mines. They had killed the acting German Army commander, General Stumme, and broken through with a massive combined force of infantry, tanks, and artillery onto higher ground in the north of the Alamein line, forcing Rommel to counterattack them. The battle had then become a desperate struggle of attrition, causing the Prime Minister to become frantically nervous, and the President — worried lest a British failure prejudice the responses of Vichy officials and military commanders to an American invasion of Morocco and Algeria on November 8 — to wish the British could have postponed their offensive for a week, as he had wanted, to synchronize with Marshall's delay of Torch.

Lieutenant General Montgomery — who had ordered the entire Eighth Army to undertake training in night fighting — had refused, however, to order his men into minefield combat (crossing the largest sewn minefield in military history to that date) without at least the light of the full October moon.

By November 2, 1942, when the Alamein battle was still not won, after eleven days, there was growing apprehension. Yet as the disappointing results of the American congressional election came in on the night of November 3, so too did Ultra intercepts of Rommel's desperate appeals to Hitler to be allowed to retreat, taking with him what was left of his once-victorious Afrika Korps.

The tide, then, *was* turning in the Middle East.

Churchill's mood — which had dipped during the last days of October, when victory was still not won[4] — changed from depression to elation.

Hitler's negative response — "siegen oder sterben" (win or die) — marked a turning point in World War II. Not even the famed Field Marshal Rommel, though, could halt the exodus of his mobile units as they fled the battlefield, leaving behind even their own Afrika Korps commander, General von Thoma, and tens of thousands of abandoned, battle-weary German and Italian troops, to surrender to Montgomery.

It was victory, at last, for the British, after three long years of defeat — and the President was as excited as Churchill — for the great pincers he had planned for over a year could soon be applied, if all went well.

Hitler, having so recently entertained and extolled Rommel in Berlin, was mortified. The Führer had moved his headquarters back to East Prussia — chagrined that, having come so close to victory in Russia and in Egypt that summer, victory seemed now to be slipping away from him by the hour.

His troops had not succeeded in swiftly capturing Stalingrad. Nor had they quite breached the vast mountain chain of the Urals, despite reaching the peak of Mount Erebus. Now, with Rommel's Panzer Army in Egypt in full retreat, the possibility of a double German envelopment of the oil fields of the Caucasus from north *and* south became a chimera — indeed, so worried was Hitler by the military situation that Goebbels was told the Führer might not be able to travel to Munich for his annual get-together with Nazi Party stalwarts on November 9, 1942.[5]

Goebbels, for his own part, remained sure that Rommel, the star performer of the German Wehrmacht, would spring something out of the bag to confound the British, as he had so often done before.[6] A German internal Security Service reported on November 4, 1942, that "the people are breathlessly following the battle for North Africa. Their trust in Rommel is so high, they cannot imagine a crisis there. The situation at Stalingrad is murky, but it's hoped the city will be in our hands before the onset of winter."[7]

It was not to be. At his Wolf's Lair headquarters in Rastenburg, "huge problems" were awaiting Hitler. "He still isn't eating either lunch or dinner with his staff," Goebbels noted in his diary on November 4. "Actually this is quite good for his health," Goebbels added, "since that way he saves four or five hours a day, hours he would otherwise need for conversation." Nevertheless, "the way things are going in North Africa are getting to one's nerves — even the Führer's. I'm getting reports he's more and more anxious about the outcome. The whole afternoon is consumed by concern. It's absolutely dreadful we have to wait so long for news. But it's the same for the Führer. Rommel doesn't send much. In these critical hours he'll have other things to do than constantly send us dispatches. We'll have to wait patiently for tomorrow, when things will be clearer."[8]

The next day's news was "somewhat bleak," however, Goebbels noted — plotting how, as Reichsminister for propaganda, he could turn defeat into a story of "calculated withdrawal" to better positions in Egypt.[9] American losses in the naval and land battle for Guadalcanal, as well as the Democratic Party's losses in the congressional elections, would keep American focus on the Far East, surely.[10] Yet even Goebbels had to wonder when he received reports, on the night of November 6, 1942, that Allied warships and troop transports were passing through the Straits of Gibraltar, and entering the Mediterranean Sea — ships whose destination was "still unknown."[11]

Was it a British relief convoy for Malta? Or an attempt to land British forces behind Rommel's front, in Libya? "We're going to do everything in our power to smash it" using air and naval forces, Goebbels recorded. "There are reconnaissance reports of three aircraft carriers and a battleship among them. If we can lure them into a naval battle, we could reverse the defeat we've suffered. . . . Everything else that's going on in the world is being overshadowed by North Africa."[12] He lamented Hitler's increasing reluctance to broadcast or be filmed for weekly newsreels, but hoped the Führer's forthcoming trip to Munich, if he went ahead with it, would give an opportunity for rabble-rousing rhetoric.

Instead he got Torch.

33

First Light

RETURNING FROM HYDE PARK on November 5, 1942, the President stayed briefly in Washington. There he finally revealed to the secretary of state, Cordell Hull, the still-secret details of Operation Torch — tasking him to do his best to keep the Spanish government from interfering from Spanish Morocco, or offering free access across Spain to the Mediterranean to the Germans, once the landings commenced. Then the President formally opened the new White House wing, where Admiral Leahy was now installed as his military chief of staff.

"At 2:20, the President laid a corner stone at the NorthEastern [*sic*] corner of the new addition to the Executive Mansion which contains my office," Leahy recorded in his diary, noting that the ceremony "involved no speeches and no formality other than the usual taking of photographs"[1] — for the press were to be given no chance to get too close to the President, or his staff, on the eve of such a momentous military undertaking, with tens of thousands of American lives at risk.

"Of course we hear no word from the great convoys that are converging on the rendezvous," Secretary Stimson noted that same day, "because they are all under radio silence. But the fact that they are coming is already foreshadowed by messages which are coming out of Germany." Enemy reconnaissance planes had "evidently spotted them in the Gibraltar Channel. Today word came through that the Germans had asked Spain for permission to go through."[2]

Thanks to Montgomery's great victory in Egypt, it seemed unlikely the Spanish, who had remained neutral for so long since 1939, would agree. "The news from Egypt is getting better and better. Rommel is in complete retreat, has lost a large number of tanks and a considerable number of prisoners and, as the day wore on today, the news indicated he was running faster and faster, and the British becoming more and more jubilant. For once matters have been timed admirably for our own action," Stimson — the former refusenik — confessed, "for Hitler's main forces are still tied up in Russia and now Rommel's force seems to have been pretty effectively smashed in the eastern Mediterranean."[3]

So far, so good. General Marshall had warned the war secretary that the President "was very snappy today and was biting off heads," but when Stimson sought an interview at the White House he found Roosevelt "in very good humor," in fact was as "amiable as a basket of chips," as he recorded afterwards with relief[4] — the President even agreeing with Stimson's solution to the problem of competition between the nation's need for soldiers and for specialists in the war industries: namely a presidential appointee to arbitrate between the Manpower Commission and the Selective Service authorities, both of which were working remarkably well.

The tension in the War Department and at the White House was, however, growing by the hour.

The next day, Friday, November 6, 1942, the President addressed the cabinet at 2:00 p.m. Stimson had a new bee in his bonnet, this time about a "military school at Charlottesville." It was designed by the secretary of war "to train officers for proconsular duties after the war was over." As the war was by no means over, and since the cabinet had been divided over the subject at its last meeting, the matter threatened to become a controversial red herring.[5]

Once again Roosevelt had to beat back the temptation to silence his secretary of war — resorting instead to his usual tactic when he didn't want a particular issue to be debated, or another to be raised. As he confided several weeks later to the Canadian premier, Mackenzie King, "I adopt the policy when asked a question that is embarrassing, of stalling to tell a story, and after a time, others forget and lose interest in the question they have asked."[6]

The tactic worked — for the most part. "I had all the typical difficulties of a discussion in a Roosevelt Cabinet," Stimson lamented after the cabinet meeting, once back at the War Department. "The president was constantly interrupting me with discursive stories which popped into his mind while we were talking, and it was very hard to keep a steady thread through, but I kept my teeth in the subject and think I finally got it across."[7]

Roosevelt knew exactly what he was doing, however; the matter was deferred. No sooner was the cabinet meeting over, then, than the President — anxious to evade the press, who might pick up rumors of the impending landings — set off for Shangri-la. With him went Harry Hopkins, Hopkins's new wife, Louise, Grace Tully, Daisy Suckley, and several more guests.

"Quite cold — large fires in the fireplaces," Daisy noted of their arrival. "There was a feeling of excitement. Telephone calls now & then, but the P. keeps conversation light — teases everyone."[8]

They went to bed early. There were "flashing lights" in the woods and some commotion, but eventually she fell asleep.[9]

It was the eve of the largest amphibious invasion launched in American history — an armada of over a hundred ships approaching French Northwest Africa and about to land more than a hundred thousand men on the shores of Morocco and Algeria: Torch.

How such a huge invasion, dispatched from two continents, could be kept so secret and timed to arrive synchronously was nothing short of miraculous.

Daisy Suckley knew something was up, but what it was even she had no idea. "For weeks," she noted in her diary afterwards, the President "has had something up his sleeve." Only a handful of people knew of the operation, she recorded, "though everything, down to the very date, has been planned since July. He spoke of an egg that was about to be laid — probably over the weekend." They might have to return to Washington on Saturday "if the hen laid an egg!" she recalled the President's warning with amusement.[10]

In the event, they remained at Shangri-la. There was little the Commander in Chief could now do. For good or ill, the invasion must go ahead — indeed, on November 1, while still in Hyde Park, Roosevelt had had to crush urgent recommendations from Robert Murphy, his presidential representative in Algiers, who pleaded for the invasion to be postponed for two weeks.

Poor Murphy had run up against a dire difficulty. "Kingpin" — i.e., General Giraud, the "hero" who had escaped from a German prison camp — had been duly contacted in Vichy, on the grounds that he was, in contrast to General de Gaulle in England, the best prospective military leader who might persuade Vichy forces in Morocco and Algeria to lay down their arms, once U.S. troops landed. However, to preserve secrecy, the President's emissaries had declined to tell Giraud in advance when exactly the invasion would take place. Once informed, the brave Frenchman had proven nothing less than a thorn in General Eisenhower's side — insisting he needed more time if he was to be the savior of France.

Murphy, hearing this at his office in Algiers on November 1, had suddenly lost faith in the whole Torch enterprise. "I am convinced that the invasion of North Africa without favorable French High Command will be a catastrophe," he had wired to the President in Washington. "The delay of two weeks, unpleasant as it may be, involving technical considerations of which I am ignorant, is insignificant compared with the result involving serious opposition of the French Army to our landing."[11]

There can have been few more "ridiculous" cables sent by a career diplomat in the days before a major amphibious invasion involving more than a hundred and thirty thousand soldiers, sailors, and airmen in its first wave — as Murphy, to his credit, admitted in retrospect. "The intricate movement of vast fleets from the United States as well as England was already under way, and a delay of even one day would upset the meticulous plans which had been meshed into one master plan by hundreds of staff officers of all branches of the armed forces of both Allied powers," the diplomat afterward reflected — complaining that no one had "briefed" him on the complexity of such an operation of modern war.[12]

General Eisenhower, who had never commanded in combat, nor been responsible for such a vast operation of war involving army, navy, and air components operating simultaneously from two continents, had been rocked by his copy of Murphy's cable, and waited for the President to decide what to do. "Of course it was a preposterous proposal," Secretary Stimson noted in his diary, "but strangely enough" Giraud and his conspirators in Vichy France had "won over 'McGowan' [Murphy's code name] to support it."[13]

In Washington, Secretary Stimson called Giraud's plea to postpone the invasion by two weeks "as impossible as a flight to the moon."[14] Roosevelt felt the same. Receiving Murphy's personal recommendation, the President had been contemptuous. Oh, the French! he'd mused — hearing that General Giraud not only wanted to delay the invasion, but had announced he wished to be made commander in chief of the entire Allied invasion forces, including the Americans, once it took place!

Admiral Leahy, in Washington, spoke with Marshall and King. All were agreed: the Frenchman was mad, and must be dumped if he did not comply with the President's wishes. "The decision of the President," Leahy signaled in an uncompromising cable sent to Murphy from the White House on November 2, "is that the operation will be carried out as now planned and that you will do your utmost to secure the understanding and cooperation of the French officials with whom you are now in contact."[15]

"I personally don't expect much enthusiasm on the part of the French African Army in opposing American troops," Leahy noted in his diary that night, "although the coast defenses of the Navy may be expected to oppose the landings."[16] Even Secretary Stimson, who was feeling daily more confident in the enterprise, called the Murphy cable in his diary "one of the crises which inevitably occur in military operations, particularly in such long and complicated ones as the one we are now launching."[17]

The invasion was still on. The Germans remained unaware of what exactly was coming. The Vichy French were either blissfully ignorant, or squabbling over who would wield power in the aftermath. General Patton, commanding the Western Task Force, thirsted for glory. General Eisenhower cursed at the complexity of dealing with French colonial defenders he needed to befriend in order to fight the real enemy, the Nazis.

And more than a hundred thousand trained assault troops fought seasickness and fear, as "D-day" and "H-hour" — the moment of touchdown — approached.

November 7, 1942, in the Catoctin Mountains, in north central Maryland, dawned chilly. "One can hear every sound from one room to another," Daisy noted. Even the "doors themselves creak & snap & groan!"[18]

She lit the fire in her bedroom from the paper and kindling outside her door. The camp's staff brought her breakfast. She read the newspaper, then took Fala, the President's dog, for a walk around the grounds. "When I got back to Shangri-La I found the P. sitting in the enclosed porch. He told me that one of the guards last night had challenged a dozen or so men with guns, in the dark. The dozen men refused to stop or answer, so he reported to headquarters. All available soldiers & S.[ecret] S.[ervice] were called out, beat the woods, etc. Much excitement!" Daisy recorded. It turned out that there were only two intruders: "two boys were looking for skunks, & being 'natives' & independent, saw no reason for answering the challenge! All's well!"[19]

The President chuckled — wondering, however, whether this was a microcosm of what would be happening in Northwest Africa. Reports had been confirmed that ships sailing from Great Britain through the Straits of Gibraltar "have been spotted by Spanish and Italian observers," as Secretary Stimson, at the War Department, noted.[20]

Torch was now in the lap of the gods.

The President remained serenely optimistic.

This, the President reflected, was the great virtue of the Torch he was lighting: that whatever transpired on the battlefield — however mixed up the invasion forces, however chaotic the scenes in North Africa, however conflicted the Vichy French defenders of France's African colonies — Torch simply could not fail.

There were still no Germans in French Northwest Africa — and given the sheer size of the secret invasion forces poised to descend on Algeria and Morocco, there was nothing the Germans, or the Vichy French, could do to stop it. Within days of the first landings there would be almost a quarter million American troops, backed by British units, established on the Atlantic and Mediterranean shores, with airfields and seaports to receive reinforcements, drawn from the vast U.S. military arsenal the President had created that year. There was no way Hitler could evict them.

How different a U.S. invasion of France, across the English Channel, would have fared that year — or, without combat experience, the next. The United States had never mounted such an amphibious operation in its history, and there was so much still to learn — even before U.S. troops actually met Germans on the field of battle. The British had been fighting Germans since the spring of 1940, when the "phony" war ended and Hitler launched his massive attack on the Western Front; it had taken them more than two long and unhappy years of combat to win a single battle. How long would it take the U.S. Army?

It didn't matter.

This, again, was something which even the smartest brains in the War Department had been unable to accept, the President reflected: namely, the time it would take for a formerly isolationist, pacifist nation not only to gird itself up for foreign war, but to learn how to fight it there, on the battlefield.

American observers had returned from the British front in Libya and

North Africa that summer with many lessons and recommendations based on desert fighting: especially the need to deal with the Wehrmacht's dreaded 88mm antiaircraft gun used in its lethal mobile antitank role; also the seamless cohesion between Rommel's infantry, panzers, artillery, and his Luftwaffe air support. But until American commanders and their units were tested in battle, such observations were simply theory. Even after years of British combat in North Africa, it had taken a commander as ruthlessly professional as General Montgomery to kick out the duds in the British Eighth Army and recast the way the citizen army of a democracy *should* fight, if it ever hoped to defeat the indoctrinated, disciplined warriors of Hitler's brutal Third Reich: a nation where killing had become the be all and end all of German vengeance for defeat in World War I; where butchering one's own people, of the wrong creed or faith, was accepted by the masses — merciless slaughter, carried out without public protest, and without even a semblance of collective conscience. That stain, that genocidal distortion of humanity, had to be brought to an end, the President was utterly determined — and by putting his first major American army into battle in an area where it could win its spurs, and hearten the free world as well as occupied nations, seemed to him a noble, realistic, and achievable aim.

It was this that caused the President to feel so confident in the days and hours leading up to the Torch invasion, as all around him attested. When Prime Minister Mackenzie King called him on November 6 — his call put straight through to Shangri-la — the Canadian premier had been amazed and delighted to hear the President's voice, immediately. "Said he was feeling very well," and was speaking "from the top of a hill" seventy miles from Washington, and almost two thousand feet "high." The President seemed untroubled by the congressional election results. In fact, "everything considered," Roosevelt remarked, "to still have control of both Houses of Congress in a third term was not too bad." Winston Churchill had called him the night before, "very pleased" with the victory at Alamein; and there would be "other things very soon," the President cautiously assured King — who'd been informed of the Torch operational details both by Churchill and by his minister of defense, since many Canadian naval vessels would be taking part in the invasion armada.

Prime Minister King had consistently argued against a cross-Channel Second Front invasion — and had been proven tragically right when so many of his compatriots were senselessly mown down at Dieppe on August 19. Torch, however, was different — and the Canadian premier was "looking forward" to it. "He said he had been so glad to hear my voice again," King described the President. "He sounded very cheerful" — so much so, in fact, that he "said he wanted to tell me a joke about some of the Italians and the Germans who had been captured in Egypt. He said that they were in terrible shape, Italians were black with dirt, and the Germans in a positively filthy condition . . ."

Mackenzie King didn't get, or lost, the point. But where, in the spring and summer that year, his own mind had been disturbed by the collapse of British forces in the Far East, Indian Ocean, and Middle East, his Canadian heart was now filled with hope.

As to the Pacific, "about all we can do there is to hold our own," Roosevelt confided, "and we are doing that" — the situation at Guadalcanal "much better."[21] But the major blow, as the President had always insisted, was now to be in the West.

The President's telephone rang constantly — Hopkins ignoring his wife, Louise, as he sought to help field the incoming reports and facilitate the President's responses. "Throughout the week-end, Harry was in & out of F.D.R.'s room from breakfast time on," Daisy noted; "Louise stayed in her room all Sunday morning," November 7.[22]

In Washington the situation was more fraught. General Eisenhower had cabled to "inform us that a landing of the American expedition will be commenced at Oran and Algiers at 1:00 a.m. Greenwich civil time, which is 9:00 p.m. Washington time," Admiral Leahy formally recorded in his diary in his new office in the White House East Wing. "Received radio information that one combat loaded ship in a convoy en route to Algeria was torpedoed before reaching the Straits of Gibraltar," he added — telephoning the news to the President at Shangri-la. "This ship, which probably carried 3000 troops, is reported to be afloat and in tow but definitely out of the operation."[23]

In his diary, Secretary Stimson dismissed all office work but that relating to the impending assault, noting that "the underlying thing in our minds is the approaching offensive in Africa." Telegrams were coming in "thick and fast" — zero hour being "early Sunday morning, November 8th in North Africa, "which means the middle of the evening tonight," November 7, in Washington. He and his wife had kindly invited General

Patton's wife, Beatrice, to dinner, "and she came with great eagerness and we three spent the evening together."[24]

At Shangri-la, the President had still said nothing to his guests — though they "couldn't fail" to have noticed "F.D.R. was on edge," Grace Tully later recalled, "and that there must be some unusual reason."[25]

In the privacy of the President's bedroom that evening, Roosevelt finally took the call from Admiral Leahy.

"Thank God. Thank God. That sounds grand. Congratulations," Roosevelt burst out. "Casualties are comparatively light — much below your predictions," he confirmed his understanding of the message.[26]

With a huge sigh of relief the President then "dropped the phone and turned to us," his secretary recalled — being one of the few to be in on the secret of the invasion. "Thank God. We have landed in North Africa," Roosevelt declared. "We are striking back."[27] He still said nothing to his guests, however.

Daisy Suckley, in the sitting room, was vaguely but distinctly aware that something momentous was taking place. "There was a feeling of suspense through dinner, though the Pres. as always was joking & teasing," she recorded. "About 8.30, we left the dining table after a delicious dinner of which the main course was *musk-ox* — It was like the most tender beef but with a tiny difference in taste," she described — prepared and served by the Filipino staff from the USS *Potomac*. "As we were getting settled in chairs & on the sofa with the P. he suddenly said that at nine 'something will break on the radio.'"[28]

The moment, then, had come.

A "portable radio was brought in, as the huge expensive one doesn't work well (quite usual!) & at nine we got the news of the landing of our troops on North Africa!" Daisy noted in her diary. "Morocco, Algiers and Tunisia — Until quite late we all sat around the P., the radio on, he getting word of dispatches by telephone from the White House. It was terribly exciting."[29]

In Washington there was the same anticipation. "At nine o'clock," having also listened to the radio and heard "the proclamations of the President and General Eisenhower which were delivered to the world coincidentally with the landings," Secretary Stimson was told by telephone from the War Department "that the three assaults were under way and the landings had been made" at Casablanca, Oran, and Algiers — successfully. This was a great relief to Stimson — a perennial worrier — who had been concerned over "the prophecies of bad weather which might prevent the landing and disjoint the whole performance." Worse still, it might have caused General Patton, "who is impulsive and brave," to "take off in an impossible sea and suffer great losses."[30]

Soon after, Secretary Stimson felt pleased enough to call the President to congratulate him.

It was a telling conversation — the man who had opposed the Torch invasion from the start to the bitter end, arguing it was too risky to undertake; a man who the previous day had told a visiting British munitions official that, in contrast to Torch, he preferred the idea of "keeping up the pounding on Germany through the air through the winter," and waiting till 1943 to mount a cross-Channel invasion.[31]

Roosevelt graciously said nothing. For one thing, it was too early to crow. Yet for a president who loved American history it was, nevertheless, a moment to savor — eleven months to the day since the Pearl Harbor defeat.

By the time Daisy wrote her diary entry the following day, November 8, 1942, she was aware the event had already passed into "History, & in the papers." Nevertheless, she reflected, it was "thrilling" to have experienced it in the presence of her cousin, the President she adored. "And for the P. it was a tremendous climax, for he had been planning it, arranging it, for months."[32]

On the way back to the White House the next afternoon, Sunday, November 8, the President was so exhausted, he slept in the car. "I had to wake him as we approached the city," Daisy recorded: "it wouldn't look well for the P. of the U.S. to be seen driving through the streets with his eyes closed and his head nodding!"[33]

34

The Greatest Sensation

TODAY EVERYTHING WAS ENTIRELY overshadowed by what was going on in Africa," Secretary Stimson recorded proudly on November 8, 1942. "The whole affair seems to have gone off admirably in respect to its execution and timing. Coming as it does, and was planned to do, on top of the British victory over Rommel in Egypt, it has taken the Nazi forces both at a surprise and at a great disadvantage, and every reaction today which came from Vichy and from the Berlin radios confirmed this."[1]

It was incredible yet true: the Führer caught with his pants down, traveling by train to Munich to give his traditional annual address to Nazi Party stalwarts in the Löwenbräukeller, when "the reports of the Allied landings in North Africa" came through to him.[2] Hitler, for once, was astounded — and furious at the failure of the Abwehr, the German foreign intelligence department.

German as well as Italian analysts had assured the Führer the Allied troop transports that had recently been reported passing Gibraltar must be on their way to Malta, or possibly a landing in Libya, in Rommel's rear. Dr. Goebbels had noted "the ultimate destination of the great armada" was "still unknown," but once it got closer to Italian- and German-dominated airspace "we will descend on it, and give it all we've got. Among other vessels it's reported to have three carriers and a battleship. If we can give it a real pounding, our poor position in North Africa can be made good again."[3]

It was not to be, however. The armada suddenly switched course, to Oran and Algiers.

Goebbels was dumbfounded. "What will happen?" he asked himself in his diary. "The landings thought to be in Italian territory or Rommel's rear" had unexpectedly "switched course in the night" to become a "vast attempted invasion of French Northwest Africa." Information had only come through at three o'clock in the morning; it was the "greatest sensation in ages" — the Americans and British seeking to "seize the initiative," and declaring "this was now the Second Front."[4]

So *that,* Goebbels recognized in shock, explained the long autumn weeks of silence in the Allied camp! The *Americans,* not the British, were coming!

"The Americans have taken the British completely under their wing," Goebbels noted. It was now "coalition warfare" — with the United States in command, and seizing the initiative on a grand scale. "This is their way to help Russia," he added, wincing at the thought. As master of Nazi deceit, he sneered at Roosevelt's proclamation that the landing of U.S. troops in French territory was merely to forestall German occupation, and that the territory would be restored to French control in due course. Yet even the Mephisto of modern propaganda had to admit "the President's appeal to the population not to counter the invasion" would probably work, "for the Americans were coming as friends and not as enemies."[5]

Marshal Pétain, in Vichy, had immediately declared that France would defend its colonies against such an invasion — yet Goebbels had his doubts. "The situation this morning is still utterly murky, not to speak of how it appeared in the night. When I got the first news at 3:30 in the night, I couldn't make any sense of it. I can't get in touch with the Führer, because he's on his way from his military headquarters to Munich. This gives me a few hours to mull things over. . . . These sensational reports have put events in Egypt completely in the shade."[6]

Suddenly the entire war seemed to have been turned on its head. "What will France do?" Goebbels wondered, "and how will it affect, even disrupt our work" in Europe and Russia, "for example if we have to checkmate the French?"[7]

Plans, he knew, had long been drawn up to abrogate the 1940 armistice and occupy the rest of metropolitan France and Corsica, if the Allies attempted an invasion of the French mainland. No war-gaming had been undertaken for the possibility of an invasion of French Northwest Africa by *Americans,* though!

"France's hour" of destiny had come. The Gallic race stood at the threshold of true greatness, if only they would now actually fight with Hitler and the Third Reich, instead of against it — indeed, Pierre Laval, Pétain's deputy, was soon on his way to Munich to propose an egregious new treaty with the Third Reich, in which France would be a full Nazi partner: a Quadripartite Pact.

Meantime, however, whatever Marshal Pétain might say about Frenchmen defending French territory in Northwest Africa "to the last drop of blood" — and hoping thereby to dissuade the Germans from occupying the entire mainland of France — Goebbels had little confidence such a statement by Pétain would prove to be effective on the field of battle, whether the French were facing the Allies or the Germans. The French were a rotten race; they would be conflicted down to their intestines. Was it not better now to simply go ahead and dump the terms of the 1940 armistice: to ignore Pétain and Laval, and overrun metropolitan Vichy France with German troops — to "have a bird in the hand rather than two in the bush?"[8]

That afternoon, November 8, 1942, the Führer finally reached the Brown House in Munich — national headquarters of the Nazi Party in Germany. There the Reichsminister for propaganda met with him.

The Führer had aged since their last meeting in the summer. Only four months before, Hitler had been in *"bester Laune"* — in fine fettle, brimming with pride.[9] The entire Western world had seemed his oyster — stretching as far as the Urals. He still had Blondi with him, the dog he'd acquired in 1941 as a gift from his loyal deputy, Martin Bormann — a German shepherd "of outstanding racial purity," as Goebbels had recorded, glad that the Führer "has at least one being with whom he can be happy." Successes "in every theater of the war put him in a wonderful mood," Goebbels had noted in the summer — Hitler talking "in the most laudatory way about Rommel, who has become the Marshal of the Desert," a good Nazi and a man to whom the Führer would ultimately entrust command of the entire German army "if things get that far."[10]

But they hadn't. Everything had now been upended — stunning Goebbels, but bearing out the Führer's lingering suspicion that the Allies might yet come up with a surprise that would compromise Operation Blue, his drive deeper into Russia.

Goebbels had not shared the Führer's premonition. How stupid it was of the British to talk of cross-Channel landings, he had sneered, since the idea of a Second Front in France had only served to harden German defenses in the coastal areas. "One should never alert people to what is supposed, later, to be a surprise," Goebbels had observed with contempt, two months before the British fiasco at Dieppe. "As a consequence our troops have been reinforced as never before, and made more mobile."[11] Moreover, if the British or Americans thought the local French population would rise up to help them, they had another think coming, Goebbels had noted, recording with satisfaction the Führer's dismissal of such a possibility. "The Führer thinks the chances of French guerillas or partisans are absolutely nil," he recorded — the Germans having shown on the Eastern Front how they dealt with such resistance, and it was not pretty. In sum, "the Führer has not a moment's doubt that an attempted British invasion, lasting possibly eight or ten days, would be a complete catastrophe," which "might lead to a transformation of the war, perhaps even an end to the war."[12]

And yet ... As Goebbels had confided in his diary, the Führer *did* worry. Churchill got under his skin. Goebbels had remained confident the British would not undertake something as stupid as a cross-Channel invasion, but the Führer had demurred. "As I noted earlier, the Führer is extraordinarily careful and remarks, in this connection, that no general has ever been criticized for having been too well prepared, only for being insufficiently so. The Führer adds that the British *have* to do something with their forty or fifty intact divisions — they can't be expected to simply capitulate to us, given the number they have. We've no idea where they might invade; but given the characters and temperaments of Churchill and Roosevelt anything is possible. Thank God the Führer is so cautious!"[13] Hitler was even having his "so-called Mountain Nest" military headquarters, situated near the Belgian border — the center from which he'd directed his 1940 invasion of the West — completely renovated, so he could move back at any sign of a major cross-Channel offensive. "He makes provision for every eventuality," Goebbels noted, "and doesn't depend on luck. You can really see how he'd love to renew a battle with the British in the West. Mr. Churchill would probably come off a lot worse than the Führer."[14]

That prediction had been made by Dr. Goebbels on June 24, 1942 — shortly after the fall of Tobruk. It had proven prophetic in terms of the disastrous British-Canadian "raid in force" on Dieppe eight weeks later. But now, on November 8, 1942, a real invasion was taking place — and not where German forces could repel them.

Such a strategic throw of the dice had actually occurred to Hitler in the summer, but the Führer had never imagined it would be an American undertaking.[15] "Whether the British might attempt an invasion of Africa is always a possibility," Goebbels had noted on June 23, but "the Führer thinks it would be pointless. What on earth would they [the British] want there? I suppose they could bring the French Vichy territories under British control; but that wouldn't be decisive, in terms of the war's likely course."[16]

Now, on November 8, 1942, the "invasion of Africa" had started — and it filled Hitler with foreboding, since it was clearly a U.S. undertaking, which the French authorities in North Africa might welcome rather than repell. What should the Germans do? Would Mussolini insist on German help? If so, where? Would Rommel's Panzerarmee Afrika be crushed between two Allied pincers, one American, one British? Should Rommel's army be withdrawn across the Mediterranean? Or would Italy then lose heart and be tempted to sue for peace?

Already the neutral countries such as Sweden were turning hostile toward the Third Reich; Spain, equally, was refusing to cooperate, despite the help Hitler had given General Franco in the Spanish Civil War . . .

Germany, which had looked to be on top of the world only three months before, suddenly looked beleaguered — evil, abandoned, vulnerable. The Führer's vaunted military caution had impressed his propaganda minister, but had not served to warn him of an American rather than British assault in Africa. Further east, Rommel's army had been smashed at Alamein and was retreating into Libya. The Russians were refusing to surrender at Stalingrad, and there was no possibility of getting across the Urals, now that snow was falling.

Everything had gone wrong. As U.S. commander in chief, Roosevelt had ignored calls for a cross-Channel Second Front — thus avoiding the catastrophe Hitler had prepared for their arrival. Instead, by landing in Morocco and Algeria, the Americans would now have a secure base from which, with their vast industrial capacity and manpower, they could prosecute the war against the Third Reich, advancing from two possible launch pads: the British Isles and North Africa — and forcing the Germans to defend from both directions.

The Führer had been outwitted. Even the most conservative French, who might have resisted a British invasion of French Northwest Africa, could not be relied upon to offer more than token resistance, since the Americans were clearly uninterested in becoming a colonial power, and were already supplying copious amounts of food to the Vichy authorities.

Hitler's worst nightmare — a major war on two fronts — had now come to pass, with Morocco and most of Algeria too distant for even the Luftwaffe to reach, let alone armored forces.

Hitler's first response was to quash any possibility of panic among his staff. The foreign minister, Joachim Ribbentrop, had, for example, joined the Führer's train at Bamberg, in Bavaria — having received news of the American landings at his office on the Wilhelmstrasse in Berlin and flown down immediately. Not surprisingly, Ribbentrop had clutched at straws. It was he, after all, who had negotiated the infamous Nazi-Soviet peace pact with the Russians in 1939 — allowing Hitler to invade the West with impunity, while the Russians watched; he who had been less than enthusiastic, however, about the Führer's decision to declare war on Russia in the summer of 1941; he who had not followed the Führer's logic about the United States being confined to fighting only in the Pacific after Pearl Harbor; he who had opposed the Führer's decision to therefore declare, with supposed impunity, war on America — a decision Ribbentrop had argued vainly against, he later claimed. In any event, it was Ribbentrop the Nazi diplomat who once again attempted to get the Führer to be sensible — begging the Nazi leader to allow him to put out peace feelers to Stalin via Stockholm, while there was still time to negotiate an end to the war of annihilation in the East.

Hitler had brushed away such a proposition.

"From now on," the Führer had snarled, "there will be no more offer of peace."[17]

Absent a miracle, the people of the Third Reich would no longer be asked to fight for *Lebensraum* — living space. It would be *Todesraum* — room to die.

As Führer of the Third Reich, unaccountable to anyone but his own demonic agenda, Hitler was adamant. General Paulus would be denied permission to pull his almost encircled army back from Stalingrad. And though his "siegen oder sterben" order to Rommel at Alamein had been disobeyed, that did not mean he would allow the Marshal of the Desert to bring his Panzer Army back to Europe or Germany. Rather, it would be made, like Field Marshal Paulus's army, to fight until it was destroyed or surrendered.

Torch had thus ignited a veritable funeral pyre, upon which Hitler would prefer to see his nation immolated rather than that he should seek to negotiate a way out or step down as führer — knowing he himself would be tried as a war criminal and executed.

Thus did the Nazi dream meet reality, at last — Europe's largest nation having willingly followed his banner of anti-Semitism and ruthless conquest, yet now facing on November 8 the stark reality that, despite Germany's triumphant victories in the summer of 1942, it was not going to work; that Winston Churchill had inspired his country to hold out, and that, far from focusing exclusively on dealing with the Japanese in the Pacific, the great United States of America, under President Roosevelt, was moving to Europe to bring the thousand-year Third Reich to an inevitable end.

At the Brown House in Munich, addressing his old Nazi Party colleagues and veterans, Hitler did not even mention the American landings, confining himself to a tirade against the Jews — the source of all Germany's misfortunes. In the meantime, however, he had given orders via his High Command Headquarters that German units were immediately to seize and occupy all of Vichy-controlled France, the Pyrenees, and Corsica, as per Case Anton. More, that a fresh German army be assembled to go to Tunisia under General von Arnim, and deny the Americans easy eviction of Rommel's German or Italian forces in North Africa. It was impossible now for Nazi Germany to win the war, Hitler knew — but with luck and stout German hearts, it might not lose it.

If only, he rued, he had not banked on America concentrating upon the Pacific.

35

Armistice Day

AMERICAN FORCES LAND IN FRENCH AFRICA;
BRITISH NAVAL, AIR UNITS ASSISTING THEM;
EFFECTIVE SECOND FRONT, ROOSEVELT SAYS.

SUCH WAS THE *New York Times* banner headline on November 8, 1942.

"SECRET CLOSELY GUARDED — Reporters Locked in Office in White House to Bar Leak Before Release Hour," another headline ran, much to the President's amusement.

As congratulatory messages from world leaders streamed in to the Oval Office — from Stalin, Churchill, Chiang Kai-shek, Mackenzie King, and dozens of others — the President had good reason to be proud.

At his office in the War Department, Secretary Stimson congratulated General Marshall, telling him that Torch "was the most difficult and complex and large expeditionary plan that the United States had ever undertaken in its history — that it had been planned for execution and carried out in a most wonderful and perfect manner, and that I thought that the chief credit belonged to him. He seemed touched by what I said," Stimson noted — having withheld from Marshall "my very grave misgivings as to the hazards of the whole plan strategically."

Stimson was still tormented by the many things that might yet go wrong — and which had caused him to make "my protest to the President last spring or summer and repeated it again to Marshall several times while they were getting ready until I really think he got rather tired of me. But now when we get it out on maps, the hazard of it seems to be more dangerous than ever," the secretary confided in his diary. "It is a hazard that can be met by good luck and by the superb execution of our own men; but when I look at the map and see how easy it would be for

Germany, if she makes a compromise and arrangement with Spain to come down quickly through Spain and with the aid of the 140,000 men in Spanish Morocco, to pinch off the Straits and cut our lines of communication to the eastward, I shiver. . . ."[1]

Stimson's concerns regarding Spain proved groundless. Given his anxiety, it seemed incredible that he had so doggedly pressed for a cross-Channel assault that year, within swift striking distance of more than twenty-six German divisions, insisting upon such an invasion even to the point of mutiny.

For his own part the President had never credited a "compromise arrangement" between Nazi Germany and Franco's Spain, let alone a German drive through the Iberian Peninsula — an armored offensive that would have added yet another enemy to Hitler's ample roster without actually contesting the landings in Morocco or Algeria. (During the Arcadia Conference in January that year the Joint Planning Committee had, in examining prospects for operations in Northwest Africa, determined that "it would take the Germans six weeks to prepare to invade Spain" and a "further six weeks to become firmly established with land and air forces in the South of Spain after they had crossed the Pyrenees.")[2] Yet the hazards of mounting, with only a few weeks to prepare, the largest amphibious undertaking in human history, had certainly been real — and remained so for several days. In the hours that followed the Torch invasion there would, the President knew, be a thousand mistakes, untold misunderstandings, and awkward negotiations with leading French officials, officers, and insurgents, who were expected to help administer the territories liberated by America's legions.

It didn't matter! That was the beauty of Torch. It could not fail — too far from German forces to be extinguished, as a cross-Channel attack could so easily have been by Hitler's air, naval, and ground forces in France and northern Europe.

Above all, there was the simple, clear, and symbolic message that the Torch invasion would send across the occupied world: *The Americans are coming!*

As the President explained to White House correspondents, off the record, on November 10, 1942, "where hundreds of thousands of lives are involved," it was "a pretty good rule of all wars" that you "couldn't find a second front offensive in a department store, ready made." What he didn't say was that Stimson and Marshall's "ready made" cross-Channel Second

Front would have led to a catastrophe, with untold American casualties, and have helped Hitler win the war. It hadn't been viable, not only because the British wouldn't fight, but because the Germans *would* have — the lunacy of such an operation forcing the President, as commander in chief, to look for something else that *was* possible.[3]

Operation Torch had required, he was willing to tell White House reporters, "a great deal of study, a great deal of coordination, a great deal of preparation of all kinds" — in secret, while half the world was demanding a cross-Channel invasion. "And so in succeeding months both Mr. Churchill and I have had to sit quietly and take with a smile, or perhaps you might say take it on the chin," the President said, as the reporters laughed, "as to what all the outsiders were demanding."[4]

And insiders.

For his part, Secretary Stimson remained a bundle of nerves. During the early hours on November 10, "while I lay sleepless," Stimson confided in his diary, "I had one of my bogy fits. This time it hitched around the situation," he moaned, "which the American army was getting itself into in North Africa."

What if "the Germans should force their way or make any arrangement with Spain to come through without opposition and shut the Straits of Gibraltar on us"? he queried yet again. "It was the old objection which I have always had to the plan showing itself up and it seems worse now, in the light of my examination of the maps yesterday, than ever before. I called in General Handy this morning when I got to the office and went over the matter with him. He is the Chief of the Operations Division. He didn't feel any better than I did and the cold facts and figures showed a very serious situation in case the Germans came through."[5]

General Handy did his best to be respectful, but to calm down the Republican secretary, who was, yet again, full of foreboding. Handy showed him the latest reports "showing the vigor and initiative and general efficiency of our troops." These were, Stimson accepted, enough "to reconcile anybody to hazard. Those men can meet almost any danger," he was assured.[6] Still, Stimson could not refrain from calling the secretary of state, Cordell Hull — pouring out his fears and imploring Hull to speak to the President about his anxieties regarding Spain.

The President duly saw Hull at 3:45 p.m., and telephoned Stimson to reassure him. Spain was *not* going to get involved, the President maintained. The invasion was too big, too sudden, too unrelated to Spain's own interests for General Franco to cooperate with Hitler now, when he had failed to do so for two long years since Hitler's invasion of the West.

Overall, the President told them, Torch had gone rather well — despite some troops being landed on wrong beaches, despite French coastal battery fire, despite French submarines, destroyers, and even cruisers as well as air defense going into action, and despite myriad other problems associated with an invasion. The majority of French officers and administrators seemed worried about their pensions, he heard, if they turned against the Vichy government. It would all work out, however.

Now seventy-five, Stimson was, as he confessed, "feeling very tired. The unconscious strain has been pretty heavy on me."[7]

By contrast, President Roosevelt, aged sixty, was feeling at the top of his form.

Torch — *his* Torch — had been lit, and the United States was established in force on the threshold of Europe, with a Vichy cease-fire order already in effect in Algiers and a general cease-fire applicable to the whole of French Northwest Africa in the works, if all went well. The United States had beaten Hitler to the punch — Torch victorious in a matter of only three days.[8]

Admiral Hewitt had shepherded his armada across the Atlantic and put the men of General Patton's Western Task Force ashore with remarkable precision — the French clearly unaware, until the landing craft appeared, of any threat from the sea. Even the ocean had complied — the usual rough winter sea glacially calm and only the quietest surf, as if by biblical command. (The meteorological officer who predicted this was awarded the Legion of Merit by a grateful General Eisenhower.) Much handwringing had concerned the fifteen-inch guns of the latest French battleship *Jean Bart*, in harbor at Casablanca, but dive-bombers from the USS *Ranger* and shells from the sixteen-inch guns of the USS *Massachusetts* silenced it; when it began firing yet again on November 10, more dive-bombers from the *Ranger* sank it.

Aboard the USS *Augusta* — the heavy cruiser on which President Roosevelt had signed the Atlantic Charter the previous year — General Patton had alternately fumed, sworn, and prayed: amazed to see the shore lights, harbor lights, and even lighthouse lights still burning as the U.S. vessels approached the Moroccan coast after a two-week voyage. It was "almost too good to be true. Thank God. He Stays on our side," he'd jotted in his diary[9] — mortified that the gun blasts from the after-turret of the *Augusta* had blown his thirty-two-foot plywood launch to bits, with all his communications equipment, though not his ivory-handled revolvers, which he retrieved.

Once ashore at Fedala, shortly after midday on November 8, he had earned his monicker "Blood and Guts" — delighted at General Harmon's capture of Safi, and General Truscott's seizure of the port and airfield at Lyautey — leaving only Casablanca to be taken. However, in the confusion of the Torch battle he had seen for himself how fortunate his troops were not to have been fighting Germans, rather than the French. He had spent most of the first two days of the invasion literally "kicking ass" — "The French bombed the beach and later strafed it," he wrote in his diary on November 9, describing operations at Fedala. "One soldier who was pushing a boat got scared and ran onto the beach and assumed the Fields [fetal] position and jiberred. I kicked him in the arse with all my might and he jumped right up and went to work. Some way to boost morale. As a whole the men were poor, the officers worse; no drive."[10]

Patton certainly radiated drive, and when the French commander refused to surrender the city of Casablanca, he arranged for an all-out American naval and air blitz to begin at 7:00 a.m. on November 10 — General Eisenhower having sent a chastening cable telling him the Eastern Task Force landings had meantime met almost no resistance. "Algiers has been ours for two days. Oran crumbling rapidly. The only tough nut left is in your hands. Crack it open."[11]

Patton did so — only calling off the devastating firepower of his naval and air support a mere ten minutes before the attack was due to go in, when the French sent word they would surrender, which their senior commanders subsequently did at Patton's headquarters.

"People say that Army Commanders should not indulge in such practices" as "kicking ass" on invasion beaches, Patton later reflected. "My theory is that an Army commander does what is necessary to accomplish his mission and that nearly 80 per cent of his mission is to arouse morale in his men."[12] He and his chosen field commanders had certainly earned the faith the President had vested in them. Early on November 11, Armistice Day, Admiral Leahy reported to the President he'd received a report from London that "the French Military force in Casa Blanca capitulated at 7 a.m. today and that the city of Oran was occupied by American troops last night."[13] Morocco and Algeria were in the Allied bag; there was nothing the Germans could now do about it.

General Giraud, unfortunately, had proven a great disappointment, despite an American team under General Mark Clark that had brought Giraud by submarine from Vichy France to Eisenhower's advance headquarters at Gibraltar, and then to Algiers, where he was supposed to persuade Vichy forces to lay down arms in order to limit the bloodshed. He had failed abysmally to do so — indeed, whether he would have the authority to order his fellow Frenchmen to cease contesting American landings, and even inspire the 140,000 French troops in North Africa to fight the Nazis rather than the American forces, was now a very open question.

General Eisenhower — badgered day and night by Churchill, who could not resist meddling[14] — could only shake his head at news the Germans were landing troops by air in Tunis without a single shot being fired by the Vichy French to stop them, while the latter were continuing in many places to oppose American forces. The French resident-general, Vice Admiral Jean-Pierre Estéva, had even ordered that "German planes be given a friendly reception in eastern Algerian ports."[15]

It was too awful. "If they would only see reason at this moment, we could avoid many weeks of later fighting," Eisenhower railed in a message to his chief of staff in London from his headquarters still in Gibraltar. Unfortunately, "they are not thinking in terms of a cause, but of individual fortunes and opportunities. Consequently, Darlan, Juin, Giraud and the rest cannot combine to place their composite influence behind any particular project. Right this minute they should all be making it impossible for Admiral Estava," the French commander in chief in Tunis, "to permit the German into Tunisia." Instead the French had virtually welcomed the Germans. "He apparently has the equivalent of three divisions down there, and without the slightest trouble, could cut the throat of every German and Italian in the area and get away with it. . . . A situation like this creates in me so much fury that I sometimes wish I could do a little throat-cutting myself!"[16]

Was General Giraud, though, a better hope for getting a general ceasefire to even hold, let alone ginger French forces to fight the incoming Germans? Admiral Leahy thought not — in fact, for his own money, Leahy thought it a godsend that Admiral Darlan, the right-wing commander in chief of all Vichy French forces under Marshal Pétain, had happened to be in Algiers on the night of the Torch invasion, visiting his disabled son who had polio.

Despite being profoundly anti-British and an appeaser of Hitler, Darlan at least seemed to be pro-American, and have real authority over French forces in Morocco, Algeria, and Tunisia. However, he too proved to be a broken reed — declining to break with his head of state, Marshal Pétain, who nevertheless relieved him of his post as commander in chief and made General Nogues in Morocco, an even more egregious appeaser, Darlan's successor, with orders to continue to repel the American forces — while declining to order Frenchmen to lift a finger to resist the German and Italian forces, even as they invaded the remaining Vichy-controlled region of metropolitan France and Corsica, abrogating the 1940 armistice.

In sum, the indifference of Vichy French officers toward the Nazis, in comparison with their intransigence and hostility toward American forces, would have been comical had it not been so disgraceful for a once-great nation, both Leahy and the President reflected.

It didn't matter, though. That was the vantage of Torch: that American force majeure would carry the day, in spite of Vichy French perfidy, Roosevelt was certain — though it now pained him to watch as the French refrained from firing a single bullet to stop the Germans from occupying Tunisia by air and then by sea, while French Vichy forces continued to kill Americans (over five hundred), even as they listened to news of the rest of their homeland being invaded and occupied by the Nazis.[17]

Such, however, was the darker side of war and of alliances.

By contrast the British, who had initially fought so feebly in the Far East and had shot thousands of their own colonial subjects in India rather than accept them as fellow fighters,[18] seemed to have gotten a sort of second wind, once reinforced in Egypt with American armaments and air force groups. In Egypt, under Montgomery's generalship, they had trounced Erwin Rommel's seemingly invincible Panzerarmee Afrika. And in the Torch invasion under an American supreme commander, they had dovetailed their naval, air, and land contributions in remarkably successful fashion . . .

Coalition warfare, then, might yet work. Over time, perhaps, even the French might rediscover their native courage, and fight alongside American forces to defeat Hitler.

This, in sum, was the other subtext of Torch: the first coalition molding of Allied forces against the Axis powers, on the field of battle. It was no longer simply a political front — Roosevelt's twenty-six free nations, speaking as the United Nations opposed to Axis tyranny — but a new, all-powerful assembly of national military forces, fighting under American supreme leadership and command.

There would doubtless be much to learn, commencing with the blooding of American troops in combat with the professional killers of the Wehrmacht, in Tunisia. But with the successful American invasion of North Africa, a start had been made. The Americans were coming.

Reading the messages and reports that came into the White House Map Room, the President felt humbled by the enormity of what had taken place — thankful it had, in the end, borne out his most fervent hopes. At 11:00 a.m. that day, Armistice Day 1942, he therefore went to Arlington Cemetery, Admiral Leahy accompanying him to the Tomb of the Unknown Soldier, across the Potomac.[19]

"Old General Pershing, although he wasn't really fit to do it, he came along and went [in the car] with the President, while Knox and I followed behind," Secretary Stimson recorded in his diary.[20] General Marshall, Admiral King, and the commanding officer of the Marines also attended.

Stimson was feeling a great deal better, having heard that, although the "Germans this morning invaded unoccupied France and are rushing through it towards the south coast in an attempt to get to Marseilles and the French fleet at Toulon,"[21] there was no chance that they could now halt or throw back the American forces in Algeria and Morocco. At last Admiral Darlan, Stimson noted, "has ordered all resistance in North Africa to cease."[22]

Torch was over; the pincer campaign to defeat or evict Axis forces from the southern Mediterranean could now proceed.

In the circumstances, the President's address was deeply moving.

"Here in Arlington we are in the presence of the honored dead," Roosevelt, standing with the aid of his fourteen-pound steel leg braces, reminded his audience. "We are accountable to them — and accountable to the generations yet unborn for whom they gave their lives.

"Today, as on all Armistice Days since 1918, our thoughts go back to the first World War; and we remember with gratitude the bravery of the men who fought and helped to win that fight against German militarism. But this year our thoughts are also very much of the living present, and of the future which we begin to see opening before us — a picture illumined by a new light of hope.

"Today, Americans and their British brothers-in-arms are again fighting on French soil. They are again fighting against a German militarism which transcends a hundred-fold the brutality and the barbarism of 1918.

"The Nazis of today and their appropriate associates, the Japanese, have attempted to drive history into reverse, to use all the mechanics of modern civilization to drive humanity back to conditions of prehistoric savagery.

"They sought to conquer the world, and for a time they seemed to be successful in realizing their boundless ambition. They overran great territories. They enslaved — they killed.

"But, today, we know and they know that they have conquered nothing.

"Today, they face inevitable, final defeat.

"Yes, the forces of liberation are advancing."

The President looked around. "Britain, Russia, China, and the United States grow rapidly to full strength," he stated. "The opponents of decency and justice have passed their peak.

"And — as the result of recent events — very recent — the United States' and the United Nations' forces are being joined by large numbers of the fighting men of our traditional ally, France," he declared — hopefully! "On this day, of all days, it is heartening for us to know that soldiers of France go forward with the United Nations."

Which brought the President to the mission of the United States.

"The American Unknown Soldier who lies here did not give his life on the fields of France merely to defend his American home for the moment that was passing. He gave it that his family, his neighbors, and all his fellow Americans might live in peace in the days to come. His hope was not fulfilled," he declared candidly.

Roosevelt was coming to the crux of his vision of the United States as a global guardian of liberty, in a world where it was too easy for the forces of violence, intolerance, and savagery to get their way unless effectively challenged. "American soldiers are giving their lives today in all the continents and on all the seas in order that the dream of the Unknown Soldier may at last come true. All the heroism, all the unconquerable devotion that free men and women are showing in this war shall make certain the survival and the advancement of civilization."[23]

As the spectators and participants in the little ceremony made their way back from Arlington National Cemetery to their cars in the chilling cold, they recognized that, in a sense, America's new journey had just begun. It would not be an easy road, but it was a noble challenge Roosevelt was setting. Moreover, they could take comfort in the fact that the President, who had saved the nation at a time of the worst economic depression it had ever suffered, was now, on a global stage, proving to be perhaps the greatest commander in chief in American history.

Returning to his office at the White House, Admiral Leahy was certainly proud of his commander in chief — the man who liked to call himself "a pig-headed Dutchman."[24] The President had, he noted in his diary, "made a very impressive five minute address to a large gathering of people," with spectators "seated in an amphitheater and standing about in the clear cold morning. Except the President and myself, all of the official party wore heavy overcoats."[25]

Torch had set the tone and determination of the United States in prosecuting the war against the Axis powers. In overruling his generals, the President had, Admiral Leahy reflected, undoubtedly saved his nation from the military catastrophe that would have awaited them on the shores of mainland France. Instead they could now learn in comparative safety the dark arts of modern war — with every chance of ultimate victory. Vast American forces were, after all, now safely established on the threshold of Europe — and of greatness on behalf of their nation, if they could translate that triumph, step by step, into the defeat of Mussolini's Italy, Hitler's Nazi Germany, and finally of Emperor Hirohito's Japan.

More difficulties would arise with the French, and with a rejuvenated Winston Churchill, now that his British Empire stood to be restored, thanks to American might. And there would be the problem of Stalin, the Russians — and the Chinese.

It would all work out, the President assured Leahy. It had been quite a journey over the past eleven months, since December 7, 1941.

Most moving of all to the widower admiral, though, had been the President's prayer, at the end of his address. "Our thoughts," Roosevelt had proclaimed in his unmistakable, lilting tenor voice, "turn in gratitude to those who have saved our Nation in days gone by. God, the father of all living, watches over these hallowed graves and blesses the souls of those who rest here. May He keep us strong in the courage that will win the war, and may He impart to us the wisdom and the vision that we shall need for true victory in the peace which is to come."[26]

Acknowledgments

The study of leadership — moral, literary, political, and military — has been my abiding interest for almost forty-five years as a biographer and historian.

My particular fascination with FDR goes back to *American Caesars,* a Suetonian-style biography of the last twelve U.S. presidents, which I published in 2010. Researching the opening chapter on President Roosevelt, I found it hard to believe that no military biographer or military historian had tackled his military leadership in World War II as commander in chief in a full-scale work. Once I completed *American Caesars* I was able to examine the literature and original documentation more closely. I became even more intrigued — especially at the difference in command styles adopted by Churchill and Roosevelt in directing World War II.

I knew perhaps more than many people of my generation about Winston Churchill as a military leader, and as a striking personality, for I had stayed with him and Lady Churchill at their home at Chartwell, in Kent, while a student at Cambridge University. Moreover, I had spent many, many hours discussing Churchill's leadership with my quasi godfather, Field Marshal Bernard Montgomery, who revered the former prime minister — but lamented his intrusions into the battlefield, and his failure to understand the principles of effective modern command. Later on, over the period of a decade, I spent yet more time interviewing men and women who had known or served under the Prime Minister in World War II for *Monty,* my official life of Montgomery, published in three volumes in the 1980s — in each of which Winston Churchill played a major part.

On the American side, I was also lucky to have interviewed many of the senior surviving World War II commanders and staff officers, from

General Mark Clark to Generals "Lightning Joe" Collins, Max Taylor, and Jim Gavin; from General Al Gruenther to General Freddie de Guingand. In the course of my work I had also gotten to know many senior American World War II military writers and historians, from Forrest Pogue to Russell Weigley, Steve Ambrose, and Carlo D'Este.

And on the German side I was fortunate, too. Thanks to a semester at Munich University and my first marriage to a German (who died tragically in 1973), I had good command of the German language, and sources not available or translated for use by many British or American writers.

In short, I felt confident enough in 2010 to tackle such a project afresh.

The result, *The Mantle of Command: FDR at War,* presents a very different portrait than the conventional characterization of President Roosevelt as commander in chief in World War II. In this respect I was blessed by being able to interview the last living member of FDR's White House team in World War II, Commander George Elsey, who worked in the Map Room, as well as several members of FDR's family, including his granddaughter Ellie and his step-grandson Tom Halsted. Working my way through the many diaries, memoranda, and correspondence kept by the members of the President's staff and military officials, held in various archives in the United States and United Kingdom, I tried my best to reconstruct the story *wie es eigentlich gewesen ist* — how it really was.

For reasons of length I had decided from the beginning to focus on selected landmark moments or episodes in FDR's performance as commander in chief in World War II that best illustrate his responses both to defeat and to victory in war, for good or ill. Unfortunately, even this attempt at condensation proved a failure. The eleven-month period between Pearl Harbor and the first landings of American troops on the threshold of Europe — Operation Torch — seemed to me too important not to reconstruct and get right, given the many alternative, often misleading, accounts that have been given over the years: in particular, that of Winston Churchill in his monumental opus, *The Second World War.*

Interviewing so many World War II commanders and their staffs, I had learned how much of history, in the end, is dependent on the perspective or point of view of the participant. The main perspective of *The Mantle of Command,* let us be clear, is unabashedly that of Franklin D. Roosevelt and the White House he used as his command post in 1941 and 1942. The story, moreover, is a quite fatal one, in terms of world history. Had FDR, in the first year of America's involvement in World War II, not learned to wear the mantle of command so firmly, and to overrule his generals, it is quite possible Hitler would have achieved his aim when declaring war on the United States on December 11, 1941: winning the war in Europe. It is a sobering reflection.

Naturally, in retelling and recasting this extraordinary story I have subjected certain reputations to revision, from those of Winston Churchill and General George Marshall to General Douglas MacArthur and the war secretary, Colonel Henry Stimson. I hope I am not unsympathetic to their memories, serving to the best of their abilities in a world crisis such as we hopefully will never have occasion to repeat or replicate; nevertheless, it seemed important to me to recount the saga from FDR's perspective with absolute if compassionate honesty, since the President did not live to do so. Every other major military participant managed to impart his own account, either autobiographically or via a chosen plaidoyer; only President Roosevelt's POV as commander in chief has remained dark since his death in 1945.

In researching and writing this account — which will be followed by a concluding work — I was helped by a small but wonderful army of professional colleagues, friends, and family. I'd like first to thank my educator wife, Dr. Raynel Shepard, for her everlasting patience in the book's genesis, research, writing, and preparation. Next: Ike Williams, my literary agent in Boston, who saw immediately the potential importance of the undertaking — and found me a well-tempered, experienced commissioning publisher and editor in Bruce Nichols of Houghton Mifflin Harcourt. Bruce not only cut and clarified my often prolix prose, but recognized the need for two separate books to do justice to FDR's wartime story.

To Ike and his associates Katherine Flynn and Hope Denekamp, therefore, and to Bruce Nichols and Melissa Dobson, my copyeditor, my deep gratitude. In terms of colleagues, I have been fortunate to have been a Senior Fellow in the John W. McCormack Graduate School of Policy and Global Studies of the University of Massachusetts, Boston, for many years, and wish to thank Steve Crosby, his successor, Ira Jackson, the staff, and my colleagues there for their constant support — as also the University Provost, Winston Langley, and the ever-helpful staff of the University Library.

The staff and facilities of the Widener Library and Microfilm Department in the Lamont Library, Harvard University, have also been outstanding, as has been the staff of the Boston University Microfilm Department, and the Franklin D. Roosevelt Presidential Library at Hyde Park.

I'm deeply grateful, too, to those colleagues and friends who were willing to read and offer criticism of sections of the growing manuscript, as it evolved, beginning with my oldest Cambridge University friend, Robin Whitby; Professor Mark Schneider; Lieutenant Colonel Carlo D'Este; Professor David Kaiser; James Scott; and Professor Mark Stoler. I'd also like to record my thanks to members of my Boston club, The Tavern, who listened to my early readings from the manuscript and offered advice and encouragement — especially Stephen Clark, Frinde Maher, Alston Purvis, Ed Tarlov, David Scudder, David Amory, and Clive Foss.

Two conferences at which I gave papers based upon chapters of the manuscript were extremely helpful to my work. They were a Raymond E. Mason Jr. Distinguished Lecture on FDR's "Great Spat" with Winston Churchill over India in 1942, delivered at the National World War II Museum in New Orleans as part of the second annual Winston S. Churchill Symposium in July 2012; and a paper on Torch, given at the invitation of Professor David Reynolds to the Guerre des Sables Conference of international World War II scholars at the École Française de Rome in November 2012. The 2012 International Conference on World War II, held at the National World War II Museum in December 2012, was also fruitful, and I thank the director, Dr. Nick Mueller (and conference organizer Jeremy Collins), for inviting me to speak along with fellow panelists Rick Atkinson, Gerhard Weinberg, Allan Millett, Christopher Browning, Conrad Crane, and Mark Stoler.

In the U.K. I would like to thank Allen Packwood, Director of the Churchill Archives Centre in Cambridge, for his help on my visit there, and especially Professor David Reynolds for his hospitality and intellectual support in reexamining the fateful year, 1942, and the story of the collapse of the British Empire, together with its ramifications for FDR.

In London I would like to thank the wonderful staff of the Imperial War Museum's Department of Documents: the former Curator, the late Rod Suddaby, and current Curator, Anthony Richards, for pointing me to useful Churchill and FDR material; also Phil Reid, Director of the IWM's Cabinet War Rooms below Whitehall, for a wonderful personal tour. Also the Liddell Hart Military History Centre at King's College — and my research assistant in London, Jean Simpson, for her help in obtaining documents.

Back in the U.S., I want to record my thanks to the staff of the Manuscript Division Reading Room at the National Archives in Washington, D.C., especially Jeff Flannery, the Head of Reference and Reader Services Section in the Manuscript Reading Room. Also the staff of the Operational Archives of the U.S. Naval History and Command, Washington Navy Yard, D.C., especially John Greco for his help. In Oakland, California, I'd like to thank the volunteers and staff of the presidential yacht, the USS *Potomac,* for their tour — and cruise in San Francisco Bay — in August 2012. And in Boston, my research assistant, Eric Prileson, a graduate of Northeastern University.

As President of BIO — Biographers International Organization — from 2010 to 2012 I was privileged to work with a wonderful committee of fellow biographers, and to participate in excellent annual conferences in Boston, Washington, D.C., Los Angeles, and New York. Thanks to them, the craft of biography has seemed vastly less isolating than in my earlier years, and I want to thank especially Elizabeth Harris and my fellow members of the Boston Biographers Group (BBG), who meet once a month to share progress on their individual projects. Listening to and comparing the practical challenges of biography of fellow practitioners, working on an extraordinary array of different life stories across different centuries, has been, over the past five years, a veritable lifeline to me, and I cannot too highly recommend joining such an organization to anyone contemplating or already working on a biography.

I'd like finally to acknowledge the memories of two women who died recently: Margery Heffron, who cofounded the Boston Biographers Group, but managed to complete her masterpiece, *The Other Mrs. Adams,* before she passed; and my mother, Olive Hamilton, who first invested me with my love of biography, and wrote many herself before passing in January 2012, at age ninety-six — twenty two years after my father, Lieutenant Colonel Sir Denis Hamilton, DSO, who landed as a twenty-five-year-old battalion commander on D-day, four months after my birth — and inspired my fascination with leadership.

Photo Credits

The Plan of Escape. FDR in Oval Office, summer 1941: Corbis / © Arthur Rothstein; USS *Potomac* off New England coast, Aug. 1941: Corbis / Bettmann

Placentia Bay. USS *Augusta* before the onset of war: U.S. Navy Official / National Archives; FDR welcomes Winston Churchill (WSC) aboard *Augusta*, Aug. 9, 1941: FDR Library; FDR, WSC, and their staffs on board *Augusta*, Aug. 9, 1941: FDR Library

The Atlantic Charter. FDR walks from USS *McDougal* onto HMS *Prince of Wales*, Aug. 10, 1941: FDR Library; WSC greets FDR aboard *Prince of Wales*, Aug. 10, 1941: FDR Library; Divine service aboard *Prince of Wales*, Aug. 10, 1941: FDR Library

Pearl Harbor. Hopkins and FDR in Oval Study, 1941: FDR Library; Japanese bomber's photo of Pearl Harbor, Dec. 7, 1941: National Archives; Burning U.S. battleships, Dec. 7, 1941: FDR Library

A Date Which Will Live in Infamy. White House, night of Dec. 7, 1941: Getty / © Thomas D. McAvoy; FDR before Congress, Dec. 8, 1941: Corbis / Bettmann; Hitler before Reichstag, Dec. 11, 1941: Getty / Keystone-France

Coalition War. FDR greets WSC in Washington, Dec. 22, 1941: FDR Library; FDR and WSC give White House press conference, Dec. 23, 1941: FDR Library; FDR broadcast to nation from White House, Feb. 23, 1942: FDR Library

Spring of '42. Close-up of Commander in Chief, 1942: FDR Library; the Map Room, White House: FDR Library; communicating with MacArthur, Map Room: FDR Library; "Field Marshal" MacArthur and President Quezon in the Philippines: FDR Library

The Raid on Tokyo. Lt. Col. Jimmy Doolittle flies B-25 off USS *Hornet*, April 18, 1942: FDR Library; FDR decorates Doolittle in Oval Office, May 19, 1942: FDR Library

Hawaii Is Avenged. Aircraft carrier *Agaki*, sunk in Battle of Midway, June 4, 1942: FDR Library; Marine General Thomas Holcombe shows FDR Japanese flag at White House, Sept. 17, 1942: FDR Library

The Fall of Tobruk. FDR with WSC at Hyde Park, June 20, 1942: FDR Library, Margaret Suckley Collection; Rommel in triumph, British surrender of Tobruk fortress and port, June 21, 1942: Bundesarchiv, Federal Archives of Germany; FDR, with Canadian premier Mackenzie King behind him, at Pacific Council, June 25, 1942: FDR Library

Dieppe. General Marshall and War Secretary Stimson plot against the President to insist on cross-Channel landings in 1942: U.S. Signal Corps / National Archives; Canadian dead litter beaches of Dieppe, Aug. 19, 1942: National Archives of Canada; Admiral Bill Leahy, new chief of staff to the Commander in Chief, July 21, 1942: FDR Library / Life

FDR Inspects the Nation. FDR aboard his touring train, Sept. 17–Oct. 1, 1942: FDR Library, Margaret Suckley Collection; FDR disembarking at Fort Lewis, Sept. 22, 1942: FDR Library; FDR waves from rear platform: FDR Library

Gearing Up for Victory. FDR watches launch of *Joseph N. Teal*, Kaiser Shipyard, Oregon, Sept. 23, 1942: FDR Library; inspects aircraft carrier construction, Bremerton Naval Shipyard, Sept. 22, 1942: FDR Library; receives clip at Federal Cartridge Plant, Minnesota, Sept. 19, 1942: FDR Library; reviews tank unit at Fort Lewis, Washington, Sept. 22, 1942: FDR Library; inspects bomber production, Douglas Aircraft Corp., Long Beach, California, Sept. 25, 1942: FDR Library; inspects Ford bomber production, Willow Run, Michigan, Sept. 18, 1942: FDR Library; inspects army units, Fort Lewis, Washington, Sept. 22, 1942: FDR Library; watches rehearsal landings of U.S. Marines, San Diego: FDR Library

Waiting for Torch. FDR dining with staff at Shangri-la, Aug. 1942: FDR Library, Margaret Suckley Collection; close-up of FDR, fall 1942: FDR Library

Torch. General Patton, on Desert Training Center maneuvers prior to Torch invasion: National Archives; General Eisenhower before appointment as supreme commander, Torch invasion: Eisenhower Library; U.S. troops landing near Surcouf, Algeria, Nov. 8, 1942: National Archives; U.S. troops marching toward Algiers, Nov. 8, 1942: National Archives

Armistice Day. President gives address at Arlington Cemetery on Nov. 11, 1942, accompanied by General Pershing: FDR Library; a wreath is laid, Nov. 11, 1942: FDR Library

Notes

PROLOGUE

1. Ross T. McIntire, *White House Physician* (New York: G. P. Putnam's Sons, 1946), 141.
2. See David Reynolds, "FDR's Foreign Policy and the Construction of American History, 1945–1955," in *FDR's World: War, Peace, and Legacies*, ed. David B. Woolner, Warren F. Kimball, and David Reynolds (New York: Palgrave Macmillan, 2008), 7.
3. Viz. Eric Larrabee, *Commander-in-Chief: Franklin Delano Roosevelt, His Lieutenants, and Their War* (New York: Harper & Row, 1987), in which only one of the work's eleven chapters is devoted to the Commander in Chief. Joseph E. Persico's more chronological and wide-ranging narrative of the generals who served under FDR, and their relations with the Commander in Chief, *Roosevelt's Centurions: FDR and the Commanders He Led to Victory in World War II* (New York: Random House, 2013), was published as *The Mantle of Command* went to press.
4. Alan Brooke, *War Diaries, 1939–1945: Field Marshal Lord Alanbrooke*, ed. Alex Danchev and Daniel Todman (Berkeley: University of California Press, 2001), 247.
5. For a recent brief summary and refutation of the "mythology" surrounding the relationship between FDR and his chiefs of staff, see Mark Stoler, "FDR and the Origins of the National Security Establishment," in *FDR's World*, ed. Woolner, Kimball, and Reynolds, 69–78.
6. Barbara Tuchman, *Stilwell and the American Experience in China, 1911–45* (New York: Macmillan, 1970), 241.
7. Mark Stoler, *The Politics of the Second Front: American Military Planning and Diplomacy in Coalition Warfare, 1941–1943* (Westport, CT: Greenwood Press, 1977), 26.
8. Brooke, *War Diaries*, 273.
9. Kenneth Pendar, *Adventure in Diplomacy: Our French Dilemma* (New York: Dodd, Mead, 1945), 152.

1. BEFORE THE STORM

1. "The White House, Washington: Memorandum of Trip to Meet Winston Churchill, August 1941," August 23, 1941, Franklin D. Roosevelt Presidential Library, Hyde Park, NY.
2. Ian Kershaw, *Hitler 1936–1945: Nemesis* (New York: Norton, 2000), 385.
3. Stetson Conn and Byron Fairchild, *The Framework of Hemisphere Defense* (Washington, DC: Office of the Chief of Military History, Department of the Army, 1960), 98.
4. Ibid.
5. See inter alia Hadley Cantril, ed., *Public Opinion 1935–1946* (Princeton, NJ: Princeton University Press, 1951), 1061, 1128, and 1162; Robert Dallek, *Franklin D. Roosevelt and American Foreign Policy, 1932–1945* (New York: Oxford University Press, 1979), 210 and 289; and James MacGregor Burns, *Roosevelt: The Soldier of Freedom* (New York: Harcourt Brace Jovanovitch, 1970), 98–99.
6. Franklin D. Roosevelt, *The Public Papers and Addresses of Franklin D. Roosevelt,* comp. Samuel I. Rosenman, vol. 9, *War — And Aid to Democracies* (New York: Russell & Russell, 1969), 488.
7. The Neutrality Act forbade American flagged vessels from sailing into war zones; permitted belligerents, of any nationality, to be supplied on a cash-and-carry basis only; and mandated that such supplies be carried in non-American shipping, to avoid the United States being drawn into hostilities. At President Roosevelt's request, the Lend-Lease Act of March 1941 had modified the financial terms of trade to belligerents such as Britain, who had been confronting the Nazi menace to the great profit of the American armament industry. No deeper political commitment to war than that, however, was contemplated by Congress.
8. The U.S. Army Air Forces, amalgamating the Army Air Corps and the General Headquarters (GHQ) Air Force, was created on June 20, 1941.
9. Robert Sherwood, *Roosevelt and Hopkins: An Intimate History* (New York: Harper, 1948), 351.
10. Entry of August 3, 1941, John Colville, *The Fringes of Power: 10 Downing Street Diaries, 1939–1955* (New York: Norton, 1985), 424.
11. Martin Gilbert, *Winston S. Churchill,* vol. 6, *Finest Hour: 1939–1941* (Boston: Houghton Mifflin, 1983), 1148.
12. Ibid., 1155.
13. Conn and Fairchild, *The Framework of Hemisphere Defense,* 124.
14. Ibid., 119.
15. Mark A. Stoler, *The Politics of the Second Front: American Military Planning and Diplomacy in Coalition Warfare, 1941–1943* (Westport, CT: Greenwood Press, 1977), 9.
16. Conn and Fairchild, *The Framework of Hemisphere Defense,* 137; and Mark A. Stoler, *Allies and Adversaries: The Joint Chiefs of Staff, the Grand Alliance, and U.S.*

Strategy in World War II (Chapel Hill: University of North Carolina Press, 2000), 51.

17. Stoler, *Allies and Adversaries,* 52–53.

18. "Our Chiefs of Staff believe that the Battle of the Atlantic is the final, decisive battle of the war and everything has got to be concentrated on winning it. Now, the President has a somewhat different attitude. He shares the belief that British chances in the Middle East are not too good. But he realizes that the British have got to fight the enemy wherever they find him. He is, therefore, more inclined to support continuing the campaign in the Middle East": Hopkins to the Prime Minister and British Chiefs of Staff at 10 Downing Street, July 24, 1941, in Robert Sherwood, *Roosevelt and Hopkins,* 314. See also Mark A. Stoler, *Allies in War: Britain and America Against the Axis Powers, 1940–1945* (London: Hodder Arnold, 2005), 31.

19. Hitler later told Mussolini he would prefer to have "three or four teeth pulled" than endure another nine hours' negotiation with the Spanish generalissimo, Franco: Kershaw, *Hitler: Nemesis,* 330.

20. Stoler, *Allies and Adversaries,* 41.

21. Letter of August 2, 1941, in *F.D.R., His Personal Letters,* ed. Elliott Roosevelt (New York: Duell, Sloan and Pearce, 1947–50), vol. 2, 1197.

22. Geoffrey C. Ward, ed., *Closest Companion: The Unknown Story of the Intimate Friendship Between Franklin Roosevelt and Margaret Suckley* (Boston: Houghton Mifflin, 1995), 140.

23. Theodore A. Wilson, *The First Summit: Roosevelt & Churchill at Placentia Bay, 1941* (Boston: Houghton Mifflin, 1969), 34.

24. Entry of August 9, 1941, Henry Harley Arnold, *American Airpower Comes of Age: General Henry H. "Hap" Arnold's World War II Diaries,* ed. John W. Huston (Maxwell Air Force Base, AL: Air University Press, 2002), 226.

25. Ibid., entry of August 4, 1941, 218.

26. Ibid.

27. Ibid., 61.

28. "Operation Riviera, Atlantic Meeting, August, 1941," entry of August 8, Diary of Ian Jacob, Liddell Hart Centre for Military History, King's College London.

29. Ward, *Closest Companion,* 140.

30. Stark Diary, in Mitchell Simpson III, *Admiral Harold R. Stark: Architect of Victory, 1939–1945* (Columbia: University of South Carolina Press, 1989), 92.

31. Ward, *Closest Companion,* 140.

32. The toadfish proved hard to label definitively and was sent to the Smithsonian for further identification.

33. Henry H. Arnold, *Global Mission* (New York: Harper, 1949), 186.

34. Entry of August 8, 1941, Arnold, *American Airpower Comes of Age,* 221.

35. Ibid., 221–22.

36. George C. Marshall, *George C. Marshall: Interviews and Reminiscences for Forrest*

C. Pogue, 3rd ed. (Lexington, VA: George C. Marshall Research Foundation, 1991), 285.

37. Wilson, *The First Summit,* 71.
38. Entry of August 8, 1941, Arnold, *American Airpower Comes of Age,* 223.
39. Ibid., entry of August 10, 1941, 228.
40. Ibid., entry of August 8, 1941, 223.
41. Benjamin Welles, *Sumner Welles: FDR's Global Strategist* (New York: St. Martin's, 1997), 303.
42. Sumner Welles, *Where Are We Heading?* (New York: Harper, 1946), 6. See also Wilson, *The First Summit,* 32 and footnote 65, 275.
43. Delivered to Congress January 6, 1941. See also Wilson, *The First Summit,* 154.
44. Conn and Fairchild, *The Framework of Hemispheric Defense,* 125.
45. Ibid., 126.
46. Wilson, *The First Summit,* 185. See also Forrest Pogue, *George C. Marshall,* vol. 2, *Ordeal and Hope, 1939–1942* (New York: Viking, 1966), 153–54.
47. Wilson, *The First Summit,* 71.
48. Elliott Roosevelt, *As He Saw It* (New York: Duell, Sloan and Pearce, 1946), 22.
49. Ibid.
50. Ibid., 22–23.
51. Ibid., 24.
52. Ibid., 24–25.
53. Ibid., 25.
54. H. V. Morton, *Atlantic Meeting* (London: Methuen, 1943), 90–91.
55. "Operation Riviera, Atlantic Meeting, August, 1941," entry of August 9, Jacob Diary.
56. Ibid.
57. Ibid.
58. Ward, *Closest Companion,* 141.
59. Entry of August 10, 1941, Arnold, *American Airpower Comes of Age,* 224.
60. Ibid.
61. Dallek, *Franklin D. Roosevelt and American Foreign Policy,* 285.
62. Morton, *Atlantic Meeting,* 85.
63. Ward, *Closest Companion,* 141.
64. Sherwood, *Roosevelt and Hopkins,* 365.
65. Alexander Cadogan, "Atlantic Meeting," record of 1962, in *The Diaries of Sir Alexander Cadogan, O.M., 1938–1945,* ed. David Dilks (London: Cassell, 1971), 398.
66. Sherwood, *Roosevelt and Hopkins,* 354.
67. Wilson, *The First Summit,* 163.
68. Ward, *Closest Companion,* 141.
69. Since May 10, 1940, Hopkins — whom FDR had once seen as a possible successor to him as president — had lived at the White House as special assistant to the President. In December 1937 he underwent surgery for stomach cancer, and

though the cancer did not recur, he suffered many postgastrectomy problems and relapses. See James A. Halsted, "Severe Malnutrition in a Public Servant of the World War II Era: The Medical History of Harry Hopkins," *Transactions of the American Clinical and Climatological Association* 86 (1975): 23–32.

70. Cadogan, "Atlantic Meeting," *The Cadogan Diaries,* 398; and David Reynolds, *The Creation of the Anglo-American Alliance, 1937–41* (London: Europa, 1981), 258 and footnote 28, 364.

71. Elliott Roosevelt, *As He Saw It,* 29.

72. Ibid., 28.

73. Morton, *Atlantic Meeting,* 86–87.

74. Elliott Roosevelt, *As He Saw It,* 29.

75. Entry of August 10, 1941, *The Cadogan Diaries,* 397.

76. Arnold, *Global Mission,* 252.

77. Entry of August 10, 1941, Arnold, *American Airpower Comes of Age,* 226.

78. Arnold, *Global Mission,* 252.

79. Entry of August 10, 1941, *The Cadogan Diaries,* 397.

80. Wilson, *The First Summit,* 136–37.

81. Winston S. Churchill, *The Second World War,* vol. 3, *The Grand Alliance* (Boston: Houghton Mifflin, 1950), 386.

82. David Reynolds, *In Command of History: Churchill Fighting and Writing the Second World War* (New York: Random House, 2005), 261.

83. Ibid.

84. Ibid.

85. "Operation Riviera, Atlantic Meeting, August, 1941," entry of August 10, Jacob Diary, 22–23.

86. Wilson, *The First Summit,* 98.

87. "Operation Riviera, Atlantic Meeting, August, 1941," entry of August 10, Jacob Diary, 21.

88. Ward, *Closest Companion,* 141.

89. Morton, *Atlantic Meeting,* 113–14.

90. Ward, *Closest Companion,* 141.

91. "Operation Riviera, Atlantic Meeting, August, 1941," entry of August 10, Jacob Diary, 24.

92. Ward, *Closest Companion,* 141.

93. "Operation Riviera, Atlantic Meeting, August, 1941," entry of August 10, Jacob Diary, 25–26.

94. Ibid., 26.

95. Entry of August 10, 1941, Arnold, *American Airpower Comes of Age,* 228.

96. "Operation Riviera, Atlantic Meeting, August, 1941," entry of August 12, Jacob Diary, 36.

97. Stoler, *The Politics of the Second Front,* 10. American planners felt the British paper amounted to "groping for panaceas," in an effort to "bring the United States into the war at the earliest possible date": ibid.

98. "Operation Riviera, Atlantic Meeting, August, 1941," entry of August 11, Jacob Diary, 27.
99. Ibid.
100. Churchill to Eden, May 24, 1941, regarding "Memorandum by Maynard Keynes on British War Aims," Churchill Papers, 20/36, Churchill College, Cambridge, UK.
101. Elliott Roosevelt, *As He Saw It,* 35.
102. Thomas B. Buell, *Master of Sea Power: A Biography of Admiral Ernest J. King* (Boston: Little, Brown, 1980), 130.
103. Elliott Roosevelt, *As He Saw It,* 35.
104. Ibid., 35–36.
105. Ibid., 36.
106. Ibid., 37.
107. Ibid., 38.
108. Ward, *Closest Companion,* 142.
109. Ibid.
110. Ibid.
111. Elliott Roosevelt, *As He Saw It,* 41–42.
112. "Operation Riviera, Atlantic Meeting, August, 1941," entry of August 12, Jacob Diary, 31.
113. Opinion polls showed no change in American reluctance to intercede in the war in Europe following the Atlantic Charter meeting: Stoler, *Allies in War,* 27.
114. Ward, *Closest Companion,* 142.
115. Ibid.
116. "Operation Riviera, Atlantic Meeting, August, 1941," entry of August 12, Jacob Diary, 33. The departure of the Prime Minister's battleship proved more dramatic than expected. The two accompanying U.S. destroyers failed to notice the *Prince of Wales* slowing down, ahead of them, which the battleship did to pass an anchored American vessel. The destroyers almost collided with the battleship's stern. Then, about an hour and a half into the voyage, one of the destroyers suddenly veered across the bow of the *Prince of Wales.* "Our captain ordered full speed astern and missed the destroyer by about 40 or 50 yards," Colonel Jacob recorded with relief. "Apparently the destroyer's helm had jammed hard over, and she came across quite out of control . . .": Ibid., 34.
117. Ward, *Closest Companion,* 142.

2. THE U.S. IS ATTACKED!

1. Eleanor Roosevelt, *This I Remember* (New York: Harper, 1949), 232.
2. Ibid.
3. See Ronald A. Spector, *Eagle Against the Sun: The American War with Japan* (New York: Free Press, 1985), 93–100; Robert B. Stinnett, *Day of Deceit: The Truth About*

FDR and Pearl Harbor (New York: Free Press, 2000); and Christopher Andrew, *For the President's Eyes Only: Secret Intelligence and the American Presidency from Washington to Bush* (New York: HarperCollins, 1995), 105–22, inter alia.

4. Gordon W. Prange, *At Dawn We Slept: The Untold Story of Pearl Harbor* (New York: McGraw-Hill, 1981), 487.

5. Ibid., 467.

6. Ibid., 468.

7. Ibid., 446.

8. Ibid., 468.

9. Ibid., 446.

10. Ibid., 485.

11. Robert E. Sherwood, *Roosevelt and Hopkins: An Intimate History* (New York: Harper, 1948), 426–27.

12. Ibid., 427.

13. Kenneth S. Davis, *FDR, the War President, 1940–1943: A History* (New York: Random House, 2000), 398.

14. Sherwood, *Roosevelt and Hopkins,* 427.

15. Eleanor Roosevelt, *This I Remember,* 233.

16. Station HYPO or Fleet Unit Radio Pacific was the U.S. Navy signals cryptographic unit in Pearl Harbor, but it had no Purple machine equivalent, and received no Purple signals to decrypt. Instead, the unit worked to break some of the Japanese Imperial Navy two-book code JN-25 — which was changed on December 1, 1941, forcing U.S. code breakers in Hawaii to begin from scratch.

17. Prange, *At Dawn We Slept,* 294; Stinnett, *Day of Deceit,* 234.

18. Prange, *At Dawn We Slept,* 294.

19. Ibid.

20. Ed Cray, *General of the Army: George C. Marshall, Soldier and Statesman* (New York: Norton, 1990), 255.

21. Gordon W. Prange, *Dec. 7, 1941: The Day the Japanese Attacked Pearl Harbor* (New York: Wings Books, 1991), 98.

22. Cordell Hull, *The Memoirs of Cordell Hull* (New York: Macmillan, 1948), vol. 2, 1095.

23. Prange, *Dec. 7, 1941,* 28.

24. Signal from Admiral Stark, priority, in Stinnett, *Day of Deceit,* 172–73.

25. Prange, *Dec. 7, 1941,* 247.

26. Ibid., 247–48.

27. Sherwood, *Roosevelt and Hopkins,* 430.

28. B. Mitchell Simpson III, *Admiral Harold R. Stark: Architect of Victory, 1939–1945* (Columbia: University of South Carolina Press, 1989), 114. Hopkins, in a memo that night, noted that it was "at about 1.40 p.m.": Sherwood, *Roosevelt and Hopkins,* 430.

29. Simpson, *Admiral Harold R. Stark,* 114. Hopkins noted: "a radio from the

Commander-in-Chief of our forces there advising all our stations that an air raid attack was on and that it was 'no drill.'": Sherwood, *Roosevelt and Hopkins,* 430–31.

30. See Ted Morgan, *FDR: A Biography* (New York: Simon and Schuster, 1985), 186–90 and 200.

31. Marshall, *George C. Marshall Interviews and Reminiscences for Forrest C. Pogue,* 610–11.

32. "FDR Visits Hawaii," Navy History Hawaii, http://navyhistoryhawaii.blogspot. com/2010/07/fdr-visits-hawaii_28.html, accessed April 29, 2011.

33. Franklin D. Roosevelt, "Remarks in Hawaii," July 28, 1934. John T. Woolley and Gerhard Peters, *The American Presidency Project*, http://www.presidency.ucsb. edu/ws/?pid=14729, accessed April 29, 2011.

34. Sherwood, *Roosevelt and Hopkins,* 431.

35. Chris Bellamy, *Absolute War: Soviet Russia in the Second World War* (New York: Knopf, 2007), 140.

36. Ibid., 107.

37. Ibid., 148.

38. Davis, *FDR, the War President,* 339.

39. Hull, *The Memoirs of Cordell Hull,* vol. 2, 1096.

40. Henry L. Stimson and McGeorge Bundy, *On Active Service in Peace and War* (New York: Harper and Brothers, 1948), 391.

41. Sherwood, *Roosevelt and Hopkins,* 431.

42. Prange, *Dec. 7, 1941,* 383; Linda Lotridge Levin, *The Making of FDR: The Story of Stephen T. Early, America's First Modern Press Secretary* (Amherst, NY: Prometheus Books, 2008), 252.

43. Levin, *The Making of FDR,* 252.

44. "The announcement of the attack was made in a brief statement by President Roosevelt. Naval and military targets on the principal island of Oahu have also been attacked." W. Averell Harriman and Elie Abel, *Special Envoy to Churchill and Stalin, 1941–1946* (New York: Random House, 1975), 111.

45. Martin Gilbert, *Winston S. Churchill,* vol. 6, *Finest Hour, 1939–1941* (Boston: Houghton Mifflin, 1983), 1267.

46. John G. Winant, *A Letter from Grosvenor Square: An Account of a Stewardship* (Boston: Houghton Mifflin, 1947), 198–99.

47. Gilbert, *Finest Hour,* 1268.

48. David Reynolds, *In Command of History: Churchill Fighting and Writing the Second World War* (New York: Random House, 2005), 264.

49. Sherwood, *Roosevelt and Hopkins,* 431.

50. Ibid.

51. Ibid., 432.

52. Grace Tully, *F.D.R., My Boss* (New York: Scribner's, 1949), 254.

53. Maurice Matloff and Edwin M. Snell, *Strategic Planning for Coalition Warfare,*

1941–1942 (Washington, DC: Office of the Chief of Military History, Dept. of the Army, 1953), 18.

54. Simpson, *Admiral Harold R. Stark,* 109.
55. Henry H. Arnold, *Global Mission* (New York: Harper, 1949), 193.
56. Tully, *F.D.R., My Boss,* 255.
57. Ibid.
58. Prange, *Dec. 7, 1941,* 255.
59. Tully, *F.D.R., My Boss,* 255.
60. Ibid., 256.
61. Ibid.
62. Draft No. 1, December 7, 1941, Proposed Message to the Congress, Franklin Delano Roosevelt Library, Hyde Park, NY.
63. Tully, *F.D.R., My Boss,* 256.
64. Magic intercept of Tokyo Foreign Office Purple message to the Japanese Embassy in Washington, D.C., dated January 30, 1941, translated on February 7, 1941. Such intercepts could not, of course, be made public by the Roosevelt administration, but the gist of them was shared among all State Department and military authorities.
65. Hull, *The Memoirs of Cordell Hull,* vol. 2, 1098.
66. Tully, *F.D.R., My Boss,* 256.
67. Sherwood, *Roosevelt and Hopkins,* 432.
68. Levin, *The Making of FDR,* 252.
69. Richard Strout, in *Christian Science Monitor,* December 7, 1951, quoted in Prange, *Dec. 7, 1941,* 385.
70. John Morton Blum, ed., *From the Morgenthau Diaries,* vol. 3, *Years of War, 1941–1945* (Boston: Houghton Mifflin, 1967), 2.
71. Eleanor Roosevelt, *This I Remember,* 234.
72. Prange, *At Dawn We Slept,* 557.
73. Sherwood, *Roosevelt and Hopkins,* 433.
74. Ibid.
75. Prange, *At Dawn We Slept,* 556.
76. Ibid.
77. Ibid., 557.
78. Ibid.
79. Ibid., 557–58.
80. Sherwood, *Roosevelt and Hopkins,* 433.
81. Prange, *At Dawn We Slept,* 558.
82. Frances Perkins, Columbia University Oral History, quoted in Lynne Olson, *Citizens of London: The Americans Who Stood with Britain in Its Darkest Hour* (New York: Random House, 2010), 145; Andrew, *For the President's Eyes Only,* 118–19.
83. Morgan, *FDR: A Biography,* 617.

84. Sherwood, *Roosevelt and Hopkins,* 433.
85. Prange, *At Dawn We Slept,* 559.
86. Morgan, *FDR: A Biography,* 618.
87. Prange, *Dec. 7, 1941,* 389.
88. Prange, *At Dawn We Slept,* 560.
89. Ibid.
90. Prange, *Dec. 7, 1941,* 390.
91. Ibid., 384.
92. Prange, *At Dawn We Slept,* 516.
93. Davis, *FDR, the War President,* 347.
94. Sherwood, *Roosevelt and Hopkins,* 433.
95. Ibid., 434.
96. Stinnett, *Day of Deceit,* 3.
97. A. M. Sperber, *Murrow: His Life and Times* (New York: Freundlich Books, 1986), 207.

3. HITLER'S GAMBLE

1. Robert E. Sherwood, *Roosevelt and Hopkins: An Intimate History* (New York: Harper, 1948), 435–36.
2. Ibid., 437.
3. Franklin D. Roosevelt, *The Public Papers and Addresses of Franklin D. Roosevelt,* ed. Samuel Rosenman, vol. 10, *The Call to Battle Stations, 1941* (New York: Russell and Russell, 1969), 514–16.
4. Martin Gilbert, *Churchill and America* (New York: Free Press, 2005), 246.
5. Alan Brooke, "Notes on My Life," in *War Diaries, 1939–1945: Field Marshal Lord Alanbrooke,* ed. Alex Danchev and Daniel Todman (Berkeley: University of California Press, 2001), 209.
6. Cable C-138x, in Warren Kimball, ed., *Churchill & Roosevelt: The Complete Correspondence,* vol. 1, *Alliance Emerging, October 1933–November 1942* (Princeton, NJ: Princeton University Press, 1984), 283.
7. Entry of Tuesday, December 9, 1941, "Secret Diary" of Lord Halifax, Papers of Lord Halifax, Hickleton Papers, Borthwick Institute of Historical Research, University of York, Yorkshire, England.
8. Letter to the Prime Minister, December 9, 1941, Papers of Lord Halifax, Hickleton Papers, Borthwick Institute of Historical Research, University of York, Yorkshire, England.
9. Ibid.
10. Ibid.
11. Letter to Hiram Johnson Jr., December 13, 1941, in Hiram W. Johnson, *The Diary Letters of Hiram Johnson, 1917–1945,* vol. 7 (New York: Garland, 1983).
12. Letter to the Prime Minister, December 9, 1941, Papers of Lord Halifax.
13. Ibid.

14. Andrew Roberts, *The Holy Fox: A Biography of Lord Halifax* (London: Weidenfeld and Nicolson, 1991), 287.

15. Ibid., 280.

16. Ibid.

17. Cable R-73x, draft A, in Kimball, *Churchill & Roosevelt,* vol. 1, 285.

18. Entry of Wednesday, December 10, 1941, Halifax Diary.

19. David Reynolds, *In Command of History: Churchill Fighting and Writing the Second World War* (New York: Random House, 2005), 266.

20. Winston S. Churchill, *The Second World War,* vol. 3, *The Grand Alliance* (Boston: Houghton Mifflin, 1950), 551.

21. Cable C-139x, in Kimball, *Churchill & Roosevelt,* vol. 1, 284.

22. Cable R-73x, draft B, in Kimball, *Churchill & Roosevelt,* vol. 1, 286.

23. Ibid.

24. Cable R-73x, in Kimball, *Churchill & Roosevelt,* vol. 1, 286.

25. Linda Lotridge Levin, *The Making of FDR: The Story of Stephen T. Early, America's First Modern Press Secretary* (Amherst, NY: Prometheus Books, 2008), 262.

26. Entry of December 3, 1941, Galeazzo Ciano, *Diary 1937–1943* (New York: Enigma Books, 2002), 470.

27. Ibid.

28. Ibid., entry of December 8, 1941, 472.

29. Ian Kershaw, *Hitler 1936–1945: Nemesis* (New York: Norton, 2001), 345.

30. Guderian was dismissed on December 26, 1941.

31. Henry Picker, *Hitlers Tischgespräche im Führerhauptquartier, 1941–42,* ed. Gerhard Ritter (Bonn: Athenäum Verlag, 1951), 75.

32. Ian Kershaw, *Fateful Choices: Ten Decisions That Changed the World, 1940–1941* (New York: Penguin Press, 2007), 417, quoting Walter Warlimont, *Inside Hitler's Headquarters, 1939–45* (Novato, CA: Presidio, 1964), 207–8.

33. Kershaw, *Hitler: Nemesis,* 953.

34. Entry of December 8, 1941, Ciano, *Diary,* 472.

35. Gordon W. Prange, *At Dawn We Slept: The Untold Story of Pearl Harbor* (New York: McGraw-Hill, 1981), 428.

36. Hitler to Franz Halder, March 17, 1941, in Kershaw, *Hitler: Nemesis,* 355.

37. Kershaw, *Fateful Choices,* 401.

38. Nikolaus von Below, adjutant to the Führer, in Kershaw, *Hitler: Nemesis,* 954.

39. Kershaw, *Hitler: Nemesis,* 442.

40. Kershaw, *Fateful Choices,* 418.

41. Max Domarus, ed., *Hitler, Speeches and Proclamations 1932–1945: The Chronicle of a Dictatorship,* vol. 4, *The Years 1941 to 1945* (Wauconda, IL: Bolchazy-Carducci, 1997), 2531–51. Notable Americans had sympathized. "There is no question of the power, unity and purposefulness of Germany," Anne Morrow Lindbergh had written her mother after her first trip to Germany in 1936, "it is terrific. I have never in my life been so conscious of such a directed force. It is thrilling when one sees it manifested in the energy, pride and morale of the people — especially

the young people. But also terrifying in its very unity — a weapon made by one man but also to be used by one man. Hitler, I am beginning to feel, is like an inspired religious leader, and as such fanatical — a visionary who really wants the best for his country." Anne Morrow Lindbergh, *The Flower and the Nettle: Diaries and Letters of Anne Morrow Lindbergh, 1936–1939* (New York: Harcourt Brace Jovanovich, 1976), 100.

42. Domarus, *Hitler, Speeches and Proclamations,* vol. 4, 2531–51.
43. Ibid.
44. Letter to Hiram Johnson Jr., December 13, 1941, in Johnson, *The Diary Letters of Hiram Johnson,* vol. 7.
45. Ibid.

4. THE VICTORY PLAN

1. Eleanor Roosevelt, *This I Remember* (New York: Harper, 1949), 233.
2. Mrs. Roosevelt may have misremembered; as AP's White House reporter, A. Merriman Smith, claimed in 1946, "knowledge that Churchill was en route to the White House was generally known among Washington reporters, but not a word was printed or broadcast until he arrived": A. Merriman Smith, *Thank You, Mr. President: A White House Notebook* (New York: Harper and Brothers, 1946), 129.
3. Eleanor Roosevelt, *This I Remember,* 237.
4. Entry of Sunday, December 21, 1941, "Secret Diary" of Lord Halifax, Papers of Lord Halifax, Hickleton Papers, Borthwick Institute of Historical Research, University of York, Yorkshire, England.
5. Ibid., entry of Monday, December 22, 1941.
6. Mary Soames, ed., *Speaking for Themselves: The Personal Letters of Winston and Clementine Churchill* (New York: Doubleday, 1998), 461.
7. Entry of Monday, December 22, 1941, Halifax Diary.
8. Ibid.
9. Entry of December 22, 1941, in Lord Moran, *Winston Churchill: The Struggle for Survival, 1940–1965* (London: Constable, 1966), 11.
10. Ibid.
11. Ibid.
12. See Mark A. Stoler, *The Politics of the Second Front: American Military Planning and Diplomacy in Coalition Warfare, 1941–1943* (Westport, CT: Greenwood Press, 1977), 23.
13. Winston S. Churchill, *The Second World War,* vol. 3, *The Grand Alliance* (Boston: Houghton Mifflin, 1950), 589.
14. Ibid., 589–60.
15. For an excellent summary see Mark A. Stoler, *Allies and Adversaries: The Joint Chiefs of Staff, the Grand Alliance, and U.S. Strategy in World War II* (Chapel Hill: University of North Carolina Press, 2000). See also Mark A. Stoler, *Allies in War: Britain and America Against the Axis Powers, 1940–1945* (London: Hodder Arnold,

2005); and Christopher Thorne, *Allies of a Kind: The United States, Britain, and the War Against Japan, 1941–1945* (New York: Oxford University Press, 1978).

16. Barbara Tuchman, *Stilwell and the American Experience in China, 1911–45* (New York: Macmillan, 1970), 241; Stoler, *The Politics of the Second Front*, 25.

17. Stoler, *The Politics of the Second Front*, 13.

18. Letter to Hiram Johnson Jr., February 19, 1942, in Hiram W. Johnson, *The Diary Letters of Hiram Johnson, 1917–1945*, vol. 7 (New York: Garland, 1983).

19. Churchill, *The Second World War*, vol. 3, *The Grand Alliance*, 588.

20. Stoler, *Allies and Adversaries*, 47–50.

21. The final report, with appendices, was only formally submitted to the President on September 25, 1941, though still dated September 11. "Joint Board Estimate of United States Over-all Production Requirements, September 11, 1941," "Safe" and Confidential Files, Franklin D. Roosevelt Presidential Library, Hyde Park, NY. See also Kenneth S. Davis, *FDR, the War President, 1940–1943: A History* (New York: Random House, 2000), 295.

22. "Joint Board Estimate," "Safe" and Confidential Files, FDR Library. Author's italics.

23. Ibid.

24. Lord Halifax to Prime Minister, October 4, 1941, Papers of Lord Halifax, Hickleton Papers, Borthwick Institute of Historical Research, University of York, Yorkshire, England.

25. "We lunched together, as usual, on his writing table, among his papers and knickknacks, and he talked about everything with great freedom, from Russia to the Philippines": entry of Friday, October 10, 1941, Halifax Diary.

26. Lord Halifax to Prime Minister, October 11, 1941, Papers of Lord Halifax.

27. Churchill, *The Second World War*, vol. 3, *The Grand Alliance*, 482–83.

28. Entry of December 18, 1942, Stimson Diary, Henry L. Stimson Papers, Yale University Library, New Haven, CT.

29. Ibid.

30. Ibid.

31. Jon Meacham, *Franklin and Winston: An Intimate Portrait of an Epic Friendship* (New York: Random House, 2003), 141.

32. Michael F. Reilly and William Slocum, *Reilly of the White House* (New York: Simon and Schuster, 1947), 125.

33. President's Press Conference, White House, December 23, 1941, FDR Library.

34. Smith, *Thank You, Mr. President*, 67.

35. President's Press Conference, White House, December 23, 1941.

36. Smith, *Thank You, Mr. President*, 262.

37. "Operation Arcadia: Washington Conference, December 1941," entry of December 23, Diary of Ian Jacob, 11, Liddell Hart Centre for Military History, King's College London.

38. Ibid., 13.

39. Entry of December 23, 1941, Stimson Diary, 140.

40. Ibid., 140–41.
41. "Operation Arcadia: Washington Conference, December 1941," entry of December 23, Jacob Diary, 15–16.
42. Ibid., 17.
43. "What India was for England, the eastern territory will be for us": Hitler monologues, August 8–11, 1941, quoted in Ian Kershaw, *Hitler 1936–1945: Nemesis* (New York: Norton, 2000), 402.
44. Charles Wilson, Moran Papers, Wellcome Library, London, typescript notes.
45. Ibid., typescript notes, marked "29."
46. Entry of Monday, November 10, 1941, Halifax Diary.
47. Charles Wilson, Moran Papers, typescript notes.
48. Hankey Papers, Churchill College, Cambridge, quoted in David Irving, *Churchill's War*, vol. 2, *Triumph in Adversity* (London: Focal Point, 2001), 339.
49. Thorne, *Allies of a Kind*, 116.
50. Ibid.
51. Andrew Roberts, *Eminent Churchillians* (New York: Simon and Schuster, 1994), 205.
52. Charles Wilson, Moran Papers, typescript notes.
53. Ibid.
54. Ibid.
55. Ibid.
56. Ibid.
57. "Operation Arcadia: Washington Conference, December 1941," entry of December 25, Jacob Diary, 15–16.
58. Ibid.
59. Ibid.
60. Entry of December 25, 1941, Stimson Diary, 145–46.
61. Ibid.
62. Ibid., 145.
63. Ibid., 146.
64. Ibid., 147.
65. Stephen Ambrose, *Eisenhower*, vol. 1, *Soldier, General of the Army, President-Elect, 1890–1952* (New York: Simon and Schuster, 1985), 137–38.
66. Eleanor Roosevelt, *This I Remember*, 242–43.
67. Meacham, *Franklin and Winston*, 144.
68. Ibid., 145.
69. Eleanor Roosevelt, *This I Remember*, 243–44.
70. John Morton Blum, ed., *From the Morgenthau Diaries*, vol. 3, *Years of War, 1941–1945* (Boston: Houghton Mifflin, 1967), 122.
71. Entry of Monday, December 24, 1941, Halifax Diary.
72. Entry of December 27, 1941, Stimson Diary, 144–45.
73. Entry of December 25, 1941, Halifax Diary.
74. Charles Wilson, Moran Papers, typescript notes.

75. Vivian A. Cox, *Seven Christmases*, ed. Nick Thorne (Seven Oaks, Kent, UK: Nickay Associates, 2010), 117.

76. Carlo D'Este, *Warlord: A Life of Winston Churchill at War, 1874–1945* (New York: Harper, 2008), 560.

77. Charles Wilson, Moran Papers, typescript notes.

78. Entry of Monday, December 26, 1941, Halifax Diary.

79. David Lilienthal, *The Journals of David E. Lilienthal* (New York: Harper and Row, 1964), vol. 1, 418.

80. Entry of Monday, December 26, 1941, Halifax Diary.

81. Winston S. Churchill, *The Unrelenting Struggle: War Speeches by the Right Hon. Winston S. Churchill, C.H., M.P*, comp. Charles Eade (Boston: Little, Brown, 1942), 337.

82. Ibid.

83. Smith, *Thank You, Mr. President,* 67.

84. Charles Wilson, Moran Papers, typescript notes.

85. Copy in Stimson Papers, Yale University Library.

86. "Report on the meetings of the nucleus of America First," December 17, 1941, in the home of Edwin S. Webster, copy in Stimson Papers, Yale University Library.

87. Rudolf Schröck, with Dyrk Hesshaimer, Astrid Bouteuil, and David Hesshaimer, *Das Doppelleben des Charles A. Lindbergh* [The double life of Charles A. Lindbergh] (Munich: Heyne Verlag, 2005). See also Joshua Kendall, *America's Obsessives: The Compulsive Energy That Built a Nation* (New York: Grand Central, 2013), 184–94.

88. Cordell Hull, *The Memoirs of Cordell Hull* (New York: Macmillan, 1948), 1117 et seq.

5. SUPREME COMMAND

1. Eleanor Roosevelt, *This I Remember* (New York: Harper, 1949), 243.

2. "Operation Arcadia: Washington Conference, December 1941," "Some Personalities," Diary of Ian Jacob, 26 and 24, Liddell Hart Centre for Military History, King's College London.

3. Ibid., 24.

4. Entry of December 27, 1941, "Secret Diary" of Lord Halifax, Papers of Lord Halifax, Hickleton Papers, Borthwick Institute of Historical Research, University of York, Yorkshire, England.

5. Doris Kearns Goodwin, *No Ordinary Time: Franklin and Eleanor Roosevelt; The Home Front in World War II* (New York: Simon and Schuster, 1994), 320. See also Alonzo Fields, *My 21 Years in the White House* (New York: Coward-McCann, 1961), 82, 88–89.

6. "The President's Secretary to the Secretary of State," with attachment, in Documents and Supplementary Papers, The First Washington Conference, in U.S. Department of State, *Foreign Relations of the United States, The Conferences at*

Washington, 1941–1942, and Casablanca, 1943 (Washington, DC: US Government Printing Office, 1941–43), 375.

7. Kenneth S. Davis, *FDR: The War President, 1940–1943: A History* (New York: Random House, 2000), 372.

8. "Operation Arcadia: Washington Conference, December 1941," "Some Personalities," Jacob Diary, 37–38. President Roosevelt later verified the story to Canadian prime minister Mackenzie King: entry of December 5, 1942, Diaries of William Lyon Mackenzie King, Library and Archives Canada, Ottawa, ON.

9. War Cabinet verbatim report, January 18, 1942, Papers of Lawrence Burgis, in Andrew Roberts, *Masters and Commanders: How Four Titans Won the War in the West, 1941–1945* (New York: Harper, 2009), 87.

10. Forrest Pogue, *George C. Marshall*, vol. 2, *Ordeal and Hope, 1939–1942* (New York: Viking, 1966), 276.

11. Entry of December 27, 1941, Stimson Diary, Henry L. Stimson Papers, Yale University Library, New Haven, CT, 148.

12. "Operation Arcadia: Washington Conference, December 1941," "Sunday, December 28th to Wednesday, December 31st," Jacob Diary, 20.

13. Ibid.

14. Alan Brooke, *War Diaries 1939–1945: Field Marshal Lord Alanbrooke,* ed. Alex Danchev and Daniel Todman (Berkeley: University of California Press, 2001), 215.

15. Ibid.

16. Cable of December 28, 1941, quoted in Winston S. Churchill, *The Second World War,* vol. 3, *The Grand Alliance* (Boston: Houghton Mifflin, 1950), 598.

17. Ibid.

18. Brooke, *War Diaries,* 215.

19. Ibid.

20. "Address to the Congress on the State of the Union," January 6, 1942, Franklin D. Roosevelt, *The Public Papers and Addresses of Franklin D. Roosevelt,* vol. 11, *Humanity on the Defensive 1942* (New York: Russell and Russell, 1969), 32–42.

21. Entry of January 4, 1942, Halifax Diary.

6. THE PRESIDENT'S MAP ROOM

1. Richard Holmes, *Churchill's Bunker: The Secret Headquarters at the Heart of Britain's Victory* (London: Profile Books; Imperial War Museum, 2009), 55.

2. Ibid., 72.

3. Ibid., 83.

4. "Re: Air Raid Shelter," December 15, 1942, Morgenthau Office Diaries, Franklin D. Roosevelt Presidential Library, Hyde Park, NY.

5. Winston S. Churchill, *The Second World War,* vol. 2, *Their Finest Hour* (Boston: Houghton Mifflin, 1949), 331.

6. "Re: Air Raid Shelter," Morgenthau Office Diaries.

7. Ibid.

8. Ibid.
9. Vivian A. Cox, *Seven Christmases,* ed. Nick Thorne (Seven Oaks, Kent, UK: Nickay Associates, 2010), 127–28.
10. Ibid., 284.
11. Ibid., letter of 24.1.41, 134.
12. Ibid., letter of 30.1.41, 285.
13. Ibid., 134.
14. Commander George Elsey, interview with author, September 10, 2011. All Elsey quotes in chapter are from this interview.
15. Cox, *Seven Christmases,* 130.
16. Sublieutenant Cox stayed in Washington until early February 1942. His report to the British Admiralty, detailing the site, the room, its construction, the charts, the personnel, information displayed, manner of display, etc., is reproduced in his memoir: Cox, *Seven Christmases,* 311–19. Cox was distressed, initially, by the failure of the U.S. Navy to cooperate in providing "anything like the complete picture of the [war] situation" that the President "could and should have had": ibid., 314.

7. THE FIGHTING GENERAL

1. Alonzo Fields, *My 21 Years in the White House* (New York: Coward-McCann, 1961), 52–53.
2. *Baltimore Sun,* February 1, 1942, Office of the Coordinator of Information (COI), Press Excerpts, January 27–February 1942, Papers of General Douglas MacArthur, Record Group (RG) 2, MacArthur Memorial Archives [hereafter MMA]; Richard Connaughton, *MacArthur and Defeat in the Philippines* (Woodstock, NY: Overlook Press, 2001), 258.
3. February 2, 1942, COI Press Excerpts, January 27–February 1942, MacArthur Papers, RG 2, MMA; Connaughton, *MacArthur and Defeat in the Philippines,* 258.
4. Connaughton, *MacArthur and Defeat in the Philippines,* 257.
5. Ibid.
6. January 27, 1942, COI Press Excerpts, January 27–February 1942, MacArthur Papers, RG 2, MMA; Connaughton, *MacArthur and Defeat in the Philippines,* 257.
7. January 27, 1942, COI Press Excerpts, January 27–February 1942, MacArthur Papers, RG 2, MMA; Connaughton, *MacArthur and Defeat in the Philippines,* 257.
8. Douglas MacArthur, *Reminiscences* (New York: McGraw-Hill, 1964), 93.
9. William Manchester, *American Caesar: Douglas MacArthur 1880–1964* (Boston: Little, Brown, 1978), 152, quoting Rexford Tugwell, *The Democratic Roosevelt* (Garden City, NY: Doubleday, 1957), 348–51.
10. MacArthur, *Reminiscences,* 101.
11. Ibid.
12. Tugwell, *The Democratic Roosevelt,* 349–50.

13. One of the star performers in establishing the Conservation Corps was Lieutenant Colonel George C. Marshall. Instead of making Marshall a brigadier general, as General Pershing, Marshall's former commanding officer in World War I, had requested, MacArthur — who was known to be pathologically jealous of able subordinates — made him an instructor with the National Guard, without promoting him.
14. Michael Schaller, *Douglas MacArthur: The Far Eastern General* (New York: Oxford University Press, 1989), 13–14 and 18–20; Manchester, *American Caesar,* 156.
15. MacArthur, *Reminiscences,* 96.
16. Carlo D'Este, *Eisenhower: A Soldier's Life* (New York: Holt, 2002), 238.
17. Connaughton, *MacArthur and Defeat in the Philippines,* 109.
18. James Leutze, *A Different Kind of Victory: A Biography of Admiral Thomas C. Hart* (Annapolis, MD: Naval Institute Press, 1981), 218.
19. Schaller, *Douglas MacArthur,* 26.
20. War Department 749 to MacArthur: "Reports of Japanese attacks show that numbers of our planes have been destroyed on the ground. Take all possible steps at once to avoid such losses in your area, including dispersion to maximum possible extent, construction of parapets and prompt take-off on warning": Records of Headquarters, United States Army in the Far East (USAFFE), years 1941–42, USAFFE, Chief of Staff and Commanding General, Radios and Letters Dealing with Plans and Policies, MacArthur Papers, RG 2, MMA. MacArthur also had his own code-breaking unit that had broken the Japanese diplomatic codes (Magic) and a number of Japanese naval codes.
21. William Hassett, *Off the Record with F.D.R., 1942–1945* (New Brunswick, NJ: Rutgers University Press, 1958), 88.
22. Leutze, *A Different Kind of Victory,* 212.
23. Theodore Friend, *Between Two Empires: The Ordeal of the Philippines, 1929–1946* (New Haven, CT: Yale University Press, 1965), 207.
24. Manchester, *American Caesar,* 215; D. Clayton James, *The Years of MacArthur,* vol. 2, *1941–1945* (Boston: Houghton Mifflin, 1975), 33.
25. Telegram of December 22, 1941, MacArthur Papers, RG 2, MMA.
26. James, *The Years of MacArthur,* vol. 2, 54.
27. Schaller, *Douglas MacArthur,* 72.
28. Connaughton, *MacArthur and Defeat in the Philippines,* 225.
29. James, *The Years of MacArthur,* vol. 2, 89.
30. Hassett, *Off the Record with F.D.R.,* 88.
31. Entry of January 29, 1942, in Dwight D. Eisenhower, *The Eisenhower Diaries,* ed. Robert H. Ferrell (New York: Norton, 1981), 46.
32. Letter of November 9, 1941, in Leutze, *A Different Kind of Victory,* 218.
33. Ibid., 212.
34. Telegram of December 13, 1941, MacArthur Papers, RG 2, MMA.
35. Ibid., telegram of December 22, 1941.

36. Ibid., telegram of January 2, 1942.

37. Ibid., telegram of January 7, 1942.

38. Leutze, *A Different Kind of Victory,* 265.

39. "Message from General MacArthur, To All Unit Commanders" (100 copies), MacArthur Papers, RG 2, MMA.

40. Manchester, *American Caesar,* 237.

41. Telegram of January 17, 1942, to General Marshall, MacArthur Papers, RG 2, MMA.

42. See Marshall telegrams to MacArthur 913, 917, 855, 949, 991, inter alia, MacArthur Papers, RG 2, MMA.

43. Entry of January 29, 1942, *The Eisenhower Diaries,* 46.

44. Ibid., entry of February 3, 1942.

45. Telegram 855, December 22, 1941, Records of Headquarters, USAFFE, MacArthur Papers, RG 2, MMA.

46. Telegram 1024, February 8, 1942, MacArthur Papers, RG 2, MMA.

47. Manuel Quezon, *The Good Fight* (New York: D. Appleton-Century, 1946), 261–62.

48. Robert E. Sherwood, *Roosevelt and Hopkins: An Intimate History* (New York: Harper, 1948), 492.

49. Leutze, *A Different Kind of Victory,* 240.

50. General George McClellan was dismissed as general in chief of the Union Army by President Lincoln on November 13, 1862, having failed to exploit his victory at Antietam, and having referred, it was said, to the President and Commander in Chief as a "gorilla." General McClellan later stood against Lincoln in the 1864 presidential election, where he "met with no better success as a politician than as a general": James M. McPherson, *Tried by War: Abraham Lincoln as Commander in Chief* (New York: Penguin, 2008), 141.

51. Sherwood, *Roosevelt and Hopkins,* 492.

52. Ibid.

53. Hassett, *Off the Record with F.D.R.,* 8.

54. Ibid., 14.

55. Ibid., 17.

56. "We've got to go to Europe and fight, and we've got to quit wasting resources all over the world, and still worse, wasting time," Eisenhower noted in his diary on January 27, 1942 — reversing his earlier views. "If we're to keep Russia in, save the Middle East, India, and Burma, we've got to begin slugging with air at West Europe. To be followed by a land attack as soon as possible": Entry of January 27, 1942, *The Eisenhower Diaries,* 43.

57. Ibid., entry of January 23, 1942, 44.

58. Connaughton, *MacArthur and Defeat in the Philippines,* 236.

59. James, *The Years of MacArthur,* vol. 2, 66.

60. Leutze, *A Different Kind of Victory,* 265.

61. Telegram of February 4, 1942, in MacArthur Papers, RG 2, MMA.

62. "Another long message on 'strategy' from MacArthur. He sent one on extolling

the virtues of the flank offensive. Wonder what he thinks we've been studying for all these years. His lecture would have been good for plebes": Entry of February 8, 1942, *The Eisenhower Diaries,* 47.

63. Entry of December 31, 1941, 161, Stimson Diary, Henry L. Stimson Papers, Yale University Library, New Haven, CT.
64. Quezon, *The Good Fight,* 248.
65. MacArthur, *Reminiscences,* 136; full text in MacArthur Papers, RG 4, MMA.
66. Transcript copy of telegram of January 30, 1942, MacArthur Papers, RG 2, MMA. The original wording is different from the paraphrase published in Quezon, *The Good Fight,* 261–63.
67. Telegram to General Marshall of January 31, 1942, MacArthur Papers, RG 2, MMA.
68. MacArthur, *Reminiscences,* 137.
69. Telegram of February 8, 1942, to General Marshall "from President Quezon for President Roosevelt," MacArthur Papers, RG 2, MMA.
70. Entry of February 8, 1942, Stimson Diary.
71. Ibid.
72. Ibid., entry of January 5, 1942.
73. Leutze, *A Different Kind of Victory,* 209.
74. Entry of January 5, 1942, Stimson Diary, 12.
75. Ibid.
76. *Congressional Record,* March 5, 1942. Several congressmen urged the appointment of Congressman John Wadsworth of New York — who wrote to Stimson blaming the *Washington Times Herald* for stoking the Washington "hot bed of rumors . . . It is a dirty business": Letter to Stimson of March 5, 1942, Stimson Papers.
77. Entry of February 9, 1942, Stimson Diary.
78. Ibid.
79. Ibid.
80. Telegram of February 8, 1942, to General Marshall "from President Quezon for President Roosevelt," in MacArthur Papers, RG 2, MMA.
81. Ibid.
82. Entry of February 9, 1942, Stimson Diary.
83. Forrest Pogue, *George C. Marshall,* vol. 2, *Ordeal and Hope, 1939–1942* (New York: Viking, 1966), 247–48.
84. Entry of February 9, 1942, *The Eisenhower Diaries,* 47.
85. Stimson's earlier draft for a cable to President Quezon gave an unfortunate indication of the war secretary's unprepossessing language. "I am much distressed . . . we endeavored to defeat the aggression of Japan . . . we have been marshaling our forces. . . . These difficulties have been accentuated . . . The British have been most co-operative . . . we have every hope . . . our plans are comprehensive but must not be jeopardized by reckless or hasty steps . . . You must rest assured that we shall proceed continuously and with all possible speed. . . .": "Draft for

president's reply to Quezon, prepared by HLS February 9, 1942," Stimson Papers. In his diary on February 13 Stimson was still worried about "the President's rather severe telegram of two or three days ago" and "the President's castigation": Stimson Diary, February 13, 1942.

86. Telegram 1029 of February 10, 1942, from President Roosevelt to General MacArthur, MacArthur Papers, RG 2, MMA.
87. Ibid.
88. Ibid.
89. Ibid.
90. Ibid.
91. Arguably, World War II had begun not in Europe but in Asia, in 1937, when Japan invaded China.
92. Telegram 1029 of February 10, 1942, to Commanding General, USAFFE, Fort Mills, February 10, 1942, MacArthur Papers, RG 2, MMA.
93. Entry of February 9, 1942, *The Eisenhower Diaries,* 47.
94. Telegram of February 10, 1942, MacArthur Papers, RG 2, MMA.
95. Ibid., telegram 1037.
96. Ibid., telegram 1031, February 10, 1942.
97. Entry of January 13, 1942, Papers of Paul P. Rogers, Corregidor Diary and Selected Letters, RG 46, 1941–1989, 20 October 1941–11 March 1942, MMA.
98. Ibid., entry of February 12.
99. Telegram from General MacArthur to AGWAR, "For President Roosevelt," February 11, 1942, MacArthur Papers, RG 2, MMA.
100. Ibid.
101. Ibid.
102. Ibid. In fact, General Marshall had already twice raised the issue of MacArthur's own evacuation, cabling first on January 13, then on February 4, 1942, stating that "under these conditions the need for your services there [in the Philippines] might be less pressing than at other points in the Far East": see Connaughton, *MacArthur and Defeat in the Philippines,* 259. Jean MacArthur was adamant she would not leave without her husband, declaring, "We have drunk from the same cup, we three shall stay together": Manchester, *American Caesar,* 249.
103. Manchester, *American Caesar,* 249.
104. James K. Eyre, *The Roosevelt-MacArthur Conflict* (Chambersburg, PA: printed by author, 1950), 40.
105. Ibid., 41.
106. Ibid.
107. Carlos P. Romulo, *I Walked with Heroes* (New York: Holt, Rinehart, and Winston, 1961), 219.
108. Ibid., 223.
109. Eyre, *The Roosevelt-MacArthur Conflict,* 40.
110. Ibid., 42.

111. Ibid.
112. "Secret Priority" Telegram No. 262 to General George C. Marshall, War Department, February 12, 1942, MacArthur Papers, RG 2, MMA.
113. Quezon, *The Good Fight,* 274.
114. Ibid., 275.
115. The matter of MacArthur's controversial payment, solicited from President Quezon, was first raised by Carol M. Petillo in the *Pacific Historical Review* in 1979, later republished as "Douglas MacArthur and Manuel Quezon: A Note on an Imperial Bond" in William M. Leary, ed., *MacArthur and the American Century: A Reader* (Lincoln: University of Nebraska Press, 2001), 52–64.
116. Paul P. Rogers, *The Good Years: MacArthur and Sutherland* (New York: Praeger, 1990), 165; entry of February 13, 1942, Rogers Diary, in Papers of Paul P. Rogers, Corregidor Diary and Selected Letters, RG 46, 1941–1989, 20 October 1941–11 March 1942, MMA. In a memorandum describing his diary, Rogers noted that the money was ordered to be given to MacArthur in a Philippine Presidential "Executive Act Number One," backdated on February 13, 1942, to January 1, 1942. In retrospect Rogers — who admired MacArthur — wondered if possibly he had that day typed an earlier version of the executive order, which was later amended, and the numbers increased — for he specifically recalled MacArthur "at the time saying to Sutherland that the amounts hardly compensated for the salaries they had lost by serving on the Military Mission" — even though MacArthur had been the highest-paid military officer in the world. There was "uproar in Washington," Rogers later learned, for the "radio went from Marshall to Stimson. After some discussion the request was transmitted to Chase National Bank for action, and a copy was sent to the Department of the Interior. [Secretary] Ickes apparently refused to sanction the transfer, and the action seems to have been taken over his head": Rogers, *The Good Years,* 166. For forty years the matter was then hushed up, but looking back, long after the general's death, Rogers, in his note accompanying the donation of his wartime diary to the MacArthur Memorial Archives, was minded to believe that he had "intentionally changed the dollar amount in the diary entry" to protect MacArthur's reputation. "I am sure," he wrote, "in making the entry I changed the $500,000 to $50,000; then I changed [Lieutenant General] Sutherland's figure to $45,000 [instead of $75,000] to keep it in line with MacArthur. The amounts given to [Brigadier General Richard] Marshall and [Lieutenant Colonel Sidney] Huff, being relatively minor as compared with $500,000, were recorded without change": Notes on "The Diary" filed in Papers of Paul P. Rogers, Corregidor Diary and Selected Letters, RG 46, 1941–1989, 20 October 1941–11 March 1942, MMA. Rogers published his account of the matter in *The Good Years,* 165–69.
117. MacArthur later removed his copy of the cable — MacArthur to Adjutant-General, War Department, Washington, #285, February 15, 1942 — but a copy was kept by President Roosevelt in his "Safe" and Confidential Files.
118. Rogers, *The Good Years,* 166.

8. SINGAPORE

1. "Bring Gen MacArthur Home," Speech by Wendell Willkie at the Lincoln birthday dinner of the Middlesex Club in Boston, February 12, 1942, *Vital Speeches of the Day*, vol. 10, no. 4. 297–99.

2. Ibid.

3. Stimson Diary, Henry L. Stimson Papers, Yale University Library, New Haven, CT, entry of February 12, 1942.

4. Ibid., entry of February 13, 1942.

5. Eight Hundred and Sixth Press Conference, February 17, 1942, *The Public Papers and Addresses of Franklin D. Roosevelt*, vol. 11, *Humanity on the Defensive* (New York: Russell and Russell, 1969), 103.

6. Article 7 of the "Preliminary Agreement Between the United States and the United Kingdom" called for the "elimination of all forms of discriminatory treatment in international commerce, and to the reduction of tariffs and other trade barriers; and, in general, to the attainment of all the economic objectives set forth in the Joint Declaration made on August 14, 1941, by the President of the United States of America and the Prime Minister of the United Kingdom."

7. Cable C-25, February 7, 1942, Warren F. Kimball, ed., *Churchill & Roosevelt: The Complete Correspondence*, vol. 1, *Alliance Emerging, October 1933–November 1942* (Princeton, NJ: Princeton University Press, 1984), 351.

8. Correlli Barnett, *The Collapse of British Power* (London: Eyre Methuen, 1972), 107.

9. Winston S. Churchill, *The Second World War*, vol. 4, *The Hinge of Fate* (Boston: Houghton Mifflin, 1950), 88.

10. Cable C 141x, Kimball, *Churchill & Roosevelt*, vol. 1, 287.

11. Cable C-145x, "Part II — The Pacific Front," Kimball, *Churchill & Roosevelt*, vol. 1, 299.

12. Cable C-25, Kimball, *Churchill & Roosevelt*, vol. 1, 349.

13. Alan Brooke, *War Diaries 1939–1945: Field Marshal Lord Alanbrooke*, ed. Alex Danchev and Daniel Todman (Berkeley: University of California Press, 2001), 225.

14. Ibid., entry of February 2, 1942, 226.

15. Ibid., entry of February 3, 1942, 226.

16. Ibid., annotation by Lord Alanbrooke, 226.

17. Martin Gilbert, *Winston S. Churchill*, vol. 7, *Road to Victory: 1941–1945* (London: Heinemann, 1986), 47.

18. Entry of February 9, 1942, Brooke, *War Diaries*, 228.

19. Ibid.

20. Ibid., entry of February 11, 1942, 228–29.

21. Ibid., entry of February 13, 1942, 229.

22. Alexander Cadogan, *The Diaries of Sir Alexander Cadogan*, ed. David Dilks (London: Cassell, 1971), 433.

23. Ibid., entry of February 12, 1942.

24. Entry of February 13, 1942, Brooke, *War Diaries*, 229.

25. Clifford Kinvig, *Scapegoat: General Percival of Singapore* (London: Brassey's, 1996), 208.
26. Sugata Bose, *His Majesty's Opponent: Subhas Chandra Bose and India's Struggle Against Empire* (Cambridge, MA: Belknap Press of Harvard University Press, 2011), 242. There had already been a mutiny in 1940 by Sikh artillerymen tasked with defending Hong Kong: Lawrence James, *The Rise and Fall of the British Empire* (London: Little, Brown, 1994), 492.
27. Cable C-25, Kimball, *Churchill & Roosevelt*, vol. 1, 355.
28. "On the State of the War" (British Library of Information title), or "Through the Storm: A Broadcast Survey of the War Situation," February 15, 1942, in *War Speeches by the Right Hon. Winston S. Churchill, C.H., M.P.,* comp. Charles Eade, vol. 3, *The End of the Beginning* (London: Cassell, 1942), 201–7.
29. Ibid.
30. Ibid.
31. Ibid.
32. Robert Sherwood, *Roosevelt and Hopkins: An Intimate History* (New York: Harper, 1948), 501.
33. "On the State of the War" (British Library of Information title) or "Through the Storm: A Broadcast Survey of the War Situation," February 15, 1942, *The War Speeches of Winston S. Churchill,* vol. 2, 204.
34. In the *Sook Ching,* General Yamashita's order to "clean up" anti-Japanese Chinese captured in Singapore, military cordons were erected around Chinese residential areas to stop Chinese males aged between twelve and fifty from escaping. "The Japanese admitted to responsibility for 6,000 deaths. The figure most commonly quoted by the Chinese community was 40,000": Peter Thompson, *The Battle for Singapore: The True Story of Britain's Greatest Military Disaster* (London: Portrait, 2005), 375. Another source claimed 100,000 deaths, a figure Thompson, comparing it with other Japanese massacres, found "quite credible." "Chinese were beheaded or shot," wrote Brian Farrell in his 2005 account of the fall of Singapore. "The Japanese later admitted to killing at least 6,000. Singapore Chinese claims after the war ranged up to 50,000. An accurate figure might be near the 25,000 [Colonel] Sugita [Head of Intelligence, Japanese Twenty-fifth Army] supposedly admitted to a Japanese reporter": Brian P. Farrell, *The Defence and Fall of Singapore, 1940–1942* (Stroud, Gloucestershire, UK: Tempus, 2005), 385.
35. "Reliable Information from Manila shows American and British civilians subjected to concentration. All have been removed from their homes and families have been separated. All women and children confined in one place and men in another. Living conditions severe. MacArthur": Headquarters, SAFFE to AGWAR, Washington, January 18, 1942, RG 4, MMA. "All reports confirm my previous statements as to the extremely harsh and rigid measures taken against American and English in occupied areas in the Philippines. Such steps are not only unnecessary but are unquestionably dictated by the idea of abuse and special humiliation. I earnestly recommend that steps be taken

through the State Department to have these conditions alleviated. The negligible restrictions apparently applied in the United States to the many thousands of Japanese nationals there can easily serve as the lever under the threat of reciprocal retaliatory measures to force decent treatment for these interned men and women. The only language the Japanese understands [*sic*] is force and it should be applied mercilessly to his nationals if necessary . . . I urge this matter be handled immediately and aggressively through the proper diplomatic channels MacArthur": Cable 179 to AGWAR, Washington, February 1, 1942, RG 4, MMA. General John Dewitt, commander of U.S. Army forces on the West Coast, pressed the secretary of war for evacuation of all Japanese from the vulnerable California defense-industry areas on February 3, and after several weeks of discussion and legal consultation, the evacuation and internment of some 110,000 Japanese Americans from California was ordered under Executive Order 9066 on February 19, 1942.

36. See "1981 Report of the Presidential Commission on the Wartime Location and Internment of Civilians," which concluded that a "grave injustice was done to American citizens who, without individual review or any probative evidence against them, were excluded, removed and detained by the United States during World War II": Roger Daniels, *Prisoners Without Trial: Japanese Americans in World War II* (New York: Hill and Wang, 1993), 3–4.

37. Memorandum of February 16, 1942, in Sherwood, *Roosevelt and Hopkins,* 502–3.

38. "At the Atlantic meeting," Churchill stated before Parliament in London on September 9, 1941, "we had in mind, primarily, the restoration of the sovereignty, self-government, and national life of the [white] States and nations of Europe now under the Nazi yoke . . . So that is a quite separate problem from the progressive evolution of self-governing institutions in the regions and peoples which owe allegiance to the British crown": Richard Toye, *Churchill's Empire: The World That Made Him and the World He Made* (New York: Henry Holt, 2010), 214.

9. THE MOCKERY OF THE WORLD

1. Entry of 14.2.1942, Joseph Goebbels, *Die Tagebücher von Joseph Goebbels* [The diaries of Joseph Goebbels], ed. Elke Fröhlich (Munich: K. G. Saur, 1995), Teil II, Band 3, 308. Quotes from this source have been translated by the author.

2. Entry of 15.2.1942, Goebbels, *Die Tagebücher,* Teil II, Band 3, 321.

3. Ibid., 314.

4. Ambassador Winant to Roosevelt, February 17, 1942, "Safe" and Confidential Files, in Warren F. Kimball, ed., *Churchill & Roosevelt: The Complete Correspondence,* vol. 1, *Alliance Emerging, October 1933–November 1942* (Princeton, NJ: Princeton University Press, 1984), 362.

5. See Carlo D'Este, *Warlord: A Life of Winston Churchill at War, 1874–1945* (New York: Harper, 2008), inter alia.

6. In Harold Nicolson, *Diaries and Letters 1939–1945* (London: Collins, 1967), 211.

7. Ibid., 211.

8. Entry of February 9, 1942, Alexander Cadogan, *The Diaries of Sir Alexander Cadogan, O.M., 1938–1945,* ed. David Dilks (London: Cassell, 1971), 433.

9. Ibid., entry of February 15, 1942, 434.

10. Entry of February 27, 1942, Nicolson, *Diaries and Letters,* 214.

11. Entry of 16.2.1942, Goebbels, *Die Tagebücher,* Teil II, Band 3, 326.

12. Ibid., 326, 325.

13. Ibid.

14. Ibid., entry of 19.2.1942, 340.

15. Cable R-106, February 18, 1942, in Kimball, *Churchill & Roosevelt,* vol. 1, 362–63.

16. Ibid., Cable C-30, February 20, 1942, 364.

17. Entry of 16.1.1942, Goebbels, *Die Tagebücher,* Teil II, Band 3, 120.

18. Secret File, 2-3-42, RG 2, MacArthur Memorial Archives, in Paul P. Rogers, *The Good Years: MacArthur and Sutherland* (New York: Praeger, 1990), 183.

19. See Douglas Lockwood, *Australia's Pearl Harbour: Darwin, 1942* (Melbourne: Cassell Australia, 1966).

20. W. Averell Harriman and Elie Abel, *Special Envoy to Churchill and Stalin, 1941–1946* (New York: Random House, 1975), 126.

10. THE BATTLEGROUND FOR CIVILIZATION

1. Samuel I. Rosenman, *Working with Roosevelt* (New York: Harper, 1952), 1–2.

2. Ibid., 4.

3. Ibid., 330.

4. Ibid., 5.

5. Ibid., 329.

6. Ibid., 5.

7. Ibid., 6.

8. Ibid., 7.

9. Washington's Birthday was on February 22, but since the 22nd fell on a Sunday, the talk was given on February 23, 1942.

10. The Japanese submarine, I-17, under command of Nishino Kozo, shelled oil installations ten miles north of Santa Barbara, California, as well as aimlessly firing shells inland. The attack lasted only fifteen minutes. No one was killed or injured.

11. "We Must Keep On Striking Our Enemies Wherever and Whenever We Can Meet Them" — Fireside Chat on Progress of the War, February 23, 1942, in Franklin D. Roosevelt, *The Public Papers and Addresses of Franklin D. Roosevelt,* comp. Samuel I. Rosenman, vol. 11, *Humanity on the Defensive* (New York: Russell and Russell, 1969), 105–17.

12. Kenneth S. Davis, *FDR: The War President, 1940–1943* (New York: Random House, 2000), 435.

13. Entry of February 24, 1942, Galeazzo Ciano, *Diary 1937–1943* (New York: Enigma Books, 2002), 497.
14. Ibid.
15. Ibid.

11. NO HAND ON THE WHEEL

1. "Safe" and Confidential Files, DC 740.0011, Franklin D. Roosevelt Presidential Library, Hyde Park, NY. See also "India" annotation in Warren F. Kimball, ed., *Churchill & Roosevelt: The Complete Correspondence*, vol. 1, *Alliance Emerging, October 1933–November 1942* (Princeton, NJ: Princeton University Press, 1984), 373.
2. Ibid.
3. Alexander Cadogan, *The Diaries of Sir Alexander Cadogan, O.M., 1938–1945*, ed. David Dilks (London: Cassell, 1971), 438.
4. Ibid.
5. Cable C-34, March 4, 1942, in Kimball, *Churchill & Roosevelt*, vol. 1, 374.
6. Entry of March 5, 1942, *The Cadogan Diaries*, 440.
7. W. Averell Harriman and Elie Abel, *Special Envoy to Churchill and Stalin, 1941–1946* (New York: Random House, 1975), 126–27.
8. Ibid.
9. Letter of March 18, 1942, in Richard Toye, *Churchill's Empire: The World That Made Him and the World He Made* (New York: Henry Holt, 2010), 223.

12. LESSONS FROM THE PACIFIC

1. Entry of January 2, 1942, McCrea Diary, Papers of Captain John McCrea, Box 2, Library of Congress. McCrea had been assistant to Admiral Stark in 1941, and was then appointed naval secretary for the Joint Chiefs of Staff conversations with the British in January 1942, meeting Churchill and President Roosevelt for the first time on January 4, 1942.
2. Ibid., entry of January 16, 1942. McCrea relieved Captain Beardall, who had been made commandant of the U.S. Naval Academy.
3. Ibid., entry of January 18, 1942.
4. Ibid., entry of March 31, 1942.
5. Entry of February 6, 1942, Hart Diary, Papers of Admiral Thomas Hart, Operational Archives Branch, Naval Historical Center, Washington, DC.
6. Ibid.
7. The Battle of the Java Sea took place between February 27 and March 1, 1942. The Combined (Dutch, British, and U.S.) Striking Force, under Rear Admiral Doorman, was ordered into combat by Admiral Helfrich without air cover and with minimal intership communication; in suicidal combat it was annihilated,

suffering the loss of ten warships, including no fewer than five Allied cruisers sunk, while the Japanese Navy did not lose a single warship, or delay its invasion of Java by a single day. Admiral Ernest King called it "a magnificent display of very bad strategy": Samuel Eliot Morison, *History of United States Naval Operations in World War II,* vol. 3, *The Rising Sun in the Pacific, 1931–April 1942* (Boston: Little, Brown, 1948), 132. See Samuel Eliot Morison, *The Two-Ocean War: A Short History of the United States Navy in the Second World War* (Boston: Little, Brown, 1963), 88–98; Ian W. Toll, *Pacific Crucible: War at Sea in the Pacific, 1941–1942* (New York: Norton, 2012), 255–63.

8. Entry of March 10, 1942, Hart Diary.

9. Ibid.

10. Ibid., entries of February 18–19, 1942.

11. Ibid.

12. Ibid.

13. Ibid., entries of March 8 and 9, 1942.

14. "The Secretary, clearly having my appearance before his weekly press conference very much on his mind, sent for me even before I had finished my screed, and I read it to him. He said 'fine' . . . He obviously was much relieved. So I became then and there very decidedly committed to a line as regards participation in publicity" — in print, on radio, and in filmed interviews. Ibid., entry of March 11 et seq.

13. CHURCHILL THREATENS TO RESIGN

1. Entry for March 9, 1942, in Breckinridge Long, *The War Diary of Breckinridge Long: Selections from the Years 1939–1944,* ed. Fred L. Israel (Lincoln: University of Nebraska Press, 1966), 253.

2. United States Department of State, *Foreign Relations of the United States, Diplomatic Papers 1942* [hereafter *FRUS 1942*], vol. 1, *General, The British Commonwealth, The Far East* (Washington, DC: Government Printing Office, 1942), 606.

3. Ibid.

4. Ibid.

5. Christopher Thorne, *Allies of a Kind: The United States, Britain, and the War Against Japan, 1941–1945* (New York: Oxford University Press, 1978), 235.

6. Memorandum of a Conversation by Mr. Calvin H. Oakes of the Division of Near Eastern Affairs, May 26, 1942, *FRUS 1942,* vol. 1, 660. The American ambassador to China in Chungking, after a visit to India, reported the same to the U.S. State Department, recording that "there is bitterness against the Churchill Government for having sabotaged the Cripps Mission" — thus confirming "reports from other sources that there was sabotaging": M. S. Venkataramani and B. K. Shrivastava, *Quit India: The American Response to the 1942 Struggle* (New Delhi: Vikas, 1979), 143.

7. Cable R-116, Warren Kimball, ed., *Churchill & Roosevelt: The Complete Correspondence*, vol. 1, *Alliance Emerging, October 1933–November 1942* (Princeton, NJ: Princeton University Press, 1984), 403–4.
8. Sir Ian Jacob, unpublished autobiography, 73a and 73b, Churchill College Archives, Cambridge.
9. Alexander Cadogan, *The Diaries of Sir Alexander Cadogan, O.M., 1938–1945*, ed. David Dilks (London: Cassell, 1971), 437.
10. "Churchill and Amery had disavowed the possibility of a Cabinet convention. They had reacted against the term 'National Government,' . . . They recoiled from the full Indianization of the Executive . . . Finally they denied Cripps the status of a negotiator": R. J. Moore, *Endgames of Empire: Studies of Britain's Indian Problem* (New York: Oxford University Press, 1988), 97. See also Sarvepalli Gopal, *Jawaharlal Nehru: A Biography* (Cambridge, MA: Harvard University Press, 1976), vol. 1, 279–84; M. S. Venkataramani and B. K. Shrivastava, *Roosevelt, Gandhi, Churchill: America and the Last Phase of India's Freedom Struggle* (New Delhi: Radiant, 1983), 26–28. Most British historians blamed Churchill. "A Viceroy bitterly distrustful of the Congress leadership and lacking political finesse joined forces with a Prime Minister who had no wish to see Indian independence, and for whom the mission was primarily a device to deflect American criticism": Judith M. Brown, *Nehru: A Political Life* (New Haven, CT: Yale University Press, 2003), 148.
11. Cable C-62, Kimball, *Churchill & Roosevelt*, vol. 1, 438.
12. Sir Ian Jacob, unpublished autobiography.
13. Ian W. Toll, *Pacific Crucible: War at Sea in the Pacific, 1941–1942* (New York: Norton, 2012), 255.
14. The Personal Representative of the President in India to the Secretary of State, *FRUS 1942*, vol. 1, 627.
15. The Acting Secretary of State to the Officer in Charge at New Delhi, Personal for President's personal representative, *FRUS 1942*, vol. 1, 627–28.
16. Venkataramani and Shrivastava, *Quit India*, 108–9.
17. Alan Brooke, *War Diaries 1939–1945, Field Marshal Lord Alanbrooke*, ed. Alex Danchev and Daniel Todman (Berkeley: University of California Press, 2001), 245.
18. Telegram C-65, Kimball, *Churchill & Roosevelt*, vol. 1, 443.
19. The most succinct account of the viceroy's obstructionism, the secretary of state for India's change of mind, and Churchill's sheer perfidy (including Churchill's insincerity in claiming Britain would withdraw from overall control of the Raj) is to be found in Moore, *Endgames of Empire*, 94–105.
20. Venkataramani and Shrivastava, *Quit India*, 117.
21. Moore, *Endgames of Empire*, 96–97.
22. Cordell Hull, *The Memoirs of Cordell Hull* (New York: Macmillan, 1948), vol. 2, 1484. See also Venkataramani and Shrivastava, *Quit India*, 44.
23. Winston S. Churchill, *The Second World War*, vol. 4, *The Hinge of Fate* (Boston: Houghton Mifflin, 1950), 185–96. David Reynolds, in his dissection

of Churchill's Second World War memoirs, called Churchill's account of the episode "breathtakingly disingenuous": David Reynolds, *In Command of History: Churchill Fighting and Writing the Second World War* (New York: Random House, 2005), 337.

24. Sir Ian Jacob, unpublished autobiography.

25. Brown, *Nehru: A Political Life*, 148.

26. Cable R-132, Kimball, *Churchill & Roosevelt*, vol. 1, 445.

27. The Personal Representative of the President in India to the Secretary of State, *FRUS 1942*, vol. 1, 631.

28. Venkataramani and Shrivastava, *Quit India*, 141. On April 1, 1942, Halifax predicted that the Cripps mission would fail. When Welles asked Halifax what he thought would happen, in that case, the ambassador had said, "Nothing" — an example of fatal British complacency in view of the riots and deaths that followed: Memorandum of Conversation by the Acting Secretary of State, *FRUS 1942*, vol. 1, 623.

29. Warren Kimball, *Forged in War: Roosevelt, Churchill, and the Second World War* (New York: Morrow, 1997), 140; Warren Kimball, *The Juggler: Franklin Roosevelt as Wartime Statesman* (Princeton, NJ: Princeton University Press, 1991), 134. See also Venkataramani and Shrivastava, *Quit India*, 142.

30. Letter of July 26, 1941, Papers of Lord Halifax, Hickleton Papers, Borthwick Institute of Historical Research, University of York, Yorkshire, England.

31. Ibid., Letter of May 25, 1942.

32. Kimball, *Churchill & Roosevelt*, vol. 1, 446.

33. Winston S. Churchill, *The Second World War*, vol. 4, *The Hinge of Fate*, 219.

34. Cable R-132, Kimball, *Churchill & Roosevelt*, vol. 1, 446.

35. Ibid.

36. Ibid., 446–47.

37. Robert Sherwood, *Roosevelt and Hopkins: An Intimate History* (New York: Harper, 1948), 512.

38. Entry of April 22, 1942, Stimson Diary, Henry L. Stimson Papers, Yale University Library, New Haven, CT.

39. Sherwood, *Roosevelt and Hopkins*, 512.

40. Ibid.

41. Cable C-68, draft A, not sent, April 12, 1942, Kimball, *Churchill & Roosevelt*, vol. 1, 447.

42. Stanley Wolpert, *Nehru: A Tryst with Destiny* (New York: Oxford University Press, 1996), 308–9.

43. Cable C-68, draft A, not sent, April 12, 1942, Kimball, *Churchill & Roosevelt*, vol. 1, 447.

44. Ibid., 447–48.

45. Entry of April 22, 1942, Stimson Diary.

46. Personal Representative of the President in India to the Acting Secretary of State. For the President and Acting Secretary Welles, *FRUS 1942,* vol. 1, 635–37.
47. Ibid.
48. Cable C-68, Kimball, *Churchill & Roosevelt,* vol. 1, 448.
49. Lord Ismay, *The Memoirs of General Lord Ismay* (New York: Viking, 1960), 249.
50. Andrew Roberts, *Masters and Commanders: How Four Titans Won the War in the West, 1941–1945* (New York: Harper, 2009), 152.

14. THE WORST CASE OF JITTERS

1. Entry of Wednesday, April 15, 1942, 308, Diaries of William Lyon Mackenzie King, Library and Archives Canada, Ottawa, ON.
2. Entry of April 1, 1942, McCrea Diary, Papers of Captain John McCrea, Box 2, Library of Congress.
3. Entry of Wednesday, April 15, 1942, 309, King Diary.
4. Ibid., 310.
5. Ibid., 310(h).
6. Ibid., 310(e) and (f).
7. Ibid.
8. Ibid., 309.
9. Churchill himself recounted the "disconcerting" episode in his memoirs: Winston S. Churchill, *The Second World War,* vol. 3, *The Grand Alliance* (Boston: Houghton Mifflin, 1950), 617. See also Jon Meacham, *Franklin and Winston: An Intimate Portrait of an Epic Friendship* (New York: Random House, 2003), 161.
10. Entry of Wednesday, April 15, 1942, 309, King Diary.
11. Ibid.
12. Ibid., 310.
13. Ibid., Memorandum of conversation Mr. King had with President Roosevelt, White House, Washington, DC, 311–12.
14. Ibid.
15. Ibid.
16. Ibid., entry of April 16, 1942, 317.
17. Ibid., 323.
18. Ibid., 318.
19. Ibid.
20. Ibid., 325.
21. Ibid., 315.
22. Ibid.
23. Ibid., 319.
24. Cable C-69, Warren F. Kimball, ed., *Churchill & Roosevelt: The Complete Correspondence* (Princeton, NJ: Princeton University Press, 1984), vol. 1, 454.

25. Ibid., 452–53.
26. Entry of April 16, 1942, 235, King Diary.
27. Ibid, 326.
28. Cable R-134, Kimball, *Churchill & Roosevelt,* vol. 1, 455.
29. Entry of April 16, 1942, 326, King Diary.
30. Ibid.

15. DOOLITTLE'S RAID

1. James H. Doolittle, with Carroll V. Glines, *I Could Never Be So Lucky Again: An Autobiography* (New York: Bantam Books, 1991), 265–66.
2. Entry of April 18, 1942, Stimson Diary, Henry L. Stimson Papers, Yale University Library, New Haven, CT.
3. "Notes written by VADM John L. McCrea, USN (Ret.), Naval Aide to President Roosevelt from 16 Jan. 1942 to 3 Feb. 1943," Papers of John L. McCrea, Library of Congress.
4. Werner Gruhl, *Imperial Japan's World War Two, 1931–1945* (New Brunswick, NJ: Transaction, 2007), 79.
5. Ian W. Toll, *Pacific Crucible: War at Sea in the Pacific, 1941–1942* (New York: Norton, 2012), 296.
6. Entry of April 18, 1942, Stimson Diary.
7. Toll, *Pacific Crucible,* 299.
8. Ibid., 272.

16. THE BATTLE OF MIDWAY

1. Geoffrey C. Ward, ed. *Closest Companion: The Unknown Story of the Intimate Friendship Between Franklin Roosevelt and Margaret Suckley* (Boston: Houghton Mifflin, 1995), diary entry of May 12, 1942, 159.
2. Ibid., 158.
3. Ibid., entry of May 10, 1942, 158.
4. Ibid., entry of June 1, 1942, 164.
5. Commander George Elsey, interview with the author, September 10, 2011.
6. Ibid.
7. Entry of April 12, 1942, Stimson Diary, Henry L. Stimson Papers, Yale University Library, New Haven, CT.
8. Ian W. Toll, *Pacific Crucible: War at Sea in the Pacific, 1941–1942* (New York: Norton, 2012), 370.
9. Cable C-86 of May 7–8, 1942, Warren Kimball, ed., *Churchill & Roosevelt: The Complete Correspondence,* vol. 1, *Alliance Emerging, October 1933–November 1942* (Princeton, NJ: Princeton University Press, 1984), 483.
10. Entry of April 12, 1942, Stimson Diary.

11. Eric Larrabee, *Commander-in-Chief: Franklin Delano Roosevelt, His Lieutenants, and Their War* (New York: Harper & Row, 1987), 360–67; Toll, *Pacific Crucible,* 387.

12. Entry of May 26, 1942, in Ward, *Closest Companion,* 159.

13. William D. Hassett, *Off the Record with F.D.R., 1942–1945* (New Brunswick, NJ: Rutgers University Press, 1958), 54.

14. Entry of May 26, 1942, in Ward, *Closest Companion,* 1159.

15. On April 8, 1942, General Wainwright had wired that exhaustion and malnutrition in his beleaguered forces would, after almost four months of combat, make it impossible to break out of Bataan, with no hope of relief or evacuation. There was great concern in Washington lest the Japanese, who had refused to sign the Geneva Agreements on conduct in war, would massacre the U.S.-Filipino troops, if they did surrender. Roosevelt delegated the decision to General Wainwright — who was all for fighting to the last man standing. Not even he could control events, however, when General King, commanding the U.S. and Filipino troops on the Bataan mainland, fatefully decided his starving, exhausted soldiers could no longer fight, and commenced surrender negotiations, without Wainwright's authority. "Apparently the decision of bitter-end fighting with a possible massacre had been taken out of our hands," Secretary Stimson noted the next morning, when he went in person to Pennsylvania Avenue to tell the President, "who was still asleep. I got in about nine o'clock when he had just awakened and told him the news." The number of troops surrendering totaled 36,853, as of last count taken, two days before, Stimson recorded. At the press conference that the President asked him to give, "I took occasion to point out that there were Navy troops there that had behaved very well; also the fine behavior of the Filipino scouts and the fighting together with the Philippine Army and ourselves in a common cause, as well as a pledge that we would come back and drive the invaders out eventually": entry of April 9, 1942, Stimson Diary.

16. D. Clayton James, *The Years of MacArthur,* vol. 2, *1941–1945* (Boston: Houghton Mifflin, 1975), 169.

17. James MacGregor Burns, *Roosevelt: The Soldier of Freedom* (New York: Harcourt Brace Jovanovitch, 1970), 226.

18. Hassett, *Off the Record with F.D.R.,* 57.

19. Ibid.

20. E. B. Potter, *Nimitz* (Annapolis, MD: Naval Institute Press, 1976), 90–91.

21. Toll, *Pacific Crucible,* 409.

22. Potter, *Nimitz,* 107.

23. Larrabee, *Commander-in-Chief,* 394. The Grumman F6F Hellcat, six months later, provided the answer.

24. Toll, *Pacific Crucible,* 447.

25. Ibid., 446.

26. Ibid., 462.
27. Ibid., 455.
28. Ibid., 478.
29. Ibid., 462.
30. Frank Knox, Memo for the President, enclosing letter to the Attorney-General, June 9, 1942, Franklin D. Roosevelt Presidential Library, Hyde Park, NY.
31. James, *The Years of MacArthur,* vol. 2, 170.

17. CHURCHILL'S SECOND COMING

1. Entry of June 11, 1942, Diaries of William Lyon Mackenzie King, Library and Archives Canada, Ottawa, ON.
2. Ibid.
3. Ibid.
4. Ibid.
5. Ibid.
6. Ibid.
7. Ibid.
8. Cable C-101, June 13, 1942, in Warren Kimball, ed., *Churchill & Roosevelt: The Complete Correspondence,* vol. 1, *Alliance Emerging, October 1933–November 1942* (Princeton, NJ: Princeton University Press, 1984), 510.
9. Carlo D'Este, *Eisenhower: A Soldier's Life* (New York: Henry Holt, 2002), 303.
10. Ibid., 307.
11. Entry of June 17, 1942, Stimson Diary, Henry L. Stimson Papers, Yale University Library, New Haven, CT.
12. Ibid.
13. Ibid.
14. Entry of Thursday, June 18, 1942, "Secret Diary" of Lord Halifax, Papers of Lord Halifax, Hickleton Papers, Borthwick Institute of Historical Research, University of York, Yorkshire, England.
15. Ibid.
16. Ibid.
17. Entry of June 13, 1942, in Alan Brooke, *War Diaries, 1939–1945: Field Marshal Lord Alanbrooke,* ed., Alex Danchev and Daniel Todman (Berkeley: University of California Press, 2001), 265.
18. Prime Minister's Personal Minute to Lord Linlithgow, June 13, 1942, in Martin Gilbert, *Winston S. Churchill,* vol. 7, *Road to Victory, 1941–1945* (Boston: Houghton Mifflin, 1986), 123.
19. Entry of June 19, 1942, Halifax Diary.
20. Entry of June 19, 1942, Stimson Diary.
21. Ibid.
22. Ibid., entry of June 20, 1942.
23. Ibid., entry of June 21, 1942.

24. Ibid., entry of June 20, 1942.
25. Ibid.
26. Ibid.
27. Ibid.
28. Ibid.
29. Ibid., 3.
30. "Safe" and Confidential Files, undated, but probably June 13, 1942, Franklin D. Roosevelt Presidential Library, Hyde Park, NY.
31. Ibid.
32. Diary entry of June 20, 1942, in William D. Hassett, *Off the Record with F.D.R., 1942–1945* (New Brunswick, NJ: Rutgers University Press, 1958), 68.
33. Ibid.
34. Hugh L'Etang, *Fit to Lead?* (London: Heinemann Medical, 1980).
35. Franklin D. Roosevelt Day by Day, Pare Lorentz Center, FDR Library. www .fdrlibrary.marist.edu/daybyday.
36. Winston S. Churchill, *The Second World War,* vol. 4, *The Hinge of Fate* (Boston: Houghton Mifflin, 1950), 338–39.
37. Hassett, *Off the Record with F.D.R.,* 67.
38. Letter to the President, June 19, 1942, para 81, Henry L. Stimson Papers, Yale University Library.
39. Churchill, *The Second World War,* vol. 4, *The Hinge of Fate,* 342.
40. Ibid.
41. Ibid., 343.
42. Hassett, *Off the Record with F.D.R.,* 68.
43. Ibid.

18. THE FALL OF TOBRUK

1. Entry of June 20, 1942, "Secret Diary" of Lord Halifax, Papers of Lord Halifax, Hickleton Papers, Borthwick Institute of Historical Research, University of York, Yorkshire, England.
2. Martin Gilbert, *Winston S. Churchill,* vol. 7, *Road to Victory, 1941–1945* (Boston: Houghton Mifflin, 1986), 123.
3. Robert Sherwood, *Roosevelt and Hopkins: An Intimate History* (New York: Harper, 1948), 589–90.
4. Entry of June 22, 1942, Breckinridge Long, *The War Diary of Breckenridge Long: Selections from the Years 1939–1944,* ed. Frank L. Israel (Lincoln: University of Nebraska Press, 1966), 274.
5. Winston S. Churchill, *The Second World War,* vol. 4, *The Hinge of Fate* (Boston: Houghton Mifflin, 1950), 344.
6. Entry of June 20, 1942, Halifax Diary.
7. Entry of June 21, 1942, Alexander Cadogan, *The Diaries of Sir Alexander Cadogan, O.M., 1938–1945,* ed. David Dilks (London: Cassell, 1971), 458.

8. Ibid.
9. W. Averell Harriman and Elie Abel, *Special Envoy to Churchill and Stalin, 1941–1946* (New York: Random House, 1975), 144.
10. Lord Ismay, *The Memoirs of General Lord Ismay* (New York: Viking, 1960), 254.
11. Alan Brooke, *War Diaries, 1939–1945: Field Marshal Lord Alanbrooke,* ed. Alex Danchev and Daniel Todman (Berkeley: University of California Press, 2001), 269.
12. Ibid.
13. Charles Moran, *Winston Churchill: The Struggle for Survival, 1940–1965* (Boston: Houghton Mifflin, 1966), 37–38.
14. Ibid.
15. Ibid.
16. Entry of 22.6.1942, Joseph Goebbels, *Die Tagebücher von Joseph Goebbels* [The diaries of Joseph Goebbels], ed. Elke Fröhlich (Munich: K. G. Saur, 1995), Teil II, Band 4, 569–70. Quotes from this source have been translated by the author.
17. Ibid., 571.
18. Ibid., entry of 23.6.1942, 575.
19. Ibid., entry of 21.6.1942, 565.
20. Ibid., entry of 23.6.1942, 575, 581, and 589.
21. Ibid., 582 and 581.
22. Ibid., 577.
23. Ibid., entry of 21.6.1942, 563.
24. Ian Kershaw, *Hitler 1936–1945: Nemesis* (New York: Norton, 2000), 515–17.
25. Entry of 24.5.1942, Goebbels, *Die Tagebücher,* Teil 2, Band 4, 357.
26. Kershaw, *Hitler: Nemesis,* 516–17.
27. Entry of 24.5.1942, Goebbels, *Die Tagebücher,* Teil 2, Band 4, 356.
28. Ibid., 357.
29. Ibid., entry of 24.6.1942, 605.
30. Ibid.
31. Ibid., entry of 24.5.1942, 362.
32. Ibid., 363.
33. Ibid., 361–64.
34. Ibid., 359.
35. Ibid., 354.
36. Ismay, *The Memoirs of General Lord Ismay,* 255.
37. Entry of 25.6.1942, Goebbels, *Die Tagebücher,* Teil II, Band 4, 614.

19. NO SECOND DUNQUERQUE

1. Forrest Pogue, *George C. Marshall,* vol. 2, *Ordeal and Hope, 1939–1942* (New York: Viking, 1966), 337.
2. Entry of June 23, 1942, Diaries of William Lyon Mackenzie King, Mackenzie King Papers, Library and Archives Canada, Ottawa, ON.

3. Ibid., entry of June 25, 1942.
4. Ibid.
5. Ibid.
6. Ibid.
7. Ibid.
8. Entry of Saturday, June 13, 1942, "Secret Diary" of Lord Halifax, Papers of Lord Halifax, Hickleton Papers, Borthwick Institute of Historical Research, University of York, Yorkshire, England.
9. Entry of June 25, 1942, King Diary.
10. Ibid.
11. Ibid.
12. Ibid.
13. Ibid., entry of April 16, 1942.
14. Meeting of Pacific War Council at Washington, D.C., Wednesday, April 15, 1942, Mackenzie King Papers.
15. Entry of June 25, 1942, King Diary.

20. AVOIDING UTTER CATASTROPHE

1. Entry of 4.7.1942, Joseph Goebbels, *Die Tagebücher von Joseph Goebbels* [The diaries of Joseph Goebbels], ed. Elke Fröhlich (Munich: K. G. Saur, 1995), Teil II, Band 5, 53. Quotes from this source have been translated by the author.
2. Ibid., entry of 21.7.1942, 160.
3. Ibid.
4. As far back as March 9, 1942, the President had met with his U.S. ambassador to Spain, Alexander Weddell, asking him to consider the disadvantages versus advantages "were an expeditionary force sent to effect a landing 'either in Algeria or on the northwest coast of Africa,'" as Weddell quoted Roosevelt's instructions. There were the four "Favorable results" to be had, Weddell acknowledged when responding on March 24, 1942 — two of which were: "to provide a base from which Europe might be invaded" and "To place hostile elements [Rommel's army] between United Nations' forces in East and West": Weddell Memorandum for the President, March 24, 1942, in "Safe" and Confidential Files, Franklin D. Roosevelt Presidential Library, Hyde Park, NY.
5. William D. Leahy, *I Was There* (New York: Whittlesey House, McGraw-Hill, 1950), 116.
6. The final vote, taken on July 1, 1942, was 475 to 25 in favor of Churchill's government.

21. CITIZEN WARRIORS

1. "Shangri-la," Papers of Captain John McCrea, Box 11, Library of Congress.
2. Ibid.

3. Ibid.
4. Geoffrey C. Ward, ed., *Closest Companion: The Unknown Story of the Intimate Friendship Between Franklin Roosevelt and Margaret Suckley* (Boston: Houghton Mifflin, 1995), diary entry of July 5, 1942, 168.
5. Ibid.
6. Ibid., undated entry, week of June 21, 1942, 167.
7. Ibid.
8. Ibid.

22. A STAGGERING CRISIS

1. Cable C-107, July 8, 1942, Warren Kimball, ed., *Churchill & Roosevelt: The Complete Correspondence,* vol. 1, *Alliance Emerging, October 1933–November 1942* (Princeton, NJ: Princeton University Press, 1984), 520–21.
2. Ibid.
3. Ibid.
4. Ibid., 520.
5. Maurice Matloff and Edwin M. Snell, *Strategic Planning for Coalition Warfare, 1941–1942* (Washington, DC: Office of the Chief of Military History, Dept. of the Army, 1953), 268.
6. Michael Schaller, *Douglas MacArthur: The Far Eastern General* (New York: Oxford University Press, 1989), 70–71.
7. Ibid.
8. Ibid.
9. "Memorandum for the President, July 10, 1942, Washington D.C.," *The Papers of George Catlett Marshall,* vol. 3, *The Right Man for the Job, December 7, 1941–May 31, 1943,* ed. Larry Bland (Baltimore: Johns Hopkins University Press, 1991), 271.
10. Ibid.
11. William D. Hassett, *Off the Record with F.D.R., 1942–1945* (New Brunswick, NJ: Rutgers University Press, 1958), 87.
12. Entry of July 10, 1942, p. 2, Stimson Diary, Henry L. Stimson Papers, Yale University Library, New Haven, CT.
13. "Memorandum for the President, July 10, 1942," *The Papers of George Catlett Marshall,* vol. 3, 271.
14. Matloff and Snell, *Strategic Planning for Coalition Warfare,* 270.

23. A ROUGH DAY

1. Entry of July 12, 1942, Stimson Diary, Henry L. Stimson Papers, Yale University Library, New Haven, CT.
2. Ibid.
3. Ibid., 2.
4. Ibid.

5. Ibid.
6. Leonard Mosley, *Marshall: Organizer of Victory* (London: Methuen, 1982), 151.
7. George C. Marshall, *George C. Marshall: Interviews and Reminiscences for Forrest Pogue*, rev. ed. (Lexington, VA: G. C. Marshall Research Foundation, 1991), 546.
8. Carlo D'Este, *Patton: A Genius for War* (New York: HarperCollins, 1995), 416.
9. Marshall, *George C. Marshall: Interviews and Reminiscences*, 546.
10. Entry of July 12, 1942, 2, Stimson Diary.
11. "Memorandum for the President, Subject: Pacific Operations," July 12, 1942, Stimson Papers.
12. Entry of July 13, 1942, Stimson Diary.
13. Ibid., handwritten annotation on typed Marshall-King Memorandum to the President of July 12, 1942.
14. Andrew Roberts, *Masters and Commanders: How Four Titans Won the War in the West, 1941–1945* (New York: Harper, 2009), 233. FDR was also aware that in the North Atlantic, with almost two million tons a month of merchant shipping being sunk by German U-boats (a figure that doubled by the fall), sinkings were exceeding Allied ship-construction, and would make a cross-Channel Second Front that year impossible to support logistically: B. J. C. McKercher, *Transition of Power: Britain's Loss of Global Pre-eminence in the United States, 1930–1945* (Cambridge: Cambridge University Press, 1999), 317. The President declined to use that argument, however, lest it lend credence to Marshall and King's case for a switch to the Pacific.
15. Maurice Matloff and Edwin M. Snell, *Strategic Planning for Coalition Warfare, 1941–1942* (Washington, DC: Office of the Chief of Military History, Dept. of the Army, 1953), 272.
16. Ibid.
17. Ibid., 272–73.
18. Entry of July 15, 1942, Stimson Diary.
19. Ibid., entry of July 13, 1942.
20. Ibid., entry of July 15, 1942.
21. Ibid., pp. 1–2.
22. Henry Stimson, *On Active Service in Peace and War* (New York: Harper, 1948), 425.
23. Entry of July 15, 1942, Stimson Diary.
24. Ibid.
25. Forrest Pogue, *George C. Marshall*, vol. 2, *Ordeal and Hope, 1939–1942* (New York: Viking, 1966), 346; Mark A. Stoler, *George C. Marshall: Soldier-Statesman of the American Century* (Boston: Twayne, 1989), 101.

24. STIMSON'S BET

1. Maurice Matloff and Edwin M. Snell, *Strategic Planning for Coalition Warfare, 1941–1942* (Washington, DC: Office of the Chief of Military History, Dept. of the Army, 1953), 272–73.

2. Viz. Andrew Roberts, *Masters and Commanders: How Four Titans Won the War in the West, 1941–1945* (New York: Harper, 2009).
3. Entry of July 18, 1942, Leahy Diary, William D. Leahy Papers, Library of Congress.
4. Ibid., entry of July 22, 1942.
5. Entry of July 20, 1942, Stimson Diary, Henry L. Stimson Papers, Yale University Library, New Haven, CT.
6. Ibid., entry of July 23, 1942.
7. Ibid.
8. Ibid.
9. Ibid.
10. Personal and Confidential letter of July 23, 1942, Stimson Papers.
11. Entry of July 24, 1942, Stimson Diary.
12. Entry of July 24, 1942, Leahy Diary.
13. Entry of July 24, 1942, Stimson Diary.
14. Ibid.
15. Ibid.
16. Ibid., entry of July 25, 1942.
17. Ibid.
18. Ibid.
19. Matloff and Snell, *Strategic Planning for Coalition Warfare*, 282.
20. Entry of July 25, 1942, Stimson Diary.
21. Ibid.
22. Ibid.
23. Ibid.
24. "Memorandum for the President: My Views as to the Proposals in Message 625 [message from General Marshall in London]," attached to Stimson Diary, July 25, 1942.
25. Entry of July 25, 1942, Leahy Diary.
26. Forrest Pogue, *George C. Marshall*, vol. 2, *Ordeal and Hope, 1939–1942* (New York: Viking, 1966), 347.
27. Henry Stimson, *On Active Service in Peace and War* (New York: Harper, 1948).
28. Annotations to entry of July 27, 1942, Stimson Diary.
29. Ibid., entry of July 27, 1942.

25. A DEFINITE DECISION

1. Forrest Pogue, *George C. Marshall*, vol. 2, *Ordeal and Hope, 1939–1942* (New York: Viking, 1966), 348.
2. According to American concentration camp historian Roger Daniels, "more than 120,000 individuals were held in relocation centers at one time or another," and the "camp population peaked at a little over 107,000" by early 1943. "By the beginning of the following year it was down to 93,000," and by January 1, 1945, "it had dropped to just 80,000," ending the war at 58,000. By the end of 1945, "every

camp but Tule Lake had been emptied," leaving 12,545 detainees: Roger Daniels, *Prisoners Without Trial: Japanese Americans in World War II* (New York: Hill and Wang, 1993), 73. President Roosevelt opposed the idea of such camps, reasoning that it was far better to arrange that Japanese immigrants and Japanese Americans "whose loyalty to this country has remained unshaken through the hardships of the evacuation which military necessity made unavoidable" should be dispersed and distributed across the country: "75,000 families scattered around on the farms and worked into the community" were "not going to upset anybody"; while Roosevelt declared himself deeply impressed by "the very wonderful record that the Japanese in that battalion in Italy have been making in the war. It is one of the outstanding battalions that we have": White House Press Conference of November 21, 1944, in *Complete Presidential Press Conferences of Franklin D. Roosevelt* (New York: Da Capo Press, 1972), vol. 24, 245–47.

3. Stimson Diary, Henry L. Stimson Papers, Yale University Library, New Haven, CT. President Roosevelt had authorized establishment of the Uranium Committee in October 1939 to coordinate research on nuclear fission, and on October 9, 1941, he created the Top Policy Group comprising himself, Vice President Wallace, Dr. Vannevar Bush, Dr. James Conant, General George Marshall, and War Secretary Henry Stimson to expedite development of an atomic bomb. Concerned lest the Germans outrace the Allies, the President demanded tougher supervision and on September 18, 1942, Colonel Leslie Groves of the Corps of Engineers was promoted to the rank of lieutenant general and formally placed in command of the Manhattan Project, with Secretary Stimson having overall responsibility under the President.

4. "Safe" and Confidential Files, Franklin D. Roosevelt Presidential Library, Hyde Park, NY.

5. Ibid.

6. Stimson Diary.

7. Entry of July 28, 1942, Leahy Diary, Papers of Admiral William D. Leahy, Library of Congress.

8. Ibid.

9. Maurice Matloff and Edwin M. Snell, *Strategic Planning for Coalition Warfare, 1941–1942* (Washington, DC: Office of the Chief of Military History, Dept. of the Army, 1953), 283.

10. Ibid.

11. Ibid.

26. A FAILED MUTINY

1. Robert Sherwood, *Roosevelt and Hopkins: An Intimate History* (New York: Harper, 1948), 615.

2. Forrest Pogue, *George C. Marshall*, vol. 2, *Ordeal and Hope, 1939–1942* (New York: Viking, 1966), 349.

3. Sherwood, *Roosevelt and Hopkins,* 612.
4. Pogue, *Ordeal and Hope,* 349.
5. Entry of August 7, 1942, Stimson Diary, Henry L. Stimson Papers, Yale University Library, New Haven, CT.
6. Ibid.
7. Ibid.
8. Ibid.
9. Ibid., 4.
10. Ibid., entry of August 7, 1942.
11. "DRAFT," Letter to the President, August 10, 1942, Stimson Papers.
12. Entry of August 7, 1942, Stimson Diary.
13. Ibid., entry of August 10, 1942.
14. Ibid., entry of August 11, 1942.

27. STALIN'S PRAYER

1. Winston S. Churchill, *The Second World War,* vol. 4, *The Hinge of Fate* (Boston: Houghton Mifflin, 1950), 428.
2. Robert Dallek, *The Lost Peace: Leadership in a Time of Horror and Hope, 1945–1953* (New York: Harper, 2010), 31. A full account of Churchill and Harriman's trip to Moscow is in Martin Gilbert, *Winston S. Churchill,* vol. 7, *Road to Victory, 1941–1945* (Boston: Houghton Mifflin, 1986), 172–208.
3. Samuel I. Rosenman, *Working with Roosevelt* (New York: Harper, 1952), 349.
4. Ibid.
5. Robert Sherwood, *Roosevelt and Hopkins: An Intimate History* (New York: Harper, 1948), 62; W. Averell Harriman and Elie Abel, *Special Envoy to Churchill and Stalin, 1941–1946* (New York: Random House, 1975), 168.
6. Ibid., 169.
7. Entry of September 3, 1942, Stimson Diary, Henry L. Stimson Papers, Yale University Library, New Haven, CT.
8. "Meeting at the Kremlin on Wednesday, August 12, 1942," in Gilbert, *Road to Victory,* 181.
9. Harriman and Abel, *Special Envoy,* 169.
10. Entry of October 21, 1942, Diaries of William Lyon Mackenzie King, Library and Archives Canada, Ottawa, ON.
11. "Meeting at the Kremlin on Wednesday, August 12, 1942," in Gilbert, *Road to Victory,* 182.
12. Ibid., 181.

28. A TRIP ACROSS AMERICA

1. Cable R-180, Draft A, not sent, initialed GCM, in Warren Kimball, ed., *Churchill & Roosevelt: The Complete Correspondence,* vol. 1, *Alliance Emerging,*

October 1933–November 1942 (Princeton, NJ: Princeton University Press, 1984), 581.

2. Ibid., Cable R-180, 584.

3. Ibid., 583.

4. August 31, 1942, quoted in Stephen Ambrose, *Eisenhower: Soldier, General of the Armies, President-elect* (New York: Simon and Schuster, 1983), 191.

5. Cable R-183, in Kimball, *Churchill & Roosevelt,* vol. 1, 590.

6. Mark W. Clark, *Calculated Risk* (New York: Harper, 1950), 36; Carlo D'Este, *Patton: A Genius for War* (New York: HarperCollins, 1995), 419; Piers Brendon, *Ike, His Life and Times* (New York: Harper and Row, 1986), 86.

7. Arthur L. Funk, *The Politics of TORCH: The Allied Landings and the Algiers Putsch, 1942* (Lawrence: University Press of Kansas, 1974), 100.

8. Cable C-144 of September 5, 1942, in Kimball, *Churchill & Roosevelt,* vol. 1, 591.

9. Ibid., Cable R-185 of September 5, 1942, 592.

10. Franklin D. Roosevelt, *The Public Papers and Addresses of Franklin D. Roosevelt,* comp. Samuel I. Rosenman, vol. 11, *Humanity on the Defensive, 1942* (New York: Russell and Russell, 1969), 350–51.

11. Linda Lotridge Levin, *The Making of FDR: The Story of Stephen T. Early, America's First Modern Press Secretary* (Amherst, NY: Prometheus, 2008), 294–97.

12. Geoffrey C. Ward, ed., *Closest Companion: The Unknown Story of the Intimate Friendship Between Franklin Roosevelt and Margaret Suckley* (Boston: Houghton Mifflin, 1995), 174.

13. Ibid., 175.

14. James MacGregor Burns, *Roosevelt: The Soldier of Freedom* (New York: Harcourt Brace Jovanovitch, 1970), 268.

15. Ward, *Closest Companion,* 175.

16. Arthur Herman, *Freedom's Forge: How American Business Produced Victory in World War II* (New York: Random House, 2012), 200.

17. Ibid.

18. Ward, *Closest Companion,* 175.

19. Ibid.

20. Ibid.

21. Ibid., entry of September 23, 1942, 179.

22. Herman, *Freedom's Forge,* 67.

23. Ibid., 200.

24. Entry of September 29, 1942, in Ward, *Closest Companion,* 182.

25. Ibid., 183.

29. THE PRESIDENT'S LOYAL LIEUTENANT

1. Geoffrey C. Ward, ed., *Closest Companion: The Unknown Story of the Intimate Friendship Between Franklin Roosevelt and Margaret Suckley* (Boston: Houghton Mifflin, 1995), entry of September 29, 1942, 183.

2. Cable R-187, September 26, 1942, in Warren Kimball, ed., *Churchill & Roosevelt: The Complete Correspondence,* vol. 1, *Alliance Emerging, October 1933–November 1942* (Princeton, NJ: Princeton University Press, 1984), 613.
3. Ibid., 645.
4. W. Averell Harriman and Elie Abel, *Special Envoy to Churchill and Stalin, 1941–1946* (New York: Random House, 1975), 166.
5. Arthur Herman, *Gandhi & Churchill: The Epic Rivalry That Destroyed an Empire and Forged Our Age* (New York: Bantam, 2008), 495. For an account of Churchill's use of propaganda in the United States to cast the Quit India movement in the worst possible light, see Auriol Weigold, *Churchill, Roosevelt, and India: Propaganda During World War II* (New York: Routledge, 2008), 140–60.
6. Harriman and Abel, *Special Envoy,* 172.
7. Cable C-148, September 14, 1942, in Kimball, *Churchill & Roosevelt,* vol. 1, 594.
8. Harriman and Abel, *Special Envoy,* 172.
9. Cable C-148, September 14, 1942, in Kimball, *Churchill & Roosevelt,* vol. 1, 594.

30. A CANADIAN BLOODBATH

1. "Meeting at the Kremlin on Wednesday, August 12, 1942," in Martin Gilbert, *Winston S. Churchill,* vol. 7, *Road to Victory, 1941–1945* (Boston: Houghton Mifflin, 1986), 181.
2. Ibid.
3. "Cairo, August, 1942," in Lord Moran, *Winston Churchill: The Struggle for Survival, 1940–1965* (Boston: Houghton Mifflin, 1966), 66.
4. For a full account, see Nigel Hamilton, *The Full Monty,* vol. 1, *Montgomery of Alamein, 1887–1942* (London: Allen Lane, 2001), 427–73.
5. Entry of 20.7.1942, Joseph Goebbels, *Die Tagebücher von Joseph Goebbels* [The diaries of Joseph Goebbels], ed. Elke Fröhlich (Munich: K. G. Saur, 1995), Teil II, Band 5, 348. Quotes from this source have been translated by the author.
6. Ibid., 349.
7. Ibid., 352.
8. Ibid.
9. Ibid.
10. Ibid., 353.
11. Ibid., 371.
12. Ibid., 354.
13. Ibid.
14. Entry of August 19, 1942, Diaries of William Lyon Mackenzie King, Library and Archives Canada, Ottawa, ON.
15. Ibid., entry of August 21, 1942.
16. Ibid., entry of August 24, 1942.

31. SOMETHING IN WEST AFRICA

1. Franklin D. Roosevelt, *The Public Papers and Addresses of Franklin D. Roosevelt,* comp. Samuel I. Rosenman, vol. 11, *Humanity on the Defensive* (New York: Russell and Russell, 1969), 417–18.

2. Entry of 8.9.1942, Joseph Goebbels, *Die Tagebücher von Joseph Goebbels* [The diaries of Joseph Goebbels], ed. Elke Fröhlich (Munich: K. G. Saur, 1995), Teil II, Band 5, 460. Quotes from this source have been translated by the author.

3. Ibid., 464.

4. *The Public Papers and Addresses of Franklin D. Roosevelt,* vol. 11, 417–18.

5. Entry of 16.10.1942, Goebbels, *Die Tagebücher,* Teil II, Band 6, 133–34.

6. Ibid., 134.

7. Ibid., entry of 15.10.1942, 125.

8. Ibid., entry of 26.9.1942, 571–72.

9. Ibid., entry of 9.9.1942, 464.

10. Ibid., 465.

11. Ibid., entry of 17.10.1942, 138.

12. Ibid.

13. William D. Leahy, *I Was There* (New York: Arno Press, 1979), 116.

14. On February 26, 1942, the President had written to Stimson regarding Stimson and General Marshall's order concerning the "reorganization of the Army," but wanted it reworded to "make it very clear that the Commander-in-Chief exercises his command function in relation to strategy, tactics and operations directly through the Chief of Staff. You, as Secretary of War, apart from your administrative responsibilities, would, of course, advise me on military matters": "Safe" and Confidential Files, Franklin D. Roosevelt Presidential Library, Hyde Park, NY.

15. Entry of September 17, 1942, Stimson Diary, Henry L. Stimson Papers, Yale University Library, New Haven, CT.

16. "My own feeling," Stimson confided in his diary, "is that Eisenhower has acted rather precipitately and inquiry should be made as to whether they [U.S. bomber forces] cannot carry on a while longer [in Britain] and perhaps carry on with some bombing right through. It is just another part of the price we are having to pay for this expedition to the south," he railed, "and to pay out of coin most precious to us": entry of September 9, 1942, Stimson Diary.

17. Ibid., entry of September 8, 1942.

18. Carlo D'Este, *Patton: A Genius for War* (New York: HarperCollins, 1995), 421.

19. Martin Blumenson, ed., *The Patton Papers* (Boston: Houghton Mifflin, 1972–74), vol. 2, 94.

20. Eric Larrabee, *Commander in Chief: Franklin Delano Roosevelt, His Lieutenants, and Their War* (New York: Harper & Row, 1987), 486.

21. Blumenson, *The Patton Papers,* vol. 2, 95.

22. Ibid., vol. 2, diary entry of October 21, 1942, 94.
23. Ladislas Farago, *The Last Days of Patton* (New York: McGraw-Hill, 1981), 191–92.

32. ALAMEIN

1. In the House of Representatives the Democrats lost forty-five seats, and in the Senate, eight seats.
2. Nigel Hamilton, *The Full Monty,* vol. 1, *Montgomery of Alamein, 1887–1942* (London: Allen Lane, 2001), 494.
3. Nigel Hamilton, *Monty: The Making of a General, 1887–1942* (New York: McGraw-Hill, 1981), 770.
4. Ibid., 744.
5. Entry of 4.11.1942, Joseph Goebbels, *Die Tagebücher von Joseph Goebbels* [The diaries of Joseph Goebbels], ed. Elke Fröhlich (Munich: K. G. Saur, 1995), Teil II, Band 6, 230. Quotes from this source have been translated by the author.
6. Ibid., 230–31.
7. Ibid., 233.
8. Ibid., 236.
9. Ibid., entry of 6.11.1942, 242–43.
10. Ibid., 244.
11. Ibid., entry of 7.11.1942, 246.
12. Ibid., 246–47.

33. FIRST LIGHT

1. Entry of November 5, 1942, Leahy Diary, William D. Leahy Papers, Library of Congress.
2. Entry of November 5, 1942, Stimson Diary, Henry L. Stimson Papers, Yale University Library, New Haven, CT.
3. Ibid.
4. Ibid.
5. Ibid., entry of November 6, 1942.
6. Entry of December 4, 1942, Diaries of William Lyon Mackenzie King, Library and Archives Canada, Ottawa, ON.
7. Entry of November 6, 1942, Stimson Diary.
8. Entry of November 8, 1942, in Geoffrey C. Ward, ed., *Closest Companion: The Unknown Story of the Intimate Friendship Between Franklin Roosevelt and Margaret Suckley* (Boston: Houghton Mifflin, 1995), 184.
9. Ibid.
10. Ibid.
11. Robert Murphy, *Diplomat Among Warriors* (Garden City, NY: Doubleday, 1964), 121.

12. Ibid.
13. Entry of November 2, 1942, Stimson Diary.
14. Ibid., entry of November 5, 1942.
15. Cable of November 2, 1942, in Murphy, *Diplomat Among Warriors*, 121.
16. Entry of November 2, 1942, Leahy Diary.
17. Entry of November 2, 1942, Stimson Diary.
18. Entry of November 7, 1942, in Ward, *Closest Companion*, 184.
19. Ibid.
20. Entry of November 6, 1942, Stimson Diary.
21. Entry of November 6, 1942, King Diary.
22. Entry of November 8, 1942, in Ward, *Closest Companion*, 185.
23. Entry of November 7, 1942, Leahy Diary.
24. Entry of November 7, 1942, Stimson Diary.
25. Grace Tully, *F.D.R., My Boss* (New York: Scribner's, 1949), 264.
26. Ibid.
27. Ibid.
28. Entry of November 8, 1942, in Ward, *Closest Companion*, 185.
29. Ibid., 186.
30. Entry of November 7, 1942, Stimson Diary.
31. Ibid., entry of November 6, 1942.
32. Entry of November 8, 1942, in Ward, *Closest Companion*, 185–86.
33. Ibid.

34. THE GREATEST SENSATION

1. Entry of November 8, 1942, Stimson Diary, Henry L. Stimson Papers, Yale University Library, New Haven, CT.
2. Ian Kershaw, *Hitler 1936–1945: Nemesis* (New York: Norton, 2000), 541.
3. Entry of 11.7.1942, Joseph Goebbels, *Die Tagebücher von Joseph Goebbels* [The diaries of Joseph Goebbels], ed. Elke Fröhlich (Munich: K. G. Saur, 1995), Teil II, Band 5, 346. Quotes from this source have been translated by the author.
4. Ibid., entry for "Yesterday," drawn up November 9, 1942, Teil II, Band 6, 254.
5. Ibid.
6. Ibid., 256.
7. Ibid., 257.
8. Ibid.
9. Ibid., entry of 23.6.1942, Teil II, Band 4, 594.
10. Ibid., entry of 24.6.1942, 604.
11. Ibid., entry of 23.6.1942, 591.
12. Ibid., entry of 24.6.1942, 605.
13. Ibid.
14. Ibid., 610.

15. Jacques Belle, *L'Opération Torch et la Tunisie* (Paris: Economica, 2011), 65–72.
16. Entry of 23.6.1942, Goebbels, *Die Tagebücher,* Teil II, Band 4, 592.
17. Kershaw, *Hitler: Nemesis,* 539.

35. ARMISTICE DAY

1. Entry of November 9, 1942, Stimson Diary, Henry L. Stimson Papers, Yale University Library, New Haven, CT.
2. Annex 2, Project Gymnast, U.S. Serial ABC-42, in United States Department of State, *Foreign Relations of the United States: The Conferences at Washington, 1941–1942, and Casablanca, 1943* (Washington, DC: Government Printing Office, 1941–1943), 240–43.
3. Eight Hundred and Fifty-Ninth Press Conference, November 10, 1942, in *The Public Papers and Addresses of Franklin D. Roosevelt,* comp. Samuel I. Rosenman, vol. 11, *Humanity on the Defensive* (New York: Russell and Russell, 1969), 462–63.
4. Ibid.
5. Entry of November 10, 1942, Stimson Diary.
6. Ibid.
7. Ibid., entry of November 9, 1942.
8. Allied casualties in the three days, November 8–11, 1942, were 530 killed, 887 wounded, and 52 missing — far lower than the Dieppe fiasco, despite Dieppe having been a vastly smaller operation: George F. Howe, *Northwest Africa: Seizing the Initiative in the West* (Washington, DC: Office of the Chief of Military History, Dept. of the Army, 1957), 173.
9. Entry of November 7, Martin Blumenson, ed, *The Patton Papers* (Boston: Houghton Mifflin, 1974), vol. 2, 102.
10. Ibid., 108.
11. Ibid., 109.
12. Carlo D'Este, *Patton: A Genius for War* (New York: HarperCollins, 1995), 437.
13. Entry of November 11, 1942, Leahy Diary, William D. Leahy Papers, Library of Congress.
14. On November 11, 1942, Eisenhower informed General Marshall of Churchill's "extraordinary impatience," but insisted, "I am not repeat not allowing anything to interfere with my clean cut line of subordination to the Combined Chiefs of Staff": Cable #320, in *The Papers of Dwight David Eisenhower,* ed. Alfred D. Chandler, vol. 2, *The War Years* (Baltimore: Johns Hopkins University Press, 1970), 691.
15. Ibid., 685.
16. Ibid., Cable to Major-General Walter Bedell Smith, November 11, 1942, 693.
17. For a French version of events, see Jacques Belle, *L'opération Torch et la Tunisie* (Paris: Economica, 2011), 44–53.

18. Sugata Bose, *His Majesty's Opponent: Subhas Chandra Bose and India's Struggle Against Empire* (Cambridge, MA: Belknap Press of Harvard University Press, 2011), 223.

19. Entry of November 11, 1942, Leahy Diary.

20. Entry of November 11, 1942, Stimson Diary.

21. Ibid.

22. Ibid.

23. "The Forces of Liberation Are Advancing" — Armistice Day Address, November 11, 1942, *The Public Papers and Addresses of Franklin D. Roosevelt,* vol. 2, 468–70.

24. William D. Leahy, *I Was There* (New York: Arno Press, 1979), 136.

25. Entry of November 11, 1942, Leahy Diary.

26. "The Forces of Liberation Are Advancing," *The Public Papers and Addresses of Franklin D. Roosevelt,* vol. 2, 468–70.

Index